Second Edition

Contemporary Field Research

Second Edition

Contemporary Field Research

Perspectives and Formulations

Robert M. Emerson

University of California, Los Angeles

WAVELAND

PRESS, INC.

Prospect Heights, Illinois

For information about this book, write or call:
Waveland Press, Inc.
P.O. Box 400
Prospect Heights, Illinois 60070
(847) 634-0081
www.waveland.com

Contents

PART III
Producing Ethnographies:
Theory, Evidence and Representation   281

Preface to the Second Edition

When the first edition of *Contemporary Field Research* was published in 1983, the reflexive turn in ethnography—the recognition that fieldwork itself is a social phenomenon, inescapably part of the very social worlds it seeks to discover, describe, and analyze—was well under way. Deeply critical of much of the apparatus of the natural sciences, field researchers had begun to reformulate, or discard entirely, procedures that had previously grounded much empirical social science, procedures including hypothesis testing, formulation of specifically defined variables, and statistically-based models of reliability and replicability. In turning away from prior positivist approaches field researchers took up and began actively articulating explicitly interpretive paradigms of ethnographic theory and research. In these paradigms "facts" and "data" were understood not as "objective entities," but rather as social meanings attributed by social actors—including the fieldworker—in interaction with others.

Deepening concern with the personal, interactional, moral, and political processes of doing fieldwork had also fed into and helped accelerate the reflective turn in ethnography. Emphasis on the inevitably social character of field research dissolved the unexamined assumption that fieldworkers could somehow avoid or transcend the sorts of practical concerns and personal involvements that pervade everyday social life. Personal and interactive processes came to be appreciated as lying at the core of fieldwork. Fieldwork accounts took increasing care to document what the field researcher actually said and did in the field, how those "hosting" the research defined and responded to the fieldworker's words and deeds, and how all these doings influenced the fieldworker's on-the-spot interpretations and more polished analyses of meanings and events.

In the nearly two decades since 1983, appreciation of these reflexive qualities of fieldwork not only has become widely established but also has significantly expanded in scope. In particular, the deepening concern with interpretive and reflexive processes has been complemented by a development only on the horizon in the early 1980s—recognition of ethnography as a form of writing and representation. Building on Geertz's early insistence on inscription as a core ethnographic activity, scholars began to examine the rhetorical and persuasive properties of ethnographies as texts. Indeed, by the late 1980s qualitative research generally and ethnography specifically confronted a significant "crisis of representation" (Denzin and Lincoln 1994). Ethnographic concerns with interpretation, reflexivity and representation coalesced with postmodernist sensitivities and approaches to produce a fundamental reorientation within fieldwork: Whereas in the 1960s and 1970s fieldwork defined itself by contrast with the positivist assumptions of survey and quantitative research, by the 1990s its primary dialogue engaged radically anti-positive postmodern theories that challenged many of its core notions, including "description," "theory," and even "the field."

These developments have shaped ethnographic field research as it enters the twenty-first century in two significant ways: First, ethnography has been transformed from a method of research standing on the edges of mainstream social science to an enterprise positioned at the cutting edge of contemporary social science theory and research. Ethnography now attracts widespread interest, drawing increasing numbers of advocates and practitioners—and critics and detractors—not only from anthropology and sociology, but also from cultural studies, women's studies, critical theory, and queer theory. As a result, there are more researchers who think of themselves as ethnographers, and greater interest in ethnographic findings and methods, than there were several decades ago.

Second, these developments have drastically complicated the face of contemporary ethnography, heightening diversity in stance, style and substance in ways barely anticipated twenty years ago. Gubrium and Holstein (1997), for example, identify four distinctive "idioms of qualitative inquiry"—naturalism, ethnomethodology, emotionalism and postmodernism—each using field research to pursue different questions and concerns, each positing different versions of "the field," and each specifying different methods as appropriate for so doing. Furthermore, fieldworkers advocate and pursue a greater variety of moral and political goals than in the past. Some have extended earlier recognition of the human core of fieldwork into a concern with the personal and the emotional to be realized through "autoethnography." Others call upon a wide variety of methods—intensive interviews, life histories, and narrative analyses—to study a dizzying array of social and cultural phenomena. And still others experiment with a variety of textual forms to present their ethnographies to readers and other audiences.

The increased acceptance of and the growing divergences among current approaches to ethnography have made compiling an overview of contemporary field research a difficult and daunting task. By way of response to these difficulties I have expanded and deepened the introductory materials into more comprehensive reviews of core issues in contemporary ethnography. In these introductory reviews I have tried to cover concerns central both to earlier periods of field research, particularly those marking the beginnings of the reflexive turn in the 1960s and 1970s, and to those raised by contemporary, more radically representational and postmodern approaches to ethnography.

Needless to say, other formulations of and balances between these different themes and diverse ethnographies are possible. The content and emphases evident in the introductory reviews and selected readings that follow inevitably reflect my evaluations of the multiplicity of approaches to ethnography on the current scene. In the following paragraphs I would like to explicate the understandings of fieldwork that have influenced (and, in part, emerged from) my efforts to overview recent developments in ethnography. I expect that this second edition of *Contemporary Field Research* will have particular appeal to ethnographers who share at least some of these understandings, although I hope that the volume will raise issues and suggest possibilities for those who advocate and practice ethnography resting on other principles and assumptions.

First, I share many of the concerns of postmodern approaches to ethnography, including the "doubt that any discourse has a privileged place, any method or theory a universal and general claim to authoritative knowledge" (Richardson 1991:173). However, I see danger in ethnography becoming preoccupied primarily or exclusively with textual and representational processes, whether from adopting "skeptical postmodernist" positions in which "reality is pure illusion" and "everything is intertextual" (Rosenau 1992) or from making texts the primary objects of scholarly attention. For the distinctive value of ethnographic fieldwork derives from its insistence that the researcher quit academic settings, moving out to make direct, close contact with people and the social circumstances within which they live their lives. So viewed, the core of ethnography lies in a set of research practices—practices based on immersion in and firsthand familiarity with varied social worlds—that can generate *discoveries* of new, unappreciated or unacknowledged processes underlying social life. In this respect I share the preferences of a growing collection of "neo-realist" ethnographers who remain committed to at least some of the naturalistic and realist premises that have classically provided warrant for field research.

Second, the possibility of discovery requires openness to the unexpected and the un-hypothesized. One source of such openness derives from ethnography's appreciation of indigenous processes, local categories and concerns, and subjectively meaningful experience. But this openness is also facilitated by analytic approaches that honor and preserve as much as possible of these indigenous meanings and local concerns even while linking them to broader, more general theoretical issues. The materials that follow not only assume that ethnographic fieldwork should make important theoretical contributions, but also that the theory it generates should be closely grounded in what the fieldworker has seen, heard and experienced.

Third, this volume remains committed to the value of self-consciousness at all stages of ethnographic research. Too much fieldwork continues to be carried out naively, borne ahead solely by the enthusiasm of the fieldworker and lacking sustained, considered reflection on just how "data" and "findings" are generated. Yet ethnography is inevitably produced in and through the relations formed by

the ethnographer as an individual and as social actor. Ethnography should examine and explicate the development, impact, and implications of these relations as
they shape both general understanding and specific findings. In so doing, ethnographies need to present the ethnographer in full, rounded form, not simply as
a disembodied textual voice or as a "researcher" but as a whole person with a distinctive personality, preferences and commitments who in part shapes the scene
studied and whose life is affected by doing the study. These deeply personal
qualities, viewed not as liabilities but as mechanisms enhancing deep, original
insight into the lives and concerns of others, should be subject to self-conscious
description and analysis in their own right.

Fourth, while addressed to practicing ethnographers, the examination of
ethnographic issues and concerns in the following pages is not intended primarily as a "how-to-do-it" manual. A number of excellent such manuals exist and
are useful for many purposes. But doing fieldwork is not primarily a matter of
acquiring a set of techniques and specific methods, but an engaged, multi-
phased process of going out, mixing with people and encountering moments and
pieces of their lives, writing accounts of those encounters as some form of "data,"
and thinking about their meaning and theoretical import. These processes are
necessarily highly situational and contextual in character, making it difficult to
identify meaningful principles for proceeding that hold across different settings,
projects, and fieldworkers. In this light, the value of guides to field methods
probably lies less in the recipes they provide on how to proceed in the field and
more in the reassurance they offer that other fieldworkers have encountered
some of the same uncertainties, problems, and dilemmas and have worked out
more or less adequate responses to them. The overviews and readings that follow, by extension, are intended to highlight the underlying assumptions and
implications of fieldwork methods and analytic procedures, addressing not the
issue of how to do it but of just what it is that is being done—that is, the focus is
on fieldwork as methodology, not as method or substance.

Finally, I continue the efforts noted in the first edition to keep bridges open
between sociological and anthropological fieldwork. Despite widespread awareness of ethnography as the study of "the Other" and increasing common ground
in studies of contemporary urban societies, this is an increasingly difficult task.
Sociology and anthropology remain deeply divided by disciplinary traditions and
politics; indeed, I think the two disciplines have grown even further apart during
the past two decades, if only because the increased volume of ethnographic work
makes it more and more difficult for a sociologist to keep abreast of developments in anthropological ethnography and vice versa. Hence, while I have tried
to include extensive discussions and a number of selections from anthropological ethnographers, I expect that this collection will resonate more with sociological as opposed to anthropological field researchers.

My final concern in these prefatory remarks is to acknowledge my debt both
to those who have influenced my understanding and practice of fieldwork and to
those who have provided more immediate help in preparing this volume. I
received my initial training in fieldwork in the 1960s at Brandeis University

under the guidance of Everett C. Hughes, Robert S. Weiss, and Irving K. Zola. Their teachings are reflected in many of the concerns and issues addressed in the following pages. Since coming to UCLA my concerns with ethnography have been shaped and redirected by my exposure to ethnomethodology, particularly as mediated through continuing collaboration with my friend and colleague, Melvin Pollner; Mel's insights inform much of my understanding of ethnography. But over the past several decades I have also been pulled back to and reminded of my Chicago School roots by my other close UCLA colleague, Jack Katz, whose insistently original takes on field research are frequently evident in the pages that follow. I have also benefited from the suggestions and comments of a number of former and current graduate students at UCLA, including Tiffani Chin, Amy Denissen, Bob Garot, Katherine Hill, David Morrison, Julie Peggar, Darin Weinberg, and Sal Zerilli. Similarly, I have frequently sought feedback and support from fieldworkers in other universities, recurrently drawing sustenance in this regard from Robert Dingwall, Jay Gubrium, Jim Holstein, David Snow, Barrie Thorne, Diane Vaughan and Carol Warren. Finally, this project would never have been completed without the encouragement of my wife, Ginger, and the forbearance of our children, Kenny, Nat, Kristin, Eva and Ethan.

Introduction
The Development of
Ethnographic Field Research

In its most inclusive sense, field research is simply research conducted in natural social settings, in the actual contexts in which people pursue their daily lives. The fieldworker ventures into the worlds of others in order to learn firsthand how they live, how they talk and behave, what captivates and distresses them. Whether it is the classic anthropologist trekking across the world to live with some remote tribe, the urban ethnographer moving into some hidden segment of the modern city, the participant observer sharing in and observing the lifeways of a local community or joining the rush-hour commute to study the lifeworlds of modern bureaucrats, the fieldworker's first commitment is to enter the ongoing worlds of other people to encounter their activities and concerns firsthand and close up.

Despite a common commitment to carrying out research in natural settings, fieldworkers' practices for doing fieldwork, and their understandings of these practices, are hardly uniform. In general terms, the practice and theory of fieldwork vary along three dimensions.

First, while all fieldworkers emphasize going to the field—"being there" (Gubrium and Holstein 1997) in some specific local setting—different researchers organize and understand their "being there"—what they actually do in the field—in different ways. In these terms, one major continuum ranges from detached observation on the one hand to full-fledged, active participation in local affairs on the other.

Second, fieldworkers may have different understandings, not only of how to "be there" but also of the major benefits conferred by "being there"—what distinctively can be gleaned and taken away from time spent in the field. At one extreme, going into the field is valued because it affords direct access to events and activities that otherwise would remain undetected or unobservable; at the other, going to the field provides the fieldworker with distinctive access to others' worlds of experience and meaning.

Third, fieldworkers differ in the sense they make of the deeper enterprise in which they are engaging. At one extreme, fieldwork is understood as a relatively unproblematic process of observing, recording and analyzing behaviors and events; at the other, fieldwork is seen as a deeply reflexive process in which "findings" are inseparable from the methods used to generate them.

Those doing fieldwork do not make one-time, in-principle decisions about where to locate themselves on these continua. Rather, fieldworkers continually grapple with the issues underlying these dimensions of difference: where and how to draw lines between detachment and involvement; when to focus on observations of specific actions and behaviors and when to attend empathetically to differing perceptions and understandings; when and where to carry out research as a straightforward matter of describing and analyzing an objectively given, "real" world; and when to direct attention to the ways in which people, including the fieldworker, represent and construct worlds as meaningful.

Nonetheless, sensitivity to these dimensions of difference arose at different "moments" in the historical development of ethnographic field research. In this section I provide an overview of the development of ethnographic fieldwork (at least in the English-speaking world) from the last decades of the nineteenth century. This narrative will focus on the emergence and changing understandings of how the fieldworker positions herself vis-à-vis local settings, of the distinctive value or payoff of fieldwork, and of the positivistic or reflexive character of this overall enterprise. Historically these developments involved the emergence of fieldwork in early anthropology as a form of naturalism, the transformation of naturalistic observation in both anthropology and sociology into full-blown participant observation, increasing emphasis on immersion and empathetic understanding as core processes in participant observation, and finally, deep questioning of prior positivistic assumptions with the turn toward reflexivity.

NATURALISM AND THE BEGINNINGS OF ANTHROPOLOGICAL FIELDWORK

The beginnings of fieldwork in early anthropology took somewhat different forms in Britain and the United States. In nineteenth-century Britain the scholars who developed what eventually became anthropology took up broadly comparative ethnological studies of the distribution and classification of races/peoples within a social evolutionary framework. Evolutionary ethnology assumed a distinctive stance toward these "primitive races":

> These exotic peoples were "savages," "Stone Age men," who bore the rem-
> nants of primitive antiquity. They merited study, not in their own right as
> human beings, but because such study might illuminate the origins of civi-
> lized, European Society and might help explain such puzzling, less civilized
> features of that society as its religious institutions. (M. Wax 1972:2)

Initially scholars of social evolution, such as McLennan, Tylor and Frazer, did
not consider it important to go into the field to collect their own data; they were
armchair theorists who delegated the tasks of data collection to nonscholars
who were on the spot and had some firsthand acquaintance with other peoples—explorers, traders, missionaries, and colonial officials (Stocking 1992:17).

However, the later years of the nineteenth century in British anthropology
saw concern with improving the quality of the materials to be used in evolutionary theorizing. The first efforts to address these problems sought to improve the
data-collection techniques of travelers, missionaries and colonial administrators.
The first edition of the British Association for the Advancement of Sciences'
(BAAS) *Notes and Queries on Anthropology* (1874), for example, sought to "promote
accurate anthropological observation on the part of travelers, and to enable
those who are not anthropologists themselves to supply the information which
is wanted for the scientific study of anthropology at home" (BAAS 1874:iv; cited
in Stocking 1992:17–18). Indeed, British anthropologists continued to work
closely with travelers, missionaries and colonial administrators into the first
decades of the twentieth century, frequently seeking to improve the sensitivities
and data-collecting procedures of those on the front lines (Stocking 1988).

A second approach to improving the quality of information available on
"primitive" peoples emphasized having academically trained scholars directly
organize and oversee the collection of materials. By the end of the nineteenth
century, several important expeditions, modeled on the earlier natural history
exploring and surveying tradition and staffed by academically trained natural
scientists, had collected ethnological artifacts and data. For example, Alfred
Haddon, trained as a zoologist, had intended to study fauna and coral reefs while
on an expedition to the Torres Straits in 1888 but became intrigued by native life
and artifacts. He then devoted his efforts to collecting artifacts on the distribution of material culture, as well as more general ethnological data (Stocking
1992:21). On his return to Britain, Haddon trained himself in physical anthropology and folklore, and from a position at Cambridge in 1898 led a five-man field
expedition to the Torres Straits, organized to have specialists collect physical
measurements as well as data on native psychology, language and social organization (Stocking 1992:22). These and other such expeditions generally involved
short-term stops at a succession of islands where colonial officials and missionaries served as intermediaries in setting up contacts with native peoples. On the
model of biology, these first field naturalists were primarily interested in determining the distribution of native artifacts, skull and other bodily measurements,
local psychology, language, and folklore.[1]

The beginnings of British anthropology were pervaded by concerns with the
dissolution of native societies and traditional ways of life, a stance contemporary

anthropologists characterize as "salvage ethnography" (Gruber 1970). The early development of American anthropology followed a somewhat different course: While also motivated by a concern to create some scientific record of rapidly disappearing native ways of life, particularly with the founding of the Bureau of American Ethnology (BAE) in 1879, American ethnology was very much a "government science" concerned with developing information upon which to base enlightened policies toward Native Americans (Hinsley 1981:145ff). The collection of ethnological material on Native American peoples was directed by and large by the BAE from Washington, combining concerns with both developing "more efficient and humane government policy" toward native peoples and acquiring "better knowledge of civilization through study of its antecedent forms" (Hinsley 1983:54).

Centralizing information on Native American archeology, artifacts and language, BAE also planned and coordinated a series of field surveys of Indian areas, concentrating largely on language and tribal groupings. While the BAE made major improvements in the collection of materials and data on Native Americans and established a group of trained fieldworkers, these fieldworkers worked very much in the survey tradition, collecting information about language and folklore over wide regions through limited contacts with selected informants, visiting rather than living for extended periods of time among those they studied.[2] Moreover, the division of labor within this enterprise minimized the importance of fieldwork, emphasizing the distinction between "the lower, preliminary work of exploration, observation, and collection, and the higher tasks of synthesis" (Hinsley 1981:154), the latter occurring out of the field in museums.

This tradition of fieldwork surveys of Native Americans was transformed in the first decades of the twentieth century largely through the efforts of Franz Boas. Boas had received university training in Germany in physics but undertook a geographically oriented fieldwork project with the Eskimo in 1883 and subsequently became an ethnologist. Moving to the United States, Boas began research on Vancouver Island in 1886, marking the beginning of a lifetime of field research among the Indians of the Northwest Coast. Establishing himself at Columbia University in 1896, Boas became the dominant figure in American anthropology until his death nearly half a century later. Boas articulated and led the anthropological critique of evolutionism, advocating theory and research that would "account for human variability in all its aspects" (Stocking 1992:124). He played a major role in moving the center of American ethnological research from the BAE to academic anthropology based in the universities, in the process upgrading the value of fieldwork and training several generations of academic fieldworkers.

Throughout his career Boas emphasized the importance of rigorous anthropological theorizing driven by data collected systematically through fieldwork. But Boasian fieldwork was fundamentally a process of collecting materials and observations, including artifacts, physical measurements and native-language texts. Boas did insist that fieldworkers become fluent in the native language, in part "because much information can be gained by listening to conversations of the natives and by taking part in their daily lives" (1911:60). Nonetheless Boas continued to subordinate fieldwork to anthropological theory: "Comparing, analyzing, and interpreting sources was considered scholarship; working in the field was *merely* collecting" (Rohner 1966:211).

Furthermore, observation of the talk and activities of everyday life played a minor role in Boas's fieldwork, which typically involved expeditions with stays of relatively brief duration and with frequent movement between settlements and language groups.[3] Until later in his career when his theoretical concerns shifted from historical diffusion, Boas's primary concerns lay in texts and the past, not in current social life and organization. "The observation of behavior in the present was less important than the informant's memory of the way things were, or the details of psychic life as they 'had become fixed in language, art, myth and religion'" (Stocking 1992:124, citing Voget 1968:333–35). As R. Wax observed, "In what was actually going on before their eyes, Boas, and many of the fieldworkers trained by him, evinced relatively little interest" (1971:33). As a result, in the field Boas relied heavily on finding a native informant "who was fluent in English and the native language, knew the old stories and customs, and was willing to dictate and translate texts by the hour, day, week, or month" (R. Wax 1971:32). In these ways Boas remained physically distant from—outside of—the daily lives of "his people." In particular,

> Boas rarely lived in an Indian household or community unless circumstances required that he do so. He usually stayed in a hotel or some other public accommodation within walking distance from the village where he wanted to work. (Rohner 1966:210)

On the eve of World War I, then, both British and American anthropology advocated having academically trained fieldworkers collect ethnographic data. But in addition to decreased reliance on missionaries and other untrained fieldworkers, these years also saw increasing emphasis on another dimension of fieldwork: The fieldworker was no longer conceived as simply an "inquirer" relying upon interviews and questionnaires, usually focused on past events and routine happenings. The fieldworker should also act as *observer*, making direct observations of natives' actual behavior in a variety of circumstances.[4] In part anthropologists turned away from an exclusive reliance on interviews and questionnaires because of increasing uneasiness with the European evolutionary theories that framed these devices. Rivers' "concrete method" in particular valued observation as a way of collecting data uncontaminated by problematic evolutionary assumptions. In the 1912 revision of *Notes and Queries* Rivers insisted that "native terms must be used whenever there is the slightest chance of a difference of category," and urged "the greatest caution . . . in obtaining information by means of direct questions, since it is probable that such questions will inevitably suggest some civilized category" (BAAS 1912:110–11). He also urged investigators to supplement verbal accounts by actually witnessing ceremonies, arguing that "the thorough study of a concrete case in which social regulations have been broken may give more insight . . . than a month of questioning" (BAAS 1912:116).

Fieldwork as observation was also promoted by growing disenchantment with social evolutionary-inspired "survey" expeditions—often based on ship-deck interviews with native informants provided by officials or missionaries—in favor of the "intensive study of limited areas" involving more prolonged stays with a single people. Spencer and Gillen, for example, directly observed an extended religious ritual among the Australian Arunta beginning in late 1896, and subsequently published a highly influential, detailed ethnographic account of their observations (Spencer and Gillen 1899; Stocking 1992:26). Similarly, Radcliffe-Brown spent almost two years in the field among the Andaman. The shift toward this style of "intensive work," involving not only direct observation but also prolonged contact with those studied, is also apparent in Rivers' (1913:7) advocacy of fieldwork

> . . . in which the worker lives for a year or more among a community of perhaps four or five hundred people and studies every detail of their life and culture; in which he comes to know every member of the community personally; in which he is not content with generalized information, but studies every feature of life and custom in concrete detail and by means of the vernacular language.

MALINOWSKI AND FIELDWORK AS SUSTAINED PARTICIPATION

The model of fieldwork as a means for direct observation requiring intensive, prolonged stay in the midst of the daily life of those studied was proclaimed and promoted by Bronislaw Malinowski's publication of *Argonauts of the Western Pacific* (1922). A Polish émigré uprooted by World War I, Malinowski had conducted fieldwork more or less as an exile on several New Guinea islands after the war began: the Mailu Islands from 1914–1915 and the Trobriands in 1915–1916 and 1917–1918. Dissatisfied with earlier fieldwork because "I have rather little to do with the savages on the spot, do not observe them enough" and did not speak their language (Stocking, 1992:43), Malinowski felt he had his most productive time on Mailu when the absence of the local missionary left him "quite alone with the natives" (Malinowski 1915:109). On coming to the Trobriands in 1915, Malinowski soon moved away from the colonial center of Kiriwina to stay six months at the remote village of Omarakana, deliberately isolating himself from contact with all Europeans. As Murray Wax has pointed out, to forsake European society to live among the natives was a highly significant social and personal act: "Between the world of the Melanesian natives and [that] of the British colonial administration was a steep barrier of status, wealth, and power" (1972:5). Later published writings and Malinowski's diary from the period (1967) reveal a deep antipathy to the colonial structure and to its representatives. Malinowski frequently felt out of place in their company and put off by "the manner in which my white informants spoke about the natives and put their views" (1922:5). Entries in his diary reveal that he was often unhappy and depressed on first coming to the Trobriands, when he initially lived in the colonial world, walking daily to native villages to do his work and returning at night. Gradually he began to spend more time alone with the natives, and he reported occasional stays in native villages from early 1915, both activities appearing to have lifted his spirits. By the end of his first field trip Malinowski concluded that "living among the natives (was) personally more pleasant and scientifically more productive" (M. Wax 1972:7).

Upon his return to the Trobriands in late 1917, Malinowski deepened the break from colonial society by setting up permanent residence in the middle of the village of Omarakana, pitching his tent immediately adjacent to the residence of the village chief. Subsequently, in the methodological first chapter of *Argonauts* Malinowski emphasized the major research breakthrough resulting from living "right among the natives" (1922:6). As a general methodological principle ethnographic fieldwork should proceed by "cutting oneself off from the company of other white men, and remaining in as close contact with the natives as possible, which really can only be achieved by camping right in their villages" (1922:6).

In this way Malinowski refocused ethnographic fieldwork toward "living intimately and for a prolonged period of time within a single native community whose language he had mastered" (M. Wax 1972:7). By "living intimately" with those studied the fieldworker's daily life approximates their daily rounds, and exposure and mutual influence increase. Malinowski noted, for example, his natural tendency to spend time with other Europeans when he was bored or depressed by contacts with the natives.

> But if you are alone in a village beyond reach of this [white society], you go for a solitary walk for an hour or so, return again and then quite naturally seek out the natives' society, this time as a relief from loneliness, just as you would any other companionship. And by means of this natural intercourse, you learn to know him, and you become familiar with his customs and beliefs far better than when he is a paid, and often bored, informant. (1922:7)

Malinowski emphasized his deeper appreciation of "the imponderabilia of actual life" afforded by living in the midst of native society:

> Here belong such things as the routine of a man's working day, the details of his care of the body, of the manner of taking food and preparing it; the tone of conversational and social life around the village fires, the existence of strong friendships or hostilities, and of passing sympathies and dislikes between people; the subtle yet unmistakable manner in which personal vanities and ambitions are reflected in the behavior of the individual and in the emotional reactions of those who surround him. (Malinowski 1922:18–19)

Yet while Malinowski lived in the midst of native life, and recurrently described "the Trobriand natives, and by implication all natives, as rational moral human beings in whose society a civilized man would be content to live" (M. Wax 1972:11), he did not participate deeply or intimately, or fully share in that life. While he wrote extensive fieldnotes on his observations and interviews, "recorded to a considerable extent in the native language" (Stocking 1992:46), he was extremely assertive and often imperious in his questioning of natives, in some sense perpetuating veranda-style fieldwork in the midst of the village. More importantly, Malinowski did not live on a level of parity with most villagers: his status was closer to that of the paramount chief, adjacent to whose compound he pitched his tent, and he was served by a small retinue of servants, including two or three New Guinea "cook boys" (Stocking 1992:58). Finally, while Malinowski did develop strong personal ties with some Trobrianders, emphasizing the importance of "personal friendships [to] encourage spontaneous confidences and the repetition of intimate gossip" (1929:282–83), and generally seemed to have been liked and respected (Stocking 1992:50), on some level he continued to regard and refer to natives as "savages."

Malinowski's negative feelings toward the natives were given vivid and direct expression in his posthumously published diaries (1967). However, these sentiments should be understood in context, as Stocking urges: "Without minimizing the pervasive tone of loneliness, frustration, and aggression or the evolutionary racial terms in which these feelings were often expressed, without denying the explicit racial epithets, one must keep in mind that the diary functioned as a safety valve for feelings Malinowski was unable or unwilling to express in his daily relations" (1992:49). Perhaps more critically, despite his methodological commitment to "integrate native behavior into native significance" (1935:86), Malinowski all too often seemed oblivious to native understandings of his own actions, exempting his behavior from native interpretation, in this way only partially and selectively coming to share the perspective of even those Trobrianders with whom he had frequent contact.[5]

Despite these limitations, Malinowski proposed and developed a method and rationale for fieldwork that fundamentally shaped the development of subsequent ethnography. As Stocking summarizes this contribution:

> [Malinowski's fieldwork] involved a shift in the primary locus of investigation, from the deck of the mission ship or the verandah of the mission station to the teeming center of the village, and a corresponding shift in the conception of the ethnographer's role, from that of inquirer to that of participant "in a way" in village life. It also required a shift in theoretical orientation, since as long as "the aim of anthropology [was] to teach us the history of mankind (Rivers 1913:5) the bustle of village activity could only have mediate rather than intrinsic interest." (Stocking 1992:39–40)

Malinowski's influence was direct and immediate on British social anthropology. Receiving an appointment at the London School of Economics in 1925, he trained or influenced such figures such as Evans-Pritchard, Raymond Firth and Hortense Powdermaker, all of whom were carrying out long-term field research on Malinowski's principles by the 1930s. Malinowski appears to have had little influence on American anthropology during the 1920s, as Boas's style and influence remained strong. While Boas's students, notably Ruth Benedict, Margaret Mead, Robert Lowie, and Alfred Kroeber, carried out fieldwork reflecting his theoretical shift of interest from historical diffusion toward the more present-oriented issues of acculturation and the individual and culture, they generally relied more on interviewing than on observation, working from bases near but not in the midst of the lives of those they studied. By the 1940s, however, after a period of increasing interest in Malinowski and the work of his students in the

1930s, American anthropology made ethnographic fieldwork conducted along Malinowski's lines its signature method. But before considering the further development of anthropological fieldwork, it is necessary to turn to the separate yet not unrelated emergence of fieldwork within sociology.

SOCIOLOGICAL FIELDWORK AND THE CITY: THE SOCIAL SURVEY AND THE CASE STUDY

The roots of sociological fieldwork extend back to late nineteenth-century social reform movements, in which observers sought to describe the life and conditions of the urban poor in order to change and better them. Particularly significant for later sociological fieldwork was the social survey movement. Charles Booth's *Life and Labour of the People in London* (1902) remains the best known of these massive surveys, one more systematic form of the "social exploration" (Keating 1976:11ff) following the dramatic changes produced by rapid industrialization and urbanization. The surveys of Booth and others aimed at penetrating and understanding the unknown worlds of the poor. As Booth wrote in *Life and Labour* (cited in Keating 1976:137):

> East London lay hidden from view behind a curtain on which were painted terrible pictures: starving children, suffering women, overworked men, horrors of drunkenness and vice; monsters and demons of inhumanity; giants of disease and despair.

Booth's efforts lay in "showing how things are" behind this curtain, appreciating forms of life fundamentally misconstrued from the outside. Rather than treating the poor as one homogeneous class, for example, Booth distinguished four separate classes of the "poor" and "very poor" and carefully separated Class A, "the lowest class of occasional laborers, loafers, and semi-criminals," from "the criminal class" (Keating 1976:113ff). He also described in detail and with appreciation such key institutions of the East End as the pubs, noting their central place in the life of the community.

In his studies, Booth combined statistical data, widespread interviewing, and direct observation to amass an extremely detailed and systematic description of the lives of the London poor. In their use of direct observation Booth and his colleagues at times entered directly into the world of the poor. In reporting on his initial work in the East End, for example, Booth noted (Keating 1976:125):

> For three separate periods I have taken up quarters, each time for seven weeks, where I was not known, and as a lodger have shared the lives of people who would figure in my schedules as belonging to classes C, D, and E. Being more or less boarded, as well as lodged, I became intimately acquainted with some of those I met, and the lives and habits of many others came naturally under observation.[6]

There was also a vigorous social survey movement in the United States in the first decades of the twentieth century, the most notable examples of which included DuBois's adaptation of Booth's methods for *The Philadelphia Negro* (1899), and the Pittsburgh Survey published between 1910 and 1914 (Bulmer 1984:65–67).

The classic Chicago school of sociology that dominated the discipline during the first decades of the twentieth century first brought this concern with the hidden social life of the city and reforming impulse into the academic establishment (Bulmer 1984). The first sociologists at the University of Chicago were familiar with the social survey movement, and many were actively involved in social reform movements outside the university.[7] But Chicago sociologists, while building on the empirical focus of the social survey movement, significantly modified and added to its program in developing distinctively sociological methods for conducting research on the city and its diverse populations.

Robert E. Park played the central role in this process. A former journalist who came to Chicago Department of Sociology in 1913, Park had deep interests both in race relations and in the city as a distinctive form of social life. Echoing the concerns of the nineteenth-century social surveyors, Park urged exploration of the city's various "natural areas," its tightly knit ethnic settlements and neighborhoods of anonymous rooming-house dwellers, its distinctive occupational and institutional forms, and its underlying patterns of development and change (see Hannerz 1980:23–26). But unlike the social survey movement, Park, while maintaining a lively but "Olympian" interest in social reform, was highly skeptical of moralistic "do-gooding" (Bulmer 1984). Instead he urged an explicitly *scientific* approach aimed at identifying "the processes and forces" that produced social problems (Bulmer 1984:89). The research methods Park helped develop at Chicago thus aimed not at collecting "facts" in order to identify and eradicate specific problems and pathologies, but at collecting broader sets of data relevant to the theoretical understanding of social processes. This empirical bent required tempering reform zeal: Park, for example, insisted that effective response to the rising racial tensions in Chicago culminating in the 1919 riot would be provided not by the morally indignant race-relations crusader but by "the calm, detached scientist who investigates race relations with the same objectivity and detachment with which the zoologist dissects the potato bug" (Bulmer 1984:76; citing Burgess 1961).

During the 1920s Park and his colleague, Ernest W. Burgess, supervised field research leading to a number of classic monographs describing social life in the city. Drawing parallels between procedures of the journalist and the sociologist, Park and Burgess regularly taught an influential graduate course on field studies that quickly propelled students out into the "moral regions" and distinctive social worlds found within the sprawling metropolis. In contrast to the prevailing preference for library research, Park emphasized the value of "firsthand observation" and experience, of having students directly gather sociological data on life in the city's distinctive enclaves and locales:

> You have been told to go grubbing in the library, thereby accumulating a
> mass of notes and a liberal coating of grime. You have been told to choose
> problems wherever you can find musty stacks of routine records based on
> trivial schedules prepared by tired bureaucrats and filled out by reluctant
> applicants for aid or fussy do-gooders or indifferent clerks. This is called
> "getting your hands dirty in real research." Those who counsel you are wise

> and honorable; the reasons they offer are of great value. But one more thing is
> needful: firsthand observation. Go and sit in the lounges of the luxury hotels
> and on the doorsteps of the flophouses; sit on the Gold Coast settees and on
> the slum shakedowns; sit in the Orchestra Hall and in the Star and Garter
> Burlesque. In short, gentlemen, go get the seat of your pants dirty in real
> research. (McKinney 1966:71)[8]

Going out into the field offered another important advantage: It gave the
researcher access to the subjective point of view of those studied. Park was
deeply influenced by William James's "On a Certain Blindness in Human Beings"
(1899), later in his life writing:

> The "blindness" of which James spoke is the blindness each of us is likely to
> have for the meaning of other people's lives. At any rate, what sociologists
> most need to know is what goes on behind the faces of men, what it is that
> makes life for each of us either dull or thrilling. . . . Otherwise we do not
> know the world in which we actually live. (Park 1950:vi–vii)

Concern with examining the subjective elements of social life lay at the center of
the intensive "case study," the eclectic, multi-method approach to field research
Park and Burgess developed in the 1920s. While the case study could include going
into the field to collect existing documents (newspaper stories, official records
from courts, social agencies, and other institutional sources), more emphasis was
given to methods that involved direct contact with those studied, particularly the
collection of "personal documents," interviewing, and direct observation.

The value placed upon personal documents reflected the influence of Thomas and Znaniecki's major monograph on Polish immigration and adaptation to
life in the United States, *The Polish Peasant in Europe and America* (1917). This study
relied heavily upon letters, diaries and life histories written by ordinary people
to capture the subjective aspect of their lives. Thomas maintained that these personal documents were a prime form of sociological data because they allowed
distinctive access to the subject's point of view "in his own words.[9] Park and
Burgess placed similar value upon personal documents, as reflected in the latter's
support of the use of life histories in his preface to Shaw's *The Natural History of a
Delinquent Career* (1931:ix):

> No one will question the value of the life history as a human document when
> written freely and frankly. It admits the reader into the inner experience of
> other men, men apparently widely different from himself: criminals, hobos,
> and other adventurers.

Interviewing comprised a second important tool in the case study method
repertoire. Interviews were not only used to elicit life histories (although many
life histories were autobiographies composed for other than research purposes;
Bennett 1981), but also to collect systematic data on community members, delin-
quents and criminals, and residents of rooming houses (see Bulmer 1984:103–104
for a copy of the formal interview guides used by Zorbaugh in his study of the
near North Side). Little distinction was made between formal and informal
interviewing; both were regarded as part of the case study method, "very much

integrated with other objectives such as gathering personal documents" (Bulmer 1984:102).

Direct observation, combined with informal interviewing, comprised the final method used in the case study. Observation played a key role in two classic Chicago monographs—Nels Anderson's *The Hobo* (1923) and Paul G. Cressey's *The Taxi Dance Hall* (1932)—and less obviously in a third, Frederic Thrasher's *The Gang* (1927). In all these instances the field researcher entered local settings covertly, avoiding open identification as a researcher and seeking to engage "in informal interaction in a situation of anonymity" (Bulmer 1984:105) in order to get behind ordinary appearances and activities.

While these observational procedures anticipated many features of what later became identified as participant observation, they also differed in significant ways. In general, observation was an optional component of the case study approach, which valued going to the field primarily to find or assemble personal documents, only secondarily to make direct observation and conduct informal interviews. Indeed, in some instances observational data were conceived as a specific form of personal document: Thus, the "Documents and Materials" appended to Anderson's *The Hobo* (1923:278–86) lists "Recital of an evening spent by Nels Anderson in a flophouse, April 1922," as well as numerous composite sketches of hobos (e.g., 90, "Home-guard bum, sixty-nine, works at odd jobs, often mendicant, drinks some") and interviews (e.g., 131, "Description of life with 'slum proletariat' by one of them"). Even where observation was emphasized, as in the studies of Anderson and Cressey, the primary value of direct contact and observation lay in allowing the researcher to see for him or herself rather than in providing access to subjective meanings or perspectives. Contact with those studied was typically short-term, situationally specific, and involved little effort to get close on a sustained, everyday basis. Indeed, field researchers' contacts with those studied were frequently mediated through local institutions; for example, fieldworkers used reports of settlement house and other charity workers to describe the community and personal life of specific segments of the poor, deprived, foreign, or delinquent, as well as frequently relying upon life histories and other personal documents assembled in and for these settings.

Overall, then, while the first Chicago sociologists were concerned with the subjective concerns and personal "point of view" of those they studied, personal documents and life histories rather than observation were the primary tools allowing access to these subjective understandings and local meanings. In the case study method, "[a]ccess to personal experience and its meanings is a concern, but this is certainly not seen as achieved by the investigator's sympathetic participation in a role" (Platt 1983:386).

THE EMERGENCE OF PARTICIPATION OBSERVATION IN SOCIOLOGICAL FIELD RESEARCH

In the late 1930s in Chicago sociology the practice of fieldwork couched in terms of the intensive case study began to give way to a model of field research as participant observation. Participant observation asserted that by empathetically participating in an intimate and sustained fashion the fieldworker gained privileged access to the meanings that infuse the daily lives and activities of those studied. Whereas the case study had tended to separate observation on the one hand and understanding the point of view of those studied through personal documents on the other, participant observation displaced this dichotomy, transforming the prior heavily naturalistic conception of observation into a more experiential one emphasizing empathetic involvement as a means for grasping local and subjective meanings.

This transition is reflected in the changing meaning of "participant observer" in the Chicago tradition (Platt 1983). In the 1920s participant observer referred to "a natural insider recruited by the investigator as an informant, not the investigator himself" (Platt 1983:386); thus, a sociologist of religion commented in a 1926 article:

> The minister can be a "participant observer" in religious experience, and if he reports faithfully what he observes we can build up a body of material on the basis of which theological education can be remade. (Holt 1926:227)

While Anderson, Cressey and Thrasher certainly used observational methods, none wrote of "participant observation" but conceived of their research as using the case study or personal documents method, and participated in ways "quite as much oriented to facts as to meanings" (Platt 1983:382).

Platt locates the first contemporary use of the term "participant observation" in Lohman's 1937 article, "The Participant Observer in Community Studies," which contended that "the sympathies and identities established through a close familiarity will reveal meanings and insights denied the formal investigator" (891). The concept was also emphasized by anthropologist Florence Kluckholn in a 1940 article that included a lengthy first-person account of her experiences as a woman fieldworker in a Mexican village. By the 1950s, the term became commonplace in characterizing field research methods (Miller 1952; Vidich 1955; Schwartz and Schwartz 1955; Becker 1958; Gold 1958).

The substantive exemplar of participant observation fieldwork in sociology was William Foote Whyte's *Street Corner Society*, originally published in 1943. Whyte explicitly used the term "participant observation" only in the lengthy methodological Appendix added to the second edition (1955). But his brief discussion of field methods in the 1943 edition did insist that the only way to gain "intimate knowledge of local life" was to "live in Cornerville and participate in the activities of its people" (xv–xvi), and he described these activities in detail, focusing on "particular people and . . . the particular things they do" rather than "people in general" (xix).

Describing the evolution of his study and moving to Cornerville in the 1955 Appendix, Whyte reports that, having received a graduate fellowship at Harvard, he began to pursue a vague idea to study a slum; finding no models for such a community study in sociology, he eventually "began reading in the social anthropology literature, beginning with Malinowski," concluding that this literature "seemed closer to what I wanted to do even though the researchers were studying primitive tribes and I was in the middle of a great city district" (286). After several abortive efforts to make contact with community members and feeling very much an outsider, Whyte only began to gain access to local activities when sponsored by Doc, a local cornerboy introduced to him by a settlement house worker.[10] He quickly concluded that he would not be able to conduct the kind of community research he desired from nearby Harvard:

> To meet people, to get to know them, to fit into their activities, required spending time with them—a lot of time day after day.... Only if I lived in Cornerville would I ever be able to understand it and be accepted by it. (293–94)

Eventually Whyte was able to rent a room with a family in Cornerville, spending some time learning Italian with the father.

Street Corner Society begins very specifically with a description, relying heavily upon detailed fieldnote observations and dialogue as well as informal interviews, of the group activities of "Doc and His Boys." There follows a comparison chapter on a group of "college boys," "Chick and His Club," and then a chapter analyzing the differences between these groups and their effects on individual social mobility. Later chapters expand the scope of analysis, looking at racketeering and political activities in the community, but always dealing with specific groups and individuals and their actual activities. The result is a close-up picture of specific segments of life in this community, a picture clearly reflecting personal relations sustained over an extended period of time with those studied. These qualities gave *Street Corner Society* a strong and immediate impact upon sociological fieldwork; Gusfield, for example, notes that Whyte's field study provided a "newer model" of Chicago sociology for the graduate students entering the Department at the end of World War II (personal communication, Fine 1995:6).[11]

Participant observation fieldwork in the 1940s and 1950s remained predominantly naturalistic in tone. Going to the field required the researcher to participate in local life, such participation affording direct access to events and activities that otherwise would remain undetected or unobservable by outsiders. Thus, participant observation initially involved "observation *in situ*" (Hughes 1971:496), getting into some natural setting in order to observe activities and events close up, as they naturally occur. In this view field research was defined by where it occurs (in the field), a style which persists in some contemporary participant-observation fieldwork in the emphasis on "being there" and on conveying the immediacy and detail of local scenes and activities (Gubrium and Holstein 1997). Moreover, this style of fieldwork could be carried out in a somewhat detached, distanced fashion. The typology of fieldwork roles developed by Gold (1958) and Junker (1960), for example, recognized degrees of involvement, allowing for the possibility of fieldwork as "complete observer" and as "observer as participant," as well as for more active participation.

Similarly, considerations of methods in early participant-observation field research were often instrumental in tone and character, treating participation more as a means of getting close than as an end in itself in providing distinctive experiences. Key methodological issues thus included gaining *access* to specific settings, establishing *rapport* with those studied as a way to create and extend such access, and learning to how explain oneself and one's research concerns in order to "fit in" and minimize the reactive effects of one's presence. Whyte's discussion of "Training in Participant Observation" in the Appendix to *Street Corner Society* (299–309), for example, focused on "learning how to conduct myself" in the different relations and situations he encountered in the field—how to "fit in" to the streetcorner group, how to engage in informal street banter, how and when to ask questions, the complications of managing relations with two somewhat antagonistic groups. While Whyte does provide an account of daily, continuing involvement with different people and groups, it is less an account of immersion than of passing and "fitting in" in order to manage emerging field problems and interpersonal tensions.

A variety of factors influenced this transition from field research as case study to field research as participant observation. First, by late 1930s anthropological ethnographies employing the field research procedures advocated by Malinowski began to appear, providing models for sociological fieldwork. At the University of Chicago, ties between sociology and anthropology remained strong even after the separation (Bulmer 1984:204), with younger anthropologists practicing a Malinowski-style fieldwork based upon immersion and close familiarity.[12] At Harvard, Whyte introduced himself to fieldwork by reading Malinowski and by discussing methods with Conrad Arensberg, an anthropologist who had just completed field research on a rural community in Ireland. Around the time he made contact with Doc and streetcorner life in Cornerville, Whyte also took a course on anthropological community studies taught by Arensberg and Eliot Chapple and had some familiarity with Lloyd Warner's Yankee City field research.

Second, the rise of participant observation coincided with growing criticism of and dissatisfaction with the core of the case study, personal documents and life histories, the prior source of data on people's "subjective experience." Blumer's (1939) critique of Thomas and Znaniecki's use of personal documents in *The Polish Peasant* appears to have been particularly influential in this regard. While Blumer acknowledged that the letters and life histories were of value in representing the "subjective" side of Polish-American experience, he criticized Thomas and Znaniecki's frequent failure to link their theoretical claims convincingly to this data. Blumer also expressed reservations about the evidentiary strength of personal documents, questioning the assumption that those studied could directly convey their own meanings and experiences through such materials. He noted, for example, that the letters were "fragmentary," represented events at single moments in time, and reflected highly situational concerns (e.g., immigrants' preoccupation with money), while life-history interviews produced polished and dramatic accounts incorporating distinctive versions of informant self.[13]

Third, increased awareness of the limitations of personal documents coincided with rising sociological interest in face-to-face interaction, processes particularly suited to the procedures of participant observation. Whyte was influenced by Harvard social scientists, including Arensberg, Mayo, Roethlis-berg and Dickson, who emphasized the primacy of social interaction for the study of communities and organizations. *Street Corner Society* is devoid of life his-tory and personal document data. Whyte advocated observing interaction as an "objective" method for collecting field data on social structure. More consequen-tially for participant observation, Blumer at the same time was beginning to for-mulate his version of symbolic interactionism, which eventually came to provide a major theoretical justification for field methods. Blumer emphasized the need for sociological theory and method to grasp and incorporate the meanings people assigned to objects in their world, since all social action was organized on the basis of these meanings. While Blumer did not publish a fully elaborated state-ment of his symbolic interactionist approach until 1969 (Colomy and Brown 1995), symbolic interactionist sensitivities are clearly evident in many of the leading participant observation studies published in the 1950s and 1960s.

Fourth, self-conscious use of the term "participant observation" and its explicit elaboration as a distinctive method were closely linked with the success within sociology of the new survey research methods associated with Lazarsfeld and Merton at Columbia in the 1940s (R. Wax 1971; Platt 1983). Proponents of sur-vey research claimed strict scientific rigor in the use of statistical techniques, experimental design, and other such methods. As Wax suggested (1971:40), "Faced with this challenge, a cluster of Chicagoans came to scrutinize their methodology more closely and to reconceptualize it around the term 'participant observation.'" The result was the crystallization of a dichotomy between "quantitative" and "qualitative" methods, accompanied by the elaboration and explicit justification of the latter in the methodological writings on fieldwork and participant observation produced in the 1950s (e.g., Vidich 1955; Vidich and Bensman 1954; Dean 1954).

Finally, the rise of self-conscious participant observation reflected signifi-cant changes in the social status and backgrounds of many sociological field-workers. Early Chicago fieldworkers came to sociology from established places in the worlds they studied. Hughes has noted, for example, that Park frequently took established "insiders" and converted them to sociology (1971:547):

> The First World War had broken the careers of many young Americans of religious and reforming bent. For a number of them who turned up in the department of sociology at Chicago, Park made an object of study and a new career out of what had been a personal problem or a crusade. Two, Frederic Thrasher and Clifford Shaw, probation officers, wrote *The Gang* and *The Natu-ral History of a Delinquent Career*, groundbreaking monographs. Wirth, a social worker, became a sociologist and wrote *The Ghetto*.

The career of Nels Anderson perhaps best exemplifies this practice of field research by established insiders. Anderson had been raised in and on the edges of the hobo world, and he had been a hobo for a number of years before attending college and then beginning graduate study in sociology at the University of Chi-cago (1923/1961:v–xiii). As he remarked retrospectively on his field research for *The Hobo* (xiii):

> I did not descend into the pit, assume a role there, and later ascend to brush off the dust. I was in the process of moving out of the hobo world. To use a hobo expression, preparing the book was a way of "getting by," earning a living while the exit was under way. The role was familiar before the research began.

In other instances, sociologists had established ties with settings of interest before beginning their research. Through his connections at Hull House, for example, W. I. Thomas developed ties with settlement house workers and others working with "unadjusted girls." In many cases, then, early Chicago fieldworkers had established places in the worlds to be studied, places that were created independently of their research concerns but could be used to do ground fieldwork.

Where people are already intensely involved in activities and groups that they then come to study, the typical problems seem to involve creating sufficient distance and detachment to begin to look at these matters sociologically. Park, in particular, emphasized this sort of detachment and "objectivity" in his teachings. In contrast, participant observation emphasized gaining access, creating trust and rapport, getting close—in short, immersion. This emphasis reflected the fact that fieldworkers were increasingly from middle-class and academic backgrounds and necessarily began as *outsiders* to the settings and activities they studied. Again, Whyte provides the model here, in his Appendix self-consciously talking about his middle-class origins, his brief glimpse of a Philadelphia slum on a college fieldtrip, his deep commitment to social reform (1955:280–83). Clearly, Whyte was able to cross significant class and ethnic barriers more fully than many of the earlier Chicago fieldworkers, entering as an outsider and becoming immersed in a world strange and unknown to him.

As the fieldworker increasingly began as an outsider to the groups and settings under study, directly crossing major ethnic, class, and status barriers, the processes of establishing trust and rapport, of sustaining ongoing personal relations under difficult circumstances, became more problematic. Field relations had to be negotiated and hence became more overtly problematic, increasing fieldworker sensitivity to the salience of personal ties and reactions, and to the difficulties of grasping the meanings and understandings of new and strange peoples. Moreover, as familiarity and closeness became more problematic, fieldworkers increasingly emphasized and self-consciously addressed processes of involvement and sympathetic understanding rather than detachment and distance.

IMMERSION AND REFLECTION
IN LATER PARTICIPANT OBSERVATION

As participant observation was elaborated as *the* method of field research, emphasis on immersion and sympathetic understanding, on grasping the particular feel and constraints of some of local scene or way of life, came to complement and sometimes supersede the earlier emphasis on social proximity and observation in situ. By the 1970s, participant observation fieldwork was strongly linked with identifying and describing the subjectively meaningful worlds of others (see Emerson 1981:354–57). As Lofland insisted, "In order to capture the participants 'in his own terms' one must learn their analytic ordering of the world, their categories for rendering explicit and coherent the flux of raw reality" (1971:7). Increasingly, fieldworkers found that the key to good participant observation was not simply in "physical presence at the location where interaction occurs," but in close, intimate and active involvement in the routines, rhythms and intricacies of people's daily lives. Goffman provided a forceful statement of this approach in his preface to *Asylums*:

> My immediate object in doing fieldwork at St. Elizabeth's was to try to learn about the social world of the hospital inmate, as this world is subjectively experienced by him. . . . It was then and still is my belief that any group of persons—prisoners, primitives, pilots, or patients—develop a life of their own that becomes meaningful, reasonable, and normal once you get close to it, and that a good way to learn about any of these worlds is to submit oneself in the company of the members to the daily round of petty contingencies to which they are subject. (1961a:ix–x)

Through intense participation and immersion, the fieldworker could "grasp the symbolic nexus between thought and action in a particular social milieu" (Schwartz and Merten 1971:280–81). Thus, the participant observer enters the worlds and activities of others, not primarily to be there in a physical sense, but to experience *their* "matrix of meanings . . . , to participate in their system of organized activities, and to feel subject to their code of moral regulation" (M. Wax 1980:272–73).[14]

Adoption of the term "ethnography" to characterize sociological fieldwork provides one indication of this change in the participant observers' self-understanding. While anthropological fieldworkers had described themselves as ethnographers from at least the 1920s (as in Malinowski's famous photo titled "The Ethnographer at Work"), and ethnography had become synonymous with anthropology by the 1940s, sociological fieldworkers adopted the term much later. A key moment occurred in 1972 with the publication of *Urban Life and Culture*, a journal explicitly devoted to publishing "works of urban ethnography."[15] Lofland's introduction to the first issue characterized the research style of urban ethnography as "the close-up study of the urban world." Such study required sustained "face-to-face proximity" and "faithfully representing the meanings—the phenomenology—of the people in the circumstances [the fieldworker] seeks to understand" (Lofland 1972:4). General acceptance of the term ethnography to characterize sociological fieldwork led to the change in name to *Journal of Contemporary Ethnography* in 1987.

Increased emphasis in participant observation on immersion as a means of understanding local meanings involved a number of further changes in and refocusing of fieldwork methods. First, field research became assertive in claiming a distinctive approach to the acquisition of knowledge. Ethnographers began to argue that interpretive understanding based on participation did not produce merely intuitive insight or personal "hunches" that at best could serve as hypotheses to be verified by more systematic, quantitative methods. Rather, field research produced rigorous knowledge of the social world that is held in common by members of a particular society or social group. Drawing upon Blumer's fully elaborated statement of symbolic interactionism and other sources, participant-observation fieldwork claimed to generate rigorous knowledge of social life in that it was founded upon "the perspectives of the actors themselves and upon the categories of distinctions which the actors recognize and respond to" (M. Wax 1967:329).

Participant-observation fieldwork emphasizing immersion and local meanings also accelerated the greater self-conscious about methodological issues that had begun in sociological fieldwork in the late 1940s and 1950s. Explicit considerations of the validity of field data continued to appear (e.g., Schwartz and Schwartz 1955; Becker 1958; Zelditch 1962). Fieldworkers began to publish detailed reflections on the problems of establishing and maintaining field roles (e.g., Gold 1958; Junker 1960), and they began to provide increasingly elaborate accounts of the methods used to collect data for monographs (e.g., Vidich, Bensman and Stein 1964).

Along with this heightened concern with formal methods, more assertive participant-observation fieldwork developed stronger commitment to using field data for sociological theorizing. Initially field research's growing theoretical sophistication centered on evaluations of the procedures of analytic induction developed by Znaniecki (1934) and elaborated by Cressey in his study of embezzlement (1953). But the 1960s brought both a general statement of the grounded theory approach to the analysis of qualitative data (Glaser and Strauss 1967), and a number of substantive studies employing and illustrating the use of the grounded theory method (Glaser and Strauss 1965, 1968, 1971). Lofland (1974, 1976) similarly emphasized the importance of producing general theory from field data while continuing to base such study on close observation of particular groups and settings.

Finally, this period saw growing interest in and concern with participant observation as a personal, experiential process. This coincided with a gradual shift away from an earlier concern with the distorting effects of participant observation. Anthropological accounts first appearing in the late 1930s urged that the personal biases of the fieldworker be brought into the open (e.g., Dollard 1937; Mead 1949; Redfield 1953; Lewis 1953); somewhat later attention turned to the ways in which the researcher's role and relations shaped and restricted what information he or she could collect (Paul 1953; Berreman 1962). In sociology, Schwartz and Schwartz (1955) in particular emphasized that fieldwork involves "affective participation," often of a very deep and profound sort, which had to be recognized in order to overcome its "distorting" tendencies. By the 1950s these warnings were accompanied by growing recognition of the positive consequences of affective involvement and immersion. Thus, Whyte argued in the Appendix to *Street Corner Society* that his analyses "grow up in part out of our immersion in the data and out of the whole process of living. . . . [M]uch of this process of analysis proceeds on the unconscious level" (1955:280). Schwartz and Schwartz insisted that affective participation, directed in balanced, self-conscious ways, could produce "sympathetic identification" and "more meaningful and valid data" (1955:100). Similarly, fieldworkers took note of the profoundly personal dimensions of fieldwork. Whyte's "Appendix" again played a key role here, as he maintained that the "real explanation . . . of how the research was done necessarily involves a rather personal account of how the researcher lived during the period of study" (1955:279), in this way helping establish the personal account as a genre of ethnographic writing.

THE REFLEXIVE TURN

As commitment to active research participation involving immersion, empathy and shared experience spread, ethnographers began to explore and elaborate the implications of these qualities for field research. These efforts took two interrelated forms: first, increasing questioning of the realist presuppositions that underlay the earlier model of fieldwork as detached observation in situ; and second, growing appreciation of the implications of *reflexivity* for ethnographic fieldwork.

By the 1960s there were clear indications that ethnographers had begun to problematize, and sometimes reject outright, key realist tenets that had undergirded earlier fieldwork theory and practice. Observational field research had assumed that fieldwork involved straightforwardly and "objectively" looking at and recording objects that possessed pre-established, fixed and invariant meanings. Ethnographers increasingly questioned these realist assumptions, often rejecting the idea that "the world 'out there' is isomorphic in every respect with the image the detached observer will form of it" (Nash and Wintrob 1972:529). Instead, fieldworkers began to understand reality as complex, allowing multiple interpretations, shifting in meaning, depending upon the researcher's theoretical concerns and orienting questions.

Indeed, many ethnographers moved to the position that social reality is at least in part a product of an investigator's efforts to apprehend and describe it. This view fundamentally reconceptualizes what had previously been seen as a one-way relation between reality and representation. Reality is not a pre-existing, objective entity, and representation a more or less accurate mirroring of that entity; rather, reality and representation are related *reflexively*, each shaping and hence constituting the other. Reflexive approaches thus view social reality as constructed or accomplished exactly by efforts to capture and represent it rather than as something that is simply "there."

The questioning and at least partial rejection of simple realism and the related turn toward reflexivity have reverberated throughout contemporary ethnographic field research. These developments can be characterized as producing a contemporary "crisis" (e.g., Lincoln and Denzin 1994), implying a clear-cut, radical break with prior practice. But it is probably more useful to note that ethnographic sensitivity to these matters emerged gradually, as fieldworkers recognized and explored a variety of puzzles and issues arising within full-blown participant observation and its emphasis on immersion as a method for acquiring experiential knowledge of other social worlds. These issues involved changing understandings of three key processes: detachment, observation and representation.

The Limits of Detachment

Participant-observation urgings to get "close" to those studied, to achieve empathetic involvement in their lives, generated numerous tensions with prior, more impersonal and distanced models of field relations. In many cases fieldworkers began to question the assumptions of professional distance and careful,

nonreactive presence that had marked prior fieldwork practice, frequently opt-
ing for "increasing personal involvement . . . with their subjects" (Nash and Wintrob 1972:529). This tendency is strikingly evident in the publication of extended
accounts of the personal processes and problems arising in fieldwork (e.g., R.
Wax 1960; Maybury-Lewis 1965; Powdermaker 1966; Briggs 1970; Johnson 1975).
In detailing the relational, personal and emotional aspects of fieldwork, these
personal accounts depicted the fieldworker not as "a self-effacing creature without any reactions other than those of a recording machine," but rather as "a *human*
scientist whose own self and relationships with subjects have become important
factors in evaluating his observations" (Nash and Wintrob 1972:527, 528).[16]

Relatedly, ethnographers increasingly rejected notions of fieldwork as
detached observation in favor of the imagery of fieldwork as a profound, experiential encounter with the lives, behaviors, and thoughts of those from different
social worlds. Such appreciation of the worlds and concerns of others was characterized as a form of *verstehen, or interpretive understanding,* a mode of inquiry
leading to "the perception of action as meaningful" (M. Wax 1967:332). Such
understanding required grasping holistically "the vast background of shared
meanings" through which the social world is organized into socially recognized
categories in the first place (M. Wax 1967:326). The ethnographer

> . . . begins "outside" the interaction, confronting behaviors he finds bewilder-
> ing and inexplicable. . . . the fieldworker finds initially that he does not under-
> stand the meanings of the actions of this strange people, and then gradually
> he comes to be able to categorize peoples (or relationships) and events: e.g.,
> this man who is visiting as a brother-in-law to my host; last week his wife
> gave mine a gift; today he is expecting some reciprocity. (M. Wax 1967:325)

Indeed, ethnographers began to characterize fieldwork as a process of resocialization: Sharing the lives of others, the field researcher comes "to enter into the
matrix of meanings of the researched, to participate in their system of organized
activities, and to feel subject to their code of moral regulation" (M. Wax
1980:272–73). Actively participating in another way of life, the ethnographer
learns what is required to become a member of that world, to experience events
and hence to understand what they mean and portend to others.

Finally, discomfort with the idea of detachment also appeared in responses to
accusations of significant "reactive effects" in fieldwork resulting from high levels of
immersion and involvement. For example, Becker consistently defended participant
observation methods with the argument that reactive effects tend routinely to be
neutralized; that is, those studied are interactionally and institutionally constrained
in ways that make it difficult if not impossible for them to consistently present a
false front to the fieldworker over the long term. Other fieldworkers offered radical
reframings of reactive effects, taking the position that researchers could learn more
by describing and analyzing just what their effects were on those studied than by
trying to minimize or eliminate them (Gussow 1964). It is a short step from this
stance to questioning the very conception and possibility of total detachment and
elimination of reactive effects in fieldwork (Katz 1983; Pollner and Emerson 1983).

The Complexities of Observation

Earlier fieldwork had assumed that observation was a simple, straightforward process: The observer looked and saw "things"—"real objects" that were fixed, stable, and inherently meaningful—that could be more or less faithfully reported to others. Moreover, since objects had fixed and invariant meaning, these objects could be apprehended by anyone who cared to look at or for them. Later fieldworkers, however, increasingly recognized the limitations and inadequacies of these assumptions, becoming more and more sensitive to previously unappreciated complexities of observation (see Part I).

Questions about a simple realist understanding of observation assumed direct salience to a key ethnographic task—assembling richly textured and accurate *descriptions* of other social worlds. Producing such descriptions was not a simple matter of observing and recording what was "there," since it quickly became clear that if two observers looked at the same social reality, they could well come up with two essentially different ethnographic descriptions. Observation, then, could only occur through specific lenses, and descriptions involved complex and problematic processes of understanding and interpretation filtered through these lenses. These lenses were provided not only by the ethnographer's theoretical commitments and by the cultural categories used to observe, order, and describe events, but also more generally by how the ethnographer attended to what was to be observed and described.

Field researchers then had to reassess prior understandings of the nature of observation and description. As multiple descriptions of the same scene, activity or culture came to be recognized as legitimate, ethnographers moved from conceptualizing such descriptions as independent, objective reports to seeing them as products of the describer and his or her actual methods for making and reporting observations. And from here, it was often a short step from pointing to observer effects on descriptions of social reality to contending that the observer created or constituted these realities exactly through these descriptions.

Ethnographic Writing and Representation

Recognition that ethnographies did not provide "literal descriptions" mirroring the reality of other ways of life also led to new appreciation of the salience of writing and representation for the ethnographic enterprise. Geertz's (1973a and this volume) early insistence on the centrality of *inscription* in ethnography sparked growing recognition that the ethnographer "writes into being," as well as explores, exotic and familiar social worlds. This insight fundamentally transformed ethnography's self-understanding. Field research was not simply going to the field, but also (and more critically) generating written accounts of what had been seen and experienced in the field. As Clifford (1986b:115) and others insisted, the ethnographer "translates experience into text," continually and successively writing accounts *"re-presenting"* moments and slices of ongoing social life to various readers. Again, ethnographic writing was not just a straightforward account on paper of what had been observed, but more deeply and fundamentally a partial, selective and purposed re-presentation of these ways of life gleaned through the researcher's efforts to get physically and socially close. Doing ethnography, then, was not simply a matter of "grasping what's there through close participation," but of actively interpreting ongoing social life and transforming those experiences and interpretations into texts that could be made available to others as versions or representations of "what's there."

This reflexive turn in ethnography was fueled by and intricately linked to changes in the structure and practice of fieldwork. These changes destroyed the sheltered environments that had sustained simple realist assumptions by enabling ethnographers to disregard the infrastructures that supported and facilitated fieldwork.

First, the years following the end of World War II saw the decline of the colonial regimes that had created and maintained the conditions for conducting field research (Maquet 1964; Asad 1973). The pervasive and yet often unspoken power of the colonial presence could be relied on to facilitate many of the nitty-gritty tasks of fieldwork, such as securing access and cooperation. Yet under most conditions, the fieldworker tended to remain oblivious to this power.[17] Indeed, Barnes (1967) argued that the colonial system provided a structure that had allowed anthropological fieldworkers to view the field and those in it with complete detachment, as if it were a natural science laboratory: "The field of inquiry was perceived as exterior to themselves, something which could be observed by an outsider without significant distortion" (194).

With the decline of colonialism, conditions that had been taken for granted became uncertain and problematic. Researchers had to obtain more direct approval of the people to be studied, without implicit or explicit reliance upon colonial power. As Nash and Wintrob suggested, the fieldworker "had to take the native point of view into account before, during, and after his field research. It became more important than ever before to be aware of what the natives were thinking" (1972:531). As access and the day-to-day process of fieldwork became more problematic, more dependent on actively establishing working relations with particular people, personal and relational self-consciousness inevitably increased. Under these conditions it is difficult for the fieldworker to avoid confronting his or her own activities and uses of power, or to maintain an image of the field as essentially independent of such activities (Gupta and Ferguson 1997a). The notion of the field as scientific laboratory, a notion that maximizes distance between studier and studied by positing (and creating!) essential differences between them, becomes much more effortful to maintain.

Second, fieldwork experience in sociology became denser and more complex as mediated contact with those studied and initial insider status declined. The field researcher not only had to work at establishing close relations directly with those studied, as noted earlier, but also became more sensitive to the quality and uncertainty of these relations. In such fully participant-observational field research the fieldworker's own experiences were recognized as more central to the actual processes of collecting data. Closer attention to the fieldworker's own interactional and role problems was also encouraged by symbolic interactionism's concern with the creation of meaning in and through interaction.

Finally, fieldworkers were forced to confront the fact that their research could be read by those it was about, and they increasingly had to anticipate and deal with these reactions. In anthropology, with the decline of colonialism and the spread of literacy, ethnographic monographs began to attract the attention of governmental administrators and of the people studied. Similarly, a number of sociological fieldworkers found they could no longer count on their subjects remaining ignorant of or uninterested in ethnographic accounts of their lives (although this assumption does persist; see Ellis 1995b). Vidich and Bensman's *Small Town in Mass Society* (1958), for example, generated intense criticism both from the community studied and from academics; they responded by issuing a revised edition (1968) that specified their methodological procedures and elaborated their theoretical position. Under these conditions, the previously unexamined assumption that fieldwork occurred in but not necessarily as *part of* the field became increasingly untenable. Fieldworkers were hard pressed to depict even highly descriptive ethnographies as simply "scientific" accounts and to maintain that these accounts had no significant impact on those they studied. A simple, realist version of ethnography as objective, fact-based reports—created independently of, and without significant effects for, those observed and described—assumed that the subjects of these accounts would neither read them nor respond to them effectively. These changes, then, tended to break down "the division between those under the microscope and those looking scientifically down the eyepiece" (Barnes 1967:197).

PLAN OF THE BOOK

The introductory material and readings that follow explore the expressions and implications of the reflexive turn in fieldwork. Part I, "The Face of Contemporary Ethnography," takes up in detail the issues made problematic by the reflexive turn in ethnography—the processes of observing and describing others' social realities, and the nature of ethnographic writing, representation and authority. Part II picks up ethnographers' efforts to develop the implications of actually doing involved, participatory fieldwork. Departing from Cicourel's (1964) insistence that "the observer is part of the field of action," and hence *what* is known can never be grasped independently of *how* it is known, this section considers the relevance of field relations for "findings," and the implications of the emerging, more humanistic conception of fieldwork practice. These matters are directly related to the further ethical and political issues that fieldwork inevitably generates. Finally, Part III turns to issues of producing and evaluating fieldwork accounts. It addresses three major issues: (1) how fieldworkers generate theory of general scope and applicability from data that seek to capture the distinctive meanings of events and objects in a particular social world; (2) what kinds of criteria are appropriate for appraising the adequacy of the findings and theoretical claims at which we ultimately arrive through field research; and (3) how ethnographers assemble and convey, in different textual forms, significant aspects of their field experience and knowledge of other social worlds.

NOTES

[1] Haddon subsequently introduced the term "field-work" into anthropology in promoting the training of "field-anthropologists" (Haddon 1903; cited in Stocking 1992:27).

[2] The intensive fieldwork conducted by Frank Cushing at a single Zuni pueblo for two and a half years beginning in 1879 provides a major exception. Cushing lived in the quarters of the Zuni governor of the pueblo when the BAE survey expedition of which he was part moved on, was adopted by a Zuni family, and participated in daily life (he was given his Zuni name, Medical Flower, because of his efforts to treat ill pueblo children), eventually learning the language and participating in and observing Zuni religious ceremonies (Hinsley 1981, 1983). Recent analyses (e.g., Clifford 1997) argue that Cushing's intensely participatory fieldwork practice was marginalized and ignored as a model of participant observation because of its incompatibility with developing scientific justifications of fieldwork.

[3] Between 1886 and 1930 Boas made thirteen field trips to the Northwest Coast, spending a total of just less than two and a half years in the field (Rohner 1966:152).

[4] One of the earliest instances of distinctively observational fieldwork is provided by Alice Fletcher, who spent some time living with and observing a group of Sioux Indians in 1881 self-consciously using a model of astronomy, employing "long periods of looking (and listening) and meticulous recording of what one saw and heard" (Reinharz 1992:49–50, quoting Mark 1988).

[5] Malinowski's failure to share the natives' perspective is strikingly revealed in a series of passages from his diary, quoted by M. Wax (1972:11), in which he expresses irritation with two aristocratic natives for taking too much of his supply of betel-nut. As Wax suggests, "To help themselves to his supply was impudence from the European perspective. Yet to withhold his supply was, for the natives, failure to acknowledge native norms of generosity. The native view is evident in Malinowski's comment (1935/1965:40–41) on the Paramount Chief: were his stores of tobacco or betel-nut "exposed to the public gaze, he would, on the principles of *noblesse oblige*, have to distribute them among the surrounding people." Clearly, Malinowski failed to apply the "native" patterns he analyzed so closely with his own situation and experience in the field.

[6] Similarly, Beatrice Potter, a coworker of Booth's who later married social reformer Sidney Webb, regularly ventured into the day-to-day life of the poor, working as a seamstress in order to experience sweatshop conditions firsthand (Webb 1926). Park was familiar with and favorably disposed toward both Booth's survey (Bulmer 1984:71) and the substantive and methodological writings of the Webbs (R. Wax 1971:39).

[7] The reform efforts of Albion Small are well known, as are Robert Park's pre-University of Chicago participation in the Congo Reform Association and his long-term connection with Booker T. Washington and the Tuskegee Institute. In addition, both W. I. Thomas and George Herbert Mead regularly participated in the reform activities centered around Hull House, the leading social settlement house in the country and a source of great intellectual and social ferment (see Deegan and Burger 1978, 1981). Thomas, for example, was a personal friend of Hull House founder and leader Jane Addams and was closely connected with a variety of reform movements radiating from Hull House, including the juvenile court movement, child protection, and a variety of reform efforts concerned with prostitution, immigration, and race relations (Deegan and Burger 1981).

[8] In his influential article "The City" (1915/1952:15), Park cited not only the methods of the social survey movement but also the work of contemporary anthropologists, including Boas and Lowie, as examples of how to carry out the sociological exploration of the city. W. I. Thomas was similarly familiar with the work of Boas and remained deeply interested in comparative studies, ethnography, and evolutionary issues right up to his death in 1941 (Janowitz 1966:xx). Indeed, at the University of Chicago sociology and anthropology were a combined department until 1929, and after formal separation Park worked closely with a number of students who became well-known anthropologists, notably Robert Redfield.

[9] Indeed, Thomas preferred personal documents to interviews, feeling that the latter "manipulated the respondent excessively" (Janowitz 1966:1).

[10] As noted above, early Chicago fieldworkers had relied on the settlement house and the social worker for access to groups with whom the latter worked, and had remained relatively oblivious

to the limited place of social agencies and reform groups in urban ethnic communities. Thus, Whyte's approach to the field in *Street Corner Society* is also significant in that he left the settlement house through which he initially made contact with his main informant, Doc (1955:290ff), and ventured out directly onto the streets to become immersed in the everyday world of the cornerboys. Indeed, it was only with the perspective gained from the streets that Whyte came to recognize that the primary function of the settlement house was "to stimulate social mobility, to hold out middle-class standards and middle-class rewards to lower-class people" (1955:104). Again, to leave the settlement house was also to leave the pre-established set of relations it provided and to enter into the highly problematic and uncertain task of developing working personal relations on the street.

[11] Boelen (1992) has recently raised questions about Whyte's fieldwork methods and had challenged a number of his substantive findings, including his account of group structure and leadership and the position of the racketeer in the local community. Boelen's "reexamination" of Cornerville based on interviews with some of those described in *Street Corner Society*, Whyte's response, and several commentaries and reflections on their differences, appeared in a special issue of the *Journal of Contemporary Ethnography* (v. 21, n. 1).

[12] Blanchard (1979:423), for example, recounts how Sol Tax sought to emulate Malinowski's fieldwork by setting up "a camp of my own in the midst of native camps" among the Fox Indians in Iowa in 1932. The Fox, however, thought Tax foolish to "stay out there and cook for myself like a squaw when I could get to town in five minutes."

[13] In later years this line of criticism was expanded to emphasize that the Chicago School fieldwork in general evinced little or no concern with the circumstances and constraints under which personal documents were produced; hence, classic Chicago criminology treated life histories written by or for probation officers as essentially equivalent to those written by the subject for the researcher or elicited via interviews from the subject (Bennett 1981).

[14] This development was part of a wider sociological commitment to what Matza (1969:25) characterized as *appreciation*, that is, seeking "to comprehend and to illuminate the subject's view and to interpret the world as it appears to him."

[15] Indeed, the first editor, John Lofland, originally proposed the title *Journal of Urban Ethnography*. In response to the publisher's objection that "the word 'ethnography' was often confused with the word 'ethnology' and, by extension, 'ethnic studies,'" Lofland accepted the title *Urban Life and Culture* "as the closest equivalent to 'ethnography'" (1987:26).

[16] The proliferation of such accounts is primarily a function of the increased importance accorded personal and relational processes in fieldwork. Nash and Wintrob suggest that the generation of anthropological fieldworkers who followed Boas and Malinowski certainly became involved in the lives of the peoples they studied; but adhering to prevailing notions of scientific objectivity, they were unwilling or unable to publish accounts of these personal experiences.

[17] Such obliviousness characterized Malinowski's fieldwork in the Trobriands (M. Wax 1972). Malinowski simply assumed that he had the right to pitch his tent in the middle of Omarakana and that the local authorities would cooperate with his efforts. Wax suggests that this cooperation was forthcoming from the paramount chief on the assumption that Malinowski would reciprocate in some way by influencing the British colonial administration favorably toward him, an obligation to which Malinowski simply seemed blind.

PART I

The Face of Contemporary Ethnography

Coming to terms with the implications of full-blown participant observation and its emphasis on immersion has propelled the recent development of ethnographic field research. As suggested previously, key issues arose with the problematization of simple realism and the related reflexive turn in ethnography. This section will map the contours of these issues. It will begin by tracing the growing recognition of the complexities of the core ethnographic activity—observing and *describing* other ways of life. It will then consider the deeply reflexive turn in ethnography arising from recognizing ethnography as a form of *representation* involving distinctive forms of interpretation and writing. Finally, it will consider responses to emerging tensions between relativism and realism in contemporary ethnography.

DOING ETHNOGRAPHIC DESCRIPTION

In a generic sense an ethnography provides "a description of the way of life, or culture, of a society" that identifies "the behaviors and the beliefs, understandings, attitudes, and values they imply" in that social world (Berreman 1968:337). Ethnographic field research assembles the sorts of data that can be used to construct rich, empirically based descriptions of such social life and activities. Field researchers, however, now recognize that describing the activities and realities of other people is not as straightforward a task as it had initially appeared. First, there are problems inherent in the description of even the most commonplace or "obvious" events and activities, problems noted earlier with regard to the limitations of strict realist assumptions. Second are the perhaps more vexing problems which derive both from the distinctive character of social realities and from the ethnographer's specific interest not simply in "events" and "activities" them-

selves but in the ways in which they are engaged, guided, described, and generally assigned significance by group members.

The Limits of "Literal Description"

As noted previously, realist approaches had rested on a model of "literal"
description. Two fundamental assumptions sustained this model: First, description involves stable "real objects" that can be straightforwardly observed and
recorded because they possess inherent meanings. On looking, the observer sees
"things"—"brute data"—that can be more or less faithfully reported to others.
Second, since objects have fixed and invariant meaning, these objects can be
apprehended by anyone who cares to look at or for them. Thus, if two observers
look at the same "thing," they will come up with essentially the same descriptions
of it. Fieldworkers concerned with ethnographic description found the notion of
literal description unsatisfactory and have increasingly questioned these assumptions regarding inherent meaning and observer-independent means of discovery.

In the first place, where to look, what to look at, and how to report what has
been observed are not the almost mechanical processes that the model of literal
description implies. It is impossible to observe everything that takes place in a
particular scene, as there is simply too much happening on too many different
levels. Perceptual matters aside, it is impossible—or more relevantly, without
purpose—to describe everything that could be seen. These features mean that
any and all description is inevitably *partial and selective*; descriptions include some
traits, features, or aspects and exclude others.

What is included or excluded, however, is not randomly determined; rather,
processes of looking and recording are guided by the observer's implicit or
explicit concepts that make some details more important and relevant than others. As Berreman has argued, theory is always "inherent in ethnography":

> The underlying assumptions by which [the researcher] selects what he will
> observe from the mass of stimuli with which he is confronted in his research,
> what he will record from the innumerable observations he has made, and
> what he will report from the multitudinous records he has kept, comprise
> his theory or theories. If he regards it as more important to record a cere-
> mony than a bull session, a song than an epithet, how and where people eat
> than how and where they defecate, the rules by which they marry rather
> than the infractions of these rules, the circumstances in which they take
> grievances to court than the circumstances in which they become embar-
> rassed, what they do when someone dies than when someone belches (or
> vice versa), it is because he has a set of understandings or assumptions about
> the nature of human society, how it works and what is important in it. A
> theory is nothing more than a coherent set of assumptions. (1968:339)

Thus, to insist on a sharp polarity between description and analysis is deeply
misleading: *description is necessarily analytic.*

The inevitable analytic component of descriptions in general has crucial
implications for ethnographic descriptions in particular. First, an ethnographic
description can never be an exact, literal picture of some "thing" such as an event

or social action. It is always a theory-informed *re-presentation* of that "thing," a rendering of the event that transforms it in particular ways (e.g., by presenting "what happened" in purposive, partial and selective ways). A description of shooting heroin (or "fixing") in the street world of the junkie, for example, is inevitably partial and selective (compare the different descriptive accounts provided by Agar 1973:52–55 and Gould et al. 1974:26–30). Such a description re-presents some set of activities that has taken place in ways that inevitably differ from the actual experience of "shooting up" or even from the direct experience of observing such "shooting up."

Second, descriptions of the same social scene will vary depending on the theoretical constructs that observers bring to and use in their witnessings and representations. Thus, in an influential early study, Bennett (1946) argued that different ethnographers produced strikingly different descriptions and interpretations of Pueblo Indian culture depending upon their theoretical preferences: Those committed to an organic theory highlighting social integration and harmonious values, and those preferring a repression theory alive to "*covert* tension, suspicion, anxiety, hostility, fear, and ambition" (363), described and analyzed the "same events" in very different ways. Viewed with the first concept, work among the Hopi represents "an example of 'harmonious' and spontaneous cooperative attitudes toward fulfillment of the universal plan of Nature" (366). In the light of the second concept, work is not a product of voluntary cooperation, but of a pervasive, harsh socialization necessitated by the demands of irrigation.[1]

In using concepts, whether explicit or implicit ones, the ethnographer organizes what might otherwise be irrelevant and unconnected events and features into some pattern or order. This interpretive process of ordering begins immediately with perception; we perceive not the "things in themselves" but something made meaningful by being seen in relation to some known category, generally coded into language:

> Almost immediately what is perceived is interpreted by the addition of concepts, the conceptualization assimilating sensory stimuli to ideas derived from the anthropologist's own cultural experience or from the society being studied. An investigator noting that "the officiant shaves some hair from the girl's temples and the back of her neck," by applying concepts (the officiant, hair, the act of shaving, etc.) to parts of a total event, in effect conceptualizes the whole event by organizing the parts into a single activity. (Honigmann 1976:245)

Several different issues are involved here. First, the observer uses categories to identify and interpret certain things as meaningful (e.g., "shaves"). Second, the observer links these features together, organizing them as parts of a single activity, thereby making a higher-level interpretation of meaning.

In sum, ethnographers have come to see descriptions not only as influenced by value and theoretical commitments and by cultural categories used to observe, order, and describe events, but more generally as products of how an observer *attends* to what is to be observed and described. Attending includes but is not limited to the use of concepts and categories to order and interpret. It also ranges from the basic ways in which the describer engages with the world as a condition for describing it to the fieldworker's actual practice of inquiry. Such decisions as exactly where and when to go to observe, and how to present yourself and your observations to those being watched, can critically shape descriptions. In this respect, no description is independent of the describer and her actual methods for making and recording observations, and multiple descriptions of the same scene, activity or culture are both likely and legitimate.

Describing Meanings

Providing ethnographic descriptions, however, faces additional complications because of the distinctive problems of describing social as opposed to physical reality. Social theorist Alfred Schutz, for example, drew the following contrast between physical reality as described by the natural scientist and social reality as described and analyzed by the social scientist (1962:58–59):

> It is up to the natural scientist and to him alone to define, in accordance with the procedural rules of his science, his observational field, and to determine the facts, data, and events within it which are relevant for his problem or scientific purpose at hand. Neither are those facts and events pre-selected, nor is the observational field pre-interpreted. The world of nature, as explored by the natural scientist, does not "mean" anything to molecules, atoms, and electrons. But the observational field of the social scientist—social reality—has a specific meaning and relevance structure for the human beings living, acting, and thinking within it. By a series of common-sense constructs they have pre-selected and pre-interpreted this world which they experience as the reality of their daily lives. It is these thought objects of theirs which determine their behavior by motivating it. The thought objects constructed by the social scientist, in order to grasp this social reality, have to be founded upon the thought objects constructed by the common-sense thinking of men, living their daily life within their social world.

Ethnography, then, does not seek to represent social "things in themselves"—if indeed there are such things—but things as they are grasped and shaped through the meaning-conferring response of members. Ethnographic descriptions of the social world, therefore, must identify and convey the *meanings* that actions and events have for actors in that world, their distinctive interpretations of reality. Indeed, this mandate to "understand the way that group members interpret the flow of events in their lives" (Agar 1980:194) lies at the core of contemporary ethnography.

Producing descriptions, not only of significant events and activities, but also of the meanings that these events and activities have for those studied, is a complex and subtle enterprise on a number of counts. First, this stance requires avoiding "objective," behaviorist procedures which treat human action as a physiological process in favor of fuller, more "subjective" descriptions of socially meaningful behavior. For as Geertz argues (this volume, pp. 57–58), description of the social world is not concerned with contractions of the eyelids, but with the interpreted significance of winks, parodied winks, and the like. Thus ethnographic description seeks to identify the subjective meanings people attribute to events rather than the "objective" characteristics of such events.

By way of illustration, consider the problem of describing illicit drug use. Pharmacologists generally describe methadone and heroin as essentially similar drugs and contend that street addicts cannot tell the difference between them under double-blind conditions. Yet as Gould et al. (1974:xix) have insisted, in describing the world of the heroin user, what is critical is not pharmacological reality but "the reality that is experienced by the research subjects." For addicts methadone is a fallback drug, used to prevent sickness or cut down on a habit, while heroin is used to get high. On the level of meaning, pharmacological reality is irrelevant to understanding and describing street-drug worlds, since it is the addicts' beliefs about the drugs, rather than existing scientific knowledge of their effects, that is critical for addicts' behaviors.

Describing events and activities based in other cultures poses further complications. Most significantly, such descriptions can easily become *ethnocentric* from implicit reliance upon standards or criteria drawn from the ethnographer's own culture. Consider the seemingly straightforward descriptive claim, "The Thai are noisy in temple" (Moerman 1969:464). This statement may simply mean, "The Thai I saw in temple were noisier than Methodists are supposed to be in church"; if so, it frames Thai behavior in temples against an external criterion, almost caricaturing rather than describing that behavior on its own terms. To establish the claim that the Thai are noisy in temple, Moerman argues, requires the development of intracultural contrasts, that is, comparison of the noise (and other aspects of social behavior) in this setting with the noise in other locally comparable situations (among the Thai, for example, dispute hearings, village meetings, and casual conversations). The observer is then led to a comparison of public behaviors in different settings in Thai society, and to contrasting organizational and interactional patterns found within them. Thus the goal is to ground descriptions on distinctions consistently drawn from within the culture being described rather than from an outside culture.

Anthropologists originally addressed the problems of cross-cultural description by distinguishing between *etic* descriptions on the one hand and *emic* descriptions on the other. The former involves descriptive accounts based on concepts that come from outside the culture studied; the latter involves descriptions that use categories from within that culture that would be used or recognized by its members. These terms derive from the work of the linguist Kenneth Pike (1954:8–28), who contrasted *phonetics*, the classification of sound bits according to their acoustic properties, and *phonemics*, the classification of sounds on the basis of their internal function in the language in question. In a parallel way, those who stress etics insist that descriptions should be based on concepts that allow cross-cultural comparisons. The ethnographer may well derive such concepts not from the native culture but "from his own mind, from ethnological theory, or from other particular cultures, including his own" (Naroll 1967:511). Advocates of emic approaches, in contrast, see the goal as description of a particular culture in its own terms; native categories should not be ignored even if they

do not lend themselves to comparison with other cultures. To return to the nois-
iness of Thai temples: One could measure decibel levels in a Thai temple and in a
Methodist church, but such a comparison does not describe behaviors in locally
meaningful terms. As Moerman insists (1969:464), "If I am correct in asserting
that the Thai are quieter in temple than they are in other locally delimited situations, then however loud they sound to Methodists and however quiet to [Jamai-
can] Pocamanians, the Thai whether ethnographically or for purposes of
comparative ethnology . . . are quiet in temple."

Ethnographers pursuing emic approaches came to recognize that the initial
specification of native categories raises complex problems. In the effort to avoid
imposing exogenous categories, ethnographers sought to produce cross-cultural
descriptions by "finding the 'things' that go with the words" (Frake 1962a) (i.e.,
point to an object, elicit the native's name for it, then match this name with one's
own word for that object). "The logic of the operation is: if the informant calls
object X a *mbubu* and I call object X a *rock*, then mbubu means rock" (Frake
1962a:73). Not only is such a "name-getting" approach methodologically uncertain (the ethnographer assumes, among other things, that the native understands
that his finger points to "rock" as opposed to its color, size, texture, etc.), it also
provides only limited understanding of the native culture: to learn that the
Eskimo have many words for snow while English-speaking people have only one
not only tells us very little about their world and how it is meaningful, but also
describes that world only by contrast with our own society and its concepts.

Work in cognitive anthropology and ethnoscience sought to move beyond
this approach by reconceiving ethnographic description as a process of "finding
out what are in fact the 'things' in the environment of the people being studied"
(Frake 1962a:74). Frake, then, insisted that no object "has been described *ethnographically* until one has stated the rules for its identification in the culture being
studied" (1962b:55). To return to the illustration of Eskimos and snow: For
Frake an ethnographic description would identify the rules the Eskimo themselves use in making the distinctions between these different kinds of snow, and
hence the practical purposes for making such distinctions. Taking this approach
a step further, when describing more complex social activities, these ethnographers sought to specify the *background cultural knowledge* needed to perform particular action in another culture—for example, to enter a Yakan house (Frake 1975)
or to ask for a drink in Suburan (Frake 1964b)—in ways that would be recognized as appropriate by members of that culture. Goodenough (1967:1203) suggested that these sorts of descriptions in fact specified the local culture:

> What does a person need to have learned if he is to understand events in a
> strange community as its members understand them and if he is to conduct
> himself in ways that they accept as conforming to their expectations of one
> another? To describe the contents of such a body of knowledge is to describe
> a community's culture.

Frake (1964a:133) proposed a similar understanding of ethnographic description:
"The model of an ethnographic statement is not: 'if a person is confronted with

stimulus X, he will do Y,' but: 'if a person is in situation X, performance Y will be judged appropriate by native actors.'"

Thick Description

Ethnography's distinctive commitment to describing local, folk or members' meanings provides the point of departure for Geertz's influential concept of "thick description," developed in his introduction (this volume, pp. 56–57) to *The Interpretation of Cultures* (1973a). Drawing the term "thick description" from the British analytic philosopher Gilbert Ryle, Geertz argues that the foundational task of ethnography is to describe the specific "meaningful structures" through which local actors produce, perceive and interpret their own and others' actions. Such "thick descriptions" are first and foremost "actor oriented," demanding that the ethnographer grasp and convey how members of the studied society or setting make sense of—interpret, find the meaning of—the flow of events that makes up their lives. Given this commitment to local meanings, the key to thick description lies not in reporting, collecting and assembling "facts," but in *interpretively* understanding and representing the subtleties and complexities of meaning. Geertz's thick description of a series of events involving a Jewish trader, Berber tribesmen and French officials in Morocco in 1912, for example, is "cast in terms of the constructions we imagine Berbers, Jews, or Frenchmen to place upon what they live through, the formulae they use to define what happens to them."

In this way, Geertz understands ethnographic description as a thoroughly *interpretive* enterprise. A thick description is not simply a collection of events and activities, nor even a collection of the local meanings of such events and activities; rather, such a description is a complex interpretation of local meanings— the ethnographer's effortful, imaginative rendering of these meanings. Echoing Schutz's characterization of sociological theories and descriptions as "constructs of the second degree, namely constructs of the constructs made by the actors on the social scene" (1962:5–6), Geertz argues that thick description provides "our own constructions of other people's constructions of what they and their compatriots are up to" (this volume, pp. 59–60). In short, ethnographic description involves interpretations of interpretations.

In highlighting the interpretive character of ethnographic description, Geertz also called attention to a critical yet neglected procedure through which ethnographers produce descriptions—"*inscription*." Insisting that ethnographic descriptions are not reality but representations of reality, not straightforward renderings of social things "in themselves" but deeply and unavoidably interpretive accounts of reality, Geertz pointed to the deep significance of writing in ethnography:

> The ethnographer "inscribes" social discourse; *he writes it down*. In so doing, he turns it from a passing event, which exists only in its own moment of occurrence, into an account, which exists in its inscriptions and can be reconsulted. (emphasis in original)

Whereas ethnographers had previously treated writing as at most a peripheral fieldwork skill, regarding it as a straightforward process of recounting "what happened," Geertz drew upon the hermeneutic tradition, specifically the work of Paul Ricoeur, to highlight writing as a constitutive rather than an accidental feature of ethnography. Thus, as interpretation ethnographic description "consists of trying to rescue the 'said' of [social] discourse from its perishing occasions and fix it in perusable terms" (this volume, pg. 68).

In that thick descriptions provide interpretive understanding of local meanings, such descriptions are necessarily context sensitive and context preserving. Thick descriptions present in close detail the context and meanings of events and scenes that are relevant to those involved in them. This task requires the ethnographer to identify and communicate the connections between actions and events, especially those salient to the variety of local actors themselves. In this sort of descriptive enterprise, actions are not stripped of locally relevant context and interconnectedness but are tied together in textured and holistic accounts of social life.

This sensitivity to, and even preoccupation with, locally meaningful context contrasts sharply with many standard social science procedures, in which observers typically try either to ignore or to reduce contextual meanings in the interests of standardization and comparability.[2] Consider the differences between description in this thick vein and observational methods that employ fixed, predetermined categories for coding behavior. In studies of police decision making (Reiss 1971; Lundman 1974; Black 1980), observers were sent into the field, riding along with patrol officers, armed with code sheets for recording all interactions between officers and civilians. Such code sheets were essentially predetermined questions that the observer/coder was to ask of each and every incident qualifying for observation. Each question was in fact a variable, and the value of each variable could be determined for every incident observed. One variable examined in this way, for example, was the use of physical force by each police officer (e.g., Reiss 1968). Based on a prespecified definition of force (here, one that excluded instances of "simple restraint"), all observed cases were classified on the basis of specific criteria into either "necessary" or "unnecessary" uses of force (Reiss 1968:12).

These procedures produced data that are extremely useful for many purposes; for example, the researchers can specify the frequency with which such events occur, then explore the correlations between these variables.[3] Yet such standardization necessarily restricts the appreciation of meaningful contexts and the complexity of social life; it demands that the observer orient to any particular incident primarily to decide how its features fit within predetermined categories.

Thick ethnographic description, in contrast, does not seek to reduce observed happenings to a specific categories or variables (although it does reduce these happenings to textual form and hence to data). Rather, it seeks to represent the local meanings and contexts of complex human actions as experienced and interpreted by the ethnographer. Consider two fieldwork accounts of police use of force—Van Maanen's (1983:217–73) fieldnotes on the arrest and violent loading of a drunken bar patron into a police van, and Hunt's (1985:329–31) extended interview account from a patrol officer who repeatedly blackjacked a

driver who had embarrassed her by twice driving away when she had tried to
ticket him. These accounts trace out in detail the interactional sequences leading
up to the officer's use of force, describe the emotions observed or experienced as
these acts are occurring, present the on-the-spot talk normalizing and justifying
the use of such force, and recount the reactions of various others during and after
these violent incidents. These descriptions convey a sense of police work as
patrol officers might themselves understand and talk about it—at least to (some
of) their peers. The use of force in circumstances not prescribed by law is not
only viewed matter-of-factly, as part of the job, but is assumed to be justified or
"normal" in particular contexts and under certain circumstances (e.g., presumptive challenges to police authority), but not in any and all. Indeed, Hunt's analysis delineates the situational contexts in which the police view the use of force as
legitimate or normal, even if exceeding the limits prescribed by law, and those
which the police themselves recognize the use of force as excessive or "brutal."

Geertz's "thick description" treatment of local meaning and context
reframes and deepens the standard emic/etic distinction, highlighting the relation between members' constructs and the ethnographer's construction of those
constructs. Emic accounts are not literally members' constructs, but rather second-order renderings of those constructs produced in one fashion or another by
the ethnographer; and the ethnographer's reconstruction of these local meanings
may well import exogamous (etic) qualities. Rather than a sharp dichotomy,
then, Geertz suggests a continuum between what he elsewhere (1976:223) terms
"experience-near" and "experience-distant" concepts. The former are emic-like
concepts that a member of a society would "naturally and effortlessly use to
define what he or his fellows see, feel, think, imagine, and so on, and which he
would readily understand when similarly applied by others." The latter are
etic-like concepts employed by specialists "to forward their scientific, philosophical, or practical aims" (1976:223). Specifically, "'Love' is an experience-near
concept, 'object cathexis' is an experience-distant one." Thick description starts
with—but does not restrict itself to—experience-near concepts (see pp. 72–73).
Purely emic descriptions, even if possible, would seem useless and uninteresting
for social science. The task, rather, is to "grasp concepts which, for another people, are experience-near, and to do so well enough to place them in illuminating
connection with experience-distant concepts theorists have fashioned to capture the general features of social life" (Geertz 1976:224). The critical question
here, Geertz suggests, is

> ... how, in each case, ought one to deploy them so as to produce an interpre-
> tation of the way a people lives which is neither imprisoned within their
> mental horizons, an ethnography of witchcraft as written by a witch, nor
> systematically deaf to the distinctive tonalities of their existence, an ethnog-
> raphy of witchcraft as written by a geometer. (1976:223)

Geertz's notion of thick description struck a responsive chord with ethnographers, providing a general model of and justification for pursuing mean-
ing-rich, context-sensitive, and holistic descriptions of social activities. It has led

to understanding ethnographic description as a fundamentally interpretive process in which the ethnographer is not simply a fieldworker, but also and simultaneously a writer, artfully representing her understanding of indigenous interpretations of some piece of the social world. As a result the dynamic of ethnography is transformed from the realist discovery, collection and ordering of "facts" to the subtle interpretation and communication of indigenous concerns and symbolic meanings. As Leach (1976:1) has depicted this change, "Ethnography has ceased to be an inventory of custom, it has become the art of thick description; the intricate interweaving of plot and counterplot as in the work of a major novelist."

The Reflexivity of Descriptions

Ethnographic description faces further complexities when it is recognized that all social actors—not just ethnographers or other social scientists—routinely produce descriptions and that such descriptions can be consequential in and for social life. These issues have been addressed in particularly telling ways in the ethnomethodological writings of Garfinkel, Cicourel and Wieder.

Following Schutz (1962), ethnomethodology holds that the social world is preinterpreted, or alternatively, "predescribed." These *member descriptions* are of central concern to ethnomethodologists. In a major statement of this approach, Harold Garfinkel (1967) argues that members' descriptions of their social worlds create or constitute those social worlds as meaningful phenomena. Members' descriptions are not "'mere words' but are ways of doing things with words." A description characterizes members' circumstances in particular ways for particular purposes; in this way it identifies specific meanings and thereby excludes other meaning possibilities.

Consider this concrete example: When Melvin Pollner and I began fieldwork on psychiatric emergency teams (PET teams) operating out of community mental health clinics, a number of PET workers described their job as "shit work" (Emerson and Pollner 1976). The term provided a description—albeit an encapsulated and negative one—of what PET was doing. But on reflection we came to realize that this "dirty work" description is misunderstood if it is treated as a neutral, detached, "factual" characterization of what PET was up to. Rather, we came to see PET talk of dirty work as providing a set of instructions to us and to others, instructions on how to "see" the "real meaning" of PET activities, particularly in circumstances that might well have been read otherwise. For example, despite strong commitment to crisis intervention modes of therapy and to community treatment, "day after day PET hospitalized people who did not want to be hospitalized, used coercion in effecting hospitalization, and so forth" (252). Yet in describing such actions as dirty work, PET workers provided a narrative instructing observers to attribute certain meanings and not others to them:

> Talk of shit work, for example, formulates involuntary hospitalization and the use of coercion as exceptions to the "real" purpose of PET. Through such talk PET personnel made themselves and others aware that the actual treat-

ment accorded cases ought not to be taken as representative of what they would prefer to do or what PET, at heart, was designed to do. (252)

Moreover, these descriptions were *consequential* in and for the organizational context within which PET workers operated. To invoke the notion of dirty work as a resistant patient was physically restrained and taken off to the hospital, for example, communicated that the worker knew that this was not "helping," yet he remained committed to the value of providing therapy. Thus, these descriptions provided *accounts* (Garfinkel 1967) that instructed those in the setting (including field researchers) in how to appreciate its situationally specific meanings and order, and simultaneously, invoked and created those very meanings and order.

Descriptions, then, are not simply *about* some social world but are also *part of that world.* In this sense descriptions are *reflexive* in character: "Descriptions about some aspect of the social world are simultaneously within (part of) the very world that they described" (Schwartz and Jacobs 1979:51). Since descriptions are reflexive in this way, fieldworkers cannot treat members' descriptive talk as "objective reporting" of "factual data." To do so would involve treating such talk as independent of the social world that produced it, as somehow transcending the specific social situation within which it was generated.

The selection from D. Lawrence Wieder, "Telling the Convict Code," analyzes description as a reflexive, socially consequential process of providing meaning-creating accounts. Wieder found that residents of a halfway house for ex-drug addicts often referred to the "convict code" in describing events in the house. When a resident invoked the code and its specific tenets, he was not offering a neutral, transcendent description; rather, reference to the code was a way of *taking action* in the social organization of the house, an organization made relevant to this particular occasion by these very statements. Thus, when a resident drew upon the code to justify his refusal to talk to staff (or to Wieder!) about personal matters, this action (a sort of description) made a statement about his relations with others in the house. It indicated, for example, that he stood with residents against staff, or that within the house the fieldworker was to be treated as staff.

Wieder's specific analysis of the telling of the code, and ethnomethodological concerns with description in general, have a number of important implications for ethnography. To begin, the relationship between members' descriptions and the accounts that the fieldworker comes to offer must be explicitly examined. In fact, ethnomethodologists suggest that many fieldworkers take over members' accounts and descriptions as their own analyses, using these accounts to explain events in that particular social world. To cite an example from Wieder's study, the classic sociological literature on prisons (e.g., Sykes 1958) used the prisoners' own description of the convict code as a resource for explaining how prison life was organized—for example, to suggest that rehabilitative efforts were bound to fail because they ran counter to the requirements of the code. In this way, the code is turned from a member's description into the sociologist's explanation; just as members explain behavior by reference to the code and its provisions, so too does the sociologist.

This happens, of course, because the sociologist treats the member's description as fact, as a report about "real" events standing outside the social order described. Ethnomethodologists suggest an alternative view: that members' descriptions are inevitably embedded in and part of the order they describe. They then recommend the investigation of these descriptions as phenomena in their own right. Cicourel's (1968) analysis of how probation officers write up reports of contacts with delinquent youth provides a case in point. These reports provided not "pure descriptions" of delinquent behavior, but rather a heavily selected recounting of such behavior intended to further certain practical organizational concerns of the probation officer. In looking at how probation officers assembled such reports, the ethnographer treats descriptive partiality, selectivity, and perspective as topics as well as problems.

Furthermore, since descriptions are integral parts of the social worlds they describe, descriptions will vary with the describer's particular "practical or theoretical problem at hand" (Schutz 1964:235). As these problems or purposes vary, so will the nature of the descriptions provided. Members with different responsibilities in the same organization, for example, will provide descriptions of the organization that reflect their distinctive problems. Hence, attendants in mental hospitals, whose work centers on ordering the flow of daily life on the wards, describe patients in terms that reflect these practical demands; as "tidy" or "untidy," "mobile" or "feeble," "cooperative" or "bad," and "working" or "idle" (Bucher and Schatzman 1962:340–43). Psychiatrists in these settings would tend to describe the same patients in terms of their psychodynamics or their degree of "insight," descriptions reflecting their diagnostic and therapeutic responsibilities.

Since members' descriptions are formulated for particular purposes, ethnomethodologists suggest that close attention be paid to these purposes. As a result, ethnographic accounts should not be limited to describing members' general concepts, categories, or perspectives. Rather, ethnographers should seek to describe the *actual use* of such concepts and categories in specific social interactions (see also Emerson et al., 1995:126–30). Merely describing these concepts is of limited utility, since knowing only these categories abstractly and in principle we still do not know exactly how members apply them in real social situations.[4] By way of illustration: as Wieder suggests, the ethnographer cannot assume in advance exactly how the convict code will be applied or invoked in particular situations in the halfway house. The code, for example, contains no specific provisions about how to treat fieldworkers; its provisions will have to be expanded, changed, modified, or extended in one way or another to cover this situation. Similarly, even if we know that PET workers describe much of what they do as "shit work," we cannot predict exactly what situations they would so characterize until they actually do so. Descriptions that are limited to member categories without reference to actual use thus remain incomplete and empty.

Finally, ethnomethodologists are inclined to turn ethnographic description back on itself by insisting that the ethnographer's accounts are in no fundamental way different from those members provide. Both reflect the describer's purposes at hand; that the ethnographer's purposes are perhaps more "theoretical" does not make her descriptions any less partial, selective, or perspectival than member descriptions—only different. Similarly, both ethnographic and folk descriptions make frequent use of specific interpretive procedures to find and convey meaning and regularity. As Garfinkel explains one such procedure, the "documentary method of interpretation":

> The method consists of treating an actual appearance as "the document of," as "pointing to," as "standing on behalf of" a presupposed underlying pattern. Not only is the underlying pattern derived from its individual documentary evidences, but the individual documentary evidences, in their turn, are interpreted on the basis of "what is known" about the underlying pattern. Each is used to elaborate the other. (1967:78)

The convict code provides an instance of such a pattern, used by member and fieldworker alike to interpret a variety of specific actions in the halfway house. All descriptions employ such procedures; hence, for ethnomethodologists, ethnographic as well as member methods for assembling descriptions should be examined in terms of their use of such procedures.

REPRESENTATION AND ETHNOGRAPHIC AUTHORITY

The reflexive turn in contemporary ethnography not only is evident in more sophisticated understandings of the nature of observation and description; it also has led to consideration of ethnography as a form of representation intricately tied to processes of writing and interpretation. This interest in representation was fed in part by deepening appreciation of the complexities confronting efforts to grasp and convey others' worlds of meaning. But active interest in the doing of ethnography also contributed to this concern with representation. Moving beyond confessional accounts of personal relations and other processes in the field, ethnographers have begun to problematize the very notion of "the field" and hence of "fieldwork." Finally, following Geertz's insistence that writing comprises an essential part of doing ethnography, ethnographers have begun to examine the previously neglected textual properties of ethnographic accounts. The following sections will examine these contemporary, increasingly reflexive approaches to ethnography as representation: greater sophistication in representing indigenous meanings, problematization of the field and fieldwork, and textual properties of ethnographies.

The Complexities of Representing Indigenous Meanings

As noted earlier, grounding ethnography upon local, members' meanings changes drastically with the recognition that the ethnographer's renderings of those meanings possess a different ontological status than members' lived understanding and use of them. This recognition undermines the straightforward realist stance that "I know because I was there and have come to experience things from the members' perspective." Such a claim assumes that the fieldworker's experience of members' worlds is essentially isomorphic with the members' own experiences. Yet, as Bittner (1973) and others have insisted, the ethnographer's experience can never exactly duplicate that of a member. At the very least, the member has grown up in that culture, whereas the fieldworker comes upon it as a "second culture" apprehended in light of his first culture. For these and other reasons, "the ethnographer does not, and, in my opinion, largely cannot, perceive what his informants perceive" (Geertz 1976:224). Since the ethnographer can, at best, only approximate rather than completely replicate members' lived experience, ethnographic representations of local meanings cannot be grounded simply on claims of direct participation, personal intimacy, or empathetic experience.

Furthermore, to conceive of ethnography as simply describing "the actor's perspective" or "the native's point of view" fares no better as a solution to this problem, for the ethnographer elects to go to the setting, is in it only temporarily, and knows she can leave when the research ends. The fieldworker's experience is thus *freer*, ultimately a product of choice and decision; the experience of the member, and even of the stranger who has come to stay in a new culture, is surrounded by necessity. As Karp and Kendall note (1982:257):

> Fieldworkers . . . are not subject to the same constraints, and this must inevitably affect the quality of their experience. Rosemary Firth (1972) recounts a nightmare she had shortly before leaving the field. She dreamt that she really was a Malay woman, "squatting in front of a smoky fire." The participation that the fieldworker gives is neither as committed nor as constrained as the native's.

This lack of experienced commitment and constraint inheres in the very formulation of members' realities as "perspectives" or "points of view." The fieldworker's relatively unconstrained presence can produce a tendency to slip "in and out of points of view," to treat the "meanings of objects as more or less freely conjured" by members (Bittner 1973:122). Their conceptual categories depict social life as *perceived* events and meanings, ignoring or distorting the lived reality of members' worlds that are characterized by "traits of depth, stability, and necessity that people recognize as actually inherent in the circumstances of their existence" (Bittner 1973:123). Thus, as Geertz (1976:224) suggests, what the ethnographer *sees* as a "concept" the native *experiences* more immediately:

> People use experience-near concepts spontaneously, unselfconsciously, as it were colloquially; they do not, except fleetingly and on occasion, recognize that there are any "concepts" involved at all. That is what experience-near means—that ideas and the realities they inform are naturally and indissolubly bound up together. What else could you call a hippopotamus?

In sum, the ethnographer does not grasp members' perspectives "in themselves," but as mediated through his or her own theoretical, cultural, and personal constructs, which tend to reconfigure and perhaps distort members' meanings.

The issues addressed to this point have centered on members' and ethnographers' asymmetrical experiences of local worlds. A related line of criticism identifies ethnographers' *theoretical commitments* as fundamental impediments to grasping and representing local meanings. On a general level, one factor in the declining faith in the authority and legitimacy of generalizing or totalizing paradigms for analyzing contemporary social life, particularly Marxism and Parsonianism, was recognition that such paradigms ignored, obscured, and/or distorted local meanings. The response within ethnography, Marcus and Fischer suggest (1986:12), frequently involved a shift of attention to "the interpretation of the details of a reality that eludes the ability of dominant paradigms to describe it, let alone explain it." Specifically within anthropological ethnography, the concept of culture that had dominated and helped organize research on other peoples for much of the twentieth century came under increasing scrutiny. Highlighting ethnography's longstanding preoccupation with "the primitive" as cultural alien or "other," critics insisted that constructing those studied as "the other" deeply and fundamentally obscured local meanings and indigenous senses of social life. Said (1979) in particular drew attention to the ways in which representing those studied as "the other" simultaneously exoticizes and depicts them as passive rather than as active subjects. Even self-conscious attempts to avoid these problems, such as cognitive anthropology's strategy of mapping "cultural categories against 'objective' grids of culturally neutral categories," were ultimately unconvincing; these frameworks appeared "not at all culturally neutral, but . . . shot through with the analyst's own cultural categories and assumptions" (Marcus and Fischer 1986:28, 29).

Somewhat similar concerns appear in ethnomethodology's condemnation of sociological theorizing's imposition of exogenous meanings on the here-and-now achievement of the "lived order" (Goode 1994:127ff). Ethnomethodologists view society as consisting of the ceaseless, ever-unfolding transactions through which members concertedly accomplish the order and meaning they take as sensible, rational, or intelligible. The orderliness of social life is thus a practically achieved phenomenon "incarnate" in the interactions and activities of social actors in actual particular circumstances (Lynch et al., 1983). Casting this phenomenon in terms of standard social science theories either diverts attention from the lived order, formulates it as epiphenomena, and/or imposes concepts and mechanisms variously irrelevant or unintelligible to participants. The alternative, Garfinkel insists, is to explicate the interactional accomplishment of order by capturing its endogenously relevant "details." On a general level this requires that the ethnographer abandon ethnography and become an adept practitioner (see pp. 42, 125, this volume). More concretely it also requires the avoidance of any "end-point object" or ultimate outcome as a resource for retrospectively describing/analyzing "events-to-start-with" (Garfinkel et al., 1981:136–37). Ethnomethodology instead seeks to provide "real time" descriptions of events and actions—that is, descriptions which use only what is known by members at each point as an event unfolds and which thus preserves the in-process sense of indeterminacy, uncertainty and contingency (Emerson et al. 1995:60–63).

From these different criticisms follow very different approaches to the representation of local meanings. Geertz's interpretive ethnography insists that understanding indigenous worlds does not derive directly from "acceptance" by those studied, but from soaking up their symbolic sensitivities as a result of prolonged, close contact:

. . . whatever accurate or half-accurate sense one gets of what one's informants are, as the phrase goes, really like, does not come from the experience of that acceptance as such, which is part of one's own biography, not of theirs. It comes from the ability to construe their modes of expression, what I would call their symbol systems, that such an acceptance allows one to work toward developing. Understanding the form and pressure of, to use the dangerous word one more time, natives' inner lives is more like grasping a proverb, catching an illusion, seeing a joke—or, as I have suggested, reading a poem—than it is like achieving communion. (1976:236–37)

Marcus and Fischer (1986:31) highlight dialogue and translation as core processes in grasping and conveying indigenous meanings:

In cross-cultural communication, and in writing about one culture for members of another, experience-near or local concepts of the cultural other are juxtaposed with the more comfortable, experience-far concepts that the writer shares with his readership. The act of translation involved in any act of cross-cultural interpretation is thus a relative matter with an ethnographer as mediator between distinct sets of categories and cultural conceptions. . . . The first juxtaposition and negotiation of concepts occur in the dialogues of fieldwork; the second in the remaking of the former as the anthropologist communicates with his readership through writing an ethnographic account.

Developing new forms and styles of representation provides the key to more authentically incorporating indigenous meanings (through experience-near concepts) into ethnographies; experimental "ethnographies of experience" have "improve(d) accounts of the long sought-after 'native point of view' . . . (employing) different textual strategies to convey to their readers richer and more complex understandings of their subjects' experience" (1986:43).

In contrast, recent statements of ethnomethodology by Garfinkel and others hold that the divide between indigenous order and sociological theory is unbridgeable. In order to avoid using sociological concepts in descriptions of the lifeworld of others, ethnomethodologists are urged to abandon sociology as an audience, avoid any and all of the analytic impulses of conventional sociology, and instead produce writings in the local vernacular that are instructive to practitioners. In this vein, Garfinkel et al. (1988:11) fault Lynch's research on lab science for producing findings that "are not results in neurobiology," but praise Livingston's seven years of graduate training as a mathematician in that it allowed him to undertake "the work of proving mathematical structures and (of gathering) analytically descriptive details of it."

Problematizing "the Field" and "Fieldwork"

Anthropological approaches to the field point to the lasting impact of implicit assumptions and practices deriving from "the classical Malinowskian image of fieldwork (the lone, white, male fieldworker living for a year or more among the native villagers)" (Gupta and Ferguson 1997b:11; see also Stocking

1992:57–59). In recent years ethnographers have begun to question this realist understanding of "the field" as simply the place the ethnographer went to conduct research. Extending initial examinations of the relational processes and power dynamics involved in doing fieldwork, ethnographers now conceive of "the field" not as "a pre-given natural entity" but as "something we construct, both through the practical transactions and activities of data collection and through the literary activities of writing fieldnotes, analytic memoranda, and the like" (Atkinson 1992:5). Specifically:

> . . . the field is produced (not discovered) through the social transactions engaged in by the ethnographer. The boundaries of the field are not "given." They are the outcome of what the ethnographer may encompass in his or her gaze; what he or she may negotiate with hosts and informants; and what the ethnographer omits and overlooks as much as what the ethnographer *writes.* (Atkinson 1992:9)

In this sense, the ethnographer's "field" "enables certain kinds of knowledge while blocking off others, authorizes some objects of study and methods of analysis while excluding others" (Gupta and Ferguson 1997b:4).

What specific practices are used to construct and sustain "the field" in the course of research? Clifford (1997:186) views fieldwork as "an embodied spatial practice" involving both "displacement" (i.e., "physically going out" from "home" to some other "different" place or setting) and "focused, disciplined attention." The latter component highlights the ways in which the ethnographer finds and attends to local scenes and events through a distinctive theoretical lens constituted by specific methodological practices (learning a local language, systematic observation, attending to deep or implicit structures). Similarly, Gupta and Ferguson (1997b:4) note that the field is defined by its radical separation from "home": the former is distant and exotic, the latter familiar, safe, and known. Anthropological fieldwork in other cultures in particular has strongly accented the field/home distinction, conceiving of the former as a far-away, exotic, and pastoral place unaffected by contemporary development and technology in which data collection ("fieldwork") takes place, and of the latter as "where analysis is conducted and the ethnography is written up" (Gupta and Ferguson 1997b).[5] But in addition, the field is defined as a domain of face-to-face relations, typically located in local communities, as ethnographers prefer "field" settings that are "agrarian, pastoral, and maybe even 'wild'" (Gupta and Ferguson 1997b:8). In so doing they ignore prominent features of contemporary social life, including the outcomes of cross-cultural contacts and the more general relevance of "translocal" relations and phenomena.[6]

Ethnographers point out that these unexamined assumptions about the field and fieldwork exaggerate the separation of and differences between field and home, foist notions of purity and "naturalism" on those studied, assume separate, isolated local cultures, and ignore broader social processes and forces. Indeed, Gupta and Ferguson urge abandoning the notion of the field as a (local) site, urging instead that the field be conceived as encounters between people exposed to transformative cultural and social processes. In their view fieldwork becomes "a self-conscious shifting of social and geographical location," that is, "a form of motivated and stylized dislocation" pursued by a researcher to increase sensitivity to other ways of life (1997b:36–37).

Identifying the ways in which ethnographers construct particular situations and encounters as "the field" focuses attention on the implicit assumptions and routine practices that guide, constrain, and shape ethnographic understanding and analysis. Moreover, different approaches to research lead to different understandings of what the field involves: classic ethnographic naturalism views the field as geographical place, whereas ethnomethodology's "field" lies "wherever reality-constituting interaction takes place" (Gubrium and Holstein 1997:52). Those concerned with examining the emotions focus on inner lived experience in ways which blur any distinction between "the field and its representational venue" (71), while postmodern conceptions of "hyperreality" displace any equation of "the field" with fixed, spatial location (77–79). These different core assumptions about "the field" not only shape general methods of inquiry but also provide specific taken-for-granted ways of orienting to ongoing social life; different moments and happenings, for example, become significant candidates for observation and analysis.

The Textual Properties of Ethnographies

In 1980, George Marcus noted that few ethnographers had followed the lead provided by Geertz's interpretive treatment of ethnography as inscription: While ethnographers had begun to give attention to "the experience of doing fieldwork . . ., they have virtually ignored the activity through which anthropologists determine and represent what they know in the writing of ethnographies" (Marcus 1980:507). But in the following two decades ethnographic self-consciousness expanded to open new lines of inquiry into *writing* as a core component of the ethnographic enterprise. Indeed, previously marginal and unappreciated, writing descriptive and analytic accounts has come to be recognized as a defining ethnographic activity.

Examinations of ethnographic writing drew heavily from the philosophical traditions of hermeneutics and phenomenology, and from classic and emerging approaches in literary criticism. Geertz's emphasis on inscription derives directly from the hermeneutical writings of Paul Ricouer that focused on "the theory of rules that govern an exegesis, that is to say, an interpretation of a particular text" (Palmer 1969:43). The phenomenological concept of the "lifeworld" from Husserl focused attention on the distinctive character of everyday human experience. Coming from different sides, both traditions highlighted the fundamental distinction between lived experience and renderings or re-presentations of such experience—in Ricouer's terms, between "the saying" and "the said." Other ethnographers saw parallels between ethnographic writing and established and developing traditions of literary criticism, including considerations of the structure and uses of rhetoric in literature (e.g., Burke 1945; Frye 1957; Booth

1961) and of the literary conventions of realist fiction (e.g., Frye; Auerbach 1953; Stern 1973).[7] Concern with rhetoric, authority and narrative has guided much of the intensive, reflexive scrutiny of ethnographic texts that resulted.

Analysis of rhetoric—the means by which language achieves its persuasive effects—had long been restricted to fiction and other forms of art. But social scientists began to see significant possibilities in Frye's suggestion for "literary analysis of scientific knowledge," a proposal premised on the argument that "anything which makes a functional use of words will always be involved in all the technical problems of words, including rhetorical problems" (1957:331). In a 1976 article ("The Literary Rhetoric of Science"), for example, Gusfield applied the concept of rhetoric to social science literature on drunk driving. Gusfield argued that rhetoric had been dismissed as relevant to science through what he termed the "windowpane" theory of scientific writing:

> ... [This theory] insists on the intrinsic irrelevance of language to the enterprise of Science. The aim of presenting ideas and data is to enable the audience to see the external world as it is. In keeping with the normative prescriptions of scientific method, language and style must be chosen which will approximate, as closely as possible, a pane of clear glass. (16–17)

The windowpane theory, then, maintains that scientific writing persuades not by literary devices but by the weight of the "facts" it provides and by the power of its theoretical framing (see also Geertz 1988).

However, rhetoric is not absent in scientific analyses: ". . . words, sentences, paragraphs and larger units are a major tool for reporting, and therefore persuading," so that "the language and literary style of science" should be made an object of study (Gusfield 1976:17). But scientific rhetoric assumes distinctively self-effacing forms that, like the transparent windowpane, are easily ignored. The "literary art involved in scientific presentation" tends to obscure itself; as writer the scientist "must persuade the audience that the results of the research are *not* literature, are *not* a product of the style of presentation," but simply the way things are; hence the literary style of science is an ironic one, a "style of non-style" (17). The rhetorical style of social science studies of "problem drinking" and the "drunken driver," for example, involves accounts that appear to be "untainted by the obvious presence of the observer" (20). This effect is achieved through "an emphasis on the externality of the source of action" (produced by such phrasings as "Differences were found . . ." and "This finding necessitates the reevaluation . . .") and by minimizing the presence of the observer in the text (through the use of passive rather than active verbs and of impersonal rather than personal terms) in ways that establish "a reality outside the observer."

Pursuing these lines of inquiry, "a growing appreciation of rhetoric" marks contemporary ethnography (Gubrium and Holstein 1997:89–92). This appreciation involves a shift of interest to *how* ethnographies are presented rather than simply *what* they present. "The fundamental question concerning rhetoric . . . is the characteristic manner by which a text's language and organization convinces its readers of the truth, or at least the credibility, of its claims" (Marcus 1980:508). Analysis of the rhetoric of ethnographic texts thus directs attention away from the truth or accuracy of particular ethnographic accounts to the literary or textual means by which such accounts convince or persuade readers that their depictions of local life capture the everyday realities, perspectives and meanings of those studied.

Rhetoric also moves *readers* and the reading of ethnographic writing to the foreground. Earlier conceptions assumed that ethnographic texts more or less spoke for themselves, their meaning residing in the words themselves with the reader playing a passive role at most. But the very notion of rhetoric shifts attention to how texts persuade readers, and hence generates interest in readers not only as audiences but as active, consequential interpreters of meaning and import. While few ethnographers accept without reservation extreme "reader-oriented postmodernism" and its insistence that "meaning originates *not* in the production of a text (with the author), but in its reception (by the reader)" (Rosenau 1992:37), many recognize readers' reactions and understandings as an intrinsic part of ethnography. Indeed, Atkinson argues that the field is constituted through the ethnographer's gaze, through the ethnographer's writing a text-of-the-field, and "*through the reader's work of interpretation and contextualization*" (1992:9; emphasis added; see also Atkinson 1990, chapter 2).

Furthermore, an appreciation of rhetoric directs attention to texts and their persuasive structure as significant sources of power. For example, in his critique of Western representations of non-Western societies, Said (1979)

> . . . attacks particularly the rhetorical devices which make Western authors active, while leaving their subjects passive. These subjects, who must be spoken for, are generally located in the world dominated by Western colonialism or neocolonialism; thus, the rhetoric both exemplifies and reinforces Western domination. Moreover, the rhetoric is itself an exercise in power, in effect denying subjects the right to express contrary views, by obscuring from the reader the recognition that they might view things *with equal validity*, quite differently from the writer. (Marcus and Fischer 1986:1)

Examining the rhetorical properties of classic ethnographies, it is readily apparent that these texts rely upon a distinctively realist rhetoric, a rhetoric that has come to be identified as *ethnographic realism*. Ethnographic realism is "a mode of writing that seeks to represent the reality of the whole world or a form of life" (Marcus and Cushman 1982:29). Just as the realist novels of Dickens could be examined for the ways in which his writing produces "that sense of assurance and abundance and reality that speaks to us from every page and every episode" (Stern 1973:2), so too classic ethnographic texts can be analyzed for how they convey a sense of having been to and understood life and activities in unfamiliar worlds and settings.

The rhetorical effects of realist ethnography are produced through writing practices that convey the sense that the ethnographer has directly and deeply experienced another way of life, and that this way of life is authoritatively represented in the text. Marcus and Cushman (1982) discuss realist ethnography as a distinctive genre analyzable in terms of standard literary conventions of plot, point of view, characterization, content and style. In these terms realist ethnographies employ "the narrative structure of total ethnography" (seeking "the complete description of another culture or society"), "the unintrusive presence of the ethnographer in the text," "common denominator people" (i.e., characterization of those studied not as individuals but in global, composite terms), and a "focus on everyday life situation" (Marcus and Cushman 1982:31ff). Van Maanen (1988:47) identifies "studied neutrality" as a core convention in realist ethnography; here "the narrator . . . poses as an impersonal conduit, who unlike missionaries, administrators, journalists, or unabashed members of the culture themselves, passes on more-or-less objective data in a measured intellectual style that is uncontaminated by personal bias, political goals, or moral judgments." In a selection from *The Ethnographic Imagination* (this volume), Atkinson examines some ways in which ethnographers persuade their readers "of the authenticity, plausibility and significance of representations of social scenes or settings." Focusing on "how the text creates an 'introduction' to a 'spirit of place,'" Atkinson compares the opening paragraph of a Hemingway short story with that of a classic ethnography of a bar (Spradley and Mann 1975), showing the use of similar writing devices to produce "reality-like effects."

Concern with the rhetorical organization of ethnographies also generates interest in the ways in which the *authority* of a specific text is established. Examinations of authority ask how a text asserts or warrants its implicit claim to provide an "authoritative representation of the experience and social world under investigation" (Denzin 1997:7); that is, what establishes the ethnographic account as credible, believable, trustworthy? Clifford identifies the deeply problematic character of authority in ethnographic writing in the following fashion:

> If ethnography produces cultural interpretations through intense research experiences, how is unruly experience transformed into an authoritative written account? How, precisely, is a garrulous, overdetermined, cross cultural encounter shot through with power relations and personal cross purposes circumscribed as an adequate version of a more-or-less discrete "other world," composed by an individual author? (1983:120)

Clifford argues that the means of establishing ethnographic authority have changed since the 1970s and are now in a state of flux and experimentation. Classic participant-observation ethnography rested on *experiential authority*, invoking the personal knowledge and experience of the researcher in conveying a distinctive "feel" or sense of the style of a people or place: "Experience evokes a participatory presence, a sensitive contact with the world to be understood, a rapport with its people, a concreteness of perception" (Clifford 1983:130). Following Geertz, much contemporary ethnography involves *interpretive authority* highlighting "the creative (and in a broad sense, poetic) processes by which 'cultural' objects are invented and treated as meaningful" (1983:130). Through interpretation, for example, "we say a certain institution or segment of behavior is typical of, or a communicative element within, a surrounding culture" (1983:131).

Both experiential and interpretive authority are deeply "monologic" in that such texts are monopolized by the voice of the ethnographer, despite concerns to represent the point of view of those studied. Such texts reveal "the unreciprocal quality of ethnographic interpretation" which results when ethnographies "portray the cultural realities of other peoples without placing their own reality in jeopardy" (Clifford 1983:133; citing Leiris 1950; Maquet 1964; and Asad 1973).[8] In response, a variety of textual experiments seek to minimize monologic authority by infiltrating ethnographic accounts with dialogue. *Discursive authority* tries to minimize "any sharp separation of an interpreting self from a textualized other" (Clifford 1983:134), making heavy use of conversational exchanges between informant and ethnographer. *Polyphonic authority* preserves multiple, different voices, emphasizing heterogeneity and "the collaborative production of ethnographic knowledge" (139).

⌐   While analyses of rhetoric and authority seek to specify how ethnographic writing persuades or convinces readers, ethnographic texts can also be examined for the ways in which such writing is formatted, structured or organized. One such structuring device typical of ethnographies is the *narrative* or story. In technical terms, a narrative "presents a sequence of events," while a story connects a narrative to "a point," that is, to "a reason for being told that goes beyond, or is independent of, any need for the reporting of events" (Johnstone 1990:18). In most instances, however, ethnographers use the terms more or less interchangeably (e.g., Denzin 1997:158, citing Polkinghorne 1988:13).

Narratives allow ethnographers to transform experience into meaningful texts. Even the seemingly simple process of organizing a series of happenings into some sequence is not a straightforward, mechanical matter. Narrative involves "the representation of events" (Atkinson 1990:104): The writer decides not only which particular events are significant, which are merely worthy of inclusion and which are absolutely essential, and how to order these events, but also what is counted as an "event" in the first place. Such an ordering accords events different "evaluative connotations," as "the narration of people's doings not only arranges them in sequence, but also conveys consequence" (105). For example, narratives that extend "backward" from some critical incident to locate "predisposing" factors or conditions tend to exonerate or excuse misconduct, while narratives that focus upon subsequent consequences tend to accent fault and blame. Thus, narrative creates meaning, not by specifying universal truth conditions but by establishing particular connections between events:

> Narrative is the primary way through which humans organize their experiences into temporally meaningful episodes (Polkinghorne 1988:1). People link events narratively. The meaning of each event is produced by its temporal position and role in a comprehensible whole. Narratively, to answer the question "What does something *mean*?" requires showing how the something contributed to the conclusion of the episode. The connections between the events is the meaning. (Richardson 1990b:21)

As constructions, narrative can link or sequence events in many different ways, and can move toward any number of very different points. Such linkages and points tend to be conventionalized, leading to recurrent narrative styles in ethnography. Often these styles only become evident retrospectively, the emergence of a new narrative revealing the unnoted structuring of the prior narrative.

Van Maanen provides this illustration:

> Bruner (1986) provides a sharp example of how the implicit narrative struc-
> ture surrounding ethnographies of Native American cultures shifted radi-
> cally in the post-World War II years. Prior to the war, Bruner notes that the
> dominant story both Indians and ethnographers told was one in which the
> past was glorified, the present disorganized, and the future promised assim-
> ilation. After the war, this melting-pot tale rapidly lost credibility, and a
> new narrative emerged in which the past was viewed as exploitation and the
> present resistance, and the future promised ethnic resurgence. (1988:11)

In sum, ethnographic writing relies on narrative in a variety of forms as
devices for organizing or structuring accounts of social life. In this sense, narratives provide ethnographers with standardized models or "[t]extual formats
[which] make the social world readable." But structuring or making social life
readable has its costs: "Readable narratives . . . necessarily reduce and subsume
the complexities and indeterminacies of social life" (Atkinson 1990:11, 14).
Indeed, some contend that the reduction of social life to structured narrative,
wrought by the ethnographer's representational choices, perpetrates a kind of
"symbolic violence" (Bourdieu and Passeron 1977).

NAVIGATING THE REALIST/RELATIVIST DIVIDE

As ethnographers take up and seriously engage matters of representation,
they encounter epistemologically complex if not dangerous issues. These issues
arise from the possible "eclipse of the real by the representational" (Gubrium and
Holstein 1997:105), that is, by the radically relativist claim that there is no "reality" beyond or independent of its specific representations. Extreme versions of
"skeptical" postmodernism (Rosenau 1992), for example, question the need for a
concept of reality and the value of representation:

> Skeptical postmodernists argue that reality is pure illusion: everything is
> intertextual, not causal or predictive. . . . [They] refuse to enter the discus-
> sion on the nature of reality; they either doubt that a conception of reality
> need exist at all (Fokkema 1984:45) or argue that if it does it is "the conse-
> quence rather than the cause of scientific activity" (Latour and Woolgar
> 1979:153). (Rosenau 1992:22, 110)

> Representation is politically, socially, culturally, linguistically, and episte-
> mologically arbitrary. It signifies mastery. . . . In the absence of truth one
> must welcome multiple interpretations, whereas representation assumes
> something out there is true or valid enough to be re-presented. Modern rep-
> resentation assumes "meaning or truth preceded and determined the repre-
> sentation that communicated it." Postmodernists argue that it is the other
> way around; representations create the "truth" they supposedly reflect
> (Ryan 1988:560). (Rosenau 1992:94, 95)

While ethnographers generally remain committed to the idea of empirical
research, they come down very differently with regard to these issues of reality

and representation. Two major stances are evident. Those more influenced by postmodern ideas insist on rejecting any strong version of realism and instead turn to new representational forms and procedures. In contrast, others maintain that rejecting all realist assumptions deprives ethnography of its distinctive warrant—discovering and describing social worlds—and hence seek ways of maintaining some grounding notion of reality while also providing a place for issues of representation.

Denzin's postmodern-influenced "interpretive ethnography" provides one of the most elaborated examples of the first approach to the realist/representation tension. Denzin consistently rejects any "postpositivist" practice that assumes the existence of social reality independently of its textual representations, insisting on the unbridgeable differences between lived experience and representation of that experience. Ethnographies can never provide direct access to others' lived experience, but only textually mediated versions of experience; ethnographic accounts thus rest on "textually constructed presence" rather than "pure presence" (1997:5). Appeals to "reality" are thus chimerical, as Denzin rejects any possibility of determining the truth or accuracy of ethnographic accounts: "There can never be a final, accurate representation of what was meant or said—only different textual representations of different experiences" (1997:5).[9] Denzin thus finds the core of ethnography in its representational practices, a position Tyler (1986:138) articulated as follows: "No object of any kind precedes and constrains the ethnography. It creates its own objects in its unfolding and the reader supplies the rest."

But for Denzin, abandoning reality is not equivalent to foregoing empirical research. Indeed, he disavows postmodernist disinterest in the empirical, particularly its claim that there are no criteria for assessing accounts/representations of social life. But he also wants an ethnography that can empirically apprehend the distinctive "hyperreality" of postmodern society, that is, a reality marked by rapid change, blurred boundaries, pervasive images. To this end he proposes a representationally oriented ethnography that is careful, self-conscious and experimental in representing social life in as open, nonauthoritative ways as possible. The key here is

> . . . to strip any text of its external claims to authority. Every text must be taken on its own terms. The desire to produce a valid and authoritative text is renounced. The unmasking of validity as authority now exposes the heart of the argument. If validity is gone, values and politics, not objective epistemology, govern science. (1997:9)

Such nonauthoritarian representation must first make explicit its own theoretical, political and moral commitments:

> An antifoundational, critical social science project seeks its external grounding not in science, in any of its revisionist, postpositivist forms, but rather in a commitment to post-Marxism and feminism with hope but no guarantees (Hall 1986:58). It seeks to understand how power and ideology operate through systems of discourse. . . . A good text is one that invokes these com-

mitments. A good text exposes how race, class, and gender work their ways
into the concrete lives of interacting individuals. (1997:9–10)

Denzin's ethnography thus seeks not "accurate description" but "emotionality,
caring, subjective understanding, dialogic texts, and the formation of long-term
relationships with those studied" (1997:28).

Many ethnographers, however, remain uneasy with this eliding of reality
into representation. Gubrium and Holstein's position is typical of those with
this concern:

> Not only are we reluctant to fully embrace the unbridled relativism . . . of
> skeptical postmodernism, but we don't want to give up on reality, so to
> speak. . . . [We remain committed] to documenting the social world, to the
> possibility of empirically based description of everyday life. For us, this is
> the enduring stuff of qualitative inquiry. (1997:99)

These ethnographers cite a number of specific concerns in rejecting the view
that ethnographic description "amounts only and entirely to representation"
(Gubrium and Holstein 1997:87). First, as Hammersley (this volume) notes, such
a position dissolves ethnography's distinctive, longstanding warrant—its ability
"to discover and represent faithfully the true nature of social phenomena." Secondly and relatedly, prioritizing textual realities promotes an "out of the streets,
into the armchairs" mentality (Best 1995) and an abandonment of direct, first-
hand research. As Gubrium and Holstein develop this concern (1997:88): "[Post-
modernism] portends the transformation of social experience into a postmodern
field of nothing but texts, with the likelihood of that field turning into yet
another field of texts, where the real is less grounded in lived experience than
embedded in the written page."

Finally, some ethnographers contend that an emphasis on representation promotes a profound self-centeredness that devalues learning about the social world:

> After all, if the analyst inevitably shapes the analysis, the reasoning goes, we
> should focus our attention, not on the subject of analysis, but on the analytic
> act. The focus shifts from social life to the analyst's self, a shift which is self-
> centered, self-congratulatory, and self-indulgent. Anything—but especially
> anything personal—is grist for the postmodernist mill: sexual memories,
> reactions to movies or fast-food restaurants, recollections of life's disap-
> pointments. All musings are equally worthy. (Best 1995:128–30)

Such concerns lead these ethnographers to combine some core assumptions
of realism with key relativist methodological tenets, including "a radical questioning of the certainty and authority of the scholarly text, a rejection of the
search for 'truth' and reason as absolutes, a denial of the intellectual and moral
distance between the academic and his or her human 'subjects,' (and) a suspicion of 'big' narratives of totalizing theory (historical, Marxist, sociological)"
(Atkinson 1992:38). Thus these approaches retain a commitment to some version
of realism but at the same time pursue postmodern representational issues in
ways that encourage critical examination of "their methodological assumptions

and choices with an eye to expanding their own epistemological and empirical horizons" (Gubrium and Holstein 1997:97).

Several such approaches focus on revising key realist assumptions in light of relativist concerns. Altheide and Johnson (1994:489), for example, propose an *analytic realism*, "based on the value of trying to represent faithfully and accurately the social world or phenomena studied," but understanding social reality "as interpreted world, not a literal world, always under symbolic construction." Similarly, Martyn Hammersley's concept of *subtle realism* (see "Ethnography and Realism," this volume) rejects a consistently realist approach as requiring the abandonment of analysis of the worlds of those studied as social constructions. But a consistently relativist position undermines the viability of the research process, generating a series of insoluble problems—circularity, infinite regress, recognition of "as many realities as there are people." His solution is to reformulate key tenets of both "naive" realism (the possibility of absolute or certain knowledge of the social world) and of relativism (that because the ethnographer is unable to conduct research from a position outside the social world, there are no phenomena independent of her claims about them). His subtle-realist ethnography thus recognizes "multiple, noncontradictory and valid" representations of reality, each framed from a particular "point of view which makes some features of the phenomenon represented relevant and others irrelevant."

Gubrium and Holstein take a somewhat different tack, seeking "the reflexive middle ground of qualitative inquiry" (1998:416) by successively bracketing a "reality" to look at *how* it is constructed, then turning around and reexamining *what* is being constructed. The result is a qualitative sociology that seeks to preserve rather than resolve the distinctive impulses of both realism and reflexive relativism: "We maintain that the tension within the enterprise— between the desire to describe and understand the social, on the one hand, and a growing realization that we ourselves are part of this enterprise, on the other—should not be expunged" (1998:417). This shifting back and forth between "the whats and the constitutive hows of social life, allowing us to shift our attention from the substantive or the contextual to the artful components of reality construction, and back again" relies on *analytic bracketing*. Gubrium and Holstein insist on the need to treat realism and relativism as inseparable processes (1997:212):

> Like two sides of the same coin, interpretive artfulness and substantive conditions mutually inform one another, so they can never be fully separated. The most the researcher can do is to temporarily bracket one or the other in order to address its counterpart. The bracketing is decidedly heuristic, because knowledge of what is confined within the brackets insists on informing the analysis. One cannot understand artfulness without reference to its circumstances; conversely, the realities of everyday life are embodied in and through meaning-making processes. It is specious and unproductive to insist that qualitative inquiry separate, or assign different priority to, phenomena that are reflexively related.

NOTES

[1] In turn, these different theories, Bennett emphasized, reflect distinctive value commitments: the organic theory values "solidified, homogeneous group life"; the repression theory values "equalitarian democracy and non-neurotic, 'free' behavior" (1946:366).

[2] Mishler (1979a:3) argues that methodological procedures that seek to discover invariant relations between discrete variables lead to "the stripping away of contexts." While experimental procedures represent one extreme in these terms, all methods that seek "pure variables," i.e., those that are "independent, free-standing, orthogonal—that is, unrelated to measures of other variables," simplify and remove contextual factors and seek to reduce social life to separate, measurable categories.

[3] Summarizing the results of this procedure, Reiss notes: "In the seven-week period [of observation], we found thirty-seven cases in which force was used improperly. In all, forty-four citizens had been assaulted. In fifteen of these cases, no one was arrested. Of these, eight had offered no verbal or physical resistance whatsoever, while seven had" (1968:12). Elsewhere (1971:142) he reports that the rate of excessive police force was on the order of three instances per every 1,000 citizen encounters.

[4] Ethnomethodological researchers suggest that many ethnographers treat members' perspectives or categories as a set of "rules" with which to explain member behavior. Ethnomethodology holds that such categories or rules do not "cause" behavior so much as make it meaningful, and that like all rules their application to particular situations is problematic and not specified or specifiable by these rules themselves.

[5] This field/home separation takes a somewhat different and diluted form in sociological ethnographies. While in some instances sociologists interested in the urban underlife of slums or gangs moved to and lived in the settings studied (e.g., Whyte 1955), much sociological fieldwork involves "subway ethnography" in which the researcher visits the field for brief, discrete periods. As a result the tension between home and field is less extreme and pervasive.

[6] This tendency traces back to classic "salvage anthropology" and was perpetuated by Malinowski's insistence on finding a people to study who continued to live in their "pristine, natural condition," thus marginalizing and ignoring urban scenes and the mixings of peoples and cultures. "Wild" field settings complement romanticized notions of the ethnographer as engaged in a "heroized journey into Otherness" as suggested by Sontag's (1966) characterization of the work of Lévi-Strauss (Gupta and Ferguson 1997b:16ff).

[7] These efforts were also influenced by Hayden White's (1973) use of the approaches of literary criticism to analyze historical theorizing and writing.

[8] Asad (1973:17) provides one indicator of this lack of reciprocity in the fact that "virtually no European anthropologist has been won over personally to the subordinated culture he has studied; although countless non-Europeans, having come to the West to study its culture, have been captured by its values and assumptions, and also contributed to an understanding of it."

[9] Thus Denzin criticizes "postpositivist" efforts to specify distinctive criteria for evaluating ethnographies because they "cling to the conception of a 'world-out-there' that is truthfully and accurately captured by the researcher's methods" (1997:6).

Thick Description
Toward an Interpretive Theory of Culture

Clifford Geertz

I

In her book, *Philosophy in a New Key*, Susanne Langer remarks that certain ideas burst upon the intellectual landscape with a tremendous force. They resolve so many fundamental problems at once that they seem also to promise that they will resolve all fundamental problems, clarify all obscure issues. Everyone snaps them up as the open sesame of some new positive science, the conceptual center-point around which a comprehensive system of analysis can be built. The sudden vogue of such a *grande idée*, crowding out almost everything else for a while, is due, she says, "to the fact that all sensitive and active minds turn at once to exploiting it. We try it in every connection, for every purpose, experiment with possible stretches of its strict meaning, with generalizations and derivatives."

After we have become familiar with the new idea, however, after it has become part of our general stock of theoretical concepts, our expectations are brought more into balance with its actual uses, and its excessive popularity is ended. A few zealots persist in the old key-to-the-universe view of it; but less driven thinkers settle down after a while to the problems the idea has really generated. They try to apply it and extend it where it applies and where it is capable of extension; and they desist where it does not apply or cannot be extended. It becomes, if it was, in truth, a seminal idea in the first place, a permanent and enduring part of our intellectual armory. But it no longer has the grandiose, all-promising scope, the infinite versatility of apparent application, it once had. The second law of thermodynamics, or the principle of natural selection, or the notion of unconscious motivation, or the organization of the means of production does not explain everything, not even everything human, but it still explains something; and our attention shifts to isolating just what that something is, to disentangling ourselves from a lot of pseudoscience to which, in the first flush of its celebrity, it has also given rise.

Whether or not this is, in fact, the way all centrally important scientific concepts develop, I don't know. But certainly this pattern fits the concept of culture, around which the whole discipline of anthropology arose, and whose domination that discipline has been increasingly concerned to limit, specify, focus, and contain. It is to this cutting of the culture concept down to size, therefore actually insuring its continued importance rather than undermining it, that the essays in *The Interpretation of Cultures* (1973) are all, in their several ways and from their several directions, dedicated. They all argue, sometimes explicitly, more often merely through the particular analysis they develop, for a narrowed, specialized, and, so I imagine, theoretically more powerful concept of culture to replace E. B. Tylor's famous "most complex whole," which, its originative power not denied, seems to me to have reached the point where it obscures a good deal more than it reveals.

The conceptual morass into which the Tylorean kind of *pot-au-feu* theorizing about culture can lead, is evident in what is still one of the better general introductions to anthropology, Clyde Kluckhohn's *Mirror for Man.* In some twenty-seven pages of his chapter on the concept, Kluckhohn managed to define culture in turn as: (1) "the total way of life of a people"; (2) "the social legacy the individual acquires from his group"; (3) "a way of thinking, feeling, and believing"; (4) "an abstraction from behavior"; (5) a theory on the part of the anthropologist about the way in which a group of people in fact behave; (6) a "storehouse of pooled learning"; (7) "a set of standardized orientations to recurrent problems"; (8) "learned behavior"; (9) a mechanism for the normative regulation of behavior; (10) "a set of techniques for adjusting both to the external environment and to other men"; (11) "a precipitate of history"; and turning, perhaps in desperation, to similes, as a map, as a sieve, and as a matrix. In the face of this sort of theoretical diffusion, even a somewhat constricted and not entirely standard concept of culture, which is at least internally coherent and, more important, which has a definable argument to make is (as, to be fair, Kluckhohn himself keenly realized) an improvement. Eclecticism is self-defeating not because there is only one direction in which it is useful to move, but because there are so many: it is necessary to choose.

The concept of culture I espouse, and whose utility the essay below attempts to demonstrate, is essentially a semiotic one. Believing, with Max Weber, that man is an animal suspended in webs of significance he himself has spun, I take culture to be those webs, and the analysis of it to be therefore not an experimental science in search of law but an interpretive one in search of meaning. It is explication I am after, construing social expressions on their surface enigmatical. But this pronouncement, a doctrine in a clause, demands itself some explication.

II

Operationalism as a methodological dogma never made much sense so far as the social sciences are concerned, and except for a few rather too well-swept corners—Skinnerian behaviorism, intelligence testing, and so on—it is largely dead now. But it had, for all that, an important point to make, which, however we may feel about trying to define charisma or alienation in terms of operations, retains a certain force: if you want to understand what a science is, you should look in the first instance not at its theories or its findings, and certainly not at what its apologists say about it; you should look at what the practitioners of it do.

In anthropology, or anyway social anthropology, what the practitioners do is ethnography. And it is in understanding what ethnography is, or more exactly *what doing ethnography is*, that a start can be made toward grasping what anthropological analysis amounts to as a form of knowledge. This, it must immediately be said, is not a matter of methods. From one point of view, that of the textbook, doing ethnography is establishing rapport, selecting informants, transcribing texts, taking genealogies, mapping fields, keeping a diary, and so on. But it is not these things, techniques and received procedures, that define the enterprise. What defines it is the kind of intellectual effort it is: an elaborate venture in, to borrow a notion from Gilbert Ryle, "thick description."

Ryle's discussion of "thick description" appears in two recent essays of his (now reprinted in the second volume of his *Collected Papers*) addressed to the general question of what, as he puts it, "*Le Penseur*" is doing: "Thinking and Reflecting" and "The Thinking of Thoughts." Consider, he says, two boys rapidly contracting the eyelids of their right eyes. In one, this is an involuntary twitch; in the other, a conspiratorial signal to a friend. The two movements are, as movements, identical; from an I-am-a-camera, "phenomenalistic" observation of them alone, one could not tell which was twitch and which was wink, or indeed whether both or either was twitch or wink. Yet the difference, however unphotographable, between a twitch and a wink is vast; as anyone unfortunate enough to have had the first taken for the second knows. The winker is communicating, and indeed communicating in a quite precise and special way: (1) deliberately, (2) to someone in particular, (3) to impart a particular message, (4) according to a socially established code, and (5) without cognizance of the rest of the company. As Ryle points out, the winker has done two things, contracted his eyelids and winked, while the twitcher has done only one, contracted his eyelids. Contracting your eyelids on purpose when there exists a public code in which so doing counts as a conspiratorial signal is winking. That's all there is to it: a speck of behavior, a fleck of culture, and—voila! —a gesture.

That, however, is just the beginning. Suppose, he continues, there is a third boy, who, "to give malicious amusement to his cronies," parodies the first boy's wink, as amateurish, clumsy, obvious, and so on. He, of course, does this in the same way the second boy winked and the first twitched: by contracting his right eyelid. Only this boy is neither winking nor twitching, he is parodying someone else's, as he takes it, laughable, attempt at winking. Here, too, a socially established code exists (he will "wink" laboriously, overobviously, perhaps adding a grimace—the usual artifices of the clown); and so also does a message. Only now it is not conspiracy but ridicule that is in the air. If the others think he is actually winking, his whole project misfires as completely, though with somewhat different results, as if they think he is twitching. One can go further: uncertain of his mimicking abilities, the would-be satirist may practice at home before the mirror, in which case he is not twitching, winking, or parodying, but rehearsing; though so far as what a camera, a radical behaviorist, or a believer in protocol sentences would record he is just rapidly contracting his right eyelids like all the others. Complexities are possible, if not practically without end, at least logically so. The original winker might, for example, actually have been fake-winking, say, to mislead outsiders into imagining there was a conspiracy afoot when there in fact was not, in which case our descriptions of what the parodist is parodying and the rehearser rehearsing of course shift accordingly. But the point is that between what Ryle calls the "thin description" of what the rehearser (parodist, winker, twitches . .) is doing ("rapidly contracting his right eyelids") and the "thick description" of what he is doing ("practicing a burlesque of a friend faking a wink to deceive an innocent into thinking a conspiracy is in motion") lies the object of ethnography: a stratified hierarchy of meaningful structures in terms of which twitches, winks, fake-winks, parodies, rehearsals of parodies are produced, perceived, and interpreted, and without which they would not (not even the zero-form twitches, which, as a cultural category, are as much nonwinks as winks are nontwitches) in fact exist, no matter what anyone did or didn't do with his eyelids.

Like so many of the little stories Oxford philosophers like to make up for themselves, all this winking, fake-winking, burlesque-fake-winking, rehearsed-burlesque-fake-winking, may seem a bit artificial. In way of adding a more empirical note, let me give, deliberately unpreceded by any prior explanatory comment at all, a not untypical excerpt from my own field journal to demonstrate that, however evened off for didactic purposes, Ryle's example presents an image only too exact of the sort of piled-up structures of inference and implication through which an ethnographer is continually trying to pick his way:

> The French [the informant said] had only just arrived. They set up twenty or so small forts between here, the town, and the Marmusha area up in the middle of the mountains, placing them on promontories so they could survey the countryside. But for all this they couldn't guarantee safety, especially at night, so although the *mezrag*, trade-pact, system was supposed to be legally abolished it in fact continued as before.
>
> One night, when Cohen (who speaks fluent Berber), was up there, at Marmusha, two other Jews who were traders to a neighboring tribe came by to purchase some goods from him. Some Berbers, from yet another neighboring tribe, tried to break into Cohen's place, but he fired his rifle in the air. (Traditionally, Jews were not allowed to carry weapons; but at this period things were so unsettled many did so anyway.) This attracted the attention of the French and the marauders fled.

The next night, however, they came back, one of them disguised as a woman who knocked on the door with some sort of a story. Cohen was suspicious and didn't want to let "her" in, but the other Jews said, "oh, it's all right, it's only a woman." So they opened the door and the whole lot came pouring in. They killed the two visiting Jews, but Cohen managed to barricade himself in an adjoining room. He heard the robbers planning to burn him alive in the shop after they removed his goods, and so he opened the door and, laying about him wildly with a club, managed to escape through a window.

He went up to the fort, then, to have his wounds dressed, and complained to the local commandant, one Captain Dumari, saying he wanted his 'ar—i.e., four or five times the value of the merchandise stolen from him. The robbers were from a tribe which had not yet submitted to French authority and were in open rebellion against it, and he wanted authorization to go with his mezrag-holder, the Marmusha tribal sheikh, to collect the indemnity that, under traditional rules, he had coming to him. Captain Dumari couldn't officially give him permission to do this, because of the French prohibition of the mezrag relationship, but he gave him verbal authorization, saying, "If you get killed, it's your problem."

So the sheikh, the Jew, and a small company of armed Marmushans went off ten or fifteen kilometers up into the rebellious area, where there were of course no French, and, sneaking up, captured the thief tribe's shepherd and stole its herds. The other tribe soon came riding out on horses after them, armed with rifles and ready to attack. But when they saw who the "sheep thieves" were, they thought better of it and said, "all right, we'll talk." They couldn't really deny what had happened—that some of their men had robbed Cohen and killed the two visitors—and they weren't prepared to start the serious feud with the Marmusha that a scuffle with the invading party would bring on. So the two groups talked, and talked, and talked, there on the plain amid the thousands of sheep, and decided finally on five hundred sheep damages. The two armed Berber groups then lined up on their horses at opposite ends of the plain, with the sheep herded between them, and Cohen, in his black gown, pillbox hat, and flapping slippers, went out alone among the sheep, picking out, one by one and at his own good speed, the best ones for his payment.

So Cohen got his sheep and drove them back to Marmusha. The French, up in their fort, heard them coming from some distance ("Ba, ba, ba" said Cohen, happily, recalling the image) and said, "What the hell is that?" And Cohen said, "That is my 'ar." The French couldn't believe he had actually done what he said he had done, and accused him of being a spy for the rebellious Berbers, put him in prison, and took his sheep. In the town, his family, not having heard from him in so long a time, thought he was dead. But after a while the French released him and he came back home, but without his sheep. He then went to the Colonel in the town, the Frenchman in charge of the whole region, to complain. But the Colonel said, "I can't do anything about the matter. It's not my problem."

Quoted raw, a note in a bottle, this passage conveys, as any similar one similarly presented would do, a fair sense of how much goes into ethnographic description of even the most elemental sort—how extraordinarily "thick" it is. In finished anthropological writings, including those collected here, this fact—that what we call our data are really our own constructions of other people's constructions of what they and their compatriots are up to—is obscured because most of what we need to comprehend a particular event, ritual, custom, idea, or whatever is insinuated as background information before the thing itself is directly examined. (Even to reveal that this little drama took place in the high-lands of central Morocco in 1912 and was recounted there in 1968—is to deter-mine much of our understanding of it.) There is nothing particularly wrong with this, and it is in any case inevitable. But it does lead to a view of anthropological research as rather more of an observational and rather less of an interpretive activity than it really is. Right down at the factual base, the hard rock, insofar as there is any, of the whole enterprise, we are already explicating: and worse, explicating explications. Winks upon winks upon winks.

Analysis, then, is sorting out the structures of signification—what Ryle called established codes, a somewhat misleading expression, for it makes the enterprise sound too much like that of the cipher clerk when it is much more like that of the literary critic—and determining their social ground and import. Here, in our text, such sorting would begin with distinguishing the three unlike frames of interpretation ingredient in the situation, Jewish, Berber, and French, and would then move on to show how (and why) at that time, in that place, their copresence produced a situation in which systematic misunderstanding reduced traditional form to social farce. What tripped Cohen up, and with him the whole, ancient pattern of social and economic relationships within which he functioned, was a confusion of tongues.

I shall come back to this too-compacted aphorism later, as well as to the details of the text itself. The point for now is only that ethnography is thick description. What the ethnographer is in fact faced with—except when (as, of course, he must do) he is pursuing the more automatized routines of data collec-tion—is a multiplicity of complex conceptual structures, many of them superim-posed upon or knotted into one another, which are at once strange, irregular, and inexplicit, and which he must contrive somehow first to grasp and then to render. And this is true at the most down-to-earth, jungle fieldwork levels of his activity: interviewing informants, observing rituals, eliciting kin terms, tracing property lines, censusing households . . . writing his journal. Doing ethnography is like trying to read (in the sense of "construct a reading of") a manuscript—for-eign, faded, full of ellipses, incoherencies, suspicious emendations, and tenden-tious commentaries, but written not in conventionalized graphs of sound but in transient examples of shaped behavior.

III

Culture, this acted document, thus is public, like a burlesqued wink or a mock sheep raid. Though ideational, it does not exist in someone's head; though unphysical, it is not an occult entity. The interminable, because unterminable, debate within anthropology as to whether culture is "subjective" or "objective," together with the mutual exchange of intellectual insults ("idealist!"—"material-ist!"; "mentalist!"—"behaviorist!"; "impressionist!"—"positivist!") which accompanies it, is wholly misconceived. Once human behavior is seen as (most of the time; there *are* true twitches) symbolic action—action which, like phonation in speech, pigment in painting, line in writing, or sonance in music, signifies—the question as to whether culture is patterned conduct or a frame of mind, or even the two somehow mixed together, loses sense. The thing to ask about a bur-lesqued wink or a mock sheep raid is not what their ontological status is. It is the same as that of rocks on the one hand and dreams on the other—they are things of this world. The thing to ask is what their import is: what it is, ridicule or chal-lenge, irony or anger, snobbery or pride, that, in their occurrence and through their agency, is getting said.

This may seem like an obvious truth, but there are a number of ways to obscure it. One is to imagine that culture is a self-contained "superorganic" real-ity with forces and purposes of its own; that is, to reify it. Another is to claim that it consists in the brute pattern of behavioral events we observe in fact to occur in some identifiable community or other; that is, to reduce it. But though both these confusions still exist, and doubtless will be always with us, the main source of theoretical muddlement in contemporary anthropology is a view which developed in reaction to them and is right now very widely held—namely, that, to quote Ward Goodenough, perhaps its leading proponent, "culture [is located] in the minds and hearts of men."

Variously called ethnoscience, componential analysis, or cognitive anthro-pology (a terminological wavering which reflects a deeper uncertainty), this school of thought holds that culture is composed of psychological structures by means of which individuals or groups of individuals guide their behavior. "A society's culture," to quote Goodenough again, this time in a passage which has become the *locus classicus* of the whole movement, "consists of whatever it is one has to know or believe in order to operate in a manner acceptable to its mem-bers." And from this view of what culture is follows a view, equally assured, of what describing it is—the writing out of systematic rules, an ethnographic algo-rithm, which, if followed, would make it possible so to operate, to pass (physical appearance aside) for a native. In such a way, extreme subjectivism is married to extreme formalism, with the expected result: an explosion of debate as to whether particular analyses (which come in the form of taxonomies, paradigms, tables, trees, and other ingenuities) reflect what the natives "really" think or are merely clever simulations, logically equivalent but substantively different, of what they think.

As, on first glance, this approach may look close enough to the one being developed here to be mistaken for it, it is useful to be explicit as to what divides them. If, leaving our winks and sheep behind for the moment, we take, say, a Beethoven quartet as an, admittedly rather special but, for these purposes, nicely illustrative, sample of culture, no one would, I think, identify it with its score, with the skills and knowledge needed to play it, with the understanding of it pos-sessed by its performers or auditors, nor, to take care, *en passant*, of the reduction-ists and reifiers, with a particular performance of it or with some mysterious entity transcending material existence. The "no one" is perhaps too strong here, for there are always incorrigibles. But that a Beethoven quartet is a temporally developed tonal structure, a coherent sequence of modeled sound—in a word, music and not anybody's knowledge of or belief about anything, including how to play it, is a proposition to which most people are, upon reflection, likely to assent.

To play the violin it is necessary to possess certain habits, skills, knowledge, and talents, to be in the mood to play, and (as the old joke goes) to have a violin. But violin playing is neither the habits, skills, knowledge, and so on, nor the mood, nor (the notion believers in "material culture" apparently embrace) the violin. To make a trade pact in Morocco, you have to do certain things in certain ways (among others, cut, while chanting Quranic Arabic, the throat of a lamb before the assembled, undeformed, adult male members of your tribe) and to be possessed of certain psychological characteristics (among others, a desire for distant things). But a trade pact is neither the throat cutting nor the desire, though it is real enough, as seven kinsmen of our Marmusha sheikh discovered when, on an earlier occasion, they were executed by him following the theft of one mangy, essentially valueless sheepskin from Cohen.

Culture is public because meaning is. You can't wink (or burlesque one) without knowing what counts as winking or how, physically, to contract your eyelids, and you can't conduct a sheep raid (or mimic one) without knowing what it is to steal a sheep and how practically to go about it. But to draw from such truths the conclusion that knowing how to wink is winking and knowing how to steal a sheep is sheep raiding is to betray as deep a confusion as, taking thin descriptions for thick, to identify winking with eyelid contractions or sheep raiding with chasing woolly animals out of pastures. The cognitivist fallacy—that culture consists (to quote another spokesman for the movement, Stephen Tyler) of "mental phenomena which can [he means "should"] be analyzed by formal methods similar to those of mathematics and logic"—is as destructive of an effective use of the concept as are the behaviorist and idealist fallacies to which it is a misdrawn correction. Perhaps, as its errors are more sophisticated and its distortions subtler, it is even more so.

The generalized attack on privacy theories of meaning is, since early Husserl and late Wittgenstein, so much a part of modern thought that it need not be developed once more here. What is necessary is to see to it that the news of it reaches anthropology; and in particular that it is made clear that to say that culture consists of socially established structures of meaning in terms of which people do such things as signal conspiracies and join them or perceive insults and answer them, is no more to say that it is a psychological phenomenon, a characteristic of someone's mind, personality, cognitive structure, or whatever, than to say that Tantrism, genetics, the progressive form of the verb, the classification of wines, the Common Law, or the notion of "a conditional curse" (as Westermarck defined the concept of 'ar in terms of which Cohen pressed his claim to damages) is. What, in a place like Morocco, most prevents those of us who grew up winking other winks or attending other sheep from grasping what people are up to is not ignorance as to how cognition works (though, especially as, one assumes, it works the same among them as it does among us, it would greatly help to have less of that too) as a lack of familiarity with the imaginative universe within which their acts are signs. As Wittgenstein has been invoked, he may as well be quoted:

> We...say of some people that they are transparent to us. It is, however, important as regards this observation that one human being can be a complete enigma to another. We learn this when we come into a strange country with entirely strange traditions; and, what is more, even given a mastery of the country's language. We do not *understand* the people. (And not because of not knowing what they are saying to themselves.) We cannot find our feet with them.

IV

Finding our feet, an unnerving business which never more than distantly succeeds, is what ethnographic research consists of as a personal experience; trying to formulate the basis on which one imagines, always excessively, one has found them is what anthropological writing consists of as a scientific endeavor. We are not, or at least I am not, seeking either to become natives (a compromised word in any case) or to mimic them. Only romantics or spies would seem to find point in that. We are seeking, in the widened sense of the term in which it encompasses very much more than talk, to converse with them, a matter a great deal more difficult, and not only with strangers, than is commonly recognized. "If speaking *for* someone else seems to be a mysterious process," Stanley Cavell has remarked, "that may be because speaking *to* someone does not seem mysterious enough."

Looked at in this way, the aim of anthropology is the enlargement of the universe of human discourse. That is not, of course, its only aim—instruction, amusement, practical counsel, moral advance, and the discovery of natural order in human behavior are others; nor is anthropology the only discipline which pursues it. But it is an aim to which a semiotic concept of culture is peculiarly well adapted. As interworked systems of construable signs (what, ignoring provincial usages, I would call symbols), culture is not a power, something to which social events, behaviors, institutions, or processes can be causally attributed; it is a context, something within which they can be intelligibly—that is, thickly—described.

The famous anthropological absorption with the (to us) exotic—Berber horsemen, Jewish peddlers, French Legionnaires—is, thus, essentially a device for displacing the dulling sense of familiarity with which the mysteriousness of our own ability to relate perceptively to one another is concealed from us. Looking at the ordinary in places where it takes unaccustomed forms brings out not, as has so often been claimed, the arbitrariness of human behavior (there is nothing especially arbitrary about taking sheep theft for insolence in Morocco), but the degree to which its meaning varies according to the pattern of life by which it is informed. Understanding a people's culture exposes their normalness without reducing their particularity. (The more I manage to follow what the Moroccans are up to, the more logical, and the more singular, they seem.) It renders them accessible: setting them in the frame of their own banalities, it dissolves their opacity.

It is this maneuver, usually too casually referred to as "seeing things from the actor's point of view," too bookishly as "the *verstehen* approach," or too technically as "emic analysis," that so often leads to the notion that anthropology is a variety of either long-distance mind reading or cannibal-isle fantasizing, and which, for someone anxious to navigate past the wrecks of a dozen sunken philosophies, must therefore be executed with a great deal of care. Nothing is more necessary to comprehending what anthropological interpretation is, and the degree to which it is interpretation, than an exact understanding of what it means—and what it does not mean—to say that our formulations of other peoples' symbol systems must be actor-oriented.[1]

What it means is that descriptions of Berber, Jewish, or French culture must be cast in terms of the constructions we imagine Berbers, Jews, or Frenchmen to place upon what they live through, the formulae they use to define what happens to them. What it does not mean is that such descriptions are themselves Berber, Jewish, or French—that is, part of the reality they are ostensibly describing; they are anthropological—that is, part of a developing system of scientific analysis. They must be cast in terms of the interpretations to which persons of a particular denomination subject their experience, because that is what they profess to be descriptions of; they are anthropological because it is, in fact, anthropologists who profess them. Normally, it is not necessary to point out quite so laboriously that the object of study is one thing and the study of it another. It is clear enough that the physical world is not physics and *A Skeleton Key to Finnegan's Wake* not *Finnegan's Wake*. But, as, in the study of culture, analysis penetrates into the very body of the object—that is, *we begin with our own interpretations of what our informants are up to, or think they are up to, and then systematize those*—the line between (Moroccan) culture as a natural fact and (Moroccan) culture as a theoretical entity tends to get blurred. All the more so, as the latter is presented in the form of an actor's-eye description of (Moroccan) conceptions of everything from violence, honor, divinity, and justice, to tribe, property, patronage, and chiefship.

In short, anthropological writings are themselves interpretations, and second- and third-order ones to boot. (By definition, only a "native" makes first-order ones: it's *his* culture.)[2] They are, thus, fictions; fictions, in the sense that they are "something made," "something fashioned"—the original meaning of *fictiō*—not that they are false, unfactual, or merely "as if" thought experiments. To construct actor-oriented descriptions of the involvements of a Berber chieftain, a Jewish merchant, and a French soldier with one another in 1912 Morocco is clearly an imaginative act, not all that different from constructing similar descriptions of, say, the involvements with one another of a provincial French doctor, his silly, adulterous wife, and her feckless lover in nineteenth-century France. In the latter case, the actors are represented as not having existed and the events as not having happened, while in the former they are represented as actual, or as having been so. This is a difference of no mean importance; indeed, precisely the one Madame Bovary had difficulty grasping. But the importance does not lie in the fact that her story was created while Cohen's was only noted. The conditions of their creation, and the point of it (to say nothing of the manner and the quality) differ. But the one is as much a *fictiō*—"a making"—as the other.

Anthropologists have not always been as aware as they might be of this fact: that although culture exists in the trading post, the hill fort, or the sheep run, anthropology exists in the book, the article, the lecture, the museum display, or, sometimes nowadays, the film. To become aware of it is to realize that the line between mode of representation and substantive content is as undrawable in cultural analysis as it is in painting; and that fact in turn seems to threaten the objective status of anthropological knowledge by suggesting that its source is not social reality but scholarly artifice.

It does threaten it, but the threat is hollow. The claim to attention of an ethnographic account does not rest on its author's ability to capture primitive facts in faraway places and carry them home like a mask or a carving, but on the degree to which he is able to clarify what goes on in such places, to reduce the puzzlement—what manner of men are these?—to which unfamiliar acts emerging out of unknown backgrounds naturally give rise. This raises some serious problems of verification, all right—or, if "verification" is too strong a word for so soft a science (I, myself, would prefer "appraisal"), of how you can tell a better account from a worse one. But that is precisely the virtue of it. If ethnography is thick description and ethnographers those who are doing the describing, then the determining question for any given example of it, whether a field journal squib or a Malinowski-sized monograph, is whether it sorts winks from twitches and real winks from mimicked ones. It is not against a body of uninterpreted data, radically thinned descriptions, that we must measure the cogency of our explications, but against the power of the scientific imagination to bring us into touch with the lives of strangers. It is not worth it, as Thoreau said, to go round the world to count the cats in Zanzibar.

V

Now, this proposition, that it is not in our interest to bleach human behavior of the very properties that interest us before we begin to examine it, has sometimes been escalated into a larger claim: namely, that as it is only those properties that interest us, we need not attend, save cursorily, to behavior at all. Culture is most effectively treated, the argument goes, purely as a symbolic system (the catch phrase is, "in its own terms"), by isolating its elements, specifying the internal relationships among those elements, and then characterizing the whole system in some general way—according to the core symbols around which it is organized, the underlying structures of which it is a surface expression, or the ideological principles upon which it is based. Though a distinct improvement over "learned behavior" and "mental phenomena" notions of what culture is, and the source of some of the most powerful theoretical ideas in contemporary anthropology, this hermetical approach to things seems to me to run the danger (and increasingly to have been overtaken by it) of locking cultural analysis away from its proper object, the informal logic of actual life. There is little profit in extricating a concept from the defects of psychologism only to plunge it immediately into those of schematicism.

Behavior must be attended to, and with some exactness, because it is through the flow of behavior—or, more precisely, social action—that cultural forms find articulation. They find it as well, of course, in various sorts of artifacts, and various states of consciousness; but these draw their meaning from the role they play (Wittgenstein would say their "use") in an ongoing pattern of life, not from any intrinsic relationships they bear to one another. It is what Cohen, the sheikh, and "Captain Dumari" were doing when they tripped over one another's purposes—pursuing trade, defending honor, establishing dominance—that created our pastoral drama, and that is what the drama is, therefore, "about." Whatever, or wherever, symbol systems "in their own terms" may be, we gain empirical access to them by inspecting events, not by arranging abstracted entities into unified patterns.

A further implication of this is that coherence cannot be the major test of validity for a cultural description. Cultural systems must have a minimal degree of coherence, else we would not call them systems; and, by observation, they normally have a great deal more. But there is nothing so coherent as a paranoid's delusion or a swindler's story. The force of our interpretations cannot rest, as they are now so often made to do, on the tightness with which they hold together, or the assurance with which they are argued. Nothing has done more, I think, to discredit cultural analysis than the construction of impeccable depictions of formal order in whose actual existence nobody can quite believe.

If anthropological interpretation is constructing a reading of what happens, then to divorce it from what happens—from what, in this time or that place, specific people say, what they do, what is done to them, from the whole vast business of the world—is to divorce it from its applications and render it vacant. A good interpretation of anything—a poem, a person, a history, a ritual, an institution, a society—takes us into the heart of that of which it is the interpretation. When it does not do that, but leads us instead somewhere else—into an admiration of its own elegance, of its author's cleverness, or of the beauties of Euclidean order—it may have its intrinsic charms; but it is something else than what the task at hand—figuring out what all that rigmarole with the sheep is about—calls for.

The rigmarole with the sheep—the sham theft of them, the reparative transfer of them, the political confiscation of them—is (or was) essentially a social discourse, even if, as I suggested earlier, one conducted in multiple tongues and as much in action as in words.

Claiming his 'ar, Cohen invoked the trade pact; recognizing the claim, the sheikh challenged the offenders' tribe; accepting responsibility, the offenders' tribe paid the indemnity; anxious to make clear to sheikhs and peddlers alike who was now in charge here, the French showed the imperial hand. As in any discourse, code does not determine conduct, and what was actually said need not have been. Cohen might not have, given its illegitimacy in Protectorate eyes, chosen to press his claim. The sheikh might, for similar reasons, have rejected it. The offenders' tribe, still resisting French authority, might have decided to regard the raid as "real" and fight rather than negotiate. The French, were they more *habile* and less *dur* (as, under Mareschal Lyautey's seigniorial tutelage, they later in fact became), might have permitted Cohen to keep his sheep, winking—as we say—at the continuance of the trade pattern and its limitation to their authority. And there are other possibilities: the Marmushans might have regarded the French action as too great an insult to bear and gone into dissidence themselves; the French might have attempted not just to clamp down on Cohen but to bring the sheikh himself more closely to heel; and Cohen might have concluded that between renegade Berbers and Beau Geste soldiers, driving trade in the Atlas highlands was no longer worth the candle and retired to the better-governed confines of the town. This, indeed, is more or less what happened, somewhat further along, as the Protectorate moved toward genuine sovereignty. But the point here is not to describe what did or did not take place in Morocco. (From this simple incident one can widen out into enormous complexities of social experience.) It is to demonstrate what a piece of anthropological interpretation consists in: tracing the curve of a social discourse; fixing it into an inspectable form.

The ethnographer "inscribes" social discourse; *he writes it down.* In so doing, he turns it from a passing event, which exists only in its own moment of occurrence, into an account, which exists in its inscriptions and can be reconsulted. The sheikh is long dead, killed in the process of being, as the French called it, "pacified"; "Captain Dumari," his pacifier, lives, retired to his souvenirs, in the south of France; and Cohen went last year, part refugee, part pilgrim, part dying patriarch, "home" to Israel. But what they, in my extended sense, "said" to one another on an Atlas plateau sixty years ago is—very far from perfectly—reserved for study. "What," Paul Ricoeur, from whom this whole idea of the inscription of action is borrowed and somewhat twisted, asks, "what does writing fix?"

> Not the event of speaking, but the "said" of speaking, where we understand by the "said" of speaking that intentional exteriorization constitutive of the aim of discourse thanks to which the *sagen*—the saying—wants to become *Aus-sage*—the enunciation, the enunciated. In short, what we write is the *noema* ["thought," "content," "gist"] of the speaking. It is the meaning of the speech event, not the event as event.

This is not itself so very "said"—if Oxford philosophers run to little stories, phenomenological ones run to large sentences; but it brings us anyway to a more precise answer to our generative question, "What does the ethnographer do?"—he writes.[3] This, too, may seem a less than startling discovery, and to someone familiar with the current "literature," an implausible one. But as the standard answer to our question has been, "He observes, he records, he analyzes"—a kind of *veni, vidi, vici* conception of the matter—it may have more deep-going consequences than are at first apparent, not the least of which is that distinguishing these three phases of knowledge-seeking may not, as a matter of fact, normally be possible; and, indeed, as autonomous "operations" they may not in fact exist.

The situation is even more delicate, because, as already noted, what we inscribe (or try to) is not raw social discourse, to which, because, save very marginally or very specially, we are not actors, we do not have direct access, but only that small part of it which our informants can lead us into understanding.[4] This is not as fatal as it sounds, for, in fact, not all Cretans are liars, and it is not necessary to know everything in order to understand something. But it does make the view of anthropological analysis as the conceptual manipulation of discovered facts, a logical reconstruction of a mere reality, seem rather lame. To set forth symmetrical crystals of significance, purified of the material complexity in which they were located, and then attribute their existence to autogenous principles of order, universal properties of the human mind, or vast, a priori *weltanschauungen*, is to pretend a science that does not exist and imagine a reality that cannot be found. Cultural analysis is (or should be) guessing at meanings, assessing the guesses, and drawing explanatory conclusions from the better guesses, not discovering the Continent of Meaning and mapping out its bodiless landscape.

VI

So, there are three characteristics of ethnographic description: it is interpretive; what it is interpretive of is the flow of social discourse; and the interpreting involved consists in trying to rescue the "said" of such discourse from its perishing occasions and fix it in perusable terms. The *kula* is gone or altered; but, for better or worse, *The Argonauts of the Western Pacific* remains. But there is, in addition, a fourth characteristic of such description, at least as I practice it: it is microscopic.

This is not to say that there are no large-scale anthropological interpretations of whole societies, civilizations, world events, and so on. Indeed, it is such extension of our analyses to wider contexts that, along with their theoretical implications, recommends them to general attention and justifies our constructing them. No one really cares anymore, not even Cohen (well . . . maybe, Cohen), about those sheep as such. History may have its unobtrusive turning points, "great noises in a little room"; but this little go-round was surely not one of them.

It is merely to say that the anthropologist characteristically approaches such broader interpretations and more abstract analyses from the direction of exceedingly extended acquaintances with extremely small matters. He confronts the same grand realities that others—historians, economists, political scientists, sociologists—confront in more fateful settings: Power, Change, Faith, Oppression, Work, Passion, Authority, Beauty, Violence, Love, Prestige; but he confronts them in contexts obscure enough—places like Marmusha and lives like Cohen's—to take the capital letters off them. These all-too-human constancies, "those big words that make us all afraid," take a homely form in such homely contexts. But that is exactly the advantage. There are enough profundities in the world already.

Yet, the problem of how to get from a collection of ethnographic miniatures on the order of our sheep story—an assortment of remarks and anecdotes—to wall-sized culturescapes of the nation, the epoch, the continent, or the civilization is not so easily passed over with vague allusions to the virtues of concreteness and the down-to-earth mind. For a science born in Indian tribes, Pacific islands, and African lineages and subsequently seized with grander ambitions, this has come to be a major methodological problem, and for the most part a badly handled one. The models that anthropologists have themselves worked out to justify their moving from local truths to general visions have been, in fact, as responsible for undermining the effort as anything their critics—sociologists obsessed with sample sizes, psychologists with measures, or economists with aggregates—have been able to devise against them.

Of these, the two main ones have been: the Jonesville-is-the-USA "microcosmic" model; and the Easter-Island-is-a-testing-case "natural experiment" model. Either heaven in a grain of sand, or the farther shores of possibility.

The Jonesville-is-America writ small (or America-is-Jonesville writ large) fallacy is so obviously one that the only thing that needs explanation is how people have managed to believe it and expected others to believe it. The notion that one can find the essence of national societies, civilizations, great religions, or whatever summed up and simplified in so-called typical small towns and villages is palpable nonsense. What one finds in small towns and villages is (alas) small-town or village life. If localized, microscopic studies were really dependent for their greater relevance upon such a premise—that they captured the great world in the little—they wouldn't have any relevance.

But, of course, they are not. The locus of study is not the object of study. Anthropologists don't study villages (tribes, towns, neighborhoods . . .); they study *in* villages. You can study different things in different places, and some things—for example, what colonial domination does to established frames of moral expectation—you can best study in confined localities. But that doesn't make the place what it is you are studying. In the remoter provinces of Morocco and Indonesia I have wrestled with the same questions other social scientists have wrestled with in more central locations—for example, how comes it that men's most importunate claims to humanity are cast in the accents of group pride?—and with about the same conclusiveness. One can add a dimension—one much needed in the present climate of size-up-and-solve social science; but that is all. There is a certain value, if you are going to run on about the exploitation of the masses in having seen a Javanese sharecropper turning earth in a tropical downpour or a Moroccan tailor embroidering kaftans by the light of a twenty-watt bulb. But the notion that this gives you the thing entire (and elevates you to some moral vantage ground from which you can look down upon the ethically less privileged) is an idea which only someone too long in the bush could possibly entertain.

The "natural laboratory" notion has been equally pernicious, not only because the analogy is false—what kind of a laboratory is it where *none* of the parameters are manipulable?—but because it leads to a notion that the data derived from ethnographic studies are purer, or more fundamental, or more solid, or less conditioned (the most favored word is "elementary") than those derived from other sorts of social inquiry. The great natural variation of cultural forms is, of course, not only anthropology's great (and wasting) resource, but the ground of its deepest theoretical dilemma: how is such variation to be squared with the biological unity of the human species? But it is not, even metaphorically, experimental variation, because the context in which it occurs varies along with it, and it is not possible (though there are those who try) to isolate the y's from x's to write a proper function.

The famous studies purporting to show that the Oedipus complex was backwards in the Trobriands, sex roles were upside down in Tchambuli, and the Pueblo Indians lacked aggression (it is characteristic that they were all negative—"but not in the South"), are, whatever their empirical validity may or may not be, not "scientifically tested and approved" hypotheses. They are interpretations, or misinterpretations, like any others, arrived at in the same way as any others, and as inherently inconclusive as any others, and the attempt to invest them with the authority of physical experimentation is but methodological sleight of hand. Ethnographic findings are not privileged, just particular: another country heard from. To regard them as anything more (*or anything less*) than that distorts both them and their implications, which are far profounder than mere primitivity, for social theory.

Another country heard from: the reason that protracted descriptions of distant sheep raids (and a really good ethnographer would have gone into what kind of sheep they were) have general relevance is that they present the sociological mind with bodied stuff on which to feed. The important thing about the anthropologist's findings is their complex specificness, their circumstantiality. It is with the kind of material produced by long-term, mainly (though not exclusively) qualitative, highly participative, and almost obsessively fine-comb field study in confined contexts that the mega-concepts with which contemporary social science is afflicted—legitimacy, modernization, integration, conflict, charisma, structure, . . . meaning—can be given the sort of sensible actuality that makes it possible to think not only realistically and concretely *about* them, but, what is more important, creatively and imaginatively *with* them.

The methodological problem which the microscopic nature of ethnography presents is both real and critical. But it is not to be resolved by regarding a remote locality as the world in a teacup or as the sociological equivalent of a cloud chamber. It is to be resolved—or, anyway, decently kept at bay—by realizing that social actions are comments on more than themselves; that where an interpretation comes from does not determine where it can be impelled to go. Small facts speak to large issues, winks to epistemology, or sheep raids to revolution, because they are made to.

VII

Which brings us, finally, to theory. The besetting sin of interpretive approaches to anything—literature, dreams, symptoms, culture—is that they tend to resist, or to be permitted to resist, conceptual articulation and thus to escape systematic modes of assessment. You either grasp an interpretation or you do not, see the point of it or you do not, accept it or you do not. Imprisoned in the immediacy of its own detail, it is presented as self-validating, or, worse, as validated by the supposedly developed sensitivities of the person who presents it; any attempt to cast what it says in terms other than its own is regarded as a travesty—as, the anthropologist's severest term of moral abuse, ethnocentric.

For a field of study which, however timidly (though I, myself, am not timid about the matter at all), asserts itself to be a science, this just will not do. There is no reason why the conceptual structure of a cultural interpretation should be any less formulable, and thus less susceptible to explicit canons of appraisal, than that of, say, a biological observation or a physical experiment—no reason except that the terms in which such formulations can be cast are, if not wholly nonexistent, very nearly so. We are reduced to insinuating theories because we lack the power to state them.

At the same time, it must be admitted that there are a number of characteristics of cultural interpretation which make the theoretical development of it more than usually difficult. The first is the need for theory to stay rather closer to the ground than tends to be the case in sciences more able to give themselves over to imaginative abstraction. Only short flights of ratiocination tend to be effective in anthropology; longer ones tend to drift off into logical dreams, academic bemusements with formal symmetry. The whole point of a semiotic approach to culture is, as I have said, to aid us in gaining access to the conceptual world in which our subjects live so that we can, in some extended sense of the term, converse with them. The tension between the pull of this need to penetrate an unfamiliar universe of symbolic action and the requirements of technical advance in the theory of culture, between the need to grasp and the need to analyze, is, as a result, both necessarily great and essentially irremovable. Indeed, the further theoretical development goes, the deeper the tension gets. This is the first condition for cultural theory: it is not its own master. As it is unseverable from the immediacies thick description presents, its freedom to shape itself in terms of its internal logic is rather limited. What generality it contrives to achieve grows out of the delicacy of its distinctions, not the sweep of its abstractions.

And from this follows a peculiarity in the way, as a simple matter of empirical fact, our knowledge of culture . . . cultures . . . a culture . . . grows: in spurts. Rather than following a rising curve of cumulative findings, cultural analysis breaks up into a disconnected yet coherent sequence of bolder and bolder sorties. Studies do build on other studies, not in the sense that they take up where the others leave off, but in the sense that, better informed and better conceptualized, they plunge more deeply into the same things. Every serious cultural analysis starts from a sheer beginning and ends where it manages to get before exhausting its intellectual impulse. Previously discovered facts are mobilized, previously developed concepts used, previously formulated hypotheses tried out; but the movement is not from already proven theorems to newly proven ones, it is from an awkward fumbling for the most elementary understanding to a supported claim that one has achieved that and surpassed it. A study is an advance if it is more incisive—whatever that may mean—than those that preceded it; but it less stands on their shoulders than, challenged and challenging, runs by their side.

It is for this reason, among others, that the essay, whether of thirty pages or three hundred, has seemed the natural genre in which to present cultural interpretations and the theories sustaining them, and why, if one looks for systematic treatises in the field, one is so soon disappointed, the more so if one finds any.

Even inventory articles are rare here, and anyway of hardly more than biblio-
graphical interest. The major theoretical contributions not only lie in specific
studies—that is true in almost any field—but they are very difficult to abstract
from such studies and integrate into anything one might call "culture theory" as
such. Theoretical formulations hover so low over the interpretations they govern
that they don't make much sense or hold much interest apart from them. This is
so, not because they are not general (if they are not general, they are not theoretical), but because, stated independently of their applications, they seem either
commonplace or vacant. One can, and this in fact is how the field progresses conceptually, take a line of theoretical attack developed in connection with one
exercise in ethnographic interpretation and employ it in another, pushing it forward to greater precision and broader relevance; but one cannot write a "General
Theory of Cultural Interpretation." Or, rather, one can, but there appears to be
little profit in it, because the essential task of theory building here is not to cod-
ify abstract regularities but to make thick description possible, not to generalize
across cases but to generalize within them.

To generalize within cases is usually called, at least in medicine and depth
psychology, clinical inference. Rather than beginning with a set of observations
and attempting to subsume them under a governing law, such inference begins
with a set of (presumptive) signifiers and attempts to place them within an
intelligible frame. Measures are matched to theoretical predictions, but symptoms (even when they are measured) are scanned for theoretical peculiarities—
that is, they are diagnosed. In the study of culture the signifiers are not symptoms or clusters of symptoms, but symbolic acts or clusters of symbolic acts, and
the aim is not therapy but the analysis of social discourse. But the way in which
theory is used—to ferret out the unapparent import of things—is the same.

Thus we are led to the second condition of cultural theory: it is not, at least
in the strict meaning of the term, predictive. The diagnostician doesn't predict
measles; he decides that someone has them, or at the very most *anticipates* that
someone is rather likely shortly to get them. But this limitation, which is real
enough, has commonly been both misunderstood and exaggerated, because it has
been taken to mean that cultural interpretation is merely post facto: that, like the
peasant in the old story, we first shoot the holes in the fence and then paint the
bull's-eyes around them. It is hardly to be denied that there is a good deal of that
sort of thing around, some of it in prominent places. It is to be denied, however,
that it is the inevitable outcome of a clinical approach to the use of theory.

It is true that in the clinical style of theoretical formulation, conceptualization is directed toward the task of generating interpretations of matters already in
hand, not toward projecting outcomes of experimental manipulations or deducing
future states of a determined system. But that does not mean that theory has only
to fit (or, more carefully, to generate cogent interpretations of) realities past; it has
also to survive—intellectually survive—realities to come. Although we formulate
our interpretation of an outburst of winking or an instance of sheep-raiding after
its occurrence, sometimes long after, the theoretical framework in terms of which
such an interpretation is made must be capable of continuing to yield defensible

interpretations as new social phenomena swim into view. Although one starts any effort at thick description, beyond the obvious and superficial, from a state of general bewilderment as to what the devil is going on—trying to find one's feet—one does not start (or ought not) intellectually empty-handed. Theoretical ideas are not created wholly anew in each study; as I have said, they are adopted from other, related studies, and, refined in the process, applied to new interpretive problems. If they cease being useful with respect to such problems, they tend to stop being used and are more or less abandoned. If they continue being useful, throwing up new understandings, they are further elaborated and go on being used.[5]

Such a view of how theory functions in an interpretive science suggests that the distinction, relative in any case, that appears in the experimental or observational sciences between "description" and "explanation" appears here as one, even more relative, between "inscription" ("thick description") and "specification" ("diagnosis")—between setting down the meaning particular social actions have for the actors whose actions they are, and stating, as explicitly as we can manage, what the knowledge thus attained demonstrates about the society in which it is found and, beyond that, about social life as such. Our double task is to uncover the conceptual structures that inform our subjects' acts, the "said" of social discourse, and to construct a system of analysis in whose terms what is generic to those structures, what belongs to them because they are what they are, will stand out against the other determinants of human behavior. In ethnography, the office of theory is to provide a vocabulary in which what symbolic action has to say about itself—that is, about the role of culture in human life—can be expressed. . . .

It is not only interpretation that goes all the way down to the most immediate observational level: the theory upon which such interpretation conceptually depends does so also. My interest in Cohen's story, like Ryle's in winks, grew out of some very general notions indeed. The "confusion of tongues" model—the view that social conflict is not something that happens when, out of weakness, indefiniteness, obsolescence, or neglect, cultural forms cease to operate, but rather something which happens when, like burlesqued winks, such forms are pressed by unusual situations or unusual intentions to operate in unusual ways—is not an idea I got from Cohen's story. It is one, instructed by colleagues, students, and predecessors, I brought to it.

Our innocent-looking "note in a bottle" is more than a portrayal of the frames of meaning of Jewish peddlers, Berber warriors, and French proconsuls, or even of their mutual interference. It is an argument that to rework the pattern of social relationships is to rearrange the coordinates of the experienced world. Society's forms are culture's substance.

VIII

There is an Indian story—at least I heard it as an Indian story—about an Englishman who, having been told that the world rested on a platform which rested on the back of an elephant which rested in turn on the back of a turtle, asked (perhaps he was an ethnographer; it is the way they behave), what did the turtle rest on? Another turtle. And that turtle? "Ah, Sahib, after that it is turtles all the way down."

Such, indeed, is the condition of things. I do not know how long it would be profitable to meditate on the encounter of Cohen, the sheikh, and "Dumari" (the period has perhaps already been exceeded); but I do know that however long I did so I would not get anywhere near to the bottom of it. Nor have I ever gotten anywhere near to the bottom of anything I have ever written about. <u>Cultural analysis is intrinsically incomplete.</u> And, worse than that, the more deeply it goes the less complete it is. It is a strange science whose most telling assertions are its most tremulously based, in which to get somewhere with the matter at hand is to intensify the suspicion, both your own and that of others, that you are not quite getting it right. But that, along with plaguing subtle people with obtuse questions, is what being an ethnographer is like.

There are a number of ways to escape this—turning culture into folklore and collecting it, turning it into traits and counting it, turning it into institutions and classifying it, turning it into structures and toying with it. But they are escapes. The fact is that to commit oneself to a semiotic concept of culture and an inter-pretive approach to the study of it is to commit oneself to a view of ethnographic assertion as, to borrow W. B. Gallie's by now famous phrase, "essentially contest-able." Anthropology, or at least interpretive anthropology, is a science whose progress is marked less by a perfection of consensus than by a refinement of debate. What gets better is the precision with which we vex each other. . . .

My own position in the midst of all this has been to try to resist subjectiv-ism on the one hand and cabbalism on the other, to try to keep the analysis of symbolic forms as closely tied as I could to concrete social events and occasions, the public world of common life, and to organize it in such a way that the con-nections between theoretical formulations and descriptive interpretations were unobscured by appeals to dark sciences. I have never been impressed by the argument that, as complete objectivity is impossible in these matters (as, of course, it is), one might as well let one's sentiments run loose. As Robert Solow has remarked, that is like saying that as a perfectly aseptic environment is impossible, one might as well conduct surgery in a sewer. Nor, on the other hand, have I been impressed with claims that structural linguistics, computer engineering, or some other advanced form of thought is going to enable us to understand men without knowing them. Nothing will discredit a semiotic approach to culture more quickly than allowing it to drift into a combination of intuitionism and alchemy, no matter how elegantly the intuitions are expressed or how modern the alchemy is made to look.

The danger that cultural analysis, in search of all-too-deep-lying turtles, will lose touch with the hard surfaces of life—with the political, economic, stratifica-tory realities within which men are everywhere contained—and with the biolog-ical and physical necessities on which those surfaces rest, is an ever-present one. The only defense against it, and against, thus, turning cultural analysis into a kind of sociological aestheticism, is to train such analysis on such realities and such necessities in the first place. It is thus that I have written about nationalism, about violence, about identity, about human nature, about legitimacy, about revolution, about ethnicity, about urbanization, about status, about death, about time, and most of all about particular attempts by particular peoples to place these things in some sort of comprehensible, meaningful frame.

To look at the symbolic dimensions of social action—art, religion, ideology, science, law, morality, common sense—is not to turn away from the existential dilemmas of life for some empyrean realm of deemotionalized forms; it is to plunge into the midst of them. The essential vocation of interpretive anthropology is not to answer our deepest questions, but to make available to us answers that others, guarding other sheep in other valleys, have given, and thus to include them in the consultable record of what man has said.

NOTES

[1] Not only other peoples' anthropology *can* be trained on the culture of which it is itself a part, and it increasingly is, a fact of profound importance, but which, as it raises a few tricky and rather special second-order problems, I shall put to the side for the moment.

[2] The order problem is, again, complex. Anthropological works based on other anthropological works (Lévi-Strauss', for example) may, of course, be fourth-order or higher, and informants frequently, even habitually, make second-order interpretations—what have come to be known as "native models." In literate cultures, where "native" interpretation can proceed to higher levels— in connection with the Maghreb, one has only to think of Ibn Khaldun; with the United States, Margaret Mead—these matters become intricate indeed.

[3] Or, again, more exactly, "inscribes." Most ethnography is in fact to be found in books and articles, rather than in films, records, museum displays, or whatever; but even in them there are, of course, photographs, drawings, diagrams, tables, and so on. Self-consciousness about modes of representation (not to speak of experiments with them) has been very lacking in anthropology.

[4] So far as it has reinforced the anthropologist's impulse to engage himself with his informants as persons rather than as objects, the notion of "participant observation" has been a valuable one. But, to the degree it has led the anthropologist to block from his view the very special, culturally bracketed nature of his own role and to imagine himself something more than an interested (in both senses of that word) sojourner, it has been our most powerful source of bad faith.

[5] Admittedly, this is something of an idealization. Because theories are seldom if ever decisively disproved in clinical use but merely grow increasingly awkward, unproductive, strained, or vacuous, they often persist long after all but a handful of people (though *they* are often most passionate) have lost much interest in them. Indeed, so far as anthropology is concerned, it is almost more of a problem to get exhausted ideas out of the literature than it is to get productive ones in, and so a great deal more of theoretical discussion than one would prefer is critical rather than constructive, and whole careers have been devoted to hastening the demise of moribund notions. As the field advances one would hope that this sort of intellectual weed control would become a less prominent part of our activities. But, for the moment, it remains true that old theories tend less to die than to go into second editions.

Telling the Convict Code

D. Lawrence Wieder

In the following pages Wieder analyzes the nature and course of his efforts to carry out fieldwork in a halfway house for paroled ex-addicts in East Los Angeles. From his very first contacts in the house Wieder found that residents referred to the same "convict code" that researchers had described as fundamental to prison subcultures. Wieder identified the following specific "maxims" that made up the code: (1) do not snitch (inform); (2) do not cop out (admit that you have done anything illegal or against the house rules); (3) do not take advantage of other residents; (4) share what you have; (5) help other residents; (6) do not mess with other residents' interests; (7) do not trust staff—staff is heat; and (8) show your loyalty to the residents (Wieder 1974:115–118). In the materials included here Wieder examines the various ways this "convict code" was invoked and used by all those present in the halfway house—setting residents, staff, and researcher alike—to structure and create meaning in routine activities.   RME

INTERACTIONAL USES OF THE CODE

The Code as Told by Residents

My first contact with the project came about because I was looking for some kind of research position on a project dealing with deviance. I had heard through colleagues that the Department of Corrections might have something, so I called them. I was invited to their research offices in downtown Los Angeles and told that they had a position open. My colleague-to-be, Mr. Don Miller, said that his section of the Research Division had been charged with studying the halfway house in East Los Angeles. They had already made outcome studies and, there-fore, knew that a stay at the halfway house did not improve a parolee-addict's chances of abstaining from drug use. However, they did not know why this was the case. Miller and some of the members of the administration of the depart-ment thought that an exploratory study of the structure of the organization and of the lives of the residents might shed light on why the organization was not "working." The job promised considerable freedom, and it appeared quite appealing to me, so I arranged to take it.

I want to stress that I knew nothing about correctional establishments, that I had read none of the literature in this area, and at that point decided with other researchers in the Department of Corrections research office (Don Miller and Al Himmelson) that it would be desirable, at least at first, for me to remain ignorant in that regard. We felt that my ignorance was desirable, because equipped with the literature, my observations might be pushed in the direction of the results of previous studies. However, we did have brief discussions concerning the possi-bility of the existence of some kind of oppositional subculture in the halfway house and that that was one of the things I might look for.

Miller, who had already spent one day a week at the halfway house for six months or so, took me there and introduced me to the staff and a few of the resi-dents he had come to know. I was given an office in the upstairs of the building in an area where none of the staff had their offices. I had planned to try to avoid identification as a staff member, to observe what I could of the organization by being around it in as many places as I could, and to become friends with resi-dents so as to spend time with them in order to see what it was that they were doing and saying. To assist in doing this, I wore casual clothes, i.e., a sport shirt and cotton slacks, while the staff wore coat and tie, and intended not to locate myself next to staff while in the presence of the residents.

My first contact with the residents was provided by Miller, who introduced me to a resident with whom he had become friendly. He told the resident, whom I will call Sanchez, that I was going to study what was going on at the halfway house. Sanchez said that he would like to help, so the next time I was at the half-way house, I asked him to come to my office to tell me about the place. After he had sketched out the program for me and explained the difficulty in finding jobs for ex-convicts, I asked him how the residents got along with one another; partic-ularly, were there things that they should do and should not do. He said that "guys" should not snitch (inform on each other) or steal from one another. I asked if there were anything else, and he replied that, yes, there was more to *the code* than that. When I first heard that, I wondered if he had had so much contact with researchers that they had taught him to speak about moral expectations as form-ing a code, although later experience with other informants, who said essentially the same thing, led me to think that that was not the explanation. In any case, I was struck with the extent to which those expectations were verbally formalized.

I tried to get my informant to tell me more. For example, were there parts of the code that had to do with the use of drugs in the house. I said that I had heard that there were a lot of drugs at the halfway house. What had seemed up to that point to be a conversation that was filled with "good rapport" and was teaching me much, suddenly was destroyed. For a moment he said nothing. Then he told me that I could not ask that—at least not now. He said that for me to do research in the halfway house would require my making it clear that I was on the side of the residents. He suggested that I should publicly argue with the staff about their treatment of the residents, that I should not spend time with the staff, and that I should take guys out for beer and the like. I later came to see that he was telling me to behave like a good resident by showing my loyalty to the residents. He suggested that if I followed his instructions, then perhaps after several weeks I might find out something. Even then, however, he was unsure about the possibility of learning very much from the residents. After giving me this piece of advice, he then said he had to go set up the tables for dinner, and the conversation which had lasted for nearly an hour ended. I realized later that the very matters being talked about in the conversation with Sanchez made the course of that conversation understandable as a rule-governed dialogue. I saw why the conversation had halted—because for him to tell me about drug use would have amounted to or come close to snitching.

Following Sanchez's advice, in part, I then began my attempts at observing life at the halfway house. I went to the meetings the residents went to, sitting as they sat, and saying nothing. I went to lunch and dinner with them. I stayed with them when they washed the dishes and did other work around the house, sat on the front porch with them, and talked with them in the front room. When it seemed appropriate, I asked them to join me for a beer outside the house, though this was not a common occurrence. . . .

. . . [M]y contact with the residents was erratic at best. The very routines of the halfway house made contact difficult. The residents were rarely there when they did not have to be. This meant that during the day, only those that were at the house to work off board and room were typically there. The others would come in for dinner, sometimes for lunch, and for meetings, and then leave until curfew. I could never count on seeing a particular resident, since anyone with whom I had already talked would most likely not be around again except at meetings and meals.

Nevertheless, some halting and some extensive conversations were held, especially with residents who were working around the house, and sometimes with others immediately before dinner and after meetings. When these conversations did occur, I found the residents very ready to tell me something of their history, their complaints about parole, the halfway house, the police, the difficulty in finding good jobs, and what it was like in prison, but exceedingly little about life in the halfway house aside from relations with staff, and practically nothing at all about relations between residents and what the particular resident was doing besides working or looking for work.

. . . I began to see that the difficulty I was experiencing was produced by the same phenomenon that I was trying to investigate. I came to see that my experience of not being able to join conversations over the dinner table, although conversations were going on all around me, was being produced by the code that I was trying to explicate. When I was having a conversation with a resident and other residents passed by and said something in Spanish to him, followed by the conversation coming to a quick halt, I came to understand that this too was a sanctioning of the code.

In the third to fourth week of the study, my understanding of the code as it applied to me (that it applied to me and how it applied to me) was strengthened by some residents who explicitly pointed out the relevance of the code in and for their dealings with me. A point I wish to emphasize is that resident recitations of the code, or some element of it, were done in such a way that the residents were not simply describing a set of rules to me, but were also simultaneously sanctioning my conduct by such a recitation. I experienced their "telling the code" as an attempt to constrain my conduct by telling me what I could and could not appropriately do. In particular, they were often engaged in persuading me that some questions I might ask and some questions I did ask were "out of order" and that there were some areas of resident "underlife" that I should not attempt to explore. To show this in more detail, some concrete examples will be cited.

In my fifth or sixth week at the house, I encountered a younger resident, whom I will call Arnaldo, in the hall, who asked me if I knew of any jobs that were available. We were walking down the hall toward his dormitory, and both of us walked into it, when I said that I didn't know of any. Then he began to tell me of the pressure staff was putting on him because he was not yet employed. We talked about the ways staff was suspicious of him because he had not yet found work and what his social life was like without any money. The house manager came past and asked us to help unload a truck of toys for the annual Christmas party. While we unloaded the truck, Arnaldo told me about "kiss asses" who volunteered to do favors for staff, which, he explained, unloading the truck was not, since he was more or less ordered to do it. After we finished the unloading, I asked him if he would like a beer, and he said, "Sure, if you're buying." We continued our talk about "regulars," "snitching," and "kiss asses," and about getting stopped by the police because one lives at a halfway house, while we walked to a nearby tavern which reputedly catered to addicts. Though our conversation had been long and friendly, when I started to ask him about the clientele of the bar and the fact that I had heard that there were lots of guys "holding" (possessing drugs) there, Arnaldo said, "I don't know, but you'd be the last one I'd tell if I did." I was taken aback by this remark, for our talk during the past two hours had led me to think that I could ask such a question. I did not know what to say and did not press the matter further, as I might have done by asking him why I would be the last one he would tell. "The reason" seemed immediately obvious, since we had been talking about the code—for him to have told me would have bordered on snitching. He changed the topic by asking me if I had read a lot of books about addicts, and what I thought about what they had to say. At that point another resident, whom I will call Miguel, popped his head in the door for a moment and then left. We had resumed talking, when Miguel returned and came in. I said hello to him, at which point Arnaldo said that he had to get back to the house to set up for dinner, leaving me with Miguel, who sat down at the bar next to me.

I said that I had seen him just a moment ago, to which he replied that he had seen me, decided that he did not want to be "grouped" by me, and started to leave, but had seen the "fuzz" (police) patrolling the block outside and decided to come back, even if that meant talking to me. I had talked to Miguel several times in the house prior to this. I said, "What do you mean, be 'grouped' by me?" He said that when he was in the house talking to me that other guys would come past and say to him in Spanish, "Hey man, cut loose of that guy or he'll group you," which meant "talk to you about what is your business and none of his." At about this point, a girl he knew came up and started talking to him, and though he introduced me to her, when he turned to talk to her, I was not part of their conversation. A resident who was a parolee-at-large (one who breaks parole by deliberately avoiding all contact with his agent) walked in, spotted me, and left. I said to my "informant" Miguel that I was sorry that I could not convince residents that I would not let the staff know I had seen them, to which he replied, "Do you think that they would believe you?", as if to say that, of course, they would not. I said that I supposed they could not afford to. I asked him if he could tell me more about that, but we had to leave if we were to eat dinner at the halfway house. I suggested that we might go out for a beer that evening, and he said "Fine; we can talk more about your work then."

. . . [After dinner, when Miguel was ready to leave] I asked him where he would like to go, and he said that he would prefer somewhere outside the neighborhood, because my presence in a local bar would make other guys uncomfortable, and he did not want to be seen with me there. So we "headed" for a bar near the place where he worked. The ride in my car to the bar provided a stream of conversational topics—that he got a ride to work every day from another employee of the place where he worked; that he had that guy pick him up a block away from the halfway house so that his friend would not see him coming out of the halfway house; what kind of a bar we were going to; its bikini-clad waitresses; and, when we arrived, the fact that aside from the waitresses, there were no women in the bar. Then he turned his attention to what I was doing in the halfway house. He said that I was "fucking up" and "ranking" my job by talking to guys about themselves and the house. He said it was foolish to try to talk to convicts about personal matters like that, unless I knew them very well, and that that would not happen because guys were not there long enough. When I asked him what I could do, if that were the case, his response indicated that it was not "really" a problem of "establishing rapport," as he had previously seemed to indicate. Instead, he said that my "problem" was the kind of event it was for residents to be talking to me in the setting of the halfway house as that conversation would be construed by other residents. That is, it was an issue of residents' being seen by other residents as violating maxims of the code or appearing to be about to violate maxims of the code, especially prohibitions against snitching, copping out, and messing with other residents' interests, and prescriptions calling for a show of loyalty among residents and a show of distrust for staff.

He said that guys would rather not lie to me if they could help it, so they would try to steer clear of me if they could. He said that what I had been told was largely a lot of "bullshit." When I asked what was going on that kept guys from talking to me, he replied that they would tell each other not to talk to me, but more than that, every one of them had the following fear, though he, Miguel, talked to me in spite of it: every ex-con knows that he is very likely to go back to prison sometime, and that is especially so for addicts. On the return trip, the ex-con might meet others he had seen and known at the halfway house. That other guy might be there on a fifteen-year sentence and count himself as dead, that is, he would not care what happened to him. If the "dead man" recalled that someone had spoken to me at the halfway house, he could take that as an instance of someone's gossiping to me about the "dead man's" business and, in turn, attack and perhaps kill the supposed gossip. Therefore, it was dangerous to talk to a researcher. My attempts to get people to talk to me were "stupid" and were endangering persons who were helpful to me. . . .

. . . My data gathering efforts with the residents altered the character of my own circumstances as I knew them. As I obtained new materials about the residents' social world, my own field of action was progressively developed. By "telling the code," residents gave me a schema for seeing the sensible, factual, and stable properties of that part of my social world which intersected theirs. Residents' "telling the code" was consequential for the ways in which I saw my research circumstances. In this consequentiality, "telling the code" was not merely about the halfway house and events in it but was, as well, an active element of that same setting. . . .

The Code as Told by Staff

As I continued my observational work, I increasingly watched staff-resident encounters, the round of staff's activities, and the character of staff's talk. These observations showed me that staff had been taught the code by residents and each other and employed it in ways that paralleled its uses both by sociologists and by residents and inmates. Staff "told the code" in describing, interpreting, explaining, and finding the patterned character of resident conduct. They also used the code in giving advice to each other, in devising strategies, and in justifying their own actions and decisions. For staff, "telling the code" identified the meaning of resident behavior, portrayed situations from the point of view of residents, and defined staff's own situation and the meaning of staff's actions.

Some of my conversations with staff were tape recorded. Excerpts from . . . these conversations[1] show some of the ways that staff "knew" and "told" the code.

> W: Suppose a guy discovered that his jeweled watch had been stolen from him here in the house; what do you think he should do about it?
>
> PA: I think he should do a little investigating on his own and find out who took it. Okay, and then after he did that, he should confront the guy with it and tell him to give back his watch, or otherwise he will take care of the justice himself. I do not think he should tell staff.
>
> W: Okay, why?
>
> PA: Okay, well, if he tells staff about it, he's going to be branded as a fink.

The majority of them [the residents] would think that way. Any time you tell staff anything like that, you're a fink, you know.

W: What consequences do you see for him?

PA: Oh, you know, he's liable to get killed. Yeah, that's a sixty-forty possibility. There's a sixty-forty possibility he'd be a—his status in the eyes of the rest of the people—it would diminish because he did something you're not supposed to do, and staff would have feelings about it too. They wouldn't know whether they should take his side or say, "What the hell is the matter with you—you violated the rules."

The parole agent's response is almost identical to resident advice about the same matter. Staff elaborated the meaning of the situation from the standpoint of the residents by invoking the code as relevant to the possible alternatives a victim of theft would face. The moral and consequential meanings of a situation of action—what to do about a stolen watch—are generated by imagining the possible actions that a resident could take and then assessing those actions in terms of their likely meanings when defined by reference to the code.

. . . Like residents and sociologists, staff "told the code" to identify or name individual acts and patterns of repetitive action and to collect diverse actions under the rubric of a single motive and, in turn, to name them as the same kind of act. They rendered resident action sensible or rational by noting the ways in which resident action was rule-governed and directed toward achieving goals that were specified by the code. In this way staff offered a folk version of Weber's adequate causal analysis by showing that the typical patterned actions of residents followed from a "correct" course of reasoning. Staff portrayed the reasonable character of resident action by using the code and its elements to define the residents' situation. By "telling the code" as the residents' definition of their situation, staff showed that patterns of resident action had Durkheim's social-fact properties of exteriority and constraint. Residents' actions were reasonable in the sense that they had no choice but to behave in the fashion that they did.

In "telling the code," staff implicitly and explicitly used a wide range of social scientific conceptions, e.g., rule-governed action, goal-directed action, the distinction between the intended and unintended outcomes of action, the distinction between normatively required and normatively optional means of achieving a morally valued end, roles, role-bound behaviors, and definition of the situation. The use of these ethno-social scientific conceptions in "telling the code" structured staff's environment. It did this by identifying the meaning of a resident's act by placing it in the context of a pattern. An equivocal act then becomes "clear" in the way that it obtains its sense as typical, repetitive, and more or less uniform, i.e., its sense as an *instance* of the kind of action with which staff was already familiar. Staff's environment was also structured by the flexibility of "telling the code," which could render nearly any equivocal act sensible in such a way that it was experienced as something familiar, even though the act might not be "expected" or "predicted" in any precise meaning of those terms. For example, when the parole agent portrayed a diverse collection of actions—a resident's ridiculing the agent and other group members in a committee meeting, being late to the meeting, giving inadequate excuses, never siding with staff on any issue, and playing one staff member off against another—as instances of a familiar pattern of behavior (demonstrating one's opposition to staff as a display of one's loyalty), he made them parts of an already known pattern, even though the specific behaviors might not have been predicted. "Telling the code" also structured staff's environment by *connecting* a given act to its possible goal or to some specific consequence of the act among its many consequences. For example, one staff member identified a case of a resident's (possibly accidental) burning his own mattress as an attack on staff. This consequence was only one among many consequences, e.g., it created much smoke that would bother his dorm mates, and it could have served as a "cover" for some illegitimate activity. By seeing the potential code-relevance of the act as an attack on staff, the staff member identified "the" specific meaning of the act. Acts were also rendered sensible by connecting them to the activities of others (especially staff) in terms of role-bound reciprocities.

. . . Staff's "telling the code" also rendered important features of staff's environment *trans-situational* and *non-situation specific* in character. It rendered parts of staff's environment trans-situational by depicting them as recurrent and produced by a constantly operative set of motives (provided by the code) which were acted upon in every staff-resident encounter. Non-situation specificity was an accompaniment of trans-situationality, for in staff's hands, "telling the code" drew attention away from the specific features of the situation of an act (e.g., that it was *this* resident acting toward a specific staff member who had treated him in a particular way), while giving it a trans-situational explanation. By explaining the varieties of unpleasant gestures that residents directed toward them in terms of "the (trans-situational) principles by which these men live," staff "avoided" the possible interpretation of those unpleasant actions in such situation-specific terms as "getting back at a staff member for the way he treated the resident the day before" or "responding to an obvious attack on the resident's integrity." . . .

"Telling the code" among staff occurred with greatest regularity when residents were doing something troublesome or unusual. On the occasion that a staff member had to tell of the trouble, explain it, or propose some remedy for it, the code was frequently invoked to account for the source of the trouble. The most common trouble staff was called on to explain was the lack of progress in committees and groups. Once a week, a staff meeting was held in which the staff members who led committees reported on what their committee had done. When a staff member reported that his committee had not accomplished much, he explained that the residents could not and would not participate in any active way and that there was nothing that staff could do to alter that fact. Therefore, whatever the committee could accomplish had to be done by staff, and staff did not have enough time. Frequently other staff members would join in with sympathetic remarks (such as, "They regard group as a crock of shit . . . They think it's square to participate in committees," "They say going to a pool tournament at halfway house is for kids"), showing that they understood that the men would not participate and that they were deliberately motivated not to participate. When those in charge attempted to reject these accounts, they did so not by arguing against the claim that residents refused to cooperate, but by arguing against the claim that staff did not have enough time to do what residents would not do. In many cases, a staff member's explanation for nonproductivity which was based on resident refusal to participate was accepted and obtained the acknowledgment of others that the staff member was properly doing his job, even though his committee had not accomplished anything.

. . . Through these examples, it can be seen that the code was usable by staff in explaining, describing, and strategizing about resident behavior, not only in talking with the researcher, but also in dealings between themselves. On the occasions in which the code, its categories, and analogues of the code were offered by staff to staff, they were accepted as factual. That is, "telling the code" was unquestioned, and to the extent it suggested action, it was usable as the socially sanctioned grounds of action.

Through these accounts, staff identified actual or anticipated actions and events as instances of the same kinds of troublesome occurrences they had seen before and already knew how to deal with. Couching the accounts in the language of the code portrays the occurrences as independent of the particular resident personnel that were involved, e.g., it was not simply that those particular ten new residents were "testing the limits," but that any group of new residents would "test the limits." The occurrences were also thereby characterized as independent of the particular issues over which they had occurred, e.g., resident resistance to a committee was independent of the particular work of that committee, or disputes with staff over transportation were independent of residents' actual needs for transportation money, etc. The occurrences that were accounted for by use of the code and its analogues were also thereby seen as independent of the staff member who was involved. That is, it was not that this particular staff member had done something to the residents that obtained hostility or resistance in response. Instead, the code account provided that residents would behave that way toward any staff member.

The trans-situational and non-situation specific character of "telling the code" made it useful for staff in managing their relationships with each other. It served to relieve staff members of some of their responsibilities for motivating residents to participate in the program. It accounted for the relative lack of productivity in those aspects of the program which called for staff and residents to work together. It served to defend staff and staff ideas against the complaints of residents. It did these things by focusing attention away from the substance of the interactions, the substance of staff-resident work, and the substance of resident complaints about staff and staff programs. By "telling the code," staff could discount resident talk and action as not "really" substantive complaints and resistance to something in particular. Instead, they could interpret that talk and action as compelled by the residents' code-required need to show their loyalty to each other and to show their lack of trust in staff. . . .

PERSUASIVE AND REFLEXIVE FORMULATION: THE CODE AS ABOUT AND A PART OF THE SETTING

One *could* say that the "telling of the code" was a formulation of the organized character of resident life which residents and staff provided as a narrative which accompanied their affairs. The fact that the code was titled would make it appear to be some kind of "oral tradition" which had the moral force to govern the affairs of contemporary residents. Indeed, as I have indicated, residents spoke of the long-standing, "what-I-was-taught-as-a-child" character of the code. It was also the case that the code was "told" in showing the organized character of resident life. This was so in the ways that the reciting of the code "formulated" a particular occurrence being presently talked about as an instance of a typical occurrence. For example, the staff-aide's resistance to going to a neighborhood bar with parole agents was a show of his loyalty to the residents and was analyzed by him as an instance of avoiding the possibility of being seen as a snitch or other kind of turncoat.

It would appear that one *could* speak of the code as an "oral tradition" which was employed to instruct outsiders (like myself and staff) as to the organized character of what they had seen, were seeing, or would see. That is, one *could* say that residents employed this narrative to point out that an event, or "our relationship," or the behavior of that other resident, or the resident's own behavior were instances of patterns which were long-standing, which had been seen before, and which would be seen again. One would also then say that residents were "telling the code" in showing, or perhaps to show, that the particular event under consideration would have been enacted by "any resident," because persons who were residents were morally constrained to act in that fashion. That is, the code was employed to explain why someone had acted as they had and that that way of acting was necessary under the circumstances. In brief, one would be saying that the code was employed by residents to analyze for outsiders and perhaps for themselves the "social-fact" character of their circumstances, for they were noting particular occurrences as instances of regular-patterns-of-action-which-are-produced-by-compliance-to-a-normative-order.

While one *could* propose such an analysis of the code as an exegetical organizing narrative, that would be something like a narrative which is offered by the tour guide of a museum or the narration for a travelogue film; to do so would be misleading. Such an analysis, if it simply left the matter here, would be misleading in precisely the ways that a travelogue narrative differs from the "telling of the code." Since I find the travelogue narrative helpful by contrast, let me indicate what I understand as its features. In the travelogue story of a voyage, one encounters the story shown on the screen and the identifications, explanations, and descriptions of the narrative heard over a loudspeaker as discrete occurrences—narrative and picture. One hears the narrative as an outside commentary on the events depicted visually. In the case of "purely narrative films," the soundtrack never cuts to ongoing conversation or other sounds of events shown visually. Whatever talk comes over the loudspeaker, and all of that which comes over the loudspeaker, is narrative. The narrative begins with the beginning of the film and "completes itself" by the end. Whoever speaks on the soundtrack is doing narration. Typically, explanations are temporally juxtaposed to the scenic occurrences they explain. Finally, one listens to the narration and sees the film passively as a depicted scene for one's enjoyment or edification, not as an object that one must necessarily actively encounter and immediately deal with. Coupled with the feature of the passive audience, the narrator speaks for whomever listens. The parties hearing him are unknown to him, do not act upon his fate, and indeed have no involvement with him beyond their listening.

"Telling the code" contrasts with each of the above enumerated features of the travelogue narration. The crucial difference is that the code was not encountered "outside" the scene it was purportedly describing, but was told within that scene as a continuous, connected part of that scene by being manifested as an active consequential act within it.

The talk occurring in the halfway house that invoked the code, referred to the code, or relied on the code for its intelligibility, then, was not simply or merely a description of life in a halfway house. Instead, this talk was at the same time part of life in the halfway house, and it was a part that was itself included within the scope of things over which the code had jurisdiction. It is in this sense that talk involving the code was reflexive within the setting of its occurrence. . . .

"Telling the code" was not heard as a "disinterested" report delivered in the manner of a narrator who was speaking to unknown and distant persons about matters upon which they could not act. Instead, the code was being "told" about matters which were critical to hearer and listener, because "the telling" formulated and fed into their joint action. In contrast to that sort of narrative which is a description of the events displayed on a screen, the code was often "told" about the immediate behavior of the hearer and teller. It was multi-formulative and multi-consequential in the immediate interaction in which it was told and multi-formulative and multi-consequential in and for the occurrence of that interaction as an aspect of the social organization of the halfway house.

As a first step in explicating this multi-consequential and multi-formulative character of "telling the code," let us examine the range of "work" that a single utterance can accomplish. When talking with residents, staff and I often had a relatively friendly line of conversation terminated by a resident's saying, "You know I won't snitch." Hearing such an utterance functioned to recrystallize the immediate interaction as the present center of one's experiential world. "You know I won't snitch," multi-formulated the immediate environment, its surrounding social structures, and the connections between this interaction and the surrounding social structures. It (a) told what had just happened—e.g., "You just asked me to snitch." It (b) formulated what the resident was doing in saying that phrase—e.g., "I am saying that this is my answer to your question. My answer is not to answer." It (c) formulated the resident's motives for saying what he was saying and doing what he was doing—e.g., "I'm not answering in order to avoid snitching." Since snitching was morally inappropriate for residents, the utterance, therefore, formulated the sensible and proper grounds of the refusal to answer the question. It (d) formulated (in the fashion of pointing to) the immediate relationship between the listener (staff or myself) and teller (resident) by relocating the conversation in the context of the persisting role relationships between the parties—e.g., "For *you* to ask *me* that, would be asking me to snitch." Thus saying, "You know I won't snitch," operated as a renunciation, or a reminder of the role relationships involved and the appropriate relations between members of those categories. It placed the ongoing occasion in the context of what both parties knew about their overriding trans-situational relationships. It (e) was *one more* formulation of the features of the persisting role relationship between hearer and teller—e.g., "You are an agent (or state researcher) and I am a resident-parolee. Some things you might ask me involve informing on my fellow residents. Residents do not inform on their fellows. We call that snitching." Besides reminding the participants of a trans-situational role relationship, the features of that trans-situational role relationship were originally and continuously formulated through such utterances as, "You know I won't snitch."

Beyond the multi-formulative character of this single utterance, it was also a consequential move in the very "game" that it formulated. As a move in that field of action which it formulated, it pointed to the contingencies in that field as they were altered by *this* move. Furthermore, the utterance as a move obtained its sense and impact from those altered contingencies. Much of the persuasiveness of "telling the code" consisted in its character as a move in the field of action which it also defined. By saying, "You know I won't snitch," (a) the resident negatively sanctioned the prior conduct of the staff member or myself. Saying that the question called for snitching was morally evaluating it and rebuffing me or the staff. The utterance (b) called for and almost always obtained a cessation of that line of the conversation. It was, therefore, consequential in terminating that line of talk. In terminating that line of talk, it (c) left me or staff ignorant of what we would have learned by the question had it been answered. And it (d) signaled the consequences of rejecting the resident's utterance or the course of action it suggested. By saying, "You *know* I *won't* snitch," the resident pointed to what he would do if the staff persisted. He "said" he would not comply, irrespective of the staff's wishes. He thereby warned that the conversation would turn nasty if staff or I did not retreat from the question. He also pointed to the staff's obligation (or my obligation) to be competent in the affairs of residents. To refuse to acknowledge the sense and appropriateness of the resident's response was to risk being seen as incompetent in the eyes of all other residents and staff. Finally, by noting that what was being requested was *snitching*, a resident pointed to the consequences for himself if he were to go ahead and answer the question. The potential consequences for him could include beatings and even death. Since staff was obliged to protect residents, this fate was also consequential for them. The potential consequences of refusing to accept the credibility of the resident's response made that response persuasive.

Note

[1] I encountered innumerable instances of staff's "telling the code." For a more lengthy presentation of tape-recorded protocols of staff's "telling the code" and an analysis of the varieties of the modes of "telling the code," see Wieder (1969:235–50).

3

Ethnography and the Representation of Reality

Paul Atkinson

In this chapter I shall deal with various key features whereby the ethnographer constructs versions of social reality, and persuades his or her reader of the authenticity, plausibility and significance of representations of social scenes or settings. To begin with one should note that the ethnographic text conveys the authority of its account very largely through its persuasive force. The sociological message is conveyed through the use of descriptive writing, in which implicit analysis and "point of view" are inscribed. Second, the "data"—from which the published text is constructed—themselves frequently (not exclusively) consist of authored representations of social scenes. In other words, there is a process of translation and transcription that goes through several stages. The first stage of conventional, textual representation is the construction of "fieldnotes." The ethnographer records the scenes and settings that have been observed and engaged with, "writing down" what goes on: The imagery is that of transcription uninterrupted by self-conscious intervention or reflection. In contrast, the second phase of producing ethnographic texts, "writing up," carries stronger connotations of a constructive side to the writing. In this phase what was written "down" is treated as data in the writing "up."

However, both phases of the work involve the creation of textual materials; both are equally matters of textual construction. The text that is constructed out of the fieldnotes and whatever other data are at hand (such as interview transcripts, documents and so on) constructs and describes a social world. It conveys to the reader a sense of place and of persons. The physical space of the social world is peopled with actors who go about their daily lives and whose culture is portrayed. It is, therefore, part of the rhetorical work of the ethnography to persuade the reader of the existence of the world so represented and of the reasonableness of the account itself. Here therefore I shall deal with some aspects whereby ethnographers can construct "descriptions" which warrant the plausible, factual nature of their accounts, and which artfully foreshadow important thematic elements in the sociology itself. My argument is that we are dealing not with mere descriptive writing (whatever "mere" description might connote). It contains within it the *analytic* message of the sociology itself. In other words, when we talk of the role of "understanding" or "interpretation" in interpretative, qualitative studies, we are often dealing with something other than or additional to explicitly stated propositions. Often, the argument is conveyed at a more implicit level, through the very textual organization of accounts: in the way we select and write descriptions, narratives and so on; how we organize texts in thematic elements; how we draw upon metaphorical and metonymic uses of language; how, if at all, we shift point of view, and so on.

This descriptive work is accomplished throughout the ethnographic text, but it is especially important towards the beginning. Together with other bits of the textual apparatus, such as the title, it is crucial in establishing a framework of expectations and trust between the text and its reader. We often find that ethnographies begin with passages that "set the scene" by way of introduction to the entire work. One of the most important functions performed by introductory or prefatory passages is the provision of certain sorts of warrant for the account it precedes. A term widely used in structuralist and post-structuralist literary theory, *vraisemblance,* captures part of this function particularly well. That is, the production of "reality-like" effects—the ways in which an account's "authenticity," grounded in an everyday shared reality, is guaranteed. In general terms, it is not usually sufficient for a text/author simply to announce that a given account is to be read as a "factual" one. For a text to "come off" in that way then it normally has to conform to what we (conventionally) take to be realistic and factual texts.

What I have said so far applies equally well to what we normally think of as "literary" rather than scholarly or scientific products. This is certainly the case for varieties of "realistic" fiction. Indeed, this is one particular focus for a good deal of attention on the part of literary theorists. In theorizing about the textual conventions and codes of the novel and the short story, critical theorists have sought to uncover some of the ways in which texts achieve their reality-like effects, and can be read as plausible accounts of the everyday world of shared mundane experience. This is how Todorov puts it:

> One can speak of the vraisemblance of a work in so far as it attempts to make
> us believe that it conforms to reality and not to its own laws. In other words,
> the vraisemblance is the mask which conceals the text's own laws and which
> we are supposed to take for a relation with reality. (1968:2–3)

This is not a simple relation. As Todorov also remarks, "there are as many versions of vraisemblance as there are genres." There is, therefore, another facet to such verisimilitude: the extent to which texts recognizably conform to the canons of an appropriate mode of organization for a given genre.

As I have remarked at much greater length elsewhere (Atkinson 1983), there is a long, but often ambivalent, relationship between the literary and the ethnographic. It is abundantly clear that while they differ in many respects, such texts share many similar stylistic devices, used to achieve parallel effects. In the rest of this chapter I intend both to illustrate and to exploit such parallelism. For obvious reasons, the great majority of critical studies have been undertaken on works of "literature." It is, therefore, a handy heuristic device—at bare minimum—to take comparable extracts from literary and sociological texts, and to see what mileage may be gained from the use of "literary" insights towards an understanding of the ethnographic.

I intend, therefore, to take comparable extracts from the *openings* of texts, with particular emphasis on how the text creates an "introduction" to a "spirit of place." This is by no means the only sort of opening which is conventionally available, and as we shall see, it has sub-types. It is, however, a style of opening which is common in many realist novels and stories; it is also used by authors of ethnographic texts.

LITERARY AND SOCIOLOGICAL ACCOUNTS

Rather than pre-empting much of the later discussion by offering general propositions about such textual elements, let me now continue by presenting some specific examples. I have chosen two opening paragraphs from published works. They comprise a "literary" and a "sociological" exemplar. The choices are far from random. They have surface similarities in the subject-matter and treatment. Furthermore, the "literary" example has already been considered by critical theorists. Hence my own approach here is somewhat artful. It will no doubt tend to exaggerate similarities between the literary and the sociological but, initially at any rate, I would seek to justify it on heuristic grounds. In defense of the strategy, furthermore, I add that the pairing was in no sense hard to find. I did not have to spend a great deal of time and effort rummaging through the literature in order to come up with relevant examples.

The pair of extracts has been selected because the two extracts apparently describe similar scenes and settings—the first a lunch-room and the second a cocktail bar—and both describe similar social activities of "ordering." Moreover, as will become apparent, both do a great deal more than that. Furthermore, as I have already said, both extracts have the textual function of opening or introducing a longer written account: in one case a short story, and in the other an ethnographic account.

The first of the extracts is taken from a short story by Hemingway ("The Killers"); the second is the opening of the ethnography *The Cocktail Waitress* by Spradley and Mann (1975). The opening of the Hemingway is chosen primarily because it has already received critical consideration from a number of authors, including Fowler (1977). For ease of reference I have adopted the convention of numbering the separate sentences in each of the passages. First, then, the Hemingway extract, "Henry's Lunch-Room":

1. The door of Henry's lunch-room opened and two men came in.
2. They sat down at the counter.
3. "What's yours?" George asked them.
4. "I don't know," one of the men said.
5. "What do you want to eat, Al?"
6. "I don't know," said Al.
7. "I don't know what I want to eat."
8. Outside it was getting dark.
9. The street-light came on outside the window.
10. The two men at the counter read the menu.
11. From the other end of the counter Nick Adams watched them.
12. He had been talking to George when they came in.
13. "I'll have a roast pork tenderloin with apple sauce and mashed potatoes," the first man said.
14. "It isn't ready yet."
15. "What the hell do you put it on the card for?"
16. "That's the dinner," George explained.
17. "You can get that at six o'clock."
18. George looked at the clock on the wall behind the counter.
19. "It's five o'clock."
20. "The clock says twenty minutes past five," the second man said.
21. "It's twenty minutes fast."
22. "Oh, to hell with the clock," the first man said.
23. "What have you got to eat?"
24. "I can give you any kind of sandwiches," George said.
25. "You can have ham and eggs, bacon and eggs, liver and bacon, or a steak."
26. "Give me chicken croquettes with green peas and cream sauce and mashed potatoes."
27. "That's the dinner."
28. "Everything we want's the dinner, eh?"
29. "That's the way you work it."
30. "I can give you ham and eggs, bacon and eggs, liver."
31. "I'll take the ham and eggs," the man called Al said.
32. He wore a derby hat and a black overcoat buttoned across the chest.
33. His face was small and white and he had tight lips.
34. He wore a silk muffler and gloves.

(Hemingway, quoted in Fowler 1977:48–49)

In order to establish at least a preliminary framework, I shall rely heavily on Fowler's commentary on this extract. First, Fowler (1977) shows how the organization of the text achieves certain kinds of *effect*. The text is highly ordered and stylistically coherent, while the repetitive style, he suggests, contributes to a sense that the main "action" of the narrative is being postponed. This is achieved in large measure by the arrangement of nouns and pronouns. This, Fowler argues, "simultaneously holds the text together, and holds it up." In other words, it contributes to an overall effect of "suspense." This tight, repetitive ordering is evident, for instance, with respect to the thematic content of "food." As Fowler himself puts it:

"What's yours" in sentence 3 implies a deleted object naming a choice of food; in 4 the deletion is sustained; the food-choice is named by the referentially opaque "what," echoing George's "what" in 3; 6 and 7 repeat the refusal-to-name of 3–5 (note that 7 is an echoic syntactic transformation of the sum of 4 and 5). 13 implies a proverb "have" to "eat" in 5 and 7 and fills in the previously unspecified object-position "a roast pork tenderloin"; this object is then pronominalized as "it" and "that" in 14 and 15, 16 and 17. A new routine figuring the same topic begins with "what" in 23 (recalling 3, 3, 7) which is replaced by fully lexicalized noun phrases specifying items of food in 24, 25, 26, 30 and 31, and pronominalized in 27 and 28. (Fowler 1977:50)

The fragment of text also reveals a general stylistic feature of Hemingway's writing; that is, a tendency to write as an "impersonal" author who neither discloses himself, nor claims privileged insight or knowledge concerning the characters. Certainly the extract from the story is marked by a minimal degree of overt "interpretation" on the part of the author/narrator. As Fowler points out, there are

no verbs such as "feel" which would suggest an inner view, or "seem" which would draw attention to a narrator tentatively judging from outside a character ("He felt nervous" or "he seemed nervous" are taboo here); no sentence adverbs indicating degree of commitment ("probably," "definitely"); no evaluative adjectives. (Fowler 1977:53)

As Fowler also remarks, this general stylistic feature is paralleled by the minimal use of verbs introducing the dialogue (almost entirely "asked" and "said"). The only hints we get of the author/narrator's knowledge and allegiance are these:

The very first phrase, "The door of Henry's lunch-room," which, because it is definite, refers to an institution we assume to be already familiar to the narrator; sentence 12 which relates information about the Nick-George group's behavior anterior to the entry of the gangsters, and so suggests the narrator's membership of the group; and 31, "the man called Al," by which the narrator disclaims knowledge of "Al's" real identity. (Fowler 1977:53)

Overall, then, this brief and rather spare opening of "The Killers" achieves a good deal, in terms of style and narrative. The textual organization, coupled with the narrator's apparent lack of knowledge about "Al" and his companion, suggest an element of suspense. The two newcomers are not simply that—they are "outsiders": not known to the narrator and the other "insiders," they themselves do not "know the ropes" (hence the wrangle over what food is available). As the actors are introduced to the reader, so they are separated into the two opposed groups. Fowler concludes his brief analysis:

The action and the characters begin to receive some more specific, and at the same time mythological, symbolic, semantic content. I have already spoken of "intrusion," "aggression"; there is an opposition between the familiar and the alien, the inside or domestic and the outside or foreign, a stock thematic opposition expressed here by the polarization of the characters. (Fowler 1977:54)

Even without further detailed analysis one can glimpse here how the various elements of the text combine to produce the coherence and effect that they do by way of introducing the story.

When we turn to the second fragment, from *The Cocktail Waitress* (1975), we find that we are dealing with a not dissimilar text. Although I am not for one moment claiming that they are "the same" in content, style or author's intentions, there are certainly instructive similarities.

Brady's bar

1. It is an ordinary evening.
2. Outside a light spring rain gives softness to the night air of the city.
3. Inside Brady's the dim lights behind the bar balance the glow from the low-burning candles on each table.
4. A relaxed attitude pervades the atmosphere.
5. Three young men boisterously call across the room to the waitress and order another round of beer.
6. For one of them, recently come of age, tonight marks his legal entry into this sacred place of adult drinking.
7. A couple sits at a secluded corner table, slowly sipping their rum and Cokes, whispering to one another.
8. An old man enters alone and ambles unsteadily toward the bar, joining the circle of men gathered there.
9. The bartender nods to the newcomer and takes his order as he listens patiently to a regular customer who talks loudly of his problems at home.
10. Four men pick up their drinks and move away from the commotion at the bar to an empty table nearby.
11. The cocktail waitress brushes against a shoulder as she places clean ashtrays and napkins in front of them.
12. "Would you care to order another drink here?"
13. Her smile is pleasant, yet detached.
14. Her miniskirt and knee-high boots add silently to the image that her smile conveys.
15. "Scotch and water."
16. "Same."
17. "Manhattan."
18. "Gin and tonic."
19. She remembers the orders easily and on her way back to the bar stops to empty dirty ashtrays and retrieve the used glasses and bottles.
20. Two customers at the next table are on their third round, and as the waitress passes their table, one reaches out, touching her waist.
21. "What are you doin' after work, honey?"
22. The other man at the table laughs, she steps out of reach, ignoring the question, and continues on her way.
23. Seconds later, she gives the bartender her order, bantering with him about the customers.
24. In a few minutes she is back, effortlessly balancing a tray of drinks, collecting money, making change and always smiling.

(Spradley and Mann 1975:1–2)

Without for a moment suggesting that the authors of the sociological monograph were deliberately modeling themselves on Hemingway or any other specific author of fiction, one can immediately note some similarities in the respective treatments of similar social settings. There are differences too, of course. One immediate difference is that the narrator is willing to commit him or herself to greater freedom in describing the action: "a relaxed attitude"; "boisterously call"; "listens patiently"; "her smile is pleasant yet detached" and so on. Nevertheless, the overall impression conveyed in the passage is that of the observer. Although the narrator remarks on the participants, he or she does so from the point of view of an interpreter of observable actions and attributes— the waitress's clothing, "effortlessly balancing drinks" and so forth. Apart from the readily observable work of the bartender and the waitress, the narrator offers only two pieces of information which may not be observable directly: one young man has recently come of age, and one customer is identified as a "regular." Either we must assume that the narrator is claiming privileged prior knowledge, or that these were directly inferred from their behavior at the bar.

These two tidbits of information about the people in the bar serve only to highlight how little we are told about a relatively large number of customers. By and large they are identified for us by means of the most general and anonymous of categories: "three young men"; "one of them"; "a couple"; "an old man"; "the circle of men"; "the newcomer"; "a regular customer"; "four men." Similarly, "the bartender" and "the waitress" are not identified any further. The only name which is mentioned is Brady's, the name of the bar itself.

The repetitious nature of this fragment lies in the series of more or less anonymous characters about whom little more is learned. The only thematic coherence which is used to link them together as a series of "attributes" lies in the drinks which at least some of them are described as having or are heard ordering. In large measure this stylistic feature parallels the thematic coherence of the Hemingway passage, generated through the ordering (or not ordering) of food. Here we find the separate, minimally identified characters with: "another round of beer" (5): "their rum and Cokes" (7); "four men pick up their drinks" (10); "Scotch and water" (15); "Same" (16); "Manhattan" (17); "gin and tonic" (18); "on their third round" (20). In the stretch of dialogue in 15 to 18 ("an order") the naming of drinks is all that is done; and, apart from Brady's, drink names are the only names which appear.

Presumably, the ethnographer/narrator, having completed the research to be reported, knows more than is given away here. There is, one assumes, a good deal which could be divulged at the outset. For example, the bartender, the waitress and the regular should be known, at least by name. More "privileged," "inside" information could be vouchsafed the reader. In fact, in refraining from mentioning such things, this introduction is quite artfully managed, in much the same way that the Hemingway extract is constructed.

Neither extract is explicitly labeled as a "preface" or "introduction," or "setting the scene"; but quite clearly each of these extracts can be read as an opening passage. Both have a certain economy of style, and within a relatively brief span each accomplishes basic and important prefatory work. As already suggested, the Hemingway extract achieves a degree of "suspense." In a rather similar fashion, the opening of the *The Cocktail Waitress* deftly sets the scene by simultaneously establishing significant themes and holding back potentially available information.

Although clearly trading off accumulated knowledge (by virtue of the research to be reported in the monograph) the narrator in *The Cocktail Waitress* introduces the reader to the setting as if both were relative strangers, observing the scene from the outside, as it were. Hence the work is introduced with the expectation that there will be further exploration and discovery of "inside" knowledge. At the same time, as I have hinted already, themes are introduced and foreshadowed implicitly. Briefly, we might characterize them thus: Brady's is a relatively anonymous place, where customers have in common only their shared pursuit of drinking. It is characteristic of such a setting, then, that the only episode of social interaction which is reported here—apart from the ordering of drinks—is the waitress's refusal of an invitation and avoidance of social engagement. The way in which the waitress coolly disengages from this advance thus pinpoints the anonymity and lack of overall cohesion among the various parties. Similarly, the variety of the customers in Brady's bar is hinted at—again by virtue of the way in which they are introduced as a series, with no overt linkage, with only a bare amount of information. Other than the bar itself, the reader has no further framework in which to locate this collection of, apparently, randomly selected customers.

At this stage in the reading, an inspection of the text does not guarantee that such thematic strands will be confirmed. For all we know, the author/narrator will overturn our expectations. It is, however, instructive to note the paragraph which immediately follows this introductory scene-setting. Here the style shifts abruptly, from a "literary," descriptive mode to a discussion which is more clearly and recognizably "sociological":

> Ritually, this scene is repeated millions of times each night in bars and cocktail lounges throughout the country. Here one finds a wide range of behavior to observe: lonely individuals seeking human companionship for a few hours, people hustling for a little action, business men conducting interviews and closing deals, others gambling, dancing, holding wedding celebrations, and even attending birthday parties—those individual rites of passage by which our culture marks off the transition from child to adult. From corporation executive to college student, to skid-row bum, nearly every kind of person can be found in one or another type of bar. (Spradley and Mann 1975:2)

Here, then, at least one of the themes which has been presented implicitly in the first-hand "observational" account is now generalized into an explicitly sociological observation and related to recognizably sociological or anthropological concepts, such as "rites of passage." The *local* in Brady's bar is thus transformed into the *archetypal*, a thoroughly familiar and pervasive aspect of contemporary American culture.

What, then, of the relationship between these two paragraphs from *The Cocktail Waitress*? Arguably, perhaps, the first is redundant. The authors state their sociological themes explicitly and succinctly enough in the second section. But such a view would mistake the textual function of the introductory passage. It serves to warrant the subsequent sociological discourse, by establishing its vraisemblance. It furnishes the "guarantee" of an eyewitness report, couched in terms of the dispassionate observer, using the conventional style of the realist writer of fiction, or documentary reporter.

The Cocktail Waitress and "The Killers" share one further specific feature relevant to their vraisemblance. Each contains a passing reference to conditions "outside." In the Hemingway: "Outside it was getting dark. The street-light came on outside the window" (8 and 9). In the Spradley and Mann: "It is an ordinary evening. Outside a light spring rain gives softness to the night air of the city" (1 and 2). Again, one might at first glance think that such remarks were gratuitous, but in the context of the two descriptions these two fleeting observations are far from insignificant.

In the first place they both have a function in helping to establish the contrast between "inside" and "outside"—a basic theme in both narratives, where the arrival of unknown outsiders to a place of familiarity and "regulars" is of some significance. Further, these references are all that link the enclosed settings to the world beyond their confines. They have an important function in these texts quite disproportionate to their length or complexity. Indeed, it is their very "mundane" or "matter-of-fact" expression which contributes to their force.

Roland Barthes (1968) indicates for us the function of these two very similar passages, in identifying the importance of the "reality effect" (l'effet de réel). Such descriptive elements function to establish the "narrative contract" whereby the reader is, at least provisionally, guaranteed that the narrative refers to a recognizable world of shared everyday reality: "Elements of this kind confirm the mimetic contract and assure the reader that he can interpret the text as about a real world" (Culler 1975:193). Appositely enough for the particular examples considered here, Culler cites a counter-instance from Robbe-Grillet, in which mutually contradictory statements about conditions "outside" are made, so that the mimetic contract of the natural attitude is rendered problematic: "Outside it is raining . . . outside it is cold . . . outside it is sunny . . . " There, in the opening paragraph of Dans le labyrinthe, it is the arrangement—the symmetry and development—of the text itself which is of prime importance. A realistic referential function is subordinated and disrupted here. As Heath (1972) remarks in this context:

> The vraisemblance of traditional narrative is "brought to the surface," the expectations of the novel, so much a part of our Real, are demonstrated in the forms on which they depend; the "subject" of the novels is their composition, the structuration of the text itself which is present(ed) as such, strictly "un roman qui se pense lui-même."

This contrast, then, helps throw into relief the conventional character of the sort of vraisemblance and reality-effect achieved by the short passages referred to from "The Killers" and The Cocktail Waitress. They are by no means arbitrary or insignificant.

In general terms, therefore, a preliminary inspection of our first pair of examples helps to illuminate some features of ethnographic writing as exemplified in The Cocktail Waitress. We have seen how stylistic elements are used to "set the scene," to foreshadow sociological themes and arguments, and to establish a mimetic contract with the reader. The introductory passage provides the warrant of first-hand, authentic and "realistic" reportage, whereby the reader is introduced to a convincingly plausible reality.

Establishing the Narrative Contract

One of the important devices whereby the narrative contract is invited in the text is via the rhetorical device known as *hypotyposis*; that is, the use of a highly graphic passage of descriptive writing, which portrays a scene or action in a vivid and arresting manner. It is used to conjure up the setting and its actors, and to "place" the implied reader as a first-hand witness. The opening section of *The Cocktail Waitress* exemplifies it.

Crapanzano (1986) has discussed the role of ethnographic hypotyposis in relation to the writing of George Catlin's early descriptions of North American Indian scenes: "His aim is to impress his experience of what he has *seen* so strongly, so vividly, on his readers that they cannot doubt its veracity. It is the visual that gives authority" (57). Likewise, Edmondson (1984:38) remarks on the use of vivid visual imagery in Rex's introduction to Rex and Moore (1967), where "the immigrant" is presented to the reader in vivid terms and visual imagery. Edmondson also notes how Willis (1976) uses varieties of hypotyposis to enable the reader to "visualize" individual "lads."

The figure of hypotyposis is not used throughout the ethnographic monograph in equal measure. It is frequently deployed at key junctures. It is used to establish and reaffirm the relationship of co-presence of reader and author "at the scene." The narrative contract is thus maintained through these vivid representations. The figure is used, as we have seen already, to introduce settings and social actors, or to establish key transitions in the text. The reader enters into a sympathetic engagement with the social scene and its characters.

The use of this figure is especially well exemplified in Gouldner's *Patterns of Industrial Bureaucracy* (1954), at a point where the text establishes a new social and physical location, and seems to invite a particular response from the reader. The scenic transition represents a crucial analytic point in Gouldner's sociological analysis. Readers familiar with Gouldner's book will recall that its subject-matter concerns rule-use and social control in a gypsum plant. Among other themes and contrasts is the distinction between miners working underground and surface workers in the factory above. Gouldner wishes to argue that social relationships, groups and uses of social rules differ in the two contrasting locations. At one point in the text Gouldner takes the reader underground. The relevant chapter starts with a passage which is remarkable for its use of graphic imagery. It stands out even against the background of a vigorously written and memorably argued book. It has perhaps elements of the "purple passage," but it functions very clearly as a transition: the reader is transported into the new physical setting.

> The two production spheres, mine and surface, were sharply contrasting parts of the total work system at the Oscar Center plant. The workers themselves saw these two divisions as vitally different in many ways. Miners and surface men, workers and supervisors, all viewed the mine as being "in another world."
>
> Access to the mine could be secured by either of two routes: One way was to take a battered, gate-enclosed elevator at the surface, down to the mine's

"foot." Another, was to walk down (what to a sedentary researcher appears to be) an interminable length of rough, wooden staircases, under a low roof which necessitated frequent bending and careful footwork. A vault-like spiral of rock entombed the staircase as it crisscrossed downward. While descending the air grows moister, and trickles of water seemingly ooze out of nowhere.

At the bottom, or "foot" of the mine, the rough offices of the mine supervisor were hewn into rock, and here, too, were the miners' locker rooms and the maintenance men's machines and equipment. The rooms were separated from each other by unfinished walls, adorned by an occasional pin-up girl and desultory office-notices. Dominating the scene with its roaring noises was the rock crusher. Into the rock crusher railroad cars dumped large lumps of gypsum which came from the mine. . . .

At the "face," in these mining rooms, the men worked in near darkness, while moving beams of light from die lamps in their helmets formed ever-changing patterns against the darkness. Generally, the light was focused on objects, gyp rock and machines, while the men peered out of the darkness which enveloped them. A low ceiling, three and one-half to five feet high, often forced the miners to work bent over, and sometimes on their knees. The noise created by the machinery in operation, which was most of the time, made communication among the men at the face difficult. The roar of the crusher at the foot was matched by the clang of the joy-loader at the face as it scooped up the gyp set free by the miners' blasts. It was frequently necessary to shout in order to be heard, and even this occasionally proved inadequate. (Gouldner 1954:105-7)

At this point Gouldner himself notes that this description of the mine was deliberately written in what he calls a "subjective" way. In that footnote Gouldner raises the analytically important issue: that he and his research team felt that, unlike the surface, "the mine was not, and could not be, bureaucratized." The sociological observation was initially tied to the researchers' personal response to the mine itself. Their "hunches," theories and responses are mutually interdependent, and Gouldner attempts to convey them in the writing which introduces the underground mine as a physical and social environment. Gouldner draws on sensory imagery—tactile emphasis on the texture of the surfaces; the play of light and dark; the enveloping noise from the machinery. Noticeably, the miners themselves remain obscure and shadowy figures in comparison with the physical scene.

The use of hypotyposis here, therefore, serves several functions in the development of Gouldner's argument. It forcefully introduces the new setting, and marks the transition between above-ground and below-ground. The arrangement of the passage and its style "take" the reader beneath the surface, recapitulating the journey of the miners, and of course of the researchers. Again, therefore, we find this rhetorical figure being used to align the reader empathetically with a particular perspective on the social setting, the actors and the action within it. It draws reader and narrator together into a complicity of shared viewpoints.

There is a close relationship between the "authenticity" of these vivid accounts and the authority of the account—and hence of the author. Authenticity is warranted by virtue of the ethnographer's own first-hand attendance and participation. It is therefore mirrored in the "presence" of the reader in the action that is reproduced through the text. The ethnographer is a virtuoso—a witness of character and credibility. It is therefore important that "eye-witness" evidence be presented which recapitulates that experience.

The graphic representation of physical or social scenes is but one important textual element that exemplifies the significance of metaphorical writing. As Crapanzano says in relation to the Cadin reportage of the O-Kee-Pa ceremony: "he is in fact no objectivist, no Robbe-Grillet, describing the ceremony laboriously, metonymous step by metonymous step" (Crapanzano 1986:56). Indeed, none of the texts of sociological or anthropological ethnography essays nonmetaphorical descriptions; and certainly the graphic descriptive passages that "place" the work are often highly metaphorical. The "realism" of such textual elements is not achieved by their purely metonymic features.

The figure of hypotyposis may be coupled with a major metaphor which simultaneously establishes the setting to be explored and the proposed way of understanding that setting. An early example from the Chicago School can be taken from the opening sequence of Thrasher's *The Gang* (1927).

> The characteristic habitat of Chicago's numerous gangs is that broad twilight zone of railroads and factories, of deteriorating neighborhoods and shifting populations, which borders the city's central business district on the north, on the west, and on the south. The gangs dwell among the shadows of the slum. Yet, dreary and repellent as their external environment must seem to the casual observer, their life is to the initiated at once vivid and fascinating. They live in a world distinctly their own—far removed from the humdrum existence of the average citizen.
>
> It is in such regions as the gang inhabits that we find much of the romance and mystery of a great city. Here are comedy and tragedy. Here is melodrama which excels the recurrent "thrillers" at the downtown theaters. Here are unvarnished emotions. Here also is a primitive democracy that cuts through all the conventional social and racial discriminations. The gang, in short, is *life*, often rough and untamed, yet rich in elemental social processes significant to the student of society and human nature.
>
> The gang touches in a vital way almost every problem in the life of the community. Delinquencies among its members all the way from truancy to serious crimes, disturbances of the peace from street brawls to race riots, and close alliance with beer running, labor slugging, and corrupt politics—all are attributed to the gang, whose treatment presents a puzzle to almost every public or private agency in the city, which deals with boys and young men.
>
> Gangs, like most other social groups, originate under conditions that are typical for all groups of the same species; they develop in definite and predictable ways, in accordance with a form of entelechy that is predetermined by characteristic internal processes and mechanisms, and have, in short, a nature and natural history. (Thrasher 1927:3–4)

Thrasher's monograph here begins with a highly colored introductory passage. (The text reproduced above is the entire "Introduction.") It establishes a special physical setting for the account, and foreshadows a particular stance towards it. The style presages a romantic and naturalistic tone that will be repeated throughout the monograph. It is especially noticeable how the author implies authoritative knowledge which is provisionally withheld from the reader. There is a constant interplay between the familiar and the strange, the mundane and the exotic, the drab, everyday surroundings and the exotic action they contain. Here, then, the descriptive scene-setting is mingled with metaphorical writing which foreshadows much of the sociological treatment: the images of the "primitive" and "elemental" are significant. Thrasher begins to weave together the urban landscape with a parallel set of images—that of the "jungle." The "introduction" thus contains an implied contract. The text will display the unknown and the exotic, and will render it comprehensible. At the outset the taken-for-granted order of experience has been questioned: what to the casual observer is repellent will be shown to be exciting and vibrant, while the life of the "average" reader will be shown to be humdrum by comparison. The reader's attention is thus solicited in this titillating introduction. Moreover, as the last paragraph of the four makes clear, this alien reality will be naturalized once more into the domain of natural entities, of species and forms and mechanisms. The reader may embark on the journey of discovery safe in the knowledge that for all its strangeness, this social world will ultimately be revealed with all the reassuring certainty of natural history.

The initial "scene-setting" of ethnographic description is just one of several introductory and prefatory elements in the text that help to establish its authenticity and foreshadow an appropriate frame of reference for its implied reader. These elements all contribute to the potential persuasiveness of the text and its sociological arguments. The rhetorical devices already alluded to combine with what we might normally think of as the more straightforwardly "scientific." The sociological reader is unlikely to be engaged and swayed by a text merely by a "factual" account of its methodology, a careful review of the literature, and so on, if the rest of the text is found severely wanting.

Ethnography and Realism

Martyn Hammersley

In this chapter I want to discuss some of the philosophical underpinnings of ethnographic research. For some ethnographers such a discussion may seem irrelevant at best. There is a strong anti-philosophical strand in ethnographic thinking that places value on the practice and products of research and has little patience with or interest in discussions *about* research.[1] I have some sympathy with this. Philosophical discussion and debate can easily become a distraction; a swapping of one set of problems for another, probably even less tractable, set. Certainly, I do not believe that philosophy is foundational, in the sense that the problems in that realm can or should be resolved before we engage in social research. Indeed, in my view empirical research, accompanied by reflection on its practice and products, has much to contribute to philosophy. But there is no escape from philosophical assumptions for researchers. Whether we like it or not, and whether we are aware of them or not, we cannot avoid such assumptions. And, sometimes, the assumptions that we make lead us into error. I believe that this is the case with some of the epistemological ideas current amongst ethnographers. These ideas are my concern in this chapter.

At the center of these problems is the doctrine of realism, by which I mean the idea that there is a reality independent of the researcher whose nature can be known, and that the aim of research is to produce accounts that correspond to that reality. There can be little doubt about the widespread acceptance of this view. It is a philosophical doctrine on which much ethnography is founded. One of the most common rationales for the adoption of an ethnographic approach is that by entering into close and relatively long-term contact with people in their everyday lives we can come to understand their beliefs and behavior more accurately, in a way that would not be possible by means of any other approach. This was the reason for the shift within social and cultural anthropology in the late nineteenth and early twentieth centuries from relying on the reports of travelers and missionaries to first-hand fieldwork by anthropologists themselves. Similarly, within sociology, the same idea motivated Robert Park's advocacy of case-study research in Chicago in the 1920s. One of the most developed versions of the argument is to be found in the methodological writings of the Chicago sociologist Herbert Blumer. He criticizes experimental and survey research for failing to grasp the distinctive nature of human social life, and the key feature of the naturalistic research strategy that he recommends is "getting close" to naturally occurring social phenomena. The metaphors he uses to describe this approach—notably, "lifting the veils" and "digging deeper"—illustrate the realist assumptions that underlie his views (Hammersley 1989:127–28). In much the same way, David Matza advocates "naturalism," arguing that its core is a commitment to capture the nature of social phenomena in their own terms. And this idea is found in explicit form in many introductions to ethnographic method (Lofland and Lofland 1995; Schatzman and Strauss 1973; Hammersley and Atkinson 1995). From this point of view the goal of ethnographic research is to discover and represent faithfully the true nature of social phenomena. And claims about the superiority of ethnography are based precisely on the grounds that it is able to get closer to social reality than other methods.

Despite this commitment to realism, however, there is an important strand in ethnography that pushes in a contrary direction. Central to the way in which ethnographers think about human social action is the idea that people *construct* the social world, both through their interpretations of it and through the actions based on those interpretations. Again, Blumer is an influential figure here, though the same idea can be found in many other sources.[2] Blumer argues at one point that even people in geographical proximity to one another may live in different "social worlds" (Blumer 1969:11). Furthermore, the implication seems to be that these worlds are incommensurable, so that one cannot be treated as superior to another (and certainly not in the sense of being a truer representation of reality because these worlds *constitute* reality for the people concerned). This same idea has long been central to social and cultural anthropology, with its attempts to understand alien belief systems "from inside," rather than judging them from a Western, scientific point of view.[3]

This constructivism is quite compatible with realism so long as it is not applied to ethnographic research itself. It can be taken simply to require ethnographers to seek to understand (rather than judge) other people's beliefs, and to document the multiple perspectives to be found within and between societies. But we must ask: why should ethnographers be treated in a different way from others? To do so implies that they are outside of society, and this is surely unacceptable. Yet, once we treat ethnographic research as itself a social activity and seek to apply the constructivist approach to it, the question of the epistemological status of ethnographic findings is immediately raised. What may seem to follow is that in their work ethnographers create a social world (or worlds), rather than merely representing some independent reality (more or less accurately). And, it may be concluded, this world is no more nor less true than others; for instance than the perceptions and interpretations of the people studied. In this way, ethnographic constructivism seems to result in a relativism that is in conflict with ethnography's commitment to realism.

Faced with this apparent contradiction within ethnography, there are two obvious candidate solutions: to apply either realism or relativism consistently across the board, to both ethnographic method and to the social life that is studied. As I shall try to show, however, neither of these strategies is satisfactory.

If we apply ethnographic realism to our understanding of the people studied as well as to the research process, this implies an approach that is at odds with what is characteristic of ethnography. It means interpreting people's beliefs as the product *either* of contact with reality *or* of cultural bias. This abandons what is in my view one of the most valuable features of ethnography: its commitment to seeking to *understand* the perspectives of others, rather than simply judging them as true or false. It also involves the adoption of an asymmetrical approach to explaining beliefs, so that we appeal to different explanatory factors, depending on whether we take the beliefs to be valid or invalid. Those that are true are explained as products of the impact of reality, while those that are false are explained as the result of causal (probably cultural) factors producing error. There are good reasons to avoid this approach. One is that it is implausible, since it is clear that true conclusions can be reached on the basis of false premises; and even vice versa, if there are *implicit* assumptions that are false. And, given that we can have no direct contact with reality, beliefs can never be a simple product of such contact. Cultural assumptions and social interests are always involved in perception and cognition, and they may mislead us or they may lead us towards the truth (or more likely they may do both at the same time, in different respects). Given this, in my view there should be no difference between the mode of explanation we employ to deal with what we take to be true beliefs (or rational actions) and those we believe to be false (or irrational). Another reason why the asymmetrical approach is counterproductive is that we can never know for sure whether beliefs are true or false. Hence, we can never be certain which of the two explanatory schemes ought to be applied in any particular case. As a result, what we treat as a sound explanation at one point in time may later need to be abandoned in favor of a different explanation, not because we have found out anything new about the production or functioning of the belief itself, but simply because our assessment of its validity has changed.[4]

The alternative strategy for solving the conflict between realism and relativism within ethnography is to apply relativism to the research process. This has been more popular among ethnographers than the first strategy, especially in recent times. And this reflects, in part, the influence of a variety of trends in philosophical ideas. In the 1960s and 1970s the impact of phenomenology often encouraged relativism.[5] What was taken from Husserl and other phenomenologists was primarily the idea that our understanding of the world is constructed on the basis of presuppositions, those presuppositions being interpreted not as universal givens (in the manner of Husserl), but as culturally relative. Particularly influential here was Schutz's discussion of multiple realities, an idea derived from William James rather than from Husserl. While Schutz specified these as the worlds of everyday life, dreams, science, and religion, his discussion has sometimes been interpreted as predicating multiple realities constituted by different cultures; and indeed this is compatible with some of what he says, and certainly with James's treatment of the idea (Schutz and Luckmann 1974:22–23; Berger and Luckmann 1966).

Similar relativistic conclusions have been drawn from the later Wittgenstein's view that our language sets the limits of our world, and his discussions of forms of life and language games. Particularly influential here was Winch's application of these ideas to the understanding of other cultures. Winch argues that we can understand the beliefs and actions of people in a society very different from our own, for example those surrounding Zande magic, only by seeing them in the context of the cultural rules characteristic of that society. Furthermore, he claims that we cannot judge those beliefs without presupposing our own mode of thinking, the validity of whose assumptions and criteria can no more be established independently of our culture than can those of the Azande (Winch 1958, 1964). In a rather similar manner to Schutz, Winch treats science and religion as different cultural worlds.

Both these philosophical traditions had an impact on ethnography during the 1960s and 1970s. Often, their influence was diffuse, blending with constructivist and relativist thinking generated within it. In the case of ethnographers influenced by ethnomethodology, though, their impact was more focused; and it led to distinctive forms of ethnographic work.[6]

Running alongside these developments, and having a similar effect, was the emergence of revisionist ideas in the philosophy of science. Up until the early 1950s there was a substantial consensus among Anglo-American philosophers of science that the distinguishing feature of science was that the knowledge it produced was based on observation and logic. However, at that time, this "received view" came under increasing criticism, to the point where there was wide recognition that it could not be sustained (Suppe 1974). A variety of alternative views were developed, though none has formed a new consensus. Much the most influential product of this debate was Thomas Kuhn's book *The Structure of Scientific Revolutions* (1962). Kuhn argued that we cannot see the history of science as the cumulative development of more accurate and precise knowledge about the physical world. Rather, what we find in each field is a sequence of periods in which research is dominated by a particular paradigm, consisting of assumptions about the phenomena investigated and how they are to be studied and understood, these being embodied in investigations treated by scientists as exemplary. These periods of paradigmatic consensus are punctuated by what Kuhn calls "scientific revolutions," in which one paradigm is gradually abandoned and a new one takes its place. Kuhn argues that the replacement of one paradigm by another is not, and cannot be, based entirely on a rational appraisal of each paradigm in terms of the evidence for and against it. This is because what counts as evidence, and its significance, are determined by the paradigms themselves; so that scientists operating in terms of different paradigms effectively see the world in different ways. There has been much debate about whether Kuhn's views are relativist, and Kuhn has sought to clarify this matter himself (1970, Appendix). However, there is no doubt that his views have been interpreted in relativistic terms by many social scientists, including ethnographers.

These developments in the philosophy of science also stimulated changes within Anglo-American philosophy more generally, and in recent years there has been intense debate over realism. Here anti-realists have drawn both on resources present within the Anglo-American tradition, such as the early phenomenalism of the logical positivists and the later work of Quine, as well as on Dewey's pragmatism and continental European ideas (especially hermeneutics and post-structuralism). This anti-realist renaissance has also recently begun to have an impact on ethnography.[7]

The consequence of all these influences has been to encourage the application of a constructivist perspective to the research process itself; and thereby to undercut the realist rationale for ethnography, with its associated claim to objective description. Instead, it has been concluded by some ethnographers, often more informally than formally, that their accounts are simply one version of the world amongst others. This view is becoming increasingly popular, for example with ethnography being presented as a research paradigm that is incommensurable with others (Smith and Heshusius 1986; Smith 1989), or ethnographic accounts being treated as *creating* cultural realities through the rhetorical devices they employ (Clifford and Marcus 1986; Tyler 1985). Here, any vestige of ethnography as representation of an independent reality is abandoned. Thus, Tyler (1986:138) suggests that "no object of any kind precedes and constrains the ethnography. It creates its own objects in its unfolding and the reader supplies the rest." Without the ethnographer there is "only a disconnected array of chance happenings." This has led some to argue for ethnographic texts to be multi-vocal or dialogical, with the voice of the ethnographer playing only an equal, or perhaps even a subordinate, role to those of the people studied. Yet others have stressed the necessarily rhetorical character of ethnographic accounts and have advocated the use of modernist and post-modernist textual devices which subvert their own claims to knowledge.[8]

In my view, however, applying relativism to ethnographic method is no less problematic than extending the realism assumed in much ethnographic methodology to our understanding of social life. The problems of relativism are well known. Central is the old question of what status we are to give to the claim that all knowledge is culturally relative. If it is true, then it applies to itself; and therefore it is only true relative to a particular culture or framework, and maybe false from the perspective of other cultures or frameworks. Moreover, how are we to identify cultures or paradigms in a way that does not result in their proliferation, with people perhaps drawing cultural boundaries simply to protect the validity of their beliefs? In fact, any claims about the nature and boundaries of particular cultures would themselves presumably have to be treated as relative. This leaves us lost in circularity (Hammersley 1991).

Over and above the self-refuting character of relativism it is also worth pointing out its practical implications for ethnography. If it is true that what ethnographers produce is simply one version of the world, true (at best) only in its own terms, what value can it have? And there is no reason to suppose that ethnographers produce just one version of the world. Given that they differ among themselves in cultural assumptions, we must surely conclude that their accounts are to be viewed as creating multiple, incommensurable worlds on the basis of the same or similar research experience. In the words of one of the advocates of anti-realism, we may have to conclude that "there are as many realities as there are persons" (Smith 1984:386). If this is so, what is the point in spawning yet more versions of "reality," especially given the relative costs of ethnography compared with, say, armchair reflection? And why should some "realities" be published and discussed at the expense of others? Of course, in place of the claim to provide true representations of the world we might appeal to the idea that our accounts, while not true, are useful in some way, for example, in providing instructive ideas or even entertainment. But do not etiquette books, books counselling how to make friends and influence people, political tracts, novels, plays, films, as well as newspaper articles and television programs, fulfill these functions? What need is there for ethnography given all this? The practical implications of relativism for ethnography are worth reflection.

It seems to me, then, that we can resolve the ambivalence towards realism that is built into ethnography neither by extending ethnographic realism to our theorizing about human social life, nor by applying relativism to ethnographic method. In what direction does a solution lie, then? The first step, I think, is to recognize that the realism often built into ethnographic methodology is of a relatively naive or crude kind. Effectively, it assumes not only that the phenomena we study are independent of us, but that we can have direct contact with them, contact which provides knowledge whose validity is certain.[9] In practice, most ethnographers probably assume a weaker version than this: that the closer we can get to reality the more likely it is that our conclusions will be true. But the implication is the same: that if we could only get rid of the barriers lying between us and reality, most obviously our cultural preconceptions, we would be able to see reality itself. Once these barriers have been overcome, once the veil has been lifted, once we have dug below the surface impressions, reality itself will be revealed. Such a view is clearly indefensible. It assumes that there is some foundation of direct knowledge to which we can get access. But what form could that foundation take? All perception and observation are assumption-laden. And even if there were such a foundation, there is no means by which we could logically induce knowledge from our observations in such a fashion that its validity would be guaranteed.

The next step in the argument is to recognize that relativism is not the only alternative to naive realism. There is a great danger of backing ourselves into a corner by deploying a dichotomy which obscures the wide range of epistemological positions available. We can maintain belief in the existence of phenomena independent of our claims about them, and in their knowability, without assuming that we can have unmediated contact with them and therefore that we can know with certainty whether our knowledge of them is valid or invalid. The most promising strategy for resolving the problem, in my view, then, is to adopt a more subtle form of realism. Let me summarize the key elements of such a view.

1. The definition of "knowledge" as beliefs whose validity is known with certainty is misconceived. On this definition there can be no knowledge, since we can never be absolutely sure about the validity of any claims; we could always be wrong. In my view, we should instead define knowledge as beliefs about whose validity we are reasonably confident. While we can never be absolutely certain about the validity of any knowledge claim, and while we may sometimes be faced with a choice between contradictory claims that are equally uncertain in validity, often we *can* be reasonably confident about the relative chances of validity of competing claims. Assessment of claims must be based on judgments about plausibility and credibility: on the compatibility of the claim, or the evidence for it, with the assumptions about the world that we currently take to be beyond reasonable doubt; and/or on the likelihood of error, given the conditions in which the claim was made (see Hammersley 1992, chapter 4).

2. There are phenomena independent of our claims about them which those claims may represent more or less accurately. And true knowledge is true by virtue of the fact that it corresponds to the phenomena it is intended to represent (though, as I indicated, we can never be *certain* that any knowledge claim is true). This assumption is clearly an essential element of any realism. However, we must consider the issue of what the term "independence" means in this basic tenet of realism. This is complex. In one sense we are all part of reality and from that point of view cannot be independent of it. The same is true of any knowledge claims we make. However, what I mean by "independence" here is simply that our making of a claim does not itself change relevant aspects of reality in such a way as to make the claim true (or false). And it seems to me that most social science accounts are neither self-fulfilling nor self-refuting. While some predictions may become self-fulfilling, even here the relationship is not entirely determinate. Whether a prediction is fulfilled as a result of its being made public always depends on other conditions: on whether it is believed and on whether other factors intervene, for example. And I suspect that most social research findings have (at best, or worst) only an extremely weak influence on what they predict or describe. Other powerful factors are always involved. In this sense, then, for the most part reality is independent of the claims that social researchers make about it.

3. The aim of social research is to represent reality, but this is not to say that its function is to *reproduce* it (that is, to represent it "in its own terms"). Rather, representation must always be from some point of view which makes some features of the phenomena represented relevant and others irrelevant. Thus, there can be multiple, non-contradictory and valid descriptions and explanations of the same phenomenon.[10]

This subtle realism retains from naive realism the idea that research investigates independent, knowable phenomena. But it breaks with it in denying that we have direct access to those phenomena, in accepting that we must always rely on cultural assumptions, and in denying that our aim is to reproduce social phenomena in some way that is uniquely appropriate to them. Obversely, subtle realism shares with skepticism and relativism a recognition that all knowledge is based on assumptions and purposes and is a human construction, but it rejects these positions' abandonment of the regulative idea of independent and knowable phenomena. Perhaps most important of all, subtle realism is distinct from both naive realism and relativism in its rejection of the notion that knowledge must be defined as beliefs whose validity is known with certainty.[11]

What are the implications of subtle realism for the way we think about and practice ethnography? For one thing, subtle realism requires us to be rather more vigilant regarding the dangers of error than naive realism would lead us to be. We must accept that we necessarily rely on cultural assumptions, and that these can lead us astray, just as easily as leading us in the right direction. Certainly, we cannot legitimately claim that simply because we were "there" we "know." Yet this is the fundamental rhetorical strategy employed by ethnographers, as Geertz points out:

> The ability of anthropologists to get us to take what they say seriously has less to do with either a factual look or an air of conceptual elegance than it has with their capacity to convince us that what they say is a result of their having actually penetrated (or, if you prefer, been penetrated by) another form of life, of having, one way or another, truly "been there." And that, persuading us that this offstage miracle has occurred, is where the writing comes in. (1988:4–5)

Nor can we rely on the fact that because participants are "there" that *they* "know," as do those who define credibility in terms of respondent validation (Guba and Lincoln 1982). What we have here are rhetorical appeals to naive realism, and they are not sustainable because of the weakness of that philosophical position. However, the fact that the observer was there and/or that participants believe the account to be true are important sorts of *evidence* for the validity of an account. As researchers, we must develop the ways in which we monitor our assumptions and the inferences we make on the basis of them, and investigate those we judge not to be beyond reasonable doubt. This is not suggesting something that is new or novel. Ethnographers have become increasingly concerned with ways of checking their conclusions. Subtle realism simply encourages greater concern with this.[12] However, it runs counter to the implications of relativism, which undercut the rationale for such checks by denying that there is any reality to be known and implying that this rationale is based on arbitrary philosophical or political assumptions; assumptions which might, with equal warrant, be replaced by others, such as those generating fictional accounts.

What is implied by subtle realism is not, then, a complete transformation of ethnographic practice. We must still view people's beliefs and actions as constructions, and this includes their accounts of the world *and* those of researchers. At the same time, though, we should not assume that people's accounts are necessarily "true" or "rational" in their own terms. Whether we should be concerned with the truth or falsity of any account depends on how we plan to use it. There are two sorts of interest we can have in accounts, implying different require-ments. First, we may treat them as social phenomena that we are seeking to understand and explain, or as indicators of cultural perspectives held by the peo-ple producing them. Here we must ignore our judgments about their validity or rationality, since this is not relevant to the task of understanding them. Indeed, the ethnographer should suspend any of her/his own beliefs that conflict with those being described and explained; otherwise there is a danger of misunder-standing. As I argued earlier, the question of the truth or falsity of an account carries no implications for how it should be explained. On the other hand, we may use accounts as a source of information about the phenomena to which they refer. They may, for example, provide us with information about events that we could not ourselves witness (for example that happened in the past or in settings to which we do not have access). Or they may allow us to check our own or oth-ers' observations through triangulation. Here we *must* be concerned with the truth or otherwise of the accounts, and we must judge this as best we can, both in terms of the likelihood of error of various kinds and according to how the information relates to our other knowledge. We can, of course, apply both these approaches to the same account; indeed, understanding an account may well help us in assessing its validity. However, it is very important to maintain the distinction between these two ways of analyzing informants' accounts. Only if we do so can we retain the valuable ethnographic approach of seeking to under-stand and explain people's behaviour and beliefs independently of their sup-posed rationality or truth, while not lapsing into relativism.[13]

There is one area where subtle realism does imply something of a break with conventional ethnographic practice founded on naive realism. This arises from its abandonment of the ideal of reproduction in favor of selective representation. Given that what is produced is, at best, only one of many possible valid accounts of the phenomena studied, it is a requirement that ethnographers make explicit the relevancies on which their accounts are based. This is not always done.

CONCLUSION

In this chapter I have addressed what seems to me to be one of the central ambiguities in ethnography: between a commitment to a methodology based on naive realism and a theoretical approach founded on constructivism that is often taken to imply relativism. I looked at each of the two most obvious solutions to this problem: the adoption of a consistent (naive) realism or a consistent relativ-ism. However, I concluded that neither of these offered an adequate solution. The first involves unacceptable assumptions about the asymmetry of explana-tions of true and false beliefs and of actions based upon them. The second leads to all those problems that usually follow from the adoption of a relativist episte-mology, notably internal inconsistency. I argued that satisfactory resolution of this problem requires us to recognize that we are not faced with a stark choice between naive realism and relativism, that there are more subtle forms of realism that avoid the problems of these two positions. I outlined what seem to me to be the main components of such a subtle realism, and sketched some of its implications for the principles and practice of ethnographic method.

Notes

[1] Something of this attitude is to be detected, for example, in Geertz's attack on "anti-relativism" (Geertz 1984).

2 Blumer draws this idea from pragmatism, but it can also be found in one or another form in nineteenth-century historicism and in the eighteenth century in the writings of Vico and Herder (Berlin 1976).

[3] For useful discussions of this idea in anthropology, see Jarvie (1964, 1983), Winch (1964), Tennekes (1971) and Herskovits (1972). See also Geertz (1984).

[4] For an application of this argument to social scientists' use of the concept of ideology, see Hammersley (1981).

[5] This is ironic since the origins of phenomenology lie in Husserl's attempt to ground knowledge in fundamental essences that are constitutive of human experience and therefore of the world, an enterprise resolutely opposed to skepticism and relativism. see Kolakowski (1975) and Bell (1990).

[6] See, for example, Sudnow (1967) and Wieder (1974). For a useful general discussion of ethnomethodology in this respect, see Atkinson (1988).

[7] Bernstein (1983) provides a useful overview of anti-realist trends. An example of the impact of these ideas on ethnography is the recent work of Denzin which seems to combine them in a relatively indiscriminate fashion (see, for example, Denzin 1989, 1990). The differences and inconsistencies among the sources I have outlined are at least as important as the similarities. And, as I have indicated, many of them are by no means unambiguously relativistic, even though that is often how they have been interpreted.

[8] See the discussion of anthropological examples of "experimental" ethnographic writing in Marcus and Fischer (1986). In sociology, Krieger (1983) provides an example of a text in which the voice of the researcher is suppressed in favor of those of the people studied.

[9] It is also worth noting that to think of the phenomena studied as consisting of a reality independent of the ethnographer is misleading. We can treat them as independent of the researcher while recognizing that both are part of the same reality.

[10] Here I am adopting the neo-Kantian idea that reality is infinitely extensive and intensive (Rickert 1986). However, I do not believe that reality is structureless. In constructing our relevancies we must take account of what we know and can discover about that structure if we are to get the information we need to serve our purposes (that is, in part at least, we must *discover* what is relevant).

11 Relativists' attitude to this definition is often ambivalent. On the one hand, they adopt it in arguing against realism, claiming that because there can be no knowledge of reality in this strong sense there is no sense in which we can reasonably claim to understand phenomena that are independent of us. In more constructive mode, however, relativists define knowledge in terms of what is taken to be certain within a particular culture or paradigm. While my conception of knowledge shares something with this latter view, it differs from it in treating agreement as an indicator not as a definition of validity; and like all indicators it is subject to error.

[12] For a more extended account of the assessment of ethnographic claims, see Hammersley (1998).

[13] Once again, this is not to recommend something that is entirely novel. Ethnographers have long employed both these forms of analysis, though they do not always distinguish between them sufficiently clearly. Something like this distinction is to be found in McCall and Simmons (1969.4). The sort of subtle realism I have outlined clarifies the basis, and underlines the need, for this distinction.

PART II

Fieldwork Practice
Issues in Participant Observation

Participant-observation fieldwork begins with the process of "getting into place," that is, getting close to those studied "while they are responding to what life does to them" (Goffman, this volume). Ethnographers have long regarded these distinctively in-the-field practices—developing relations with others, immersing oneself in their social worlds—as the core of really "doing fieldwork." In recent years, ethnographers have also come to recognize writing—the transformation of observations and experiences into data—as a core fieldwork practice. Relating/observing in the field and writing about these matters raise a series of ethical and political issues that continue to receive close attention. This section and its accompanying readings explore issues which recurrently arise in and from these in-the-field practices for developing close relations; for understanding, experiencing and writing up data; and for dealing with the moral and political issues thereby generated.

FIELD RELATIONS

Participant-observation methods possess a strikingly social character. In Cassell's words, "The interaction is the method; the ethnographer is the research instrument" (1980:36). Appreciating these interactions and the relationships they create and sustain provides a critical task for fieldworkers:

> Good fieldwork . . . depends crucially upon discovering the meaning of social relations, and not just those characterizing the "natives'" relations with each other. It depends equally upon discovering the meanings of anthropologists' relations with the people they study. (Karp and Kendall 1982:250)

The ethnographer's interactions and personal relations shape key aspects of the fieldwork process. First, "getting into place"—more a continuing series of negotiations rather than a one-shot agreement to entree (Johnson 1975)—puts the fieldworker in the presence of the ongoing social life to be observed and recorded. Thus field relations generate distinctive sorts of fieldwork *data*:

> The role assumed by the observer largely determines where he can go, what he can do, whom he can interact with, what he can inquire about, what he can see and what he can be told. (McCall and Simmons 1969:29)

Second, the longer-term relations established with those studied determine how the fieldworker will experience their social world, in this way shaping her *empathic understanding* of local ways of life. Gaining deeper intuitive appreciation of others' social worlds—not only, as Goffman suggests, catching their humor but also coming "to engage in the same body rhythms"—is a product of ongoing field interactions and relations. Such participatory understandings, as Kondo (this volume) recounts, can deeply influence and transform the ethnographer's theoretical and substantive concerns.

Third, the very processes of getting on in the field, of dealing with recurrent problems such as entree, access, and trust, reveal critical substantive and theoretically relevant features of the setting under study. In fieldwork, *methodological procedures are intricately linked with substantive findings*. Indeed, Cicourel (1964:65) has argued that "the participant observer interested in obtaining 'good' contacts in the field and the social scientist interested in studying basic patterns of social interaction" share a concern with the styles of interaction and social types found in any particular setting.[1]

Finally, given the interdependence of method and substance, what the fieldworker actually does in the field provides one way of *assessing ethnographic evidence*, for evaluating the quality of both the data collected and the analysis made of that data. For if data, description, and analysis are products of modes of participating in a broad sense, then understanding such participation can aid in evaluating substantive and analytic ethnographic claims (see Part III).

Fieldwork Roles

Field relations have traditionally been analyzed in terms of fieldwork roles. In his classic statement of this approach, Gold (1958) suggested that such roles fall along a continuum from complete observation (at an extreme, observing from behind a one-way mirror) to complete participation (the researcher gone native). Gold emphasized the different qualities of the two roles falling at the midpoints of this continuum, the observer as participant and the participant as observer. Gans (1968) made a similar distinction between the total participant, the researcher-participant, and the total researcher. More recently, Adler and Adler (1987:34) contrast a range of more or less detached observer roles, many of which involve some participation, with more involved "membership" roles in which the fieldworker "participate(s) in the routine practices of members, as one of them, to naturalistically experience the members' world."

Others locate the core dimension of field relations in the overt or covert character of the research rather than in the extent of participation. Here the key distinction lies between fieldworkers who are overtly identified as researchers and those who covertly assume roles natural to that setting. Thus, Lofland and Lofland (1995:31–41) contrast the *unknown* with the *known investigator* as two basic fieldwork styles, while Schwartz and Jacobs (1979:57) maintain that whether others think the researcher is a "scientist" or a "bona fide member" is a critical variable in field relations. The latter also suggest that whether a role is overt or covert does not automatically determine how the researcher participates in the setting; both types of fieldwork may be conducted by means of detached obser-vation or "normal, natural" participation.

Ethnographers cite several circumstances that may make covert fieldwork particularly advantageous. First, fieldworkers may adopt a covert role in order to gain access to settings that would exclude an openly identified researcher. Covert fieldwork can help penetrate the various fronts, lies, and evasions that groups put up to keep outsiders, including fieldworkers, from learning the truth. Secondly, covert field roles may help minimize reactive effects and circumvent likely efforts to hide important matters from observers. The fieldworker will be treated as just another member in the setting, so that any effects from one's pres-ence or behavior may be regarded as "natural" for this setting.

Some forms of covert fieldwork explicitly assume a conflict model of field relations. This model rejects the inevitability of common interests between field-worker and those studied, holding instead that

> . . . many of the people one deals with, perhaps all people to some extent, have good reason to hide from others what they are doing and even to lie to them. Instead of trusting people and expecting trust in return, one suspects others and expects others to suspect him. Conflict is the reality of life; suspi-cion is the guiding principle. (Douglas 1976:55)

As a result covert fieldwork may assume a probing, even antagonistically "inves-tigative" form (Douglas 1976).

In recent years, ethnographers have become increasingly uneasy with the sometimes overly rational and impersonal accounts of field relations as field-work "roles." Snow et al. (1986) propose a flexible understanding of roles as products of emergent, interactionally specific negotiations, distinguishing the structural or generic dimension of roles from their "derived" or locally achieved features. The former provides only a general "skeletal-like frame" for organizing field relations; the latter include the more variable, situationally specific pro-cesses through which actual relations are created and maintained (380–81). Identifying three derived roles from their own research—the controlled skeptic, the ardent activist, and the buddy-researcher—Snow et al. examine the differen-tial "informational yields" of each for three primary categories of field data: reports of direct experience, observation, and members' narrations.

Other fieldworkers have questioned the utility of any sort of fixed role imag-ery for analyzing highly variable field relations. Schatzman and Strauss (1973:58–63), for example, talk not about mutually exclusive roles but about distinct modes of participation in ongoing situations, including: watching from outside; passive presence in the situation; limited interaction (aimed at clarifying actors' intents and meanings); active control; full participation as a researcher; and participation with a hidden identity. They view these modes of involvement not as mutually exclusive options (except for the last) but as tactical choices, all of which may be selected at different times and occasions in the course of a particular study.

In practice, many fieldworkers have more or less abandoned the notion of fieldwork roles as a primary conceptual framework. As reflected in the selections from Duneier, Kondo and Thorne which follow, contemporary fieldwork accounts explore the significance of situational and local features of field settings and emphasize variations and shifts in field relations from situation to situation, person to person, and over time. These analyses also insist that field relations are often only marginally under the control of the researcher (Johnson 1975), and hence must be viewed as mutual, collaboratively produced exchanges between fieldworker and those studied. Such exchanges, marked by frequent misunderstandings, enduring cross-purposes, and continuing negotiations, are unavoidably affected by the mesh of the fieldworker's social and personal characteristics with those of the people and groups studied, and hence are deeply contingent and unpredictable.

Social Attributes of the Fieldworker: Race/Ethnicity, Gender, Age

The fieldworker's social characteristics fundamentally affect the kinds of interactions and relations that develop, and hence the character and degree of immersion in the lives of those studied. Johnson (1975:91) in particular emphasized the critical if often unnoted relevance of "the observer's sexual status, racial status, socioeconomic background, appearance, abilities, goals" in shaping the way those studied define, evaluate, and react to the researcher. Substantial bodies of writing examine the significance of three major ascribed statuses for fieldwork relations—racial/ethnic identity, gender, and age.

Racial/Ethnic Identity and Insider/Outsider Research. While in much anthropological research the ethnographer's race and ethnicity differ from those of the people studied, this is not necessarily the case in sociological fieldwork. Not only can the sociological fieldworker often assume covert research roles, "passing" as or becoming a member; but also the "fit" between key social attributes of the fieldworker and those of the groups studied can become matters of self-conscious choice in selecting and making a place in the field. These possibilities have assumed particular importance with regard to the match of the fieldworker's ethnicity/race in research in minority communities.

Some fieldworkers advocate "insider research," in which fieldwork is conducted by persons of the same race or ethnicity as those studied (see Baca Zinn, this volume). Zavella (1996:139) summarizes the arguments of some Chicano scholars:

> . . . insiders are more likely to be cognizant and accepting of complexity and internal variation, are better able to understand the nuances of language use, will avoid being duped by informants who create cultural performances for their own purposes, and are less apt to be distrusted by those they study.

> Some assert that ethnic insiders often have an easier time gaining access to a
> community similar to their own, and that they are more sensitive to framing
> questions in ways that respect community sensibilities.

Indeed, shared racial status seems to have played an important if implicit role in
Eli Anderson's (1978) ability to become part of the social world inside Jelly's bar
and liquor store on the South Side of Chicago. As Anderson describes this world:

> In the social setting of Jelly's both working and nonworking black people
> can gather among others enough like them to matter socially. Here they seek
> out certain others to spend their leisure time with—friends and companions
> with whom they can act sociably, talking, laughing, arguing, and joking. It is
> in this setting that they can feel themselves among equals, especially in rela-
> tion to the wider society. (29)

Anderson entered this world by becoming friendly with Herman in the more
open and anonymous bar side of the establishment. With Herman's sponsorship
("going for cousins"), he was able to move to the more informal, peer-group
liquor store side. Herman characterized Anderson as a "decent" man getting his
PhD in introducing him to Jelly's regulars, men who worked regularly and
sought to be "treated as respectable" (55). With Herman's guidance and protection, Anderson actively participated in the loose, often confrontational and pro-
fane "laughing, arguing and joking" that took place there, helped by his
knowledge (sometimes upgraded on site!) of these ways of socializing.

Despite the advantages it may offer, however, "insider" fieldwork can
encounter distinctive complications. Insider fieldwork can generate distinctive
relational problems and tensions, "different in kind, but by no means different in
severity" (Maykovich 1977:118) from those encountered by "outsider" fieldworkers. In conducting fieldwork on marital roles, power and ethnicity in Chicano
families through a parent education program, Baca Zinn (this volume) describes
the tensions she experienced on receiving an appeal for support based on ethnic
loyalty that could well have undermined her field entree. Similarly, Zavella
(1996:143) found that sharing the ethnic identity (and class background) of the
working women she studied only went so far. The women were acutely aware,
for example, of Zavella's educational status and position in the world of the university. Furthermore, the questions she asked—how they made decisions, "how
they organized the household division of labor, how they felt about being working mothers" (143)—signaled significant political differences:

> With a few notable exceptions, these were women who "happened to
> work," and whose seasonable employment did not challenge the traditional
> notions that their husbands should be the breadwinners and heads of the
> family and that they should do most of the domestic work, although some
> did contest these notions somewhat. My feminist questions, then, pointed
> out the contradictions of their constructions of their selves and led to some
> awkward moments when women preferred silence to full discussion of
> problems in their families or with their husbands. It was at these times that
> my outsider status seemed glaring. (Zavella 1996:143)

The complexities of ethnic identification are also revealed in Kondo's experiences in doing fieldwork as a Japanese American woman in Japan (this volume). Kondo emphasizes that the Japanese employ "an eminently biological definition of Japaneseness." As a result,"My physical characteristics led my friends and coworkers to emphasize my identity as Japanese, sometimes even against my own identities and desires."

While "insider" fieldwork can give rise to its own set of problems, it is also evident that racial/ethnic "outsiders" have produced excellent studies of minority communities, from Whyte's fieldwork among 1930s Italian cornerboys to Duneier's (1999) and Wacquant's (1995, 1998a, b) ethnographies of 1990s African-American book venders and prizefighters. Fieldwork conducted under these conditions both requires and generates special sensitivity to the dynamics of race and ethnic relations. In *Tally's Corner*, for example, Liebow noted that the racial difference was always present (1967:248), in all likelihood more markedly so for the men studied than for himself: "When four of us sat around a kitchen table, for example, I saw three Negroes; each of them saw two Negroes and a white man." On occasion, he felt that the racial differences had been transcended:

> Sometimes, when the word "nigger" was being used easily and conversationally or when, standing on the corner with several men, one would have a few words with a white passerby and call him a "white mother-fucker," I used to play with the idea that maybe I wasn't as much of an outsider as I thought. (248–49)

But on closer reflection, Liebow noted that even conversations in which his black friends would talk openly of the irrelevance of his being white ultimately served to call attention to the distance race created (see the two incidents on pp. 249–50). As he concluded (250–251):

> . . . the wall between us remained, or better, the chain-link fence, since despite the barriers we were able to look at each other, walk alongside each other, talk and occasionally touch fingers. When two people stand up close to the fence on either side, without touching it, they can look through the interstices and forget that they are looking through a fence.

Mitchell Duneier reports similar experiences in "On the Evolution of *Sidewalk*" (this volume). Duneier describes the suspicion with which his initial informant, Hakim Hasan, responded to his requests to observe his street bookvending activities. Persistence, sensitivity to the race and class differences between them, gradual revision of his initial presumptions about Hakim (that he was unhoused, relatively uneducated and engaged in street-vending by necessity), and open discussion of these issues eventually led to more comfortable relations and to acceptance as a regular observer. After several years Duneier and Hasan even achieved a quasi-collaborator relationship, with Hasan co-teaching a course and contributing an appendix to *Sidewalk* (Duneier 1999:319–30).

As Duneier expanded the scope of his project beyond Hakim's domain, he encountered some indications of continuing distrust from street vendors as a white academic. Duneier accepts some such distrust as inevitable and irremediable, recommending that the fieldworker's response must involve sustained, self-conscious analysis of his "social position" and its influence on relations with those studied. Indeed, in addition to analyzing exactly how his "outsider" position influenced his research, Duneier deliberately exploited this position to identify by contrast distinctive features of street vendors' worlds: "I try to use myself as a kind of control group, comparing the way I am treated in particular situations with the way people on the street are treated." Coming to recognize his own taken-for-granted access to public restrooms, for example, led him to appreciate and to investigate systematically the obstacles that poor, black street vendors encountered in this regard.

   Gender.   Fieldwork is fundamentally shaped and constrained by the gender lines that permeate and organize all social worlds. Early twentieth-century ethnography tended to ignore gender, treating male-dominated domains as representing all of local social life and almost completely neglecting female-centered activities and spaces (Warren, this volume). But beginning in the 1930s ethnographers began to examine the gendered worlds of those they studied, as women fieldworkers in particular began to direct attention to previously ignored areas of social life organized and maintained primarily by women in many societies—family, child-raising, health and illness. Subsequently, as Warren emphasizes, ethnographers began to pay close attention to the workings and influence of gender in their own dealings with those they studied, a development spurred both by the increasing recognition of the interactional and relational grounding of fieldwork and by the emergence of feminist approaches to qualitative research. While gender structures and relations shape and influence the conduct of fieldwork by both male and female ethnographers, the latter have by and large developed explicit analyses of gender relations in fieldwork. As Warren notes, "most of the twentieth-century writing about gender and ethnography has been done by and about women," in large part because women fieldworkers routinely have to navigate their way through restrictive gender arrangements.

   Women fieldworkers have reacted in two different ways to the typically gender-segregated worlds they encounter in the field. Some women ethnographers bring "deeply feminine interests and abilities" to the field, exploring the worlds and activities of women and children (Warren and Hackney 2000:7, citing Mead 1986). In general, these fieldworkers establish a local place by accepting and accommodating to local, conventional gender expectations. Kondo (this volume), for example, essentially became the adopted daughter of the local family with whom she initially lived, using these relations as a base for exploring situations and selves as encountered and experienced by a variety of Japanese women. Other women ethnographers, more "masculinely oriented," avoid local women's worlds in order to gain what idiosyncratic access they can to male worlds and activities (Warren and Hackney 2000:7). In so doing they typically resist conventional gender expectations, ignoring or violating local gender-appropriate forms of behavior in negotiating a place from which to ask questions and make observations as an androgynized "honorary male" (Warren, this volume).

The field experiences of Arlene Daniels in studying military psychiatrists provides an example of the first process. In this all-male, hierarchically organized world, Daniels remained a "low-caste stranger," an "amusing and ornamental mascot, treated with friendly affection but little respect" (1967:295). This position is evident in the following exchange:

> On another occasion, at a convention meeting, I joined a group of officers at a party. One member of the group was not known to me. He asked the person standing next to him who I was. That officer clapped us both on the back and said: "What? You don't know Arlene? Then you ought to meet her. She's a great girl. She's our mascot. She studies us." (1967:285–86)

Jennifer Hunt's (1984) fieldwork among police patrol officers exemplifies the processes of negotiating a sexually ambiguous "honorary male" role. Hunt resisted easy incorporation into the standard female roles within the patrol subculture—"dyke," "whore," and moral woman. To avoid marginalization and exclusion, she sought to negotiate an identity and set of relations as a liminal "street-woman-researcher" (289), playing off of while simultaneously contradicting elements of these conventional roles. For example, Hunt describes acting in ways male officers subsequently characterized as "hard," "pinch hungry," and "crazy," all qualities associated with being "a 'good man' whose skills and personality conformed with 'street cop' rather than 'management cop' culture" (290). She also openly cursed, but turned down sexual overtures, sometimes politely, occasionally menacingly (e.g., in one instance responding to a groping officer with "Do you wanta get kicked in the balls?"), soon becoming known as a woman who "won't go out with cops" (292).

The insider/outsider problematic discussed previously with regard to race/ethnicity arises with regard to gender as well. Clearly women ethnographers can gain entree and learn about aspects of women's lives where men would have been excluded or responded to in very different, limiting ways. Some literature ascribes a distinctive nurturing, emotional sensitivity to women fieldworkers, whose presumed special abilities as "nurturers, communicators, emotional laborers" make them attractive as "sociability specialists" (Warren, this volume). Similarly, Devault (1999) emphasizes drawing upon her own experience as a woman in talking to women about their routine activities and subjective concerns in "provisioning" and "feeding" their families. Devault thus suggests that her gender experiences provided a specific, theoretically cultivated sensitivity to partially articulated nuances of meaning and concern in women's lives.

Of course, there are also situations in which gender is not enough, where the assumptions of understanding because of common gender and gender-based experiences prove inadequate. Riessman (1987:179–88), for example, contrasts interviews she conducted with a white middle-class and a working-class Puerto Rican woman, emphasizing the ways in which class and cultural differences led her initially to miss the distinctive way the latter organized her narrative account of marital separation as a series of *recurring situations* within the family (rather than by recounting a sequential development of personal stresses with her husband).

Age. A number of anthropological studies have emphasized that the age of the fieldworker has important implications for field relations. The effects of age, however, are often impossible to separate from those of gender. Thus Warren reports that a number of middle-aged women anthropologists were able to establish a quasi-male, androgynous status. Similarly, R. Wax (1979) emphasized that her matronly status and appearance allowed her to go places and raise issues among the Sioux that would have been difficult or impossible for younger fieldworkers.

It would seem that much sociological fieldwork is conducted with those who fall into roughly equivalent age groupings as the researcher. Some of the difficulties of "studying up" may derive from problems younger (as well as lower-status) fieldworkers face in fitting into the worlds of the established and powerful. In contrast, typically the dependent elderly are readily accessible to younger fieldworkers (Gubrium 1986; Diamond 1992).

Age matters most directly and dramatically in fieldwork with children. Most participant-observation fieldwork with children is conducted by adults who assume some sort of "friend" role; the dynamics of this process differ in fieldwork among preschoolers (where the research emphasis is typically on language learning), preadolescent (focused on learning and testing the limits of acceptable behavior), and adolescents (focused on deviance and rebellion) (Fine and Sandstrom 1988). Fieldwork among preschoolers poses age-based relational problems in particularly acute form. Fine and Sandstrom (1988:40–44) suggest that some fieldworkers, particularly the more observationally oriented, maintain a more or less strictly adult role (e.g., Sluckin 1981); others try to avoid identification with adult authorities, making themselves available for informal and playful exchanges with children while still acting in recognizably adult ways (e.g., Corsaro 1985); and finally, some fieldworkers attempt to minimize distance from the children studied by pursuing what Mandell (1988) terms the "least-adult role." This approach involves "participating in children's social world as a child" (Mandell 1988:435), recognizing that the adult's greater physical size poses a significant obstacle but one which can be so managed as to become "inconsequential in interaction."

In "Learning from Kids" (this volume), Barrie Thorne reflects on her fieldwork practices and experiences with children in two fourth-grade classes. She describes relating to these children as a sympathetic adult outside the lines of school authority—expressing interest in their informal activities, participating in playground games, dodging overt alignment with school staff. Despite her identification with the kids and her concern "to uncover and document kids' points of view and meanings," her fieldwork depended upon a freedom of choice and movement unavailable to those studied; for example, she relied upon the "free-lancing privilege of an adult visitor" to follow the flow of classroom and playground action. Indeed, the key to her fieldwork lay less in participating like a child, more in abandoning common ethnocentric (Fine and Sandstrom 1988:35) or "adult-centric" (Goode 1986) assumptions about children: "that children's daily actions are mostly trivial, worthy of notice only when they seem cute or irritating; that children need to be actively managed or controlled; that children are relatively passive recipients of training and socialization." This theoretical sensitivity allowed her to appreciate whole domains of meaningful activity marginalized and neglected in adult views of children, such as children's "secret and oppositional" use of food and other objects in the school setting.

Reconsidering the Insider/Outsider Dichotomy. The insider/outsider dichotomy highlights the relative advantages of racial/ethnic, gender and age similarities and differences. The advantages of insider fieldwork are readily apparent—more facile entree, a higher degree of trust, easier access to the nuances of local interaction and meaning. The advantages of conducting fieldwork as an outsider are initially less apparent but can nonetheless be compelling. First, outsiders may not be held accountable to the demands for local in-group solidarity, such as appeals to ethnic loyalty, or to the restrictions of local status distinctions. Fieldworkers who are "insiders" to the local society may encounter problems on both counts. Consider the efforts of third-world anthropologists to conduct "indigenous" ethnography in their own cultures: Fahim and Helmer (1980:646–47) describe an instance in which an Egyptian anthropologist generated profound distrust in attempting fieldwork among the Nubian people in the Sudan because of his sponsorship by the Egyptian government and his cultural view of the Nubians as a low-status group; yet a Norwegian anthropologist, unencumbered by these local expectations, successfully completed a detailed ethnographic study of these people.

Second, outsider fieldworkers may be able to pursue lines of inquiry and to ask questions closed off to insiders. For example, sociologist Jennifer Platt (1981) encountered incomprehension when interviewing sociologists about their own research projects; her questions appeared incongruous when respondents knew that she knew many of the things she was asking about. The cultural outsider, in contrast, may well be able to ask direct questions about taken-for-granted or quasi-taboo matters.[2]

Third, outsider fieldwork often generates distinctive sensitivity to and methodological self-consciousness about relational processes. Warren and Hackney (2000:ix), for example, suggest that women field researchers have tended to become acutely aware of methodological issues because they "experienced the field differently from the androcentric fieldwork representations within which they had been trained," a pattern apparent in fieldwork spanning racial/ethnic and age differences as well. In contrast, fieldwork involving a close match between the social characteristics of fieldworker and those studied often leave relational processes implicit and unexamined.

At a deeper level, however, many ethnographers question the very insider/outsider dichotomy, contending that this distinction is artificial and overdrawn, exaggerating and reifying marginal and shifting differences. Some contend that the insider/outsider dichotomy is confining and inadequate in implicitly assuming that a single trait or attribute dominates and determines field outcomes. While race/ethnicity, gender and age can and do provide "master statuses" that structure and constrain fieldwork relations, they do not mechanically shape and determine the specific qualities of such relations. Fieldwork relations in fact involve whole persons, socially constituted as bundles of situationally relevant traits; a fieldworker is never only and simply a woman, for example, but more holistically a woman of a certain age, class, color, ethnicity, appearance, training and commitments. Similarly, a wide variety of cross-race or cross-ethnic relations can be nurtured and cultivated, although perhaps at greater cost in time and effort, and without duplicating all aspects of same race or same ethnic relations. Indeed, fieldworkers increasingly recognize that they "are almost always simultaneously insiders and outsiders" (Zavella 1996:141; see also Baca Zinn, this volume). As a consequence, while social attributes exercise a pervasive influence on field relations, there is no principled way of deciding whether the shared attributes of fieldworker and those studied should be minimized or maximized. In any case, the outcomes of such matching efforts are often beyond the control of the fieldworker. Fieldwork relations involve balances of both similarities and differences, balances that are constantly shifting as fieldwork proceeds, as at given times and places similarities are invoked and differences accentuated.

Immersion and Membership in Fieldwork

Participant observation entails immersion in the daily rounds and ordinary interactions of the social world under study. As Goffman emphasizes (this volume), fieldwork involves "subjecting yourself, your own body and your own personality, and your own social situation, to the set of contingencies that play upon a set of individuals, so that you can physically and ecologically penetrate their circle of response to their social situation." This sort of prolonged, intensive immersion provides a "deep familiarity" with others' social worlds, a profound empathic appreciation enabling the fieldworker to absorb a feel for the local "tissue of events." Even more strongly, Wolff insists that fieldwork ultimately requires *surrender* to the culture and community studied—that is, "total involvement, suspension of received notions, pertinence of everything, identification, and risk of being hurt" (1964:237). Such strong subjective engagement leads to deep understanding of the life concerns and circumstances of those studied.

Contemporary ethnography, prioritizing the methods of participant observation, recognizes different degrees and kinds of immersion. Many approaches recommend immersion accompanied and hence limited by strong research and observational priorities, thus balancing closeness with detachment in what has been termed the "respectful distance" approach (Reinharz 1992:67). Karp and Kendall (1982:261), for example, describe the paradoxical and "peculiar combination of engrossment and distance" in fieldwork, noting that both are necessary in order to deeply comprehend others' realities. This combination in turn demands empathy, not full sympathy, with the immediacy of the lives of those studied.[3]

A number of ethnographers, however, urge deeper, more thorough-going forms of immersion in which the fieldworker becomes an actively engaged, fully competent participant in the local social world of interest. A number of feminist fieldworkers, emphasizing "the ethical and epistemological importance of integrating their selves into their work" (Reinharz 1992:69), have sought total immersion in the worlds they study (see Reinharz's overview, 1992:67–71). In this vein Adler and Adler (1987) distinguish between two deeply participatory *membership roles* in fieldwork—active membership and complete membership.[4] *Active membership* occurs when fieldworkers "take part in the core activities of the group," performing some central, functional roles just as members do, but avoiding other such roles and complete or permanent commitment to the group (50). Examples include Hunt's (1984) research with the police, in which she underwent basic training and rode in patrol cars on eight-hour shifts, Rochford's (1985) study of the Hare Krishna as an engaged but not fully committed or accepted devotee, and Wacquant's (1998a) long-term, intensive training as a boxer in studying a distinctive institution of the ghetto life.

In *complete membership* fieldworkers perform the core activities that mark active group membership, doing so in a spirit of "good faith" commitment. The nature of this commitment may vary. Some fieldworkers accept the goals and values of the group while retaining strong commitment to their research and planning ultimately to make their way in the academic world. Others "become so committed to the group that they abandon their ties to the scientific community and fail to return from the field" (Adler and Alder 1987:67).[5] Furthermore, complete-member fieldworkers can take up these commitments in different ways. Some "opportunistically" (Riemer 1977) select groups and settings in which they have prior membership, then working to "forge a research role" in their previously social or collegial relations with other members (73). Hayano (1979, 1982), for example, had long been a regular player in poker card rooms before deciding to study these games and their participants. Others "select a setting for study in which they are not previously involved, and in conducting the research they become converted to group membership" (Adler and Adler 1987:68). Jules-Rosette (1975), Brown (1985) and Forrest (1986) provide examples of fieldworkers who began detached, uninvolved studies of religious groups only to find themselves increasingly attracted by and ultimately converting to their beliefs and practices.

Membership roles facilitate entree (particularly in the face of explicit resistance) and allow the fieldworker to get behind the normal fronts and facades in ways that open up use of a variety of qualitative procedures, as Wacquant (1998b:4) emphasizes with regard to participating in "the local pugilistic universe":

> Without becoming a "quasi-member" (and paying one's dues in the ring), one would not have been able to carry out direct, day-to-day observation. And without such naturalistic observation, the interview materials could not have been substantiated, filtered, and properly interpreted, let alone produced in the first instance.

Since members come to regard the fieldworker as a fellow member, this approach reduces reactive effects. But even more critically, by having fieldworkers actually do what members do, as opposed to simply observing these processes from the outside (no matter how empathically), membership fieldwork generates deeper sensitivity and insight. Actually performing core activities subjects the fieldworker to the constraints experienced by ordinary members. Taking a membership role

... forces the researcher to take on the obligations and liabilities of members. In repeatedly dealing with the practical problems members face, researchers ultimately organize their behavior and form constructs about the setting's everyday reality in much the same way as members. (Adler and Adler 1987:34)

Similar themes mark other approaches to deep-immersion fieldwork. *Auto-ethnography* seeks to draw data directly from the fieldworker's own experiences and subjective insights. Hayano (1979) originally used this term to characterize his study of poker games and players as a competent player himself. In this sense autoethnography involved fieldwork among one's "own people" where "researchers possess the qualities of often permanent self-identification with a group and full internal membership, as recognized both by themselves and the people of whom they are a part" (1979:100). Ellis (1991) places a different accent on autoethnography, viewing it as "systematic introspection" critical for exploring and documenting neglected subjective aspects of lived experience. Ellis and others use this emotion-centered form of autoethnography to "capture and evoke the complex, paradoxical, and mysterious qualities of subjectivity" (Ellis and Flaherty 1992:5), relying upon both self- and interactive introspection (e.g., Ellis, 1995a; Ronai 1992) to produce field data that is sensitive to emotional and bodily experiences as well as relational and interactive processes. Robillard (1999) similarly uses an introspective method to recount the disruptions of his ordinary bodily competences accompanying his progressive paralysis through ALS.

Reacting to the neglect of the body in much ethnography, other approaches to immersion focus on *embodied participation* in other social worlds. Some emphasize replicating the bodily experiences of those studied. Estroff (1981), for example, took psychotropic medications to experience firsthand what ex-mental patients go through; Goode (1994:25) sought physically to approximate the life-world of a child rendered deaf, dumb and blind by Rubella through several unorthodox methodological practices (e.g., simulating deaf-blindness by using ear stops and blindfolds). Others accent the acquisition and deployment of various embodied competencies. Wacquant (1995, 1998a) spent three years training as a boxer in order to experience and convey "the passion, the love, the suffering, the sensual roots of (boxers') experience of boxing" (1995:491).

Finally, recent versions of ethnomethodology also advocate a radical form of immersion in which "going native" is required, not optional. Now tending to focus on scientific and other highly technical, esoteric work settings (e.g., Garfinkel et al. 1981; Lynch 1985; Livingston 1986), ethnomethodology insists that only a competent practitioner with in-depth experience and familiarity with the work skills involved can adequately grasp and represent indigenous meanings. For ethnomethodology, adequate description requires not mere observation but embodied presence as a knowing participant in the field of action. In the words of an earlier proposal to the same effect, the researcher must "become the phenomenon" (Mehan and Wood 1975), gaining "adequate mastery of other disciplines as a precondition for making ethnomethodological descriptions" (Lynch 1993:274). The researcher who is not an active, adept and accredited participant will distort or miss entirely the experienced "depth, stability and necessity" of the lived order.

While ethnographers generally agree that the distinctive value of fieldwork derives from intimate participation in local social worlds, they are deeply divided on the degree to which that participation can in fact replicate the experience of members. Most maintain, as emphasized earlier, that the experience of even the most engaged member-researcher is never isomorphic with that of the ordinary member: The complete-membership fieldworker can always leave the setting to pursue academic careers, or to escape unbearable tensions and dilemmas (Adler and Adler 1987:79–80). On the other hand, ethnomethodology insists that under very specific conditions, notably the long-term practice of technical skills and the abandonment of all commitment to exogenous "constructive" theorizing, the inquirer can indeed become the phenomenon and provide undistorted accounts of indigenous meanings.

"No Time Out": The Limits of Trust and Immersion

Deep immersion, membership roles, and insider research all seek to maximize the trust and rapport with those studied that are frequently viewed as the sine qua non of successful fieldwork.[6] Indeed, in much fieldwork literature "trust" is conceived as "magically opening a door to collection of valid and reliable data," providing access to the backstage information and intimate secrets required for accurate ethnography (Johnson 1975:119). Fantasia's (1988) fieldwork on strikes offers a not atypical instance: Initially experiencing extreme mistrust from a tightly organized group of strikers, at a press conference Fantasia aggressively defended a pro-union priest besieged by reporters.

> At the conclusion of the press conference, the strike leaders rushed over to thank me for my comments and invited me to join them for a drink. Thereafter, the strike community seemed to open up to me to an extraordinary degree. The word had gone out that my research needs were to be met, and I was then able to arrange interviews with strikers. (Fantasia 1988:251)

However, it is easy to exaggerate and distort the implications of such "magic moments" of "full openness" in which prior suspicions, fronts and evasions drop away (see also Johnson 1975:204). Just as a fieldworker is both insider and outsider within and across collectivities, so too may a fieldworker be simultaneously trusted by some and distrusted by others. Establishing close, trusting ties with some people will inevitably generate distance and distrust with others; Fantasia's newfound rapport with the strike community, for example, prevented him from talking to employers and strikebreakers (1988:251). These outcomes often follow the lines of cliques and factions within the group studied, as the Adlers suggest in the following incident from their fieldwork on drug dealing (Adler 1985):

> [W]hen we accepted one of our key informants into our house to live for several months, our relationship with him became much more intimate. However, this alienated his ex-wife, another one of our key informants, who was involved with a different but overlapping set of associates in her own right. (Adler and Adler 1987:42)

Furthermore, even trust within a single relationship is never absolute and unconditional. Warren and Rasmussen's (1977) fieldwork on massage parlors provides an illuminating example. "A youthful, divorced, and attractive male," Rasmussen was soon able to develop close relations with some female masseuses (thereby threatening many male parlor owners, customers, and intimates of the masseuses), even becoming the boyfriend of one of the former. Yet his close, even intimate rapport with the masseuses *both generated access to some sorts of data and restricted access to others*. Defining him as a "boyfriend," for example, "[t]he women in the parlor were somewhat reluctant to tell the whole truth about their sexual involvements" (354), for "boyfriends" were not told everything (or sometimes even anything) about these sexual activities (see also Douglas 1976). Thus, even (or perhaps, especially) romantic intimacy will not open the doors to total, "magical" trust.

In sum, ethnographers often experience moments of deep, significant change in their relations with those they study, frequently viewing these moments as evidence of relational "rapport" or "trust." These new relations do not dissolve all restraints on revealing secrets, but rather establish different patterns for conveying and withholding information. Being an insider and gaining trust provide relationally situated, and hence inevitably partial, access to some secrets, to some but not all aspects of the lives and concerns of others. In field relations as in everyday life, we never learn all the secrets of others, just as we can never be sure that we are "fully trusted and accepted" (Duneier, this volume). All social relations are patterned and regulated in specific ways, and there is "no time out" from these relationally specific patterns and regulations, no totally free, transcendent position from which to study social life.[7]

Under these circumstances accounts of field relations should move beyond dramatic examples of gaining trust and simple insider/outsider dichotomies to examine in detail both "the social location of the ethnographer and informants" and the actual negotiations of difference between them (Zavella 1996:140–41). The fieldworker should self-consciously and analytically attend to the interplay of social similarities and differences in field relations, tracing in detail, as Duneier (this volume) insists, the specific ways in which "a different social position can have a serious effect on one's work." To do so requires close consideration of the pattern of interaction between fieldworker and those studied. Pollner and Emerson (this volume) take up this sort of close interactional analysis by noting that those studied act not only to exclude but also to incorporate the fieldworker into their social worlds and routine rounds of activities. Thus, "participant observation" depends upon interactional devices and strategies that allow the fieldworker to stay on the edges of unfolding social scenes rather than being drawn into their midst as a central actor. Indeed, "the field" as a site of both participation and observation must be understood as a jointly accomplished activity, one dependent upon the willingness of those studied to allow the fieldworker to be physically present but socially marginal.

PERSONAL DIMENSIONS OF FIELDWORK

Contemporary ethnographic accounts self-consciously explore the personal and emotional processes that arise in doing fieldwork. As Clarke emphasized (1975:118), "We must look then to the knower as much as to his field if we would understand what he is saying, and recognize that he has a valid part to play as a person, not just as a manipulator of techniques, in the acquisition of knowledge." Two general themes mark this literature: the implications of the fieldworker's unique personality, prior experiences and emotional responses for the research process; and the personal and emotional effects of fieldwork on the ethnographer.

Fieldworker as Person

The ethnographer's unique personal characteristics exercise an important influence on fieldwork processes. Individual traits and idiosyncratic interests may attract (and/or repel) those encountered in the field and encourage (or prevent) the development of close relations. In addition to physical attractiveness, the fieldworker's interest and liveliness, learning and/or professional status may account for some of the willingness of those studied to spend time with a researcher. Finally, features of personality may influence the style an ethnographer develops in the field. Hunt (1984), for example, resisted incorporation into a standard police role for women not simply because of its methodological limitations but also because of her personal attraction to physical action.

"The observer's biographically unique personal experiences" may also play a crucial role in fieldwork (Johnson 1975:91). This effect is clear-cut in complete-membership fieldwork, in which a researcher studies a world or setting wherein she has existing contacts and competencies; but it is also evident in fieldwork in settings with which the researcher has had little or no prior acquaintance, as when an interest in cooking is extended to fieldwork on professional cooks (Fine 1996) or a concern with one's children's experiences in school influences the decision to study elementary school classrooms (Thorne, this volume). These sorts of prior experiences may not only influence how the fieldworker presents herself, and hence the development of fieldwork relations, but <u>may also provide a lens through which she attends to and interprets events in the field</u>. Karp and Kendall (1982:252–53) in particular suggest that each fieldworker brings "a singular mixture of presuppositions, personal penchants, and past histories into the field, and these factors cannot help but color interpretations made there, . . . [predisposing] individual fieldworkers toward particular ideological or theoretical positions."[8]

Fieldwork is also shaped by the ethnographer's emotional makeup and reactions. Personal preferences on the part of the fieldworker—feeling a "natural" connection with a particular individual, becoming fascinated with and drawn into particular social situations and social worlds—play an important role in fieldwork outcomes. Similarly, personal aversions arise and influence the course of fieldwork: Thorne (this volume), for example, examined and came to terms with her initial emotional reactions to the most "popular" and to the poorest, most marginalized girls in the fourth-grade class she studied.

Fieldworkers have also been concerned with the personal consequences of conducting covert fieldwork. Some contend that the burden of sustaining a covert role inhibits the fieldworker's openness and sensitivity to the nuances of interpersonal communications. Cassell, for example, insists that "the investigator who presents a 'false' self is affecting both the ability to judge what is going on and the course of interaction by the need for constant monitoring of one's 'act' or 'front'" (1980:36).

The play of these personal and emotional qualities help make fieldwork reactive, contingent and even haphazard in character. Fieldwork involves a highly personalized set of relation-based inquiries, typically pursued in a "creative trial and blunder" fashion (Karp and Kendall 1982:260). Thus, few actually carry out field research in a pre-planned, rational manner (although methodological accounts may suggest some such rational schema after the fact); key decisions are as likely to be shaped by "personal or subjective factors" as by strictly research concerns (Johnson 1975:90).

Personal and Emotional Effects of Fieldwork

Fieldwork involves processes of "relearning and resocialization" that inevitably engender deep feelings of insecurity, anxiety, loneliness, frustration, and confusion (R. Wax 1971:20). These subjective and emotional experiences may deeply affect ethnographers, influencing research outcomes and understandings as well as changing and perhaps transforming their selves.

Fieldwork inevitably gives rise to personal involvements and identifications with those studied. Earlier treatments of the personal effects of fieldwork tended to focus on recognizing and overcoming the biases or distortions in observation and interpretation that might result. Extending Schwartz and Schwartz's earlier analysis (1955) of the distortive effects of intense anxiety on participant observation, Gans (1968) identified a number of subjective processes specific to field relations that lead to overidentification with those studied, including the experience of irremediable marginality from the group and guilt from the subtly deceptive stance assumed toward its members.

But fieldworkers increasingly view identification not only as a source of bias, but also as means to gain empathic appreciation of other's daily lives and social worlds, viewing feelings "as resources for understanding the phenomenon under study" (Kleinman 1991:184). Thorne, for example, explains that her active participation in the Vietnam War draft resistance movement influenced her fieldwork concerns and analyses in the following manner:

> My discussion of movement conflicts over strategies and tactics was anchored in my having been in the thick of the debates. At the time, I didn't suspend my emotions, as a detached observer might have done. I cared about the practical and political consequences, for example, of draft counseling, compared to the turning in of draft cards. Having myself argued the pros and cons, I gained better understanding of the strong feelings which accompanied these movement schisms. (Thorne 1983:232)

Ethnographers may also extrapolate from their own specific experiences in the field to understand and interpret members' experiences. For example, in conducting fieldwork on how families living in an Israeli town subject to terrorist shelling coped with this ever-present threat, Reinharz (1979) had first to make what provisions she could for her own physical security. In so doing she came to realize that her own strategies and reactions to the shelling were comparable to those of the Israeli families:

> Early in the process . . . I uncovered my previously unknown and unexamined responses to potential disaster. I found myself recording my own feelings to the same problem to which the families' responses were being studied. . . . I no longer considered these personal reactions internal noise that disturbed the research process. Rather, I looked to my reactions as an indicator of general patterns for coping with the continuous threat of potential destruction. (1979:336)

Similarly, an "epiphanal moment" occurred in Kondo's fieldwork (this volume) when her landlady responded to her complaint about having to reciprocate a favor requested by a local teacher who had helped her improve her Japanese, informing her that people had to do things "for the sake of maintaining good relationships, regardless of their 'inner' feelings." Here Kondo personally encountered "the lack of importance of any personal self apart from social obligations," an experience that led her to abandon her intended focus on kinship and economics in favor of inquiry into selves and social relations.

Kleinman (1991) comments on the neglect of fieldworkers' negative emotions toward those studied. She recounts experiencing strong feelings of disappointment, frustration and anger toward members of an alternative therapy center when it appeared that they spent most of their time talking about "budgets, money, and planning fundraisers rather than about holistic health, organizational ideals, or interpersonal relations" (188). As a result she lost enthusiasm for her fieldwork. Only when she recognized and clarified the sources of these feelings in her own personal experience and values was she able to empathize with the group.

The personal and emotional dimensions of fieldwork provide the central focus for those who advocate autoethnographic introspection as an important source of data. Treating their own relational and emotional experiences as typical (or at least indicative) of the experiences of others, ethnographers such as Carolyn Ellis propose making sociology an "intimate conversation about the intricacies of feeling, relating, and working," striving to integrate private and social experience by writing about the intimate details of social relations from the first-person point of view (1995a:3–4).

The subjective and emotional experiences of doing fieldwork can affect, often at a profound level, the very self of the fieldworker. As Clarke argued (1975:118):

> We must accept that social scientific research involves the researcher relating to those he investigates, and that the result is the outcome of their relationship, a relationship that, like all relationships, will change both parties.

> The knowledge thus gained from these relationships not only changes the knower; it becomes part of the knower.

Particularly when venturing into other cultures, fieldworkers are exposed to "the impact of a new way of thought and life upon their own" (Clarke 1975:104), an exposure that may fundamentally transform their sense of who and what they are. Even in less exotic field settings, personal values and beliefs are frequently challenged and questioned, and attitudes drastically changed as a result (Clarke 1975; Johnson 1975). Indeed, going into the field may lead to resocialization or even conversion experiences that deeply affect the fieldworker's personal identity. Zola (1982) provides a striking account of the impact of fieldwork on researcher identity in discussing his personal experiences in a village for the physically handicapped in the Netherlands. This field experience not only radically transformed his sociological understanding of the world of the handicapped but also had profound personal consequences, as he came to fully recognize and embrace rather than to distance himself from his own longstanding physical impairment.[9]

Fieldwork, in sum, is a deeply personal as well as a scientific project, and the subjective, emotional experiences of doing fieldwork not only may shape the interpretations and theories ultimately produced but may also change the very self of the ethnographer. But to acknowledge and explore these field-based emotional and personal experiences raises a number of unresolved issues. First, to what extent is full disclosure of the personal experiences of fieldwork a realistic possibility? There are good reasons for fieldworkers not to reveal the full extent of their field mistakes and foibles, settling at most for presenting the "second worst" misstep in their fieldwork (Lofland and Lofland 1995:224). Second, to what extent is full disclosure useful or warranted? Clarke has warned against the dangers of "vulgarization and distortion posed by highly personal accounts" and advised against including "every passing emotion" in field reports (1975:120). Similarly Geertz expresses misgivings about the capacities of "author saturated" texts "to get an I-witnessing author into a they-picturing story" (1988:97, 84). One minimal criterion might restrict inclusion to those personal and emotional experiences that significantly affect the researcher's understanding of the setting in general or of critical activities within it.

TRANSFORMING EXPERIENCE AND OBSERVATION INTO DATA: WRITING FIELDNOTES

The insights gained from immersion, trust, and deeply personal and emotional experience do not speak for themselves. These matters must be translated into textual form. This process begins in or close to the field with the writing of fieldnotes—*written accounts* that provide the core data for ethnographic analyses. The process usually culminates in writing a final, polished ethnography, a book or article intended for wider audiences. Ironically, more attention has been given to writing finished ethnographies (see Part III) than to writing fieldnotes, despite the fact that most ethnographic monographs are assembled from and incorporate these field-based texts.

Ethnographers have recently begun to examine their own varied practices for writing fieldnotes (Sanjek 1990a; Jackson 1990a; Emerson et al. 1995; Lofland and Lofland 1995). Fieldworkers hold different views of the appropriate content and organization of fieldnotes. Some produce fieldnotes as "a running log written at the end of each day" (Jackson 1990b:6); others distinguish between this kind of daily log and "fieldnote records," that is, "information organized in sets separate from the sequential fieldwork notes" (Sanjek 1990b:101). Some consider fieldnotes as their records of what others said and did, while others distinguish fieldnotes—"a record of one's reactions, a cryptic list of items to concentrate on, a preliminary stab at analysis" (Jackson 1990b:7)—from "data." Fieldworkers also differ on *when* fieldnotes should be written: The standard recommendation, particularly in sociological fieldwork, is to write elaborate notes as soon as possible after witnessing relevant events, typically sitting down to type detailed observations after every foray into the field. But many ethnographers initially produce less detailed records, filling notebooks with handwritten entries to be elaborated and "finished" upon leaving the field.[10]

Fieldnotes as initially produced in the field reveal distinctive writing qualities (Emerson et al., 2001:353–56). Produced more or less contemporaneously with the events, experiences and interactions they recount, such "raw" fieldnotes are written incrementally, set by set, without any sustained logic or underlying principle and on the assumption that not everything included will be useful for a larger/finished project. Thus:

> Fieldnotes are not written in accord with some tightly pre-specified plan or for some specifically envisioned, ultimate use. Rather, composed day-by-day, open-endedly, with changing and new directions, fieldnotes are an expression of the ethnographer's deepening local knowledge, emerging sensitivities, and evolving substantive concerns and theoretical insights. Fieldnotes are therefore unruly or "messy" (Marcus 1994), changing form and style without attention to consistency or coherence; they have the "loose," shifting quality of working, preliminary, and transitory, rather than final or fixed, texts. (Emerson et al., 2001: 355)

As a result, fieldnotes build up into a corpus having little or no overall coherence or consistency; this corpus may well contain brief accounts of unrelated incidents, different snippets of members' talk, accounts of the fieldworker's interactions and feelings, and close-to-the-ground descriptions of and reflections on matters just witnessed or overheard.

While providing the core data for most ethnography, fieldnotes are not straightforward factual accounts, but *authored representations of ongoing social life*. As such, fieldnotes inevitably reduce the welter and confusion of lived reality, translating or rendering into written form the lived complexities of others' worlds and the fieldworker's lived experience of those worlds. Hence fieldnotes are inevitably selective, never providing a "complete" record (Atkinson 1992:17). Fieldnotes are necessarily partial and incomplete in that they recount only the fleeting moments the fieldworker was able to observe, make some sense of, and reconstruct at some later point. Moreover, dialogue cannot be rendered from memory in absolutely complete form (Fine 1993:277–78), and fieldnote accounts may incorporate routine misunderstandings: "We mishear, we do not recognize what we see, and we might be poorly positioned to recognize the happenings around us"(Fine 1993:279). And finally, fieldnotes are inevitably selective in terms of which observations are written up—the ethnographer writes about some incidents that seem "interesting"or "significant,"often leaving out matters that do not.[11]

Fieldnotes are also selective in what they do include, since they inevitably *present or frame* the events and objects written about in particular ways, hence "missing" other ways that events might have been presented or framed (see Part I, pp. 27–30). To cite but one example, an event may described from an "endpoint" or in "real-time" (Emerson et al. 1995:60–63). In the former, understandings obtained later on at some "end point" involving complete (or at least greater) knowledge are used to describe what was observed earlier on. Thus, one might write about a skid-row scene by describing a "line" of homeless men waiting to get a "sleep ticket" entitling one to spend that night inside a local mission (60–61). A real-time description of this scene, in contrast, would describe this scene as it came to make sense to the writer-observer: the realization that this collection of poor men sitting, laying and standing around on a downtown sidewalk are in fact "in line"; then learning that their purpose for waiting was to get a bed for the night, and so on. Real-time descriptions thus preserve incomplete or even inaccurate interpretations that ultimately came to be discarded, but that guided or provided meaning at earlier moments.

Ethnographers have begun to examine the literary conventions characterizing fieldnotes. First, fieldnotes have a strongly *descriptive* thrust, providing accounts of people, scenes, and dialogue that minimize explicit theorizing and interpretation. "For the most part, fieldnotes are a running description of events, people, things heard and overheard, conversations among people, conversations with people" (Lofland and Lofland 1995:93). Descriptive fieldnotes can also include detailed accounts of the fieldworker's initial impressions, unusual happenings that depart from the routine and ordinary, the observer's personal reactions to events and encounters, and indigenous terms used by people in the setting (Emerson et al. 1995:26–30).[12]

Second, fieldnotes often make heavy use of stories or narrative. On the one hand, those studied frequently organize and report their experience in some narrative form, in large part because "people experience and interpret their lives in relationship to time," and "time is made human" by means of temporally ordered narratives (Richardson 1990b:22). Fieldworkers receive, elicit and write up a variety of different sorts of members' stories, including narratives of *everyday life and routines* (as in response to such questions as "what happened at work today"), *autobiography* (a telling of one's story that "gives meaning to the past from the point of view of the present and the future"), and *biography* (a narrative constructing and linking "key events" in the life of another) (Richardson 1990b:22–24; see also Holstein and Gubrium 2000).

On the other hand, ethnographers themselves frequently construct their fieldnotes in the form of a narrative. Lederman (1990:84) emphasizes that a field-worker may think about and organize observations into units as *events*, such units having "an apparent 'wholeness'" that make them "good modes of entry into fieldnotes." Emerson et al. (1995:87–90) emphasize that fieldworkers rely on narrative forms in writing both brief *episodes* (one- or two-paragraph accounts depicting an incident as one continuous action or interaction) and extended "fieldnote tales" (loosely structured strings of action chunks linked together by the ethnographer). Fieldnote tales usually have a mundane, everyday quality, rarely moving to the dramatic or even clear-cut outcomes typical of artfully crafted narratives. But fieldnote narratives are also essentially open-ended and revisable in character:

> The cohesion of fieldnote tales . . . is temporary and conditional: ethnographers' understandings of recounted events may change as fieldwork continues. In the light of further observation of related activities and reappearing characters, the ethnographer may reassess connections and disjunctions between episodes. . . . (He) may begin to see earlier tales differently than when he wrote them. He may reexamine the implicit connections, the gaps he did not understand, and the endings he inferred. . . . (Emerson et al. 1995:98)

Finally, ethnographers have come to pay increasing attention to the process of rendering emotional experience in fieldnotes. The fieldworker's own emotional reactions to events in the field may provide important analytic leads by mirroring the reactions of others in that setting, as discussed above, and have become a major concern of advocates of experiential or autoethnography. Ellis (1991, 1995a) in particular urges writing emotionally evocative fieldnotes in order to facilitate reconstruction of features of a setting or scene at some later point in time. Including these personal reactions and sensitivities ensures that the ethnographer does not write herself out of the text but remains visible as both social actor and embodied inquirer, thus enhancing "authorial responsibility" (Rosenau 1992:27). In addition, by focusing attention on emotions as aspects of social life worthy of attention in their own right, evocative fieldnotes may capture complexities of process and experience that would elude descriptions of behaviors obtained by direct observation or interview questions alone (Ellis 1991:33–34).

ETHICAL ISSUES IN THE FIELD

Those engaged in ethnographic fieldwork routinely encounter a number of often complex ethical issues. Some of these issues are endemic to all research, and indeed to social life generally. But in recent years ethnographers have given primary attention to ethical dilemmas that are specifically tied to their long-term, intimate participation in the daily lives of people who have their own distinctive interests and moral beliefs. These sorts of ethical issues can be grouped into three categories: First, overt fieldwork practice frequently involves some misdirection and deceit in relations with those studied. Second, ethical issues in covert or disguised fieldwork move beyond simple dissembling to employ more systematic deception. Finally, fieldwork activities and relationships may directly affect and change the lives and circumstances of those studied in ways that raise still further ethical issues.

Dissembling in Overt Fieldwork

Openly identified ethnographic research often involves elements of dissembling. Often, the fieldworker "pretends to participate emotionally when he does not; he observes even when he does not appear to be doing so, and . . . he asks questions with covert purposes of which his respondents are likely to be unaware" (Gans 1968:314). Indeed, Stacey (1991:114) suggests that ethnography inevitably entails some exploitation: "Conflicts of interest and emotion between the ethnographer as authentic, related person (i.e., participant), and as exploiting researcher (i.e., observer) are . . . inescapable features of ethnographic method. . . . [T]he lives, loves, and tragedies that fieldwork informants share with a researcher are ultimately data. . .".

Mild dissembling and secret-keeping often mark negotiations for access. Even while telling of research intents and plans in seeking entree, few fieldworkers fully reveal what they are about. Thorne (1980:287), for example, observes that in seeking access fieldworkers provide self-introductions that often represent "partial truths," especially "vague and even misleading initial statements of identity and purpose." Fine (1993:275) notes that ethnographers may sugarcoat their intention to study those whose cooperation they must obtain by saying, "We are interested in the problems faced by people in your condition, what you do, and how you think"—an often effective explanation with those who do indeed feel unappreciated by the public. Furthermore, fieldworkers frequently offer accounts of research purposes to some but not to all those encountered; in many situations, for example, fieldworkers tell the immediate host of the research more or less what the fieldwork is about but provide little or no such information to those they observe less frequently and more episodically. Clinic or hospital staff, for example, may know what the fieldworker is doing, but many times it will be difficult and highly intrusive to inform all patients of these matters.

Even if fieldworkers reveal the specific focus of the research—often a near necessity simply in order to obtain access to the kinds of events they wish to observe—they may withhold from those studied their basic analytic concerns and commitments (Thorne 1980). In studying psychiatric settings, for example, fieldworkers may not tell the staff of their theoretical commitment to look at events from the perspective of the patients. Bloor (this volume), for example, encountered strenuous objections when this commitment became apparent. In addition, fieldworkers may gloss over the specific methods of the research and their implications. As Thorne notes (1980:289), "People aware of a fieldworker's general purpose and presence do not realize what the methodology entails: making daily and detailed written records of ongoing behavior."

Finally, fieldworkers may engage in a variety of tactical presentations of self that are intentionally misleading or deceptive. Fieldworkers may present them-

selves as uninformed novices in order to be able to get those under study to talk
about issues and assumptions that would be taken for granted by the knowl-
edgeable. Parts of the self may be suppressed in order to appear ignorant and
harmless in these ways. Furthermore, as Fine (1993:270) emphasizes, "Most, if
not all, ethnographers make a play for their subjects, suggesting that they are
intensely sympathetic chroniclers" when their real sentiments are something
else again and anything but "kindly." Leo (this volume), for example, describes
how in seeking access to interrogations conducted by police detectives he
adopted a "chameleon strategy" in which he "fabricated a nonthreatening
research persona in order to establish rapport with the detectives in charge of
conducting suspect interrogations." An ethnographer may employ even more
extreme deception in expressing support and sympathy for personally objectionable goals and concerns of the group studied (Peshkin 1986; Klatch 1988), in
effect becoming "a spy, an undercover agent operating against the interests of the
observed group" (Fine 1993:272).

There are, of course, a number of good reasons for deceptive or less than full
informing. First, entree may not otherwise be attainable; particularly when fieldworkers seek to observe controversial activities and powerful and self-protective
groups of major sociological relevance, access may be denied if sympathy is not
expressed or feigned.[13] Second, since fieldwork often involves commitment to
indigenous meanings and local phenomena, and hence typically begins without
explicit hypotheses, ethnographers may indeed not know specifically what they
will study when they start out. Third, concern with possible reactive effects may
lead fieldworkers to avoid or "shade" telling those studied of research interests,
on the assumption that "if subjects know the research goals, their responses are
likely to be skewed" (Fine 1993:274). The danger is not primarily that such information will create "demand characteristics" on the order of laboratory experiments, but that those studied will act in stilted, self-conscious ways. Those who
have been told that a field researcher is studying their humor, for example, will
inevitably joke in very different fashion than those who have not been told of such
a research interest. Finally, explanations of the nature of the research are subject
to the interpretations of those studied and hence are not entirely under the control of the fieldworker. Thorne, for example, reports that children translated her
accounts for her presence and research concerns into terms meaningful to them.
Similarly, Duneier (this volume) shows that multiple, sophisticated and often
contradictory understandings of what the fieldworker is up to, and what the
import of his research is likely to be, can arise and persist throughout fieldwork.

There can be marked variation in the nature and degree of dissembling in
overt fieldwork relations with those studied. Within particular field projects,
some individuals never gain the fieldworker's confidence and may be uninformed or even deceived about some key matters; at the other extreme some
become effective if not quite equal collaborators in the fieldwork, as in the case
of Hakim Hasan in Duneier's research. Similarly, ethnographers vary in their
stances on these matters. Some prefer to keep some core research concerns from
those they study. Others, including feminist and postmodern ethnographers

who value equality and reciprocity their exchanges with those studied, employ *collaborative* fieldwork practices, making persistent efforts to avoid or minimize misdirection and secret-keeping in their exchanges with those they study (Stacey 1991; Devault 1999). Yet even the most collaborative-minded fieldworkers acknowledge that it is impossible to avoid completely deception in each and every situation, for all fieldwork "is secret in some ways and to some degree—we never tell the subjects 'everything'" (Roth 1962:283). The fieldworker learns much in confidence that cannot be told to others, but possessing such information can place the fieldworker in "situations of inauthenticity, dissimilitude, and potential, perhaps inevitable, betrayal" (Stacey 1991:117). As Fine (1993) emphasizes, while there are inevitably elements of convenience in limiting or shading what we tell those studied we are up to, there are also conflicting principles involved—for example, the benefits of gaining access to understudied realms of social life, the desire not to alter or destroy the phenomena of interest.

All social life—ethnographic fieldwork included—involves forms and occasions of dissembling and secrecy. Most openly identified fieldwork seeks not to avoid all secrecy on all occasions, but rather, as Roth (1962:284) has suggested, to determine "[h]ow much secrecy shall there be with which people in which circumstances." Fieldworkers can indeed try to minimize secrecy and deception but cannot take cover behind a universal principle to "always tell the truth." Issues of who will be told what must be faced as they arise in the actual circumstances of particular field relationship; in this respect, to continue Roth's observation, fieldworkers are "in the same boat with physicians, social workers, prostitutes, police, and others who must deal with information which is sometimes delicate, threatening, and highly confidential." Secrecy neither can nor should be avoided; "It is rather a problem to be faced as an integral part of one's work" (Roth 1962:284).

Ethical Issues in Covert Research

Fieldwork conducted by more deeply covert means raises further ethical issues. One form of covert fieldwork has involved the researcher assuming a *disguised identity*. The elaborateness of the disguise has varied greatly, from documenting a false identity in order to allow an officer to pass as an enlisted man (Sullivan, Queen, and Patrick 1958) and sustaining the pretense of having converted to a millennial sect (Festinger, Riecken, and Schachter 1956), to claiming to suffer from mental symptoms in order to gain mental hospital admission (Caudill et al. 1952; Rosenhan 1973), and to attending meetings of AA dressed in ways intended to elicit different social class responses (Lofland and Lejeune 1960).

A second form of covert research involves revealing actual identity but *concealing research purposes and activities*. Thus, residents of Springdale knew that Vidich was the field director of a quantitative research project from Cornell, but not that his seemingly innocuous social contacts and queries were means of collecting qualitative data about the social structure of the town (Vidich and Bensman 1958, 1964). Similarly, Ellis (1986, 1995b) hid indications of her research purposes and fieldnote writing from the Chesapeake fisher folk she intermittently visited and lived with over a nine-year period.

Some fieldworkers oppose all forms of covert research, often rejecting utilitarian ethics in favor of a Kantian principle that "persons be treated at all times as ends in themselves, never merely as means" (Cassell 1980:35). They maintain that deceit not only blunts the fieldworker's moral sensibilities (and research sensitivities) but in so doing violates the autonomy of those researched by "making the research interaction inauthentic" (Cassell 1980:35). Erikson (1967, 1995) has consistently maintained that disguised observation constitutes an ugly invasion of privacy and is, on that ground alone, objectionable. Disguised observation is also likely to bring injury, harm, and pain to those studied—from violations of trust and the exposure of personal worlds—in ways that the researcher cannot anticipate. Thus, Erikson urges the following foundational moral principle for field research: "It is unethical for a sociologist to *deliberately misrepresent* his identity for the purpose of entering a private domain to which he is not otherwise eligible" (1967:373).

Other ethnographers, however, defend covert methods in fieldwork, unequivocally supporting an ends-justifies-the-means approach in which deception and disguise are necessary to gain fieldwork access to centers of political power or illegal activity as important research settings.[14] Douglas (1976) specifically advocates fieldwork "infiltration" as an essential tactic for getting at the dirty laundry of social and political life. Similarly, Marx (1984) argues that absolutist rejections of all covert practices will exclude fieldworkers from critical "hidden and dirty data." Implicit here is the assertion that the moral standards for conducting field research "may be different from the moral standards by which we judge human beings in daily life" (Leo 1996). While not always and everywhere defending deception, Leo contends that some research projects may have sufficient value to justify deceit, particularly in the face of noncooperation and resistance from those controlling access to key settings.

Means-ends rationales are often accompanied by rejection of morally absolutist principles for deciding ethical issues in specific situations and cases. Fieldwork, it is emphasized, is a morally ambiguous enterprise fraught with moral hazards, contingencies and uncertainties (Klockars 1979). In fieldwork, as in other domains,

> [t]here are no hard-and-fast rules about what is right and what is wrong across all settings and in all situations. There are no easy answers. There will always be trade-offs, compromises, and competing considerations. (Leo 1996:126)

These ethical considerations can become particularly complex in fieldwork conducted in membership roles. Fieldworkers who assume active and complete membership roles are frequently but not always open about both their research concerns and identities (Adler and Adler 1987:83). Hayano's (1979) fellow poker players, for example, remained unaware of his research interest in their sessions; yet he was "naturally" a participant in these activities, confronting on a level of parity all the risks and dangers facing everyone else who was involved. And presumably neither his employers, co-workers or patrons knew of Goffman's sociological research activities or his position as a university professor when he trained and worked as a casino dealer to study "gambling action" in Nevada (Goffman 1967). Is the reason one decides to participate the key factor? As Roth asks, "Is it moral if one gets a job in a factory to earn tuition and then takes advantage of the opportunity to carry out a sociological study, but immoral to deliberately plant oneself in the factory for the express purpose of observing one's fellow workers?" (1962:284). Similarly, is there a significant moral difference between a sociologist who has himself admitted to a mental hospital to conduct a study when he was not "really mentally ill" (Caudill et al. 1952) and one who studies his hospital experience when he has suffered a "real" mental breakdown and been institutionalized for depression (Killian and Bloomberg 1975)? In learning the skills needed to perform some task and then carrying out that task responsibly, the fieldworker actually becomes that social being, even if concealing other aspects of his identity. In such instances notions of disguised and misrepresented identity, not to mention those of means and ends, become blurred.

Consequences and Harm in and to the Field

Further ethical issues arise from the possibility that fieldwork will have substantial if sometimes subtle effects on those studied, effects which the fieldworker often cannot anticipate and which are as likely to be harmful as neutral or beneficial. While such effects are likely to occur when finished ethnographic texts are published (see Part III), others are the specific consequence of the ethnographer's actions and relations in the field.

The literature provides a few instances of extreme harm resulting from fieldwork. Perhaps the most dramatic is that reported by Briggs (1970; cited in Appell 1978:92):

> One of the administrators I met warned me to be very circumspect in my study of shamanism among the Eskimo. He said that the Eskimo are aware that whites frown on the practice, and he related to me the consequences of one investigation into shamanism. The anthropologist had been working in a highly missionized Eskimo community and had finally persuaded some Eskimo to sing shamanistic songs for him. Shortly thereafter, one man who had recently converted to Christianity committed suicide as a result of his guilt over participating in an activity which was an important part of the native religion.

In other instances, fieldworkers have generated profound but more subtly harmful consequences. In restudying the Yucatan village of Chan Kom, Goldkind (1966, 1970) made contact with a local faction ignored by Redfield and his coworkers in their earlier research. Goldkind concluded that the rise to prominence and uncontested political hegemony of the "progressive" leader, Don Eustaguio Cime, was made possible by the support of Redfield and other Americans. Briefly, Don Eus managed to monopolize local contacts with Redfield's anthropological expedition (as he had done also with earlier archaeological expeditions) and to gain control of the important resources (jobs and money) these groups brought to the village. In addition, Eus parlayed Redfield's political support and published statements into financial and other support from the Mexican government. The presence of the anthropologist was thus highly conse-quential in ways that were not appreciated initially.

Clearly, such local consequences derived from the fieldworker's *power*, including material resources, political connections, and social prestige. Cassell (1980) has in fact argued that the relative power of fieldworker and hosts pro-vides a key consideration in evaluating the overall impact of fieldwork. She sug-gests this relation can vary on four dimensions: (1) the fieldworker's power as perceived by those studied, (2) the fieldworker's control over the wider setting of the research, (3) the fieldworker's control over the local context of the research, and (4) the extent to which fieldworker or hosts initiate specific research inter-action. Compared to other forms of research, Cassell suggests that fieldwork generally involves low degrees of control, is more reactive, and exercises minimal power, although there can be wide variation from situation to situation.

Feminist ethnographers have recently given increasing attention to the con-sequences of the sometimes close relationships formed with those they study. Stacey (1991) argues that fieldwork activities inevitably intrude into and effect the web of local relations exactly because ethnography "depends upon human relationship, engagement and attachment":

> No matter how welcome, even enjoyable, the fieldworker's presence may appear to "natives," fieldwork represents an intrusion and intervention into a system of relationships, a system of relationships that the researcher is far freer than the researched to leave. The inequality and potential treacherous-ness of this relationship is inescapable. (1991:113)

The fieldworker's frequently sympathetic, supportive stance, for example, may give rise to definite expectations about particular endeavors. Even the "neutral" presence of a fieldworker during a psychiatric interview, for example, may be read by the interviewer as a sort of validation of her procedures and emerging decision, even when the observer's opinion is not directly sought. Furthermore, by actively and sympathetically participating in local activities, the fieldworker may tacitly incur specific obligations; thus harm can result from the field-worker's failure to perform in ways that those studied had expected from their readings of the commitments implied by this relation. Pollner and Emerson (this volume) describe an instance when a situation of escalating threat made the observer aware that psychiatric emergency team members were counting on him for physical help if need be.

Additional problems surface with the disruption or severing of relations with the fieldworker's departure from the field. Many ethnographers have noted the difficulties of extrication and disengagement from the field due to the "intense interpersonal ties between fieldworker and informants" (Snow 1980:111). Leaving the field will typically transform these relationships, in some instances ending them entirely, in others diminishing contact to the point that informants feel abandoned (Adler and Alder 1987:62). Sometimes the fieldworker ends contact because of personal unease with further contact. Offended by the treatment accorded the mentally retarded in a state institution by attendants he personally liked, Taylor (1991:244–45) stopped going to the field:

> I began to feel terribly inauthentic. I found it difficult to keep up the facade, yet could not confront the attendants without blowing my cover and letting them know I had misled them about my true feelings. So, without even calling an end to the study in my own mind, I simply stopped visiting.

However, other fieldworkers continue to maintain contact with at least some of those studied even after withdrawing from the field. The Adlers note that many of those who do membership-role fieldwork "form friendships, especially with key informants, that are lasting. Through these people they can manage contact with the group for several purposes, including follow-up research and future reentry" (1987:79).

In conclusion, ethnographers regularly face a variety of personal and ethical issues arising in the course of field relations with those studied. While most of these issues can be anticipated in some general sense, the form they take varies drastically depending upon particular features of the setting and the ethnographer's relations with those in it. Moreover, the moral choices confronting the fieldworker are often not only complex, deeply troubling, and resistant to preformulated solution but may also have to be resolved without careful deliberation for "(e)thical problems in fieldwork often require an immediate resolution" (Dingwall 1980:885) and cannot be taken in for careful consultation.

POLITICAL ISSUES IN THE FIELD

Silverman and Gubrium (1989:8–10) distinguish between the politics *of* the field (the political understandings underlying the constitution of "the field" as a research site), politics *in* the field (the political processes implicit in generating fieldwork data), and politics *from* the field (the broader political uses and consequences of fieldwork data). Here I want to address politics *in* the field, focusing on the political issues fieldworkers face in entering, making a place in, and moving through the social worlds they study. These issues include the increasingly politicized conditions for conducting fieldwork, the broader implications of selecting particular groups or institutions to study, and the ramifications of fieldworker alignment within the divisions characterizing the social world studied.

Over the last half of the twentieth century the conditions for organizing and conducting fieldwork in both anthropology and sociology have become increasingly politicized. As noted earlier, in colonial circumstances the political dimensions of anthropological fieldwork remained latent and implicit. On the one hand, the fieldworker, allied with and supported by the political power of the colonial administration, could remain outside of or above local political concerns. While unacknowledged, colonial power had pacified the Trobriand Islands, allowing Malinowski to undertake his "epoch-making fieldwork . . . a decade after a permanent government station, a decade and a half after the last internal fighting and an abortive attempt at violent resistance to colonial power, two decades after the Methodist Overseas Mission headquarters had been established at Losuia" (Stocking 1992:218). On the other hand, these political arrangements created both the space within which fieldwork could be conducted and the terms on which it would be carried out: "The colonial power structure made the object of anthropological study accessible and safe—because of it sustained physical proximity between the observing European and the living non-European became a practical possibility" (Asad 1973:17).

The decline of colonialism has made visible the political underpinnings of fieldwork, frequently necessitating extended, complex and multileveled negotiations in order to begin fieldwork. As Clifford (1986a:9) notes, "[A] variety of formal restrictions are now placed on fieldwork by indigenous governments at national and local levels. These condition in new ways what can, and especially what cannot, be said about particular peoples." Thus, ethnographers may not be allowed access or may be directed to study only particular issues in desired ways. As a result, anthropological fieldwork has become politicized; or, more accurately, the conditions under which fieldwork will be carried out and upon which it had relied has been transformed so that its political underpinnings are visible and unavoidable.

Similarly in developed countries, many of the previously unorganized and relatively powerless groups traditionally studied by sociological fieldworkers have become more aware of and begun to assert more control over field research. Warren (1977) reports from her research on gay worlds in the 1970s: "I found gays sometime defined sociologists as public relations persons for deviants, and assumed that my purpose was to 'tell it like it really is' about gay life. . . . Gay organizations and individuals may screen out researchers who are non-gay, or who appear to be hostile to gays, since they fear that gay life will not be 'told as it is.'" Many fieldworkers continue to work closely with politically organized movements, and/or with related social agencies and public programs, in order to obtain access to marginalized populations. Much fieldwork on AIDS victims and prevention programs is closely linked with AIDS support and political action groups (e.g., Gamson 1989; Sandstrom 1990; Broadhead and Fox 1990). Studies of abused women, the homeless, or Alzheimer-family caregivers often rely upon access through shelters and support groups (Loseke 1992; Weinberg 1997; Gubrium 1986). These groups and programs, often deeply concerned with how they are going to be presented both to the general public and to governmental decision makers, function as de facto gatekeepers to the populations they are concerned with and may push fieldwork in directions they approve.

Ethnographers have also become more conscious of the political implications of their decisions about which groups to study. Laura Nader's (1969:289) call to "study up," to reorient fieldwork toward "the colonizers rather than the colonized, the culture of power rather than the culture of the powerless, the culture of affluence rather than the culture of poverty," has had several important consequences. First, research on elites now constitutes a distinctive subgenre within ethnography, with its own methodological literature (e.g., Cassell 1988; Aldridge 1993; Ostrander 1993; Thomas 1993) and an expanding number of substantive studies of high-status groups and powerful institutions, including upper-class women (Ostrander 1984; Daniels 1988), elite law firms (Mann 1985; Nelson 1988), and mainstream financial institutions (Smith 1981; Abolafia 1996; Harper 1998). In the same vein, spurred by labeling or societal reaction approaches, much fieldwork on deviance, branded as voyeuristic because of its preoccupation with "nuts, sluts, and perverts" and other marginal and subordinate groups in American society (Liazos 1972), has been redirected toward social control institutions and agencies—police, courts, jails, hospitals. Nonetheless, ethnographers actively continue to study the disadvantaged, including the poor, ethnic groups, immigrants, the homeless, and drug users; thus studies of elites and social control agencies have supplemented rather than replaced research on those on the margins, leading to a dual focus on the "social worlds of the elite and the admired" and "dangerous social areas and morally perverse people" (Katz, this volume).

However, in turning their sociological gaze upon the marginal and disenfranchised, ethnographers face increasingly complex issues. In his manifesto for underdog sociology, "Whose Side Are We On?" (1967), Becker suggested that fieldworkers regularly seek to convey the meanings, concerns and points of view of subordinate groups who are unrepresented or misrepresented in the larger society. But as Katz (this volume) emphasizes, acting as advocate for an underdog becomes much more complicated as these deviant or marginalized groups become politically organized, develop their own advocates, and produce their own portraits of their groups and activities. Since these portraits will generally be "far more favorable than what an innocently motivated ethnographer is likely to describe," ethnographers studying these groups encounter major dilemmas and conflicting pressures: "Now any account of the everyday realities in social worlds whose members are battling reputations as deviant is likely to uncover realities that the group's public relations agents will find embarrassing and counterproductive." To represent these realities risks putting one's ethnography at "the employ of repressive outside forces." But to move in the opposite direction, ignoring and suppressing observations that contradict publicly presented versions of reality, violates a fundamental ethnographic commitment to provide full descriptions of all social life.

Finally, ethnographers may become enmeshed in the day-to-day and long-term factional and internal politics endemic to the social worlds they study. As Becker (1967:240–41) has emphasized, some settings are marked by latent rather than overt divisions and are thus "apolitical," not in the sense that struggles and conflicts over power and legitimacy are absent, but in that they have been submerged.[15] Other settings are openly politicized, worked by clear-cut factions and well-articulated conflicts. In either case, the fieldworker will encounter situations of conflicting claims and demands, making it difficult if not impossible to maintain a stance of neutrality. Since hierarchies and factions characterize the life of almost any group, many of the most fundamental, politically laden decisions the fieldworker makes are how to move through these factions, and, ultimately, how to represent each with its distinctive concerns. Particular problems arise in settings marked by the dominance of a superordinate group or category over a subordinate group. To present the view of the latter is to challenge part of the political domination of the former, to counter its established "hierarchy of credibility" (Becker 1967) with the perspectives and concerns of the less credible group.

How the ethnographer identifies and aligns within the internal politics of a group or setting can also influence the research process in subtle yet significant ways. As Thorne observes (1983:233–34), in directing her attention and analysis to the charismatic leadership and risk-taking process in the draft resistance movement she implicitly oriented her account to the activities and concerns of the male movement leaders, neglecting the more routine, "supportive" activities of women movement participants. Similarly, Rochford's (1989, 1992) fieldwork in the Hare Krishna movement drew in part upon his ties with a number of marginal and ex-members. The central leadership subsequently criticized his work as overly identified with the "fringee community" they regarded as unrepresentative of and peripheral to the real core of the movement (Rochford 1992:109).

REGULATORY AND LEGAL ISSUES IN FIELDWORK

In preparing to go to the field and while actually engaged in fieldwork, most ethnographers contend with a variety of institutional requirements intended to regulate the conduct of research. Based in colleges and universities and frequently supported by funds from private foundations or public agencies, field researchers become subject to federal requirements for human-subjects protection and informed consent, administered by local institutional review boards. Furthermore, in recent years professional associations in both sociology and anthropology have produced elaborate codes of ethics also focused on issues of informed consent and confidentiality. Finally, some fieldworkers have become embroiled in legal actions where their fieldnotes have been subpoenaed and/or their direct testimony compelled about unpublished aspects of their fieldwork. These cases pose significant challenges to fieldworkers' abilities to protect confidential research information and sources.

Federal Human Subject Protection Regulations and IRBs

In 1978 federal regulations designed to protect human subjects in scientific research were extended to social science field research. These regulations had originally developed in reaction to Nazi medical experiments at Nuremberg and to the Tuskegee cases in the United States (where black syphilis victims were deceived about receiving treatment). Widely publicized deceptive social psychological experiments by Milgram (e.g., 1965) and others spurred application of these regulations to social science research. Thus, by 1980 federal regulations applied uniformly to all research involving "human subjects," including biomedical, psychological and social research (although subsequent years saw greater recognition of the differences involved in these fields). Fieldwork was particularly affected by several key provisions of these regulations: the need to assess the "risks" faced by research subjects, to obtain "informed consent" from all those determined to be "at risk," and to assure subject anonymity and confidentiality in research publications.

Federal regulations require a utilitarian calculation of the risks to subjects, broadly defined as "the possibility of physical, psychological or social injury," to be balanced against the possible benefits of the research. While some fieldworkers object to this risk/benefit ethic and prefer more absolute moral standards (Cassell 1980), most emphasize the irrelevance of this ethic to actual processes of field research. The harms and benefits of fieldwork are "less immediate, measurable, and serious" than those resulting from medical or social psychological research (Cassell 1980); moreover, these risks/harms and benefits derive primarily from publication of findings and not directly from the conduct of research. Hence a risk-benefit calculus is difficult to apply to fieldwork: "Weighing potential harms against benefits before research is carried out becomes an exercise in creativity, with little relevance to the ethical dilemmas and problems that may emerge during the research" (Cassell 1980:32). Klockars (1977:225), for example, argues that applying a cost-benefit equation to his study of a professional fence would have provided his informant with less than adequate protection; the process would have offered no substantively workable criteria for deciding "whether a researcher should risk injury to his subjects or should be judged guilty of this abuse."

Similarly, fieldworkers have sharply criticized federal informed consent procedures. Designed with biomedical and experimental research in mind, these procedures conflict at key points with actual fieldwork methods. As Wax (1996:238) summarizes these disjunctures:

> "Informed consent" is meaningful when a specific procedure is then to be administered at a specific time to a specific (powerless) subject. However, in much ethnographic research, the researcher is not about to administer a specific procedure, but is initiating a long-term and open-ended social process among a group that typically possesses major powers in its own right. Because the social process will be jointly constructed by the investigator and the numerous and varied members of the host community, its outcomes are unknown. . . .

Specifically, fieldwork does not involve short-term, discrete or contractual encounters between individuals but broader, long-term relations with groups of people; thus "the contours of the natural groups and settings of field research run against the individual model of informed consent" (Thorne 1980:293). The fieldworker does not relate to those studied within a narrow, researcher-subject role relation, but develops multiplex relations characteristic of primary groups. As Klockars (1977:218) emphasized in discussing his relations with his informant, "Vincent was not only my subject but also my teacher, student, fence, friend, and guide. Likewise, to Vincent I was not only researcher, but biographer, confidant, customer, friend, and student." Each of these role relations entailed "multiple obligations and responsibilities and expectations," many at odds with those involved in a research-subject relation, and hence inadequately protected by informed consent requirements. Finally, in contrast to medical or experimental researchers, the field researcher usually possesses little power, as perceived by those studied, and does not exercise (unilateral) control over the setting, conduct, or interactional contours of the research encounter (Cassell 1980).

Federal regulations for human-subjects protection are administered by local institutional review boards (IRBs). While all fieldworkers seeking official approval must go through their university-based IRBs, those seeking approval for projects to be carried out in "research-prone institutions such as hospitals, schools, prisons, mental institutions, and major corporations" will have to go through a second level of review by each such institution's local IRB (Timmermans 1995:155). Fieldworkers can file exemption from human-subjects review when studying "normal educational settings" and public places; but federal regulations now require local IRB review of such claims for exemption. If a field research project is not exempted, the fieldworker will be required to complete a standard protocol describing the risks and benefits of the research, as well as procedures to secure the informed consent of research "subjects" and to safeguard confidentiality. Research funding is conditional upon IRB approval of the project. In practice a number of fieldworkers seem simply to bypass IRB human subjects review by carrying out their fieldwork without funding.

Fieldworkers who seek formal IRB approval typically confront head-on the conflicts between actual fieldwork procedures and the assumptions and requirements of informed consent, often having to tailor their accounts of research procedures to fit the requirements of their local IRB. In some situations fieldworkers report lengthy and not always successful struggles to overcome IRB objections. Timmermans (1995:157ff) describes a series of troubling encounters with the IRB of the hospital where he sought to study cardiopulmonary resuscitation (CPR), coming away convinced that "the IRB members were mainly concerned with the promotion of a positivistic research paradigm and with shielding the medical profession from outside criticism" (166). A similar tendency toward policing research in order to protect institutional reputation surfaced in Rochford's dealings with a university IRB over his fieldwork with the Hare Krishna movement. During one session before this IRB, for example, Rochford was anonymously confronted with the charge that he might be "involved with the Krishnas" and therefore asked "to specifically address the question of your relationship with them" (1994:62). Later the IRB chair admitted that these questions arose from fear that Rochford "was about to involve the university in a possible Jonestown situation" (63).

Professional associations have recently elaborated codes of ethics adopting largely parallel positions on confidentiality, deception and informed consent. The ASA Code of Ethics approved in 1997, for example, discourages the use of deceptive techniques, endorses consent provisions except where the risks are minimal and where "the research could not practically be carried out were informed consent to be required," and urges rigorous efforts to protect confidential information in all situations except those involving "observations in public places, activities conducted in public, or other settings where no rules of privacy are provided by law or custom."

Many fieldworkers have expressed grave doubts about both the advisability and feasibility of governmental and professional regulation of research ethics. Some question the very possibility of developing meaningful codes of ethics: Dingwall (1980:883), for example, suggests that "[i]t is not possible to write an unambiguous set of rules for ethical behavior" and anticipates that such codes will become mechanisms for enforcing conventional morality. Others argue that the more and the less powerful need different kinds and degrees of protection, and fear that ethical regulations and code will effectively prevent fieldwork focused on the politically powerful (e.g., Galliher 1983). Many see such protection of human subjects regulations as adding to the power of local "gatekeepers" controlling research access to hospitals, schools, and prisons.

Human-subjects protections, procedures, and professional codes of ethics weigh particularly heavily on the planning and initial design of research. This focus, while trying to prevent problems down the road, also makes research projects subject to a distinct form of prior restraint. Indeed, Murray Wax's (1983:288) fear that "some types of valuable research are being discontinued and others radically redesigned" as the result of the "multiplication of administrative procedures" with federal regulation now appears extremely prescient. Moreover, concentrating review at the beginning of a project conflicts in a profound fashion with the emergent, adaptive qualities of field research. Fieldwork methods are not fixed in advance, but are situationally evolving and specific: Key decisions about where and what the fieldworker will observe and about who to talk to about which topics depend upon prior observations and emerging foci, and hence often cannot be predicted with any accuracy at the start of the research in designing informed consent procedures. Wax has long urged developing alternative procedures more fitted to fieldwork, including the following proposal:

> At the close of the fieldwork period, the investigator shall submit a detailed accounting: which peoples he studied, where he lived, and how he proceeded; with whom did he discuss and explain his research, and what did he say about it . . . what effects or impacts were consequence upon his presence? Were there persons or groups who disapproved of his presence; how is it that they felt that way; and how did he handle their objections? (1983:298)

However, "prior restraint" procedures for addressing informed consent and confidentiality continue to dominate the current landscape, with few signs of interest in alteratives more sensitive to the actual conduct of fieldwork.

Confidentiality in Legal Actions

Federal human-subject regulations require fieldworkers to protect the anonymity or confidentiality of those studied. Indeed, until very recently, informed consent protocols contained standard paragraphs assuring those studied that all fieldnote and other original field data would be kept private, that actual names would not be used, and that information about private matters would be presented in ways that would preserve anonymity. In the last few years, however, fieldworkers have been forced to recognize that the confidentiality of fieldnotes and other unpublished field data has no reliable legal protection. As Scarce, imprisoned for contempt of court for refusing to divulge any information about his fieldwork, found to his dismay (1994:134), "There simply are no laws, no regulations, no court precedents that are guaranteed to support confidentiality."

The lack of legal protection for fieldwork became evident by examining two cases in which legal authorities subpoenaed unpublished fieldnotes in investigating possible crimes. In the first case, in 1983 a graduate student at SUNY Stony Brook, Mario Brajuha, received both county and federal subpoenas demanding fieldnotes written while conducting dissertation research on waiters and work relations in New York restaurants (Brajuha and Hallowell 1986). Investigation focused on the apparent arson that had destroyed the restaurant where he had been working as a waiter while carrying out his fieldwork. Brajuha consistently refused to testify or to provide his fieldnotes. After extended litigation he agreed to submit edited copies of his notes from which he had removed all material he considered confidential; at this point both federal and county district attorneys withdrew their subpoenas.

The second case began in 1992 when Rik Scarce, a graduate student at Washington State University conducting fieldwork on the radical environment movement, received a subpoena to testify before a federal grand jury investigating an animal rights raid the previous year on labs at WSU (Scarce 1994). Before entering graduate school Scarce had published a popular book on the radical environmental movement which included interviews with several animal rights activists; one such activist who became a primary suspect in the WSU raid had house-sat for Scarce and his family. Although offered immunity from prosecution, Scarce asserted "academic privilege" under the freedom of the press clause of the First Amendment, refusing to provide fieldnotes or to testify; indeed, he "refused to either confirm or deny that I had conducted interviews with anyone involved in the raid. . . . I felt that the government had no right to tamper with my research in any way" (1994:129). The judge rejected this argument, ruling that "even a newspaper reporter, if placed in the same position, would have to testify" (130). When called before the grand jury Scarce persisted in refusing to answer questions regarding his research on the following grounds:

> Your question calls for information that I have only by virtue of a confidential disclosure given to me in the course of my research activities. I cannot answer the question without actually breaching a confidential communication. Consequently, I decline to answer the question under my ethical obligation as a member of the American Sociological Association and pursuant to any privilege that may extend to journalists, researchers and writers under the First Amendment. (Scarce 1994:130–31, citing In re Grand Jury Investigation and Testimony of James Richard Scarce 1993:36)

Scarce was subsequently held in contempt and then jailed for 159 days following an unsuccessful appeal.

Defense arguments in both cases asserted that unpublished fieldnotes collected as part of scholarly research should receive the protections accorded journalists under the freedom of the press and free speech provisions of the First

Amendment. The federal trial court decision in Brajuha's case supported this general claim, asserting that "[s]erious scholars are entitled to no less protection than journalists" (Brajuha and Hallowell 1986:461, citing 583 F. Supp.:993). However, by analogy with journalists' protections, this same court recognized a "limited" rather than absolute "scholar's privilege" in these matters. The appellate court also rejected the claim of absolute privilege for confidentiality, holding that "it was not the notes per se that were protected, but the relationships represented by the privileged data" (Brajuha and Hallowell 1986:461–62). This ruling then paved the way for Brajuha's submission of his edited version of the notes. The Scarce case provides even less protection for fieldwork confidentiality: Deliberately not ruling on the question of whether "scholarly inquiry enjoys the same freedom of press protections that traditional news gathering does," a federal appeals court held that Fifth Amendment provisions empowering grand juries took precedence over all First Amendment free speech and free press guarantees.[16]

Richard Leo's fieldnotes from his study of police interrogations (this volume) were subpoenaed under somewhat different circumstances. While the Brajuha and Scarce subpoenas asserted that the fieldworker might have information bearing on the commission of illegal acts, a defense attorney requested access to Leo's fieldnotes for possible evidence bearing on the procedural fairness of a client's confession. However, the decision again came to involve a balancing act, this time between a criminal defendant's due process rights and the asserted First Amendment right to protect the confidentiality of research sources. When the judge ruled in support of the former, Leo decided to provide the relevant notes and to testify. Despite his anticipation that his evidence would hurt the defense case, the defense attorney was able to turn it to his advantages in arguing to suppress the confession.

In addition to revealing the precarious standing of fieldnotes as confidential documents in criminal proceedings,[17] these cases raise a number of other significant issues. Briefly: (1) Informed consent procedures not only proved irrelevant to the confidentially issues that arise with subpoenas but actually suggested a nonexistent ability to protect confidentiality. (2) University administrators, attorneys and judges were often unaware of the centrality of assurances of confidentiality in fieldwork; Brajuha, for example, early on met *in camera* with the trial judge to "read passages from the notes selected to underscore the private and confidential nature of his material" (Brajuha and Hallowell 1986:459). In Leo's case, considerable pressure had to be mobilized in order to get university administrators and counsel to oppose the subpoena on First Amendment grounds. (3) Efforts to negotiate more flexible agreements to avoid blanket access to confidential fieldnote data met with limited success: While Brajuha was able to control the editing of his notes, parallel proposals by Scarce and Leo were rejected.[18] (4) Even if prison time were avoided, dealing with the subpoenas and the legal cases they generated came to dominate the fieldworker's life circumstances for a significant period of time. As Brajuha and Scarce became local cause celebres, they became preoccupied with legal matters, leading to deep disruptions of their professional, research and personal lives.

NOTES

[1] However, they do so for different ends. The fieldworker's concerns with these social types are practical—"how to identify them, enter into relationships with them, and engage their support"; theorists examine types with a variety of conceptual interests (Cicourel 1964.65).

[2] Again indigenous anthropology provides an illustration: Fahim and Helmer (1980:646) report that "the local anthropologist may not be taken seriously by informants if he probes types of behavior that informants view as commonly shared knowledge, such as marriage customs, or he may be considered intolerably crude in broaching other topics, such as sexual practices."

[3] Douglas specifies the distinction between empathy and sympathy as follows: "Empathy is an ability to *feel with*, to see things from the standpoint or perspective of the individual being studied rather than to identify with or act from this standpoint. There is no reason whatsoever to believe that to understand is to sympathize with or to agree with, although this may be necessary for certain individuals because of their own feelings, identifications, and so on" (1972.26).

[4] The Adlers' third category of involvement, "peripheral membership," encompasses the contemporary, experiential/reflexive understanding of participant observation described in Part I of this volume.

[5] Carlos Casteneda (1968) provides a case in point: Apprenticing himself to a Yaqui Indian curer don Juan, he "ultimately ... became the phenomenon in which he had formerly suspended belief, joining the world of mysterious seers and knowledge he had entered" (Adler and Alder 1987:67).

[6] The Adlers, for example, hold that "as the result of being fully accepted by members," complete-membership role fieldworkers "are able to gain the full openness of their subjects to an extent unknown to any other kind of fieldworker" (1987:81).

[7] In this respect trust (and distrust) in social relationships poses not simply methodological problems but sociological issues in their own right. Levy's (1968) fieldwork on whites in the Southern civil rights movement in the 1960s provides an example, examining the processes by which northern whites became aware of and tried to manage the pervasive expressions of deep mistrust they received from southern blacks. In this way Levy used his own experiences as a distrusted northern white as substantive topics for analysis.

[8] Karp and Kendall (1982) also suggest that a researcher's earlier fieldwork experiences will influence subsequent field studies. This tendency is particularly marked in anthropology, where the second culture studied by the fieldworker is often understood by contrast with the first one studied (and both by contrast with the researcher's native culture). Geertz (1995) in particular has explored the interconnections between his initial fieldwork in Indonesia and his later fieldwork in Morocco.

[9] Indeed, in some instances fieldwork may be pursued as a way of working through troubling identity-related issues. Hughes (1971.566–76) has suggested, for example, that a number of graduate students at the University of Chicago found in fieldwork a means of "sympathetic emancipation" from the immigrant culture or occupational background of their parents.

[10] Writing fieldnotes as soon as possible preserves both the "idiosyncratic, contingent character [of observed activities] in the face of the homogenizing tendencies of retrospective recall" and the subtle processes of learning and resocialization at the core of participant observation (Emerson et al. 1995:3–14). Composing contemporaneous fieldnotes is less critical for those who emphasize broader, intuitive insight over closely observed detail and who place less value upon the fieldworker's processes of learning and understanding.

[11] Many incidents fail to get into fieldnotes because of the physical demands of fieldwork. After Fine's frequent late-night sessions with fantasy game players (described in Fine 1983), "for much of the time I was simply present, barely monitoring what transpired among these gamers. My powers of observation were substantially decreased. When I drank or puffed marijuana with research subjects, my powers of concentration were altered for the worse and better. When I had a vexing day at the university or a dispute with my wife, my concentration diminished" (1993:280).

[12] Suspicion of all forms of representation (Rosenau 1992:92) leads some postmodern ethnographers to reject writing descriptive fieldnotes (e.g., Dorst 1989). Yet other ethnographers deeply influenced by postmodern ideas continue to view writing fieldnotes as a central research activity (Ellis 1995a; Richardson 1994), but shift the emphasis from describing others' words and deeds to using fieldnotes "as an opportunity to expand . . . habits of thought, and attentiveness to your senses" (Richardson 1994:525).

[13] Leo's justification of creating a deceptive persona to aid in gaining access to police interrogations drew criticism from Erikson (1995, 1996) on the grounds that "we should (not) do research that requires deliberate misrepresentation and deception" (1996:130). Leo (1996), however, insists that he openly and consistently identified himself as a researcher and hence did not engage in "disguised participant observation." He argues that acts of omission involve less deception than acts of commission: "That I withheld or concealed information about myself—such as my political views about the death penalty, my sympathy for abortion rights activists and my liberal-minded indifference to homosexuality—should not be confused with the act or intent of falsifying information" (1996:124).

[14] Goode (1996:31–32) provides a forceful statement of this position, insisting that "carefully and sensitively used, deception is not unethical . . . as long as no one's safety is threatened." Goode emphasizes that our society should "tolerate occasional intrusions . . . into the private lives of its citizens" in order to support "a skeptical, inquiring, tough-minded, challenging sociological community" (32).

[15] "No situation is necessarily political or apolitical. An apolitical situation can be transformed into a political one by the open rebellion of subordinate ranks, and a political situation can subside into one in which an accommodation has been reached and a new hierarchy been accepted by the participants" (Becker 1967:241).

[16] The U.S. Supreme Court refused to review this decision (Scarce 1994:136).

[17] Confidentiality issues also arise in civil suits. Clarke (1995), for example, received a request from a law firm defending an electrical contractor being sued by workers to gain access to 38 interviews and other field documents listed in the references for his *Acceptable Risk? Making Decisions in a Toxic Environment* (1989). But Clarke was able to negotiate and ultimately avoided a subpoena and providing any field data.

[18] Again, civil suits appear to allow fieldworkers more room to negotiate favorable outcomes. For example, after unsuccessfully trying to discourage the contractor's attorney from pursuing his notes, Clarke offered to provide only "the nonconfidential . . . parts of interviews and documents you requested" if given written assurance that this action would not waive any claim to the confidentiality of other documents (1995:19). While this tactic provided no long-term protection (the other side would not have been bound by any such agreement), defense attorneys ultimately dropped what was turning out to be an increasingly complex and expensive "fishing expedition."

5

On Fieldwork

Erving Goffman

INTRODUCTION

What follows is a transcription of a tape-recorded talk given by Erving Goffman during the 1974 Pacific Sociological Association Meetings, where he was a member of a panel of successful fieldworkers discussing their data collection and analysis procedures. John Lofland, who organized the session, had invited Sherri Cavan, Fred Davis, and Jacqueline Wiseman, as well as Goffman, to talk candidly and informally about how they went about doing their work. Claiming that his remarks had been too informal to warrant publication, Goffman asked not to be included in the publication of several other revised presentations from this session.

Erving Goffman liked neither to be photographed nor to be "taped" and, very much in keeping with his usual practice, at the beginning of his talk he asked that no recordings be made. However, appropriate to an overflow audience composed heavily of enthusiastic, if not totally ethical, fieldworkers, surreptitious recordings were, in fact, made and the transcription that follows is one result.

While Goffman was alive, there was every reason to hope he might eventually turn these informal remarks into a published piece. With his premature death in 1982, however, this hope was shattered. For oddly enough, despite the many students whose fieldwork he supervised and despite his own numerous experiences, Goffman never published anything on the topic. He had a great deal to say about the matter, as his many students can certainly attest, but what he had to say was communicated orally and remains only in the memories of a small number of social scientists. What he said that day in March 1974 may not be earthshaking. He was, in this instance, a creative carrier of a tradition, not its inventor. But what he had to say was, as

From *Journal of Contemporary Ethnography*, Vol 18 No. 2, July, 1989, 123–32. (Transcribed and edited by Lyn H. Lofland). Copyright © 1989 Sage Publications, Inc. Reprinted with permission. All rights reserved.

one would expect from Goffman, thoughtful, uniquely insightful, and, in places, eloquent. I am grateful to his widow, Gillian Sankoff, who agreed with us that the value of this "oral essay" overrode Goffman's expressed wish that it not be preserved, and who gave permission for its publication.

A final word about the accuracy and editing of the transcription. Unsurprisingly, given the "undercover" manner in which it was recorded, the quality of the tape is poor. Despite the use of techniques that improved that quality somewhat, portions of the talk are not sufficiently intelligible to include. Fortunately, it is clear from the tape that these portions consist entirely of "asides," brief forays into topics that are mentioned and then dropped, and their loss does not detract from the substance of what Goffman had to say. As I hope will be apparent to people who knew him well and/or who were present at the panel session, my editing of the transcription has been light. I have certainly not attempted to translate "spoken Goffman" into written prose (in fact, I have tried, with punctuation, to convey the cadence of his speech), but I have, for purposes of clarity, dropped an extraneous word here and there, added an occasional word (in brackets), section headings and footnotes, and, in one or two instances, slightly altered sentence structure.

Lyn H. Lofland

I am going to report on what I conclude from studies of this kind that I've done. And I can only begin by repeating John Lofland's remarks that what you get in all of this [attempt to articulate techniques] is rationalizations,[1] and we're in the precarious position of providing them. The only qualification of that precariousness is that ordinarily people go into the field without any discussion at all, so we can't be damaging the situation too much.

I think there are different kinds of fieldwork: going on digs, experiments, observational work, interviewing work, and the like, and these all have their own characters. I only want to talk about one kind and that's one that features participant observation—observation that's done by two kinds of "finks": the police on the one hand and us on the other. It's us that I want to largely talk about, although I think in many cases they do a quicker and better job than we do.

By participant observation, I mean a technique that wouldn't be the only technique a study would employ, it wouldn't be a technique that would be useful for any study, but it's a technique that you can feature in some studies. It's one of getting data, it seems to me, by subjecting yourself, your own body and your own personality, and your own social situation, to the set of contingencies that play upon a set of individuals, so that you can physically and ecologically penetrate their circle of response to their social situation, or their work situation, or their ethnic situation, or whatever. So that you are close to them while they are responding to what life does to them. I feel that the way this is done is to not, of course, just listen to what they talk about, but to pick up on their minor grunts and groans as they respond to their situation. When you do that, it seems to me, the standard technique is to try to subject yourself, hopefully, to their life circumstances, which means that although, in fact, you can leave at anytime, you act as if you can't and you try to accept all of the desirable and undesirable things that are a feature of their life. That "tunes your body up" and with your "tuned-up" body and with the ecological right to be close to them (which you've obtained by one sneaky means or another), you are in a position to note their gestural, visual, bodily response to what's going on around them and you've been pathetic enough—because you've been taking the same crap they've been taking—to sense what it is that they're responding to. To me, that's the core of observation. If you don't get yourself in that situation, I don't think you can do a piece of serious work. (Although, if you've got a short period of time, there would be all kinds of reasons why you wouldn't be able to get in that situation.) But that's the name of the game. You're artificially forcing yourself to be tuned into something that you then pick up as a witness—not as an interviewer, not as a listener, but as a witness to how they react to what gets done to and around them.

Now there are two main issues following from that. What you do after you get the data, which Jackie [Wiseman] has addressed herself to. And the other is, how you go about acquiring the data. And I think that, in turn, divides up into two general problems, that of *getting into place* so that you're in a position to [acquire data] and the second is the *exploitation of that place*. There's a minor phase of getting out—of "getting out" in your head—which we could look at later on if you want to.

GETTING INTO PLACE

I want to talk very briefly—a few minutes each—on those two major phases: that of getting into place and that of exploiting place once you get into it. There are certain rules in the trade about getting into place: you do a survey, you mess up some field situations that you're not going to use to find a little bit out about their life, you develop rationales for why you should be there. You have to anticipate being questioned by the people whom you study so you engage in providing a story that will hold up should the facts be brought to their attention. So you engage in what are sometimes called "telling" practices. (In the early years of this business, we frowned upon total participant observation, that is total passing in the field, because people had very fancy notions about what it would be like to be discredited. I don't mean moral issues, I mean concerns about the fact that they would be discovered and be humiliated. I think, at least in my experience, it's proven to be a fact that that's much exaggerated and that you can act as though you're somebody you're not and get away with it for a year or two. Whether you want to do that, of course, is another issue, one that bears on the ethical and professional issues attached to participant observation. I would be happy to talk about that, but I'm not talking about that right now.) So you have to get some story that will be—I like a story such that if they find out what you are doing, the story you presented could not be an absolute lie. If they don't find out what you're doing, the story you presented doesn't get in your way.

Now the next thing you have to do is cut your life to the bone, as much as you can afford to cut it down. Except for a few murder mysteries or something you can bring along in case you get really depressed, remove yourself from all resources. One of the problems of going in with a spouse, of course, is that while you can get more material on members of the opposite sex (especially if you go in with a kid), it does give you a way out. You can talk to that person, and all that, and that's no way to make a world. The way to make a world is to be naked to the bone, to have as few resources as you can get by with. Because you can argue—just as Jackie argued that every world makes sense to people—you can argue that every world provides substance for the people, provides a life. And that's what you're about, [that's what you're] trying to get quickly, you see. So, the way to get it is to need it. And the only way to need it is to not have anything of your own. So you should be in a position to cut yourself to the bone. But lots of people don't do that too much—partly because of the contingencies of getting a degree and all that.

Then there is the other issue, which I'll only remark on briefly and then go on to a little bit on note taking and the like, and that's the self-discipline required. As graduate students, we're only interested in being smart, and raising our hands, and being defensive—as people usually are—and forming the right associations, and all that. And if you're going to do good fieldwork, it seems to me, that's got to go by the board. You've got to really change your relationship to the way you manage [the] anxieties and stresses of the social networks around you. For one thing, you have to open yourself up to any overture. Now, you can't follow up these overtures because you may early associate yourself with the wrong person. You've got to be disciplined enough with the people to find out what the various classes of individuals are that are involved in the place. You've got to then decide which class you're going to study. Once you do that you've got to find out about the internal cleavages within the class, and then decide which internal cleavage you're going to accept as your own. So, you shouldn't get *too* friendly. But you have to open yourself up in ways you're not in ordinary life. You have to open yourself up to being snubbed. You have to stop making points to show how "smart assed" you are. And that's extremely difficult for graduate students (especially on the East Coast, especially in the East!). Then you have to be willing to be a horse's ass. In these little groups, the world consists of becoming very good at doing some stupid little things, like running a boat, or dealing, or something like that, you see. And you're going to be an ass at that sort of thing. And that's one reason why you have to be young to do fieldwork. It's harder to be an ass when you're old. And you have to engage in a strategy with respect to costume. People don't like to cut their hair, for example,[2] so they retain something of their own self, which is nonsense. On the other hand, some people try to mimic the accents of the people they're studying. People don't like to have their accents mimicked. So you have to get a mix of changing costume, which the natives will accept as a reasonable thing, that isn't complete mimicry on the one hand, and that isn't completely retaining your own identity either.

Then, there's the issue, again, as part of the way in which you discipline yourself, of what you do with confidants. People like to find a friend where [they're doing their study] and tell the friend the "true things" and discuss with their friend what's going on. Unless that friend is in a structural position of not being able to retell the stories—and there are ways in which you could find such a friend—then I don't think you should talk to anybody.

Now there are also tests that you can run on whether you've really pene-
trated the society that you're supposed to be studying and I'll mention some of
these briefly in passing. The sights and sounds around you should get to be normal. You should be able to even play with the people, and make jokes back and
forth, although that's not too good a test. People sometimes assume that if
they're told strategic secrets, that's a sign that they're "in." I don't think that's
too good a sign. One thing is, you should feel you could settle down and forget
about being a sociologist. The members of the opposite sex should become
attractive to you. You should be able to engage in the same body rhythms, rate of
movement, tapping of the feet, that sort of thing, as the people around you.
Those are the real tests of penetrating a group.

EXPLOITING PLACE

Let me talk for one minute before I quit on what you do *after* you get in the
situation. First, I'll review this business of "getting in." Remember, your job is to
get as close to some set of individuals as possible. So you've got to see that they're
aligned against some others that are around. There's no way in which, if you're
dealing with a lower group, you can start from a higher group, or be associated
with a higher group. You've got to control your associations. If you get seen in
any formal or informal conversation with members of a superordinate group,
you're dead as far as the subordinate group is concerned. So you've got to really
be strategic and militant about the way you handle these social relationships.

Now about exploitation of the place you're in. I think you should spend at
least a year in the field. Otherwise you don't get the random sample, you don't
get a range of unanticipated events, you don't get <u>deep familiarity.</u> It's deep
familiarity that is the rationale—that, plus getting material on a tissue of
events—that gives the justification and warrant for such an apparently "loose"
thing as fieldwork.

Then there is the affiliation issue. You can't move down a social system. You
can only move up a social system. So, if you've got to be with a range of people, be
with the lowest people first. The higher people will "understand," later on, that
you were "really" just studying them. But you can't start at the top and move
down because then the people at the bottom will know that all along you really
were a fink—which is what you are.

Note taking: two minutes or a minute on note taking. There is a freshness
cycle when moving into the field. The <u>first day you'll see more than you'll ever see
again. And you'll see things that you won't see again. So, the first day you should
take notes all the time.</u> By the way, about note taking, obviously you find corners
in the day when you can take notes. And every night you should type up your
fieldnotes. [And] you have to do it every night because you have too much work
to do and you'll begin to forget. Then there are various devices you can use. You
can start penetrating by going to open socials where, indeed, people might allow
you to take open notes. If you put your notebook on a larger piece of paper, people won't see your notebook. It's masked. They won't be disturbed by it. [Learn

to] fake off-phase note taking. That is, don't write your notes on the act you're observing because then people will know what it is you're recording. Try to discipline yourself to write your notes before an act has begun, or after it has started so that people won't be able to detect from when you start taking notes and when you stop taking notes what act you're taking notes about.

There's an issue about when to stop taking notes. Usually when you are merely duplicating what you've already got. Remember, you'll get, in a year, between 500 and 1,000 pages of single-spaced typed notes and this will be too much to read more than once or twice in your lifetime. So don't take too many notes.

Then there's [the matter of] what to do with information. Jackie takes seriously what people say. I don't give hardly any weight to what people say, but I try to triangulate what they're saying with events.

There's the issue of seeking multi-person situations. Two-person situations are not good because people can lie to you while they're with you. But with three people there, then they have to maintain their ties across those two other persons (other than yourself), and there's a limit to how they can do that. So that if you're in a multi-person situation, you've got a better chance of seeing things the way they ordinarily are.

Now, a point that I think is very important is this. We tend, because of our peculiar training, to try to write defensible statements, which is language written in Hemingway-type prose, defensible prose. That's the worst possible thing you can do. Write [your fieldnotes] as lushly as you can, as loosely as you can, as long as you put yourself into it, where you say, "I felt that." (Though not to too great a degree.) And as loose as that lush adverbialized prose is, it's still a richer matrix to start from than stuff that gets reduced into a few words of "sensible sentences." I'm now not [supporting] unscientific [practices] or anything like that. I'm just saying that to be scientific in this area, you've got to start by trusting yourself and writing as fully and as lushly as you can. That's part of the discipline itself, too. I believe that [other] people shouldn't read [your] fieldnotes, partly because it's a bore for them. But if they are going to read your fieldnotes, you'll tend not to write about yourself. Now don't just write about yourself, but put yourself into situations that you write about so that later on you will see how to qualify what it is you've said. You say, "I felt that," "my feeling was," "I had a feeling that"—that kind of thing. This is part of the self-discipline.

Now, these are comments on note taking. There are issues about getting out, about leaving the field so you can come back to it, [but] I think we can leave that, and—I'm going to stop right now.

Notes

1   In his introductory remarks, John Lofland had commented that it was likely difficult for fieldworkers to "know" exactly what it is they do to generate their analyses.

2   Recall that the year is 1974 and, especially for younger men, long hair was still both stylish and a symbol of distance from the "establishment."

Insider Field Research in Minority Communities

Maxine Baca Zinn

Field research conducted by minority scholars has some empirical and some methodological advantages. The most important one is that the "lenses" through which they see social reality may allow minority scholars to ask questions and gather information others could not:

> Undoubtedly, white social scientists are as capable of engaging in race research as their nonwhite colleagues even though their everyday experiences differ. However, because they come to the task with different backgrounds they are likely to see different problems and pose different questions. The intellectual and practical concerns may overlap, yet their analyses and recommendations will almost necessarily differ insofar as these are tempered by differences in the individual sense of urgency and conception of the possible. The results of these differing perspectives for what appears as interpretations of the urban world are profound. (Ellis and Orleans 1971:18)

Blauner and Wellman (1973:329) also believe that minority researchers will pose different questions and perhaps discover different answers. They contend further that there are certain aspects of racial phenomena that are difficult if not impossible for a member of the dominant group to grasp empirically and formulate conceptually. Indeed, the central criticism of past research is that traditional frameworks have not applied well to minority experiences. As Valentine and Valentine put it, most who study and report on ghetto life do so from a thoroughly external viewpoint and "this influences the kind of data and the quality of understanding that emerges" (1970:403). Such observations bring us to the question of whether traditional frameworks are inapplicable or merely insufficient for study-

From *Social Problems*, Vol. 27 No 2 (December 1979), pp. 209–19. Copyright © 1979 The Society for the Study of Social Problems. Reprinted by permission. All rights reserved.

ing racial, ethnic and cultural minorities. However that question may eventually be resolved, it is very clear by now that insiders in the minority world will undoubtedly influence their research, and often for the better. This is not to suggest that such researchers' understanding or experience will substitute for more systematic knowledge, rather that it may generate hypotheses and discovery of data precluded from traditional frameworks and the experiences of outsiders.

The unique methodological advantage of insider field research is that it is less apt to encourage distrust and hostility, and the experience of being excluded (e.g., as a white researcher) from communities, or of being allowed to "see" only what people of color want them to see. People in minority communities have developed so many self-protective behaviors for dealing with outsiders that it is quite reasonable to question whether many real behaviors and meanings are accessible to outsiders of another color. The issue here, again, is not only that minority people would consciously mislead white researchers (though they may well do so), but also that those researchers often lack insight into the nuances of behavior.

Parades, for example, explains how ethnographers frequently misrepresent Chicano culture because they are unaware of the "performance" element of Chicano behavior. He provides vivid examples of the way in which outsiders misrepresent Chicano behavior, and cautions that informants may go out of their way to tell the ethnographer what they think ethnographers want to hear:

> The informant not only has his stereotypes about the Anglo fieldworker, but he also has some very definite ideas as to what stereotypes the Anglo holds about him. Sometimes consciously, sometimes unconsciously, the informant may seek to conform to the stereotype he thinks the Anglo fieldworker has of him rather than expressing his own attitudes and opinions. (Parades 1977:29)

Despite the obvious advantages of insider research, the most frequently voiced objection is that the "subjectivity" of researchers will lead to bias in data gathering and interpretation. This repeated concern over subjectivity disregards the fact that, like their colleagues in majority groups, minority researchers are trained in the methodological rigors of their disciplines. This is not to say that such training by itself guarantees credibility, but simply that both insiders and outsiders are subject to the standards imposed by the scientific community. Research conducted by minority scholars should not be equated with subjective distortion. Even those researchers who openly take the side of the minorities they study, as opposed to the side of the dominant society, must subject their data to validity checks. Subjectivity does not disqualify work as scholarship or science as long as data gathering procedures and values are both made explicit. As long as researchers follow established procedures and logically relate their conclusions to the data, they are systematically guarding against bias, whatever their backgrounds.

Becker notes that researchers are accused of bias when they present the side of subordinates and relates this to a hierarchy of credibility: "In any system of ranked groups, participants take it as given that members of the highest group have the right to define the way things really are" (1967:241). Taking a stand doesn't itself present a problem; rather, the problem is to make sure that research meets the standards of good scientific work, "that our unavoidable sympathies do not render our results invalid" (239). Minority researchers who seek to "set the record straight" by correcting past distortions can still exhibit scientific integrity where data gathering procedures and interpretations are concerned. These are distinct dimensions of anyone's overall research effort.

METHODOLOGICAL AND ETHICAL ISSUES AND DILEMMAS: A PERSONAL EXPERIENCE

Minority researchers conducting studies in their "own" communities may experience problems common to all researchers as well as dilemmas imposed by their own racial identity. The effects of minority status on research relationships and data collection deserve serious consideration. My own experience in conducting field research among Chicano families may illuminate some of these issues as well as stimulate further discussions of insider research.

Entrance

The purpose of the research was to study marital roles, marital power and ethnicity in Chicano families. The intent was to "get inside" families and study marital interaction, using focused interviews and observation. "The private character of family interaction and the experience of others in gaining access to families for purposes of research suggested that entry would be a formidable problem" (Baca Zinn 1979b:9). Heeding Bott's (1957) methodological advice, I located families through local agencies, and "entered" the field through a local community education program. The program included workshops and activities for parents of enrolled students. Here I had the opportunity to work with program staff members and participating mothers.

My task was to establish credibility with a number of different groups in the organization as a basis for recruiting families for the research. For ethical reasons, I attempted to structure my relationships with people so as to include my role as researcher. I became a functioning participant in the program, sometimes assisting staff members with the numerous duties of running the program, and other times participating in workshops and other related activities, all the while communicating to people that I was there to conduct research on families.

Like all researchers, I found that entrance was not a one-time activity. As Warren remarks there is a "constant question about entree to different friendship cliques, different private homes, and different public places" (1977:101). Entering was a constant process because potential informants had to be negotiated with and relationships established separately (Schatzman and Strauss 1973:23). In the process of establishing relationships with individual informants and getting them to accept my role as researcher, I experienced anxieties common to fieldworkers in their initial phases of research.

In fact, the formidable nature of entering the field and establishing research relationships casts considerable doubt on the notion of minority scholars as "privileged" insiders. Though I was an insider in ethnic identity, I was not an insider in the organization or in the community in which I had chosen to conduct research. Like all researchers, I entered as an outsider and attempted to move carefully toward successful acceptance by community families.

Early in the research, two types of relationships developed, one with program staff members and another with participating mothers. These relationships were not given by my ascribed status of Chicana, but my ethnicity and gender did facilitate the ongoing negotiations with informants. Some of the staff members were paraprofessionals working toward their Bachelor of Arts degree at the local college. They had some knowledge of the portrayal of Chicanos and other minorities in the social sciences, and some exposure to new perspectives on minority groups. As a result, they showed great interest in the research and in the researcher, and went out of their way to be helpful. They made frequent remarks about my being Chicana (or Mexicana) and expressed the feeling that Chicanos should be studied by their own people.

Similarly, Maykovich (1977), a researcher of Japanese origin who did fieldwork among Japanese people, found that personal sympathy was shown to her, a young, female university professor who was working hard. Her appearance as a "researcher with professional qualifications seemed to represent a model success story Japanese style and the realization of achievement goals shared by Japanese in general" (1977:113). In my case, the paraprofessional staff women identified with me, not as a model success story but as a Chicana who was also working towards the completion of a degree.

The ease with which I established my researcher role with staff members did not, however, occur with the parent group. My early contacts with this group were less sustained than those with staff members, and often our interaction took place during a structured program activity. These women accepted my participation and my explanation that I wanted to get to know families for research purposes, but at first they were polite and somewhat distant. My relationship with them took shape in a most unusual way, one that illustrates the importance of the fieldworker's individual characteristics.

During a series of sewing workshops in the program, the women discovered that I was unskilled in the craft of sewing. They laughed at my ignorance, made fun of me, and teased me with comments like "a Mexicana like you doesn't know how to sew?" They decided that I should learn, and took it upon themselves to instruct and assist me in using the sewing machines at the program site. Over the course of several workshops, they worked with me on the construction of a blouse, each taking time from her own sewing and proudly displaying her knowledge of the craft. It was really through this interaction that our friendships began and that they began to identify with me: because of a peculiarity of mine, and their ideas about the skills that a proper Mexican woman should have, I was able to gain their acceptance. This experience provides support for Wax's (1979) contention that, in the field, the peculiarities of the individual researcher become magnified. In the process of developing interactions with strangers, characteristics of the individual fieldworker can drastically affect the process of fieldwork.

Through my participation in the community action program, I was able to find families for research. By taking an active part in program activities, I had acquired a place in the community and developed relationships with women. When I did "enter" their families, the process of negotiation with husbands and other family members had to take place again, but I entered as a friend of the wives, our relationships bolstered, no doubt, by our common ethnicity and gender.

Ethnicity and Gender in Data Collection

There is a notion sometimes expressed in the fieldwork literature that "women are more 'natural' fieldworkers since their traditional role in many societies is one of interaction and relationships" (Warren and Rasmussen 1977:351). This idea, however, has been based on the experiences of women researchers who have also been outsiders; there is very little information in the literature on the effect a woman's insider status can have on field research. Moore discovered in a recent project that middle-aged Mexican American men actually obtained more and better interview data than women, and she explained that finding as based on:

> ...the role of the traditional poverty level Mexican American family, in which women are quite subordinate. Men interviewers of middle age carry prestige. They are the peers of male dominated respondents and in male dominated households were allowed to interview women respondents more readily than women interviewers. (Moore 1977:155)

My experience was probably different because of the type of research I was conducting and because of the relationships I had established with women prior to the series of interviews with husbands and wives in families. Although the women were interviewed and observed more than men, the men did discuss marital roles and family decision making with me. A real shortcoming in most studies of Chicano families has been the tendency to assume that family roles can be explained by cultural ideals and values. In fact, family ideals often differ from actual role performance of husbands and wives. The privacy of the family setting allows members to engage in what Goffman (1959) refers to as "backstage" behavior. This informal behavior is an important part of family interaction, but it is often difficult for sociologists to study. I was able to observe both husbands and wives in different settings, and to ask them questions about specific behaviors in their families. A male Chicano researcher might not have been able to obtain this information. Given the Chicano ideal of male dominance, it is possible that informants would have felt compelled to reveal only the ideal dimensions of their family role to a researcher who was Chicano and male. As it was, both husbands and wives allowed me to examine both real and ideal dimensions of their roles.

Exchange and Reciprocity

As the fieldwork progressed and I developed research relationships with specific families, I became immediately involved in their day-to-day lives. I was gathering data on substantive research questions and I was also making an effort to create relationships of mutual exchange and reciprocity.

As Wax (1952) indicated some time ago, such exchanges are the key to maintaining good rapport. However, the issue of reciprocity may be different in research among minorities. Whatever the actual nature of the exchanges taking place, they involve what Moore refers to as the "status of minorities in American society" (1977:157). Because that status is a subordinate one, the researcher is often in total control of the research enterprise, creating most of the relationships and usually fashioning them to meet the demands of the research (Blauner and Wellman 1973). Viewing reciprocity as more than a field technique, I was concerned that the informants receive something in return for the information they provided. Sometimes reciprocity was expressed simply by spending time with informant family members, listening to their concerns, providing assistance when it was asked for, or helping their children with school work. Because some of the research families were involved in the community education program, I could also assist them in the course of the program activities. One informant continually called on me for help in carrying out her duties as chairperson of the parent group. I spent much time with her—planning meetings, working out activities and writing letters. Other informants also asked for assistance with such program activities as composing and typing letters, organizing meetings and workshops, and planning and carrying out a wide range of activities.

My direct involvement with informants did not always further the goals of the research, but it was "essential to alter the exploitative relationships which research imposes" (Blauner and Wellman 1973:323). I learned in the field that exchange and reciprocity are more than ideal notions. Informants quickly found that they could call on me for a variety of services. Often I experienced discrepancies between the needs of informants and the demands of the research. At times, my ongoing participation was all consuming, leaving me with little time for analysis of the evidence I was gathering.

Schatzman and Strauss (1973:117) instruct fieldworkers to move back and forth constantly between data gathering and analyzing the data. Sometimes several days would go by before I was able to sit at my desk and analyze the information that I had gathered, recorded and stored. My concern that the research not be exploitative may have led me to take on more responsibilities than I could handle—a problem, of course, not unique to researchers who are insiders.

Direct participation in the research setting does sharpen the researchers' sense of obligation to the people they are studying. Independent of one's racial identity, "participation leads to stronger emotional relationships and perhaps more compelling obligation to the community to do more than detached types of research" (Valentine and Valentine 1970:405).

Insider Problems

Maykovich cautions that a minority researcher is not any more *free* from problems than is a white researcher attempting to carry on a project in a minority community: "The problems are different in kind, but by no means different in severity" (1977:118). Meeting obligations to informants may also create problems which are peculiar to minority researchers based on their identification with the people they study. For example, an informant asked me to speak on her behalf in a dispute she was having with one of the program directors, an Anglo. In asking me to intervene and support her in the dispute she repeatedly used the phrase, "We Chicanos have to stick together." The expectation that minorities will stick together can put one to the severe test of acknowledging being an insider and at the same time realizing that some claims can jeopardize the long-term research goals. While I did intervene, I was aware that such action might be potentially dangerous to my research since the director could have withdrawn permission to recruit families through the program. A similar test could, of course, come up for nonminority fieldworkers who are asked for assistance in dealing with officials, but a request phrased in insider terms has a special ethical and political meaning to a researcher who has taken a consciously insider position.

Quality of the Data

Field research is always subject to problems stemming from invalidating or contaminating effects of the researcher's presence and selective perception and interpretation (McCall 1969:128). I attempted to guard against those biases by collecting information from a variety of sources and by using two methods: interviewing and observation. The use of more than one method is the best corrective against contamination "because each method reveals different aspects of empirical reality" (Denzin 1970:49). Items bearing on a given substantive point were compared using both methods and continually evaluated for consistency. Using both techniques clearly enhanced the credibility of the research.

Leaving the Field

In spite of the efforts I made to become directly involved in ways that would insure that informants received something from our interaction, I did not *alter* the political context within which the research took place. My relationships with the people I studied were not exploitative, but they were not equal. I created the relationships specifically to carry out my research. Furthermore, I brought those relationships to a close when my purposes were accomplished. During the last stages of the research, the stage of breaking off relationships and preparing to leave the field, the uneven nature of the research relationship became clear. I tried to be honest with primary informant families once the research relationships had been established. I was frank about the amount of time I would be spending in the field, for example. Still, they knew that I had accepted a university teaching position and eventually would be leaving the community. Nevertheless, some of the informants had come to depend on me. I knew this in the final stages of the research, and I felt uncomfortable when I heard the informant say at a parent meeting, "I wish she was not leaving us. I couldn't have been (Parent Activities) chair without her help. I don't know how I'll manage when she leaves." The woman was not merely complimenting me. She was expressing a real concern. She had come to depend on me, and now I was removing my services and support. The calls for reciprocity and researcher responsibility must be heeded, but it must also be recognized that researcher responsibility in meeting obligations may create problems of its own. A related problem in field research like this is that as researchers go about classifying, summarizing and analyzing, their own feelings and responses often get lost in the aggregate of data. Johnson says that "it is impossible to review the literature about methods in the social sciences without reaching the conclusion that 'having feelings' is like an incest taboo in sociological research" (Johnson 1975:147); but I do have some feelings about my research relationships which must be expressed. I had forged ties with families, and finally I had to bring our relationships to an end. Researchers do not often speak of it, but it was difficult for me to make that break. I felt uneasy, for example, when one of the primary informants revealed his feelings this way:

> Well it has been good that you came, good that we got to know you, but it's too bad that you won't stay here. Why is it that when our people get educated they have to leave us? You should stay here and teach at the College. When my children go to college they should be able to take courses from their own people.

I had an answer for the informant, an answer having to do with my career commitments and an answer which he accepted. Yet I did not have an answer for myself when faced with the disturbing question: was I, after all, one of those researchers who is never seen in the community again once the study is completed? It was and is a painful question which brings home the fact that "doing research is not a neutral encounter but a problematic, often painful human experience which changes the informant as well as the researcher" (Blauner 1977:xviii).

This ethical dilemma may be unique to insider research. The fact that "researchers tend to disappear from the field after short term expressions of concern" (Moore 1977:146) may be unavoidable. Insiders may have little choice in this matter, *if* their professional advancement requires their separation from their minority group.

CONCLUSION

The creation of a social science which has liberating rather than oppressive ramifications will require fundamental alterations in the relationships between minority peoples and conditions of research. Gestures of reciprocity do not, by themselves, alter the unequal nature of research relationships. Nor is having research conducted by insiders sufficient to alter the inequality that has characterized past research. Field research conducted by committed minority scholars may provide a corrective to past empirical distortions in that we are better able to get at some truths. However, our minority identity and commitment to be accountable to the people we study may also pose unique problems. These problems should serve to remind us of our political responsibility and compel us to carry out our research with ethical and intellectual integrity.

On the Evolution of *Sidewalk*

Mitchell Duneier

Hakim Hasan is a book vendor and street intellectual at the busy intersection of Eighth Street, Greenwich Avenue, and the Avenue of the Americas—aka Sixth Avenue. He is a sturdy and stocky five-foot-seven African American, forty-two years old. In the winter, he wears Timberland boots, jeans, a hooded sweatshirt, a down vest, and a Banana Republic baseball cap.

Hakim is one of many street book vendors throughout Greenwich Village and New York City generally. Most of these vendors specialize in one or more of the following: expensive art and photography books; dictionaries; *New York Times* best-sellers; "black books"; new quality mass-market and trade paperbacks of all varieties; used and out-of-print books; comic books; pornography; and discarded magazines.

On Sixth Avenue alone, among the vendors of new books, a passerby may encounter Muhammad and his family, who sell "black books" and an incense known as "the Sweet Smell of Success" at the corner of Sixth Avenue and Eighth Street. Down the block, an elderly white man sells best-sellers and high-quality hardcovers on the weekends. At Sixth and Greenwich (across the street), one encounters Howard, a comics vendor, also white, and Alice, a Filipina woman (Hakim's sometime business partner), who sells used paperbacks and current best-sellers.

It goes without saying, perhaps, that one good way to find out more about people is to get to know them at first hand, but this is more easily said than done. When I began, I knew that if I was to find out what was taking place on the sidewalk, I would have to bridge many gaps between myself and the people I hoped to understand. This involved thinking carefully about who they are and who I am.

I was uneasy.

One of the most notorious gaps in American society is the difference between people related to race and the discourse revolving around this volatile issue. Though there were also differences between our social classes (I was raised in a middle-class suburb, whereas most of them grew up in lower- and working-class urban neighborhoods), religions (I am Jewish and most of them are Muslim or Christian), levels of education (I hold a Ph.D. in sociology and attended two years of law school, whereas some of them did not graduate from high school), and occupations (I am a college professor of sociology and they are street vendors), none of these differences seemed to be as significant as that of race. Actually, the interaction between race and class differences very likely made me uneasy, though I was unaware of that at the time.

When I stood at Hakim's table, I felt that, as a white male, I stood out. In my mind, I had no place at his table, because he was selling so-called black books. I thought that his product formed the boundary of a sort of exclusionary black zone where African Americans were welcome but whites were not.

It is interesting that I felt this way. African Americans buy products every day from stores owned by whites, often having to travel to other neighborhoods to acquire the goods they need. They must shop among whites, and often speak of enduring slights and insults from the proprietors of these businesses (P. Williams 1991; Austin 1994, 1995). I myself rarely have to go to neighborhoods not dominated by whites in search of goods or services. None of the book vendors ever insulted, offended, or threatened me. None of them told me I was not welcome at his table. None of them ever made anti-white or anti-Semitic remarks. Yet I felt unwelcome in ways I had not felt during previous studies that had brought me into contact with African Americans. This was because many of the conversations I heard were about so-called black books and because the people participating in them seemed to be defining themselves as a people. (Actually, there were also white customers at Hakim's table, though I didn't know it at the time.) I felt out of place. Also, I wanted the trust that would be necessary to write about the life of the street, and race differences seem a great obstacle to such trust.

One day, before I knew Hakim and after I had concluded that these tables were not an appropriate place for me to hang out, I walked by his book table on my way to an appointment. I was surprised to see for sale a copy of *Slim's Table*, my own first book.

"Where did you get this from?" I asked, wondering if it had been stolen.

"I have my sources," Hakim responded. "Do you have some interest in this book?"

"Well, I wrote it," I responded.

"Really? Do you live around here?"

"Yes. I live around the corner, on Mercer Street."

"Why don't you give me your address and telephone number for my Rolodex."

His Rolodex? I wondered. This unhoused man has a Rolodex? Why I assumed that Hakim was unhoused is difficult to know for certain. In part, it was due to the context in which he was working: many of the African-American men selling things on the block lived right there on the sidewalk. There was no way for me to distinguish easily between those vendors who were unhoused and those who were not, and I had never taken the time to think much about it. I gave him my telephone number and walked off to my appointment.

A few weeks later, I ran into an African-American man who had been in my first-year class at the New York University School of Law. Purely by coincidence, he told me that he was on his way to see a book vendor from whom he had been getting some of his reading material during the past year. It was Hakim.

I told my classmate about my interest in getting to know Hakim and explained my reservations. He told me that he didn't think it would be as hard as I thought. Hakim had apparently gone through spells of sleeping in the parks during his time as a vendor and sometimes stayed at my classmate's home with his wife and children.

A few days later my classmate brought him to meet me in the law-school lounge. When I told Hakim that I wanted to get to know him and the people at his vending table, he was circumspect, saying only that he would think about it. A few days later, he dropped off a brief but eloquent note at my apartment, explaining that he didn't think it was a good idea. "My suspicion is couched in the collective memory of a people who have been academically slandered for generations," he wrote. "African Americans are at a point where we have to be suspicious of people who want to tell stories about us."

During the next couple of months, Hakim and I saw each other about once a week or so on our own. On a few occasions we met and talked at the Cozy Soup & Burger on Broadway. It seemed that we had decided to get to know each other better.

Early one morning a few months later, I approached his table as he was setting up and asked, What are you doing working on Sixth Avenue in the first place?

I think there are a number of black folks in these corporate environments that have to make this decision, he replied. Some are not as extreme as I am. Some take it out on themselves in other ways.

It had not occurred to me that Hakim had come to work on the street from a corporate environment. Learning this about him has been significant as I have worked to understand his life on the street. In the universities where I teach, I meet many African-American students who believe that it will be very difficult for them to maintain their integrity while working in corporate life. Many of them have come to this conclusion by hearing of the experiences of relatives and friends who have already had problems; others have themselves sensed racial intolerance on campus. Yet, in choosing to work on the street, Hakim had clearly made what would be a radical, if not entirely incomprehensible, decision by the standards of my African-American students. Once we had discussed some of these issues in depth over the subsequent weeks, Hakim volunteered that he felt comfortable letting me observe his table with the purpose of writing about it, and I began to do so.

***

After observing at Hakim's table for two years, I wrote and eventually completed a manuscript about the everyday life of one street vendor and the people who come to his table to buy and talk about books. In 1996, the manuscript was accepted for publication by Farrar, Straus and Giroux, which intended to bring it out the next year.

But I was uneasy, and ultimately I told the firm's editor in chief that I wanted to start the research all over again and write a new book. To explain why, I have to say more about how the research developed. In the process, I hope to give a sense of some of the most important methodological issues I faced.

CO-TEACHING A SEMINAR WITH HAKIM

After completing the draft of the original bookselling manuscript, I gave it to Hakim and asked him for his comments. He read it and brought to my attention a major limitation. As he saw it, my study focused too closely on him and not enough on the vendors who occupied other spaces on Sixth Avenue. As I listened to what he had to say, I realized that we needed to have a sustained conversation about the material in the manuscript. I proposed that we teach a course together at the University of California-Santa Barbara, where I was that year. Hakim was clearly well read, and I had admired his pedagogical relationships with [other] young men. Surely my students in Santa Barbara could benefit from working closely with him. I told my idea to Bill Bielby, the chair of my department, who arranged for Hakim to receive a lecturer's salary for the ten-week quarter.

Hakim and I taught a seminar for undergraduates called "The Life of the Street and the Life of the Mind in Black America." In it, we discussed a number of books which Hakim had sold at his table and spoke in detail from the draft manuscript, showing the students how "black books" entered into the lives and discussions of people who came to Hakim's table. As a teacher, Hakim was organized, insightful, and patient with students on subjects of race, class, and gender, although the discussions were sometimes quite heated.

In the class, Hakim felt that the focus on him did not give a wide-angle view of the sidewalk that he knew. (Some colleagues, too, suggested that I study the vendors who sell scavenged magazines.) Hakim thought we should invite his partner, Alice Morin, and Marvin Martin to participate in the seminar. The next month they joined us in Santa Barbara, and they participated in two weeks of classes.

My research focus was evolving as I came to get a sense of what might be gained if the book included a more comprehensive view of the street. I asked Marvin if he thought it would be possible for me to do interviews with the men he knew on Sixth Avenue, and he said that would not be a problem.

On Marvin's last night in Santa Barbara, we walked down Cabrillo Boulevard, by the ocean, reflecting on how much ground we had covered in this setting so different from Sixth Avenue. As he thought about going back to New York, he lamented that his business partner, Ron, was going through a stage of being unreliable. Every time Marvin left the table to place bets at Off-Track Betting, he had to depend on Ron to remain by the table; if Ron was drunk or high, he might abandon the table, and it would be taken by the police.

A thought occurred to me. I could work for Marvin during the coming summer. I would learn a lot more about the sidewalk, if I worked as a vendor myself, than I would by merely observing or doing interviews, and he would have his table covered. So I proposed that I work at his table for three months and give him the money I made. "What will the fellas think when I have a white guy working for me all summer?" he asked. We decided he should just tell them the truth—I was there to do research on a book about the block—and he said he would think about it.

When I told Hakim, he had reservations. Would I be safe on the streets? Could Marvin look after me? Would the toughest and most violent men on Sixth Avenue accept what I was doing as worthy of respect? Meanwhile, Marvin called from a pay phone in New York to accept my offer. I would begin in June. My summer internship, so to speak, had been arranged.

Getting In

On June 8, 1996, I appeared on Sixth Avenue at about 6:00 A.M. Ron, whom I recognized from the time I had spent on the block (but whom I had never met), was already there. I had heard enough about his violent episodes to think that I had better wait until Marvin arrived before I approached.

Marvin appeared half an hour later. He greeted me and introduced me to Ron, who, it turned out, had been expecting me. As the two men began unpacking magazines from crates which a "mover" named Rock had transported from Marvin's storage locker, Marvin told me to watch how the magazines are displayed, with the foreign fashion titles placed at the top of the table where they will catch the eyes of passersby.

As I joined in the work, I removed a tape recorder from my bag. Ron looked down at the machine and scowled. He hardly spoke that day. I put the tape recorder back in my bag, never having turned it on.

I was wearing the same clothes I had been wearing in the classroom a few days earlier: a blue button-down shirt, beige pants, and black shoes. Even if I had dressed differently, I would have stood out. My speech and diction alone would have made me seem different. Had I tried to downplay these differences, though, Ron would have seen through such a move immediately.

So right away on the block I was being a person not unlike the person I am with my friends in casual settings, my family at home, and my colleagues at work. Of course, in each of these settings, I adapt somewhat, accentuating some traits and downplaying others. In small ways I am not aware of, I doubtless did the same as I began my work.

Using myself as a participant observer, I was there to notice by taking part, trying to observe and retain information that others in the setting often thought unimportant or took for granted. I had research questions vaguely in mind, and I was already making mental comparisons between what I was seeing and what the sociology literature had to say. I was there simply to observe and record, and I was asking the people working the sidewalk to let me be there.

One of the most difficult situations I faced as I tried to make an entry into these blocks was avoiding the conflicts which already existed. Hakim, with whom I had become closely associated, got along well with everyone on Sixth Avenue except Muhammad. But if I was to get to know all the men on the block, it was essential that I not be viewed as especially associated with Hakim.

The act of "getting in," then, sometimes led me to be less than sincere about my connection to Hakim. Fieldwork can be a morally ambiguous enterprise. I say this even though I have never lied to any of the persons I write about. The question for me is how to show respect for the people I write about, given the impossibility of complete sincerity at every moment (in research as in life).

The gulf between the other vendors and myself was much greater than it was with Hakim. How could I expect these men to trust me? The vendors were wondering the same thing. One conversation captured on my tape recorder illustrates this. I had been interviewing one of them, who had been holding my tape recorder, when I got called away. While listening to the tapes a few months later, I came across the conversation that ensued after I left. (The participants, who forgot the tape was running, have asked me to conceal their identities in this instance.)

"What you think he's doing to benefit you?" X asked.

"A regular black person who's got something on the ball should do this, I would think," said Y.

"He's not doing anything to benefit us, Y."

"I'm not saying it's to benefit us," said Y. "It's for focus."

"No. It's more for them, the white people."

"You think so?" said Y.

"Yeah. My conversations with him just now, I already figured it out. It's mostly for them. They want to know why there's so much homeless people into selling books . . . I told him because Giuliani came in and he said nobody could panhandle no more. Then the recycling law came in. People voted on it."

"Case in point," said Y. "You see, I knew he had to talk to you. I can't tell him a lot of things 'cause I'm not a talker."

"I told him in California there's people doing the same thing that we're doing. They do it on a much more higher level. They are white people. You understand?"

"Yeah,"

"They have yard sales."

"Yeah."

"They put the shit right out there in their yard. He knows. Some of them make a million dollars a year. But what they put in their yard, these are people that put sculptures. They put expensive vases. These are peoples that drives in their cars. All week long, all they do is shop."

"Looking for stuff," said Y. "Like we go hunting, they go shopping."

"Right. Very expensive stuff. They bring it and they put it in their yard and sell it. And they do it every weekend. Every Saturday. Every Sunday. So they making thousands. He's not questioning them: How come they can do it? He's questioning us! He want to know how did the homeless people get to do it. That's his whole main concern. Not really trying to help us. He's trying to figure out how did the homeless people get a lock on something that he consider *lucrative*."

"Good point," said Y.

"You gotta remember, he's a Jew, you know. They used to taking over. They used to taking over no matter where they go. When they went to Israel. When they went to Germany. Why do you think in World War II they got punished so much? Because they owned whole of Germany. So when the regular white people took over, came to power, they said, 'We tired of these Jews running everything.'"

"But throughout time the Jewish people have always been business people."

"But they love to take over."

Y laughed.

"Of course," X said, laughing hysterically. "That's what he's doing his research on now. He's trying to figure out how did these guys got it. How come we didn't get it?"

Y laughed.

X continued laughing hysterically, unable to finish his next sentence.

"I don't think so," said Y.

"But he's not interested in trying to help us out."

"I'm not saying that, X. I'm saying he's trying to focus on the point."

"I told him that, too," said X. "Everyone he talk to, they're gonna talk to him on the level like he's gonna help them against the police or something like that. They're gonna look to him to advocate their rights."

"No. I don't think that, either. I think it's more or less to state the truth about what's going on. So people can understand that people like you and I are not criminals. We're not horrible people. Just like what you said, what happens if we couldn't do this? What would you do if you couldn't sell books right now?"

Hearing those stereotypes invoked against me made me realize that—conventional wisdom to the contrary—participant observers need not be fully trusted in order to have their presence at least accepted. I learned how to do fieldwork from Howard S. Becker, and one of the things he taught me—I call it the Becker principle—is that most social processes have a structure that comes close to insuring that a certain set of situations will arise over time. These situations practically require people to do or say certain things because there are other things going on that require them to do that, things that are more influential than the social condition of a fieldworker being present (Becker 1998). For example, most of the things in a vendor's day—from setting up his magazines to going on hunts for magazines to urinating—are structured. This is why investigators like myself sometimes can learn about a social world despite not having had the rapport we thought we had, and despite the fact that we occupy social positions quite distinct from the persons we write about.

It was hard for me to know what to make of that discussion between X and Y. Maybe they were "just" having fun, but I don't think so. Though I was not astonished by what I heard, I had no idea that X harbored those suspicions toward me as I had gone about my work on the blocks throughout the summer. In this sense, fieldwork is very much like life itself. We may *feel* fully trusted and accepted by colleagues and "friends," but full acceptance is difficult to measure by objective standards and a rarity in any case. If we cannot expect such acceptance in our everyday lives, it is probably unrealistic to make it the standard for successful fieldwork.

At the same time, participant observers like myself who do cross-race field-work must, I think, be aware that there are many things members of the different races will not say in one another's presence. For blacks in the United States, it has been necessary to "wear the mask," to quote the black poet Paul Laurence Dunbar, who wrote:

> We wear the mask that grins and lies,
> It hides our cheecks and shades our eyes,—
> This debt we pay to human guile;
> With torn and bleeding hearts we smile,
> And mouth with myriad subtleties.[1]

Dunbar's words are no less relevant today, for, as a survival mechanism, many blacks still feel that they cannot afford to speak honestly to whites. Surely, it would have been a methodological error for me to believe that apparent rapport is real trust, or that the poor blacks I was writing about would feel comfortable taking off the mask in my presence.

I believe that some of the vendors may have let me work out on Sixth Avenue with them because they eventually saw what I was doing nearly the way I did; others merely wanted to have me around as a source of small change and loans (something I discuss later); and a few others may have decided to put up with me so that there would be a book about them and the blocks. But it would be naïve for me to say that I knew what they were thinking, or that they trusted or accepted me fully, whatever that might mean.

***

DIAGNOSTIC ETHNOGRAPHY

When I went back to Sixth Avenue to work as a magazine vendor, I hadn't yet formulated a precise research question. I had no theories that I wanted to test or reconstruct, and I didn't have any particular scholarly literature to which I knew I wanted to contribute.

During my first summer working for Marvin and Ron, I began with a loose but useful sense to guide my data collection. I would take note of the collective activity between and among the vendors and others they worked with. I watched the relations between them and their customers; I went on hunts with the men to see how they acquired magazines; I watched them interact with police officers, trying to get a sense of how those encounters unfolded. I also talked to men in depth about their lives. At this stage of my research, I sought mainly to diagnose the processes at work in this setting and to explain the observed patterns of interactions of people. I also have a general theme that guides me in collecting data in all of my work; whether and how the persons I am with are or are not struggling to live in accordance with standards of "moral" worth.

The fact that I did not know my specific research question at the start may seem counter to the way sociologists are supposed to operate. I take a different view, however. In much of social science, especially much of quantitative research using large data sets, a research design often emerges after data has been collected. This is essentially what happened there to me. Like quantitative researchers who get an idea of what to look at from mulling over existing data, I began to get ideas from the things I was seeing and hearing on the street.

In Madison, Wisconsin, the following fall, at some distance from Sixth Avenue, I began the process of listening to the many tapes I had made on the street, as well as looking at all my notes. And I began to write down various topics that seemed important.

While I was in Madison, Ovie Carter, a photojournalist, made his first trip from Chicago to New York to photograph the scene on Sixth Avenue. During my summer as a vendor, I had called Ovie weekly to tell him what I had been seeing. Now it was his turn to show me how things looked to him.

As Ovie showed me the first batch of his photographs, I began to get a better sense of how things worked on the blocks, for he is committed to capturing relations among people and their environments and not mere individual acts.[2] For example, Ovie's photograph of a man sleeping in the doorway of Urban Outfitters is not a picture of just the man; it shows the man in the context of a table where he does business. This photograph led me to think about the relation between sleeping outside and saving a space, which led me to focus on how "habitat" is formed and works through contextual connections.

Ovie's photos also helped me make a more complete description. I recovered details, such as where goods were kept and how space mattered. With some of his photographs tacked on my office walls, I continued to listen to tapes and to look at my notes to try to figure out what could be said about life on Sixth Avenue. Many of the topics I realized were important back in Madison had not stood out as important when I was in New York. For example, while I was listening to a tape in my office, I heard Marvin talk about being kept out of a restaurant's bathroom. I also heard on the tapes constant references to the "Fuck it!" mentality, which was far more pervasive on the tapes than I had realized.

After fall classes ended, I returned to New York to work with Marvin and Ron until New Year's Eve. On the blocks then and on subsequent occasions, I began researching some of the above issues, now with clearer research questions in mind. The structure of the book ultimately resulted from considering alternative interpretations. I wanted to be open to new information and counterevidence in regard to my theme. The desire to look carefully at counterevidence and explore alternative interpretations was certainly helpful as I organized the book. But as Karl Popper (1968, cited in King, Keohane and Verba 1994:14) has argued, "there is no such thing as a logical method for having new ideas."

A colleague of mine who teaches courses in the philosophy of science, Erik Olin Wright, calls my approach "diagnostic ethnography," and I agree with that characterization. I begin observation by gaining an appreciation of the "symptoms" that characterize my "patient." Once I have gained a knowledge of these symptoms, I return to the field, aided by new diagnostic tools—such as photographs—and try to "understand" these symptoms (which is some amalgam of "explain" and "interpret" and "render meaningful"). I also read in more general literature, seeking ideas that will illuminate my case.

This approach might usefully be compared with the influential "extended case method" elaborated by Michael Burawoy in *Ethnography Unbound* (1991). The contrast is with research that begins with theory reconstruction as its pivotal agenda and seeks cases that cause trouble for received wisdom. Burawoy advocates an approach that begins by looking for theories that "highlight some aspect of the situation under study as being anomalous," and then proceeding to rebuild (rather than reject) that theory by reference to wider forces at work.

Burawoy is a scholar known for his theoretical agility, and such an approach understandably appeals to ethnographers of that ilk. I, by contrast, don't set out with theories that I know I want to reconstruct. So I observe patterns of interactions that I wish to explain, and move from diagnostics to theory reconstruction, almost in spite of myself.

In this way I work toward a middle ground, trying to grasp the connections between individual lives and the macroforces at every turn, while acknowledging one's uncertainty when one cannot be sure how those forces come to bear on individual lives. Thus I came to focus on how institutions of various sorts, especially institutions that organize power, affect the microsettings I studied. This entailed looking for proximate linkages and visible traces of organizational structure on the sidewalk. I call my strategy an extended place method.

This approach, too, is usefully explicated through comparison with Burawoy's extended case method. Burawoy, too, is interested in understanding the connection between the macro and the micro, and he collapses two distinct concerns—the importance of (1) reconstructing theory and (2) making the micro-macro link. My view is that theory reconstruction, while a fine objective on its own, was not the most efficient or rigorous way for me to make links between micro and macro.

What, then, *was* the most efficient way, and how was my approach an extended place method? For me to understand the sidewalk, that place could only be a starting point. Later, I needed to move my fieldwork on out, across spaces, to some of the other places where things had happened that had a role in making Sixth Avenue what it is. For example, having listened to unhoused men describe their day-to-day problems using public bathrooms, I paid visits to local restaurant owners, to learn more about the structural links between the sidewalk scene and the surrounding commercial reality. I also walked with Mudrick to Washington Square Park, to see an available public toilet and why it was unacceptable to him, which led to an interview with the park manager. In all these cases, the process of interviewing off the blocks grew out of participant observation on the blocks, out of seeing and hearing evidence of these problems in the day-to-day lives of people. It would have been difficult to understand the public urination I witnessed on the sidewalk without extending my fieldwork outward from the sidewalk itself.

Sometimes my effort to understand connections between micro and macro involved going farther from the blocks. I visited Pennsylvania Station with Mudrick, who showed me the specific places where he had slept before the authorities had rid the station of unhoused persons. It was impossible to understand the migration to Sixth Avenue without understanding Amtrak's decision, so I spent a good deal of time interviewing Penn Station officials, and traveling to Washington, D.C., to interview attorneys who understood the lawsuit which had been filed against Amtrak. It was not enough to ask the men on the sidewalk about their movements. I needed a more rounded picture. In order to understand how the sale of written matter came about on New York's streets, I tracked down Edward Wallace, the former city councilman who had worked to pass a local law protecting a poet's rights. In order to understand how space had been cut in half on the blocks, leading to space wars between the vendors, I spent a great deal of time doing fieldwork at the Grand Central Partnership, a Business Improvement District that had used its influence to cut down on space for vendors throughout the city. In order to contextualize the occasional sale of stolen goods on Sixth Avenue, I undertook to examine the underside of the sale of written matter throughout Now York City.

The most efficient way for me to understand these connections between micro and macro was through what the anthropologist George E. Marcus (1998) calls "multi-sited ethnography."[3] The key to what eventually became my extended place method was my own eventual recognition that the sidewalk was also "in" Pennsylvania Station, the City Council, the Farrar, Straus and Giroux lawsuit against the Strand, and the Business Improvement District, among many other places.

CHECKING STUFF

One of the ideas basic to my method was simply following my nose, going to great lengths to check stuff out and make sure there is a warrant for believing what I've been told. Here I was simply doing what any competent reporter would do, but something which ethnographers have not taken as seriously in their work. After all, the people I was writing about were not under oath. (And, as we know, even people under oath sometimes lie.) On points that were significant to developing the understandings that formed the basis of my book, I adopted the stance of the skeptic, often not accepting accounts at face value. Sometimes, as in the case of establishing the migration from Pennsylvania Station to Sixth Avenue, this involved asking many men to tell me their life stories. When the same events were told to me over and over again in the context of different individual lives, the stories were more convincing.

A number of vendors told me that, prior to living on Sixth Avenue, they had taken over a single train car of the Metropolitan Transit Authority. In order to find out whether this was possible, I ended up going on what seemed like a wild-goose chase until I met a Penn Station official who knew enough about this practice to tell me why this account was plausible. When Ron told me that he had given up his apartment voluntarily, I went with him to New Jersey to see if I could learn more about this story, which I knew some of my readers would find implausible.

In conducting this research, I benefited from developments in the humanities which emphasize the importance of stories and narrative, while not being so bound by those developments as to think that it is not legitimate and useful to look at stories for their factual value, depending on my purpose. I tried not to take people's accounts as history without doing some checking. Few people (housed or unhoused) are going to be completely honest with a researcher about the intimate details in their lives. And it's not always a matter of honesty. Poor memory, wishful thinking, and misinterpretation of the questions can lead to accounts I might characterize as less than useful.

There were some things which could be checked only gradually, and only after people had developed a great deal of trust in the researcher. Issues such as HIV status are private. Some people are also sensitive about their status as welfare dependents and like to keep this information to themselves so far as is possible. Over time, different men showed me their welfare cards, or letters from the State indicating that their benefits had been or would be cut off. Other persons asked me for help in dealing with the welfare system. These incidents occurred gradually over the years and were chiefly a consequence of my being there over time.

During the summer of 1998, Ishmael arranged for his mother, Joan Howard, to visit us on the block so that I could interview her. She lived a subway ride away in the Bronx, but she had never seen him working on Sixth Avenue. After she arrived, Ishmael introduced her to some of the other men and proudly showed her how his business works. When we went to lunch, she asked me about the book, saying, "Who would buy a book about Ishmael? He's not Michael Jackson or Madonna!" She said that she had always wanted to tell her story and that it was worth telling. The next day, Ishmael told me that his mother's visit was an important moment in his life. He had hurt her a great deal before he went to jail, and he knew that it comforted her to see him turning his life around and making "an honest living."

PUBLISHING ETHNOGRAPHY

The genre of books based on sociological fieldwork can be distinguished from many firsthand works by journalists by the way each genre deals with anonymity. Since the 1920s, American sociologists have generally used fictitious names for people and places they have written about, whereas most journalists make it a practice to identify their subjects by name. Sociologists say that they use pseudonyms to protect the privacy of the people they write about; journalists insist that they must name their subjects to give truthfulness to the accounts and assure the reader that these are not composite characters or made-up characters.

I decided to follow the practice of the journalists rather than the sociologists. I have not found that the people I write about ask to have their identities disguised. Some seem to enjoy the prospect of being in a book, and they are already known to hundreds of New Yorkers anyway. Moreover, it seems to me that to disclose the place and names of the people I have written about holds me up to a higher standard of evidence. Scholars and journalists may speak with these people, visit the site I have studied, or replicate aspects of my study. So my professional reputation depends on competent description—which I define as description that others who were there or who go there recognize as plausibly accurate, even if it is not the way they would have done it.

I did not believe that anyone could make an informed judgment about whether they would like their name and image to be in the book without knowing how they have been depicted. With this in mind, I brought the completed manuscript to a hotel room and tried to read it to every person whose life was mentioned. I gave each man a written release which described the arrangement whereby royalties of the book are shared with the persons who are in it. But I did not tell them that I would do so until the book was nearing completion.

It was not always easy to get people to sit and listen to the larger argument of the book and to pay attention to all the places where they were discussed. Most people were much more interested in how they looked in the photographs than in how they sounded or were depicted. I practically had to beg people to concentrate on what I was saying. It also did not help that they now knew they would share in the profits, a factor that sometimes made them feel less motivation to listen carefully, on the assumption that I could be trusted. The following conversation, while somewhat extreme, illustrates (among other things) that the effort to be respectful by showing the text to the person in it sometimes turns out not to seem very respectful at all. In this case, I end up insisting that the individual listen to me, and imposing my agenda on someone who seemed annoyed by my efforts. What follows is a transcription of a tape I made one Christmas Day, told in the third person.

Keith: Get on this. We got to talk about what life is about out here.

Mitch starts to read the release to Keith. When he gets to the end of the first line, Keith says, "Yo! It's all good, man. Far as I'm concerned, you're family. You came out here. You walked the walk with us, you talked the talk. It's all good. And you brought something to the attention of the people and let them know that it ain't easy. We not individuals lacksidasical. No way! For the simple fact that we work hard and we fight harder than your Wall Street executives. Okay? I'm keeping it real. You came out here. You bringing it to the attention of the world that we are the backbone of society because we work. We actually work. The rest of them people don't work. Sit and answer the phone? That's work? Go out and dig through the garbage and try to find some books to sell and take a chance of getting bit by a rat. They ain't working."

Mitch continues to read. He says, "As a scholar, my purpose has been to . . ."

Keith: [interrupts] I hate this kind of shit. Put this in the movie. This is real.

Mitch: . . . "and the difficult urban problems our society must confront in the years to come."

Keith: Well, I'm gonna tell you like this. I don't think it's just in suburbia. It's a worldwide situation. And in New York there is no reason why anyone should have to suffer. You don't know how deep your book is, do you?

At this point, Keith has still not heard any of the book.

Mitch: I hope that this study will. . .

Keith: [talking to a friend on the corner.] Crack the beer, Reg.

Mitch: Keith, listen.

Keith: I'm listening.

Mitch: "Though there is no way to anticipate the consequences of any work . . ."

Keith: It's cool!

Mitch: "I don't expect the book to make a lot of money."

Keith: Just give me the contract, Mitch. I told you. I'm signing. I'm just proud to be in the book. All this reading and everything is completely unnecessary 'cause I'm just proud to be in the book. Something to make my family proud.

Mitch: [continues to read] "And I would like you to share in the profits."

Keith: Thank you very much and I'm gonna accept whatever's given to me 'cause it's paper. I love this!

Mitch continues reading.

Keith: Man, do me a favor. Open the beer.

Hakim: Let's do this. Let him just finish this for one second, then you can get on with your business.

Keith: I'm celebrating Christmas, man. Kwanzaa. It's a done deal.

Mitch: [continues reading] ". . . of a biographical nature." [addresses Keith] Do you understand what that means?

Keith: Yes. Now, can you tell me how I sound in the book?

Mitch: I'm gonna show you every part you're in.

Keith: It's all good with me. After this book, I intend to get like Montel. Get my own show. We gonna call it "Keeping It Real." Me and brother Hakim are gonna be like Johnny Carson and Ed McMahon. Yo! Don King? Cut your hair and step aside because there's some new big dogs in town. Understand this here, Mitch. There's something you don't understand. To me this is not a money thing. It's something good that I did. I had to suffer to prove to my family that I could make it out here. And I don't need that. When they kick you to the curb and when they help you, it's a bunch of fucking bullshit. Because once you up on your feet, they turn their nose up at you. Hello you all. Kiss my ass. I got something good out of something bad.

Mitch: [continues reading] "If you do not receive payment, and you do not contact me, the money for you will be put in an escrow bank account for two years."

Keith: That sounds okay, too. I'd rather not know about it. That way, in the two years I got something I can go pick up. That's better than welfare!

Mitch: "If I still have not heard from you at the end of two years, you will forfeit the money."

Keith: I ain't forfeiting nothing.

Mitch: If I don't hear from you in two years, that money becomes mine.

Keith: Well, you'll hear from me. As long as I'm breathing, you'll hear from me. Mitch, give me the damn paper and the damn pen and let me sign.

Mitch: First, you gotta hear what the book says.

Keith: Oh, my God. Open the beer, please. This is getting on my nerves.

Mitch: First we gotta finish our work.

Keith: Damn that! I'm not signing nothing without no beer.

Mitch: [continues reading] "I want you to know how honored I am to have worked on this project. Thank you for your cooperation."

Keith: It was a pleasure, man. Like I said, my grandma can go to her grave and say, "That's my baby in that book."

Mitch: Okay, now we gotta go through the book.

Keith: I just wanna hear what's said about me. Yo, Reg, get the beer, please.

Mitch: [reads Keith's entry on the map to him] "Keith is a panhandler. He loves babies and dogs."

Keith: That sounds crazy.

Mitch: Does that sound crazy in a bad way?

Keith: No. It's like this here, man. A dog will stick by you one hundred percent. Family, your girl, everybody turn their back on you, a dog is still by your side. Children, they not only need to be taught by their family, with all the wickedness going on, they need to be protected. . . .

Mitch reads Keith's statement on panhandling.

Keith: I remember that. True words.

Mitch reads more.

Keith: Yo! Those are my words! Verbatim. You got me good, Mitch. You got the realness out. Does it say "fuck" in the book?

Mitch: Yes.

Keith: I like it.

Mitch reads more.

Keith: [Laughter] Oh my God! Oh my God. I've never been quoted before. My words is in print. That means it's law. . . .

Keith: You don't got to read no more, Mitch. I'd rather read the book when it comes out. It's cool. It's reality. Hard-core reality.

Keith signs the release. He picks up the microphone. "I'm in a book. I'm in a book. Yeah! Yeah! Yeah! Stan, I love you, man. Thank you for teaching me to be a man. That's my old uncle, the one in Denver. Mickey, thanks. And Nana, I love you. And I miss Papa. Merry Christmas."

Because Keith might have been drunk on this occasion, I had to go back and see him to go through the relevant parts of the manuscript a second and third time.

One of the most difficult aspects of reading people the sections they are in is the fear or nervousness I feel as I approach passages in the manuscript that they might interpret as negative or disrespectful. This might be one of the best arguments for making the people one writes about completely anonymous. Some observers may feel a greater license to tell the truth as they see it, even when it might be hurtful, if they never have to face the people they write about. But I have developed a rather thick skin when it comes to reading people passages they may not like. Ultimately, I believe I should never publish something about an identifiable person which I cannot look him or her in the eye and read. As I read the book to the people depicted in it, I was often asked to correct specific dates or facts of a person's life. These changes would be noticeable only to the person and his/her family. In a few cases, the corrections would make a difference to people who know the blocks or neighborhood. Yet it was absolutely essential that these aspects of the book be correct if the work was to have integrity to the persons in it.

A FINAL NOTE ON SOCIAL POSITION

As an upper-middle-class white male academic writing about poor black men and women, who are some of the most disadvantaged and stigmatized members of my own society, I have documented lives very different from my own.

How might this social position influence my work? I have already noted that in the United States, blacks and whites often speak differently when they are among people of their own race than when they are in the presence of members of another race. As a white person, it would be naïve for me to believe that the things blacks will say to me are the same as they would say to a black researcher. For this reason, I have relied upon the method of participant observation, rather than interviewing, to obtain the bulk of my data. Vendors would have urinated against the sides of buildings, for example, whether I was black or white, and whether I was there or not. I asked many questions, but rarely ones that assumed an honest dialogue about race. Sometimes, of course, as when Jerome told me about his experience buying black books, such discussions flowed from the context.

A second way that my social position can influence my work comes from the heightened sense on the part of the people I write about that I am "exploiting" them by appropriating their words and images for my own purposes and personal gain. I believe that this occurs intensely in some relations between white researchers and poor blacks because of the long history of whites' exploitation of blacks. I am always sensitive to this issue as I deal with the people I hope to write about, and I try to encourage discussion about it with them, which is sometimes a losing battle, given that it is difficult for us to always have honest dialogues, and some people simply don't want to offend me. Once the book was completed, I expressed my intention to the people in it that I would share my royalties with them. But even this cannot always eliminate the sense of exploitation, which grows out of the way a researcher's actions are interpreted in the context of a complex history.

A third way that my social position (or in this case the standpoint that emerges from my social position) can influence my work comes from the blindness I might have to the circumstances of people who are very different from me. During my first summer working as a magazine vendor with Marvin and Ron, for example, I routinely entered restaurants on the block to urinate and defecate. I would sometimes see vendors doing their bodily functions in public places, but I never thought twice about why they did so. I think the reason the issue didn't register on my radar is that my privileges made it a non-issue for me personally. Had the researcher been a poor black, he or she might have been excluded from local bathrooms enough times to say, "This is a process that needs to be understood."

Ultimately, I came to understand that such stigmatization and exclusion needed to be addressed. When I listened to tapes made on Sixth Avenue, I heard references to men's problems gaining access to rest rooms. I listened to these tapes while reviewing notes of interviews with local residents who complained about the tendency of some vendors to urinate in public. As a white male who took his bathroom privileges for granted, I might have looked at the people working the street as persons not unlike friends of mine who are white and rich and who urinate on the golf course because they don't want to bother going back to the clubhouse. But because I listened carefully to my tapes, I noted that the situation was more complex, and this led me to research it in some depth.

Though I constantly obsess about the ways that my upper-middle-class whiteness influences what I see, I must emphasize my uncertainty about what I do not see and what I do not know I missed.

I have endeavored to trade on the disadvantage of being from a different social position from the people I write about by maximizing the advantages that come from being in that position. I try to use myself as a kind of control group, comparing the way I am treated in particular situations with the way people on the street are treated. When the police treated an educated white male professor differently from an unhoused vendor on Christmas Day, I was in a better position to speculate on the underlying dynamics. And when I realized how effortlessly I walked into public bathrooms, I could make a useful comparison in discussing that topic. In none of these cases are the inferences made from the comparisons clear-cut, but they are comparisons that I am able to make *because* of my privileged position.

In addition to benefiting from some of the advantages of my upper-middle-class whiteness, I try to overcome my disadvantages by consulting with black scholars and intellectuals, some of whom grew up in poor families themselves. Sometimes their suggestions led me back to the field with new ideas and questions I had not thought to ask. In trying to understand why black women don't get entangled to the same extent as white women by street harassment in encounters with poor black men, for example, I was helped by the suggestion of a black sociologist, Franklin D. Wilson. He thinks that because the black women share a racial history with the men on the street, they do not feel responsible or guilty for the men's plight and so are less willing to excuse the men's behavior toward them. Surely a white scholar could have had that insight, but none of those who read my chapter did. I suspect it comes out of Wilson's particular life experience, from situations and people he has known.

Another thing that has helped me has been my collaboration with the African-American photographer Ovie Carter, whose professional and life experiences enable him to give me good advice. Ovie is fifty-two years old, was born in Mississippi, and grew up in Chicago and St. Louis, before serving in the Air Force. He joined the *Chicago Tribune* at the age of twenty-three. He has worked in Africa as a photojournalist but has spent most of his career covering poor neighborhoods in Chicago. Shortly before our work began on this book, his brother moved in with him from the streets as he made his way off crack. Consequently, Ovie has a deep appreciation for the anguish and problems associated with addiction. Ovie read and commented on all the chapters in *Sidewalk* as I wrote them, and the long hours we have spent together have helped me to understand aspects of life on Sixth Avenue that I would otherwise have been blind to.

All these circumstances have worked for me at times, but there is no simple way to overcome ingrained racial bias, inexperience, or others' suspicions. Perhaps the best starting point is to be aware that a different social position can have a serious effect on one's work, and these differences must be taken seriously.

INTERVENTIONS

One of the most difficult issues faced by social scientists and journalists who do sociological fieldwork is the question of when it is appropriate to intervene in the lives of the people they write about. This is especially true when such persons are living in states of deprivation. Some journalists have given assistance to the people they have written about, and they have found a way to do so that is consistent with their goals as researchers (Kotlowitz 1991; Finnegan 1998). Positivistic social scientists, who remain obsessed with securing unobtrusive measures of social phenomena which are not of their own creation, tend to be more uneasy about such involvements.

In my early weeks working as a magazine vendor, I found it very hard to say no to requests for money, usually small change, which came from a certain group of panhandlers and table watchers. In the methodological appendix to *Tally's Corner*, Elliot Liebow (who, like me, was thirty-seven years old when he completed his book) recalls being confronted with a similar problem. Liebow says that some people "exploited" him, not as an outsider but rather as one who, as a rule, had more resources than they did. When one of them came up with the resources—money or a car, for example—he, too, was "exploited" in the same way. Liebow "usually tried to limit money or other favors to what . . . each would have gotten from another friend had he the same resources" as the researcher (Liebow 1967:253).

I tried to maintain a similar stance. But as time went on, panhandlers and a few magazine vendors asked me, more and more often. Nobody expected me to give any more money than they might get from another vendor who had a good day, but a number of panhandlers came to expect me to give something on a regular basis.

Hakim and Marvin said these men asked me for money on a regular basis because they thought that as a college professor, and a Jew, I was "rich" enough to afford the donations. The questions for me were: Could I show my deep appreciation for their struggles and gain their appreciation for my purposes as a sociologist without paying for some simulacrum of it? How could I communicate my purposes as a researcher without dollar bills and small change in my hand? Did the constant requests for money suggest that I had not shown or earned proper "respect" and was being paid back accordingly?

In the end, out of practical necessity, I needed to find a way to tell certain persons that I could hardly afford the tapes I was using to record the street life, and that as a professor I could afford to be in New York City only due to the goodwill of friends who were allowing me to sleep in their spare bedrooms or on their couches. Yet I could never bring myself to say even this. I knew that my salary (while not very high) was quite high compared to the going rate on the sidewalk. Furthermore, the spare bedroom I was sleeping in (on the Upper East Side) was more hospitable than the places many of them would stay in that night. But with time I did learn to say no, and to communicate the anguish I felt in giving such an answer.

The question of how to avoid intervening when one cannot or should not do so is different from the question of whether and how to help when one can and should. At times, I was asked to do things as simple as telling what I knew about the law, serving as a reference for a person on the sidewalk as he or she dealt with a landlord or potential landlord, helping someone with rent when he was about to be evicted, and on one occasion finding and paying for a lawyer. In these situations, I did everything I could to be helpful, but I never gave advice, opinions, or help beyond what was asked for.

At other times, the question was whether and how to make larger efforts to intervene. One such situation occurred at the close of the summer of 1997. After I had worked as a magazine vendor during two summers, I began having discussions about my research with Nolan Zail, an architect from Australia on the frontiers of designing innovative housing alternatives for unhoused persons in New York City. One of the issues we discussed concerned the difficulty some unhoused men like Ishmael had in moving their magazines and personal belongings around, as well as the complaint made by Business Improvement Districts and police officers that the presence of these vendors was unsightly and frustrating because their merchandise and belongings were strewn on the pavement under their tables. I asked Zail whether he could design a vending cart which might address some of these concerns.

Here was an opportunity for us to use what we knew to make a small but practical contribution to improving conditions on Sixth Avenue. Surely this was not the same as helping to transform the larger structural conditions which brought about these problems, but it might make a difference in Ishmael's day-to-day life. First, though, it was necessary to find out if Ishmael wanted such a cart, and how he would feel about such an effort on his behalf. I could not ignore the fact that both Zail and I are white, and that Ishmael had described being treated in patronizing ways by many whites throughout his life.

Zail suggested that we meet with Ishmael to try to establish what kind of functional characteristics he was looking for in a vending cart. There on the sidewalk, Zail spent time with Ishmael trying to understand how his table functions within his business and life routine as an unhoused vendor.

Ishmael described his need for sufficient storage space to hold his merchandise and personal belongings safely. He also said that it would be useful if the design made provision for a separate lightweight carriage which he would use for his hunts and which could be attached to the vending cart.

After two weeks, Zail had designed a cart and presented drawings to Ishmael to get his input and reaction. Then he modified the designs to incorporate Ishmael's suggestions. In one meeting, Ishmael expressed his wish to pay back, in installments, the costs of manufacturing the cart. The cost had not yet come up (I knew it would, in due time), and we agreed that this would be a good way to do it. In the meantime, I received permission from Ishmael to try to raise the money to pay for the manufacture of the cart through donations.

When Ishmael felt satisfied with the cart's design, Zail and I scheduled an appointment with one of the large manufacturers of steel-and-aluminum food carts. He was already manufacturing a food cart which was pretty similar to the one we would ask him to make for us. His reaction to our ideas, and the difficulty we had in getting the cart built, became another kind of data for me, showing the nature of prejudice against the destitute and unhoused. It was yet another occasion when I was able to trade on the advantage of being white. Had I been black, I would likely never have heard the following:

"Okay, let's see what you got," he said as we began the meeting, which he gave me permission to record.

"This is what we have in mind," I said as Zail placed the architectural drawings in front of him.

"Did you show this to the head of Business Improvement District A?" (The head of BID A was a powerful man in New York real estate who, the manufacturer asserted, was an enemy of sidewalk vending.)

"No," I replied.

"Well, then, forget about it," he said.

"He doesn't have any say about what goes on in Greenwich Village," I said.

"Mitch, please! They own everything that's happening. The real-estate board controls New York City. They are the real-estate board. You're gonna show them this? Are you kidding? They want to get rid of these people!"

"Part of their argument for getting rid of these guys is that it looks so bad," I responded.

"It's not a question that we can't make something," he said. "It's the opposition. If we go out there with one of these carts, they would crucify us. They would nail me to the cross."

"Nail you?"

"Look! You know what started all this? Really simple. They want to get all the niggers off the street. They told me: 'We want them off. They're bad for business!' You want to put them on, Mitch! Why you making so much trouble, Mitch? You're spitting in their face with this!"

"What we are saying," Zail interjected, "is that this is what you can do to improve the image . . . It's actually not too dissimilar from the cart you have there."

"So how does this help?"

"Well, for several reasons," Zail continued, "One, it allows storage. Two is display. It can be displayed in a professional manner, rather than strewn all over."

"All we're asking is for you to make one of these for us on an experimental basis," I said. If it worked for Ishmael, we would likely order more.

"I'll make anything you want," the manufacturer replied. "If that's what you're telling me to do. But there is nothing that will change their appearance!"

"It will increase the aesthetic of this type of vending," I said.

"What about him, the homeless person?" he asked.

We seemed destined to go around in circles.

A few weeks later, Zail called to confirm a subsequent meeting with the manufacturer, but he said he had changed his mind. He wouldn't have any part of our project. He didn't want to do anything to make the "homeless" vendors look more like the food vendors, who constituted the real market for his carts. He said he was also concerned that he might antagonize the real-estate interests of the city, who he said were already trying to eliminate food vendors on sidewalks. (In fact, one year later, Mayor Giuliani tried to eliminate food vendors from hundreds of locations in lower Manhattan and midtown, but changed his mind in response to a public outpouring of support for the food vendors.)

When we told Ishmael of our trouble in getting the cart made, he was not surprised. After all, he had been dealing with such responses ever since he began working as a magazine vendor, seven years earlier.

In the end, despite my having given small change on some occasions and despite efforts to do more than that on others, the quality of my regard must be in the research work itself. To this day, I cannot say how much "acceptance," or "rapport," or "respect" I have on the sidewalk, or how much respect I have shown these men in our personal relations. But I would like to think that whatever respect I ultimately get will be based not on what I did or didn't give in the way of resources but on whether the people working and/or living on Sixth Avenue think the work I did has integrity, by whatever yardstick they use to take that measure.

NOTES

[1] Paul Laurence Dunbar, "We Wear the Mask," in *Lyrics of Lowly Life* (Secaucus, NJ: Citadel Press, 1997), p. 167. I thank Aldon Morris for bringing Dunbar's poem to my attention.

[2] For an analysis of contemporary photojournalism that has influenced my thinking on these issues, see Dianne Hagaman (1996).

[3] For a programmatic discussion of how important it is to explore the "relations of ruling," see Dorothy Smith (1988).

8

How the Problem of "Crafting Selves" Emerged

Dorinne K. Kondo

When I first made my acquaintance with the Tokyo neighborhood where I would live and carry out fieldwork for much of the next three years, the air was still warm and humid, awaiting the cleansing winds and rain of the September typhoons. I had come to study the relationship of kinship and economics in family-owned enterprises. Thinking about "kinship" and "economics" in abstract, organizational, structural-functionalist terms, but drawn by the emphasis on cultural meanings in the writings of interpretivists like Clifford Geertz, I began with questions concerning the ways people thought about and enacted the meanings of "company" and "family" in their everyday lives. By the following autumn—the time of *zansho*, the lingering summer heat—I was a resident and worker in the community I have described, and the focus of my study had shifted to accommodate my year's experiences and observations. For although it was true that company and family, economics and kinship, were vibrantly meaningful arenas of everyday life for the people I knew, the idiom in which they were cast was always, ineluctably, centered on persons and personal relationships in the factory, in the family, in the neighborhood, in language, in the use of space, in attitudes toward nature and toward material objects; the most insistent refrain, repeated over and over again and transposed into countless different keys of experience, was the fundamental connectedness of human beings to each other. It was a conception that exploded my Western ideas about the relationship between self and social world, and it was an inescapable motif in the everyday lives of people I knew. Abstract organizational charts of company hierarchies; kinship diagrams; neat divisions of social life into domains of kinship, economics, politics, and religion; and the use of abstract individuals like "the Japanese woman" or "the Japanese man," seemed less and less compelling, less and less able to capture the complexity of what I saw around me. By the time I left Japan, during *taikan*, the coldest days of the winter season, it had been twenty-six months since I first arrived, and the problematic of kinship and economics had come to pivot around precisely what I perceived to be even more basic cultural assumptions: how *selfhood* is constructed in the arenas of company and family. My work of that historical moment concentrated on delineating "the Japanese concept of self" and on trying to experiment with narrative voice, to begin to evoke some of the vividness of life as I had seen it in the factory.

Now, some years later—the luxury of reflection and memory shaping and reshaping my re-encounter with the people who shared their lives with me—the presupposition that informed my problematic at that moment is clear. I assumed my goal as anthropologist to be a description of a "concept of self "characteristic of all members of any particular culture." Collective identities like "the Japanese" or "Japanese concepts of self" no longer seem to me to be fixed essences, but rather strategic assertions, which inevitably suppress differences, tensions, and contradictions within. Given these moves toward practice, nonessentialism, and radical cultural and historical specificity, I develop in *Crafting Selves* (1990) the themes of personhood, work, and family by asking a slightly different question: How did the people I knew craft themselves and their lives within shifting fields of power and meaning, and how did they do so in particular situations and within a particular historical and cultural context? . . .

In attempting to enlarge the boundaries of what counts as theoretical, I attempt to build on feminist scholarship that expands our definitions of what counts as political. Power can create identities on the individual level, as it provides disciplines, punishments, and culturally available pathways for fulfillment; nowhere were these forces more evident to me than in my relationships with the Japanese people I knew. At stake in my narrative of emerging order are the constantly contested and shifting boundaries of my identity and the identities of my Japanese relatives, friends, and acquaintances. We participated in each others' lives and sought to make sense of one another. In that attempt to understand, power inevitably came into play as we tried to force each other into appropriately comprehensible categories. This nexus of power and meaning was also creative, the crucible within which we forged our relationship. In turn, our negotiated understandings of one another enabled me to shape the particular problematic that now animates my research. The sites of these struggles for understanding were located in what we might call salient features of "identity" both in America and in Japan: race, gender, and age.

ON BEING A CONCEPTUAL ANOMALY

As a Japanese American,[1] I created a conceptual dilemma for the Japanese I encountered. For them, I was a living oxymoron, someone who was both Japanese and not Japanese. Their puzzlement was all the greater since most Japanese people I knew seemed to adhere to an eminently biological definition of Japaneseness. Race, language, and culture are intertwined, so much so that any challenge to this firmly entrenched conceptual schema—a white person who speaks flawlessly idiomatic and unaccented Japanese, or a person of Japanese ancestry who cannot—meets with what generously could be described as unpleasant reactions. White people are treated as repulsive and unnatural—*ben na gaijin*, strange foreigners—the better their Japanese becomes, while Japanese Americans and others of Japanese ancestry born overseas are faced with exasperation and disbelief. How can someone who is racially Japanese lack "cultural competence"?[2] During my first few months in Tokyo, many tried to resolve this paradox by asking which of my parents was "really" American.

Indeed, it is a minor miracle that those first months did not lead to an acute case of agoraphobia, for I knew that once I set foot outside the door, someone somewhere (a taxi driver? a salesperson? a bank clerk?) would greet one of my linguistic mistakes with an astonished "Eh?" I became all too familiar with the series of expressions that would flicker over those faces: bewilderment, incredulity, embarrassment, even anger, at having to deal with this odd person who looked Japanese and therefore human, but who must be retarded, deranged, or—equally undesirable in Japanese eyes—Chinese or Korean. Defensively, I would mull over the mistake-of-the-day. I mean, how was I to know that in order to "fillet a fish" you had to cut it "in three pieces"? Or that opening a bank account required so much specialized terminology? Courses in literary Japanese at Harvard hadn't done much to prepare me for the realities of everyday life in Tokyo. Gritting my teeth in determination as I groaned inwardly, I would force myself out of the house each morning.

For me, and apparently for the people around me, this was a stressful time, when expectations were flouted, when we had to strain to make sense of one another. There seemed to be few advantages in my retaining an American persona, for the distress caused by these reactions was difficult to bear. In the face of dissonance and distress, I found that the desire for comprehensible order in the form of "fitting in," even if it meant suppression of and violence against a self I had known in another context, was preferable to meaninglessness. Anthropological imperatives to immerse oneself in another culture intensified this desire, so that acquiring the accoutrements of Japanese selfhood meant simultaneously constructing a more thoroughly professional anthropological persona. This required language learning in the broadest sense: mastery of culturally appropriate modes of moving, acting, and speaking. For my informants, it was clear that coping with this anomalous creature was difficult, for here was someone who looked like a real human being, but who simply failed to perform according to expectation. They, too, had every reason to make me over in their image, to guide me, gently but insistently, into properly Japanese behavior, so that the discrepancy between my appearance and my cultural competence would not be so painfully evident. I posed a challenge to their senses of identity. How could someone who *looked* Japanese not *be* Japanese? In my cultural ineptitude, I represented for the people who met me the chaos of meaninglessness. Their response in the face of this dissonance was to *make* me as Japanese as possible. Thus, my first nine months of fieldwork were characterized by an attempt to reduce the distance between expectation and inadequate reality, as my informants and I conspired to rewrite my identity as Japanese.

My guarantor, an older woman who, among her many activities, was a teacher of flower arranging, introduced me to many families who owned businesses in the ward of Tokyo where I had chosen to do my research. One of her former students and fellow flower arranging teachers, Mrs. Sakamoto, agreed to take me in as a guest over the summer, since the apartment where I was scheduled to move—owned by one of my classmates in tea ceremony—was still under construction. My proclivities for "acting Japanese" were by this time firmly established. During my stay with the Sakamotos, I did my best to conform to what I thought their expectations of a guest/daughter might be. This in turn seemed to please them and reinforced my tendency to behave in terms of what I perceived to be my Japanese persona.

My initial encounter with the head of the household epitomizes this mirroring and reinforcement of behavior. Mr. Sakamoto had been on a business trip on the day I moved in, and he returned the following evening, just as his wife, daughter, and I sat down to the evening meal. As soon as he stepped in the door, I immediately switched from an informal posture, seated on the *zabuton* (seat cushion) to a formal greeting posture, *seiza*-style (kneeling on the floor) and bowed low, hands on the floor. Mr. Sakamoto responded in kind (being older, male, and head of the household, he did not have to bow as deeply as I did), and we exchanged the requisite polite formulae, I requesting his benevolence, and he welcoming me to their family. Later, he told me how happy and impressed he had been with this act of proper etiquette on my part. "Today's young people in Japan," he said, "no longer show such respect. Your grandfather must have been a fine man to raise such a fine granddaughter." Of course, his statements can hardly be accepted at face value. They may well indicate his relief that I seemed to know something of proper Japanese behavior, and hence would not be a complete nuisance to them; it was also his way of making me feel at home. What is important to note is the way this statement was used to elicit proper Japanese behavior in future encounters. And his strategy worked. I was left with a warm, positive feeling toward the Sakamoto family, armed with an incentive to behave in a Japanese way, for clearly these were the expectations and the desires of the people who had taken me in and who were so generously sharing their lives with me.

Other members of the household voiced similar sentiments. Takemisan, the Sakamotos' married daughter who lived in a distant prefecture, had been visiting her parents when I first moved in. A few minutes after our initial encounter, she observed, "You seem like a typical Japanese woman" *(Nihon no josei, to iu kanji)*. Later in the summer, Mrs. Sakamoto confided to me that she could never allow a "pure American" *(junsui na Amerikajin)* to live with them, for only someone of Japanese descent was genetically capable of adjusting to life on *tatami* mats, using unsewered toilets, sleeping on the floor—in short, of living Japanese style. Again, the message was unambiguous: my "family" could feel comfortable with me insofar as I was—and acted—Japanese.

At first, then, as a Japanese American I made sense to those around me as a none-too-felicitous combination of racial categories. As fieldwork progressed, however, and my linguistic and cultural skills improved, my informants seemed best able to understand me by placing me in meaningful cultural roles: daughter, guest, young woman, student, prodigal Japanese who had finally seen the light and come home. Most people preferred to treat me as a Japanese—sometimes an incomplete or unconventional Japanese, but a Japanese nonetheless. Indeed, even when I tried to represent myself as an American, others did not always take heed. For instance, on my first day on the job at the confectionery factory, Mr. Sato introduced me to the division chief as an "American student," here to learn about the business and about the "real situation" (*jittai*) of workers in small enterprise. Soon it became clear that the chief remembered "student," but not "American." A week or so later, we gathered for one of our noon meetings to read from a pamphlet published by an ethics school. The owner came, and he commented on the theme of the day, *ketsui* (determination). At one point during his speech, he singled me out, praising my resolve, "If Kondō-san had been an ordinary young woman, she might never have known Japan." I stared at my shoes, my cheeks flaming. When the exercise finished, I hurried back to my work station. Akiyama-san, the division head, approached me with a puzzled expression on his face. "*Doko desu ka?*" he asked. (Where is it?—in other words, where are you from?) And after my reply, he announced loudly to all: "She says it's America!"

My physical characteristics led my friends and co-workers to emphasize my identity as Japanese, sometimes even against my own intentions and desires. Over time, my increasingly "Japanese" behavior served temporarily to resolve their crises of meaning and to confirm their assumptions about their own identities. That I, too, came to participate enthusiastically in this recasting of the self is a testimonial to their success in acting upon me.

CONFLICT AND FRAGMENTATION OF SELF

Using these ready-made molds may have reduced the dissonance in my informants' minds, but it served only to increase the dissonance in my own. What occurred in the field was a kind of fragmenting of identity into what I then labeled Japanese and American pieces, so that the different elements, instead of fitting together to form at least the illusion of a seamless and coherent whole—it is my contention that selves which are coherent, seamless, bounded, and whole are indeed illusions—strained against one another. The war was not really—or only—between Japanese and American elements, however. Perhaps it had even more to do with the position of researcher versus one of daughter and guest. In one position, my goal had to be the pursuit of knowledge, where decisive action, independence, and mastery were held in high esteem. In another, independence and mastery of one's own fate were out of the question; rather, being a daughter meant duties, responsibilities, and *inter*dependence.

The more I adjusted to my Japanese daughter's role, the keener the conflicts became. Most of those conflicts had to do with expectations surrounding gender, and, more specifically, my position as a young woman. Certainly, in exchange for the care the Sakamotos showed me, I was happy to help out in whatever way I could. I tried to do some housecleaning and laundry, and I took over the shopping and cooking for Mr. Sakamoto when Mrs. Sakamoto was at one of the children's association meetings, her flower arranging classes, or meetings of ward committees on juvenile delinquency. The cooking did not offend me in and of itself; in fact, I was glad for the opportunity to learn how to make simple Japanese cuisine, and Mr. Sakamoto put up with my sometimes appalling culinary mistakes and limited menus with great aplomb. I remember one particularly awful night when I couldn't find the makings for soup broth, and Mr. Sakamoto was fed "*miso* soup" that was little more than miso dissolved in hot water. He managed to down the tasteless broth with good grace and the trace of a smile on his lips. (Of course, it is also true that although he was himself capable of simple cooking, he would not set foot in the kitchen if there were a woman in the house.) Months after I moved out, whenever he saw me he would say with a sparkle in his eye and a hint of nostalgic wistfulness in his voice, "I miss Dōrin-san's salad and sautéed beef," one of the "Western" menus I used to serve up with numbing regularity. No, the cooking was not the problem.

The problem was, in fact, the etiquette surrounding the serving of food that produced the most profound conflicts for me as an American woman. The head of the household is usually served first and receives the finest delicacies; men—even the sweetest, nicest ones—ask for a second helping of rice by merely holding out their rice bowls to the woman nearest the rice cooker, and maybe, just maybe, uttering a grunt of thanks in return for her pains. I could never get used to this practice, try as I might. Still, I tried to carry out my duties uncomplainingly, in what I hope was reasonably good humor. But I was none too happy about these things "inside." Other restrictions began to chafe, especially restrictions on my movement. I had to be in at a certain hour, despite my "adult" age. Yet I understood the family's responsibility for me as their guest and quasi-daughter, so I tried to abide by their regulations, hiding my irritation as best I could.

This fundamental ambivalence was heightened by isolation and dependency. Though my status was in some respects high in an education-conscious Japan, I was still young, female, and a student. I was in a socially recognized relationship of dependency vis-à-vis the people I knew. I was not to be feared and obeyed, but protected and helped. In terms of my research, this was an extremely advantageous position to be in, for people did not feel the need to reflect my views back to me, as they might with a more powerful person. I did not try to define situations; rather, I could allow other people to define those situations in their culturally appropriate ways, remaining open to their concerns and their ways of acting in the world. But, in another sense, this dependency and isolation increased my susceptibility to identifying with my Japanese role. By this time I saw little of American friends in Tokyo, for it was difficult to be with people who had so little inkling of how ordinary Japanese people lived. My informants and I consequently had every reason to conspire to recreate my identity as Japanese. Precisely because of my dependency and my made-to-order role, I was allowed—or rather, *forced*—to abandon the position of observer. Errors, linguistic or cultural, were dealt with impatiently or with a startled look that seemed to say, "Oh yes, you are American after all." On the other hand, appropriately Japanese behaviors were rewarded with warm, positive reactions or with comments such as "You're more Japanese than the Japanese." Even more frequently, correct behavior was simply accepted as a matter of course. *Naturally* I would understand, *naturally* I would behave correctly, for they presumed me to be, *au fond*, Japanese.

Identity can imply unity or fusion, but for me what occurred was a fragmentation of the self. This fragmentation was encouraged by my own participation in Japanese life and by the actions of my friends and acquaintances. At its most extreme point, I became "the Other" in my own mind, where the identity I had known in another context simply collapsed. The success of our conspiracy to recreate me as Japanese reached its climax one August afternoon.

It was typical summer weather for Tokyo, "like a steam bath" as the saying goes, so hot the leaves were drooping limply from the trees surrounding the Sakamotos' house. Mrs. Sakamoto and her married daughter, Takemi, were at the doctor's with Takemi's son, so Mr. Sakamoto and I were busy tending young Kaori-chan, Takemi-san's young daughter. Mr. Sakamoto quickly tired of his grandfatherly role, leaving me to entertain Kaori-chan. Promptly at four P.M., the hour when most Japanese housewives do their shopping for the evening meal, I lifted the baby into her stroller and pushed her along ahead of me as I inspected the fish, selected the freshest looking vegetables, and mentally planned the meal for the evening. As I glanced into the shiny metal surface of the butcher's display case, I noticed someone who looked terribly familiar: a typical young housewife, clad in slip-on sandals and the loose, cotton shift called "home wear" (*hōmu wea*), a woman walking with a characteristically Japanese bend to the knees and a sliding of the feet. Suddenly I clutched the handle of the stroller to steady myself as a wave of dizziness washed over me, for I realized I had caught a glimpse of nothing less than my own reflection. Fear that perhaps I would never emerge from this world into which I was immersed, inserted itself into my mind and stubbornly refused to leave, until I resolved to move into a new apartment, to distance myself from my Japanese home and my Japanese existence.

For ultimately, this collapse of identity was a distancing moment. It led me to emphasize the *differences* between cultures and among various aspects of identity: researcher, student, daughter, wife, Japanese, American, Japanese American. In order to reconstitute myself as an American researcher, I felt I had to extricate myself from the conspiracy to rewrite my identity as Japanese. Accordingly, despite the Sakamotos' invitations to stay with them for the coming year, I politely stated my intentions to fulfill the original terms of the agreement: to stay just until construction on my new apartment was complete. In order to resist the Sakamotos' attempts to recreate me as Japanese, I removed myself physically from their exclusively Japanese environment.

Thus, both the fragmentation of self and the collapse of identity were results of a complex collaboration between ethnographer and informants. It should be evident that at this particular point, my informants were hardly inert objects available for the free play of the ethnographer's desire. They themselves were, in the act of being, actively interpreting and trying to make meaning of the ethnographer. In so doing, the people I knew asserted their power to act upon the anthropologist. This was their means for preserving their own identities. Understanding, in this context, is multiple, open-ended, positioned—although that positioning can shift dramatically, as I have argued—and pervaded by relations of power. These power-imbued attempts to capture, recast, and rewrite each other were for us productive of understandings and were, existentially, alternately wrenching and fulfilling.

"EPIPHANY" AND A SHIFT IN THE PROBLEM

This moment of collapse was followed by a distancing process. I returned to the United States for a month, and upon returning to Japan, I moved into the apartment promised me, next door to Hatanaka-san, my landlady and friend from the tea ceremony class. This arrangement turned out to be ideal, for I could enjoy the best of both worlds: the warmth of belonging to a family and the (semi) privacy of my own space. I immersed myself in research, finding contacts through Hatanaka-san. In fact, I ended up working in businesses owned by two of her grade school classmates: a hairdressing salon owned by Yokoyama-sensei, and the Satō confectionery factory, the focus of *Crafting Selves*.

I have written "collapse of identity" and "distancing process." But the distancing was only relative, for the same pressures were there, both internal and external, the pressures to be unobtrusively Japanese. In most cases my informants still guided me into these roles and at times refused to let me escape them. In moving to a different neighborhood and away from the Sakamotos, I had simply exchanged the role of daughter for other culturally meaningful positions—those of guest, neighbor, worker, young woman—that demanded participation and involvement.

Indeed, the shift in the focus of my study lay precisely in this participation. As time wore on, it seemed to me that the relationship of kinship and economics in these family-owned firms—the problem I had initially set out to study—was always filtered through an emphasis on personal relationships. An awareness of this person-centered universe impressed itself upon me in myriad ways. Certainly anyone who lives in this Shitamachi (downtown) district cannot help but be aware of the constant presence of others. In my neighborhood, the houses were so densely packed that the walls almost touched. Though I lived in my own apartment, I shared a wall with Akemi-chan, Mrs. Hatanaka's daughter, and we would try to be solicitous of each other's daily routines: I was especially careful to refrain from typing when she was practicing the piano. Whenever I opened my back window to air my *futon* or to hang up my clothes to dry, I inevitably ended up conversing with the gracious, elderly woman next door, who was always out tending her garden. "Cold, isn't it?" "Beautiful morning." "They say it's going to rain again." "Today feels like another scorcher." As the seasons passed, we exchanged the conventional yet somehow comfortable and comforting greetings about the weather, before branching off into other topics of mutual interest. Less pleasant were my next-door neighbors' fights. They quarreled every morning, and without ever really getting to know the nine-year-old son, I formed a distinctly unfavorable opinion of the young man. He complained constantly about his paltry allowance, yelling at his mother one morning, "How could this be enough?" (*Tarinē ja nē ka yo!*). The mother was able to give as good as she got, upbraiding him with great relish. Quarrels sometimes became neighborhood affairs. One summer evening, when everyone left their windows open to admit the cool night air, the screams from a family fight two houses away drifted in with the breeze. Alarming in its intensity, with the drunken father threatening to hit someone with baseball bats and beer bottles, the fight kept all of us up and prompted neighborhood concern and intervention. The next morning, everyone within a five-house radius was bleary-eyed from lack of sleep.

Minute details of everyday life also attracted people's attention. I was able to smell the cooking from the two houses nearest me, and I am certain that others could take note of my daily menu. No visitor could pass unnoticed. I could easily have kept, had I chosen to do so, a highly accurate accounting of the comings and goings from the Hatanakas and at least two other houses near mine. And the Hatanakas never failed to comment on the appearance of each of my visitors. When a former (male) student of mine from Harvard came to visit one afternoon, Akemi-chan observed, "He sure was here a long time, wasn't he?" (*Zuibun ita n desu, ne*). When my phone rang, the Hatanakas took note. If I happened to be out, a head would emerge from their door just as I arrived home, to inform me that I had received a call. People were able to observe what time everyone else arose in the morning, by the presence or absence of the morning paper in the mail slot in the front door. What is more, they never hesitated to comment, "Oh, you were up early this morning," or "You must have been tired; you took it easy today, didn't you?" In an area where early rising is equated with moral virtue, the latter statement was calculated to provoke shame and embarrassment, and I always tried to arise much earlier on the following day. Hatanaka-san and her family noticed how often I did my wash and when I aired my futon; if it were a properly sunny day, there would invariably be a tap on my door, telling me that I could, if I wished, air my futon on their laundry pole or, even better, lay it flat on top of their tiny Suzuki automobile so that the futon would be especially fluffy.

It may seem that I am describing a society where everyone meddles in everyone else's business, where privacy is breached at every turn. This is, indeed, one of the stereotypes of this Shitamachi, or downtown area, that I often heard from people who lived in the Uptown, or Yamanote, section of Tokyo. Yet I should not neglect to convey the sensitivity and care that so often animated social life in my neighborhood. The Hatanakas, for instance, were especially solicitous. After a hard day at work, I could almost always count on a tap on the door, and the cheery Mrs. Hatanaka would be there, bearing some wonderful concoction— more often than not, a delicious, hot meal. And on special occasions, I knew I could expect my favorite dish, beautifully prepared: *buri no teriyaki*, rich, buttery yellowtail in a gleaming *teriyaki* sauce. If I were sick, they looked in on me. When

I began to go to an acupuncturist for my back and neck ailments, the Hatanakas plied me with all sorts of remedies, from Tiger Balm to medicinal plasters to a piece of bamboo I was supposed to place under my feet as I stood at my sink doing dishes. "It will relax you," they reassured me. The Hatanakas' concern sometimes manifested itself in amusing ways. One summer night, a huge cockroach appeared in my kitchen (the Japanese species has a nasty way of flying at its attackers), and my piercing screech of *"Gokiburi!"* (Cockroach!) brought Mrs. Hatanaka over the next morning with a *gokiburi hoi hoi* (come here, cockroaches!)—a roach motel complete with smiling cockroaches waving a hearty welcome from their cardboard windows.

All this was more than mere passive awareness arising from sheer, unavoidable physical proximity. Rather, life in Shitamachi was animated by active involvement and interest in the lives of others. I initially feared that, in the case of the Hatanakas, curiosity about my "foreign" ways and their responsibility for my welfare perhaps exhausted the explanations for their concern for every detail of my life. Certainly these were important factors. But some of my fears on this score were laid to rest when, after I left, I received a letter from Akemi-chan, my landlady's teenage daughter, whose bedroom had been on the other side of the wall from my own. She described in hilarious detail the living habits of the young man who had inherited my apartment: "He gets up at six, takes a bath in the morning,[3] and then sings off key while he dries his hair with an unbelievably noisy blow dryer. How is a person to sleep?"

As an American accustomed to privacy, I sometimes found even the kindnesses were difficult to accept. Even in my own apartment, I was not able to totally relax, for my menu, sleeping and bathing habits, and housekeeping all seemed open for public inspection. But perhaps nothing symbolized this frustration more eloquently than the way my Shitamachi neighbors and friends had of paying calls. In this area, doors are never locked if someone is at home; delivery persons, friends, and visitors will simply open the door, enter as far as the *genkan*,[4] and announce their presence with a *"Gomen kudasai"* (Excuse me). On more than one occasion, such unexpected visits awakened me from a much-needed nap on my day off from the factory. In the winter months, this was particularly painful, for like many Japanese, I would snuggle under the *kotatsu*[5] as I napped. Not only was it an excruciatingly rude awakening to have to emerge into the freezing room (Japanese houses by and large do not have central heating), but I was embarrassed by having been caught fast asleep in the afternoon, when I should have been working or otherwise making myself useful.

One incident epitomized these encounters with Japanese notions of privacy and caring concern. I had fallen ill with the flu, exhausted by my hectic schedule. I had made plans to call on an artisan and his family, but because of my sickness I canceled our appointment. During the middle of the day, I was fast asleep on my futon. My apartment was in total chaos. For two days I had been unable to summon the energy to wash the dishes or even to hang up my clothes, which were strewn about the tatami room in utter disarray. As I lay there, blissfully lost to the world, the door was suddenly flung open and two voices chorused, "Gomen kudasai!" I leaped out of my futon, on the verge of heart failure from the shock. There were the artisan and his wife, all smiles, bearing armfuls of mandarin oranges, sweets, and loaves of bread. They announced their intentions to take care of me and urged me to go straight back to bed. I was mortified, for not only had I been caught in bed, sickness notwithstanding, I had been caught with a disorderly apartment and disheveled hair and clothes. I was even more mortified when Mrs. Hayashi began to wash my dishes. I scurried out to the kitchen, assuring her that her efforts weren't necessary, and thanked them profusely for the food and for taking the trouble to call on me. After a short time they left, leaving me with lists of suggestions on how to care for my flu. I was ready to cry from embarrassment, frustration, and exhaustion. I felt shamed at having been discovered in this *uchi* or informal, inside state, and constrained by the bonds of their caring and concern. I felt guilty, too, for I knew their concern to be genuine, yet I could not rid myself of the feeling of having been invaded by these expressions of kindness.

The demands and obligations of Japanese social life came to assume increasing importance in my life. The time I was living in my own apartment, I was an active member of many different social networks: relatives, acquaintances from work, classmates from tea ceremony lessons, and fellow participants in community activities. The hospitality and graciousness that were my initial due as guest were tempered with growing demands on my time. As I grew to be more of a participant in these relationships, rather than a mere observer, it came my turn to reciprocate. I was bombarded with requests to teach English, a story familiar to any Americans who have been in Japan. People asked me to take part in many social gatherings, commensurate with my positioning within social networks: a relative's funeral, another relative's memorial service, the coming of age of my neighbor's daughter, the elementary school graduation ceremony of Fusae-chan, Mrs. Hatanaka's younger daughter. Though at the beginning stages of my field research I welcomed all such invitations, the requests and solicitous care shown for me occasionally elicited feelings of invasion. I felt bound by chains of obligation to my sponsors, my relatives, my friends, and my co-workers, and though I appreciated their concern for me and realized my responsibility to return the kindnesses they had shown me, I simply did not have enough hours in the day to accommodate all of them.

The situation came to a climax one day when I received a phone call from a local teacher who had arranged a number of interviews for me. He began with "*Jitsu wa...*" (actually...) a phrase that almost always precedes the asking of a favor. My antennae went up, sensing danger. Well, said he, there was a student of his who would love to learn English conversation, and well, he would like to bring her over to meet me the following evening. Since he had been of so much help to me, I knew I could not refuse and still be considered a decent human being, so I agreed. But I was in a foul mood the entire evening. I complained bitterly to my landlady, who sympathetically agreed that the *sensei* should have been more mindful of the fact that I was so pressed, but she confirmed that I had no choice but to comply. She explained that the sensei had been happy to give of his time to help me, and by the same token he considered it natural to make requests of others, who should be equally giving of themselves, their "inner" feelings not-withstanding. "*Nihonjin wa ne*," she mused, "*jibun o taisetsu ni shinai no, ne.*" (The Japa-nese don't treat themselves as important, do they? That is, they spend time doing things for the sake of maintaining good relationships, regardless of their "inner" feelings.) I gazed at her in amazement, for her statement struck me with incredi-ble force. Not only did it perfectly capture my own feelings of being bound by social obligation, living my life for others, it also indicated to me a profoundly different way of thinking about the relationship between selves and the social world. Persons seemed to be constituted in and through social relations and obligations to others. Selves and society did not seem to be separate entities; rather, the boundaries were blurred. This realization, coming as it did through intense participation in social life, led me to shift my research problem from kin-ship and economics to what seemed to be an even more fundamental assump-tion: how personhood was defined in a Japanese context, and how, more specifically, people at the Satō factory crafted themselves in the practices of everyday life.

Participation in the field was thus a necessary step in the process of under-standing, and in fact it was instrumental in shifting the focus of my research. But in the cases I describe, it also produced a threat to the self—one of fusion or dis-solution in my collapse of identity, and one of invasion in the second epiphanal moment. My ambiguous insider/outsider position in the field may have made the issue of identity and threat to coherent selfhood especially acute, but other stud-ies by white female ethnographers and by Japanese American men suggest that my experience was not a unique one (cf. Bachnik 1978; Bernstein 1983; Hamabata 1983, 1990; Okimoto 1971). The ways my informants preferred to treat me, my increasing sense of ease in "belonging" to Japanese society, the recognition of cul-tural skills I had retained as a Japanese American—all led to the weighting of what my Japanese informants and I labeled my "Japanese" self. I collaborated in this attempted recreation with various degrees of enthusiasm and resistance.

In fact, my decision about when to leave Japan was linked to this re-writing of identity. The final months of fieldwork are generally the best and most pro-ductive: the months of laying groundwork pay off in the increasing intimacy and comfort in your relationships and in the depth of the insights you are able to reach. This fact made me ever more reluctant to say that my research was "fin-ished." I kept extending my stay at the factory; it became something of a joke, as the older women would tease me about my parents, whose "neck must be sooooo long," the expression one uses to describe someone who is waiting impatiently. "You must have found a boyfriend," they would tell me, or, laughing, they might suggest, "Why not find a nice Japanese boy and settle down here?" I laughed with them, but I continued to stay on as research became more and more pro-ductive, until one event convinced me that the time to depart was near. At a tea ceremony class, I performed a basic "thin tea" ceremony flawlessly, without need for prompting or correction of my movements. My teacher said in tones of approval, "You know, when you first started, I was so worried. The way you moved, the way you walked, was so clumsy! But now, you're just like an *ojōsan*, a

nice young lady." Part of me was inordinately pleased that my awkward, exaggerated Western movements had *finally* been replaced by the disciplined grace
that makes the tea ceremony so seemingly natural and beautiful to watch. But
another voice cried out in considerable alarm, "Let me escape before I'm completely transformed!" And not too many weeks later, leave I did.

My experiences of identification, fragmentation, and self-transformation eloquently demonstrated for me the simultaneously creative and distressing effects
of the interplay of meaning and power as my friends, coworkers, and I rewrote
our identities. Yet I would argue that enthusiastic participation in my friends'
lives was essential before I could step back to discern the meaningful order in
everyday life and thereby understand its significance. Engagement and openness
could throw into relief wrenching contradictions, but it was also productive of
meaning, of identity, of change. Through participation, one had to open oneself to
others and remain willing to change one's perceptions through this intimate contact. Only then could difference be truly realized. And only then could the issue
of identity and of crafting selves emerge as my central theoretical problem.

Consequently, experience, and the *specificity* of my experience—a particular
human being who encounters particular others at a particular historical moment
and has particular stakes in that interaction—is not opposed to theory; it *enacts*
and *embodies* theory. That is to say, the so-called personal details of the encounters, and of the concrete processes through which research problems emerged, are
constitutive of theory; one cannot be separated from the other. Deconstructing
the binary between personal/private/experiential/interior on the one hand, and
political/institutional/theoretical/exterior-to-the-self, on the other, is a key motif
in the critique of individualism and the self/society, subject/world distinction.

My "personal" account of the emergence of the problematic of selfhood is thus
the product of a complex negotiation, taking place within specific, but shifting, contexts, where power and meaning, "personal" and "political," are inseparable. Identity
is not a fixed "thing," it is negotiated, open, shifting, ambiguous, the result of culturally available meanings and the open-ended, power-laden enactments of those meanings in everyday situations. The crafting of this text; the crafting of my identity; and
the crafting of the identities of my Japanese friends, relatives, coworkers and acquaintances as represented in *Crafting Selves*, are the complicated outcomes of power-
fraught negotiations between "Self" and "Other"—the Western cultural baggage of
the terms themselves being highly problematic. In the anthropological hermeneutic
circle, participation eventually gives way to "observation" and reconstruction, as we
anthropologists create our ethnographic texts. Writing freezes the complex dance of
domination and counter-domination, of approaching and drawing back, which I
have attempted to evoke in these pages. The process of making sense of each other
involves active efforts to force others into preconceived categories. Just as my informants, in writing me and my identity, tried to excise traces of Americanness, I also in
the act of writing inevitably fix ambiguity, and attempt to stitch together pieces of
my "self," in order to construct an account of the lives of my co-workers and friends
and the ways I came to "understand" those lives. And in the act of writing, culturally
shaped abstractions like "theory," "power," "experience," and "identity" also emerge.

Consequently, the first-person voice is a rhetorical/theoretical strategy (again, the split between these terms is an artifact of our linguistic and cultural conventions). At stake in the choice of this strategy is the distinction between personal and political. Mine is an attempt to challenge and displace that distinction through a tactic that meshes so-called experiential and theoretical concerns. The narrative "I" is meant to problematize the very terms "first person," "personal," "private," and in its least complimentary form, "narcissistic," that might conventionally be used to characterize my writing strategy. That my book came to pivot around notions of identity is, I have argued, the result of a complex, open-ended series of interactions between a specific ethnographer, with a particular face, age, gender, "personality," and disciplinary training, and a particular agenda in mind, and specific Japanese people with their own particular faces, ages, genders, "personalities," and agendas. And these are not "merely personal," "deeply private" aspects of identity, something secret and unknowable that can never be shared, but multiple, crosscutting forces. Race, gender, age, academic training, and so on, are some of them, but others, equally important, include the historical and political agendas underlying anthropological research, the place of "East Asian Studies" in the United States and at particular institutions,[6] and the strategic, highly fraught geopolitical relationships between America and Japan, especially in the light of World War II and the recent "trade wars." These constitute the matrices of power within which, for both better and worse, my inquiry and all research done by Americans in Japan, or conversely, by Japanese in the United States, is conducted.[7]

In short, by deploying and problematizing the first-person voice, I argue that the bounded, interiorized self is a narrative convention. The "I" invoked is not clearly divisible from "the world," and no inviolable interior space, no fixed essence which we can unequivocally label "private," can be distilled out from the domains of what we call politics, economics, language, culture, and history Thus far I have deployed the "I" in order to describe the processes by which the problematic of identity emerged. But my major aim is to focus attention on the people I encountered in Japan, and for them, as for us, language and narrative conventions provide the most striking insights into the simultaneously creative and disciplinary production of "selves."

NOTES

[1] The issue of what to call ourselves is an issue of considerable import to various ethnic and racial groups in the United States, as the recent emphasis on the term "African American" shows. For Asian Americans, the term "Oriental" was called into question in the sixties, for the reasons Said (1978) enumerates: the association of the term with stereotypes such as Oriental despotism, inscrutability, splendor, exoticism, mystery, and so on It also defines "the East" in terms of "the West," in a relationship of unequal power—how rarely one hears of "the Occident," for example. Asian Americans, Japanese Americans included, sometimes hyphenate the term, but some of us would argue that leaving out the hyphen makes the term "Asian" or "Japanese" an adjective, rather than implying a half-and-half status: i e , that one's loyalties/identities might be half Japanese and half American Rather, in the terms "Asian American" and "Japanese American," the accent is on the "American," an important political claim in light of the mainstream tendency to see Asian Americans as somehow more foreign than other kinds of Americans.

2   See Merry White 1988 for an account of the families of Japanese corporate executives who are
    transferred abroad and who often suffer painful difficulties upon reentering Japan.

3   Most Japanese bathe in the evening, sometimes just after coming home from work. Among the
    people I knew, taking baths in the morning was considered a bit decadent, typical of someone
    who keeps very late hours.

4   This area, located at a lower level than the rest of the house or apartment, is where one leaves
    one's shoes before entering (literally, going up to) the house proper.

5   A *kotatsu* is a table with a quilt spread out underneath the tabletop. Electric kotatsu have a heat-
    ing unit attached underneath, and people usually sit with their hands, feet, and legs underneath
    the quilt in order to warm them. In some older houses, kotatsu are placed above a hole in the floor,
    where one can dangle one's legs, the heater or brazier is located in the middle of the recessed area.
    At least in the majority of Japanese households, which lack central heating, it would be safe to say
    that most family activity during the winter months centers around the kotatsu.

6   Mine, Harvard, has a very particular relationship to Japanese politics and society, especially
    through the presence of such well-known scholars as Edwin O. Reischauer, former ambassador
    to Japan, and Ezra Vogel, whose *Japan as Number One* was a best-seller in Japan.

7   See Miyoshi (1998) for an incisive analysis of this larger context of scholarship.

Gender and
Fieldwork Relations

Carol A. B. Warren

Fieldwork, like all social life, is gendered; this gendering is central to field relations, because the fieldworker is the (embodied) "research instrument." The kinds of experiences fieldworkers have, the observations they make, and their transformations of these experiences and observations into fieldnotes are products of their gendered and embodied relations with respondents. Hence the importance of analyzing how gender shapes field relations and the experiences and observations they generate.[1]

Gender has been a significant issue for ethnographers from the earliest days of anthropological research, when scholars began to move from their armchairs into the field, there to study highly gender-structured societies. And through at least the first half of the twentieth century in sociology, field researchers (including those of the Chicago school) focused analytically upon respondents' gender relations, less so on their own gendered place within the field. Writing about gender in one's own or other cultures was, in Van Maanen's (1988) terms, realist: the ethnographer (gendered, age-ed, class-ed, race-d, but all unnoted) was there to record "how it was" in Sumatra or in the inner city. Undoubtedly there were many gender and sexual issues encountered in these early fields, but much of what occurred was confined to corridor talk (if that), not inscribed as part of the ethnographic narrative.

Anthropologists were perforce more focused than sociologists upon the gender of both respondent and researcher; the settings they studied were highly structured by gender. Late nineteenth- and early twentieth-century anthropology was, essentially, male—male scholars studying the public and political life to which they had access, with women's domains either invisible or deemed unim-

Written expressly for *Contemporary Field Research: Perspectives and Formulations, 2/E*

portant. As early as 1885, however, Edward B. Tylor recognized the importance of women in fieldwork:

> ... to get at the confidence of the tribes, the man of the house, though he can do a great deal, cannot do it all. If his wife sympathizes with his work, and is able to do it, really half the work of investigation seems to fall to her, so much is to be learned through the women of the tribe which the men will not readily disclose. The experience seemed to me a lesson to anthropologists not to sound the "bull-roarer," and ward the ladies off from their proceedings, but rather to avail themselves thankfully for their help. (quoted in Wax 1979:517)

Despite Tylor's urgings, much early anthropology assumed that the culture of a given society was what male anthropologists experienced and observed among male informants, whether as "pure observer," marginal native, or professional stranger (Bell, 1993a:1). However, from the early twentieth century, women fieldworkers, including both wives of fieldworkers and professionally trained anthropologists, gave visibility to women's (as well as men's) domains in the highly gender-structured societies they studied. Women anthropologists, especially Margaret Mead and Ruth Benedict, sometimes examined women because they wanted to, sometimes because they found themselves confined by respondents to observing the domestic sphere (Mead 1986).

Gender relations in the field were rarely problematized in texts dealing with United States settings during the first half of the century. Those anthropologists who studied locales within their own nations, such as Hortense Powdermaker (who did fieldwork in Hollywood and Mississippi as well as in Zambia and among the Lesu), did write of gender issues in Western societies, perhaps because of their non-Western experiences (Bell 1993a:4).[2] Nevertheless, gender issues were "set aside" in anthropology for "many decades" between the writings of Margaret Mead and the late 1980s (Bell, 1993a:7).

Although some of the canonical sociological ethnographies of the 1940s–1960s discussed gender as it shaped the field (see, for example, Becker et al. 1961), the researcher's gender was not seen as part of the unfolding of fieldwork relations. Sherri Cavan, a student of Goffman, noted the pivotal place of gender in bar behavior throughout her monograph (Cavan 1966). But her own gender, as she visited one hundred San Francisco bars between 1962 and 1965, was mentioned only as it pertained to entree:

> ... being a female in what is customarily a male setting made some difference. . . . there were bars from which I was categorically excluded . . . some bars that are open to both males and females are typically patronized only by males and it would have been awkward, if not suspicion-arousing, to enter alone. In both cases I was dependent on male assistance. (1966:17)

With the cultural and rhetorical unchainings of the late 1960s and early 1970s, discussions not simply of respondents' gendered worlds but also of gendered encounters between respondents and researchers began to appear in anthropological and sociological ethnography, as exemplified by Peggy Golde's compilation of studies of gender and ethnography published in 1970. Later in the decade sociological ethnographers such as Warren and Rasmussen (1977) had begun to frame gender as a significant aspect of relations in the field, yet even today there is still no collection of American sociological works in gender and ethnography parallel to Golde's (1970) or its 1980s anthropological successors (Golde 1986; Whitehead and Conaway 1986; Bell, Caplan and Karim 1993).

In both sociology and anthropology after the 1970s, a process of gendered reinterpretation took place as scholars looked back upon various field projects. In a 1983 postscript to fieldwork on draft resistance done in the late sixties and published in the 1970s, Barrie Thorne described how her awareness, interpretation, and inscription of gender issues in the draft resistance activities of 1968 produced greater recognition of women's place in the movement (1983:233–34). Pat Caplan traced the change in her concerns with gender in three fieldwork stays in a Tanzanian coastal village (1965–1967; 1976 and 1985). During her first visit Caplan "was single and childless, and thought, as my supervisor put it, that 'the world was my oyster.' I saw the villagers, and especially the women, as 'other'" (1993:178). By the time of her second trip, Caplan was married with two children and had encountered feminist anthropology; during this trip she was committed to "filling in the gaps in the data" and "redressing the [gender] balance" by experiencing and observing Tanzanian women as economically as well as domestically powerful (1993:179–80). By 1985 she had "abandoned. . . . the rather simplistic neo-Engelian assumption that if women did productive work, their status must necessarily be higher than if they did not" and experienced the women as "overburdened," with "too many babies, not eating enough and suffering a high level of morbidity" (1993:180). She then asks the inevitable question—were my previous analyses of gender in error?—offering this answer: "This does not negate, necessarily, what I 'saw' before: autonomous and productive women, rejoicing in their own sexuality . . . women are all these things, and . . . gender is a much more complex matter than we have supposed" (1993:180).

Most of the twentieth-century writing about gender and ethnography has been done by and about women; indeed, ethnography is one of the Western intellectual enterprises in which women have been prominent. Rosalie Wax, in discussing the history of gender and age in anthropological ethnography, claims that "mature women" had an "advantage in fieldwork from the very beginning" (1979:515), adding that

> It is no accident that of the nine portraits appearing on the book cover page of *Pioneers of Anthropology* six are women. As early as 1884 two of these, Erminnie Smith and Alice Fletcher, had done fieldwork among American Indians on their own. . . . To the Indians they must have appeared to be rich, powerful and formidable beings.

Although not necessarily rich, powerful or formidable to their respondents, women fieldworkers were, by the 1970s, seen by their ethnographic colleagues as ideally suited to fieldwork. Women were "naturally" more emotional, communicative and accessible than men (Golde 1970; Warren and Rasmussen 1977), less threatening than men to other men (Hunt 1984; Warren 1982), and more socially adept—thus altogether more suited to fieldwork than men. Women in the field were essentialized in both sociological and anthropological fieldwork mythology:

> In most settings, the ultimate sociability specialists are women. . . . They are liked by and commonly share intimacies with both sexes. Men are simply more threatening to both sexes, even where they are the most sociable. (Douglas 1976:214)
> . . . women make a success of field work because women are more person-oriented; it is also said that participant-observation is more consonant with the traditional role of women. (Nader 1970:113–14)

By the late 1980s to early 1990s, the focus on gender in ethnography had shifted from relations in the field to the representations that were made of it, from the inscription of fieldnotes (Emerson, Fretz and Shaw 1995; Warren 2000) to the published ethnographic book or article (Clifford and Marcus 1986). The location of the ethnographer within not only field settings but also social science disciplines became crucial for an understanding of the way in which representations are structured, including gendered representations. Ethnographic methodologists analyzed what was included in or left out of accounts of gender (and sex) in fieldwork relations, used feminist theory to shape conceptualizations of the ethnographic field, and sought to include a multitude of voices within their representations of the Other, from minority, Third World women to homosexual men. Discussions of women studying women (especially by means of interviewing, less so through participant-observation) verged at times upon the romantic, prompting the inevitable backlash (see Bell 1993a:8; Luff 1999).[3]

Although Western, American culture—and thus its practice of ethnographic research—has changed considerably during the past three decades, there are certain continuities of gender that appear and reappear in fieldwork narratives.[4] In examining gender in fieldwork relationships, I begin with the assumption that gender is built into the social structure of Western and non-Western social orders, across time and space, permeating other hierarchies of race and status. "Going into the field" presupposes gendered interactions, conversations, and interpretations on the part of both ethnographer and respondents, against the background of disciplines which are themselves gendered. From the rituals of institutional review boards (IRBs) to the publication of ethnographic research, the language and images of the field generated by ethnographers fuse gender into the power that is ethnographic knowledge.

Relations in the field begin with entree—the stranger entering a strange land, or the member deciding to study her or his own land—and end (perhaps) with leaving the field. In between entering and leaving, the ethnographer negotiates a place within the "host culture" which may seem fairly stable or appear to shift dizzily over time and across situations; which seems to be wrested from the field by the researcher or given to her by a generous pseudo-family. In this chapter, I trace these representations of gender in the ethnographer's entree into the field, and finding a place within it.

GENDER AND ENTREE

At the intersection of field with gendered researcher, prison bars may spring up, or there may be no impediments whatsoever. There are settings which a woman cannot enter, such as a male gay bathhouse (Styles 1979), and settings where just about anyone of any gender or sexuality is grabbed on to, such as a genital piercing group (Myers 1992). There are settings where physical entree is not a problem since the ethnographer is already a member (Esterberg 1997), and fields where women are welcomed and men tolerated (Johnson 1986) and vice versa (Warren 1972). In both non-Western and Western cultures there are many places in which gender segregation is commonplace, and where, in Hannerz's words, it may be "preferable to have fieldworkers of both sexes" (1969: 209).[5]

Entree is into settings that are structured by gender . . . [and other factors]. In *Soulside* (1969) Ulf Hannerz noted that his entree into women's worlds and relationships was limited in the context of the "division of the ghetto community along sex lines . . . [and the] social cleavage which separated black from white" (1969:209). Nearly thirty years later, in his ethnography of homeless women, Elliott Liebow (1993:x) referred to entree as dependent upon the "resources" brought to the encounter by the fieldworker, including the resource of gender. Liebow describes how his gender was advantageous to entree in a setting where males were relatively valued and relatively rare; his late middle-aged Jewishness seemed to be unimportant in this gendered context. The fieldworker approaches the field as a gendered (and race-d, and age-d. . . .) body, and winds her way into its gendered places as the social self projected by that body.

The Gendered Body and the Social Self

The ethnographer seeking entree is a man or woman, locally defined as attractive or not, wearing suitable or peculiar clothing, of a particular demeanor, height, weight and age. In Goffman's (1959) terms, she bears signs given off by this social embodiment, as well as signs presented through verbal communication: professional, marital, and other credentials. The image is something like a snow-ball (not of sampling, but of the self), with the ethnographer picking up more and more social meanings, for the host society, as he makes his way into the setting.

For the stranger confronting the Other, socially meaningful characteristics such as gender, age, social class, nationality and attractiveness structure the ways in which entree is effected—embodiment as the first impression of a socially interpret-able self. Rosalie Wax, in her analysis of the place of gender and age in fieldwork during the 1940s–1970s, underscored the significance of her age and gender in vari-ous settings; she noted that in her study of a wartime Japanese interment camp, "perhaps the fact that I was a strapping five feet ten and weighed (then) about 180 pounds helped a bit" in enabling her to evade danger and threat (1979:521). Liebow said of his body that "I am 6'1" and weigh about 175 pounds. I had a lot of white hair but was otherwise nondescript" (1993:x), adding: "Most of the women probably liked having me around. Male companionship was generally in short supply and the women often made a fuss about the few male volunteers" (1993:xi).

In recent scholarship, the body has been seen as a text of culture, and culture as a textualization of the body (Foucault 1978; Lamphere, Ragone and Zavella 1997). Gender, as it is displayed by the fieldworker and interpreted by respondents, gathers together the other elements of personal appearance significant to both stranger and host, from attractiveness to proper dress and demeanor. Age joins gender in social meaningfulness, as do, in many societies, the global, postcolonial signifiers of nationality, skin color, and apparent social status.

Parts of the gendered body may also assume significance for fieldwork relationships, including such genital-social matters as male circumcision (see Oboler 1986; Caplan 1993b), female mutilation (see Fleuhr-Lobban and Lobban 1986), or piercing (Myers 1992). In India, where the left hand is reserved for "dirty" tasks, the wearing of a wedding ring on that hand may be seen as an inappropriate symbol of a woman's marital status (Vera-Sanso 1993:164). Also in India, where "the sole of the foot is one of the most polluted parts of the body," Penny Vera-Sanso's attempt to return a shoe to a poor woman caused a gender/class/body-based scandal (1993:159).

The novice fieldworker—unable, for the most part, to change her body—may attempt to modify dress and demeanor so as not to alienate the host society. Hazel Hitson Weidman describes her adoption of the typical Burmese woman's style: "I selected flowered [long robes] that appealed to their tastes, and I sat with propriety, as a modest, well-bred young woman should. I wore fragrant body lotion, lipstick, earrings . . . and flowers in my hair" (1986:256). She reports no problems with this getup. In contrast, during her fieldwork in Madras, India, Vera-Sanso inadvertently violated age norms:

> I decided initially against wearing a sari. . . . Instead, I had a tailor make up three sets of matching long dirndl skirts and blouses. . . . To my bewilderment I was continually being told I would look much better in a sari but nobody would say why. It was only after a few weeks into the research, when I noticed a young schoolgirl wearing more or less the same clothes, that I realized I had dressed myself as a prepubescent girl! (1993:162)

Western ethnographers researching Western settings have some day-to-day knowledge of attires deemed proper amongst different social and occupational groups, knowing how to dress, or at least knowing the signs given off by dress. Ruth Horowitz (1985:6ff), in her Chicano gang study, describes herself as "small, fairly dark, a woman, dressed slightly sloppily but not *too* sloppily," unwilling to mimic equality with her women respondents to the extent of borrowing her women respondents' outfits or letting them cut her hair. Liebow describes how he dressed for his research among homeless women as casual, "often in corduroy pants, shirt, and cardigan" (1993:x), contributing to what he saw as an unthreatening yet appealing appearance.

Embodied, clothed, and gendered, ethnographers enter the field, picking up social meanings as they move into the world they have chosen, thereby creating intersections with those other worlds they inhabit. Partridge's account of his male bonding with an informant in Colombia and Wax's description of Margaret Mead's entree into a new setting both evoke the insertion of gendered status and disciplinary hierarchies into the gendered field. They also, taken together, underline the differences in male and female entree experiences:

> In the company of [two male informants] I set out to rent a house. . . . On top of [the rent] *I would still have to pay a maid and cook.* . . . That evening [two male informants] and I took in the local house of prostitution and spent a pleasant evening, even though everyone got quite intoxicated. This event proved to be of no minor significance when the following morning I received compliments from [other male informants]. Apparently, such an evening is one of their great pleasures, and they were happy to see that a foreigner enjoyed himself also. (Kimball and Partridge 1979:34–37, italics added)

> At age 36, on her first walk through a village in New Guinea, she pointedly identified herself as a knowledgeable and discreet woman by remarking loudly, "No, I won't go into the House Tambaran, that's the men's house. I am a woman." This announcement pleased the old men so much that they "shouted it up and down". . . . (It would be my guess that Mead's announcement also pleased the women). (R. Wax 1979:514)

Gender and the Field of Meanings

The encounter of the gendered body and the social self with the field permits or restricts entree not only physically—entering the village or bureaucracy—but also situationally and meaningfully—entering into the discourses of kin, sexuality, or public life. Women ethnographers from the 1920s to the present, especially in anthropology, have either chosen, or have found by default, that their research is focused on the private and domestic spheres of childrearing, health, and nutrition, with their male colleagues (sometimes husbands) responsible for the public and political. Niara Sudarkasa, for example, notes that in her study of the Yoruba

> I was never expected to enter into, and never did see, certain aspects of the life of men in the town. I never witnessed any ceremonies that were barred to women. Whenever I visited compounds I sat with the women while the men gathered in the parlors or in front of the compounds. . . . I never entered any of the places where men sat around to drink beer or palm wine or to chat. (1986:181)

Sociologist Laura Adams (1999:345), in her study of Uzbekistan, found that as a young girl she was identified with—and steered into—the "safe" or cultural aspects of Uzbeki life, and expected to shun the "risky" political aspects.

Generations of women and men fieldworkers have noted the different kinds of treatment and access they experience in gendered fields, and the ways in which gender affects their representations of the field. Ann Fischer (1986:282) says of her and her husband's fieldwork on the island of Truk in Micronesia:

> . . . there was a marked contrast between the treatment of myself and my husband. When he visited me, my chair (the only one on the island) would be preempted for his use, and an informant would squat by his side, spending hours answering his questions. Formal arrangements would quickly be

made to demonstrate for him some aspect of Trukese life in which he had expressed an interest. As a result, if our field notes are compared, my husband's record is of the more formal aspects of culture in exactitude, while mine tend to be a running account of what was happening in the village or in the homes in which I observed. The difference held in most of the cultures in which we did fieldwork together (including New England). . . . [O]ur access to data was different in every culture we studied, and although our interests and personalities may have contributed to some of these differences, our sex roles were also a most important element.

Although some women ethnographers have, historically, been interested in the "male" public and political sphere (Mead 1986), few men ethnographers have been interested in women's worlds. One exception is African-American ethnographer Norris Brock Johnson's (1986) fieldwork in a Midwestern U.S. elementary school. He attributes the initial resistance of the female teachers to his research to the male hegemony in which female authority and territory were routinely undermined, and female sexual status took precedence over professional status:

> Male custodians had free access and routinely sauntered into the classroom unannounced, mostly while classes were in session. Many times the [male] principal would walk into the classroom, without knocking, to make an announcement, often blithely interrupting the teacher. . . . The role and status of the female classroom teacher involved a gender expectation of subservience. . . . The gender expectations seemed to be that males are sexually aggressive toward females irrespective of place or situation. . . . [The teachers] wanted to find out if I was safe: that is, would I recognize their professional status and act appropriately, or would I act like a man and exhibit sexually inappropriate behavior. (1986:167–68)

Johnson gained acceptance from the teachers over time by not acting like (his image of their image of) a traditional male; by respecting their authority and territory and not flirting with them.

In contemporary ethnography, males may find themselves in the field as husbands (or partners) of female ethnographers, an inversion of the situation of thirty years ago. As Vera-Sanso notes, the "husband-wife relationship is the one which most abounds with stereotypes" in both non-Western and Western societies, and thus "obscures the interaction between the many roles an individual can hold," including that of scholar (1993:166). Upon preparing to enter Indian society with her husband David, Vera-Sanso advised him "to avoid using his left hand and not to sit next to Indian women," the "two mistakes a male traveler is likely to make" (164). When David was asked by the sponsoring organization if he wanted to attend the week of introductory meetings arranged for the anthropologist and he agreed, Vera-Sanso was concerned that she would be seen as "only the assistant researcher" (164). Her subsequent field relations revolved around the tension between marital stereotypes, gender preoccupations, and fieldwork relations.

Gender-linked concerns such as marital or childbearing status may also affect access to or within the field. Nancie Gonzalez (1986) notes that married

Guatemalan women with children consider it rude and embarrassing to discuss pregnancy and childbirth with both unmarried and child-free women. Ernestine Friedl (1986) comments that in the Greek village she and her husband studied, the male role included macho boasting about sex, use of sexual swearwords, and sexual jokes. But because her husband was a professor and thus of a higher class, the Greek village men refrained from macho talk in his presence, just as they did in her presence because of her gender. Abramson (1993:67) on the other hand, because of his British nationality and consequent high status in the eastern interior of Fiji, gained entree as a chief among male chiefs, the focus of attention, "a great, mighty and fecund chief from Great Britain."

The unmarried researcher, female or male, may be difficult for non-Western respondents to "place" socially; as Angrosino (1986:68) comments: "A single person is a rarity in most societies where anthropologists have done fieldwork." An unmarried, childless young adult woman has no social place in many non-Western (and some would say Western) cultures (Golde 1986); thus, a single woman ethnographer trying to study beyond women's worlds can find this difficult. As Peggy Golde (1986:80) says of her entree into the culture of the Nahua Indians of Mexico:

> What was problematic was that I was unmarried and older than was reasonable for an unmarried girl to be. I was without the protection of my family, and I traveled alone, as an unmarried, virginal girl would never do. They found it hard to understand how I, so obviously attractive in their eyes, could still be single. . . . Being an unmarried girl meant that I should not drink, smoke, go about alone at night, visit during the day without a real errand, speak of such topics as sex or pregnancy, entertain boys or men in my house except in the presence of other people, or ask too many questions of any kind.

Returning to a Tanzanian coastal village as a married woman and therefore "social adult," Pat Caplan (1993b:174) reported a respondent as commenting: "Before you were just a young girl; now you're grown up and we can talk to you properly."

Although unmarried male anthropologists report fewer practical problems than their female counterparts, they do indicate that there is a nearly universal expectation that adult males should be sexually active (Angrosino 1986; Turnbull 1986; Whitehead 1986; Back 1993). In his research among the Mbuti of Africa, for example, Colin Turnbull was expected to be sexually active because of his gender and age. He entered into a "temporary sexual and emotional arrangement" with a woman, Amina, which "satisfied the Mbuti as to the normality of my youthfulness and my ability to live with them as a real youth, while it satisfied the villagers that I was not a sorcerer" (1986:25). Wade (1993:208) justified his sexual relations in the field during two periods of fieldwork in Colombia by noting that they enabled him to be seen as "something other than an oddity, a pryer, or a snooper." Abramson (1993:74–75) describes how his sexual desire was "cultivated" by both his male respondents and his own needs in the context of Fijian male cultural expectations for active male sexuality.[6]

Motherhood is another part of the gendered field through which entree is negotiated; Fleuhr-Lobban and Lobban (1986:188) note the significance for their fieldwork in the Sudan of both their marriage and their daughter Josina. Women ethnographers have also found that motherhood is a potentially powerful source of mutual identification between women respondents and researchers. Macintyre (1993) reported that one respondent, Edi, "seized on all similarities and denied the differences" between them, whereas male respondents generally did the opposite. In a conversation about contraception, birth and illness in young children, for example, Edi insisted:

> ... birth is the same of all women. . . . we don't use these words. But I understand what you say. I understand you. Babies are all born in the same way. What you felt, I felt. But for you, only two, for me nine times. Oh my sister! (1993:48)

Entree is different for researchers who are already members of the field they wish to study—they are already there, or they used to be there. What may become problematic is not finding a place, but keeping their place, or perhaps finding a new one. Some fieldworkers and interviewers who have chosen to make their own groups into ethnographic settings have found that they experience dislocations from these worlds in the act of doing research: they lose their place, or their place changes. Les Back (1993), for example, in his study of a South London adolescent community, began "where he was," or at least where he thought he was, in the contexts of gender, class and race: "My choice of doctoral research was closely related to my own experience. I was born in South London in the early 1960s, of white working-class parents" (1993:221). He adds: "To my present embarrassment, I used my working-class origins as a way of gaining credit for this research and thus fictitiously dissolving the division between self and other" (222). What Back no longer was, however, was an adolescent immersed in 1990s youth subculture, or a participant in the white "racialism" of that culture. Self was no longer other, or other self. Studying masculinities as a scholar who had joined a world of feminism and antiracism, his research was not only a journey into the field but a way of making sense of the relationship between self, setting, and the passage of time: "Making our 'selves' seen is about making our masculinities the subject of discussion" (230).

Ifi Amadiume, an Eastern Nigerian anthropologist trained at the University of London, returned to her extended family in Nnobi to do fieldwork, where her gendered, statused "rightful kinship place in the society" immersed her in "accepted and expected patterns of reciprocity" (1993:196). Amadiume claims that persistent accusations against anthropologists of being Eurocentric, racist or spies are grounded in the lack of place that a stranger, and his or her project, has within this local culture of kin reciprocity. "If a stranger or anthropologist is not herself or himself a social subject or part of the field of study, what could possibly justify the study of another society?" (1993:196). While Amadiume's analysis challenges the place of the (non-Western) stranger in field research, Back's analysis challenges the place of the nonstranger.

GENDER AND SOCIAL PLACE

While the processual language of entree is used to express the fluidity of fieldwork, the classificatory language of roles and relationships—of social place—has been invoked to capture its rough continuities of peace (or war). Contemporary researchers refer to the process of finding/being given a place in the field (and it is not always possible to sort out which is which) as *incorporation*. In the societies studied by anthropologists, which are structured by gender, age, marital and childbearing status, and kinship, incorporation is often through some courtesy reference to these structures (Caplan 1993a:20). In Western societies, while gender and age are also of enduring significance, "achieved" characteristics also shape incorporation. Back, for example, notes that he was defined by the adolescents he studied as a "youth worker," his activities interpreted within the context of his field's domination by educational and professional "credentialism"—setting him apart from those he wished to get close to (Caplan 1993a:21).

Over the past few decades, ethnographers have attempted to describe, through various metaphors, their experiences of gendered social place within the field. In anthropological research, both genders—but particularly women—have been named in the field as fictive kin. Other women, particularly older ones, have been treated in ways that they describe as that of honorary male, while still others find more ambiguity in gender. In sociological research, the invisibility or hypervisibility of women in male-dominated settings—especially organizations—has been the focus of a considerable literature, with women ethnographers taken either as invisible secretaries or nurses, or as hypervisible mascots or (in Barrie Thorne's felicitous phrase) dancing daughters. Not all social places into which ethnographers are cast or cast themselves are benign: Within the hierarchies of postcolonialism or bureaucracy—or even in the public places of everyday life — female and male researchers can be mistaken for sorcerers or spies.

Fictive Kin: Field Daughters and Field Sons

Anthropologists studying non-Western societies in which kinship is the basic structuring principle may find themselves "adopted" into the society as a fictive (adoptive or classificatory) brother, sister, daughter, or child (Golde 1986). Laura Nader (1986:111) said that in her study of the Shias in Lebanon, she was assigned the role of "sister to men . . . a natural role that a woman anthropologist could walk into, should she wish. I did exactly that." Other women anthropologists have become children in the field. Jean Briggs (1986:40) describes the role of Kapluna daughter she was given by the Eskimo:

> Categorization of me as a child was probably determined by several factors. I had introduced myself as one who wanted to learn . . . and I had asked to be adopted as a daughter; I was obviously ignorant of [the culture's] proprieties and skills. The fact that I am a woman may also have facilitated my categorization as a child in several respects. . . . In order to be considered properly adult a woman must have children, and I had none . . . the role of an adult woman was virtually closed to me, whereas had I been a man I might have earned an adult role as a fisherman and hunter, as some [males] who have lived among Eskimos appear to have done.

The child role, with a married couple as "field father and mother," also characterized Karim's depiction of her social place among Carey Islanders. She noted that "my single female status positioned me in the role of a daughter to Mijah my field mother. Initially a short-term arrangement, everyone found this to be acceptable, and I finally began to relax and enjoy the fieldwork experience" (1993:83).[7]

Male anthropologists sometimes—although less frequently than women[8]—describe fictive kinship. Abramson (1993:68-79), whose entree to a village in Fiji was as a triumphant chief, described his "demotion" to the "son" of another (ultimately more powerful) chief, as well as his field-mother's "domestic harness." Johnson (1986:173-74), who did research on the island of Bequia in the Grenadines, analyzed his experiences of masculinity and father-son dynamics in his relations with a key informant, a shipbuilder:

> Men use tools to manipulate the elements and bring them under control, something I think men universally tend to admire in each other. Quite consciously, then, I sought to exhibit my [competence with tools]. . . . I remember feeling quite like a child trying to get my father's attention. I was a male coming to understand and trying to acquire his approval.

Ethnographers who study Western settings refer less frequently to fictive kinship (but see Hunt 1984), perhaps because those settings are organized around a separation of the public and private spheres. British sociologist Mick Bloor described the development, over time and against the initial presumption of heterosexual interest, of a "Favourite Uncle" relationship with a group of female residents in a therapeutic community, a relationship "established across an age and gender barrier. . . which stressed (frequently in a joking way) age differences and were without any implications of sexual attractiveness" (McKeganey and Bloor, 1991:17).[9] Ethnographic research among U.S. minorities, especially African Americans, has generated some accounts of fictive kinship, especially the researcher "going for cousins" with key informants (Stack 1974; Anderson 1990). In my own research on a Los Angeles drug rehabilitation center in the early 1970s, some of the residents referred to me as the "sister" of the black man who was the head of the center.

The literature on fictive kin emphasizes that the movement toward this form of incorporation may come from the researcher, the respondents, or both. Caplan (1993a:21) pointed out that "the role" her volume contributors "adopted in the field was not necessarily one chosen by themselves but decided by their subjects": "Karim shows how she was made to be a 'real', not just a fictitious daughter, to her Ma Betise family and how a commitment was 'forced' out of her. Similarly, Otome Hutheesing, working among a Thai aboriginal group, the Lisu, was accorded the role of powerful elder in spite of her own feelings of helplessness and inadequacy." But whatever the origins or ontological status of fictive kin labels among fieldworkers and their informants, they are highly gendered, as are many other social places named and identified by ethnographers.

The Honorary Male and Other Ambiguities of Gender

The "honorary male" appears in the ethnographic literature as a strategy for gaining access to settings patrolled by men. In some non-Western settings, the androgynous, older woman (member or anthropologist) who is no longer a sexual or menstrually-polluting threat to men may be permitted access to male rituals and privileges previously forbidden to her (Golde 1986; Wax 1979). During her research in an American police department, Hunt was situationally—in the context of displays of competence and violence—an honorary male (1984:290):

> Pistol practice provided the perfect opportunity to display the esteemed characteristics of masculine aggression and heart. One day I was practicing combat shooting and, as usual, my score was abominable. Ashamed, I left the range with my target hidden so no one could see it. However, a pistol instructor and several unknown off-duty officers approached and asked how I did. I responded, "Not so good today, but tomorrow I'll blow the mother's guts out." Astonished, one officer commented, "Did you hear what she said?!" They both smiled and nodded approvingly. I had shown that I was not a passive woman but a competent man who could feel just as violent as they did.

Not only aging but also whiteness and foreignness may permit women fieldworkers more cross-gender access than "native" women, allowing the woman anthropologist to take the role of the honorary male in obtaining access to parts of male worlds. Hutheesing (1993:97) notes that in her fieldwork in Thailand:

> As a middle-aged foreign woman, I gained an extra prestige dimension to my "face." Besides being meted out the usual respect and courtesy, I was also given the privilege of entering the village shrine of the most senior ancestor spirit, an otherwise forbidden domain for women.

Other accounts stress some uncertainties of gender in women's field experiences and access to male worlds. Ethnographers report "ambiguities" of gender for white, educated women in postcolonial societies (Fleuhr-Lobban and Lobban 1986), ambiguities which could sometimes be used to the researcher's advantage. Rena Lederman (1986:378), among the Mendi, was

> . . . concerned with not aligning myself clearly with either the men or the women (as I understood the difference then). . . . I hoped to take advantage of whatever ambiguity my outsider status afforded, sidestepping the issue of my own gender and commitments for a while, if possible.

Hunt (1984:286), too, describes ambiguities in a police world dominated by a hierarchy of authority and polarizations of gender in which

> . . . gender is an essential aspect of identity . . . characterized by a structural and symbolic split between a feminine/domestic and a masculine/public domain. . . . women . . . are viewed as untrustworthy in part because their superior feminine virtue is seen as dangerous in a public world in which most members are corrupt. In contrast, men who work on the street are perceived as trustworthy mainly because they share an involvement in illicit activity.

Within this gendered field, Hunt had to convince police that she was a trustworthy person and researcher; she did this by attempting to "negotiate a gender identity that combined elements of masculine trustworthiness with feminine honesty. I . . . became a liminal person" (286). In various situations within the shifting moments of gender and authority within the police world, Hunt was seen as dyke, whore, spy, date, or traditional woman. On one occasion

> The feminine aspects of my gender identity were ritually restored in a [playful judo] game played with an academy instructor. . . . In this ritual, the sexual order of power was restored: the tough judo player was transformed into a weak helpless woman. (293)

In recent years, the idea that anthropologists either could or should participate in existing gender relations as fictive kin or honorary male has been challenged as unrealistic (Macintyre 1993). Building upon that part of the anthropological literature that stressed the anthropologist as occupying deviant or ambiguous rather than normative (fictive kin) roles in the field, the image is of the fieldworker as an "incorporated anomaly," perhaps politely called "field daughter" but not really a daughter at all.

Some ethnographers experience changes in their gendered place in the field as social relations develop. Jean Jackson (1986:271) found that "after a period of time, my femaleness had superseded my status as an affluent and high-status outsider. . . . I was both elated and irritated. . . . Although more of an insider, I was being assigned to my proper place on the inside—second place." Similarly, Hutheesing noted that among the Thai lowland people she studied, her "adjustment" to participating in Lisu womanhood increasingly involved being placed into the gender roles of that society, which "entail [my] being made to feel a lesser being in comparison with the male" (1993:976).

Invisible and Hypervisible Women: Fieldworkers in Organizations

In male-dominated Western organizations and bureaucracies, women fieldworkers have experienced both invisibility, as nurses, secretaries, and other support staff, and hypervisibility, as a mascot or dancing daughter.[10] In all my organizational fieldwork when I was young, being a female enabled me to move around settings with little or no curiosity shown from the men in charge. In the early 1970s, I moved around the common areas of a drug rehabilitation organization not much noticed. In the early 1970s to late 1980s, I was assumed by the judge, district attorneys, defense attorneys, psychiatrists and others who "counted" in Metropolitan Court to be a nursing student or legal intern, in some cases even after I had informed them that I was a researcher and professor at the University of Southern California (Warren 1982). During the same era, I "tested the waters" of invisibility by walking into the offices of an adolescent mental hospital I was studying as part of a team and looking in file drawers (Warren 1983).

At times, I became hypervisible in the court setting as a mascot or a dancing daughter to the judge—the most important and hypervisible male. The mascot and the dancing daughter are the sometimes-sexualized and maybe-desexualized sides of the same submissive role of young women fieldworkers in male-dominated Western organizations and bureaucracies.[11] The woman-as-mascot is a badge for one or more male members of the organization—small, displayed prominently, object-like, and above all attached to the male. The dancing daughter is bright and active, young and smiling, looking up to and dancing before the father to win his approval, trying to duck the more sexualized possibilities of mascoting.[12]

The hypervisibility of the mascot occurs when a powerful man takes the ethnographer in tow. It is a testament to enduring elements in Western gender relations that women fieldworkers have written about the mascot role for more than thirty years, beginning with Arlene Kaplan Daniels in 1967. Being marked as "pretty women" and "shown around" by powerful males in the setting is characteristic of mascoting. In Easterday et al.'s 1977 research:

> I asked to observe some visiting professionals at work in the morgue. One of the attendants introduced me and conveyed my request. The response was "Of course. Who wouldn't want a pretty girl watching them work?" ... efforts were made to characterize my participation . . . as "mascot" with statements like "We like your company," and "it looks good to have a pretty girl along." (343)

In a 1999 article on her research in Uzbekistan, Adams described herself as a mascot to the male bureaucrats who supervised her research visit. Her mascot status involved being a good girl—dressing and behaving modestly, "like a Uzbek woman," and expressing "approval of [her hosts'] nation-building projects" (340-42). Like Adams, Easterday et al. (1977:343) found "the mascot is accepted simply for 'being'" rather than for research competence or agendas.

The dancing daughter dances to attract her "field-father's" eye and keep it, paternally (not sexually) on her—again, affording her certain kinds of access and longevity in the setting. As a mascot to the judge of Metropolitan Court in the early 1980s (Warren 1982), I used the dancing daughter strategy to counter the judge's sexualized mascoting, with some success (he never proceeded to what we would, in the 2000s, characterize as sexual harassment). Easterday and her colleagues (1977:343) interpreted the dancing daughter as arising from a stance taken by older males in the setting "threatened by young women or unable to interact with young women as peers" and for whatever reason not inclined to sexualize them. Adams (both mascot and dancing daughter; 1999:361) reported that the former administrator of a TV company to which she was seeking access told "everyone" that she was his "little daughter," and persuaded the current director, "although he was a busy man ... to make time for a mascot."

The places of mascot or dancing daughter in Western organizations may have some surface similarity to fictive kinship in non-Western societies; however, they are situational, transitory, and (in the case of the dancing daughter) strategic rather than part of the social structure. But, like fictive kinship, both the mascot and the dancing daughter are positive social places (at least from the perspective of the respondent, if not the researcher). Not so those of the sorcerer or the spy.

The Sorcerer and the Spy

The fieldworker as sorcerer or as spy reflects the continuities of non-Western cultural beliefs on the one hand and the power of colonial or other bureaucratic hierarchies on the other. Sorcerers and other locally anomalous but apparently powerful strangers can be male or female depending upon the group's folktales; the spy, too, can be either gender, although the canonical sexualized spy, the Mata Hari, is a woman.

Sorcerers, in many cultures, blur the boundaries between man and woman, and human and animal. Nader's behavior, outside the framework of traditional female, so puzzled the Zapotec Indians that they decided she was able to turn herself into a man or woman at will (1986:104–05). The Micronesians studied by Fischer (1986:276) were afraid that if she wandered into areas where white faces were not a familiar sight, she might be mistaken for a ghost and attacked. And Karim (1993:78) learned from her field father:

> Some said you were a head hunter and had come here to collect a few heads to fortify a new bridge on the mainland. Yet others said you were merely assuming a human form and would transform in the middle of the night into a tigress and eat us all. You ... probably ... could assume animal or human forms.

When Karim asked "Why did they mistrust me, a woman?" he replied:

> What difference does it make whether you are a woman or a man? It's the intention and the motive that matters. Formerly animals tried to overrun us by assuming human forms; these humans were not [real]. But I took you in. I knew you did not have these powers. I knew you were properly human. I made you my daughter. (1993:78)

Karim was also suspected of being a spy; her field father told her: "When you came here two years ago without any warning, the village said you were a government spy. They said you had come to gather information about the land to resettle us elsewhere" (1993:78). Similarly, although Weidman (1986:255) was welcomed into the Burmese village she studied as a daughter and benefactress, she later found out that she had been seen as a spy for the Burmese or U.S Government. In the context of globalization and postcolonialism, the presence of a stranger in a Third World village can precipitate accusations of spying as well as sorcery—and instead of fictive kinship.

Both men and women may be accused of being spies, but in different gender contexts. Because in most cultures men are seen as more political, more linked to sources of power, and more dangerous than women, they may be more readily taken for spies (Wax 1979:514); Back (1993:208) notes that "in Unguia I was sometimes seen as a detective or spy, a role unlikely to be attributed to a woman in Colombia." The literature on fieldwork in Western organizations indicates that a fieldworker whose gender does not fit with prevailing assumptions may be deemed a spy (Hunt 1984); Johnson (1986) reports that in his study of elementary school teachers, all of whom were female, he was initially seen as a spy for the administration.[13]

Women are liable to accusations of spying if they are out of their gender place; Ruth Landes was suspected of being a spy in Brazil in the 1930s in part because she lacked the obligatory male protector (1986:255). Hunt (1984) notes that any stranger doing research on urban police is liable to be seen as a spy, but a woman even more so. Not only was the police department she studied embroiled in a lawsuit charging gender discrimination against female officers, but also

> ... the role of spy was consistent with my gender identity. As a civilian and a moral woman I respected the formal order of law and the inside world of the academy. As both FBI and police internal security also represented the formal order, it was logical to assume I was allied with them. In addition, no policeman believed a woman was politically capable of fighting the department to promote honest research: Instead, the dominant elite would use me for their own purposes. (1984:289)

Hunt was also taken for a "whore" or "date," and at other times for a "dyke";[14] at its edges, spying, symbolized by Mata Hari, shades into sexuality in the field.

Sex, Marriage, and Fieldwork Relations

As Caplan (1993a:23) notes, more late twentieth-century than earlier writers on gender in the field speak of their own heterosexuality, but rarely—and even more rarely (outside the specialist literature) of homosexuality or lesbianism, for which "the silence in the literature . . . is even more deafening than that concerning heterosexual relationships." A few fieldworkers have written about their own sexuality in the field: men, mainly, of heterosexuality as it validates their male place within the field (Abramson 1993; Turnbull 1986; Wade 1993; Kimball and Partridge 1979); and women, mainly, of heterosexual male dominance, although occasionally of sexual encounters—(Davis 1986) or flirtation in the field (Warren 1988). Karim (1993) was not willing to act upon her romantic feelings during her fieldwork in Malaysia, but wrote about them later for what had, by the 1990s, become an approving disciplinary audience:

> There was someone else I thought of constantly. . . . He was tall, with a rugged face burned by the sun, but he was married. He was a "cousin" of mine, through my field-father's first-born deceased brother. . . . He came by more frequently, and I could sense the growing bond between us. I had thought, in some moments of madness, that I should do what any Ma Betise woman did—that is, openly disclose my feelings for him, but cowardice and fear of disapproval by other men and women led me to avoid him eventually. (84–85)

Although only recently inscribing some of their own sexual feelings, ethnographers have spoken for several decades of the sexual labeling they encounter from respondents. Within the seemingly universal hegemony of male dominance, women and women fieldworkers are often framed sexually as virtuous—virginal, married, or otherwise unavailable for sexual encounters—or not so virtuous—unprotected by a male and therefore fair game. Virtuous women may be the subjects of attempts at incorporation through fictive kinship arrangements or marital offerings, while the less virtuous are the objects of sexual labeling (whore or dyke), persistent invitations, sexual harassment, or even sexual violence. During her research among the Nahua Indians, Golde (1986:80) was subjected to numerous attempts to persuade her to "marry in the village. . . . In trying to persuade me, they would argue that I wasn't too old for the marriagable boys of fifteen, sixteen, or seventeen, since older women quite frequently married younger boys. This was a patent untruth." Karim's Carey Island respondents "finally chose a person" for her to marry, but "He did not match up to my expectations" and she did not marry him (1993:84).

Ruth Landes was labeled a prostitute during her 1930s Brazil research in the face of inadvertent violations of gender norms. On one occasion, she checked into a hotel that, unknown to her, was frequented by prostitutes; on another, she wore a type of shoe worn locally only by streetwalkers (1986:130–32). Returning to a Rumanian village as a widow and unattached woman, Diane Freedman (1986:357) found that in comparison to her earlier fieldwork as a married woman

> . . . my behavior was interpreted differently; friendly interactions were seen as indication of illicit behavior. My need for friendship and approval led me to participate in gatherings where cross-sex joking was common, and I was often the focus of the jokes. I interpreted these events on a surface level, as jokes in a friendly spirit. But the underlying theme was more serious than I realized at the time.

Being treated as "fair game" by men in the field was a commonplace of "corridor talk" amongst female sociological ethnographers in the 1970s and 1980s, but the issue only occasionally appeared in the literature. Joy Browne (1976:78) described her problems fending off salesmen during her research in a used car lot:

> As I progressed with my project, it became important to note that I was a young woman. Irrelevant as it might have seemed at the outset, the fact that used car lots have little shacks which can cozily accommodate a salesman (nearly all are men, and all those I encountered were men) created a methodological problem. I had to develop a method of convincing a sometimes over-eager informant that I did not want to be *that* kind of participant.

By the 1990s, accounts by women fieldworkers had become less oblique, and framed as sexual harassment. Terry Williams and his colleagues (1992:363) claimed that in their urban project and in other settings

> Several female ethnographers have had their fieldwork severely constrained or have had to terminate it completely. . . . due to the sexual expectations and demands of other males in the research setting. The threat of sexual assault or rape is a real concern for most female ethnographers and staff members.

In her interview study of divorced men, similarly, Arendell (1997) found herself the object of verbal and physical harassment, ranging from personal space violations to respondents touching her on the back, shoulder, hand, wrist, or arm, and in one case choking her.

Women in the field in the 1990s, however, as they did in earlier decades, reported attempting to evade or avert sexual overtures or harassment on the part of respondents rather than challenging the behavior. Browne's strategy for responding to overeager male informants was to "leave the field for a while and let things cool down . . . rather than face a showdown and lose an informant"

(1976:78). Almost thirty years later, Williams said that, when treated as fair game, "Usually I just move away or shift to a conversation with someone else" (1992:355). And Arendell, in 1997, indicated that she did not challenge even the most aggressive respondents because she was committed to getting her study done rather than raising their consciousness; she also became empathically involved with her respondents' accounts and was grateful to them for their time and involvement (364). Similar responses and rationales have been given by women fieldworkers cast into domestic or other roles that they normally find chafing (Warren 1982). In social science as in social life, women must often keep their place; Easterday et al.'s 1977 depiction of the ethnographer as part of "the institutionalized pattern of relationships in which women are professionally, personally, and politically subject to male authority" remains relevant in the opening years of the twenty-first century.

CONCLUSION

Gender, like other embodied personal characteristics that have social meaning, is one fulcrum upon which the ethnographic enterprise pivots. Ethnography proceeds by negotiating, living, interpreting and inscribing field relations. As embodied, feeling beings—and neorealist ethnographers—we should not lose sight of the real world out there and our own place in it. In discussions of gender and fieldwork relations, women and men fieldworkers negotiate entree and find their place within the cultural maps drawn by male respondents and ethnographers, whether as field daughters, dancing daughters, honorary males, or "fair game." But gender relations in the field involve people as well as processes and places: feelings and connections that are personal and may be more than ephemeral.

The political representations of contemporary fieldwork, which often stress the colonial or bureaucratic power of the man or woman fieldworker, miss the interplay of power and vulnerability in the field within which these gendered relations are lived out. As Macintyre (1993:47) notes:

> One of the conventional images of the fieldworker is as an outsider endowed with power or status derived from identification with earlier (or current) white colonials. It is on this basis apparently that some women anthropologists assumed or were given the role of 'honorary male' (whatever that really means).

In contrast to this disembodied image, Macintyre found a quite different reality: "My initial inability to speak the language, my ignorance of basic, everyday skills, and my breaches of etiquette meant that I often felt vulnerable and demeaned" (47).

Ethnographers are vulnerable to positive as well as negative emotions in fieldwork relations. Relationships between women fieldworkers and respondents, perhaps insignificant within the larger cultural kinship and sexual maps of the ethnographic disciplines, may be significant, in Macintyre's (1993:49) terms, as "the joys of recognition and identification." Bell (1993b:39) describes her interviewing of other Australian women about conception as "richly textured, candid and intimate. The telling of the stories was informative, cathartic, redemptive, and indulgent."

Some fieldworkers' fictive kinships become real to them (and, they indicate, to their respondents as well) over time. After being gone from Tubetube Island for several months, Macintyre's adoptive sister's child (known as her own daughter) screamed in fright at Macintyre's now-unfamiliar white face. An older girl told the child firmly, "Don't be frightened, she's not a white person, she's your mother!" (1993:53). Karim (1993:80) wrote: "Feelings about one's field-family could not be conveniently structured according to fieldwork and post-field-work phases. . . . The person I could not bear to leave was my field-father, whom I had grown to love deeply. I knew that I would pine for him quietly in the Ma Betise way, and he would for me."

It is at the intersection of personal relations and the field that structural relations of power become embodied—and thus changed. It has fallen to gender relations, in particular, to illuminate and challenge—reflexively and simulta-neously—the hierarchies that shape both the field and the disciplines that study fields. As Macintyre (1993) notes, substituting the metaphor of the Other for the discredited colonial namings of the native or the primitive does little to capture the realities of gendered relations in the field. A dialectic of self and other is "woefully inadequate as a way of conceptualizing the complex relation between the fieldworker and the people with whom she lives, whom she observes, and later writes about" (58). In fieldworkers' experiencing, observing and writing about gender relations, we see the possibilities of overcoming the binary opposi-tions in our scholarship, and we might conclude, with Diane Bell (1993b), that "yes Virginia, there is a feminist ethnography."

NOTES

[1]   Some of the material in this chapter draws from Warren and Hackney (2000).

[2]   The distinction between anthropological and sociological fieldworkers is one of disciplinary training and conceptualization: References to "honorary males" or "liminality" are, for example, more likely to be found in anthropological than sociological texts, whether these are about non-Western or Western (see Hunt 1984) fields.

[3]   By the turn of the twentieth into the twenty-first century, it has become clear that a full under-standing of the place of gender in the ethnographic enterprise hinges upon issues of both represen-tation and field relationships. The postmodern as well as the feminist turn toward representation has been critiqued as overwhelming the significance of the field itself—of the worlds of the Other, and of the roles and relationships upon which ethnographic representations were grounded (Wolf 1992, Bell 1993a). Contemporary ethnographers have begun to explore what Gubrium and Hol-stein (1997) refer to as a "new language of qualitative research" that could encompass the field, as well as representations of it. Naive "realist tales" (Van Maanen 1988) are no longer possible in eth-nography; however, neo-realist tales—narratives sensitive to, but not confined by, issues of repre-sentation—are promising. It is from this neo-realist stance that I seek to explore gender and relationships in the field as they have been discussed in recent ethnographic literature.

[4]   One of the legacies of the postmodern era is the queer-theory notion of the performative rather than structural "nature" of gender; the image is that of ephemerality and malleability. But this is an etic theory, grounded neither in the emics of everyday experience nor in the feminist uncover-ing of an actual, hierarchical patriarchy as the historical foundation of that everyday life (Kneeland and Warren forthcoming).

5 There are, increasingly in the early twenty-first century, settings where entree is prohibited through elaborate governmental and local rules concerning the "protection of human subjects"— but that, of course, is another topic.

6 Even married anthropologists may not meet cultural expectations, especially if their marriage does not fit the traditional model of male dominance and female submission. Friedl, describing her fieldwork in a Greek village accompanied by her husband, comments

> At the outset . . . I was involved in a formally and publicly wife-centered enterprise in a society that was husband-centered to a degree even greater than is customary in Western Europe and America. Half deliberately and half as a matter of natural development we pragmatically compensated for this anomaly. My husband became the spokesman for the two of us in Athens and the village. (1986.198)

During her fieldwork in Rumania, similarly, the villagers Diane Freedman studied were "scandalized" by the fact that her husband did half of their housekeeping and fetched water from the well, although the men and women interpreted his actions differently:

> Men's reactions . . . were divided. Some thought it amusing, while others felt that Robert was degrading himself by doing women's work. The women, by contrast, considered it a positive sign of Robert's concern for me. Even the women, however, had limits of custom beyond which they would not be drawn. When they realized that Robert was also washing clothes, I was advised that he should do this in the house and that I should then hang the clothes outside; otherwise my reputation as a good wife would suffer. (1986.344–45)

7 At times, fieldworkers may become field mothers to adoptive children (see Macintyre 1993).

8 This may be because non-Western societies may "place" women more closely than men within kinship and other protective social linkages.

9 There is a considerable literature in anthropology on joking relationships as a way of evading sexual implications within kinship and other social networks.

10 It may be that field relations of invisibility or hypervisibility are found in settings other than organizations or bureaucracies, but at this point they have been written about in these contexts only.

11 There may be a parallel situation of the young male researcher (perhaps the minority researcher also) as a token in within-gender, cross-gender or mixed-gender (nonminority) settings, however, this possibility remains, at the present time, confined to corridor talk.

12 Although the terminology of "dancing daughter" evokes fictive kinship linguistically, the dancing daughter is not a subtype of fictive kin. Rather than a social place based on existing "roles" in the setting, the dancing daughter is a strategy adopted by mascoted women to keep the elder male's focus on age rather than gender and sexuality (and perhaps adopted by some paternalistic males, too, as in Easterday et al 's 1977 account). After all, there is an incest taboo.

13 In Johnson's case suspicion of spying seems to have been a problem of entree rather than a continuing issue. However, there is a "role" of spy in postcolonial villages, Western organizations, and even the public order, into which individuals can be consigned at any point and with any degree of permanence. Although Karim's field father seemed not to have agreed with others' assessment of her as a spy, there is no indication that those others did not continue to see her that way. Even after entree and the presumptive establishment of trust, the role of "spy" can be invoked to account for observational behavior

> One student ethnographer studying a campus bookstore who had grown quite friendly with bookstore workers—with whom she had spoken openly about her study—nonetheless reported the following incident: "One of the younger cashiers . . . approached me tentatively about me being a spy from the other campus bookstore or possibly from the administration. Trying to ease the situation with a joke, I told her I was only being a spy for sociology's sake. But she didn't understand the joke, and it only made the situation worse." (Emerson et al 1995:25)

14 Hunt (1984) refers to gender in the field as negotiated. However, it appears from reading her article that aspects of gender such as spy, dyke, whore or honorary male were negotiated situationally, while gender itself remained a background, structural feature of her interaction with the mostly male police.

Learning from Kids

Barrie Thorne

> A different reality coexisted beside my own, containing more vitality, origi-
> nality, and wide-open potential than could be found in any lesson plan. How
> was I to enter this intriguing place, and toward what end would the chil-
> dren's play become my work?
>
> —Vivian Gussin Paley, "On Listening to What the Children Say"

When I first entered the Oceanside fourth/fifth-grade classroom as a note-
taking visitor, I thought of myself as an ethnographer with an interest in gender
and the social life of children. Beyond that, I had not given much reflection to
what I was bringing to the research. But I slowly came to realize that within the
ethnographer, many selves were at play. Responding to our shared positions as
adult women and as teachers, I easily identified with Miss Bailey and the other
school staff. Being around so many children also stirred my more maternal emotions and perspectives. (When I started the fieldwork, our older child was in
preschool, and by the end of the year I was pregnant with a second child.) Occasionally I felt much like the fourth- and fifth-grader I used to be, and the force of
this took me by surprise. This jangling chorus of selves gave me insight into the
complexity of being an adult trying to learn from kids. Hearing first one, then
another, of these different selves, or types of consciousness, helped shape what I
discovered and how I put my ideas together.[1]

Like Westerners doing fieldwork in colonized Third World cultures, or academics studying the urban poor, when adults research children, they "study down,"
seeking understanding across lines of difference and inequality. When the research
is within their own culture, the "studying down" comes swathed in a sense of familiarity. Despite their structural privilege, Western ethnographers who enter a radically different culture find themselves in the humbling stance of a novice. But it is

From *Gender Play: Girls and Boys in School*, by Barrie Thorne. Copyright © 1993 by Barrie Thorne.
Reprinted by permission of Rutgers University Press.

hard to think of one's self as a novice when studying those who are defined as learners of one's own culture. To learn *from* children, adults have to challenge the deep assumption that they already know what children are "like," both because, as former children, adults have been there, and because, as adults, they regard children as less complete versions of themselves. When adults seek to learn about and from children the challenge is to take the closely familiar and to render it strange.

Adrienne Rich (1995:50) has observed that power seems to "engender a kind of willed ignorance ... about the inwardness of others." To gain intersubjective understanding, ethnographers who "study down" often have to confront and transcend their own images of the devalued "Other" (Clifford and Marcus 1986; Mascia-Lees et al. 1989). Adults who study children of their own culture may encounter similar, although perhaps less conscious, barriers of consciousness. These barriers are rooted, perhaps paradoxically, in differences of power and in the fact that identifying with children may evoke the vulnerable child within each adult. The clinician Alice Miller describes deeply unconscious processes that may lead parents, who are threatened by their own sense of vulnerability, to deny their children's separate capacities for knowing and feeling (Miller 1983). Adult interest in controlling children may be driven, in part, by fear of their own sense of uncertainty and absence of control.

In my fieldwork with kids, I wanted to overcome these barriers and to approach their social worlds as ethnographers approach the worlds of adults: with open-ended curiosity, and with an assumption that kids are competent social actors who take an active role in shaping their daily experiences. I wanted to sustain an attitude of respectful discovery, to uncover and document kids' points of view and meanings.[2] To adopt that basic stance means breaking with an array of common adult assumptions: that children's daily actions are mostly trivial, worthy of notice only when they seem cute or irritating; that children need to be actively managed or controlled; that children are relatively passive recipients of adult training and socialization.

Indeed, asking how children are socialized into adult ways, or how their experiences fit into linear stages of individual development, deflects attention from their present, lived, and collective experiences. Moving back a step, one can see "socialization" and "development" as perspectives that many parents, teachers, and other adults *bring* to their interactions with children (Speier 1976:185). As mothers and teachers of young children, women, in particular, are charged with the work of "developing the child." But children don't necessarily see themselves as "being socialized" or "developing," and their interactions with one another, and with adults, extend far beyond those models. In my fieldwork I wanted to move beyond adult-centered, individualized frameworks and learn about the daily lives of children, especially what they do together as "they mutually build social occasions and activities in each others' presence"—to quote Matthew Speier (1976:172).

When I started observing in the Oceanside School, I set out to learn about gender in the context of kids' interactions with one another. I began to accompany fourth- and fifth-graders in their daily round of activities by stationing myself in the back of Miss Bailey's classroom, sitting in the scaled-down chairs and standing and walking around the edges, trying to grasp different vantage points. I was clearly not a full participant; I didn't have a regular desk, and I watched and took notes, rather than doing the classroom work. As the kids lined up, I watched, and then I walked alongside, often talking with them, as they moved between the classroom, lunchroom, music room, and library. At noontime I sat and ate with the fourth- and fifth-graders at their two crowded cafeteria tables, and I left with them when they headed for noontime recess on the playground. Wanting to understand their social divisions and the varied perspectives they entailed, I alternated the company I kept, eating with different groups and moving among the various turfs and activities of the playground.

In Ashton, the Michigan school, I also followed the kids' cycle of activities, but I stuck less closely to one classroom and its students. I observed in a kindergarten and in a second-grade classroom, and I spent a lot of time in the lunchroom and on the playground mapping all the groups and trying to get an overview of the school and its organization.

Looking back on my presence in both schools, I see how much I claimed the free-lancing privilege of an adult visitor. I could, and did, come and go, shift groups, choose and alter my daily routines. Unlike the kids, I was relatively, although not entirely, free from the control of the principal, teachers, and aides. Without a fixed, school-based routine, I also had more spatial mobility than the teachers and aides. My spatial privileges were especially obvious during severe winter days in Michigan, when the Ashton students, even if they wore skimpy clothes and had no mittens or gloves, were forced to stay outside for forty-five minutes during the noontime recess. While some of the kids stood shivering near the school, I was free, although I usually resisted the temptation, to go into the warm building.

I entered students' interactions to varying degrees. In teaching settings like classrooms and the Oceanside music room and auditorium, I felt most like an observer. In the lunchrooms where I was more visually separate from other school-based adults since teachers ate elsewhere and aides were on patrol, I joined more fully in kids' interactions by eating, conversing, and sometimes trading food with them. On the playgrounds I usually roamed and watched from the margins of ongoing activities, although I often talked with kids and sometimes joined groups of girls playing jump rope and games like "statue buyer." Whether on the margins or joining in, I was continually struck by kids' forms of physicality and by the structures of authority that separate them from adults.

KIDS' PHYSICALITY AND IMAGINATION

When I began my concerted effort to spend time with kids, I felt oversized, like a big Alice or Gulliver trying to fit into a scaled-down world. Schools are furnished for two sizes: smaller chairs, desks, and tables; and adult-sized chairs and desks, at which kids can sit often only with special permission. Staff bathrooms have big toilets and sinks, and the separate children's bathrooms have smaller

toilets and sinks. I knew I had crossed more fully into kids' spaces when the
sense of scale diminished, and I felt too large.

Watching kids day after day, especially on the playground, I was struck by
other differences of physicality: their quick movements and high levels of energy,
the rapidity with which they formed and reformed groups and activities. Public
schools are unusually crowded environments, which intensifies the sense of
chaos; the playgrounds were often thick with moving bodies. At first I felt like a
sixteen-millimeter observer trying to grasp the speeded-up motions of a thirty-
six-millimeter movie. One of the teachers told me that groups of children
reminded her of bumblebees, an apt image of swarms, speed, and constant motion.

After I had observed for several months, I saw much more order in the chaos,
and I developed strategies for recording rapidly shifting and episodic activity.[3]
For example, when I entered the playground, I went on an initial tour, making an
inventory of groups and activities. Then I focused on specific groups or individuals, sometimes following them from one activity to another, or from formation to
dispersal. I tried to spend time in all the playground niches, including basketball
courts, bars and jungle gyms, swings, the varied activities (foursquare, zone
dodgeball, handball, jump rope, hopscotch, tetherball) that took place on the
cement near the buildings, wandering groups, chasing scenes, large playing fields
where, depending on the season, games of baseball, soccer, kickball, and football
took place. There were also sites unique to each school: at Oceanside, "the tires,"
a climbing and swinging structure made of big rubber tires, and "the hill," a small
rise of grass; and at Ashton, the school steps, where kids hung out and talked.

I was struck not only by kids' rapid movements but also by their continual
engagement with one another's bodies—poking, pushing, tripping, grabbing a
hat or scarf, pinning from behind. Since adults in our culture experience such
gestures as invasions of personal space (notably, kids never poked, pushed at, or
pinned me from behind), I initially interpreted these engagements as more
antagonistic than, I realized over time, the kids seemed to experience or intend.
Trying to sort out playful from serious intent alerted me to the nuances of kids'
meanings *and* to my personal readiness to look for trouble, a readiness magnified
by my outlooks as a teacher and a mother.

I came to relish kids' playful uses of their bodies, their little experiments in
motion and sound, such as moving around the classroom with exaggerated hob-
bling or a swaggering hula, bouncing in a chair as if riding a horse, clucking like
hens or crowing like roosters, returning to a desk by jerking, making engine
noises, and screeching like the brakes of a car. They wrote on their bodies with
pencil and pen and transformed hands into gameboards by writing "push here"
across their palms. They held contests to see who could push their eyeballs far-
thest back and show the most white, or hold their eyes crossed for the longest
time. Sometimes these performances were private, at other times, constructed
with dramatic flair and a call for an audience.

These moments struck me as little oases of imagination in dryly routinized
scenes. They led me to reflect on growing up as a process of reigning in bodily
and imaginative possibilities, a perspective shared by nineteenth-century

romantic poets like Wordsworth, and by recent social critics like Edith Cobb, Vera John-Steiner, and Ernest Schachtel. These writers argue that children are more sensuous and open to the world than adults, and that adult creativity hinges on overcoming repression and gaining access to the child within.[4] This idealization of children contrasts with the idealization of adults built into many versions of the "socialization" and "development" perspectives. In assuming exaggerated dichotomies and casting value primarily in one direction, both views are limited.

GETTING AROUND ADULT AUTHORITY

My greater size; my access to special relations with the principal, teachers, and aides; and my sheer status as an adult in an institution that draws sharp generational divisions and marks them with differences in power and authority, posed complicated obstacles to learning from kids. I knew that if I were too associated with adult authority, I would have difficulty gaining access to kids' more private worlds. Nor did I want the tasks of a classroom or playground aide. The practical constraints of keeping order and imposing an agenda would, I quickly realized, run against the open-ended curiosity and witnessing that ethnography requires.

I entered the field through adult gatekeepers. A friend introduced me to Miss Bailey, the fourth/fifth-grade Oceanside teacher, and she, in turn, agreed to let me observe in her classroom, as did Mr. Welch, the school principal, who asked only that I not "disrupt" and that I report back my findings. My more formal entry into Ashton School, via the district Title IX office, seemed to make the Ashton principal a little nervous. But Mrs. Smith, the kindergarten teacher, and Mrs. Johnson, the second-grade teacher, seemed at ease when I was in their classrooms, and I had ample latitude to define my presence to the students of both schools.

In both schools I asked kids as well as staff to call me by my first name, and I called the staff by their first names when we spoke directly with one another. But when I talked with kids, and that's where I did most of my talking as well as watching, I joined them in using titles to refer to the teachers and principals. Everyone called the Ashton lunchroom aides by their first names. In my writing, I follow the kids' use of titles or first names; the actual names, of course, have all been changed.

On the playgrounds kids sometimes treated me as an adult with formal authority. Calling "Yard duty, yard duty!" or "Teach-er!" they ran up with requests for intervention—"Make Ralph give me back my ball"; "Burt threw the rope onto the roof." I responded by saying, "I'm not a yard duty," and usually by refusing to intervene, telling those who asked for help that they would have to find someone who was a yard duty, or handle the situation by themselves.

I went through the school days with a small spiral notebook in hand, jotting descriptions that I later expanded into fieldnotes. When I was at the margins of a scene, I took notes on the spot. When I was more fully involved, sitting and

talking with kids at a cafeteria table or playing a game of jump rope, I held observations in my memory and recorded them later. I realized that note-taking had
become my special insignia when the fourth-grader who drew my name in the
holiday gift exchange in Miss Bailey's class gave me a new little spiral notebook
of the kind I always carried around. As I opened the gift, the kids speculated
about how many notebooks I had filled by then. They also marveled at my ability
to write without looking.

This continual scribbling invited repeated inquiries about my presence and
purpose. Again and again, in classrooms and lunchrooms, and on the playgrounds, kids asked me why I was taking notes. "What's that? What're you
doing?" "You still takin' notes?" Sometimes they prefaced inquiry with a guess
about my purpose: "You writin' a book on us?" "You spying on us?" "Is it like
being a reporter?" "You're gonna have a big diary!" "You gonna be a writer?"
"What are you sposed to be?" (Questions about what I was "gonna" or "sposed to
be" startled me into realizing how much kids are encouraged to cast life in the
future and subjunctive tenses.)

Responding to these queries, I tried to be as open and straightforward as I
could. But I ran into gaps of understanding. The kids' responses clued me into
the drawbacks of some of my explanations. During one of my first forays on the
Oceanside playground, a boy came over and asked, "What ya writing?" "I'm
interested in what you children are like," I responded; "I'm writing down what
you're doing. Do you mind?" He warily edged away. "I didn't do anything," he
said. Another of my early explanations—"I'm interested in the behavior of children"—also brought defensive responses. I came to see that verbs like "doing"
and "behaving," which figure centrally in the language of social science, are also
used by adults to sanction children. The social sciences and child-rearing are
both practices geared to social control.

The kids seemed to understand more fully when I explained that I was
interested in the ways that they "play" or "what it's like to be a kid." But when I
elaborated, I ended up feeling irrelevant and longwinded. For example, during
one Oceanside recess as I crouched, watching and scribbling, on the sidelines of
a basketball game, a girl came up and asked, "What are you doing?" "A study of
children and what they play." "Do you wanna be a teacher?" she asked. "I am one.
I teach sociology, ever hear of that?" "No." "It's the study of people in groups."
"Well, good-bye," she said, running off.

Sometimes the kids played with the dynamics of my constant written witnessing. When they asked to see my notes, I showed them, privately feeling relieved
that they found my scribbles mostly indecipherable. Occasionally kids calibrated
behavior and its instant representation by telling me what to write down. "Why
don't you put that John goes over and sharpens his pencil," said a fifth-grader,
pointing to a boy in motion. On another occasion, a boy I'll call Matt Washburn
hovered by my notebook and said, "Write down: 'My best kid is Matt Washburn.'"

One girl who asked if I was "taking down names" voiced what seemed to be
their major fear: that I was recording "bad" behavior and that my record would
get them into trouble. I assured them again and again that I would not use their

real names and that I would not report anything to the teachers, principal, or aides. But of course what I wrote was not under their control, and, like all field-workers, I lived with ambiguous ethics. I guarded the information from local exposure, but intended it, with identities disguised, for a much larger audience. I was the sole judge of what was or was not reported and how to alter identifying information. My fieldnotes and later writing from this project feel less guilty than the information I gathered as a participant-observer in the draft resistance move-ment of the late 1960s (Thorne 1983). This is partly because information about kids and their doings seems much less consequential than information about adults, especially adults acting in a risky public arena. But of course that percep-tion comes from adult consciousness, not identification with kids' sense of risk.

Although a note-taking adult cannot pass as even an older elementary school student, I tried in other ways to lessen the social distance between me and the kids.[5] I avoided positions of authority and rarely intervened in a managerial way, and I went through the days with or near the kids rather than along the paths of teachers and aides. Like others who have done participant-observation with chil-dren, I felt a little elated when kids violated rules in my presence, like swearing or openly blowing bubble gum where these acts were forbidden, or swapping sto-ries about recent acts of shoplifting. These incidents reassured me that I had shed at least some of the trappings of adult authority and gained access to kids' more private worlds. But my experiences with adult authority had a jagged quality. Sometimes I felt relatively detached from the lines of power that divide kids and adults in schools. At other times I felt squarely on one side or the other.

I tried to avoid developing strong allegiances with the school staff and to build up loyalty to the kids, a strategy resembling that of ethnographers who want to learn about the experiences of prison inmates or hospital patients and therefore avoid obvious alliances with the wardens or medical staff. But I was tethered to adults by lines of structure and consciousness. My presence in both schools was contingent on the ongoing goodwill of the adult staff, which made me susceptible to their requests. When Miss Bailey asked me to help a student who was having trouble in math, or when Mrs. Johnson asked me to help the second-graders as they crafted dolls out of corncobs, I couldn't refuse, and I shifted with ease into the stance of an overseeing adult. Luckily, such requests were relatively rare because of my erratic schedule and because the teachers knew I was there to observe and not to help out in the classrooms.[6]

Although the teachers made few formal demands that drew me into their orbits of authority, they sometimes turned to me for a kind of adult companion-ship in the classrooms. While the students were seated, I usually stood and roamed the back, while the teacher often stood in front. That arrangement spa-tially aligned me with the teacher, and it was easy for our adult eyes to meet, lit-erally above the heads of the kids. When something amusing or annoying happened, the teacher would sometimes catch my eye and smile or shake her head in a moment of collusive, nonverbal, and private adult commentary. During those moments, I felt a mild sense of betrayal for moving into allegiance with adult vantage points and structures of authority.

When physical injury was at stake, my intervening adult-parental-teacher sides moved to the fore. One day just before recess a physical fight broke out in Miss Bailey's fourth/fifth-grade classroom, and the substitute teacher and I rushed to pull the antagonists apart. When I was observing on the Oceanside playground, a girl fell off the bars to the ground. Several other girls rushed toward her, one calling "Get the yard duty person! She can't breathe!" I ran over and asked the girl lying on the ground if she was hurt. An official "yard duty person" joined us, and she and I walked the injured girl to the office.

I could usually rely on playground aides to be on the lookout and to handle scenes of physical injury. It was harder for me to stay detached when kids hurt one another's feelings, and I sometimes tried to soothe these situations. For example, when Miss Bailey's students were drawing pictures at their desks, several girls talked about their summer plans. Jessica said she and her sisters and brother were going to Texas to see their mother. Sherry asked, "Why did your mother leave you?" Jessica replied, "She wanted to marry a guy, but they had a fight and she didn't." Almost simultaneously, Nancy spoke up, "She left because she didn't love you." Jessica blushed, and I resonated with her stung feelings. Feeling quite maternal, I tried to comfort Jessica by putting my arm around her and saying, "I'm sure it was hard for your mother to leave."

The teachers, principals, and aides generally assumed I was a colleague who would back up their rule. But I was primarily interested in the ways kids construct their own worlds, with and apart from adults. The official agenda of the schools—the lessons, the rules, the overtly approved conduct seemed like cement sidewalk blocks, and the kids' cultural creations like grass and dandelions sprouting through the cracks. I watched eagerly for moments of sprouting and came to appreciate kids' strategies for conducting their own activities alongside and under the stated business of the hour.[7]

THE UNDERGROUND ECONOMY OF FOOD AND OBJECTS

From my position in the back of Miss Bailey's classroom, which gives a very different perspective than the front, I could see what went on when desktops were raised, presumably on official business. Some kids had customized their desks by taping drawings or dangling objects from the inside top. In addition to official school artifacts like books, papers, rulers, pencils, and crayons, the desks contained stashes of food, toys, cosmetics, and other objects brought from market and home. These transitional objects, most of them small and pocketable, bridge different spheres of life. They also provide materials for an oppositional underlife often found in "total institutions," or settings like prisons and hospitals where a subjected population is kept under extensive control.[8] Although schools maintain far less control than prisons, students have little choice about being present, and members of a smaller, more powerful group (the staff) regulate their use of time, space, and resources. Like prison inmates or hospital patients, students develop creative ways of coping with their relative lack of power and defending themselves against the more unpleasant aspects of institutional living.

Some of the objects that kids stash and trade, like "pencil pals" (rubbery creatures designed to stick on the end of pencils), rabbit feet, special erasers and silver paper, could be found in the desks of both boys and girls. Other objects divided more by gender. Boys brought in little toy cars and trucks, magnets, and compasses; and girls stashed tubes of lip gloss, nail polish, barrettes, necklaces, little stuffed animals, and doll furniture. Patterns of trade marked circles of friendship that almost never included both girls and boys. The exception was a flat pink and yellow terry cloth pillow that Kathryn, the most popular girl In Miss Bailey's class, brought in to cushion her desk chair. Invested with the manna of Kathryn's popularity, the pillow traveled around the entire room; girls and boys sat on and tossed it around in a spirit more of honoring than teasing.

Ashton School felt like a much harsher environment than Oceanside School, in part because of the difference in weather (California was spared the cold winter of Michigan), but also because Ashton had strict rules against kids bringing objects from home. Even when it was raining, Ashton students were not allowed to carry umbrellas onto the playground, and if aides spotted any personal toys or objects, they immediately confiscated them. As a result, the school had an impoverished underground economy. (School staff might describe this differently, as eliminating distractions and maintaining order.) I saw a few sneaky sharings of food, lip gloss, and, on one occasion, a plastic whistle, but nothing like the flourishing semi-clandestine system of exchange at Oceanside School.

In my subsequent analysis (Thorne 1993) I addressed the significance of material objects in kids' social relations, as a focus of provocation and dispute, as a medium through which alliances may be launched and disrupted, as sacraments of social inclusion and painful symbols of exclusion, and as markers of hierarchy.[9] But here I want to highlight the relatively secret and oppositional nature of these objects and their negotiation and exchange. Students are not supposed to eat, play with toy cars, or rub pink gloss on their lips in the middle of an arithmetic or social studies lesson. But I saw them do all these things, creating their own layers of activity and meaning alongside, or beneath, the layers they shared with the adult school staff.

When kids invited me to participate in their secret exchanges, I felt pulled between my loyalty to them and my identification with and dependence on the teacher. During a social studies lesson, the fourth/fifth-grade students were supposed to be drawing pictures of early California missions. As Miss Bailey helped someone in another part of the room, I wandered to a corner where Jeremy, Don, and Bill leaned over and loudly whispered behind their raised desktops. Jeremy asked Don, "What's your middle name?" Don replied, "Top secret." Bill chimed in, "Porkchop." Don, who was taking pins from a box in his desk and sticking them through an eraser, responded, "Porkchop! I have two nicknames, Dog and Halfbrain." Jeremy reached for some pins from Don's desk and fashioned an *X* on his pencil eraser. Bill played with an orange toy car, making "zoom" noises as he scooted it into Jeremy's open desk. Jeremy took out an almost-finished bag of potato chips, held it out to Don, and shook a few into his hands. Bill held out his hand, but Jeremy ignored the gesture. "Give me one," Bill said. "No, you're too fat;

you should be on a diet." "I am on a diet," Bill said as Jeremy shook a few chips into his hands. "Give Barrie some," Bill said. Jeremy turned (I was sitting behind him) and asked, "Do you want some?" "Yes," I said and held out my hand as he shook a few chips into it. All of this forbidden activity went on behind the screen of the open desktops. Jeremy grinned, and I grinned back, feeling conspiratorial as I quietly munched the chips.

When I sociably interacted with a group of kids during work time, Miss Bailey sometimes noticed and told them to get back to work. This made me feel a trifle guilty since I realized that she suspected I was undermining rather than affirming—or even taking a neutral relationship to—classroom order. I noticed that Miss Bailey always refused when her students offered loans or gifts and the particularized, nonprofessional relationships they entail. But, seeking closer, more lateral ties, I accepted offers of potato chips, a cookie, a nickel; and I occasionally gave kids pencils and small change, which we called loans, although they were never returned. Once Miss Bailey saw me give a pencil to Matt when he asked if I had an extra one. She firmly told him to return the pencil to me and to get his own. I understood her actions; as a teacher, she tried to maintain social distance and a guise of universalistic treatment, and when I teach, I do the same thing. The kids called her "Miss Bailey," while I asked them to call me by my first name, another set of disparate practices that set me apart from the teacher.

I came to realize that within the classroom, the teacher and I were working at cross-purposes. Miss Bailey had lessons to teach, authority to maintain, the need to construct and display an orderly classroom. I was a kind of sideline booster, rooting for the moments when kids brought out their own artifacts and built their own worlds of talk and interaction.

I had an observational feast on a day when there was a substitute teacher who "couldn't keep control," in the words of a disgusted bilingual aide who came for several hours each day. The kids made lots of noise and ran boisterously about; a group of them talked loudly about who had beat up whom in the third grade, and who could now beat up whom. They brought out objects that were usually kept relatively under cover—a skateboard magazine, a rubber finger with a long nail, bags of nuts and potato chips—and openly passed them around. As the kids walked out the door for lunch, Jessie, one of the girls who had joined in the talk about fighting, got into an angry fist fight with Allen. This was the one fight where I intervened; the substitute teacher and I jointly worked to separate their flailing bodies. In the lunchroom Jessie retreated to sit with a group of girls, and talk about the fight went on for the rest of the day. After lunch a row of girls sat on the radiator and threw an eraser at several boys, who threw it back in an improvised game of catch. Another group went to the blackboard and drew hearts encircling different boy-girl paired names.

Mr. Welch, the principal, came in once and told the class to behave, but the effect was short-lived, and the substitute teacher seemed resigned to the chaos. I observed for three hours and that night typed up eleven single-spaced pages of notes, rich with descriptions of gender boundaries and antagonism, sexual idioms, interactions among boys and among girls, and crossing between same-gender groups. When I returned to the classroom two days later, Miss Bailey lamented the students' "sub behavior." Her managerial low was my highpoint of juicy witnessing.

TUGS OF MEMORY, AND THE CHILD WITHIN

When I colluded with the kids in breaking rules, especially when the teacher was watching, I remembered how it felt to be caught in similar situations in my own elementary school days. In the spring just after the buzzer rang at the end of an Oceanside school day, Miss Bailey called out across the room, "Barrie, Mr. Welch wants to talk with you." Several kids picked up the ominous connotations and called around the room, "Mr. Welch wants to see Barrie!" For a moment, I felt like a child being brought to task, and the class laughed with a similar reaction. Mr. Welch, it turned out, wanted me to tell him how my research was going, an inquiry that drew my adult self back to the fore.

Tugs of memory pulled on other occasions as well, especially during the first few months of fieldwork. When I began observing, I also began a chain of remembering. There was a close familiarity with the scaled-down desks and tables, the blackboards and stylized graphics on classroom walls, the sight of worn-out red rubber kickballs and dirty jump ropes, smells of wax in the hallways and urine in the girls' bathroom, the loud buzzers that govern so many local routines, the lining up, the clatter of voices in the cafeteria, and the distinctive sing-song tones of teachers. Varied sights, smells, and sounds brought me back to the Woodruff School in Logan, Utah, in the early 1950s.

Memories of my own experiences in fourth and fifth grades scatter through my fieldnotes, especially when a specific girl (boys didn't evoke such remembering) reminded me of a vivid figure from my own childhood. Three of the girls in the Oceanside fourth/fifth-grade classroom continually evoked my memories of, and feelings about, specific girls from my past: the most popular girl; a girl who was quiet, whiny, and a loner; and a girl who was unkempt, smelled, and was treated as a pariah. When I made these associations, the names of their 1950s doubles came immediately to mind.

After a few days of observing, I had figured out that Kathryn was the most popular girl in the classroom. Her cute face, stylish curly brown hair, nice clothes, and general poise and friendliness were easy to notice, and she received a lot of deference from both girls and boys. In situations where individual privileges were granted, for example, to choose and touch bowed heads in games of "seven-up" or to hand out balls in preparation for recess, Kathryn got more than her share. Miss Bailey often chose Kathryn to run errands to the main office or to do other tasks that marked out favored students. After a few weeks at Oceanside, I realized that my fieldnotes were obsessed with documenting Kathryn's popularity. "The rich get richer," I thought to myself as I sorted out yet another occasion when Kathryn got extra attention and resources. Then I realized the envy behind my note-taking and analysis and recalled that many years ago when I was a fourth- and fifth-grader of middling social status, I had also carefully watched the popular girl, using a kind of applied sociology to figure out my place in a charged social network.

In the course of my fieldwork, I felt aversion rather than envy toward Beth, a quiet fourth grader, who continually asked me to sit by her at lunch. Initially I was glad for an invitation. But when I discovered that Beth had few friends, that sitting with her, rather than, say, next to Kathryn, brought minimal social yield, and that Beth also wanted me to stick by her on the playground, I felt, as I wrote in my fieldnotes, associating to my own elementary-school past, "as if Beatrice Johnson had me trapped." When Beth requested my company, I began to respond vaguely ("maybe"; "we'll see"), much as I had in fifth grade when I felt Beatrice was trying to cling to me and I didn't want her social encumbrance.

Rita, another girl in the present who evoked strong memories from my own past childhood, was from a family with thirteen children and an overworked single-parent father (Jessica, who told the story of their mother's departure, was Rita's sister). Rita, who took care of her own grooming, had tangled hair and wore dirty, ill-fitting, and mismatched clothes; she seemed withdrawn and depressed. The first time I came close to Rita, leaning over to help her with work in the classroom, I was struck by the smell. I wrote in my fieldnotes:

> Rita's hair was quite dirty, greasy at the roots, and it smelled. There was dirt on her cheek, and her hands were smudged. She wore the same clothes she had on yesterday: a too small, short blue nylon sweater with white buttons and dirt on the back, and green cotton pants that didn't zip right. Leaning over and catching the scent of her hair, I thought of Edith Schulz, whom we all avoided in the fifth grade. I remember Edith, whose parents were immigrants from Germany, wearing a cotton sleeveless blouse and dirndl skirt in the dead of winter. The smell, the incongruous clothing—the signs, I now see, of poverty—set her apart, like Rita; both were treated like pariahs.[10]

In such moments of remembering I felt in touch with my child self. I moved from the external vantage points of an observer, an adult authority, and a "least adult" trying to understand kids' interactions in a more open and lateral way, to feeling more deeply inside their worlds. This experience occurred only when I was with girls. With boys, my strongest moments of identification came not through regression to feeling like one of them, but from more maternal feelings. Sometimes a particular boy would remind me of my son, and I would feel a wave of empathy and affection. But I generally felt more detached and less emotionally bound up with the boys.

Joel, a boy who was socially isolated and overweight, often tried to tag along with me, seeking my company and cover. After several lunchtimes spent talking with him, I made excuses to give myself more room to wander, excuses like those I offered to Beth. But I staved him off without the edge of annoyance, anchored in memories of Beatrice Johnson, that I felt with Beth. The differences in my responses to girls and to boys led me to ponder the emotional legacy of my own gender-separated elementary school years.

I felt closer to the girls not only through memories of my own past, but also because I knew more about their gender-typed interactions. I had once played games like jump rope and statue buyer, but I had never ridden a skateboard and had barely tried sports like basketball and soccer. Paradoxically, however, I sometimes felt I could see boys' interactions and activities more clearly than those of girls; I came with fresher eyes and a more detached perspective. I found it harder to articulate and analyze the social relations of girls, perhaps because of my closer identification, but also, I believe, because our categories for understanding have been developed more out of the lives of boys and men than girls and women.

Were my moments of remembering, the times when I felt like a ten-year-old girl, a source of distortion or insight? Both, I believe. The identification enhanced my sense of what it feels like to be a fourth- and fifth-grade girl in a school setting. I lived that world in another time and place, but the similarities are evocative. Memory, like observing, is a way of knowing and can be a rich resource.[11]

But memories are also fragile and mysterious, continuously reconstructed by the needs of the present and by yearnings and fears of the past. Memories can distort as well as enrich present perceptions. Beth was a different person, in another time and place, than the Beatrice that I recalled and no doubt had mentally reworked and stereotyped from my childhood. When my own responses, like my obsession with documenting Kathryn's popularity, were driven by emotions like envy or aversion, they clearly obscured my ability to grasp the full social situation. As Jennifer Hunt (1989) has observed, in the course of field research, unconscious processes may both enhance and interfere with empathy.

As I got in touch with the effects of memory and emotion, I altered my strategies for observing. My memories evoked the standpoint of a girl in the middle of the social hierarchy, who envied those above, who was susceptible to but used strategies for avoiding the claims of someone below, and who felt contaminated by a girl on the margins. During my months in Miss Bailey's classroom I thought a lot about those experiences, and I worked to see kids' interactions from other, and varied, perspectives. Instead of obsessing over Kathryn and avoiding Beth or Rita, I tried to understand their different social positions and experiences, and those of other girls and boys. This emphasis on multiple standpoints and meanings came to inform my understanding of gender.

I want to mention one final paradox in this particular relationship between the knower and those she sought to know. I like to think of myself as having hung out in classrooms, lunchrooms, playgrounds, relating to kids in a friendly and sometimes helpful fashion, and treating them, in my analysis and writing, with respect. But, like all fieldworkers, I was also a spectator, even a voyeur, passing through their lives and sharing few real stakes with those I studied. Several kids asked me if I was a spy, and, in a way, I was, especially when I went in search of the activities and meanings they created when not in the company of adults. Schools are physically set up to maximize the surveillance of students, with few private spaces and a staff who continually watch with eyes that mix benign pedagogical goals, occasional affection, and the wish to control. Kids sometimes resist this surveillance, and I wanted to observe and document their more autonomous collective moments. But in the very act of documenting their autonomy, I undermined it, for my gaze remained, at its core and in its ultimate knowing purpose, that of a more powerful adult.[12]

On the other hand, "adult," like "child," is too unitary a category. A growing sense of multiplicity and context brought me to question the use of dualistic frameworks not only for understanding gender, but also for understanding categories related to age. The dichotomy between "adult" and "child" is not a given of biology or nature; chronological and developmental age are complex continua, with enormous variation between and among five-, twelve-, and thirty-five-year-olds (Thorne 1993:135–56). People often negotiate the use of labels like "child," "teen, and "adult." However, we mark and reinforce an "adult/child" dualism— we produce categories like "the adult" and "the child"—through cultural practices such as channeling young people into elementary schools where five- and eleven-year-olds are cast together in the position of students and subordinates, with adults on the other "side" (a boundary I continually encountered in my efforts to lessen social distance between me and the kids).

NOTES

[1] For interesting essays on uses of the self and personal experience in doing social science, see Susan Krieger (1991).

[2] Vivian Gussin Paley (1986), a teacher who taped and then wrote about her interactions with young children, describes a similar effort of consciousness.

[3] Nancy Mandell (1988) describes a similar shift of consciousness in her observations in a preschool.

[4] In *The Prelude: Or Growth of a Poet's Mind*, William Wordsworth wrote about the creative power that comes from reliving childhood experience, with the outer world "striking upon what is found within." Examining the biographical experiences of creative people, Edith Cobb (1997) and Vera John-Steiner (1985) argue that adult creativity is nurtured by access to the child within. In a contribution from psychoanalytic theory, Ernest G Schachtel (1959) contends that children have unique access to sensory experience.

[5] Mandell (1988) writes about her efforts to create a position of "least adult" in a preschool; similar strategies are reported by Corsaro (1985) and by Bronwyn Davies (1989). Gary Alan Fine, who was a participant-observer with ten- to twelve-year-old boys on Little League baseball teams, and Barry Glassner, who observed in an elementary school, tried to hang out, mixing friendliness with minimal authority (Fine and Glassner 1979). All these observers avoided intervening and disciplining, except when there was a chance of serious physical injury. For a review of these and other discussions of participant-observation with children, see Gary Alan Fine and Kent L. Sandstrom (1988)

[6] Corsaro (1985), Mandell (1988), and Fine and Glassner (1979) also describe their efforts to contain adult requests for help. These requests exemplify a recurring feature in our culture's organization of children's worlds: a low ratio of adults to children and an assumption that more adult hands are always welcome, and will readily be made available, in the managerial tasks.

[7] Bronwyn Davies (1982) also discusses the dual agendas of classrooms—one set by the teacher and another, running parallel and sometimes contradictory or complementary, set by students. Also see Philip A. Cusick, *Inside High School* (1973).

[8] Erving Goffman, *Asylums* (1961). Corsaro (1985) describes processes of sharing and dispute among preschool children who smuggled in forbidden objects from home

[9] For further analyses of ritualized exchanges among children, see Tamar Katriel ("'Bexibudim!': Ritualized Sharing among Israeli Children" 1987), who observed stylized sharing of treats by children on the way home from school, and Elliot Mishler, "Wou' You Trade Cookies with the Popcorn? Talk of Trades among Six Year Olds" (1979b).

10 Social class was more inscribed in the appearance of girls than of boys. In both schools boys wore mostly T-shirts and solid-colored jeans or pants, whereas girls' clothing ranged more widely in design, fit, materials, and colors, and hence could go more easily awry. Furthermore, standards of grooming are also more exacting for girls than for boys. Girls from more impoverished backgrounds, like Rita and Jessica, wore mismatched patterns and fabric, and pants whose seats bulged out from wear. In contrast, girls from more affluent families, like Kathryn, wore well-matched "outfits" (the word itself is telling)

11 In several evocative studies, adult women have drawn on their own memories as a research tool for learning about experiences of girlhood in a patriarchal culture. See Walkerdine, *Schoolgirl Fictions*, and Frigga Haug, *Female Sexualization A Collective Work of Memory*, which explains an interesting methodology of collective "memory-work."

12 Walkerdine (1990) analyzes the "adult gaze" in teaching and in research with children.

Constructing Participant/ Observation Relations

Robert M. Emerson
Melvin Pollner

The reflexive thrust of contemporary ethnography has led to ever deepening examination of the tacit practices and presuppositions of fieldwork. Early self-analyses that focused on the (typically practical) problems of accessing and exiting the field, for example, evolved into questioning the very notion of the "field" itself (see this volume, pp. 42–44). One strand of this questioning urges "reinventing the field" in order to expand the boundaries of ethnographic attention and to transform ethnographic practice: thus Gupta and Ferguson (1997:4) recommend abandoning a spatial notion of the field as bounded place and its associated practices and presuppositions. A different impulse highlights the socially constructed character of "the field." Clifford (1997) in particular has argued that while movement ("dislocation," "displacement") literally brings the ethnographer to a different place, the critical processes in constituting the field derive from the ethnographer's distinctive "professional habitus" and representational practices. Addressed through disciplinary concerns and methods and culminating in textual representation, the spaces, inhabitants and interactions of one or another "community" are consolidated and transformed into the object and site of ethnographic scrutiny—"the field."

To focus primarily upon ethnographers' practices as field-constituting activities, however, neglects the feature of fieldwork which distinguishes it from most other social science methodologies: *embodied presence in the daily lives of those who host the research.* Some form of immediate presence is the sine qua non of ethnography; some degree of participation is unavoidable in order to establish a place and identity for oneself—and one's research activities—in the local setting

Written expressly for *Contemporary Field Research: Perspectives and Formulations, 2/E*

or community. Ethnographers must create and maintain this presence in ongoing encounters and negotiations with the people who are both hosts for and
objects of research activities. As Atkinson insists: "[t]he boundaries of the field
are not given" but are the outcome of what the ethnographer "may negotiate
with hosts and informants" (1992:9). In this sense, the ethnographer constructs
the field not simply through gaze and representation but also, and more fundamentally, by negotiating interactional presence to local events and scenes that
can then be made subject to disciplinary gaze and textual representation.[1]

Not only is "the field" a negotiated construct, so too is the identity of "fieldworker": a researcher seeking to establish a social place from which to do ethnography must secure and sustain categorization and treatment as a
"fieldworker" in actual interactions with those whose lives and circumstances
are of interest. As the researcher cognitively, interactionally and inscriptively
attempts to institute the field and herself as a fieldworker, she does so in the
midst of a host able to accept, ignore and resist such impositions. In contrast to
other methodologies in which the researcher transforms a domain into a
research object merely by intention and inscription, the fieldworker *in situ* must
invite, encourage or cajole her hosts to be objects of ethnographic scrutiny—to
be the "field"—and to allow the researcher to be a "fieldworker."[2]

Ethnographers have typically addressed these issues within the framework
of participant/observation, using the term to identify a tension inherent in their
efforts to comprehend and study social life: how to strike a balance between
closeness and distance, between involvement and detachment (Reinharz
1992:67–71). On the one hand, the participant-observer seeks to get close to
those studied, to become immersed in their everyday life. The ethnographer
desires empathetic understanding of the daily routines and subjective meanings
of the researched, seeking, in Goffman's (1989:125–26) terms, to "penetrate" their
"circle of response to their social situation" at a depth that brings visceral appreciation of local scenes, smells and standards. On the other hand, the participant-
observer must at some point disengage and distance himself from local scenes
and relations. In addition to eventually leaving the field, the fieldworker often
needs to establish the distance that will allow him to observe (rather than shape
or simply experience) the naturally occurring activity. Even Goffman, who seems
to have advocated ethnographic involvement until the fieldworker felt able to
"settle down and forget about being a sociologist," advised "forcing yourself to be
tuned into something that you then pick up *as a witness*—not as an interviewer,
not as a listener, but as a witness to how they respond to what gets done to and
around them" (this volume; emphasis added).

Ethnography, then, can be examined for how ethnographers "do closeness"
on the one hand and "do distance" on the other. Yet analyses of constructing par-
ticipant/observer relations are skewed: discussions of fieldwork methods have
devoted much attention to the processes of immersing oneself in and getting
close to the lifeworlds of others, considering specific strategies for "entering"
(Schatzman and Strauss 1973:18–33), sustaining "continuing access" (Lofland
and Lofland 1995:53–63), and moving beyond "respectful distance" to intimate

closeness (Reinharz 1992:68). It should not be surprising that processes for decreasing distance have tended to preoccupy fieldworkers; this concern mirrors the ordinary sequence of priorities in most fieldwork. The researcher must, after all, get in the door and become welcome before she can begin to do fieldwork in earnest. Distance, especially at the start of the project, is often construed as an obstacle to be overcome, and later, even when desired, appears readily attained. Similarly, "observing" would initially appear to involve an unproblematic, minimalist form of being present in social happenings.

In contrast, the other constituent of participant observation—practices for "doing distance," for staying sufficiently detached to witness what life circumstances do to these others—has received little attention.[3] Reinharz has observed that "general methodological writings about participant observation have an unwarranted (male-oriented?) assumption that the researcher can control his/ her stance" (1992:59). While we might have reservations about the imputed source of this assumption, it is indeed clear that researchers must negotiate the boundaries and nature of their involvement with their hosts from *within* the social world of the host. Unlike laboratory researchers whose one-way mirrors provide distance and allow completely unengaged observation, however, fieldworkers cannot necessarily stand back and watch social interaction with absolutely no involvement with those engaged in that interaction. Nor can the fieldworker simply declare a detached position by fiat: host members may resist the researcher's definition of his level of (non-) involvement and even ignore his self-definition as a researcher, analyst or observer. The fieldworker's recurrent problem is to achieve the distance necessary to observe while physically and socially present to those who are the objects of such observation.[4] Thus, constructing distance, though rarely in the methodological spotlight, can be as complex and consequential as the more commonly considered concerns of access and rapport. Turning to "doing distance" as an interactional process, then, corrects the imbalance in the ethnographic literature and contributes to understanding how the boundary between "field" and "fieldworker," so fundamental to the possibility of ethnography, is collaboratively constituted.

Boundary Work in Participant/Observation

The slash in participant/observation symbolizes the apportionment of a fieldworker's activities between the two modes of presence in the field: participation and observation. Ethnographic precepts and perspectives encourage the researcher to position the slash at different points on the continuum—some toward the observation pole, others toward the participatory pole.[5] Regardless of whether "participation" or "observation" is emphasized, however, decisions regarding the distribution of involvement between the two poles are inherent in ethnography. These decisions, as we have suggested, are not unilateral but a collaborative achievement of host and researcher.

From the point of view of the fieldworker, hosts may pose two major challenges: initiating exclusionary pushes to the periphery as the researcher seeks presence at the center of the group, and making inclusionary pulls to the center as he seeks to remain on the margins. Prototypical forms of *exclusion* are initiated by hosts in refusing to allow the fieldworker to enter or remain in the field; a less extreme form of such exclusion involves more partial denials of fieldworker presence on particular occasions. This exclusionary impulse may take more focused, specific form in hosts' efforts to eliminate or remove certain happenings from what is to constitute the field. For example, hosts may attempt to mark certain events as "out of bounds" for observation by asking that the fieldworker not include them in her fieldnotes:

> A field researcher studying divorce mediation had been openly taking notes while interviewing a mediator about a session just completed. "[the mediator] began to apply some eye make-up while I was finishing writing down some observations. She flashed me a mock disgusted look and said, 'Are you writing *this* down too!' indicating the activity with her eye pencil." (Emerson et al. 1995:23)[6]

The fieldworker himself may delimit or restrict his field by self-consciously staying out of certain places and situations, or by deliberately abandoning the position of observer, as Johnson (1975:159) reports doing in deciding not to write notes while in the throes of an emotionally charged moment.[7]

Less appreciated is the second source of threats to "doing observation"— pressures toward increased *inclusion*.[8] Indeed, a major threat to observation is often not that the researcher will be expelled by the observed, but rather than the researcher will be accorded some more consequential presence in ongoing scenes and relations. Such excessive involvement can arise from hosts who entice the researcher into more participatory roles or who engage the researcher other than as "fieldworker." At the extreme, the researcher may be pressured to become a fully committed participant. Or excessive participation can arise from the fieldworker's enthusiastic embrace of opportunities for fuller, more central participation in local life; at an extreme, the researcher may "go native" or "become the phenomenon" (Mehan and Woods 1975). The result in either case is an erosion of the boundary that divides and distinguishes the "field" from the "fieldworker."

Participant/observation stances vary in their direct vulnerability to such challenges and, relatedly, to the task of overtly and interactionally maintaining a boundary in situ. While classic participant-observers routinely adopted more or less detached, witnessing stances toward local happenings, some contemporary ethnographers de-emphasize observation in favor of active participation. In such "complete membership" (Adler and Alder 1987) or "experiential" fieldwork (Reinharz 1979, 1992), the fieldworker seeks to participate as an active or full member in naturally occurring activities and scenes, at the moment abandoning concern with distance and detachment in favor of intense, "natural" involvement. Thus it might appear that detached observation has no place in this approach to fieldwork. But deep immersion and experiential fieldwork do not so much abandon detachment as postpone it; in subsequently writing fieldnotes, for example, the fieldworker will necessarily reflect on and achieve distance from these experiences, turning them into recorded observations. Furthermore, there may be moments and occasions in such an experiential field where the field-worker decides to forego active participation in order to observe events and actions which she had no direct part in creating, hence having to create and sustain a visible, interactionally managed observational position.[9]

Alternatively, participant/observation may not rely on negotiated arrangements between an identified "researcher" and "research subjects." The clearest instance involves ethnographic accounts based entirely on recollections of events and experiences that were not at that time matters of research interest and concern, as in Turner's (1947) analysis of the work of the navy disbursing officer. Here the field is constituted retrospectively, as past events are remembered and reconstructed as matters for description and analysis in ways that are entirely under the control of the now-ethnographer. At the time these events occurred, of course, there was no research, no field, no ethnography, and indeed, no ethnographer. More mixed examples arise with disguised fieldwork, where the fieldworker pursues research goals while those studied remain unaware that research is taking place. This can occur both in classic covert fieldwork, where the ethnographer reveals neither professional identity nor the existence of a research project to those studied (e.g., *When Prophecy Fails*); and in autoethnography where those encountering the ethnographer in the course of his daily activities have not been informed of the fact of ongoing research. Here the field is actively but asymmetrically constructed by the ethnographer, since those studied do not know there is a field; but this occurs (in the case of covert fieldwork) by means of the interactional moves and stratagems through which the ethnographer "passes" while maneuvering into places yielding the kinds of observations and information desired. Interactional negotiations take place, but what is negotiated is only understood as matters of research by one of the parties.

Our analysis, then, addresses ethnographies involving encounters between a known, identified researcher and hosts who are aware of the fact of being studied—the situation of classic participant observation. Using a variety of accounts of fieldwork experience (including our own), we consider, first, how the distance associated with the position of "observer" is sometimes transgressed or dissolved by the host group. Specifically, we inventory how a host, wittingly or not, may refuse to allow a field researcher to be merely or only a "researcher" or an "observer" (or less an "observer" than the fieldworker would prefer to be) and draw her more deeply into local matters. In contrast to the processes through which individuals are systematically excluded from participation in various settings Lemert described in his classic "Paranoia and the Dynamics of Exclusion" (1962), the practices considered here comprise what might be termed the *dynamics of inclusion*. Second, we survey the ad hoc efforts recounted by fieldworkers to sidestep deeper involvement or to extricate themselves when they find that they have become excessively active participants. Examining the practices for doing, undoing and preserving "observer" highlights the practices through which the central duality of ethnography—"fieldworker" and "field"—is constituted and, from time to time, demolished.

INCLUSIVE OVERTURES

We have argued that while exclusion can in fact be a substantial threat to participant-observation fieldwork, at least as great dangers derive from tendencies toward inclusion, from pressures to become more of a participant, less of a researcher. For although the fieldworker may plan and proffer a distribution of observation and involvement, the host group, pursuing its own concerns and understandings, may disregard or override the projected boundaries. Accounts by fieldworkers suggest three related types of overtures for increased participation that arise with particular frequency: overtures that seek to utilize the fieldworker as a resource; incorporate her as a co-member; or engage her as a person.

Fieldworker as Resource

The ethnographer often brings attributes and possessions useful to the host. The very physical presence of the researcher, for example, may prove to be a resource that the host may incorporate and use in their everyday activities. In a study of police work (Ericson 1981:37), detectives identified the fieldworker as a researcher to citizens except in encounters involving potentially troublesome suspects; here, during search and interrogations detectives remained silent about the researcher's identity, thereby implying that he was a detective in order to increase the aura of intimidation. Researchers may sometimes be identified as a superior, authority, or expert who is then called upon to support the members in dealing with dubious or recalcitrant clients. Gussow (1964:236), for example, describes several incidents in which teachers used fieldworker entry into the classroom to chide classes for their unruly behavior.

The fieldworker provides not only a body whose imputed identity can be incorporated into ongoing activities but also one capable of actual work. With some frequency fieldworkers are used as an extra pair of hands for sundry tasks. Johnson, for example, reports that over the course of his investigations of a social welfare office he served as driver, reader, luggage porter, babysitter, money lender, ticket taker, note taker, phone answerer, book reader, book lender, adviser on automobile purchases, party arranger, bodyguard, letter writer, messenger, and other roles (1975:107). Indeed, fieldworkers occasionally become useful to the hosts as an addition to or substitute for regular workers. In our research on psychiatric emergency teams (see Emerson and Pollner 1976) typically composed of two persons, for example, some team members felt that a second team member was not necessary because one of the researchers could serve as a backup. In fact, at one point it was half-jokingly suggested that, given our experience, we, the two fieldworkers, would comprise the team.

The fieldworker may also bear valued or needed resources. Although money is probably the most common asset lit upon by hosts, anthropologists may be accessible sources of medicine (McCurdy 1976). Close relations with a "key informant" often involves the ethnographer providing a wide range of resources and services; Patricia and Peter Adler (1987:41), for example, report not only having housed their primary drug-trafficking informant for seven months, "but over the six years we were involved in the research we also fed him, clothed him, took care of his children, wrote letters of reference on his behalf, helped to organize his criminal defense, visited him in jail, gave him money, and testified in child support court for him."

The fieldworker may not only be utilized in ongoing concerns and tasks but may also inspire the host to develop projects fitted to the unique possibilities afforded by his presence. In addition to being treated as a "gofer" and extra pair of hands by the residents of the teaching hospital he studied, Bosk (1979) was also enlisted as a source of information from the "outside" world from which houseofficers felt cut off; as a sounding board for various dissatisfactions; as a referee for conflicts; and as an informal group "historian." Or the ethnographer's social capital may make her attractive as an agent or spokesperson for the group. In her study of Alzheimer's day-care centers, Lyman (1993:203) came to feel a sense of responsibility to staff and patients deriving from her insider access and also from the requests made by staff and implicitly by patients; indeed, one staff member told her, "I see you as an advocate."

Fieldworkers, of course, are often willing and even eager to provide desired resources to hosts. But the consequence of doing so may be heightened involvement in activities peripheral or irrelevant to the research project, an involvement which may threaten to overrun fieldwork purposes. McCurdy (1976), for example, found his capacity to conduct his research seriously threatened by villagers who sought his modest supply of antibiotics. The medicines worked so well against local bacteria that he became besieged by requests for treatment, requests that constantly interfered with his opportunities to observe tribal life. "They would catch me," he writes, "as I hurried to meet an informant for an interview, interrupt as I tried to type fieldnotes, or pull me away from the observation of an interesting religious event" (1976:14). Greater involvement on the hosts' terms, then, directly impinged upon the fieldworker's ability to conduct the kinds of observations he intended.

Fieldworker as Member

While some fieldworkers self-consciously attempt to establish themselves as partial or complete members, even detached participant-observers may find themselves subject to inclusive pressures to become a member of the communities or organizations they study. At the extreme, a host may exert a comprehensive claim on the fieldworker's involvement through overtures to become a full member. This kind of total overture is frequently encountered in proselytizing groups for whom others—virtually any other—are prospective converts. While such groups may be readily approached and "observed," the group may ultimately ask a high price—the fieldworker's total commitment and participation. Lofland's experiences with what proved to be the beginning of the Unification Church are illustrative of how the group may regard the fieldworker first and foremost as a prospective member (1966:274):

> [Ms.] Lee [a leader] told me that she was tired of playing the "studying the movement" game. She made it clear that she was very concerned that, after

all these months and all that the members had told me, I had not become a convert. I responded that my interest was necessarily professional. Lee expressed regret: "If I had known from the beginning that you only looked at our Precepts as a scientist—why should I have bothered?"

More commonly, hosts may come to accord the fieldworker a quasi-membership role while recognizing that the researcher is not a true member. Leo (1995:121–22, and this volume), for example, received repeated invitations from detectives to "actively participate in the interrogation process" he attempted to study. Thus:

> . . . several of the robbery detectives invited me to step outside of my role as a detached observer and to interrogate suspects myself. In one instance, two detectives loaded me up with a badge, a pair of handcuffs, a beeper and an empty holster.

Beyond total or partial efforts to make a researcher a member, host groups may effect tacit conversions. Simply "hanging around" the local culture often shapes a fieldworker's sensibility and comportment to a greater degree than they initially realize. Just as an observer may surreptitiously infiltrate the host group, the host group may surreptitiously infiltrate the observer. The venerable Evans-Pritchard (1976:244) describes how living among the Azande altered some fundamental beliefs about reality:

> Azande were talking about witchcraft daily, both among them and to me; any communication was well nigh impossible unless one took witchcraft for granted. . . . I had to act as though I trusted the Zande oracles and therefore to give assent to their dogma of witchcraft, whatever reservations I might have. If I wanted to go hunting or on a journey, for instance, no one would willingly accompany me unless I was able to produce a verdict of the poison oracle that all would be well, that witchcraft did not threaten our project; and if one goes on arranging one's affairs, organizing one's life in harmony with the lives of one's hosts, whose companionship one seeks and without which one would sink into disoriented craziness, one must eventually give way, or at any rate partially give way. If one must act as though one believed, one ends in believing, or half-believing as one acts.

Clearly the attractions of membership become seductive to many ethnographers, leading to gradually increasing levels of immersion and involvement. Some may indeed ultimately "go native" and abandon the research enterprise; but more common in the fieldwork literature are reports of fieldworkers who, having reached their "personal limits" (Adler and Adler 1987:79), drew back from intense involvement or abandoned the field entirely. "Adopted by" and having functioned as part of a Japanese family, Kondo (1990:17, and this volume) describes coming to this limit and the subsequent change in her fieldwork:

> As I glanced into the shiny metal surface of the butcher's display case, I noticed someone who looked terribly familiar: a typical young housewife, clad in slip-on sandals and the loose, cotton shifts called "home wear" (homu wea), a woman walking with a characteristically Japanese bend to the knees

and a sliding of the feet. Suddenly I clutched the handle of the stroller to steady myself as a wave of dizziness washed over me, for I realized I had caught a glimpse of nothing less than my own reflection. Fear that perhaps I would never emerge from this world into which I was immersed inserted itself into my mind and stubbornly refused to leave, until I resolved to move into a new apartment, to distance myself from my Japanese home and my Japanese existence.

Similarly, severe emotional upset when she actually began to see "spirit figures or hallucinations," accompanied by drastic weight loss, led Forrest (1986:445) to abandon completely her full-membership "apprentice-participation" research on spiritualism.[10]

Fieldworker as Person

Frequently, ties with those studied draw heavily upon the fieldworker's personal attributes, particularly congeniality and personal attractiveness. A research procedure relying upon personal ties, fieldwork almost inevitably generates tendencies to expand and deepen these ties in ways that ignore and may ultimately obliterate the fieldworker's research commitments. The researcher may be able to modulate these developing personal relations by limiting intimacy, thus balancing the often conflicting pulls of personal and research relations. But the direction and intensity of a relation are not unilaterally determined and fieldworkers may find that, having taken a step in the level of intimacy, their subjects demand or expect that they will take more. In treating the fieldworker as a "friend," for example, host members may assume a relational reciprocity demanding more self-disclosure than the fieldworker had anticipated:

> And we're rapping about the situation at God's Love (commune) and where her head's at, etc., and then, just as an afterthought, she says, "Are you a Christian?" And I went into my stereotyped song and dance about "This is a study and I can't talk about," etc., and she got furious. She was very angry, and she went on about how she considered me to be a friend, and she had told me intimate things about herself and I had acted friendly and then all of a sudden I had copped out on a friendship whenever she asked a personal question of me. She also said something about how I was trying to cop out of being a Christian by doing a "scientific trip." (taped fieldnote) (Robbins et al. 1973:266)

Hosts may make claims on the personal life of the observer not simply through friendship and praise but also through emotional button-pushing which effectively pulls the researcher into their emotional orbit. Myerhoff (1989:89), for example, describes how the elderly Jewish members of the senior citizen center she studied subjected her to guilt-inducing criticisms:

> After greeting me warmly, Basha would often ask, "Never mind these other things you all the time ask about. Tell me who's with your children?" Men and women alike would admire a new skirt or dress I wore, then turn over my hem for inspection. Nathan remarked, "For a lady professor, you don't do so good with a needle."

This barrage of criticism, combined with the guilt from comparing her youth, strength and future with those of her elderly hosts, led her to consider leaving the field: "It was unbearable to abide the countless ways in which the Center people used guilt, often unconsciously," she writes, "intending not to hurt but only to make themselves feel potent." (1989:89)

Probably one of the more frequent personal overtures involves sex. Fieldwork accounts in the 1960s and 1970s broke the earlier silence about sexual happenings in the field to recount *hosts'* sexual "motivations, imputations, and unwanted overtures" (Warren and Hackney 2000:26), thereby depicting the field as a place generating at least occasional sexual provocations and dangers.[11] More recent discussion of *fieldworkers'* sexual attraction and activities (see Warren and Hackney 2000:26–35) has begun to puncture "the myth of the chaste fieldworker" (Fine 1993), suggesting that neither fieldworkers nor their hosts are exempt from the human condition, that personal relations in the field may well assume sexual dimensions. Indeed, whether or not this occurs is not a unilateral decision under the control of the fieldworker, for members of the host community may well sexualize what had been a research relation in ways that undermine further fieldwork. For example, in responding to the overly enthusiastic used-car salesmen she was studying, Brown found it necessary "to leave the field for a while and let things cool off naturally rather than face a showdown and lose an informant" (1971:78; see also Warren and Hackney 2000:31–35).

MANAGING INCLUSIVE OVERTURES

While fieldworkers frequently feel pulls toward greater involvement, whether from hosts' enticements, the attractions of immersion, or both, the participant-observer generally tries to resist or to accede only in part. The involvement may be emotionally draining, physically dangerous, or ethically and legally problematic. Acceptance of overtures to perform as part of the "team" or to support one or another local faction may delimit access to other factions. Further, increased involvement may affect the very processes one seeks to observe. Thus, in "doing participant-observation" fieldworkers rely on a variety of distancing practices to manage overtures to deeper involvement. We will consider four such practices—interactional efforts to preclude, to finesse, and to decline overtures for greater involvement, and cognitive reminders to retain the "research" framing of one's experiences in the field.

Preempting

From the point of view of sustaining fieldwork distance, the qualities and styles usually considered obstacles to rapport can ward off unwanted overtures before they begin. Many common field relations have this character: A white European among black or brown third-world peoples, women among men, a young graduate student among older, experienced workers, are effectively preempted from certain forms of involvement. The role of novice, initiate, or learner may also serve to preclude inclusionary moves, and some fieldworkers will work long and hard to hold on to their apparent ignorance of local ways exactly in order to enjoy this exemption. In general, if the fieldworker happens to be unattractive or useless in terms of group needs and interests, or can alter or minimize qualities that would attract host interest as resource, member or friend, overtures may be nipped in the bud.

Furthermore, most fieldworkers devote considerable effort right at the start to establishing an implicit contract with their hosts allowing presence at and participation in local happenings but in restricted, limited ways. In initially negotiating access to a setting, for example, fieldworkers often try to set limits on participation, proclaiming their intent to act as only partial and detached participants in these activities. Seeking to avoid involvements that could easily become all encompassing and/or that are personally and morally unacceptable to the fieldworker, the researcher may stipulate the degree of involvement in which he is prepared to indulge. Sanchez-Jankowski (1991:13) notes, for example, that as part of the "mutual understanding" with the many gangs he observed, "it was agreed that I did not have to participate in any activity (including taking drugs) that was illegal."

Within specific interactions, the fieldworker may seek a position at the edges of the unfolding event. Almost by definition, the periphery of whatever focused engagements comprise a setting's main involvement (Goffman 1963b) are attractive niches for observing. Through initial preempting moves, along the lines of "I'm here to watch you do it" and "I'm not qualified or inclined to help you do it," fieldworkers attempt to stay on the periphery, to establish a distinctively nonconsequential presence in these interactions. Johnson (1975:102), for example, after being frequently drawn into the center of client home visits on being mistaken for a welfare worker, adopted the following strategy with the social workers he accompanied into client homes:

> I would tell them that it appeared that the physical location of the furniture in nearly all the homes included at the minimum a couch and an adjacent chair. From earlier experiences, it seemed interaction would not focus on the researcher if he was positioned at either end of the couch-chair combination. So the social workers were instructed to "manage" me to one end or the other, out of the direct line of fire, to reduce the chances that my presence in the setting would disturb the ongoing interactions.

Of course, staying on the margins may require active work, and fieldworkers often show great agility in resetting themselves at the outer edge as the fore- and background regions of a setting form and shift. Moreover, sustaining noninvolvement at the periphery often requires strategic management of facial expression, eye movements, body direction, and public demeanor to minimize accessibility. In this way, fieldworkers will often employ a "looking at no one in particular" gaze to avoid engulfing engagements, or become immersed in an engrossing side-involvement (jotting fieldnotes provides a convenient one) to preclude an imminent overture.

Principled exemptions and marginal positionings, however, are never total and absolute, and initial efforts to stake out detached observer presence are precarious and routinely subject to threat and undermining in the flux of field inter-actions. Just what might be entailed in terms of participation and observation by initial agreements to let a fieldworker "hang out" in the interest of a "study" depends upon subsequent developments. Thus, initially able to sustain research relations with male Chicano gang members by gaining acceptance as a "lady reporter," Horowitz found this arrangement began to dissolve:

> After more than a year of using "lady reporter" as a key identity, some mem-bers began to flirt seriously and tried to make passes. They claimed that my age (six to eight years older) did not constitute a barrier to starting a rela-tionship. The identity of lady reporter was being replaced by my potential as a sexual partner, regardless of my efforts to deemphasize my appearance and emphasize my age and outsider status. (1986:420)

Similarly, an interactional position on the periphery is inherently unstable: a shift in concerns, a glance, a turn of the head, may reconstitute the rim as the center, as in the following fieldnote involving a psychiatric emergency team call:

> I (RME) accompanied a PET team composed of two women, a psychiatric social worker and a public health nurse, to the home of a 21-year-old black ex-mental patient named Albert Roy. The young man's mother had initiated the visit, claiming his behavior was extremely disoriented and something had to be done. After introductions and some preliminary talk about Albert's recent problems, I seated myself in an easy chair slightly removed from but with a good view of the couch where the workers and Albert sat talking. I assiduously observed and took notes on all that was said about Albert's mental condition, efforts to get a job, problems with medication, etc. At various points Albert became somewhat "agitated," at one point get-ting up and standing two feet away from one of the PET workers, shaking his fist in her face and yelling that he could take care of himself. At this point, his mother, standing in the kitchen area watching all this, pointed toward me (I had said absolutely nothing) and warned her son: "Sit down Albert! Or that man over there will get you. That's what he's here for!"[12]

If overtures are successfully preempted, the host feels no need or desire to incorporate the observer. Once an overture has been made, however, the field-worker's options change dramatically; any response is now monitored for what it may signify about the fieldworker's character, commitments, and relation to the group. Under these circumstances, the fieldworker's distancing options involve either evasion or refusal.

Finessing

Given the potential costs for the research project of direct refusal, it is not sur-prising to find fieldworkers adept in finessing overtures through evasive or ambigu-ous replies. In some situations, the overture itself is framed so indirectly that it can be responded to in kind without either party feeling publicly embarrassed or humiliated. Arendell (1997:357), for example, reports that most of the divorced men in her inter-view study who became interested in her as a "potential date" proceeded cautiously:

For the most part, inquiries were indirect, such as: "Let me know if you'd like to go to dinner sometime." "What kinds of things do you like to do in your spare time?" "Does a busy woman like yourself have time for a personal life?" Such remarks were sufficiently ambiguous so they could be side-stepped, saving face for both of us: the participant's, if he were suggesting a date which I declined, and mine, if I was misinterpreting his meaning.

In other circumstances, however, overtures may be explicit and responses closely scrutinized. The fieldworker may find her wit and diplomacy tested when she is publicly asked to commit herself to one or another "side," as in the situation described by Bosk (1979:197):

> . . . houseofficers viewed me as a "referee" in conflicts among themselves over patient management, quarrels over the equity of the division of labor, and disputes about whether or not patients understood what was happening. In the midst of such disagreements, one houseofficer would turn to me and ask: "Well, what do you think? Which of us is right?" These were not comfortable situations for me when I could hide behind the observer role. A judgment was demanded as the price for my continued presence. Moreover, any judgment was certain to alienate one of my informants. *I developed tactics for throwing the question back to the disputants or for pointing out the merits of either side, or making a joke of the entire dispute.* (emphasis added)

Evasive responses are a consummate test of the fieldworkers' ethnographic grasp of local culture, for the place that has been established must now to be preserved without wreaking havoc to the relationships that sustain it. Not only must the evasive fieldworker respond, but he must do so in such a way that members do not press for further involvement, are not offended, and do not treat the fieldworker as evasive. As part of his covert participation in the Children of God, Van Zandt (1991:14) was called upon to "litness" or sell COG literature to the public, a task he found especially odious.

> Fortunately, the structure of litnessing permitted me to develop a number of techniques to avoid these unpleasant interactions. Chief among these was to reduce my activity to the minimum acceptable limit: I litnessed very slowly and approached only a small number of people; I litnessed furiously for a very short time. I took a deep breath, attempted to desensitize my feelings, and rapidly approached people with the same statement. After such a period, I would slip out of view of my litnessing partner and take a rest. Another technique I used was to claim that I needed more "Word Time" or devotional time, and request that we take a break to read a Mo [the leader of COG] letter together. I drew on my status as a neophyte as an excuse to take more and longer breaks than most competent members.

Furthermore, these circumstances permitted a measure of overt role distance: Using devices ranging from facial expressions communicating "'Can you believe I'm doing this? I can't" to confessing to those encountered "that I was really a sociologist conducting a covert study" (1991:15), Van Zandt participated by showing that his identity was other than what his activities might imply.

Because of the indexicality of evasions it is not unusual that responses intended as hedges fail. Responses intended to be "neutral" and noncommittal, for example, may be transformed into patently partial statements. *When Prophecy Fails* (1956) provides the prototypical instance:

> At the end of the December 3–4 meeting, Bertha sat for "private consultations" between the individual members and "the Creator" who spoke through her. All the observers dutifully asked a question or two of the Creator and accepted the answers passively, quitting the situation as soon as they politely could. The last observer to go through this ritual was not allowed to be merely passive and nondirective, however. The voice of the medium droned on for a few minutes and then said: "I am the Creator." Next the voice asked our observer: "What do you see when I say 'I am the Creator'?" To this the observer replied, "Nothing", whereupon the medium's voice explained: "That's not nothing; that's the void." The medium then pressed further: "Do you see a light in the void?" Our observer struggled with this impasse by answering, "A light in the void?" and got, as a reply, a fuller explanation of the "light that expands and covers the void" together with an increasing flood of elaboration that terminated when the medium called other members into the room and asserted that the observer had just been "allowed to witness Creation"! The medium further stated that this "event" was validation of her speaking with the Creator's voice since, every time her voice said "I am the Creator" our observer saw the vision of Creation! (Festinger et al. 1956:242–43)

As these fieldworkers lamented: "Against this sort of runaway invention even the most polished technique of nondirective response is powerless" (243).

Nonetheless, evasive finessing provides one of the foundational skills of participant/observation fieldwork. Counterposing efforts to draw close and develop rapport, interactional techniques of ambiguity and avoidance, often conveyed through humor and misdirection, are standard ethnographic implements for sustaining nonconsequential presence in the face of inclusive overtures.

Declining and Withdrawing

Overtures may be so sudden and direct that the fieldworker feels compelled to respond with a more or less direct refusal. Often this is an explicit declaration asserting identity as (just) a researcher or unwillingness to participate: When asked by attending physicians for advice on life-and-death decisions on a neonatal intensive care unit, Anspach (1993:203) asserted that "as a sociologist" she "had no special expertise in resolving ethical dilemmas."[13] Such declarations, of course, may be hostilely received, as in the following reaction to Terry Williams' appeal to his researcher identity as a way of declining a sexual overture that arose in his study of cocaine users in after-hours clubs (1989:30):

> I was in a club that had been heterosexual until the Thursday night I arrived, which was "gay night." I thought I would take advantage of the situation for sociological purposes, making comparison between heterosexual and homosexual cocaine users. I was wearing black leather (the fashion in New York at the time) not realizing the role of black leather in the gay community. I noticed

a group of men sitting in the corner and moved toward them inconspicuously, or so I thought, until I was eight or ten feet away. One of them stared up at me and I of course looked toward him. His sleeves were rolled past his elbows, revealing purple and red tattoos on both arms. After looking at me for a few seconds, he walked over and offered to buy me a drink, asking if this was my first time there. I explained that I had been there before and informed him that I was a researcher and just wanted to talk to as many people as possible. He grew red in the face and said to his companions in a loud voice, hands on his hips, head cocked to one side: "Hey, get a load of this one. He wants to do research on us. You scum bag! What do we look like pal? Fucking guinea pigs? You got some nerve walking in here, talking about doing some research!"

Since declining may give offense and damage rapport, ethnographers often take care to identify indigenous methods for declining to participate in local activities. For example, in seeking to study cocaine culture without using cocaine, Williams (1989:29) "observed several patrons actually refusing cocaine that was offered them, saying 'my nose is out' or 'I'm coked out' or simply that they did not trust other people's drugs." Relying on these techniques, Williams was able to observe cocaine use in after-hours clubs without arousing suspicion.

In some situations, what is intended as an unequivocal declination by the fieldworker may be understood in an entirely different way by members. Golde (1970) noted, for example, that when her refusals of amorous propositions were filtered through indigenous cultural understandings, their meaning and implications were transformed. "The difficulty was that it was expected of the female always to appear unwilling initially," Golde writes, "so that my lack of interest and my refusals were not always taken at face value but were interpreted as typical female behavior" (1970:86). Indeed, in extreme instances, members may maintain an interpretive frame that deprives the fieldworker of any effective means of declaring distance. Snow's (1980) efforts to terminate his fieldwork in the Nichiren Shoshu Buddhist movement provides a case in point. Committed members of this group responded to those showing signs of disaffection or withdrawal with renewed contact and involvement. Snow, for example, told his group leader about his growing disillusionment only to be congratulated because such feelings were "good signs" and subsequently taken to the Community Center for "guidance." As Snow comments: "While I was thus trying to curtail my involvement and offer what seemed to be legitimate reasons for dropping out, I was yet being drawn back at the same time" (1980:110).

The overtures may be so intense or sustained that despite efforts to preempt, evade or directly decline, the fieldworker may feel that she has no recourse but to withdraw from the field. As Horowitz was increasingly seen as a sexually available "chick" by the Latino gang she observed, for example, she attempted to ward off overtures by not dancing with any of the youths and by making sure that other women were present at meetings. The persistence of the overtures, however, rendered her position as researcher untenable. "As the pressures increased to take a locally defined membership role," Horowitz writes, "I was unable to negotiate a gender identity that would allow me to continue as a researcher" (1986:423).

Subjective Anchoring

A variety of processes may lead fieldworkers to become deeply engulfed by and immersed in the worlds they came to study. Declining overtures to deeper involvement may threaten continued access to the group; as McCurdy noted, for example, refusal to dispense medications would likely have resulted in his exclusion from the village. Detached, passive observation can become strained or boring, making the fieldworker amenable to normalizing his presence by engaging in host activities. Relatedly, fieldworkers may seek opportunities to express their gratitude for what Bosk (1979) refers to as the "gift" of access by doing things with and for his hosts. Finally, deeper involvement may furnish attractive opportunities to construct selves and acquire experiences not possible in other circumstances. As Thorne (1983:222) had suggested, ethnography affords the researcher "controlled adventure" into exciting, tabooed, dangerous, enticing circumstances, while retaining the ability to control the time, extent, and costs of participation.

On many occasions, when actively involved in host events, distancing, as by establishing a publicly recognized role of "observer," is neither possible nor desired. Instead, composing oneself as an observer is primarily a matter of self-discipline: Unable to preempt, evade, or decline overtures, or to symbolically distance herself from the actions she performs, the fieldworker remains distant from her hosts only through the work whereby she recalls her "researcher" identity and commitments. In one way or another, the researcher reminds (re-minds) herself of her anchorage in the discipline, not in the activities in which she is currently engaged, much less in the host group.[14]

Writing fieldnotes provides one concrete method for re-minding and recommitting to research purposes. The fieldworker may get caught up in the moment-by-moment, day-after-day experience of living in the field, becoming immersed in the rhythms and routines of local life. In simply "participating" and "experiencing," research priorities may recede and disappear. Taking up the task of writing fieldnotes draws the fieldworker back into the space of research and observation, revitalizing fieldworker "commitment to the exogenous project of studying or understanding the lives of others—as opposed to the indigenous project of simply living a life in one way or another" (Emerson et al. 1995:36). And returning to these matters may not be easy: As one anthropological fieldworker observed (Jackson 1990a:18): "I slowed down. More concerned with the hour to hour. You forget to take notes because you feel this is your life."

Other fieldworkers may create devices for immediate self-reminding as their local involvement leads them into activities which create discomfort, anxiety and internal conflict. Van Zandt (1991:181) describes one such device:

> I thought if I could keep some perspective on my activity, it would be easier to get by. I carried two index cards. One contained a list of imperatives to help me remember my goals and to keep that perspective. The second held the words to a song that I always found particularly relaxing and reassuring.

The first card included advice such as "1. Maintain 2 distinct positions: don't let them merge and conflict. . . . 3. Maintain distance or perspective. . . . 7. Study what is happening to self" (1991:181).

As the anchorage is attenuated, the distinction between fieldworker and member may dissolve. In a section entitled "'Going Native,' Almost," Van Zandt describes the instant in a conversation with a COG leader when he felt, to invoke Goffman's words, that he "could settle down and forget about being a sociologist":

> I felt a rush to just emotionally fall on him—not Jesus—or not physically—I wanted to rest emotionally on him; things clouded up—and I was unclear about my exact relation—researcher/member—[it]came after [he] listened and understood my problem about security and answered some questions forthrightly—also after I mentioned some things Roy [Wallis] said [to me about the Family] then I realized I was trapped . . . I thought maybe the Lord was moving me. (1991:16, brackets in original)

Van Zandt tried to hide his emotional reaction and asked the leader "sociological" questions but later that evening and the next morning contemplated the possibility of joining the Family. What kept him from the "brink," as he describes it, was reminding himself not so much of the sociological project per se but of the unacceptability of the COG's overall project.[15]

CONCLUSION

The workaday practices of the human sciences vary in the extent to which the distinction between researcher/observer and subject/observed is problematic. At one extreme, studies of documents, records, and bones allow examination without fear of rebuff or rejection. In a literal sense the documents and bones are objects indifferent to investigation (though, of course, their keepers and owners may not be). When active human agents comprise the focus of study, however, the epistemological conditions of research become more problematic. Insofar as the "object" of concern can object—that is, resist or refuse the inquirer's efforts to examine and explore—the subject/object dichotomy is transformed from an abstract philosophical scheme presupposed by the researcher to a relation which must be continually and collaboratively constructed.

Excessive participation in the social world under observation—whether due to engulfment by the host and/or enthusiastic embrace by the researcher—threatens the boundary dividing and constituting the "field" from the "fieldworker." As the boundary is attenuated through enticements to, say, "go native," not only is the "field" vulnerable to dissolution but so too is the identity of the fieldworker. Appreciation of the in-situ co-constitution of fieldworker/field invites attention to the practices through which the very distinction is implicitly or explicitly invoked, used and sustained—or disregarded. As Schegloff (1987:219) notes, the common sociological practice of identifying interactional participants by reference to a particular role or status—e.g., "doctor" and "patient"—assumes that participants are treating one another in that capacity in the course of interaction. Interactants who might be appropriately categorized as "doctor" and "patient" respectively, however, may orient to other dimensions of their relation, e.g., "friends." Thus, in any particular interaction, the identification of situatedly relevant identities awaits establishing the identities to which participants are actually oriented. Similarly, the construction of "fieldworker," "ethnographer," "observer," as well as "observed," as operative categories in relations in the field ultimately refers to whether and how host and researcher collaboratively define and use these categories as a premise of interaction.

The collaborative construction and maintenance of participant/observation fieldwork, we have suggested, can be extremely precarious: any and every transaction between a fieldworker and his hosts can affirm or nullify the stance of "observer." Host actions that ostensibly do not seem to address or implicate the fieldworker—a cold shoulder, as it were—implicitly establish the latter as a non-consequential witness. Alternatively, the observer's seemingly Archimedian perch is eroded as group members find they cannot or do not want to disregard the fieldworker's presence. Thus, "observing" is a continuously negotiated posture in which fieldworker and host orchestrate their activities to allow the researcher to remain on the margins with minimal consequence and involvement. Not a position given or obtained once and for all, "doing observer" is variously reproduced, threatened, and preserved through the particulars of interaction.

Ironically, even hosts' acceptance of the definitions of themselves as observed and observable objects, and of the researcher as their observer/fieldworker, does not provide a terminal point of negotiation much less a transcendent position allowing unproblematic study. Rather, such acceptance comprises and reflects negotiations in which hosts orchestrate themselves as researchable "objects" and the researcher as "observer". Not only may hosts refrain from what they anticipate might be inappropriately inclusive overtures, but they may monitor and manipulate the researcher to make sure he conducts himself in a manner appropriate to an observer. Thus, in contrast to Kondo's family who attempted to make her look, sound and act Japanese, Whyte's Cornerville hosts cautioned him against becoming like them (1955:304):

> At first I concentrated upon fitting into Cornerville, but a little later I had to face the question of how far I was to immerse myself in the life of the district. I bumped into that problem one evening as I was walking down the street with the Nortons. Trying to enter into the spirit of the small talk, I cut loose with a string of obscenities and profanity. The walk came to a momentary halt as they all stopped to look at me in surprise. Doc shook his head and said: "Bill, you're not supposed to talk like that. That doesn't sound like you."

In doing observed/observer, hosts may invite, solicit and even stage events in which they believe the researcher is interested. Hosts may also impose their version of the appropriate focus of or framing for observable matters. Lomax and Casey (1998, para. 5.13), for example, describe how their efforts to videotape midwife practice[16] were stymied by their hosts' versions of these matters:

> Once I had set up the camera I left the room and went downstairs. After about 5-10 minutes Sarina (the midwife) shouted to me "we've finished," a

statement which I interpreted as a summons to switch off the video camera, which I did. Reviewing this experience in the context of both the events which occurred during the visit after the camera had been switched off and the consultations videoed so far, it is becoming apparent that there are certain activities which the midwives construe as "midwifery" and that they perceive I will be interested in researching (the physical examination, bathing the baby, helping mum breast-feed) and others which, although observable in each of the visits I will not be interested in ("social" talk occurring at the beginning and end of a visit, making arrangements for a subsequent visit). On this occasion, it being difficult to explain in the context of the visit that in fact I was interested in interaction other than that around the physical examination of the mother and child, I went along with the assumption and switched off the camera.

The host group may even appropriate the ethnographer in his very capacity as observer into its ongoing activity. Consider Bosk's (1992) paradoxical involvement in a project in which he was invited to do an ethnographic study of genetic counseling. Accepted and understood to be an observer of the counseling team's activities, Bosk was often requested to "witness" what the doctors were doing (1992:13): to serve as a "reality check" regarding what transpired in particular cases; to provide some measure of legal protection in complex and contested cases; and to appreciate the existential conundrums confronted by the team. Far from being unilaterally invoked, the observer/observed distinction may be appropriated, cultivated, and used by hosts.

In sum, the ethnographic field is constructed through processes that both organize encounters and relations between researcher and researched, and represent such encounters and relations. While the latter processes involve the largely unilateral constitution of field and fieldworker, the former are essentially and unavoidably mutual and collaborative. Our analysis, however, has by and large addressed the mutual construction of field and fieldworker in one-sided terms, focusing on the interactional work of "doing observer." But as our final series of reflections make clear, the "observation" of ongoing scenes and relationships requires the concerted participation of both the observer and the observed. This collaborative process can and should also be examined specifically from the latter's point of view; thus, the analysis of "doing observer" we provide here should be complemented by consideration of exactly how hosts constitute themselves as objects of study, that is, by full analysis of "doing observed."

NOTES

[1] Clifford (1997) certainly recognizes fieldwork as "embodied spatial practice" but subordinates such in-the-field "embodied participation" to subsequent textual representation. For example, he emphasizes how gender, race and sex, while deeply salient in actual field relations, are typically written out of ethnographers' representations of the field (1997:202), ignoring the processes whereby gender, race and sex enter into and affect actual, ongoing relations in ways that allow and shape the ethnographer's interactional presence with and among host members.

[2] Analyses of "the field" as a construct developed by the practices of ethnography often neglect or ignore these processes, instead depicting the field as the essentially *unilateral construction of the field-*

worker. Clifford (1997), for example, treats fieldwork as an activity initiated and controlled by the ethnographer; the core terms of his analysis—"practice," "dislocation," "attention"—all refer to actions/mindings originating from and controlled by the ethnographer. On occasion the field may indeed be the solipsistic creation of the ethnographer, arising exactly because the ethnographer thinks, speaks and writes as though it did. But in actual encounters with hosts, in attempting to "make a place" from which to participate and observe, the ethnographer generally lacks unilateral power, and "field" and "fieldworker" are co-constituted by hosts and researcher through processes of negotiation which require some (but not necessarily consistently equal) power on both sides.

3   Discussions of distance and detachment by and large have addressed two standard issues: the dangers of "overrapport" (Miller 1952), of too intimate or sympathetic identification with those studied (Douglas 1976); and a recommended sequencing of immersion and withdrawal, the latter to take place after the more active phases of fieldwork have been concluded (e.g., Schwartz and Schwartz 1955).

4   At first glance it might appear that fieldworkers could avoid the interactional conundrums of constructing an observer role simply by seeking out and adopting locally available, indigenous observer roles. Humphreys (1970:27–28) recounts such a procedure in studying sexual activities in men's public toilets: "I assumed the role of the voyeur—a role superbly suited for sociologists and the only lookout role that is not overtly sexual." But such a strategy simply pushes the problem back one step: The sociologist-as-voyeur must still enact and sustain this distanced, nonparticipatory stance in the midst of a variety of cues, invitations and overtly sexual activities.

5   Park's hoary exhortation to get the "seat of your pants dirty" by going out to "observe" neighborhoods in Chicago, for example, yields a marginally involved (i.e., sitting on the side) observer. Reinharz's more recent suggestion of an "openness to intimacy and striving for empathy," which "lays the groundwork for friendship, shared struggle, and identity change" (1992:68), promotes a far more immersed and involved researcher.

6   Often such negotiations are conducted through humor, as in the following instance:
A fieldworker in a HUD housing office reported: "The workers are talking and laughing as Sam decides where to put his desk in his new office. I hear one of the workers say, 'I hope Bob didn't write that down.' I walked up. 'What?' 'Oh, I just told Sam it's good he's got space for his machete behind his desk.' They laugh." (Emerson et al. 1995:220)

7   As Johnson explains (1975:159): "To observe sociologically means that one deliberately cedes experiencing the things in themselves to the members of the setting, observation entails seeing phenomena as 'exhibits' of the things in themselves."

8   For an exception, see Ericson (1981:36), who called attention not only to the efforts of police detectives to exclude fieldworkers from key observational sites, but also to "many attempts at *inclusion* of fieldworkers in policing tasks," notably detectives' efforts "to use fieldworkers as allies" in certain field situations.

9   Similar processes arise in autoethnography, a variant of experiential fieldwork in which circumstances of the researcher's own life are constituted as a field. Again, to the extent that one is a central figure in the focal events, "observation" becomes a form of self-reflection in which distance from events and experiences is achieved conceptually, with the fieldworker bifurcating levels of awareness or consciousness, simultaneously immersing in the activity at hand and sustaining a more detached, observational standpoint. For example, Adler and Adler (1987:70) provide this description of the complexity of orienting to poker playing while actively participating in the game:
Hayano, for instance, simultaneously had to play the cards that he was dealt, think about the other cards that had already passed through the deck, observe his fellow players to try to interpret what they were holding, look for general categories or typologies of action through which he could organize and analyze the scene, and look for behaviors that constituted specific examples of these types to draw upon in his future writings as examples.

10 As Bosk (1979:193) suggests: "In the field, the everyday life of his subjects overwhelms the researcher, threatens to obliterate his sense of self, and forces a reconsideration of deeply held personal and intellectual beliefs."

[11] As Clifford (1997) emphasizes, classic accounts of fieldwork represented the ethnographer as having a distinctive "disciplined professional body," one in which emotions are restricted, the fieldworker's gender and race are marginalized, and sex with the natives is taboo. This last taboo, Clifford suggests, arose less as a barrier against "'going native' or losing critical distance than against 'going traveling,' violating a professional habitus" (202). As he reports: "In travel practices and texts, having sex, heterosexual and homosexual, with local people was common" (202).

[12] Note also that members may perceive and react to a fieldworker's silent, watchful presence in ways that depart radically from the latter's self-understanding as "mere observer," showing once again the collaborative interactional work that underlies observation.

[13] It is our impression that such outright denials are relatively hard to find in the fieldwork literature, a fact which may well reflect members' sensitivities in what they will ask of fieldworkers, and fieldworkers' reluctance to make an outright refusal, perhaps thereby risking rapport and access. Supporting this possibility are a number of reports in which fieldworkers failed to say no when, in members' eyes or in their own retrospective evaluations, they should have; Whyte's (1955:312ff) regret for having voted under others' names provides one example. Fieldworkers do report making direct declarations of refusal when asked to report on their observations to outsiders or superordinates, but such refusals, of course, reaffirm ties to those studied by denying any obligation to these other parties.

[14] In effect, the interaction that might have been with one's hosts to preserve distance ("I am a sociologist") becomes a private interaction with oneself; in these instances, fieldworkers sustain (or reestablish) their position as "observer" without the complicity of their hosts.

[15] A variety of routine operations in the field may contribute to anchoring an individual as a researcher. From this point of view, daily note taking, letters to and from the field, contacts with chairs of dissertation committees and the like, both reflect and remind the fieldworker of her commitments.

[16] Videotaping naturally occurring interaction generates many of the same problems as faced by the participant-observer fieldworker. These problems center both around matters of where to place and when to turn on and off the camera, and around interactions between camera person and those being taped; as Lomax and Casey (1998 para. 5.2) report: "It is not possible to enter a person's home and set up camera without becoming interactionally involved."

12

Trial and Tribulations
Courts, Ethnography, and the Need for an Evidentiary Privilege for Academic Researchers

Richard A. Leo

INTRODUCTION

In our era of increasing litigation, bureaucratic controls, and obsession with the protection of human subjects (sometimes to the exclusion of other research considerations), ethical and legal issues are becoming more salient in social science research. As a result, social scientists must be aware of the legal implications of our data-gathering activities in order to understand our ethical obligations as well as to devise strategies to protect ourselves against compelled legal testimony and the seizure of our data. By describing the unique setting of my own participant observation research into police interrogation practices and the circumstances that led to the state's coercion of my testimony and private fieldnotes, I hope to contribute to the ongoing discussion of the ethical dilemmas that researchers must confront when courts and ethnography conflict. I hope this paper will also contribute to our understanding of the viable solutions to these dilemmas. In the first part of this article, I will describe the background of my participant observation fieldwork of police interrogation practices—especially the difficulties I encountered gaining access to, and overcoming the distrust of, my research subjects—in order to establish the context for my subsequent discussion of the legal events that I confronted. In the second part of

this article, I will describe the legal facts of my case and the relevant ethical issues that it raises for field researchers. Finally, in the third part of this article, I will discuss the implications of my case for social science research more generally. I will argue that we must lobby for a federal evidentiary privilege for academic researchers if we are to honor our promises of confidentiality to our research subjects in courts of law without enduring the coercive threat or reality of indefinite imprisonment. The alternative, as my case will illustrate, is to experience the stigma and feelings of betrayal that come from violating our moral and professional obligations, and, perhaps even more troubling, to risk spoiling the field for future researchers, especially in research settings where insiders are highly secretive and distrustful of outsiders.

GETTiNG INSIDE THE INTERROGATION ROOM

Police Interrogation Practices as a Hidden and Dirty Data Base

The interrogation room is—and historically has always been—the most private social space in an American police station. It is traditionally located at the rear of the station house, carefully secluded from the view of civilian outsiders and the distractions of police insiders. Interrogation rooms are notorious for their barren interior and subdued simplicity: two armless chairs and a plain table fill the small, sometimes cramped, space that exists against a nondescript and windowless white exterior. What happens inside the interrogation room—the drama of custodial questioning, the art and science of police technique—has long remained a mystery, not only to the public but also to academic criminologists, sociologists, and legal scholars. Notwithstanding the many, often sensational, portrayals of interrogation scenes in American cinema, we know very little about how custodial police questioning is routinely conducted in America.

Even among the most professional police departments, contemporary interrogation practices remain shrouded in secrecy. This may seem surprising in an era of community-oriented policing and the increasing use of video-technology to monitor police behavior. *But police interrogation is an intentionally hidden institutional practice.* Indeed, police interrogation practices constitute a hidden and dirty data base: police interrogators are human manipulators who rely on role-playing, deceit, confrontation, and outright trickery to extract admissions and confessions from criminal suspects (Leo 1994a, 1992; Simon 1991). Not only do they routinely lie during interrogation (Leo 1992; Skolnick and Leo 1992), interrogators may resort to illegal practices (Simon 1991) or fail to read the *Miranda* warnings correctly (Leo 1994a; Simon 1991). Sometimes, if rarely, American police interrogators may even resort to physical coercion (Amnesty International 1990). Although police regard psychologically manipulative and deceptive questioning methods as necessary for successful crime apprehension and control and although the courts consider such tactics legally permissible, outside observers with different values or perceptions may consider them morally inappropriate if not altogether unethical.

Outside observation or study of the hidden practices of police interrogators thus threatens to expose the gap between the ideal standards that a police department presents to the public and the actual behavior of its members. Exposure of the hidden and dirty data of police interrogation practices may also undermine group solidarity. The well-known code of silence serves to maintain both individual and group boundaries within a tightly knit and intrinsically conservative subculture. Any outside observer or researcher of interrogation practices may thus be viewed as a potential whistle-blower who threatens not only to discredit individual officers or the police organization, but also to challenge internal boundaries by potentially calling attention to indiscretions, abuses of authority, or possibly even illegalities. Police detectives and managers thus perceive that the success of their interrogation practices may often depend on maintaining the secrecy of their activities.

Though other police activities are conducted openly and subject to public scrutiny, only in exceptional circumstances will civilians or third parties be permitted to observe interrogations. There are, for example, no press privileges for police interrogations or anything comparable to ride-along programs for members of the public. Moreover, if a suspect requests an attorney prior to or during custodial questioning, interrogators will immediately terminate the session rather than open it up to the view of a potential critic. The public may read about confessions to police in high-profile cases, but rarely do the media report just how police obtained those confessions. For police, in general, do not discuss interrogation practices publicly (Thornton 1993). The discourse of interrogation remains confined to the station house and other outposts of police subculture, walled in by a code of silence that functions not so much to protect any individual cop from allegations of impropriety as to insulate an entire police practice from outside scrutiny and the possibility of public criticism. In a democratic society that has increasingly come to emphasize the public nature and purpose of its police, the interrogation room may be the last bastion of covert practice by nonundercover police. Thus, because police interrogation remains an intentionally hidden institutional practice, it is an unusually difficult subject for social scientists to research empirically, *especially through observational methods.*

From December 1992 to August 1993, I spent more than five hundred (500) hours "hanging out" as a participant observer inside the Criminal Investigation Division (CID) of the Laconia Police Department (LPD), a large, urban police department in California. The name "Laconia" is, of course, a pseudonym for the city whose police department I studied. While it may be true, as Gibbons (1975) has argued, that fictitious names are overused in general by field researchers, the use of pseudonyms remains especially important in the study of hidden and dirty data because real names may damage the reputation of the individual(s) or institution(s) under study and, as a result, may contaminate the field for future researchers who wish to study similar institutions and practices. In my case, the University of California's Human Subjects' Committee required, pursuant to federal regulations governing federally funded research and thus as a condition of the university's sponsorship of my research, that I employ pseudonyms for the police departments that I would be studying as well as the individual officers whose actions I would be observing. In addition, as a condition of my access to custodial interrogations, I promised my research subjects that I would employ fictitious names to protect their anonymity. To police officers who regularly worry about unfair criticism or sanctions from Internal Affairs, civilian review boards, police managers, external lawsuits, the media, and public defenders among others, such an assurance may be very important.

The purpose of my fieldwork was to observe custodial police questioning directly as part of a more general sociological study of police interrogation practices in America (see Leo 1994a). During nine months of field research, I sat in on and contemporaneously observed one hundred and twenty-two (122) custodial interrogations at the Laconia Police Department involving forty-five different detectives. My field research is noteworthy because of the difficulty of gaining access to such a highly secretive setting and overcoming the distrust of many police interrogators, problems that I will further discuss. Prior to my study, no participant observation or general sociological study of American police interrogation practices existed. The protection of research sources from the compulsion of courts (or any legal authorities, for that matter) is especially important in research settings such as this one, where the betrayal of promises of confidentiality will likely provide already suspicious research subjects with good reasons to deny future researchers entree. More generally, one of our most fundamental obligations as field researchers is to protect our subjects from invasions of privacy, humiliation, unwarranted exposure, internal and external sanctions or any other personal, social, legal or professional liability to which they may be subjected because we have created a data base of their activities.

Problems of Primary, Secondary, and Tertiary Access

The LPD has long held a reputation as one of the leading police departments in America, and has been the research site of several well-known academic field studies (Skolnick 1966; Muir 1977; Reiss 1985). Understandably, however, the LPD initially appeared reluctant to grant my request for research access to custodial interrogations. My dissertation advisor and I first approached the Laconia Police Department in November 1990. At the time, I was a graduate and law student in the Jurisprudence and Social Policy Program at the University of California, Berkeley. Despite several introductions to police managers and several requests for research access to custodial interrogations, LPD management did not grant me permission to study CID detectives until December 1992, more than two years later. During this time, the police chief did not return the phone calls of my dissertation advisor, and the captain of the Criminal Investigation Division told us that he could not allow me research access without the chief's permission. The captain pledged his support for my research project throughout this two-year period, yet while his offer may have been genuine it appeared to me to be a skillful run-around designed to deflect the annoying requests of a naive, if persistent, graduate student researcher.

From November 1990 through early December 1992, I regularly contacted the captain to find out whether the chief had finally granted permission to my request; each time he complained of his inability to reach the chief, yet the captain assured me that he remained hopeful of eventual approval. Although I tried always to give the captain the benefit of any doubt, several detectives subsequently informed me that both the chief and the captain had denied me research access because they feared my study could generate negative publicity for the organization, emphasizing that LPD management "would do anything" to protect LPD's public image. While I do not know it to be a fact, my personal opinion is that the sole reason I received permission to study the Laconia Criminal Investigation Division (more than two years after my initial request) was that in December 1992 the Mayor of Laconia called on my dissertation advisor to write a high-profile evaluation study of the Laconia Police Department's implementation of community-oriented policing, which suddenly created a strong incentive for the police chief to be in the good graces of my dissertation advisor. Once inside CID, however, I initially encountered additional research obstacles. With the chief's newfound blessing I promptly received a positive introduction from the captain to each of the CID section lieutenants (Robbery, Burglary, Theft, Assault, and Homicide), who in turn provided me with positive introductions to the CID detectives.[1] However, the CID detectives retained complete discretion over whether to permit me to attend their interrogations. Even with the introduction from their superiors (whom, I later learned, many of the detectives intensely disliked), most of the detectives initially distrusted my motives and the research objectives of my study; some bluntly told me so, others quietly avoided me. Despite introductions from the top layers of management, then, the burden remained on me to independently negotiate access to each interrogation I wished to observe with the individual detective(s) conducting it. In the beginning stages of my research, not surprisingly, many of the detectives refused to let me observe their interrogations. Peter Manning (1972) has referred to this as the problem of securing "secondary access," and he has argued that it may be as difficult as negotiating primary (i.e., administrative) access in police organizations. I subsequently experienced yet another threat to my research access when a managing district attorney, angry that his office had not been consulted about my study, threatened to have me thrown out of the Laconia Police Department altogether. We might call this the problem of negotiating "tertiary access."

It is worth emphasizing that the presence of a third-party observer opens police practice to potential criticism not only from outsiders such as the courts and the public, but also from insiders such as coworkers and police managers with whom a reputational interest is always at stake. The police managers who let me into CID were not the same individuals who would suffer if I had discovered and reported improprieties, illegalities or incompetence. In this context, it is significant that a couple years prior to my study a local journalist obtained research access to the case files in the Sexual Assault unit of the Assault Section, portraying herself as a benign researcher. Instead, the journalist wrote a highly critical front-page news series alleging that the section was racist and sexist in its investigation practices (Cooper 1990). The detectives in CID, as well as the Laconia County District Attorney's office, reacted with moral indignation to a front-page series that they believed was both generally unfair and factually incorrect. Nevertheless, LPD management responded to this controversial news story by publicly deflecting blame onto the Sexual Assault unit detectives, most of whom were subsequently either demoted or transferred. My presence inside the interrogation room therefore always represented a potential liability to detectives—even if they questioned suspects fairly and legally. A quote from my field notes is instructive:

> I had a conversation with detective X, and he pointed out that I am still something of a mystery to his section, and that they distrust me because I am an outsider. They were ordered by their lieutenant to cooperate with me, but they don't know what I am about, and they fear that they may say or do something in my presence that will get them in trouble. I later spoke to Detectives Y and Z (both in the lunchroom, where I was speaking to Detective X), and they echoed his sentiments. Detective Y avoids me like the plague, he said, because he is worried that if he makes an accidental wrong comment in my presence it might be in the newspapers and he could lose his job. They all explained how cops are very defensive naturally and distrustful of outsiders. And they mentioned the exposé that the *San Francisco Examiner* did on the Sexual Assault unit a year ago, and how that makes them even more distrustful of an outsider. Detective X told me that detective F was the fall guy for that, that every organization needs its martyrs in such times, and that F just happened to be the unlucky guy—even though he wasn't really doing anything wrong. Detective Y added that police departments are paramilitary organizations, and that police don't have the same rights as civilians. If I complained about a particular investigator, he said, the organization could not formally sanction the detective if he was not breaking any rule, but informally the detective may be punished by not receiving the days off or vacation time he requests—that is the kind of retaliation they would have to worry about, said detective Y.

The Sociologist as Detective: Constructing Conducive Research Roles

My strategy for overcoming the detectives' initial distrust was to spend as much time as possible getting to know them and letting them get to know me in my new research role, while seeking to blend into, and thus become accepted as a normal part of, their daily work environment. Though some of the detectives were initially receptive to small talk, most of them were guarded in my presence. In the beginning, I represented a stereotype to them: they constructed me as an academic "egghead," a Berkeley liberal (if not radical), someone whom they envisioned as a likely advocate of criminal defendants' rights and whose real agenda was to expose police misconduct. As several detectives later confirmed, they projected onto me the very qualities they distrusted most in a civilian outsider with my background.

In order to receive access to interrogations I had to break down the detectives' academic and political stereotypes while reinventing myself in a role that was nonthreatening to them and thus conducive to acquiring the data I was seeking. I accomplished this by employing two distinct fieldwork strategies: first, I attempted to integrate myself into the work routines and culture of detecting within CID at Laconia; and, second, I attempted to develop rapport with detectives based on perceived personal and political similarity. To integrate myself into the work routines and culture of the group, I had to get to know the detectives personally and socially. I asked them numerous questions about various aspects of their jobs, engaging them in broad conversations that typically led to "war stories," which often bore little, if any, relation to my specific research interests. Detectives eagerly told me of their frustrations with police work, with the inefficient bureaucracy and self-promoting hierarchy at LPD, and of their anger at other actors within the criminal justice system, frequently relaying colorful and moving stories about egocentric prosecutors, lazy judges, morally duplicitous public defenders, and an irresponsible local media. I always listened to their complaints sympathetically and without passing judgment on them, sometimes playing the role of a sounding board, while at other times plying them with my own, equally cynical, stories about the state of criminal justice in America. As we established rapport through such conversations, the detectives' superficial stereotypes of me began to break down.

I attempted to integrate myself into the group in other ways as well. Each morning I brought in a newspaper that the detectives often ended up reading; every week (at least in the beginning) I brought in expensive pastries (fearing that regular donuts would reinforce negative stereotypes); and, when I was otherwise not engaged in conversation, I frequently answered phones or offered to help out with other routine or bureaucratic office matters. As Van Maanen (1978) has pointed out, fieldworkers who do little more than hang around will appear suspicious to members of a police organization. I also posted my schedule alongside the detectives' on the daily bulletin board, so that everyone (including the secretarial staff) would know when I was coming and leaving. To my surprise, the detectives quickly began in significant ways to treat me like an insider: after only a few weeks of observations, I learned that I no longer needed to sign in and out as I came and went, nor even to wear an official visitor's tag (a significant gesture, since even newly retired officers are required to wear visitor's tags when they make the rounds). Many of the detectives began to open up to me, some enthusiastically describing the panorama of modern detective work, others simply relaying the details of their particular job assignments. The scores of informal and casual conversations—many of which, again, had little to do with my specific research interests—solidified the emergent psychological bonds of my social relationships with the detectives. Gradually, the detectives began to incorporate me into their daily rounds and routine activities, and in the process I became further integrated into the group (Leo 1994b).

The second strategy I employed might be called the "chameleon strategy" of research access: I consciously reinvented my persona to fit the attributes, biases, and worldview of my subjects. To begin with, I shaved off a nascent beard shortly before undertaking fieldwork, wore my hair short, and, like the detectives, always dressed conservatively and professionally in formal business attire. By mimicking my subjects' dress and demeanor, I drew on a strategy well known to field researchers (Galliher 1980; Stone 1962), as well as to confidence men who wish to set up their marks (Blum 1972:26):

> The best qualified is for the con man to be as near like the victim as possible. The same dress, the same speech, the same class—and the more alike in interests, the quicker the rapport.

Not only did I model my dress and demeanor after my research subjects, but I also acted as if I shared their personal, administrative, and political biases. Again, I was adopting a research strategy well known to confidence men setting up their mark (Blum 1972:34):

> Work their hatred. Everybody has hates. Just find out what it is they hate and agree with them. When the heart takes over instead of the brain, the sucker is beat.

Other social scientists (see Fielding 1982; Punch 1986) as well as journalists (see Malcolm 1990) have employed similar fieldwork strategies.

My goal, of course, was to demonstrate an empathetic understanding of the detectives' actions, problems, and outlooks. To do so, I adopted their poses, embraced their manners and exuded their worldview; ultimately, I constructed a research persona in their image. For example, I feigned conservative politics; I openly shared their bias against abortion and in favor of the death penalty; I affirmed their antipathy toward homosexuality; and I described my intimate relations with women in the same crude manner and sexist language that is common in police culture. In short, I fabricated a nonthreatening research persona in order to establish rapport with the detectives, acquire their trust, and gain observational access into the highly exclusive and secretive setting of interrogations. As the detectives' stereotypes of me began to break down, I succeeded in acquiring the access and data I was seeking.

Although all field researchers must assume social roles that fit into the worlds they are studying, there are personal and moral costs associated with enacting such role pretenses. By my personal standards, I acted in ways that I would consider morally reprehensible in other contexts. To establish rapport and gain observational access, I misrepresented my real persona; I conned the detectives into thinking I was someone other than who I really am; in effect, I intentionally manipulated my research subjects. Privately, I felt uncomfortable about my actions. Yet, to have represented myself differently would surely have confirmed some of the detectives' initial preconceptions and suspicions. To have done so surely would have blocked my ability to penetrate the code of secrecy surrounding interrogation practices inside Laconia's CID, and thus would have prevented me from acquiring the kind of data I was seeking. In some environments, strategies based on impression management and deception may be necessary in order to obtain hidden and dirty data. This is not a new argument (see Klockars 1979, Douglas 1976). As Klockars (1979) has persuasively argued, the standards necessary to carry out the role of a morally competent field researcher of deviant subjects are necessarily different than the standards by which we judge morally competent human beings.

As the robbery detectives began to trust me, my access to interrogations improved considerably. In the beginning when I asked a detective for permission to sit in on an interrogation, I was frequently denied. As they came to know me, however, many of the robbery detectives began instead to seek me out prior to questioning their in-custody suspects.[2] Even more remarkably, several of the robbery detectives invited me to step outside of my role as a detached observer and to interrogate suspects myself. In one instance, two detectives loaded me up with a badge, a pair of handcuffs, a beeper and an empty holster. Regretfully, however, the chair of my dissertation committee did not permit me to assume this role, and thus I had to decline the robbery detectives' repeated invitations to let me actively participate in the interrogation process. Nevertheless, this offer—which the detectives extended at some professional risk to themselves, for everyone knew the captain would have reprimanded them had he found out—suggested the high level of trust and respect I had achieved with robbery detectives.

Renegotiating Access, Trust, Rapport, etc.

Every fieldworker knows that establishing trust and cooperation cannot be reified as an all-or-nothing event, but instead always remains a contingent social process that must be constantly negotiated and renegotiated (Johnson 1975). This is especially true when the researcher must rotate between sectors within a large organization to accumulate his or her data. Though I began my research in the Robbery section, I eventually rotated through each of the four other sections within CID (Burglary, Theft, Assault, and Homicide). Each time, I was initially greeted with open distrust and skepticism. Each time I was once again confronted with the task of reestablishing rapport, trust, cooperation with the detectives and ultimately the legitimacy of my research role.

In the process of rotating from my second (Burglary) to third (Assault) section within CID (approximately midway through my fieldwork), I circulated a sympathetic memorandum describing my background and my research goals (along with a copy of Moston, et al.'s article (1992), "The Effects of Case Characteristics on Suspect Behavior During Police Questioning" from the *British Journal of Criminology*). The memo, whose purpose was to assuage the Assault Unit detectives' fears, read as follows:

> It has come to my attention that perhaps I have not done a good enough job
> communicating who I am, why I am studying the custodial interviewing
> process at LPD, and what I am interested in learning. I am acutely aware of
> the fact that I am an outsider, and that any police department (especially a
> [geographical location] Area police department) has good reasons to distrust outsiders. I had assumed that since [the LPD police chief] gave me permission to study CID and since the various lieutenants have introduced me
> as a trustworthy person, all of you would come to trust me as you got to
> know me. I also assumed that if I told you about my specific academic interests I would bore you. Since I now realize that both of these assumptions

may be incomplete, if not incorrect, the purpose of this memo is to tell you a little more about myself and my research project.

As you all know, I am a graduate student in a criminal justice Ph.D. Program (that goes by the awkward name of "Jurisprudence and Social Policy") at U.C. Berkeley. I am NOT a journalist, I am NOT a public defender, I am NOT a snitch for LPD management or the ACLU. Therefore, I'm NOT here to do an exposé or news story, I'm NOT here to make any moral judgments about any of you, and I'm NOT here to advance a political or ideological agenda. I am here to observe custodial interrogations for purely academic purposes. I keep confidential anything you tell me or that I observe during these custodial interrogations. Moreover, the university requires me to write up my thesis in such a way that any potentially identifying case information is also kept strictly confidential.

My dissertation (now here's the boring part) is about the history and practice of custodial interrogation in America. My fieldwork at LPD will only be one of eight chapters in a 200–300 page thesis. I am interested in the general question of what makes a good detective and an effective interviewer/interrogator. I also want to know, statistically, what the relationship is between a number of case variables (e.g., the type of crime, the amount of evidence against a suspect, the demographics of the suspect, complainant, and detective) and the rate at which admissions are obtained; what interrogation techniques work most effectively; whether and how *Miranda* helps or hurts an investigator's chances of getting a confession; how investigators work a case; and the significance of interrogation as a means of solving cases. I am also circulating (one copy for each section) an academic article that (if it doesn't put you to sleep) should give you a good idea of my academic interests.

Some of you have asked me why I chose to study Laconia. The answer is that it is the biggest department in the [geographical location] (which is where I live), and thus has the most action for me to see. However, I am also studying custodial interviewing at the Northville, Southville, and Eastville Regional Park District Police Departments. In any event, I hope to finish my fieldwork here by August 15th, 1993. If any of you have any questions about me or my research, please let me know.

This memorandum appeared to be a striking success: many detectives thanked me for laying out my research agenda more explicitly, while assuring me that they no longer distrusted my motives or aspirations. Yet as every police field researcher knows, the process of establishing trust with his research subjects can never be complete or absolute. For distrust and suspicion remain a central, immutable feature of every policeman's working identity as well as the larger police culture itself (Skolnick 1966; Reiner 1985). A certain amount of residual distrust of my activities within CID therefore remained inevitable.

As they came to know me, however, most of the detectives gradually let down their guard and permitted me to view most of their interrogations. I eventually received access to most of the interrogations at LPD most of the time, though outside of the Robbery section I often had to advertise my presence to be recognized by interrogating detectives prior to any questioning. My access to interrogations varied by each of the sections within CID, as well as by my social relationship with individual interrogators. I was most likely to be permitted to sit in on robbery interrogations, least likely to be permitted to sit in on homicide interrogations. With the exception of these homicide interrogations, eventually I received access to most of the interrogations that I knew were occurring within CID. Notwithstanding these exceptions, as a civilian outsider and potential critic, I had successfully negotiated an unprecedented, if not extraordinary, opportunity to collect contemporaneous observational data on the secret and hidden practices of police interrogators at LPD.

WHEN COURTS AND ETHNOGRAPHY CONFLICT: ANOTHER EPISODE

From the beginning I was aware of the potentially sensitive nature of any police interrogations that I might observe. In the two years during which I sought research access to the LPD's CID division, the subject of my status as a potential percipient witness arose in passing during a lunch-meeting with my dissertation chair and the captain of CID. Though we recognized that I could be called to testify about anything I observed, the three of us agreed that the likelihood of such an occurrence was low and, moreover, that if subpoenaed I would simply describe what I witnessed. The captain emphasized that I would have nothing to hide; my dissertation chair added that the police would likely be on their best behavior in my presence anyway. Yet because I assumed that the LPD would never really open its doors to me, I had no reason to give this possibility much further thought at the time.

When the Chief of LPD suddenly and unexpectedly approved my research project more than two years after our initial request, I did not worry about the possibility of eventually being called as a percipient witness, but instead turned my attention to my next, most immediate research obstacle: receiving the imprimatur of University of California Berkeley's Human Subjects Committee (HSC). Although I spent more than three months negotiating with my HSC before finally acquiring the university's permission to observe custodial interrogations (a process my research subjects considered hilariously funny for its "ivory tower absurdity"), the possibility of being called to testify never arose during any of our interactions, and therefore I was not required to discuss it in my official Human Subjects Protocol Agreement. Instead, the HSC required that I write up my research in a manner that guaranteed the anonymity and confidentiality of my research subjects and, additionally, that the police detectives (but not the custodial suspects) approve of my research activities, practices that I would have carried out even in the absence of any official directives from a university HSC. Again, I gave little thought to the possibility of a court ordering me to turn over confidential research notes or to testify about activities I observed. A fledgling graduate and law student with no prior field research experience at the time, I knew little about the politics and ethics of fieldwork.

Regardless, this is a possibility that all fieldworkers should consider well before entering the field. Under current rules of evidence, a social scientist possesses no legal right to claim a privileged or confidential relationship with his research subjects (unlike, for example, the privilege doctors, attorneys, clergy and psychotherapists possess in communications with their clients). Either a prosecutor or a defense attorney could therefore have served me with a subpoena ordering me to surrender my fieldnotes and provide oral testimony about the interrogations I had witnessed. Since I promised anonymity and confidentiality to the CID detectives at LPD both prior to and during my study, this possibility eventually began to trouble me. Like other researchers who knew of this possibility in advance (Scarce 1994; Van Maanen 1982; Humphreys 1975), I intended on strenuously objecting to turning over my research notes or providing oral testimony that could be used against my research subjects. However, as Rik Scarce's case would later illustrate, the failure to comply with the terms of a subpoena to produce records or testify may result in criminal contempt charges and indefinite incarceration. In short, field researchers who observe deviant acts that have legal consequences may find themselves in what John Van Maanen (1983) aptly called "a moral fix." There is currently no adequate solution to this ethical dilemma of field work.

During my nine months in the field, I was reminded on several occasions of the potential legal implications of my data-gathering activities and the possibility of finding myself in such a fix. As I mentioned earlier, a managing prosecutor once angrily threatened to have me kicked out of the Laconia Police Department, precisely because he feared that a defense attorney might discover my research notes and that might cause one of his deputy district attorneys to lose a suppression hearing.[3] Later in my fieldwork, the homicide detectives informed me that they would not permit me to take any notes inside their interrogations, fearing, of course, that such notes could end up in a courtroom and embarrass or contradict them. Instead, the homicide detectives provided me with a copy of their own notes to any homicide interrogations I witnessed. In one such interrogation, a suspect first invoked his right to remain silent, but immediately after the detective and I left the room the suspect called us back in, unambiguously retracted his *Miranda* rights and subsequently confessed to murder. Anticipating that the suspect's attorney would challenge the voluntariness of the suspect's waiver, the interrogating detective told me that I would likely be called as a prosecution witness in this case.

Though the detective's prediction was not realized in this case, more than six months after I had left the field I was called to testify in court as a percipient witness in a different case. During his brief interrogation, the suspect in this case had provided detectives with a full confession to his role in the armed robbery of a local food chain store and the physical assault on one of its employees. The suspect had confessed virtually spontaneously to his full participation in the crime; his interrogation lasted less than thirty minutes. During pretrial proceedings, however, the suspect maintained that he confessed only because the detectives had first threatened him with other prosecutions if he did not confess, and then prevented him from invoking his *Miranda* rights. Both detectives denied these allegations.

Upon learning that I had observed the interrogation of his client, the public defender in this case requested a personal interview from me, as well as a copy of my research notes. When I refused to cooperate with both requests, the public defender served me with a subpoena ordering me to appear at a preliminary hearing and subsequent trial to testify about my observations in his client's custodial interrogation. I immediately contacted Robert Kagan (a faculty member in my program and former chair of University of California Berkeley's HSC), Michael Smith (another former chair of Berkeley's HSC and professor of law), political science professor Austin Ranney (the chair of Berkeley's HSC at the time), and Professor Jerome Skolnick (a member of my dissertation committee) to discuss my predicament. The consensus was that we needed either to convince the judge to "quash" the subpoena or to convince the public defender to withdraw it, so that I would not have to testify or turn over confidential information. At Professor Kagan's request, on the very next day I met with the vice-chancellor of Legal Affairs, who initially questioned whether my case was significant enough to warrant legal representation at the university's expense. Professor Kagan immediately arranged for a meeting with the associate dean of Research, the vice-chancellor of Legal Affairs, Kagan, Ranney, Skolnick, and myself. During this meeting, Kagan, Skolnick and Ranney persuaded the associate dean to grant our request for university legal representation. A meeting was scheduled with the university's Office of General Counsel.

Meanwhile, Professor Skolnick attempted informally to persuade the Laconia Public Defender's Office to withdraw the subpoena. Since I was the only third-party witness to their client's interrogation and contested confession, the Public Defender's Office replied that any failure to compel my testimony would amount to legal malpractice and become a valid grounds for a legal appeal by their client in the event of a conviction. Ever creative, Professor Skolnick suggested that a third party, preferably an attorney whom the public defender trusted, read my research notes to determine whether the public defender would advance his client's case by subpoenaing me. If so, Professor Skolnick reasoned, the public defender should go forward with the subpoena, and university counsel could still attempt to quash it; if not, then the public defender could withdraw the subpoena without violating any professional obligations to his client in this case. The public defender unequivocally refused this request as well. As far as he was concerned, his client's freedom hung in the balance, and as matter of due process his client was entitled to my research notes and testimony as to what really transpired during that interrogation.

Professors Smith and Ranney, the vice-chancellor, and I attended the meeting with the Office of the General Counsel, at which four university attorneys presided. In varying degrees, each attorney expressed their skepticism about accepting my case. Although they spent much of the meeting querying me about the facts of the case, these attorneys attempted to persuade us that the university had little, if any, chance of prevailing in a case that pitted a criminal defendant's constitutional right to a fair trial against an academic researcher's professional interest in protecting privately acquired information. When the judge balanced these two interests against one another, as the law demands, surely we would lose. The attorneys continued: even in civil (as opposed to criminal) cases where there are no constitutional rights at stake and thus a defendant's (or plaintiff's) legal claim to confidential information is far less compelling, university researchers still lose virtually every balancing test in court. The attorneys reminded us that there exists no common law, constitutional or statutory privilege protecting the data university researchers acquire, however confidential. Why then, the attorneys asked, should the university expend the time and resources to defend my case when a judge would surely rule against us and, if the case were appealed, perhaps create even stronger legal precedent for future legal rulings against academic researchers?

Professors Smith and Ranney counterargued that the university had both a professional and moral obligation to defend its researchers in such situations, regardless of the chances of winning in court. If the university failed to protect its researchers from the compelled disclosure of confidential communications and observations, the very purpose of the university—the collection and public dissemination of knowledge—might be undermined. For without meaningful assurances of confidentiality, research like my own could not be conducted; research subjects would not grant us access into their private worlds if our promises of confidentiality rang hollow when put to the test. In addition, Professors Smith and Ranney argued that it was imperative for the local research community to know that the university would stand behind its principles and defend one of its members in the face of such legal compulsions. Their message was twofold: we must assure not only our research subjects of the integrity of our promises and commitments to them, but we must also assure fellow researchers that we are willing to act when those promises and commitments are threatened by third parties and/or challenged in court.

We prevailed: the Office of General Counsel agreed to assume my legal representation and fight to have the subpoena withdrawn or quashed at the upcoming preliminary hearing.

The court scheduled the preliminary hearing to run concurrently with the trial of the accused, though in a separate hearing outside the presence of the jury. At the preliminary hearing, University of California legal counsel argued that the subpoena should be quashed because the public interest in my research— research that is uniquely predicated on maintaining the assurances of confidentiality that I provided to my subjects—should outweigh any due process right the criminal defendant may possess to the discovery of my research notes or to the compulsion of my testimony. In addition, my university attorney argued that although academic researchers do not possess an evidentiary privilege shielding them from compulsory testimony, they can be analogized to journalists who enjoy a limited First Amendment right to maintain the confidentiality of their research sources. The public defender countered that the defendant's constitutional right to a fair trial unambiguously outweighed any public interest in my research; the prosecutor supported the defense's request to compel my written notes and courtroom testimony. Following the judge's skeptical, if friendly, responses to my attorney's arguments—did university legal counsel *really* believe that the public interest in my research could outweigh something so fundamental to due process as the defendant's right to a fair trial?—my attorney requested an in-camera (i.e., off-record) hearing in the judge's chambers in which I could speak in confidence to the other attorneys and the judge.

At the in-camera hearing, the public defender suggested that we resolve the matter off record simply by letting me tell the judge what happened at the defendant's interrogation; the prosecutor sharply disagreed, however, arguing that he wanted my notes and my testimony to be part of the court record. My attorney continued, unsuccessfully, to argue that the subpoena be quashed. The judge cut off my attorney's argument: the defendant's due process rights clearly outweighed any public interest in my research, he firmly declared. Since the defendant and two LPD detectives had given diametrically opposed accounts of what occurred during the interrogation in question, the judge concluded that my testimony was essential for resolving a dispute that was necessary to provide the accused with a fair trial. My attorney nevertheless continued to argue that, like journalists, I enjoyed a limited First Amendment right to the confidentiality of my research materials. The judge was not impressed by this argument either. Moreover, the judge reasoned, the First Amendment would not even shield a journalist in my identical situation from compulsory testimony, much less an academic researcher. The judge informed me that failure to testify would leave me in contempt of court, a penalty that carried a renewable five-day jail term (at least until the end of the jury trial) and a $1,000 fine.

At this point I privately consulted with my attorney. The university would support whatever decision I chose, he assured me. However, since turning over my notes would not harm my research subjects but instead help the prosecutor—the detectives had not threatened the suspect or prevented him from invoking his *Miranda* rights—there was little reason for me to risk jail. In addition, if I refused to testify, this case would likely be appealed, and surely an appellate court would rule against the establishment of an evidentiary privilege for academic researchers if it were pitted against a criminal defendant's constitutional due process rights. "Bad facts make bad law," my attorney said, echoing a familiar legal truism. Under threat of incarceration, under the mistaken impression that my research notes would do no harm to the interests of my research subjects, and believing that my failure to testify could damage the future interests of all academic field researchers, I decided to comply with the judge's order to testify at the preliminary hearing. I will always regret this decision. Although my testimony clearly established that the detectives did not threaten the suspect with prosecution prior to his confession, the public defender seized on the following section of my research notes:

> The reading of the *Miranda* admonition prior to the interrogation was impressive. After the admonition was read to him, the suspect said he wasn't sure whether, having his rights in mind, he wished to speak to the detectives. Detective X then asked the suspect why he wasn't sure, and the suspect said that, despite what he had just said (i e., that he understood each of these rights), he did not fully understand his rights. Detective X then read the *Miranda* rights from the form again to the suspect, this time very slowly, one by one, making sure that the suspect understood each of the four rights

that comprise the *Miranda* warning. After Detective X read each one, the suspect nodded his head affirming that he understood its meaning. Then, after
the four rights had been read, the suspect said he understood his rights, but
he was still not sure whether he wished to speak to the detectives. Detective
X pointed out, again, that the suspect had a legal right not to talk to the
police and if he wished he could request an attorney, which would effectively end the interrogation. Detective X then pointed out that with all the
evidence against him it was clearly in his best interest to tell the truth and
talk to the police, but if he spoke to a public defender the suspect would be
told that the best thing is not to speak to the police. This, Detective X said,
was the public defender's standard line, but it wasn't good advice, because
in this case (where the suspect had been identified, they had the gun, and
witness statements), a confession statement could only help, and not hurt,
the suspect. This was his one opportunity to tell his side of the story, said
Detective X. The suspect nodded his head in agreement and gladly signed
the admonition statement.

It is highly unusual for a detective to read a suspect his *Miranda* rights several
times and then inform the suspect that a public defender would tell him to refuse
to speak to police. One might consider such a detective to be acting in an exemplary manner, certainly within the letter, if not spirit, of *Miranda v. Arizona* (384
U.S. 436, 1966). State and lower federal courts have been divided, however, over
how to approach an arrestee's use of equivocal or ambiguous language in response
to the reading of his *Miranda* rights. As Ainsworth (1993:260–261) indicates:

> Some jurisdictions have adopted a rule requiring invocations of the right to
> counsel to be direct and unambiguous before they are given any legal effect.
> Other jurisdictions allow the police to continue questioning a suspect
> whose invocation is ambiguous or equivocal, but only to determine the sus-
> pect's intent with respect to the exercise of the right to counsel. Still others
> treat any recognizable invocation as legally sufficient to bar any further
> police interrogation.

The U.S. Supreme Court may have put this issue to rest, however, when it
recently held that police are not obligated to cease their questioning of a suspect
who makes an ambiguous request to have a lawyer present (*Davis v. United States*,
113 S. Ct. 2350, 1994).

After the preliminary hearing in which I testified, the superior court judge
decided to exclude the defendant's confession from the jury. The judge reasoned
that since Detective X had suggested that the suspect should speak to the police,
the actual waiver to his *Miranda* rights was involuntary and thus the resulting
confession must be suppressed from evidence in trial. In addition, the judge prevented the prosecutor from using the confession to impeach the credibility of the
defendant—a ruling that clearly contradicted *Harris v. New York* (401 U.S. 222,
1971), a leading case in which the Supreme Court had held that although a voluntary statement obtained in violation of *Miranda* could not be admitted into evidence as part of the prosecution's case-in-chief, it could nevertheless be used for
impeachment purposes on cross-examination if the defendant chose to take the

stand. The confession—which I believe had been properly acquired and voluntarily given—was thus suppressed solely as a result of my decision to provide the courts with my research notes and testimony.

Several weeks later I learned that the jury had convicted the suspect of one count of armed robbery, while dismissing the three other felony charges against him. We will never know the effect the suspect's confession would have exercised on the jury's verdict. I subsequently visited the Laconia Police department to apologize to Detective X for betraying my promise of confidentiality to him. Ironically, both Detective X and the second detective present at the interrogation assured me that I did the right thing by not breaking the law in response to the judge's order. Their anger was directed not at me, but at the system: "Let this be an object lesson to you in how fucked up our criminal justice system is," Detective X told me as I departed the Laconia Police Station that day. Nevertheless, I will always regret having chosen to turn over my research notes and testify, even though I was under threat of incarceration and even if my research subjects considered my actions morally appropriate. Not only had I betrayed my research subjects, but I had probably also spoiled the field for future police researchers in Laconia, perhaps elsewhere as well. As a result of my decision to testify, it is likely that my study will be not only the first *but also the last* participant observation study of American police interrogation practices for some time to come. If I am correct, future researchers may be deprived of the opportunity to replicate, test, or extend my study based on primary, especially observational, materials. While we may wish to write off this unfortunate event to the poor judgment of a naive and inexperienced field researcher, the social science community has a vested interest in preventing such a mistake from happening again.

Conclusion: The Need for a Federal Evidentiary Research Privilege

I agree with Rik Scarce (1994) that we must seek federal legislation establishing our rights as scholars to confidential communications with our research subjects if we are to protect our role as society's fact finders, educators, and questioners. Following the outcome of my case, I informally requested that the university pursue legislation protecting scholars' rights to confidentiality. The chair of the Human Subjects' Committee informed me, however, that the university did not consider this issue a high enough priority to merit the time and expense necessary to propose and lobby for such legislation. Yet, if we wish to prevent future researchers from undergoing the same indignities and intrusions that both Rik Scarce and I recently experienced, if we wish to be able to honor the promises and commitments we extend in good faith to our research subjects, and if we wish to acquire primary data and disseminate new information about controversial topics, then the sociological research community has no choice but to unite on this issue and lobby for federal legislation establishing an evidentiary privilege for academic researchers.

Rik Scarce's well-publicized case by itself should supply enough evidence to convince researchers of this conclusion. My case additionally demonstrates that even under more favorable circumstances—I went through the Human Subjects Review process, I was zealously represented by university legal counsel, and I avoided incarceration—the subpoenaed researcher will suffer personal and professional tribulations when subjected to the coercion of courts. Without a federal evidentiary privilege, all subpoenaed researchers will currently find themselves in a no-win situation, a moral fix that admits of no positive solution. As Rik Scarce (1994:147) argues, "I see no way out but to seek federal legislation that clarifies scholars' rights and those of all members of the press. This extreme, laborious step seems to me to be the only option left to us." I concur with Scarce's judgment.

However, we must acknowledge competing considerations if we are to successfully advance this cause. While I have invoked my case as additional support for Scarce's call to action, a critic might well distinguish it from Scarce's case to argue against the establishment of an evidentiary privilege for academic researchers. Such a critic might argue that one must evaluate the context and social structure of any given research setting before privileging the privacy rights of research subjects over the legitimate informational needs of third parties. The critic might contend that my principled call for an evidentiary privilege is peculiarly unsociological insofar as it emphasizes an unconditional rule over a case-by-case analysis of the various interests at issue in any given research project. The critic might, for example, point out that while Scarce was on the side of the good guys (environmental activists), I was on the side of the bad guys (cops). Even if we reject this dichotomy as simplistic, it is worth considering that Scarce resisted becoming an agent of the state to protect his research subjects from incarceration, while I tried (unsuccessfully, it turned out) to aid the state in its attempt to incarcerate someone. Perhaps more importantly, however, the critic might argue that while Scarce's research subjects merit a legitimate claim to privacy in their confidential interviews, my research subjects surely do not enjoy a similar right of privacy. For in a democratic society police are politically and publicly accountable for their actions, especially when a citizen's constitutional rights and/or freedom is at stake. Our critic could join cause with other social scientists who, more generally, have questioned whether the ASA's Code of Ethics' commitment to protecting data gathered under promises of confidentiality should be modified to account for the differences of power and position among our research subjects (Galliher 1982, 1980; Marx 1984; Punch 1986).

What these arguments fail to appreciate, however, is that political accountability may be achieved more successfully by the publication of *general* and systematic research findings—such as my own on contemporary police interrogation practices—than by exposing the misdeeds of an individual in any *specific* and idiosyncratic case. Moreover, by protecting the anonymity and confidentiality of our research subjects in the publication of general research findings, we minimize the risk of damaging the personal and professional reputations of our research subjects. If, instead, we yield to the state's compulsions and testify in courts about our confidential communications or observations, we are likely to foreclose the opportunity for similar research in the future and thus deprive the scholarly community and the public of one of the most important resources in assessing the accountability of our public officials. This will be disproportionately true for research that seeks to acquire hidden and dirty data, precisely the kind of research in which issues of accountability are most salient.

Still, I am not altogether comfortable with the implications of this argument. It was easy for me to dismiss the relevance of the public defender's subpoena because the police detectives in my case acted in an exemplary manner, despite the judge's misreading of the case law. Similarly, it was easy for Scarce to dismiss the relevance of the prosecutor's hypothetical question to him about revealing the identity of a research subject who detonated a nuclear bomb, because to environmentalists such an act would be unthinkable. Yet considering the history of third degree violence in America (see Leo 1994a: Chapter One), it is not difficult to imagine a detective physically extracting a confession from a custodial suspect. If I had observed such an event during my field research, I probably would have reacted much differently to a public defender's attempt to subpoena my testimony and research notes. Fortunately, I did not witness any physically coercive interrogations.

Nevertheless, we must not ignore the hard cases or the difficult questions. Perhaps Marquart's (1986) research should be mentioned alongside mine and Scarce's in any discussion of evidentiary privileges for academic researchers. Although Marquart (1986) was not subpoenaed by a court, his case should give us pause. Actively participating as a prison guard in research on a southern maximum security prison, Marquart witnessed (and sometimes joined in) acts of violence against prison inmates, including illegal beatings and restraining inmates while medics sutured wounds without an anesthetic. Had the inmates sued Marquart's research subjects, the prison guards, for unlawful physical brutality or for maintaining inhumane prison conditions, what would we have advised Marquart to do? Would an evidentiary privilege for academic researchers be justified in such a case?

It may be tempting for fieldworkers to fall back on Klockars's (1979) distinction between a morally competent human being and a morally competent researcher in response to such questions, but this distinction offers unsatisfactory answers in the face of human rights violations by our research subjects. While field researchers may necessarily have to suffer dirty hands and dirty roles to acquire dirty data, there is a limit to the amount of filth that is morally tolerable. We must still lobby vigilantly for the establishment of an academic research privilege, but we must recognize that there are thresholds beyond which such a privilege may no longer be justifiable. The idea of a threshold should not weaken, but rather strengthen, our claim for the establishment of an academic evidentiary privilege: after all, none of the currently existing evidentiary privileges (attorney/client, doctor/patient, psychotherapist/client, priest/penitent, and marital) are absolute. All permit exceptions in extreme situations, all contain limitations on their scope, and all can be waived by the party possessing the privilege (see Kaplan, Waltz, and Park 1992). A threshold requirement for an academic evidentiary privilege could be set according to general guidelines that would protect the fundamental human rights of third parties, and, in practice, could be evaluated on a case-by-case basis. To be sure, we cannot expect the point at which the threshold is exceeded to remain constant: there will always be competing considerations, unique circumstances, trade-offs, and room for debate; difficult cases will continue to arise and vex us from time to time. But we should not expect easy answers to the ethical issues that we encounter in our research, for fieldwork is, by its very nature, a morally ambiguous enterprise. Nevertheless, on balance, an evidentiary privilege for academic researchers is necessary if, as Rik Scarce and I have both argued, we are to achieve our primary purpose as society's factfinders, educators, and questioners.

***

I presented an earlier version of this paper to the EPOS (Ethnomethodological, Phenomenological, and Observational Sociologies) section of the Department of Sociology at the University of California, Los Angeles. For helpful suggestions about revising that talk into this paper, I thank the graduate students and faculty in attendance, especially Bob Emerson, Laura Gomez and Jack Katz. I thank Patti Adler, Peter Adler, Lauren Edelman, John Galliher, David T. Johnson, Gary Marx, Fred Pampel, Rik Scarce and Jerome Skolnick for reading an earlier draft of this paper and offering critical comments and advice.

***

NOTES

[1] In the Laconia Police Department, the detectives who work in CID are technically sergeants; no separate designation for detective even exists. For purposes of clarity, however, I will continue to refer to them as detectives.

[2] 35% of the interrogations in my sample were conducted in interrogation rooms located inside the jail and the remaining 65% were conducted in interrogation rooms located inside the Criminal Investigation Division. Since I "hung out" in the Criminal Investigation Division (which is located on the second floor of the Laconia Police Department), I was aware only of the interrogations occurring there. I became aware of interrogations occurring in the jail (which is located in the basement of the Laconia Police Department) only if the interrogating detective informed me of the event.

[3] The purpose of a suppression hearing is to evaluate whether a police officer or detective acquired alleged evidence of the accused's guilt in a legal manner: if so, judge permits the evidence to be introduced into court at trial; if not, the judge excludes the evidence from any subsequent trial proceedings.

PART III

Producing Ethnographies
Theory, Evidence
And Representation

Ethnographic writing begins rather than ends with "setting down the meaning particular social actions have for the actors whose actions they are" (Geertz, this volume, p. 73). While actively in the field the ethnographer may momentarily turn away from local scenes and relations to consider and perhaps begin to sketch patterns and analytic possibilities. But typically it is upon leaving the field that the researcher pursues these matters in sustained and focused fashion. The field researcher now seeks to compose coherent texts in which observations and experiences of particular local scenes are made to engage readers with no direct knowledge of the peoples and events recounted, usually by speaking to the concepts and traditions of a scholarly discipline.

Producing written representations of social worlds involves three interrelated processes. First, most ethnographers try to move beyond the particular situations and meanings they observed to identify general patterns and regularities in social life. They do so by developing theoretical statements of general scope and applicability, i.e., propositions which explicitly state "what the knowledge thus attained demonstrates about the society in which it is found and, beyond that, about social life as such" (Geertz, this volume, p. 73). Second, ethnographers seek to produce member-sensitive theoretical accounts that are accurate. They do so by assembling different kinds of evidence to support particular claims, and by describing the key junctures and decisions that occurred during the research process. Finally, ethnographers face a further series of complex issues in producing finished texts intended for outside audiences and publication. This section and the readings which follow will address these processes—developing analyses that stay close to the events observed, warranting and

281

appraising fieldwork claims and findings, and the representational and ethical issues that arise in producing final or published ethnographic accounts.

But first a caveat: While this section and its accompanying readings by and large take up matters of ethnographic "desk work" (Marcus 1980), the line between "fieldwork" and "desk work" is quite fluid; analysis, for example, may take place in the field as data are collected, recorded, and reviewed. But ethnographers theorize in a particularly sustained and intense fashion once they leave the field and sit down to figure what to say about their experiences. Similarly, while observing events in the field ethnographers will frequently engage issues of evidence and accuracy, or envision how some key incident or on-the-moment insight might be framed to interest future readers. But these processes too are distinctively taken up in sustained, concentrated ways when one is out of the field, sitting at a desk, committed to the actual task of writing something for broader audiences.

DEVELOPING ETHNOGRAPHIC ANALYSES

Some field researchers display little interest in theorizing, sometimes dismissing it entirely as the imposition of cultural and disciplinary interests upon local lives and experiences. But most ethnographers are committed to moving beyond more or less descriptive characterizations of those they have studied to offer explanations for observed phenomena, or to propose even more elaborate conceptual framings of these matters. This section will begin by looking at some features common to most ethnographic analysis. It will then consider several more specific approaches to developing such analyses.

The Concerns and Commitments of Ethnographic Analysis

Despite differences in how they understand the goals and procedures for analyzing ethnographic data, many field researchers share a number of deeper assumptions and sensitivities about what ethnographic analysis is and how it should be conducted.

Analysis as Craft.   Most ethnographers approach theorizing not as an intimidatingly formal, high-science endeavor but as a pragmatic craft. Becker describes Hughes' unpretentious, low-key, comparative approach to sociological theorizing in these terms (1998:1):

> Hughes had no love for abstract Theory. A group of us students once approached him after class, nervously, to ask what he thought about "theory." He looked at us grumpily and asked, "Theory of what?" He thought that there were theories about specific things, like race and ethnicity or the organization of work, but that there wasn't any such animal as Theory in general.

Becker (this volume) shares this "deep suspicion of abstract sociological theorizing." All too often it is "a tool that is likely to get out of hand, leading to a generalized discourse largely divorced from the day-to-day digging into social life that

constitutes sociological science" (Becker 1998:4). Instead he treats qualitative theorizing as a form of "sociological shop floor practice" moved forward by various
"tricks"—that is, "ways of thinking" that allow the fieldworker "to turn things
around, to see things differently, in order to create new problems for research, new
possibilities for comparing cases and inventing new categories, and the like" (7).

Minimizing Use of Received Theory.   In order to be able to make new findings
about the social world, ethnographers emphasize developing theoretical propositions after immersion in the field. Blumer long ago warned of the tendency of
the "underlying" or "initiating picture of the empirical world" to direct and
restrict sociological theorizing: "This picture sets the selection and formulation
of problems, the determination of what are data, the means to be used in getting
the data, the kinds of relations sought between data, and the forms in which
propositions are cast" (Blumer 1969:24–25). Field researchers have resisted this
tendency by minimizing or avoiding premature commitment to any theory, *a priori* concept, or system for classifying field data. Thus, grounded theorists Glaser
and Strauss (1967) contend that preconceived theories truncate empirical
inquiry "either by forcing data into preconceived conceptual categories, or by
inducing an infatuation for verification of extant theories" (Layder 1982:104).
The fieldworker should therefore enter a research setting as nearly "tabula rasa"
as possible, "without any preconceived theory that dictates . . . relevancies in
concepts and hypotheses" (Glaser and Strauss 1967:33). Similar concerns underlie Becker's (1998:123) recommendation to avoid using an established conceptual
category to define an empirical observation as a "case." For in asserting that what
we are studying is a case of *X*, we are led to assume "that everything that is
important about the case is contained in what we know about the category"; as a
result "we don't see and investigate those aspects of our case that weren't in the
description of the category we started with" (123–24).

Burawoy's (1991) proposed "extended case method" stands as the major
exception to this general ethnographic aversion to extensive theorizing in
advance of data collection. Drawing an explicit contrast with grounded theory's
commitment to "discover new theory from the ground up," Burawoy urges using
data collected through participant observation "to restructure existing theory"
(8). Existing theory provides the pivotal resource for orienting to the field site,
keying the identification of the "anomalies," "internal contradictions," and "theoretical gaps or silences" that motivate inquiry, only to then be reformulated or
"rebuilt" to explain these matters. As Burawoy outlines this process (9):

> We begin by trying to lay out as coherently as possible what we expect to
> find in our site *before* entry. When our expectations are violated—when we
> discover what we didn't anticipate—we then turn to existing bodies of aca-
> demic theory that might cast light on our anomaly. . . . The shortcoming of the
> theory become grounds for a reconstruction that locates the social situation
> in its historically specific context of determination. [emphasis in original]

Thus the field provides not opportunities to discover new or unappreciated processes of social life, but a series of sites allowing "critical tests" of existing theory.

"Rather than theory emerging from the field, what is interesting in the field emerges from our theory" (9).

Intimate Familiarity and Grounded Theorizing.   Most ethnographers insist that theorizing build on "intimate familiarity" (Blumer 1969) with and stay grounded in the setting or events under study. Theory is grounded when it grows out of, and is directly relevant to, activities occurring in the setting under study.[1] Ethnographic theory tends to be grounded in another sense: by staying close to what the people observed actually say and do, by representing their routines and dramas in something like their own terms. Thus, on the one hand ethnographers tend to avoid grand, abstract theorizing, elaborating experience-near and eschewing experience-far concepts. On the other hand, ethnographers try not to reduce lived human experience to presumably more fundamental, "deeper," beneath-the-surface processes, whether these be biological, genetic, or psychological.

Flexible Procedures and Simultaneous Data-Collection and Analysis.   Fieldwork inquiry is adaptive and flexible, as researchers modify and fit their procedures to the exigencies of the settings in which they work and to the changing directions of their analyses of those settings. As a result ethnographers do not employ pre-specified, fixed designs for data collection and analysis. Rather, in order to pursue promising empirical and theoretical leads, fieldworkers move constantly from observation and analysis to conceptual refining and reframing and then back to seek new forms of data relevant to their emerging theoretical concerns and categories. As Becker has characterized this process (1998:211–12):

> . . . analysts in this style typically assemble all the data that bear on a given topic and see what statement they can make that will take account of all that material, what generalization best encompasses what is there. If some of the data do not support a generalization, the analyst tries to reframe the generalization, complicating it to take account of the stubborn fact; alternatively, the analyst tries to create a new class of phenomena that differs from the one the datum was originally assigned to, which can have its own explanatory generalization.

In this way ethnographic analysis involves not strict induction (if such is possible), but rather "retroduction" (Bulmer 1979; Katz 1983)—a moving back and forth between observations and theory, modifying original theoretical statements to fit observations and seeking observations relevant to the emerging theory that is "simultaneously deductive and inductive" (Lofland 1976:66). Baldamus (1972:295) has suggested that this "double fitting" of fact to theory and theory to fact is analogous to

> . . . a carpenter alternately altering the shape of a door and the shape of the door-frame to obtain a better fit; . . . [in the same way] the investigator simultaneously manipulates the thing he wants to explain as well as his explanatory framework.

Constant Comparison.   Comparisons drive the development of fieldwork analyses. Of course, all forms of theorizing rely on comparison. But qualitative analysis keys on and seeks to maximize comparisons. The calls by analytic induction to pursue "negative cases" and by grounded theory to follow the "constant comparative method" (see below) both place thoroughgoing comparison at the center of efforts to generate theory from ethnographic data. Prus locates the key to the identification of generic social processes in making comparisons of "parallel activities across contexts" (1996:164): "By drawing comparisons and contrasts across settings, we not only arrive at a richer understanding of each setting, but of similar processes across a range of settings." And Vaughan's (1992) method of "theory elaboration" is propelled by making comparisons between small and large units of organized social life—for example, families and formal organizations—in order to pinpoint and explore common social processes.

Readers and Warrants.   Ethnographic texts are not immaculately conceived writings but constructed accounts subject to the concerns and interpretations of readers (Altheide and Johnson 1994). This recognition—a deep and sustained concern with actual, likely and/or envisioned audiences—underlies recent emphasis on the *relevance* of ethnographic accounts as a criterion for assessing their validity (Hammersley 1992:72–77). It also drives growing self-consciousness about ethnographic writing—how it assumes and appeals to particular audiences, how it engages their interest and enters their intellectual discourse (see below).

Katz (this volume) argues that ethnography faces a peculiar dilemma in providing new insight or original understanding to readers: Its accounts seek to represent the indigenous meanings and everyday lived realities of the people studied; why, then, in today's world of instant global communication, are "realities that are obvious to the subjects not also obvious to the ethnographer's audience?" Ethnographers respond to this dilemma by providing special *warrant* for their study—i.e., "grounds to argue that there is a need for the study in the first place." Warrant involves "the kind of *bridging work* by which ethnographers connect their subjects to their audience." Katz identifies a variety of different kinds of warrant and suggests that ethnography will become more relevant and significant if issues of audience and warrant are addressed explicitly and self-consciously.

Approaches to Ethnographic Analysis

Ethnographers have developed two general strategies for analyzing fieldwork data. One seeks to use contact with field data to stimulate new and original ideas—theoretical insights or interesting hypotheses—that can be pursued and perhaps elaborated into full-blown, systematic analyses. Another strategy, exemplified by analytic induction and grounded theory, focuses on the more general methodological logic and analytic procedures that can be used to develop and elaborate a comprehensive, integrated set of theoretical propositions from qualitative data.

Developing Analytic Insight.   Some time ago Murray Davis (1971) tried to distill the qualities or features of theorizing that led sociological readers to react, "That's interesting!" Some contemporary approaches to qualitative analysis key on the processes of coming up with an original, "interesting" idea from empirical data. Those taking this approach acknowledge, of course, that analytic insight and theoretical sensitivity involve intuition and personal qualities if not necessarily "genius," that generating interesting and original ideas from field data is not a predictable, mechanical process with guaranteed results. But they also insist that intuition and insight are at least as much skills that can be practiced and cultivated (see especially Becker 1998:215-19) as innate abilities, that field researchers can learn ways of conceptually coming at their data which increase the chances of producing interesting conceptual linkages and analyses. Acquiring these skills requires developing easy familiarity with sociological ways of thinking and with exemplars of ethnographic analysis; indeed, the necessity to get into the nitty-gritty detail and substance of specific analyses provides an underlying theme to the varied approaches to developing theoretical sensitivity that will be considered here.

A number of ethnographers emphasize the pursuit of "generic" theories as a way of developing analytic insight. Lofland and Lofland (1995) provide one such approach. The key to developing analyses, they argue, lies in asking questions of field data that will lead to generalized concepts, that is, "generic propositions that sum up and provide order in major portions of your data" (182). To proceed in this way one asks (159):

> Of what more abstract and social analytic category are these data an instance? The goal is to translate the specific materials under study into instances of widely relevant and basic social types, processes, or whatever. In its *upward categorization* generic framing finds fundamental human themes and concerns in obscure and sometimes seemingly trivial social doings. The situation under study is lifted out of its historically unique details and placed among the array of matters of interest to broad audiences.

Ethnographers draw upon three resources to generate these types of questions (160-63): First, the use of metaphor through the claim that X is (or is like) Y, in this way providing "a new way to understand that which we already know" (160, citing Brown 1977:98); second, constructing ironic contrasts between intended and actual consequences, or between official understandings and actual practice; and finally, identifying new forms of social units and/or new variations of analytic types, structure, causes, and consequences. For example, a variation on standard causal understandings of homelessness might contend that "disoriented behavior and heavy drinking among the homeless appears to emerge or increase as the homeless try to cope with the stressful and difficult exigencies of their situation rather than being the reason for their situation" (162, citing Snow and Anderson 1993).

Approaches to generic social theorizing frequently employ what Prus (1996:165) has termed "an analytic grid with which to assess and incorporate . . . research in the field . . . to facilitate conceptual stock taking." Thus Lofland and Lofland identify eight substantively different kinds or forms of generic propositions, those involving types, frequencies, magnitudes, structures, processes, causes, consequences and agency (1995:182-83). The intent here is to specify the

substantive kinds of analytic questions that are asked about field data; this typology of basic, productive questions will presumably help the ethnographer move
toward more abstract and hence generic conceptual categories. Similarly, also
drawing upon the theoretical tradition of symbolic interaction, Prus (1996:142)
proposes focusing ethnographic inquiry on "generic social processes," that is,

> ... the transsituational elements of interaction— ... the abstracted, trans-
> contextual formulations of social behavior. Denoting parallel sequences of
> activity across diverse contexts, generic social processes highlight the emer-
> gent, interpretive features of association.

To appreciate process—"the emerging, sequencing, unfolding, ongoing features
of group life" (148)—the analyst should examine the "career," "natural history"
or "life-spans" of a variety of generic processes, including acquiring perspectives,
achieving identity, being involved, doing activity, experiencing relationships,
and forming and coordinating associations (149–50).

Rather than providing an "analytic grid" of generic conceptual categories to
help generate "interesting" theory, Katz (this volume) proposes developing innovative warrants for ethnographic accounts. Articulating such warrants, Katz
suggests, would counter the tendency to view "theory" as pure concepts without
relevance for or relation to readers or audiences; instead it conceives theory as a
way of connecting empirical data and concepts to matters that interest, resonate
with or provoke an audience of readers.[2] Examining a wide range of studies,
Katz argues that ethnographic warrants often recast common understandings of
the *moral status* of those studied: thus warrants typically establish that "what is
obvious to the subjects has been kept systematically beyond the cognitive reach
of the ethnographer's audience because of the moral character of the social life
under investigation." Many classic ethnographies established warrant by focusing on the marginal, stigmatized, and disreputable—". . . dangerous social areas
and morally perverse people." But ethnographers can also provide warrant by
studying those "dripping with respectability, or charismatically inspired." Ethnographies of the morally condemned establish warrant either by normalizing—
showing how these subjects are in basic ways like others—or by exaggerating
their deviance in representing them as bohemians. Ethnographies of the morally
exceptional establish warrant either by debunking the elites—for example, by
showing how they engage in dubious, questionable practices—or by debunking
the reasons outsiders accord them deference.

Finally, Becker (1998 and this volume) identifies a series of informal practices or
"generalizing tricks" fieldworkers can use to make interesting sense of their materials. Such tricks provide "ways of expanding the reach of our thinking, of seeing what
else we could be thinking and asking, of increasing the ability of our ideas to deal
with the diversity of what goes on in the world" (1998:7). In particular, tricks help
overcome pervasively conventional ways of thinking, including those established by
existing sociological theories. Consider the trick "learning how lines are drawn"
(1998:150–58). Here the fieldworker takes common distinctions made in some organizational setting—between "us" and "them," "this" and "that"—and then treats

... these distinctions as diagnostic of that organization, those people, their situations, their careers. When your notes record such distinction making and line drawing, you know that this is something to follow up, to find out more about. Who is drawing the line? What are they distinguishing between by doing it? What do they think they will accomplish by making that distinction, drawing the line there? (150)

Becker traces his use of this trick to analyze the important place of "crocks" (patients with "multiple complaints but no discernible physical pathology") in medical students' clinical training (151–58).

Analytic Induction.   In *The Method of Sociology* (1934), Florian Znaniecki proposed the method of analytic induction as a rigorous, systematic means for deriving theoretical propositions from empirical data. Znaniecki contrasted analytic induction with statistical "enumerative induction," where conceptual categories and empirical generalizations are formulated from an existing pool of cases. With analytic induction, in contrast, the researcher begins with a rough formulation of the phenomenon to be explained and an initial hypothesis explaining the phenomenon, then goes on to examine a data set on a case-by-case basis. Analytic induction seeks to provide "perfect" explanation, that is, one that "applies to every case that fits the definition of the phenomenon to be explained" (Becker 1998:195). This can be achieved either by modifying the hypothesized explanatory factor (in the term Katz prefers, the *explanans*) or by redefining the phenomenon to be explained (the *explanandum*) in order to exclude as irrelevant cases that do not fit. By looking at every case, and by deliberately searching for and incorporating negative cases into the analysis, analytic induction "abstracts from a given concrete case the features that are essential, and generalizes them: (Bulmer 1979:661).

By way of illustration, consider the successive reformulations of both what was to be explained and the hypotheses offered as explanation in Cressey's classic study of embezzlement (1953). First, Cressey noted that since the category of convicted embezzlers included both con artists and passers of bad checks, and did not include some offenders who had in fact embezzled (e.g., a bank teller convicted of forgery but not embezzlement for forging a customer's name to a check), it was not useful sociologically. He thus redefined his phenomenon as persons who had "accepted a position of trust in good faith . . . [and then] violated that trust by committing a crime" (1953:20).

Cressey's explanation of such violations of trust began with the hypothesis that such violations occurred when those in positions of trust came to see theft as merely "technical violations." He rejected this notion on finding convicted embezzlers who admitted knowing that their behavior had been wrong and illegal. Next he explored the possibility that violations occurred when a worker "defines a need for extra funds or extended use of property as an 'emergency' which cannot be met by legal means" (28). But some violators noted even greater emergencies in the past but no violation, and others reported no financial emergency ever. The revised hypothesis focused on psychological isolation, often tied to gambling losses: "persons become trust violators when they conceive of themselves as having incurred financial obligations which are considered as nonsocially sanctionable and which, consequently, must be satisfied by a private or secret means" (28). But negative cases appeared in which there were no financial obligations and hence that condition was modified to more general "nonshare-able problems" seen as solvable by trust violation. The final negative case occurred with violators who met the above conditions but who had not earlier embezzled because of their ideas of right and wrong. Changing his hypothesis to incorporate these cases, Cressey came to the following final proposition:

> Trusted persons become trust violators when they conceive of themselves as having a financial problem which is non-shareable, are aware that this problem can be secretly resolved by violation of the position of financial trust, and are able to apply to their own conduct in that situation verbalizations which enable them to adjust their conceptions of themselves as trusted persons with their conceptions of themselves as users of the entrusted funds or property. (30)

Other classic examples of analytic induction include studies by Lindesmith (1947) of opiate addiction, by Becker (1953; 1998:204–207) of becoming a marijuana user, and by Katz (1982 and this volume) of the involvement of poverty lawyers in their work. Characteristically these studies explain "the one specific outcome of interest—opiate addiction, the criminal violation of financial trust, using marijuana for pleasure" (Becker 1998:195). As Katz (forthcoming) emphasizes, pursued in this fashion analytic induction has proved particularly useful "as a way to develop explanations of the interactional processes through which people develop homogeneously experienced, distinctive forms of social action." These explanations tend to highlight three types of explanatory mechanisms: "the practicalities of action (e.g., learning distinctive *techniques* for smoking marijuana)"; "matters of self-awareness and self-regard (e.g., *attributing* physical discomfort to withdrawal from opiates)"; and "the sensual base of motivation in desires, emotions, or a sense of compulsion to act (e.g., embezzling when *feeling pressured* to resolve a secret financial problem)" (4–5).

Analytic induction's claim to universal explanation has long proved a major point of contention. In his early critique, Turner (1953:606) argued that despite claims to universal explanation, Cressey's theory cannot be used to predict who will and will not embezzle, since it does not indicate when and how a problem becomes nonshareable, when embezzlement comes to be seen as a solution, or which violators will be able to rationalize their behavior. This critique has appeared more recently in the assertion that explanations using analytic induction identify necessary but not sufficient causes, since "there was no investigation of cases where the factors assumed to cause embezzlement were present to discover whether it always (or more frequently) occurred in those cases" (Hammersley 1998:99).

Contemporary proponents of analytic induction qualify any claim to universal explanation. Researchers now generally understand the search for perfect explanation not as a goal in itself but as a pragmatic research strategy for conceptual refinement (Ragin 1994:98). Thus Katz (this volume) maintains, "The test is not whether a final state of perfect explanation has been achieved but the *distance* that has been traveled over negative cases and through subsequent qualifications from an initial state of knowledge" (133). Furthermore, proponents argue that while analytic induction cannot identify sufficient causes with absolute certainty (as by examining a control group of nonviolators to exclude the possibility that embezzlement did not occur despite the presence of all explanatory factors), its use typically involves credible if limited tests for sufficiency. Cressey, for example, modified his preliminary hypothesis that trust violations occurred because of an "emergency" which could not be resolved by legal means on finding some eventual violators who had not violated earlier on in the face of "even greater (financial) emergencies"; this procedure thus provides an effective although not perfect comparison between violators and nonviolators. As Katz argues, if "the researcher finds data describing transition points from non-X to X, as well as data describing progressions from X to non-X (e.g., desistance studies), claims of sufficiency may be precisely tested" (8).[3]

Finally, it should be noted that systematic use of the procedures of analytic induction inevitably narrows or restricts research focus. As Becker (1998:206–207) writes, these studies

> ... consider one major hypothesis, designed to explain one specific outcome, and rigorously exclude other, "extraneous" outcomes as not being cases of the phenomenon to be explained. Thus, I ignored the people who continued to smoke marijuana even though they never learned to enjoy it. . . . Similarly, Cressey excluded cases of professional criminals who took positions of financial trust exactly so that they could violate them.

And Katz's progressive narrowing of his explanadum—from poverty lawyers who stayed, to those who stayed despite frustrating work, and finally to those who stayed despite low-status work—essentially redefined the scope of his study from a comparison of the differences between stayers and leavers to "staying as an accomplishment for those doing low-status work" (Ragin 1994:96).

It is likely that this narrowing of focus—the consequence of redefining the phenomenon to be explained in order to exclude cases that do not fit—has restricted the appeal of "rigorous analytic induction" among ethnographers:

> Ethnographers are seldom so single-mindedly interested in finding a unique solution to one specific problem as Lindesmith or Cressey were. Instead, they are typically interested in developing an interlocking set of generalizations about many different aspects of the organization or community they are studying, and much of the force of an ethnographic description comes from seeing how the various generalizations support one another. (Becker 1998:208)

An ethnographer interested in embezzlement, for example, might well focus on those working in positions of trust in banks, but examine the broader "operation of banks as social organizations" (Becker 1998:207) and how such operations both facilitate and seek to prevent any and all forms of covert theft. In general, then, many ethnographers adapt and pursue in less systematic fashion procedures advocated by analytic induction, in particular the commitment to search for and examine negative cases. Thus, analytic induction has exercised an important indirect influence of ethnography, an influence reflected in ethnographers' "refusal to write disconfirming evidence off as some sort of dismissible variation;

in their insistence on instead addressing it as evidence that has to be theoretically accounted for and included as part of the story" (Becker 1998:210).

Grounded Theory. In developing the grounded theory approach in the 1960s, Glaser and Strauss urged abandoning the then-dominant forms of sociological theorizing—the formal theories of Parsons and Blau, and hypothesis-testing theorizing exemplified by survey research—as appropriate models for analyzing qualitative data. The overly logico-deductive approach of the former gave little attention to empirical data, or simply fitted data within pre-established theoretical categories. Grounded theory in contrast should seek to derive analytic categories from close, sustained and systematic review of data: "It is necessary to do detailed, intensive, microscopic examination of the data in order to bring out the amazing complexity of what lies in, behind, and beyond those data" (Strauss 1987:10). And while quantitative survey research brought empirical data to bear on theoretical issues, the priority accorded hypothesis testing made it an unfruitful model for qualitative data analysis. In contrast, the grounded theory approach viewed data collection and analysis not as means of establishing the relation between a few key variables decided in advance, but as procedures for generating and elaborating complex, interrelated series of theoretical propositions through close, systematic examination of the data.

In this task grounded theory emphasizes four primary procedures:

1. *Simultaneous data collection and analysis.* From a very early point in data collection grounded theory instructs the researcher to make analytically explicit observed phenomena as theoretical categories, to systematically identify the properties and dimensions of these categories, to formulate provisional questions or hypotheses about the occurrence or relations between these categories, and to then seek out new data in the field specifically relevant to these refined or focused issues. Indeed, Strauss urges beginning analysis "with the very first, second, or third interview or after the first day or two of fieldwork," continuing (1987:26–27):

> It follows also that the next interviews and observations become informed by
> analytic questions and hypotheses about categories and their relationships. This
> guidance becomes increasingly explicit as the analysis of new data continues.

In this way theoretical categories derive not from the research literature, but by close, continuing examination and collection of data (Charmaz, this volume).

2. *Systematic coding of data.* Initial analysis proceeds by means of qualitative coding driven heavily by the logic of comparison. This coding is not concerned with determining the frequencies of particular events, but with developing and elaborating theoretical categories. It does so through a line-by-line reading of the data with an openness to recognizing all analytic possibilities. In coding the researcher seeks "to analyze the data minutely," an approach which "'minimizes the overlooking of important categories, leads to a conceptually dense theory, gives the feeling—to the reader as well as to the analyst—that probably nothing of great importance has been left out' of the theory, and forces both verification and qualification" (Strauss 1987:31, citing Glaser 1978). Initially this process involves simply

identifying and naming any and all phenomena or general categories. Initial categories can be elaborated by identifying their properties, dimensions and subdimensions by systematically asking about the conditions, interaction among the actors,
strategies and tactics, and consequences of these phenomena (Strauss 1987:27–28).

3. *Memoing.* Simultaneously with ongoing data collection and coding, the
grounded theorist begins to write more extended analyses—memos which
explore and elaborate ideas and concerns arising from the data and its codings
(Charmaz, this volume). While initial memos stay close to coded categories,
developing their properties and dimensions and making comparisons with
related phenomena, subsequent "integrating memos" (Charmaz 1983:123)
develop the relationships between selected, promising categories. Making comparisons between events in the data and between coded categories provides the
key to initial memoing, and to subsequently exploring and specifying the relations between categories, properties and dimensions in integrative memoing.
Indeed, the original statements of the grounded theory approach identified *constant comparison*—looking for variations and contrasts in the data—as the core
mechanism for theory generation (Charmaz, this volume).

4. *Theoretical sampling.* Comparisons are developed by reviewing existing data
or specifically collecting new data in order to elaborate, qualify and test analytic
categories and more complex theoretical propositions. This sort of theoretical
sampling provides "a way of checking on the emerging conceptual framework"
(Glaser 1978:39). Specifically it proceeds by asking, "'*What* groups or subgroups
or populations, events, activities (to find varying dimensions, strategies, etc.)'
does one turn to *next* in data collection?" (Strauss 1987:38–39, citing Glaser 1978).
These decisions are guided not by concern with statistical representativeness but
by concerns of theoretical relevance. "The aim of theoretical sampling is to sample events, incidents, and so forth, that are indicative of categories, their properties and dimensions, so that you can develop and conceptually relate them"
(Strauss and Corbin 1990:177). While grounded theorists emphasize theoretical
sampling as a procedure for enriching conceptual comparisons among data collected in a particular setting, they have also advocated its use as a focused way of
collecting data in new settings relevant to specific conceptual claims.

To illustrate this approach to analyzing qualitative data, consider a portion of
the analysis of how machines affect staff-patient interaction in a hospital setting
developed in Strauss et al. (1985) (and summarized by Strauss 1987:14–17). Fieldwork provided an initial observation: "many machines are connected to the sick
persons." The researcher then formulated this phenomenon as a general analytic
category—"machine-body connections." Considering other observations of this
category, a "dimension" of such connections was identified: The contrast between
connections through one of the body's orifices—"internal connections"—and
connections to the skin of the patient or "external connections." The researcher
then asked a variety of questions about these dimensional categories, for example,
"those orifices are sensitive, so that connection probably hurts," eventually identifying hurt, safety, discomfort, and fear as subdimensions. Using these categories

and their dimensions and subdimensions, the researcher then took up further questions about consequences, staff strategies, patient strategies, and interactions (e.g., "what went on between the personnel and the patient when he was being hooked up?"). The answers to these questions constituted provisional hypotheses to be specifically checked out through further observations or interviews—for example, are there generally safe connections that can become unsafe, as when disconnected? As Strauss sketched one such line of "directed inquiry":

> How do they become disconnected? By accident, carelessness, purposeful-
> ness (as on the part of the annoyed or uncomfortable or fearful patient)?
> What tactics and techniques are used by the personnel to minimize or pre-
> vent disconnection? Special care? Warning the patient about moving?
> Emphasizing that one's safety depends on staying immobile or in not loosen-
> ing the connection no matter how it hurts? Or by eliciting "cooperation,"
> promising that the connection will remain only for several hours or be
> removed periodically to give relief? (15–16)

These lines of inquiry and analysis can be extended by making focused comparisons, for example, between uncomfortable and comfortable machine connections, or between institutional response to dangerous as opposed to nondangerous disconnections.

This illustration highlights several salient differences between grounded theory and analytic induction. First, in contrast to analytic induction's pursuit of one specific hypothesis, grounded theory seeks to produce multiple hypotheses and sets of analytic propositions; theory then should be "conceptually dense," containing "many concepts, and many linkages among them" (Strauss 1987: 10). Second, pursuing multiple-stranded theory, grounded theory insists on the value of exhaustively identifying a wide range of phenomena and categories of interest and of systematically exploring their dimensions and properties *prior to* establishing theoretical relationships between some of these categories and dimensions. In this sense grounded theory "frontloads" the analytic process, focusing of systematic theoretical groundwork prior to formulating explicit hypotheses. In contrast, in order to begin identifying and incorporating negative cases, analytic induction requires an early specification of a hypothesis—however provisional and subject to subsequent revision. Finally, while analytic induction pursues comparison through the identification and incorporation of negative cases, grounded theorists seek a broader range of comparisons. In order to avoid narrowing and restricting theorizing, they seek only a "general fit":

> . . . one is looking to see if they fit in a general sense and in most cases, not
> necessarily in every single case exactly. Continuing modifications and
> changes can be made in the statements until a general match is made.
> (Strauss and Corbin 1990:139)

Glaser and Strauss's original insistence on characterizing grounded theory as a process of "discovering" theory in qualitative data has spawned recurring criticism. One major concern has been grounded theory's separation and prioritizing of the "discovery" over the "verification" of theory, particularly evident in *The Dis-*

covery of Grounded Theory (1967). Some insist that the distinction between "discov-ery" and "verification" (or "justification") is invalid and useless since "we are dealing with a single uniform domain of procedures all of which are equally important for the growth of science" (Feyerabend 1975:167). Others emphasize that the position that theory can be "discovered" independently of and prior to validation appears to abandon any claims to developing valid theory (Katz 1983).[4]

The language and arguments of *The Discovery of Grounded Theory* certainly pro-vide grounds for these criticisms. But in some part the strong accent these initial statements gave to the discovery/verification contrast might be read less as an abandonment of any concern with validity and more as an attempt to evade the limitations of then-dominant survey research procedures. In the 1950s "verifica-tion" was a quantitative enterprise focused on statistical frequencies and distri-butions in testing hypotheses; distinguishing discovery and verification and emphasizing the former thus provided a way of separating and exempting grounded theory from such procedures.

Subsequent statements of the grounded theory approach offer some support for this interpretation. In recent work Strauss (1987) frequently writes of "gener-ating" rather than "discovering" theory (see also Charmaz 1983). When men-tioned, "discovery" may be closely linked with validity; for example, "the theory is not just discovered but verified, because the provisional character of the link-ages—of answers and hypotheses concerning them—get checked out during the succeeding phases of inquiry, with new data and new coding" (Strauss 1987:17). But most significantly, discussions of determining the validity of theoretical propositions figure prominently in recent expositions of the approach. For example, having decided on a "core category" (the central phenomenon around which all the other categories are integrated) for focused or "selective" coding, Strauss and Corbin (1990:116) urge the researcher to relate it systematically to other categories and then begin "validating the relationships" between these cat-egories by going back to the data or returning to the field to collect new data.

Grounded theory has also received criticism for flirting with pure induction in its insistence on deriving concepts from the data, exacerbated by its injunc-tion to avoid all established concepts or theories in developing concepts. Critics point out that pure induction along these lines is impossible: On the one hand, data don't speak themselves; concepts are inevitably involved and presupposed in making sense of data (Bulmer 1979:667–68). On the other hand, the processes whereby "data" are assembled build concepts into the data from the very start; thus data are pre-theorized, products of the fieldworkers' interpretive and con-ceptual decisions in the ways considered previously in Part I.

Again, in recent statements grounded theorists have challenged these cri-tiques as "misconceptions" (Strauss 1987:55). As noted, Strauss now places less emphasis on "discovery" and takes care to distance himself from narrowly empir-icist positions; for example, "the researcher will be making a number of interest-ing, if at first quite provisional, linkages among the *'discovered' (created) concepts*" (1987:17; emphasis added). Similarly, Charmaz (this volume) views the researcher as actively constructing or generating data in the field, and recommends tying analysis directly to data collection in order to make theoretical assumptions explicit and useful for determining what kinds of data to collect. Strauss (1987:6) also gives particular weight to personal experiences as a source of analytic insight, insisting that researchers should be "fully aware of themselves as instruments for developing that grounded theory." And Strauss and Corbin (1990:51–52) provide a place for existing literature not only in cultivating theoretical sensivitity, but also in stimulating questions to begin inquiry and later in directing theoretical sampling.

As Charmaz (this volume) emphasizes, Glaser and Strauss's approach to grounded theory drew together and made explicit analytic procedures and research strategies that had previously comprised an unarticulated part of fieldwork practice. Over the years grounded theory has served as a rallying point for many ethnographic field researchers, providing a coherent, concise codification and extension of practices for analyzing fieldwork data. Yet there are definite points of tension between grounded theory's priority on generating theory and the often more descriptive emphases of ethnography, a tension Glaser and Strauss (1971:183) accented at one time in contrasting their model of the researcher as primarily "an active sampler of theoretically relevant data" with that of "an ethnographer trying to get the fullest data on a group."

Assessing Ethnographic Accounts

In developing analyses that stay close to observed events and indigenous meanings, ethnographers also confront complex issues in deciding how to warrant and assess descriptive and theoretical accounts. Initially leery of assessment criteria and procedures drawn from quantitative social science, ethnographers sought to develop ways of assessing the strength or adequacy of their findings that avoided criteria and procedures ill-matched to the nature of ethnographic goals and methods. But in recent years widespread acceptance of social constructivist views of social reality has brought into question underlying realist assumptions and hence the very possibility of making meaningful assessments of ethnographic accounts.

In the 1950s, in response to the influence of survey research and experimental psychology, many fieldworkers turned to criteria developed for assessing quantitative research to evaluate qualitative research: validity, the extent to which the researcher has accurately represented or measured the phenomenon of interest; and reliability, whether two researchers would reach the same result. But ethnographers gradually came to emphasize differences between the goals and procedures of quantitative and qualitative research. Quantitative research seeks to provide explanation by specifying differences between groups or categories possessing different characteristics or traits, framing these differences as specific variables. Qualitative research tends to look at social life holistically and in context, at least initially avoiding breaking up observed actions and events into discrete variables. Quantitative procedures typically employ preset, fixed designs in order to test clearly formulated hypotheses. Qualitative procedures involve emerging, situationally specific modes of inquiry that are not fixed in advance and that are often difficult to specify even after the fact. As a result ethnographers began to insist that different criteria, vocabulary and procedures of evaluation, fitted to the distinctive purposes and procedures of ethnographic research, were needed.[5]

In the past several decades, however, the pursuit of distinctively qualitative criteria has merged with the deeper paradigm shift toward constructivist understandings of social reality. Constructivism in turn had led some field researchers to reject the feasibility of specifying any criteria for assessing the accuracy of empirical inquiry. As Hammersley (1992:57) notes, such researchers maintain that "the very notion of assessing research products in terms of a set of criteria is itself incompatible with the nature of the social world and how we understand it." Thus as Silverman (2000:188) suggests, a completely relativist position "would rule out any systematic research since it implies we cannot assume any stable properties in the social world"; for if reality is socially constructed and constituted by multiple perspectives, there can be no fixed, "gold standard" of reality (against which to determine accuracy), only claims about or representations of reality produced from one or another partial perspective (Altheide and Johnson 1994). In short, efforts to determine whether ethnographic findings correspond to "events in the real world" are fundamentally misguided, since there is no transcendent way—a procedure independent of all partial perspectives and of some specific, reality-creating method—to determine the character of such events.

While sympathetic to constructionist views of social reality, many ethnographers are extremely reluctant to abandon completely all realist assumptions and the possibility of assessing accuracy. To do so would fundamentally contradict a number of core ethnographic assumptions—for example, that ethnography has a distinctive capacity to make discoveries about the social world that had been unknown or misknown, that social reality has an obdurate quality such that not just anything goes. In response ethnographers in recent years have articulated approaches involving "subtle realism" (Hammersley, this volume) or "analytic realism" (Altheide and Johnson 1994). Such approaches seek to provide assessment criteria and procedures that both are sensitive to a constructivist view of reality and the distinctive qualities of ethnographic inquiry on the one hand, and provide grounds for assessing the truth or accuracy without presuming a transcendent "gold standard" of reality against which to hold up specific ethnographic accounts on the other.

In initial efforts to develop distinctively qualitative criteria, field researchers paid particular attention to procedures involving "member validation" and theoretical originality.[6] Ethnographers took two different approaches to the former. Conceptualizing culture as what a person has to know in order to act appropriately in the eyes of its members, some proposed that ethnographic accounts were adequate when they could be used as instructions by an outsider to pass as a member. Douglas (1976:123), for example, held that tests of "interaction effectiveness" provide presumptive evidence of the fieldworker's grasp of appropriate behavior in the setting and hence of field findings. Wiseman (1970:280–81) reported that she "tested" her findings on skid row life by having several novices read her descriptions and then "successfully" pass as skid row drunks for short periods of time. In a somewhat different strategy, variously termed "member validation" (Gould et al. 1974), "member tests of validity" (Douglas 1976), or "host verification" (Schatzman and Strauss 1973), ethnographers took their findings directly back to the members whose worlds they had described and analyzed. As Bloor (this volume) indicates, this procedure recognizes that fieldwork accounts are second-order constructs, formulated for different purposes and to different ends than member accounts; thus the expectation is not that the accounts would be absolutely identical but rather that members would "recognize, understand, and accept one's description of the setting" (Douglas 1976:131).

Both of these procedures encountered difficulties as methods for assessing ethnographic accounts. First, it became evident that one may "pass" as a member without actually performing as a competent insider, due to the politeness or face-saving graces of members, for example. Second, presenting one's findings to those studied does not allow straightforward, unequivocal determinations of accuracy (Bloor, this volume). In particular, the fieldworker must inevitably interpret the meaning and import of members' evaluations of her findings. As Bloor suggests, positive member reaction may come to be seen as the product of friendship, disinterest, or civility, negative reaction as the result of ideological preconceptions or local institutional commitment. Under these conditions, member support or rejection of fieldwork findings may reveal very little about the "validity" of these findings and a great deal about what is significant and meaningful to members.

A second effort to specify distinctively qualitative criteria focused on the *theoretical* originality and contribution of an ethnographic account. Qualitative researchers (Lofland and Lofland 1995; Athens 1984) have regularly listed generic theory, developed or elaborated theory, and novel theoretical claims as criteria for evaluating ethnographic accounts (see Hammersley's summary 1992:64). But there are significant limitations to making theoretical contributions the exclusive or even a primary cornerstone for assessing ethnographies. In the first place, not all ethnographers are or should be concerned with developing formal or generic theory (Hammersley 1992:64). Secondly, ethnographers usually offer theoretical contribution as one of several assessment criteria involving accuracy or consistency; Athens (1984), for example, insists formal theoretical claims should be "consistent with the empirical observations from which they were derived" and "scientifically credible." Thus the fundamental tension between constructionism and assessing accuracy remains.

Recognizing the limitations of taking findings back to the field as a means for assessing ethnographic adequacy, and of theoretical originality as an exclusive criterion for such assessments, ethnographers have articulated two further approaches to this issue. One involves a variety of procedures for assessing the adequacy of the evidence offered in support of ethnographic claims; the other emphasizes providing detailed accounts of the critical junctures and choices that marked the research process.

Assessing Evidence

Procedures for weighing and evaluating *the adequacy or sufficiency of evidence* lie at the core of current strategies for assessing the accuracy of ethnographic accounts. Hammersley, for example, emphasizes that an ethnographic account should represent "accurately those features of the phenomena that it is intended to describe, explain, or theorize"; the accuracy of such claims are judged "on the basis of the adequacy of the evidence offered in support of them." Similarly, Becker (this volume) holds that the accuracy of descriptions of the subjective concerns and "point of view of the actor" is enhanced by collecting data (evidence) close to actual occasions in which people confer meaning: "The nearer we get to the conditions in which (people) actually do attribute meanings to objects and events the more accurate our descriptions of those meanings are likely to be."

Determining the adequacy of evidence, however, involves complex judgment and interpretive work, not the simple, straightforward sifting of "facts" or comparing of account and reality often connoted by terms like "truth" and "accuracy." Assessments of the adequacy of evidence are subject to several sources of indeterminacy. First, "all judgments about the truth of knowledge claims rest on assumptions, many of which we are not consciously aware, and most of which have not been subjected to rigorous testing" (Hammersley 1992:69). Second:

> Given that there is no bedrock of truths beyond all doubt which we can use as a basis for our assessments, the process of assessment is always potentially subject to infinite regression. Whatever evidence is offered for a claim, the validity of that evidence may always be challenged; and any further evidence provided may in turn also be challenged; and so on, *ad infinitum.* (ibid.)

Finally, even if clearly defined, evaluative criteria can only be applied to specific ethnographic claims by making additional judgments and interpretations not specified by the criteria themselves. In sum, evidentiary adequacy is not a matter of subjecting ethnographic claims to specific "tests" which can determine validity with absolute certainty; rather it is an open-ended interpretive process of providing or identifying "good reasons for believing that something is true or false" (Hammersley 1998:59).[7]

Ethnographers have tended to discuss the interpretive assessment of evidence by considering standard, recurrent challenges that can be brought against particular evidence-based claims. These challenges include the possibilities of blatant misrepresentation and of subtle reactive effects, of potential researcher bias and selectivity, and of failing to provide grounds for generalizing from the case studied to wider contexts.

Misrepresentation and Reactive Effects.   Ethnographers have devoted a great deal of attention to the possibilities that their data can be inaccurate because of deception or misrepresentation: Those studied may tell out-and-out lies, self-consciously misrepresent or distort the meaning and significance of events, and/or behave in blatantly atypical ways exactly because of the presence of the ethnographer. Ethnographers are similarly concerned with possible reactive effects—that is, that what is done and said in natural settings can be significantly shaped by the presence and actions of the observer. Do the fieldworker's words and deeds influence—however subtly and perhaps even unconsciously—what those studied say and do?[8]

While discussions of field methods usually separate issues of deception and misrepresentation from those of reactivity, ethnographers approach both issues in similar terms. Initially consider the problem of reactivity. From the perspective of quantitative methods, field data appear particularly subject to reactive effects since they are not collected by prespecified, fixed procedures. But in recent years ethnographers have moved away from viewing reactive effects as necessarily sources of distortion and bias. As Gussow (1964:231) argued early on, "Ordinarily, in good fieldwork, researchers are not greatly concerned about whether they have disturbed the natural field or not, provided that they can analyze how they affected it structurally. Indeed, by affecting it, they often get to know better what it is they are studying." Fieldwork is inherently social in character, and the fieldworker must then be treated as part of the social reality being studied (Altheide and Johnson 1994). In this way, the field researcher is viewed as "a source for the result, [not] as a contaminant of it" (Clarke 1975:99); the effects of the researcher's words and deeds are data, not interference.

Ethnographers generally see lies and misrepresentations in the same light. Of course fieldworkers constantly ask themselves, "Does the informant have reason to lie or conceal some of what he sees as the truth?" (Becker 1970a:29) and in a variety of ways seek to decide when they have been lied to and deceived (see below). But lies, like reactive effects, can be understood as "data" rather than "contaminant." To do so, however, requires recognizing lies and reactive effects when they occur. In order to maximize the chances of identifying deception and reactivity, ethnographers try to amass a large, diverse body of data collected at different times and places by different procedures.

In order to identify possible reactive effects on answers to their questions, fieldworkers advise comparing the answers to such questions to "volunteered statements" about the same topic or subject matter addressed either to them or to others present (Becker 1970a:30). This tactic presupposes sufficiently intimate, long-term involvement in a setting to allow witnessing a variety of such statements.

Fieldworkers routinely conduct supplementary investigations to determine the truth of key descriptive or analytic claims. Upon receiving particular accounts of important events or developments, ethnographers may undertake further focused inquiries to help decide whether or not to accord factual status of these accounts. Duneier reports how he conducted a number of extended investigations checking reported details he regarded as critical from the life histories of the street vendors he studied. Of course even additional evidence did not allow him to decide these questions with absolute certainty; but he became more confident about treating these as factual reports rather than as simply accounts presenting his informants' current understandings of their biographies.

Continuing presence close to key events, sustained over time and on different occasions, allows the ethnographer to collect a rich and varied set of observations with which to detect both blatant deceptions and subtle reactive effects. Becker's insistence that, in general, fieldwork evidence is highly credible in that it incorporates "rich detailed data" invokes just this point (1970a:52). Rich data are a result of the fieldworker spending a long period of time studying the particular setting, collecting a variety of observations on any particular topic, and using many different procedures. Any particular conclusion or interpretation the fieldworker reaches "has therefore been subjected to hundreds and thousands of tests" (1970a:53), which may not be readily apparent, however, in the formal presentation of findings.

The fieldworker's presence over time in naturally occurring, ongoing social life makes it difficult for those studied to sustain deliberate deceptions and misrepresentations. Despite the presence of the observer, people in their natural habitats are subject to the everyday constraints which naturally operate in the situation studied:

> They are enmeshed in social relationships important to them, at work, in community life, wherever. The events they participate in matter to them. The opinions and actions of the people they interact with must be taken into account, because they affect those events. All the constraints that affect them in their ordinary lives continue to operate while the observer observes. (Becker 1970a:46)

The result is not simply that it is difficult to maintain a consistent deception over time, but also that the field researcher may well eventually be present to observe incidents that those studied would generally hide but which they feel constrained to reveal in particular circumstances (see Becker's analysis of his observation of a student cheating on an exam, this volume, p. 325).

Again, determining the truthfulness of a particular claim or the reactive character of particular statement involves complex processes of interpretation in identifying, assembling and weighing evidence. There are no formulae for deciding whether or not to believe what those in the field tell us or others. Rather, we conclude that an informant told the truth or lied only by comparing what we were told with other observations and tellings and by judging (interpreting) what fits and what seems contradictory. When unfamiliar with a setting, we cannot tell the lies from the truths or discern what is said cynically to please superiors from what is said in good-faith community with coworkers. Deciding these matters depends on what we have learned about the ways and concerns of those observed.

Furthermore, while concerned with the accuracy or truth value of what informants have said, ethnographers are not interested in throwing out "contaminated" pieces of data, eliminating from analytic consideration events identified as deceptions and reactive effects. Once recognized, a lie—as therapists maintain—may be more revealing than the truth, making all too apparent the deceiver's self-protective interests, deep-running undercurrents in local social relations, or muted tensions in researcher-informant exchanges. Similarly, Becker (1970a:30) does not dismiss as reactive effects the "deeply 'idealistic' sentiments about medicine" medical students expressed when alone with the observer in the face of their very "cynical" talk and behavior among themselves. As he insists, "We would err if we interpreted one or the other of these expressions as the 'real' one, dismissing the other as mere cover-up" (1970a:48); the solution lies rather in reconciling the apparent conflict between these "cynical" and "idealistic" statements by recognizing that medical students held both attitudes but expressed them differently depending upon the situation.

Finally, in actual fieldwork practice, ethnographers display some ambivalence toward reactivity. On the one hand they contend that solutions to reactivity lie not in restricting, cutting off or regularizing field interactions, but in trying to become sensitive to and perceptive of how one is perceived and treated by others. But on the other hand, many fieldworkers are reluctant to intervene too actively or assertively in the settings they study, in this sense preferring to restrict and minimize the ways in which they influence these settings. A major injunction of fieldwork relations is to "fit in," to adopt as many local ways as possible, to act like a member as closely as possible. While some seek minimally consequential presence (Pollner and Emerson, this volume) for ethical reasons—it would be highly presumptuous to go in and take over indigenous settings—there are good methodological reasons for doing so as well. First, the less the researcher actively intervenes in life in the setting studied, the fewer and presumably more easily identified any reactive effects. Secondly, trying to fit in and minimize the effects of one's presence increases the likelihood that whatever effects do arise are those that would tend to occur in other interactions in the setting.

Researcher Bias and Selectivity.   Fieldwork findings are subject to additional challenges, deriving not from possible distortions in how those studied behave toward the ethnographer, but from distortions in how the ethnographer understands, processes and assembles data and evidence in making descriptive and analytic claims. These challenges take the form of questions: How do we know that the observer did not simply "restrict his observations so that he sees only what supports his prejudices and expectations?" (Becker 1970a:52) How do we know that the fieldworker considered all relevant events, and interpreted and categorized events in a consistent fashion? How do we know that different researchers would not have interpreted events in different ways?

There are several responses to the first question. One begins with the claim that sustained, detailed and varied observations create a rich set of data that make it difficult for the researcher to only observe and record what supports her preconceptions. Extensive, varied methods of data collection at least in principle should create a data set that has not simply assembled anticipated and supportive findings. This stance is reinforced by two further ethnographic principles: The fieldworker is not restricted to recording only those events which fit within some predefined theoretical framework or set of categories; fieldnotes should not be filtered through some specific, invariant frames of relevance, and researchers should be open to unanticipated findings. Second, the ethnographer should avoid strong initial theoretical commitments, in part to avoid observing selectively in predetermined ways to confirm existing theory. Moreover, if the ethnographer has not yet worked out the direction and details of the analysis, self-deception and biased selectivity will be difficult in recording data, since "the researcher will often be unable to grasp immediately whether what he is recording is supporting or contradicting his current analysis" (Katz 1983).

Similar concerns have expressed the possibility of "anecdotalism" in final texts. As Mehan (1979:15) has argued:

> Conventional field studies tend to have an anecdotal quality. Research reports include a few *exemplary* instances of the behavior that the researcher has culled from fieldnotes. . . . Researchers seldom provide the criteria or grounds for including certain instances and not others. As a result, it is difficult to determine the typicality or *representativeness* of instances and findings generated from them.

Silverman (2000) similarly asks how fieldworkers "convince themselves (and their audience) that their 'findings' are genuinely based on critical investigation of all their data and do not depend on a few well-chosen 'examples'."

One proposed solution is "comprehensive data treatment"; i.e., all of the data collected must, at some point, be inspected and analyzed, so that any generalization applies "to every single gobbet of relevant data you have collected" (Silverman 2000:180). Comprehensive data treatment addresses the reliability or "consistency with which instances are assigned to the same category by different observers or by the same observer on different occasions" (Hammersley 1992:67). Silverman argues that reliability can be strengthened by systematizing conventions for writing fieldnotes, such that such data sources "record what we can see as well as what we hear" and are expanded beyond immediate observations to create a more comprehensive record. He also supports efforts to achieve intercoder agreement in the analysis of field data (see Glassner and Loughlin 1987).

But Silverman also endorses another set of strategies to achieve consistency, strategies tied to systematically trying to falsify or refute initial assumptions and evidence by means of constant comparison, deviant-case analysis and the like. As Katz (this volume) emphasizes, such efforts commit the researcher to seeking out and considering all data relevant to a particular issue in order to modify the analysis to incorporate initially counter instances. This procedure thus assures consistent treatment of the data in that any evidence relevant to a particular theoretical claim is examined; this consistency is made evident by the complex, multiple strands of data and analysis created as concepts are qualified and explanatory propositions generated by converting "disconfirming into confirming data." The resulting analytic framework may be illustrated by "what may seem superficially to be casually selected 'anecdotes'"; but in fact these incidents have been selected on analytic grounds.

Transferability and Generalizing.   Ethnographers generally study a single case, or at most a small number of cases. Issues arise of how to generalize with efforts to make claims that extend beyond the particular case studied. In qualitative research such generalization usually proceeds not by establishing the general representativeness of case findings but by demonstrating their *transferability* to other specific contexts (Lincoln and Guba 1985:296–98). Transferability depends on evidence of the similarity between the context studied and those to which findings are to be transferred. That is, the question of whether findings hold "in some other context, or even in the same context at some other time, is an empirical issue, the resolution of which depends upon the degree of similarity between sending and receiving (or earlier and later) contexts" (316).[9]

Hammersley (1992, 1998) suggests that matters are more complicated in that ethnographers generalize in two very different ways, by empirical generalizations and theoretical inferences, each of which requires different kinds of evidence in support of transferability. With empirical generalizations, evidence should indicate how and why findings in the case studied apply to a larger population or "are transferable to other settings" (again, usually without statistical measures of representativeness) (Hammersley 1998:56). The key here is to specify both "the larger whole to which generalization is being made, and . . . the reasons why such generalization is believed to be sound" (51). The latter often involves developing the claim and providing evidence that the case(s) studied "are typical in relevant respects of larger aggregates that are of interest" (103). This may require narrowing or restricting these aggregates. For example, it might be implausible to claim that a school studied is typical of all secondary schools in England and Wales in 1970s, but not to assert it is "typical of small, boys' inner-city secondary moderns in the early 1970s" (124–25). Or the researcher may argue that the case studied in its very atypicality represents the likely direction of future development (as did Cicourel and Kitsuse (1963) in contending that their highly professional, bureaucratic college counselors represented the wave of the future). In general, empirical generalization is useful for establishing the broader relevance of the findings of a particular case study, and requires ethnographers "to make rational decisions about the populations to which generalization is to be made, and to collect and present evidence about the likely typicality of the case(s) they study" (Hammersley 1992:93).

Generalization based on theoretical inference has a very different character. Theoretical statements do not refer to "particular phenomena occurring in particular places at particular times," but rather to "why one type of phenomenon tends to produce another (other things being equal) wherever instances of that type occur" (1998:48). Hence the problem is not one of the fit with larger populations or aggregates, but of the appropriateness or reasonableness of basing theoretical claims on the case studied and its particular features. With theoretical conclusions, then, "we need to be clear about the theory the case(s) have been used to develop and/or test and about why they are believed to provide the basis for theoretical inference" (1998:51). The latter involves making an argument that what was studied provides a "critical case" with regard to the specific theoretical claims made; this in turn will require both comparison with other cases to justify the asserted difference (criticalness) and eliminating other factors that might account for the theoretical relationship claimed. By way of illustration: the theory that "pressure on schools for 'good' examination results reduces the degree of choice they give students in selecting courses well in advance of the examination" (Woods 1979) would require both comparative evidence about "how heavy was the pressure on this school to achieve good examination results" and "attention to other factors that might have produced limited course choice for students" (Hammersley 1998:102).

Finally, some ethnographers emphasize that theoretical density and internal variety create high levels of transferability. Thus Katz (1983:147) argues that analytic induction's "single-minded pursuit of qualifications" increases internal variation, which in turn enhances "the prospects of accurate application to other times and places. . . . [T]he more differences discovered within the data, the greater the number of possible negative cases, and thus the more broadly valid the resulting theory." Strauss and Corbin (1990:253) take a similar position:

> The purpose of a grounded theory is to *specify* the conditions that give rise to specific sets of action/interaction pertaining to a phenomenon and the resulting consequences. It is generalizable to those specific situations only. Naturally, the more systematic and widespread the theoretical sampling, the more conditions and variations that will be discovered and built into the theory, therefore the greater its generalizability. . . .

Explicating the Research Process

Many researchers contend that assessing of the credibility of ethnographic findings requires not only nuanced interpretation of the adequacy of evidence, but also detailed understanding of how these findings were actually produced. Altheide and Johnson (1994:485) in particular locate the key to contemporary ethnographic practice in "assessing and communicating the interactive process through which the investigator acquired the research experience and information," a process they term "validity-as-reflexive-accounting." Their approach builds on and extends earlier recommendations that field researchers provide "natural histories" of their projects (Becker 1970) and that conveying the credibility of findings requires accounts of the actual research processes used (Glaser and Strauss 1967:230; Athens 1984). Explicating the research process is critical to make available to evaluation key junctures in assembling and analyzing data. By describing procedures for collecting data, making comparisons, finding and incorporating disconfirming evidence, and developing theoretical categories and propositions, the researcher makes visible processes and decisions that would only appear in truncated and abbreviated form in the analyses themselves.[10]

In some sense explicating the research process represents an alternative to attempting to replicate ethnographic findings. The history of ethnography is certainly marked by a number of well-known restudies—Lewis (1953) and Goldkind (1966) of Redfield (1930, 1941), Freeman (1983) of Mead (1928), Boelen (1992) of Whyte (1955). But these projects, based on different sets of field relations generating different data and organized around other theoretical concerns, uniformly produced new studies, not replications—albeit studies pointedly critical of the earlier work. Indeed, viewing findings as (at least in part) the result of the procedures used to produce them, ethnographers have generally concluded that literal replication is an impossibility, since any restudy will necessarily employ different methods and procedures (if only because it is conducted at a different time and as a second study; see Bloor, this volume). In this sense, explicating key phases of the research process is not a means of replicating findings, but a recognition that describing the actual methods and critical junctures in this process allows a reader to understand and assess how the researcher came up with these findings.

Ethnographers urge examination of three specific aspects of the research process: Theory, field relations, and the tacit practices involved in transforming lived experience and observation into field data. First, it is an ethnographic truism that theory guides observation, such that observers with different theoretical commitments will focus and observe differently and come up with very different findings. Consequently ethnographers need to recognize and make explicit their core theoretical interests and commitments as they determine what is looked at and what is treated as significant in the process of data collection. Sanjek (1990c) terms this process "theoretical candor." One canon of ethnographic validity, theoretical candor requires self-conscious examination of the broad, discipline-based, social, political or economic theories which shape the planning and conduct of fieldwork; it also demands awareness of the local, "terrain-specific theories of significance about people, events and places" arising and pursued through focused inquiry in the field. In the same spirit Strauss and Corbin (1990:252–54) hold that readers should be able to "accurately judge how the researcher carried out the analysis"; thus the field researcher should address not only what major categories emerged and which were used to guide theoretical sampling, but also when and how hypotheses were formulated and the core category selected (1990:253).

A second emphasis shifts attention from analytic commitments and procedures to what Sanjek (1990c:398–400) has aptly termed "the ethnographer's path" into and through relationships and interactions in the field. Anthropologists tend to characterize this path in terms of relations with informants, wherein the fieldworker "meets people, is introduced to still others, locates a range of informants, develops a variety of relationships, and enters data about and from this set of persons into fieldnotes" (Sanjek 1990c:398). Indeed, Heath (1972, quoted in Sanjek 1990c:398) holds that "any effective anthropologist develops his own social network in the process of fieldwork," the character of this network acting simultaneously as "both a determinant and an outcome of the research enterprise." Sociologists place less emphasis on specific relations, characterizing this path as an interactional process of making a place as researcher and person in a specific social world. Thus, Glaser and Strauss (1967:230) hold that the credibility of field studies requires descriptions of "what range of events the researcher saw, whom he interviewed, who talked to him, what diverse groups he compared, what kinds of personal experiences he had, and how he might have appeared to various people whom he studied." And noting that "good ethnographies show the hand of the ethnographer," Altheide and Johnson (1994:493) identify "accounting for ourselves" as a core component of explicating research process. Addressing "how a given observer resolved the inevitable field problems" that arise in ethnographic research requires special attention (491); for example, reflexive accounting would trace how a given observer met and responded to problems generated by the mesh between her age, gender, ethnicity, class and other personal qualities and local systems of social stratification.

Finally, some field researchers focus on explicating the actual procedures, analytic assumptions, and interpretive devices used to collect, interpret, and organize field data. Cicourel (1964, 1978) in particular has sought to ground fieldwork on the self-conscious explication of the tacit resources and practices used to transform experiences and observations in the field into textual forms of data. For example, fieldworkers rely upon various kinds of "background knowledge" to decide on the import and meaning of any particular scene or action. Some of this background knowledge derives from familiarity with the setting studied and the people in it; other parts come from the more global, common-sense knowledge about social life we possess as members of society. Fieldworkers' interpretations of the meaning of specific incidents also rest on and invoke implicit "models of the actor" (Cicourel 1974a:27). The solution lies not in avoiding these procedures, but in making their nature and use explicit in presenting field data. In his fieldwork analyses Cicourel (e.g., 1968) takes great care to identify both the background knowledge and the model of the actor he relies upon to come to and ground his interpretation of particular events.

In addition to the self-conscious explication of one's interpretive resources, Cicourel has also given close consideration to specific fieldwork procedures for transforming observations and experiences into textually represented data. These procedures typically involve complex forms of information processing and can be understood, Cicourel maintains, by studying comparable processes in other settings. The comparison of transcripts of medical interviews with physicians' subsequent written summaries of these exchanges (1974b), for example, can shed light on how ethnographers produce fieldnotes through similar "summarizations" of recalled exchanges, mediated through the structure of memory. More precise field data can be collected, Cicourel maintains, through "the explicit study of interpretational and summarization procedures, as they occur during interaction, interviews, and taking notes or elaborating upon them" (1978:29).

ISSUES IN WRITING ETHNOGRAPHIES

Ethnographic inquiry culminates with writing some finished, generally published text. Contemporary ethnographers have addressed three major issues centered around this production of such more or less coherent, polished ethnographic accounts: recognizing and expanding the conventions for writing ethnography; confronting concrete writing choices in producing such texts; and anticipating the distinctive ethical and political issues that arise from making such texts available to wider audiences.

Ethnographic Conventions and Experimental Texts

As emphasized in Part I, recognition of rhetorical properties of ethnographies and increasing awareness of ethnographies as texts have led to new concern with ethnographic writing and to increased self-consciousness about writing practices. Among sociologists Atkinson (1990:180) insists that a "fully mature ethnography requires a reflexive awareness of its own writing, the possibilities and limits of its own language, and a principled exploration of its modes of representation." Such self-consciousness, allowing the ethnographer to choose rather than to take for granted specific modes of writing, requires recognition of the specific literary and disciplinary conventions that underlie different forms and styles of representation. In practice field researchers have expanded their writing options by radically transforming and/or rejecting outright core conventions of realist ethnography (Marcus and Cushman 1982; Van Maanen 1988). Experimenting with new textual forms and unorthodox substance, ethnographers now produce finished ethnographies that depart in marked ways from the classic realist monographs of the mid-twentieth century:

> The surface of the text has become more fragmented and more diverse; there is an emphasis on "dialogic" forms of representation; elements of parody and pastiche have been allowed to enter the intellectual field. The scholarly text has itself become a more "open" one, repudiating the closure and certainty of the orthodox work. (Atkinson 1992:41)

Three general trends mark efforts to move beyond the conventions of realist ethnography: (1) bringing the person of the ethnographer to the center of the text; (2) innovative representations of indigenous worlds and/or "the Other"; and (3) self-conscious experimentation and variation of literary forms.

"I-Witnessing" Ethnography. One key convention of realist ethnography involved the unintrusive presence of the ethnographer in the text (Marcus and Cushman 1982). In recent years many ethnographers have stood this convention on its head, placing the ethnographer at the center of the constructed text. Richardson (1994:520) pinpoints the influence here of the postmodernist insistence that "writing is always partial, local, and situational, and that our Self is always present, no matter how much we try to suppress it." Geertz (1988:78) terms this introspective, first-person, biographical form of ethnographic writing, exemplified in anthropologist Malinowski's posthumously published *A Diary in the Strict Sense of the Term* (1967), the "I-witnessing approach to the construction of cultural descriptions." One intent of this approach is

> ... to represent the research process in the research product; to write ethnography is such a way as to bring one's interpretations of some society, culture, way of life, or whatever and one's encounters with some of its members, carriers, representatives, or whomever into an intelligible relationship. (Geertz 1988:84)[11]

"I-witnessing" can take somewhat different forms. Some fieldworkers describe personal relations, experiences and insights as these shaped and influenced to the course of the fieldwork (e.g., Johnson 1975; Rabinow 1977). A slightly different tack is to highlight the ethnographer's inner life and social experiences in the field as a personal story, providing less personal narratives of the research than "narratives of the self" (Richardson 1994:521)—that is, narratives which "connect the personal experiences of the writer to the ethnographic project at hand" (Denzin 1997:227; examples include Read 1965; Zola 1982; Kondo 1990; Krieger 1991). Sociological autoethnography (e.g., Ellis 1995a) has taken these processes to an extreme, providing deeply personal, emotion-focused first-person accounts in which the ethnographer is an active and central character. This approach to ethnography provides privileged access to the ethnographer's feelings and perceptions, framing these not as personal biases but as a critical, previously neglected source of data for certain kinds of analyses.

Innovative Representations of Indigenous Worlds and/or "the Other." Reacting to the "interpretive omniscience" convention characteristic of realist ethnography, field researchers have also experimented with creating texts that provide more meaningful access to others' worlds. Some move in this direction by avoiding monologic ethnography "dominated by the voice of the privileged narrator" (Atkinson 1992:40), constructing discursive or polyphonic texts that bring in and highlight indigenous voices (Clifford 1983). Discursive texts provide "a process of dialogue where interlocutors actively negotiate a shared vision of reality" (Clifford 1983:134). In some instances the ethnography consists entirely of transcribed conversations between ethnographer and informant (e.g., Dwyer 1982, presenting such conversations with a Moroccan farmer); others, such as Dumont (1978), build the ethnography around the collaborative negotiation of meaning and understanding represented as more selected, ongoing dialogue. Polyphonic texts are built of lengthy stretches of talk from a number of informants in order to represent the "voices" of those studied, to reproduce and present in detail their actual words and modes of thinking.[12] Ethnographies "in their own voices" assume highly biographical forms, as in Crapanzano's (1985) work on whites in South Africa and Stacey's (1990) ethnography of two working women and their families in the Silicon Valley in the 1980s. More radical forms of polyphony "do the natives and the ethnographer in different voices" (Clifford 1983:139).

Others have sought to construct texts that present the ways of life and thinking of other peoples as much in their own terms as possible by minimizing the intrusion of the ethnographer's concerns and cultural categories into the text. Emerson et al. (1995:112–33) discuss ways of writing fieldnotes to capture and represent local concerns and meanings. By attending to and writing notes incorporating everyday questions and answers, naturally occurring members' descriptions, members' stories, indigenous terms, types and typologies, indigenous contrasts, and members' explanations and theories, ethnographers can accumulate data on people's indigenous ways of ordering and interpreting their worlds. Ethnomethodological studies (e.g., Sudnow 1978; Livingston 1986; Goode 1994; Robillard 1999) abandon any standard researcher role, urging the fieldworker to gain embodied competence on becoming a skilled participant and to avoid any sort of "constructive analysis" that would impose exogenous concerns and categories on the local "lived order" (Pollner and Emerson 2001). Such studies are subject to the "unique adequacy requirement" (Garfinkel and Wieder 1992:182) in that the researcher should become "competent in the local production and reflexively natural accountability of the phenomenon of order he is 'studying.'"[13]

A final approach to indigenous representation turns back to the spirit of Boasian fieldwork to reframe ethnography as a collecting and assembling of "indigenous ethnographic texts." Dorst's (1989:5) "post-ethnography" of a small Pennsylvania community of Chadds Ford presents a "collection/collage" of local "autoethnographies and souvenirs"—"postcards, texts from brochures, the words of Chadds Ford natives, . . . excerpts from travel literature, fiction and popular history, photographs, reproductions." As Dorst characterizes his approach:

> I have treated a Site "out there" as a kind of library, or better, an apparatus that exists for and through the management of texts; and I have imagined my task as twofold: first, the formation of a collection—selecting and arranging; and then reading, or more specifically, reading critically as a rhetorician, looking for the "motivations" of the texts, reading them as historically situated. . . . Conceptually, this gathering of native texts, rethought as autoethnographic fragments, now becomes the main activity, not just one source of "data" among many. (206–07)

The completed text thus seeks to soften the voice of the ethnographer by making minimal use of interview data and fieldnotes, instructing the reader to treat any such account as "just another textual fragment of the same order as the other souvenirs" (1989:5).

Using New Literary Formats.   Classic realist ethnography relied upon a standard literary format marked by the impersonal, third-person voice and a documentary style of presenting the worlds of others through concrete details of observation and talk. Contemporary ethnographers have experimented with a wide variety of literary forms for organizing and presenting their accounts. Thus, in recent years ethnographic texts have been framed as personal narratives (e.g., Krieger 1991; Ellis 1995a), poems (e.g., Richardson 1992a), plays (e.g., Mulkay 1985; Paget 1990; McCall and Becker 1990), playful dialogues (e.g., Mulkay 1985), and fictional stories (e.g., Wolf 1992). Such experimentation draws upon a broad range of writing conventions to try to convey more dramatically and effectively the insights gained from spending time and talking with people and the ordinary routines and exceptional dramas that mark social life. As Richardson (1994:521–22) has emphasized, ethnographers draw on standard devices in narrative fiction in order "to tell a 'good story' . . . about the group or culture studied," turn to "poetic representation" as a way of writing up interviews to reveal and accent the speaker's cadence and rhythms, and create "ethnographic dramas" in order to "reconstruct the 'sense' of an event from multiple 'as-lived' perspectives."

The variety of uses of such forms is well illustrated by Mulkay's innovative study of "the interpretative practices observable in scientific discourse" concerning technical disagreements, experimental replications, and discoveries (1985:3). Mulkay rejects exclusive use of the "empiricist monologue" for presenting sociology, arguing instead that sociology "needs a form of analytic discourse which is appropriate to its analytical perspectives" (9). He continues:

> If you accept, as I do, that every "social action" and every "cultural product" or "text" has to be treated as a source of or as an opportunity for creating multiple meanings, or further texts (Gilbert and Mulkay 1984), then forms of analytic discourse which were designed to depict the singular, authoritative, supposedly scientific meanings of social phenomena can never be entirely satisfactory. They must be supplemented by new analytic forms which use two or more textual voices to re-present and display the ever-present possibility of interpretative multiplicity. (1985:9–10)

Thus, in the Introduction, the Author is confronted by the Reader as questioner, as in the following exchange:

> *My first question is about monologue and dialogue. Am I right in thinking that you want to abandon the monologic form completely in both written and spoken texts and replace it with various forms of dialogue?*
>
> No, I doubt whether we could do away with monologues completely, even if we wanted to. . . . [B]oth dialogic and monologic forms rely on conventions of discourse. Neither form is superior in any ultimate sense. There is no point, therefore, in trying entirely to replace one form with the other. However, the two forms do enable you to do rather different things. (9–10)

Similarly, dialogue is introduced into the analysis of an exchange of "letters" between two biochemists when the "Textual Commentator" "interrupts" to point out how the Author "writes in a way which draws attention to the textual organization of these letters and away from the organization of his own text" (1985:20).

Mulkay's text also ignores conventional boundaries between fact and fiction, mixing straight-ahead monologic exposition with literary forms involving "invention," including frequent dialogues between a variety of "characters," a short play (chapter 5, "The Scientist Talks Back"), and fictionalized speeches and exchanges (an "analytic parody" of the ceremonial receipt of the Nobel Prize). As analyst, Mulkay "explicitly claims the right to fashion the materials into new arrangement and to mold them into a range of different formats" (Atkinson 1992:46). Yet the relationship between the factual and the fictional in this text is no simple matter:

> As with all Mulkay's inventions, the fictional versions are put together out of fragments of "real" utterances and exchanges. As with all "analyses," the texts are arranged and constructed by the author out of shards of evidence. . . . Throughout Mulkay's textual inventions there is a constant recognition that the original "data" are themselves "textual" products. . . . Mulkay is not, therefore, simply interested in "making up" his own "fictional" versions; rather, he uses his rhetorical skills to explore the textual productions of social actors *and* sociologists. Consequently, Mulkay argues, the work of the social scientist is to construct "secondary" texts that use and build on the "original" texts of everyday life. (Atkinson 1992:46)

In a similar vein, a number of experimental ethnographies refashion fieldnotes and other accounts of "'real' utterances and exchanges" . . . "into new arrangements and . . . mold them into a range of different formats" (Atkinson, 1992:46). Ellis, for example, advocates using original fieldnotes as resources to create texts that lead readers "through a journey in which they develop an 'experiential sense' of the events . . . and come away with a sense of 'what it must have felt like' to live through what happened" (Ellis and Bochner, 1992:80). Thus, in *Final Negotiations* (1995a), she substantially reworks fieldnotes—constructing unwitnessed conversations, condensing several experiences into a single episode—in order to intensify the emotional impact of the final text. Similarly, Moeran (1990) relies on the "literary" format of his *Okubu Diary* (1985) to authorize not only significant changes in chronological sequences and the creation of composite characters, but also the depiction of his experiences as occurring during "one continuous period of fieldwork." His fieldnotes thus provide a flexible set of materials for writing in which, for example, "what had been said by one . . . person in the course of a 'real' conversation could . . . be expressed by a different, or at least composite, character" (1990:348).

Creating Texts: Writing Choices in Producing Ethnographies

Writing an ethnography is not simply a matter of reviewing experiences and data with a view toward their theoretical implications. While some analysis can be carried out strictly in the head, the actual details and complexities are handled only upon putting ideas into words on paper. As Richardson (1994:516) emphasizes:

> Although we usually think about writing as a mode of "telling" about the social world, writing is not just a mopping-up activity at the end of a research project. Writing is also a way of "knowing"—a method of discovery and analysis. By writing in different ways, we discover new aspects of our topic and our relationship to it.

With growing appreciation of writing conventions and of the possibilities of experimenting with ethnographic formats, contemporary field researchers confront a wide range of concrete, practical writing choices in sitting down to produce their polished texts. In addition to selecting an appropriate literary format, the ethnographer as writer may have to make explicit decisions about a number of key aspects of the emerging text.

Overarching Frameworks for Organizing Ethnographic Texts. In analyzing the styles or "frames" preferred and recommended by reviewers for the ethnographic journal *Urban Life and Culture*, Lofland (1974) identified five primary *frames* for organizing ethnographic texts: generic (developing a generic conceptual framework), novel, elaborated, eventual or abundantly documented, and the frame interpenetrated by rich empirical materials. More recent approaches identify more formal, rhetorical organizing devices; Hammersley and Atkinson (1995:245–53) consider four "master-tropes," including *metaphor*—depicting "a relationship of similarity in difference" (Atkinson 1990:51), *synecdoche*—using a part to stand for the whole (see also Richardson 1990:17–18), *metonymy*—linking topics through "contiguity" rather than on the basis of similarity (see also Atkinson 1990:50–53)—and *irony*.

The Use of Narration. Ethnographies are built around narratives (Richardson 1990a, 1990b). Field researchers both elicit and record lay narratives as a primary form of field "data," and then rewrite and reconstruct these narratives into polished ethnographic texts. Ethnographers thus face choices in determining when and how to use different narratives to create and structure ethnographic texts. At one extreme, narrative can be used to organize whole ethnographies: *When Prophecy Fails* (Festinger, Riecken and Schachter 1956) and *Hip Capitalism* (Krieger 1979) provide examples, as ethnographic narrators "weave their own and others' observations and accounts into more extended accounts of social action" (Atkinson 1990:104). At another extreme, the ethnographer may rely upon narrative forms to write up brief episodes or to craft more extended "fieldnote tales" (Emerson et al. 1995:87–99). Or the researcher may reconstruct the stories people tell about the course of their lives as extended life-history narratives.

Using Interview and Fieldnote Data. Richardson (1990b:39–44) explores different options for incorporating interview quotations into biographical narratives, identifying different uses of a series of short direct quotations, brief quoted phrases embedded within an analytic narrative, and longer, extended quotations. Similar writing choices arise in incorporating fieldnotes into finished texts. Emerson et al. (1995:179–80) distinguish between *excerpt strategies*, in which fieldnotes are set off from the surrounding text (by indentation and/or italics), and *integrative strategies*, which weave fieldnotes into one smooth, thematically focused text with minimal spatial markings between fieldnote and interpretation. The former highlights the discursive contrast between descriptive fieldnotes and analytic writing, framing the former as "evidence," as "originally recorded" voices and events, standing in contrast to subsequent interpretation (Atkinson 1990:103).[14] The latter facilitates consistently writing in the first person, as well as the construction of complex, extended narratives linking a wide range of data.

Ethical and Political Implications of Final Ethnographies

The ethical and political implications of making ethnographic accounts available to wider audiences have long concerned field researchers. Disseminating ethnographic accounts can have direct and dramatic implications for those whose lives, words and deeds are recounted, whether openly or in some disguised fashion, in these writings. Published ethnographies may have less direct but still important effects on broader collectivities and social processes.

The problems of identifying settings, groups and individuals stand at the core of standard considerations of the ethical consequences of publishing (or disseminating) research reports. It is at this point that groups and individuals described in such accounts might be identified and suffer direct harm as a consequence; those familiar with the setting, for example, may recognize themselves and others, leading to significant disruptions of interpersonal relations as a result (Becker 1964:267). Typically fieldworkers have addressed this possibility by taking steps to preserve confidentiality and anonymity, assigning pseudonyms to people and places and changing distinguishing features of situations and settings in their written accounts.

Clearly, problems may arise with this anonymity strategy. The researcher may not anticipate the need to change or disguise particular features of a setting. Warren (1980:295), for example, thought she had disguised the identity of the court she had studied, only to receive vociferous complaints from the field six months after publishing an article based on this research that her unnamed "metropolitan mental health court" was the only mental health court in the nation! It is often difficult to keep insiders from determining individual identities, or from assuming that they have been recognized by other insiders (Ellis 1995b). The results may be deep feelings of ill will and hostility that disrupt local community bonds or exacerbate existing interpersonal tensions. There can be significant trade-offs in accuracy in making radical changes to details and circumstances in order to enhance anonymity. And academic institutions and research review boards may sometimes thwart researcher efforts to protect confidentiality. Rochford (1994:65), for example, reports that his university denied his request to hold his dissertation out of circulation for one year to prevent it from fueling internal tensions within the Hare Krishna movement then undergoing a period of deep crisis.

But there is a deeper issue involved here: The people whose lives and activities have been described and analyzed in ethnographic reports may have strong and sometimes negative reactions to how they have been presented in these texts. "Springdalers" apparently felt demeaned and betrayed by Vidich and Bensman's (1958, 1964) depiction of the shallowness of their small-town life. Warren (1980:294) reports that the public defender office she studied in fieldwork on involuntary mental hospitalization proceedings felt betrayed and harmed by her depiction of them as "nonadversarial." And a number of community members angrily denounced Ellis for her characterizations of local sexual and birth control practices; one woman she had known for seventeen years drove her from her home, yelling, "I don't want you steppin' foot in my trailer again" (1995b:83).

But encountering ethnographic accounts about one's own life and activities can be more subtly upsetting and disenchanting, for there is often a deep tension between ethnographic accounts of scenes and events and the perspectives that members hold:

> Everett Hughes has often pointed out that the sociological view of the world—abstract, relativistic, generalizing—necessarily deflates people's view of themselves and their organizations. Sociological analysis has this effect whether it consists of a detailed description of informal behavior or an abstract discussion of theoretical categories. (Becker 1964:273)

Ethnographic accounts may have just these effects (although a member may also have the experience of "catching sight of himself in the mirror"; see Bloor, this volume). When the field researcher treats as problematic what members take for granted or view as sacred, even highly descriptive accounts may jar or outrage those they are about. Consider, for example, the reaction of a psychiatric emergency team member to an ethnographic account intended to represent his work concerns from "his point of view" (Emerson and Pollner 1992:84). After noting the paper "captured a lot of PET," he continued:

> The other thing too, it's interesting to read about yourself working, from somebody else's point of view. [Right, yeah] I thought wow! That's probably true! That's an outside view.

In this respect ethnographic accounts may have deeply personal implications. They may not accord with members' views of themselves and their moral worth, whether the public view, professed views, or their private views. In this instance reading the ethnographic account appeared to shake the worker's personal faith in PET's value and integrity (Emerson and Pollner 1992:95):

> My initial impression, I really felt bad. I really said, God, PET is really in bad
> shape. I mean . . . then I said to myself, there's every grounds for discontinu-
> ing, as is. It's irrational.[15]

Ethnographers cannot escape recognizing these and other consequences of the
inescapable differences between their concerns and understandings and those of
the people they study (Richardson 1992b).

Some contemporary ethnographers urge abandoning the standard practice
of anonymity in favor of openly identifying the specific site of their study and
using the real names of those studied in their accounts. Over the years Whyte
has explicitly identified the North End of Boston as "Cornerville," provided the
real names for many of the key figures in *Street Corner Society*, and published an
appendix written by former informant and co-fieldworker Angelo Ralph Orlan-
dello (Whyte 1981). Duneier (1999, this volume) abandons the usual social science practices of anonymity in his original publication, citing both the
willingness of those studied to be identified by name and photograph, and the
desirability of holding descriptions to "a higher standard of evidence" (pg. 178).
This approach, however, brings with it an ethical obligation to present one's
descriptions and accounts of others to these people in a direct and effective way.
Indeed, while Bloor describes the earlier impulse to taking findings back to those
they are about as primarily a mechanism for validating those findings,
ethnographers like Duneier now emphasize taking findings back primarily as an
ethical commitment to those studied. Such a collaborative stance lies at the core
of feminist ethnography's commitment to minimize control and harm in the
research process (Devault 1999). Stacey (1990:272–78), for example, discussed
drafts of her chapters with the two Silicon Valley women she studied as a means
of decreasing the asymmetry of ethnographic research and of increasing the
involvement of and collaboration in the ethnographic enterprise.

Finally, published ethnographies may have broader effects exactly by making those studied and their ways of life open public knowledge. Some field
researchers have suggested that ethnographic study of the lives and worlds of
the marginal in particular may have harmful consequences, for example, breaking the protective secrecy of the marginal and powerless. Becker (1964) has
pointed out the potential harm that publication might bring to stigmatized
groups whose habits or even existence may not have been known by the public
at large. Warren (1980:292) provided a concrete example raised by gay men in
response to her study of the gay community:

> Several respondents expressed the fear that if I published a "true" account of
> the gay world as one in which effeminacy stereotypes do *not* prevail, then non-
> effeminate homosexuals might suffer by being suspected. . . . While my gay
> respondents did not argue that it was not "true" that most gay males are not
> effeminate, they did argue that it would be preferable for them—they would
> suffer less adverse effects—if the "false" stereotypes continued to prevail.

To the extent that disadvantaged or hidden groups become of interest to governmental agencies, ethnographic findings may have direct political and social consequences. Fieldworkers have become more sensitive and aware of the outside

and official uses of their findings. Revelation of past instances of deceptive, politically motivated support of research (see, for example, Saunders' (1999:135) account of the CIA's use of the Ford, Rockefeller, and Carnegie foundations as "funding cover" for "cultural cold war" objectives), and of blatantly exploitative funding of social science research (Horowitz 1967), makes it difficult to present fieldwork as nonpolitical and of only intellectual relevance.

NOTES

[1] Again, the extended case method, seeking to specify "some particular feature of the social situation that requires explanation by reference to particular forces external to itself" (Burawoy 1991:9), departs from this practice

[2] In addition to using warrants to direct or focus the analysis of data, ethnographers may also use warrants to help choose sites and topics for research, as well as to make in-the-field decisions about how to carry out the study.

[3] Analytic induction has also been criticized as tautological. Turner, for example, noted that the causes of embezzlement Cressey pointed out cannot be fully specified apart from the outcomes they presumably produced As he asked, "Is it possible, for example, to assert that a problem is nonshareable *until* a person embezzles to get around it?" (606) In response, Katz (forthcoming) has argued that the criticism tends to assume cross-sectional as opposed to temporally organized data The latter, deriving from interaction and lived experience, is only broken down into discrete variables by arbitrary, imposed distinctions. Thus, "it should be expected that in some cases the development of the explanatory factors will be depicted as continuous with the emergence of the target phenomenon" (8), as in "the development of addiction after an explicit and abrupt recognition that a long-standing pattern of distress has been due to repeated opiate withdrawal" (9)

[4] Katz (1983:128–30) also contends that by treating discovery as separate from and prior to verification, grounded theory perpetuates the image of fieldwork as insightful but not rigorous

[5] Some ethnographers propose qualitative criteria while retaining the terms and categories of quantitative assessment, especially validity and reliability (e.g., Silverman 2000). Others explicitly reject validity and reliability in favor of other assessment procedures, insistent on avoiding assessment procedures that privilege quantitative assumptions, goals and criteria, Becker in particular has proposed that the question that should be asked is "how credible are the conclusions derived from data gathered by fieldwork?" (1970a:39)

[6] Two other related procedures included "triangulation"—applying different methods to study the same phenomenon (see Bloor, this volume) and more implicit claims to ethnographic validity based on the fieldworker's direct experience ("I know because I was there")—a position strongly critiqued by Bittner, Geertz and others (see Part I)

[7] Moreover, different kinds of claims require different sorts of evidentiary assessments (Hammersley 1992:85ff) Those central to the argument or analysis require more convincing evidence than do more marginal claims, descriptive claims require evidence related to "location, events, fit between the phenomena and categories built into that description," while analytic claims ("theories"), concerned with relationships between types of phenomena, require evidence of the correlation between these two phenomena

[8] For example, the questions asked may lead informants to provide answers that are responsive to categories or assumptions built into the question but that are alien or irrelevant to local concerns, accounts will then be developed and elaborated, but specifically in response to the investigator's concerns, and would presumably not normally occur on other occasions in local life. Similarly, those studied may engage in certain acts, or assume certain stances, because of the field researcher's evident interest in that particular area of social life

[9] Lincoln and Guba also maintain that the original investigator is only partially responsible for providing evidence pertaining to transferability, since she "cannot know the sites to which transferability might be sought, but the appliers can and do" (1985.298). The original investigator, however, should provide enough evidence to allow subsequent researchers to take up these matters of similarity.

[10] Some ethnographers see little or no additional value in explicating the research process. Katz (1983), for example, prefers to examine the finished research product—fully developed, qualified theoretical propositions—for indications of the research process. He also sees less value in recounting past practice than in encouraging other researchers to take up a theory at any point in the future and apply or test it against new data, modifying it if need be.

[11] Geertz also stresses the distinctive problems of writing research experiences in the first person, thereby constructing the "comprehension of the self by the detour of the other" (1988.92, quoting Rabinow 1977). Bruner (1993.6) similarly warns of the danger of "putting the personal self so deeply back into the text that it completely dominates, so that the work becomes narcissistic and egotistical." Berger (1981) provides a model for effective first-person writing ("I have put the author, myself, front and center in this book instead of bunkering him behind devices such as the passive voice, the Royalist We, and the presentation of findings with no visible, sentient finder ") by directing such I-witnessing toward showing how he came to "the interpretive frame which shaped the meaning I gave to the data" (1981:ix).

[12] In providing access to the "voices" of those studied, ethnographers decenter not only the privileged voice of the narrator/ethnographer, but also the realist convention of composite "common denominator people" (Marcus and Cushman 1982). Of course, writing "in-their-own-voice" ethnographies is not a straightforward matter of simply "retelling their stories" (Riessman 1993). As Atkinson (1992.23) points out, "Informants cannot 'speak' for themselves. In order to give an impression of it we have to select, edit and *represent* their spoken narratives." At every turn, the ethnographer recreates voices, whether or not she quotes from fieldnotes, tapes, or film, or if she reconstructs her memory of voices.

[13] Garfinkel et al.'s (1988.11) criticisms of Lynch's study of a neurobiological laboratory illustrate the level of competence envisioned by "unique adequacy": Lynch "was not taken seriously" by laboratory researchers (12); "described the technical specifics of discovering axon sprouting though he did not know that work and could not recognize it for himself", and was not required to and could not teach practices to practitioners as the latter did among and to one another.

[14] In addition, the excerpt strategy allows the ethnographer to speak in two different voices—as fieldworker describing the experience depicted in the excerpt ("here is what I heard and observed") and as author now explaining those events to readers ("here is the sense that I *now* make of it") (Atkinson 1990).

[15] As this statement attests, ethnographic accounts may also be seen to have important political implications in and for the local setting and those studied of which the ethnographer may have been unaware (Emerson and Pollner 1988).

13

The Epistemology of Qualitative Research

Howard S. Becker

QUALITATIVE AND QUANTITATIVE

It is rhetorically unavoidable, discussing epistemological questions in social science, to compare qualitative and ethnographic methods with those which are quantitative and survey: to compare, imaginatively, a field study conducted in a community or organization with a survey of that same community or organization undertaken with questionnaires, self-administered or put to people by interviewers who see them once, armed with a printed form to be filled out.

Supposing that the two ways of working are based on different epistemological foundations and justifications leads to asking the question: What's the epistemology of qualitative research? To me, it's an odd question. I'm an intellectual descendant of Robert E. Park, the founder of what has come to be called the Chicago school of sociology. Park was a great advocate of what we now call ethnographic methods. But he was equally a proponent of quantitative methods, particularly ecological ones. I follow him in that, and to me, the similarities between these methods are at least as, and probably more, important and relevant than the differences. In fact, I think that the same epistemological arguments underlie and provide the warrant for both.

How so? Both kinds of research try to see how society works, to describe social reality, to answer specific questions about specific instances of social reality. Some social scientists are interested in very general descriptions, in the form of laws about whole classes of phenomena. Others are more interested in understanding specific cases, how those general statements worked out in this case. But there's a lot of overlap.

From Jessor et al. (eds.), *Ethnography and Human Development*, pp. 53–70. Copyright © 1996, by The University of Chicago Press. Reprinted with permission.

The two styles of work do place differing emphasis on the understanding of specific historical or ethnographic cases as opposed to general laws of social interaction. But the two styles also imply one another. Every analysis of a case rests, explicitly or implicitly, on some general laws, and every general law supposes that the investigation of particular cases would show that law at work. Despite the differing emphases, it all ends up with the same sort of understanding, doesn't it?

That kind of ecumenicism clearly won't do, because the issue does not go away. To point to a familiar example, although educational researchers have done perfectly good research in the qualitative style for at least sixty years, they still hold periodic conferences and discussions, like this one, to discuss whether it's legitimate and, if it is, why it is. Surely there must be some real epistemological difference between the methods that accounts for this continuing inability to settle the question.

SOME THOUGHTS ABOUT EPISTEMOLOGY

Let's first step back and ask about epistemology as a discipline. How does it see its job? What kinds of questions does it raise? Like many other philosophical disciplines, epistemology has characteristically concerned itself with "oughts" rather than "is's," and settled its questions by reasoning from first principles rather than by empirical investigation. Empirical disciplines, in contrast, have concerned themselves with how things work rather than what they ought to be, and settled their questions empirically.

Some topics of philosophical discussion have turned into areas of empirical inquiry. Scholars once studied biology and physics by reading Aristotle. Politics, another area philosophers once controlled, was likewise an inquiry in which scholars settled questions by reasoning rather than by investigation. We can see some areas of philosophy, among them epistemology, going through this transformation now, giving up preaching about how things should be done and settling for seeing how they are in fact done.

Aesthetics, for instance, has traditionally been the study of how to tell art from nonart and, especially, how to tell great art from ordinary art. Its thrust is negative, concerned primarily with catching undeserving candidates for the honorific title of art and keeping such pretenders out. The sociology of art, the empirical descendant of aesthetics, gives up trying to decide what should and shouldn't be allowed to be called art, and instead describes what gets done under that name. Part of its enterprise is exactly to see how that honorific title—art—is fought over, what actions it justifies, and what users of it can get away with (Becker 1982:131–64).

Epistemology has been a similarly negative discipline, mostly devoted to saying what you shouldn't do if you want your activity to merit the title of science, and to keeping unworthy pretenders from successfully appropriating it. The sociology of science, the empirical descendant of epistemology, gives up trying to decide what should and shouldn't count as science, and tells what people who claim to be doing science do, how the term is fought over, and what people who win the right to use it can get away with (Latour 1987).

So this chapter will not be another sermon on how we ought to do science, and what we shouldn't be doing, and what evils will befall us if we do the forbidden things. Rather, it will talk about how ethnographers have produced credible, believable results, especially those results which have continued to command respect and belief.

Such an enterprise is, to be philosophical, quite Aristotelian, in line with the program of the *Poetics*, which undertook not to legislate how a tragedy ought to be constructed but rather to see what was true of tragedies which successfully evoked pity and terror, producing catharsis. Epistemologists have often pretended to such Aristotelian analysis, but more typically deliver sermons.

WHY DO WE THINK THERE'S A DIFFERENCE?

Two circumstances seem likely to produce the alleged differences between qualitative and quantitative epistemologies. One is that the two sorts of methods typically raise somewhat different questions at the level of data, on the way to generalizations about social life. Survey researchers use a variant of the experimental paradigm, looking for numerical differences between two groups of people differing in interesting ways along some dimension of activity or background. They want to find that adolescents whose parents have jobs of a higher socioeconomic status are less likely to engage in delinquency, or more likely, or whatever—a difference from which they will then infer other differences in experience or possibilities that will "explain" the delinquency. The argument consists of an "explanation" of an act based on a logic of difference between groups with different traits (see Abbott 1992).

I don't mean to oversimplify what goes on in such work. The working out of the logic can be, and almost always is, much more complicated than this. Researchers may be concerned with interaction effects, and with the way some variables condition the relations between other variables, in all this striving for a complex picture of the circumstances attending someone's participation in delinquency.

Fieldworkers usually want something quite different: a description of the organization of delinquent activity, a description which makes sense of as much as possible of what they have seen as they observed delinquent youth. Who are the people involved in the act in question? What were their relations before, during, and after the event? What are their relations to the people they victimize? To the police? To the juvenile court? Fieldworkers are likewise interested in the histories of events: How did this start? Then what happened? And then? And how did all that eventually end up in a delinquent act or a delinquent career? And how did this sequence of events depend on the organization of all this other activity?

The argument rests on the interdependence of a lot of more or less proved statements. The point is not to prove, beyond doubt, the existence of particular relationships so much as to describe a system of relationships, to show how things hang together in a web of mutual influence or support or interdependence or what have you, to describe the connections between the specifics the ethnographer knows by virtue of having been there (Diesing 1971). Being there produces a strong belief that the varied events you have seen are all connected, which is not unreasonable since what the fieldworker sees is not variables or factors that need to be "related" but people doing things together in ways that are manifestly connected. After all, it's the same people and it's only our analysis that produces the abstract and discrete variables which then have to be put back together. So fieldwork makes you aware of the constructed character of "variables." (Which is not to say that we should never talk variable talk.)

A second difference which might account for the persistent feeling that the two methods differ epistemologically is that the situations of data gathering present fieldworkers, whether they seek it or not, with a lot of information, whether they want it or not. If you do a survey, you know in advance all the information you can acquire. There may be some surprises in the connections between the items you measure, but there will not be any surprise data, things you didn't ask about but were told anyway. A partial exception to this might be the use of open-ended questions, but even such questions are usually not asked in such a way as to encourage floods of unanticipated data suggesting new variables. In fact, the actual workings of survey organizations discourage interviewers from recording data not asked for on the forms (see Peneff 1988).

In contrast, fieldworkers cannot insulate themselves from data. As long as they are "in the field" they will see and hear things which ought to be entered into their fieldnotes. If they are conscientious or experienced enough to know that they had better, they put it all in, even what they think may be useless, and keep on doing that until they know for sure that they will never use data on certain subjects. They thus allow themselves to become aware of things they had not anticipated which may have a bearing on their subject. They expect to continually add variables and ideas to their models. In some ways, that is the essence of the method.

MANY ETHNOGRAPHIES

The variety of things called ethnographic aren't all alike, and in fact may be at odds with each other over epistemological details. In what follows, I will concentrate on the older traditions (for example, participant observation, broadly construed, and unstructured interviewing) rather than the newer, more trendy versions (for example, hermeneutic readings of texts) even though the newer versions are more insistent on the epistemological differences. What I have to say may well be read by some as less than the full defense of what they do that they would make. So be it. I'll leave it to less middle-of-the-road types to say more. (I will, however, talk about ethnographers or fieldworkers somewhat indiscriminately, lumping together people who might prefer to be kept separate.)

A lot of energy is wasted hashing over philosophical details, which often have little or nothing to do with what researchers actually do, so I'll concentrate less on theoretical statements and more on the way researchers work these positions out in practice. What researchers do usually reflects some accommodation to the realities of social life, which affect them as much as any other actor social scientists study, by constraining what they can do. Their activity thus cannot be accounted for or explained fully by referring to philosophical positions (see Platt, unpublished manuscript). In short, I'm describing practical epistemology, how what we do affects the credibility of the propositions we advance. In general, I think that the arguments advanced by qualitative researchers have a good deal of validity, but not in the dogmatic and general way they are often proposed. So I may pause here and there for a few snotty remarks on the excesses ethnographers sometimes fall into.

A few basic questions seem to lie at the heart of the debates about these methods. First, must we take account of the viewpoint of the social actor and, if we must, how do we do it? And how do we deal with the embeddedness of all social action in the world of everyday life? And how thick can we and should we make our descriptions?

THE ACTOR'S POINT OF VIEW: ACCURACY

One major point most ethnographers tout as a major epistemological advantage of what they do is that it lets them grasp the point of view of the actor. This satisfies what they regard as a crucial criterion of adequate social science. "Taking the point of view of the other" is a wonderful example of the variety of meanings methodological slogans acquire. For some, it has a kind of religious or ethical significance: if we fail to do that we show disrespect for the people we study. Another tendency goes further, finding fault with social science which "speaks for" others, by giving summaries and interpretations of their point of view. In this view, it is not enough to honor, respect, and allow for the actors' points of view. One must also allow them to express it themselves.

For others, me among them, this is a technical point best analyzed by Herbert Blumer: all social scientists, implicitly or explicitly, attribute a point of view and interpretations to the people whose actions we analyze (Blumer 1969). That is, we *always* describe how they interpret the events they participate in, so the only question is not whether we should, but how accurately we do it. We can find out, not with perfect accuracy, but better than zero, what people think they are doing, what meanings they give to the objects and events and people in their lives and experience. We do that by talking to them, in formal or informal interviews, in quick exchanges while we participate in and observe their ordinary activities, and by watching and listening as they go about their business; we can even do it by giving them questionnaires which let them say what their meanings are or choose between meanings we give them as possibilities. To anticipate a later point, the nearer we get to the conditions in which they actually do attribute meanings to objects and events, the more accurate our descriptions of those meanings are likely to be.

Blumer argued that if we don't find out from people what meanings they are actually giving to things, we will still talk about those meanings. In that case, we will, of necessity, invent them, reasoning that the people we are writing about must have meant this or that, or they would not have done the things they did. But it is inevitably epistemologically dangerous to guess at what could be observed directly. The danger is that we will guess wrong, that what looks reasonable to us will not be what looked reasonable to them. This happens all the time, largely because we are not those people and do not live in their circumstances. We are thus likely to take the easy way and attribute to them what we think we would feel in what we understand to be their circumstances, as when students of teenage behavior look at comparative rates of pregnancy, and the correlates thereof, and decide what the people involved "must have been" thinking in order to behave that way.

The field of drug use, which overlaps the study of adolescence, is rife with such errors of attribution. The most common meaning attributed to drug use is that it is an "escape" from some sort of reality the drug user is said to find oppressive or unbearable. Drug intoxication is conceived as an experience in which all painful and unwanted aspects of reality recede into the background so that they need not be dealt with. The drug user replaces reality with gaudy dreams of splendor and ease, unproblematic pleasures, perverse erotic thrills and fantasies. Reality, of course, is understood to be lurking in the background, ready to kick the user in the ass the second he or she comes down.

This kind of imagery has a long literary history, probably stemming from De Quincey's 1856 *Confessions of an English Opium Eater* (a wonderful nineteenth-century American version is Fitz Hugh Ludlow's 1857 *The Hashish Eater*). These works play on the imagery analyzed in Edward Said's dissection of *orientalia*, the Orient as mysterious other (Said 1978). More up-to-date versions, more science-fictiony, less oriental, and less benign, can be found in such works as William Burroughs's *Naked Lunch* (1966).

Such descriptions of drug use are, as could be and has been found out by generations of researchers who bothered to ask, pure fantasy on the part of the researchers who publish them. The fantasies do not correspond to the experiences of users or of those researchers who have made the experiments themselves. They are concocted out of a kind of willful ignorance.

Misinterpretations of people's experience and meanings are commonplace in studies of delinquency and crime, of sexual behavior, and in general in studies of behavior foreign to the experience and lifestyle of conventional academic researchers. Much of what anthropological and ethnographic studies have brought to the understanding of the problems of adolescence and growing up is the correction of such simple errors of fact, replacing speculation with observation.

But "don't make up what you could find out" hardly requires being dignified as an epistemological or philosophical position. It is really not much different from a more conventional, even positivist, understanding of method (see Lieberson 1992), except in being even more rigorous, requiring the verification of speculations that researchers will not refrain from making. So the first point is that ethnography's epistemology, in its insistence on investigating the viewpoint of those studied, is indeed like that of other social scientists, just more rigorous and complete. (I find it difficult, and don't try very hard, to avoid the irony of insisting that qualitative research is typically more precise and rigorous than survey research, ordinarily thought to have the edge with respect to those criteria.)

One reason many researchers who would agree with this in principle nevertheless avoid investigating actors' viewpoints is that the people we study often do not give stable or consistent meanings to things, people, and events. They change their minds frequently. Worse yet, they are often not sure what things do mean; they make vague and woolly interpretations of events and people. It follows from the previous argument that we ought to respect that confusion and inability to be decisive by not giving things a more stable meaning than the people involved do. But that makes the researcher's work more difficult, since it is hard to describe, let alone measure, such a moving target.

An excellent example of the instability of "native" meanings is given in Bruno Latour's (1987) analysis of science. Conventionally, social scientists accord a special status to the knowledge created by scientists, treating it as better than conventional lay knowledge, as being more warranted. Latour notes this paradox: scientists themselves don't always regard science that way. Sometimes they do, treating a result as definitive and "blackboxing" it. But scientists often argue with each other, trying to keep others from putting a result in a black box or, worse yet, opening black boxes everyone thought were shut for good. His rule of method is, we should be as undecided as the actors we study. If they think a conclusion, a finding, or a theory is shaky, controversial, or open to question, then we should, too. And we should do that even if what we are studying is a historical controversy whose outcome we now know, even though the actors involved at the time couldn't. Conversely, if the actors involved think the piece of science involved is beyond question, so should we.

People who write about science prescriptively—epistemologists—could avoid misconstruing the ideas of those they study if they followed the simple rules anthropologists have invented for themselves about fieldwork. It was once thought good enough to visit your tribe for a month or two in the summer and to get all your information from informants interviewed with the help of translators. No one thinks that any more, and now there is a minimum standard—know the native language, stay a year to eighteen months, use some sort of rudimentary sampling techniques. Applied to the study of science, these rules would require that epistemologists learn the native language fully, not just the high church version trotted out on formal occasions but the language of daily work as well, not just the views of "eminent scientists" and those who speak for the science, but of the ordinary scientists who actually do the work. Which is what Latour and the other students of "shop-floor practice" in science have done (and what Diesing [1971], an unusual epistemologist, did), and many other sociologists of science did not.

Epistemologically, then, qualitative methods insist that we should not invent the viewpoint of the actor, and should only attribute to actors ideas about the world they actually hold, if we want to understand their actions, reasons, and motives.

THE EVERYDAY WORLD: MAKING ROOM FOR THE UNANTICIPATED

A second point, similar to the emphasis on learning and understanding the meanings people give to their world and experiences instead of making them up, is an emphasis on the everyday world, everyday life, the *quotidian*. This catch phrase appears frequently in ethnographic writing, often referring to the ideas of Alfred Schutz. In Schutz's writings (see Schutz 1962), and in the elaborations of those ideas common among ethnomethodologists, the everyday world typically refers to the taken-for-granted understandings people share which make concerted action possible. In this, the idea resembles the notion of culture one finds in Redfield—"shared understandings made manifest in act and artifact" (1941:132)—and the similar emphasis on shared meanings in Meadian (George Herbert Mead, that is) thought as interpreted by Blumer.

The general idea is that we act in the world on the basis of assumptions we never inspect but just act on, secure in the belief that when we do, others will react as we expect them to. A version of this is the assumption that things look to me as they would look to you if you were standing where I am standing. In this view, "everyday understandings" refers not so much to the understandings involved, say, in the analysis of a kinship system—that this is the way one must behave to one's mother's brother's daughter, for instance—but to the deep epistemological beliefs that undergird all such shared ideas, the meta-analyses and ontologies we are not ordinarily aware of that make social life possible.

Much theoretical effort has been expended on this concept. I favor a simpler, less controversial, more workaday interpretation, either as an alternative or simply as a complement to these deep theoretical meanings. This is the notion of the everyday world as the world people actually act in every day, the ordinary world in which the things we are interested in understanding actually go on. As opposed to what? As opposed to the simpler, less expensive, less time-consuming world the social scientist constructs in order to gather data efficiently, in which survey questionnaires are filled out and official documents consulted as proxies for observation of the activities and events those documents refer to.

Most ethnographers think they are getting closer to the real thing than that, by virtue of observing behavior *in situ* or at least letting people tell about what happened to them in their own words. Clearly, whenever a social scientist is present, the situation is not just what it would have been without the social scientist. I suppose this applies even when no one knows that the social scientist is a social scientist doing a study. Another member of a cult who believes flying saucers from other planets are about to land is, after all, one more member the cult would not have had otherwise and, if the cult is small, that increase in numbers might affect what the observer is there to study.

But given that the situation is never exactly what it would have been otherwise, there are degrees of interference and influence. Ethnographers pride themselves on seeing and hearing, more or less, what people would have done and said had the observers not been there. One reason for supposing this to be true is that ethnographers observe people when all the constraints of their ordinary social situation are operative. Consider this comparatively. We typically assure people to whom we give a questionnaire or who we interview that no one will ever know what they have said to us, or which alternatives on the questionnaire they have chosen. (If we can't make that assurance, we usually worry about the validity of the results.) This insulates the people interviewed from the consequences they would suffer if others knew their opinions. The insulation helps us discover people's private thoughts, the things they keep from their fellows, which is often what we want to know.

But we should not jump from the expression of a private thought to the conclusion that that thought determines the person's actions in the situation to which it might be relevant. When we watch someone as they work in their usual work setting or go to a political meeting in their neighborhood or have dinner with their family—when we watch people do things in the places they usually do them with the people they usually do them with—we cannot insulate them from the consequences of their actions. On the contrary, they have to take the rap for what they do, just as they ordinarily do in everyday life. An example: when I was observing college undergraduates, I sometimes went to classes with them. On one occasion, an instructor announced a surprise quiz for which the student I was accompanying that day, a goof-off, was totally unprepared. Sitting nearby, I could easily see him leaning over and copying answers from someone he hoped knew more than he did. He was embarrassed by my seeing him, but the embarrassment didn't stop him copying, because the consequences of failing the test (this was at a time when flunking out of school could lead to being drafted, and maybe being killed in combat) were a lot worse than my potentially lowered opinion of him. He apologized and made excuses later, but he did it. What would he have said about cheating on a questionnaire or in an interview, out of the actual situation that had forced him to that expedient?

Our opinions or actions are not always regarded as inconsequential by people we study. Social scientists who study schools and social agencies regularly find that the personnel of those organizations think of research as some version of the institutional evaluations they are constantly subject to, and take measures to manipulate what will be discovered. Sometimes the people we find it easiest to interview are on the outs with their local society or culture, hoping to escape and looking to the ethnographer for help. But although these exceptions to the general point always need to be evaluated carefully, ethnographers typically make this a major epistemological point: when they talk about what people do they are talking about what they saw them do under the conditions in which they usually do it, rather than making inferences from a more remote indicator such as the answer to a question given in the privacy of a conversation with a stranger. They are seeing the "real world" of everyday life, not some version of it created at their urging and for their benefit, and this version, they think, deserves to be treated as having greater truth value than the potentially less accurate versions produced by other methods, whatever the offsetting advantages of efficiency and decreased expense.

A consequence of finding out about the details of everyday life is that many events and actions turn out to have mundane explanations seldom accounted for in our theories. A student in a fieldwork class I taught in Kansas City studied letter carriers. Under my prodding, he tried to find out what sorts of routes the carriers preferred, which parts of town they chose to work in when they had a chance to make a choice. Having done his research, he invited his fellow students to guess the answer and, budding social scientists that they were, their guesses centered on social class: the carriers would prefer middle-class areas because they were safer; the carriers would prefer working-class areas because the inhabitants would be on fewer mailing lists and thus there would be less mail to carry; and so on. All these clever, reasonable guesses were wrong. What the carriers he talked to preferred (and this is not to say that other carriers elsewhere might not have different preferences and reasons for them) were neighborhoods that were flat. Kansas City is hilly and the carriers preferred not to climb up and down as they moved from street to street. This is not an explanation that would make sense from a "stratification" point of view; a follower of Bourdieu, for instance, might not think to include such an item in a survey. But that was the reason the carriers gave, a homely reason waiting to be discovered by someone who left room for it to come out.

FULL DESCRIPTION, THICK DESCRIPTION: WATCHING THE MARGINS

Ethnographers pride themselves on providing dense, detailed descriptions of social life, the kind Geertz (1973a) has taught us to recognize as "thick." Their pride often implies that the fuller the description, the better, with no limit suggested. At an extreme, ethnographers talking of reproducing the "lived experience" of others.

There is something wrong with this on the face of it. The object of any description is not to reproduce the object completely—why bother when we have the object already? —but rather to pick out its relevant aspects, details which can be abstracted from the totality of details that make it up so that we can answer some questions we have. Social scientists, for instance, usually concentrate on what can be described in words and numbers, and thus leave out all those aspects of reality that use other senses, what can be seen and heard and smelled. (How many monographs deal with the smell of what is being studied, even when that is a necessary and interesting component—and when isn't it? [cf. Becker 1986:121–35].)

Ethnographers usually hail "advances" in method which allow the inclusion of greater amounts of detail—photographs, audio recording, video recording. These advances never move us very far toward the goal of full description; the full reality is still a long way away. Even when we set up a video camera, it sits in one place at a time, and some things cannot be seen from that vantage point; adding more cameras does not alter the argument. Even such a small technical matter as the focal length of the camera's lens makes a big difference: a long lens provides close-up detail, but loses the context a wide-angle lens provides.

So full description is a will-o'-the-wisp. But, that said, a fuller description is preferable to, and epistemologically more satisfying than, a skimpy description. Why? Because, as with the argument about the actor's point of view, it lets us talk with more assurance about things than if we have to make them up—and, to repeat, few social scientists are sufficiently disciplined to refrain from inventing interpretations and details they have not, in one way or another, observed themselves. Take a simple example. We want to know if parents' occupations affect the job choices adolescents make. We can ask them to write down the parents' occupations on a line in a questionnaire; we can copy what the parents have written down somewhere, perhaps on a school record; or we can go to where the parents work and verify by our own observation that this one teaches school, that one drives a bus, the other one writes copy in an advertising agency.

Is one of these better than another? Having the children write it down on a form is better because it is cheap and efficient. Copying it from a record the parents made might be better because the parents have better knowledge of what they do and better language with which to express it than the children do. Seeing for ourselves would still be open to question—maybe they are just working there this week—but it leaves less room for slippage. We don't have to worry about the child's ignorance or the parents' desire to inflate their status. Epistemologically, I think, the observation which requires less inference and fewer assumptions is more likely to be accurate, although the accuracy so produced might not be worth bothering with.

A better goal than "thickness"—one fieldworkers usually aim for—is "breadth": trying to find out something about every topic the research touches on, even tangentially. We want to know something about the neighborhood the juveniles we study live in, and the schools they go to, and the police stations and jails they spend time in, and dozens of other things. Fieldworkers pick up a lot of incidental information on such matters in the course of their participation or lengthy interviewing but, like quantitative researchers, they often use "available data" to get some idea about them. They usually do that, however, with more than the usual skepticism.

It is time to mention, briefly, the well-known issue of "official statistics" or, put more generally, the necessity of looking into such questions as why records are kept, who keeps them, and how those facts affect what's in them. (None of this is news to historians, who would think of this simply as a matter of seeing what criticisms the sources they use have to be subjected to.) As Bittner and Garfinkel (1967) told us years ago, organizations don't keep records so that social scientists can have data but, rather, for their own purposes. This is obvious in the case of adolescents, where we know that school attendance records are "managed" in order to maximize state payments; behavioral records slanted to justify actions taken toward "difficult" kids; and test scores manipulated to justify tracking and sorting. Similarly, police records are kept for police purposes, not for researchers' hypothesis testing.

Ethnographers therefore typically treat data gathered by officials and others as data about what those people did: police statistics as data about how police keep records and what they do with them, data about school testing as data about what schools and testers do rather than about student traits, and so on. That means that ethnographers are typically very irreverent, and this makes trouble.

It makes trouble where other people don't share the irreverence but take the institution seriously on its own terms. Qualitative researchers are often, though not necessarily, in a kind of antagonistic relationship to sources of official data, who don't like to be treated as objects of study but want to be believed (I have discussed this elsewhere under the heading of the "hierarchy of credibility" [Becker 1967]).

CODA

There's not much more to say. Practitioners of qualitative and quantitative methods may seem to have different philosophies of science, but they really just work in different situations and ask different questions. The politics of social science can seduce us into magnifying the differences. But it needn't, and shouldn't.

FURTHER THOUGHTS

After the foregoing had been discussed at the conference, some people felt that there were still unresolved questions that I ought to have dealt with. The questions were ones that are often raised and my answers to them are not really "answers," but rather responses which discuss the social settings in which such questions are asked rather more than the questioners may have anticipated....

One such question dealt with validity, noting that my paper did not speak to that question, but instead talked about credibility. Do I really think that that's all there is to it, simply making a believable case? Isn't there something else involved, namely, the degree to which one has measured or observed the phenomenon one claims to be dealing with, as opposed to whether two observers would reach the same result, which was one of the ways some people interpreted my analysis of credibility?

We come here to a difference that is really a matter not of logic or scientific practice but of professional organization, community, and culture. The professional community in which quantitative work is done (and I believe this is more true in psychology than in sociology) insists on asking questions about reliability and validity, and makes acceptable answers to those questions the touchstone of good work. But there are other professional communities for whose workers those are not the major questions. Qualitative researchers, especially in sociology and anthropology, are more likely to be concerned with the kinds of questions I raised in the body of my paper: whether data are accurate, in the sense of being based on close observation of what is being talked about or only on remote indicators; whether data are precise, in the sense of being close to the thing discussed and thus being ready to take account of matters not anticipated in the original formulation of the problem; whether an analysis is full or broad, in the sense of being based on knowledge about a wide range of matters that impinge on the question under study, rather than just a relatively few variables. The paper contains a number of relevant examples of these criteria.

Ordinarily, scholarly communities do not wander into each other's territory, and so do not have to answer to each other's criteria. Operating within the paradigm accepted in their community, social scientists do what their colleagues find acceptable, knowing that they will have to answer to their community for failures to adhere to those standards. When, however, two (at least two, maybe more) scholarly communities meet, as they did in this conference, the question arises as to whose language the discussions will be conducted in, and what standards will be invoked. It is my observation over the years that quantitative researchers always want to know what answers qualitative researchers have to *their* questions about validity and reliability and hypothesis testing. They do not discuss how they might answer the questions qualitative researchers raise about accuracy and precision and breadth. In other words, they want to assimilate what others do to their way of doing business and make those other ways answer their questions. They want the discussion to go on in their language and the standards of qualitative work translated into the language they already use.

That desire—can I say "insistence"? —presumes a status differential: *A* can call *B* to account for not answering *A*'s questions properly, but *B* has no such obligation to *A*. But this is a statement about social organization, not about epistemology, about power in hierarchical systems, not about logic. When, however, scholarly communities operate independently, instead of being arranged in a hierarchy of power and obligation, as is presently the case with respect to differing breeds of social science, their members need not use the language of other groups; they use their own language. The relations between the groups are lateral, not vertical, to use a spatial metaphor. One community is not in a position to require that the other use its language.

That has to some extent happened in the social sciences, as the growth of social science (note that this argument has a demographic base) made it possible for subgroups to constitute worlds of their own, with their own journals, organizations, presidents, prizes, and all the other paraphernalia of a scientific discipline.

Does that mean that I'm reducing science to matters of demographic and political weight? No, it means recognizing that this is one more version of a standard problem in relations between culturally differing groups. To make that explicit, the analogies to problems of translation between languages and cultures (neatly analyzed, for instance, in Talal Asad's essay, "The Concept of Cultural Translation in British Social Anthropology" [1986]) are close. Superordinate groups in situations of cultural contact (for example, colonial situations) usually think everything should be translated so that it makes sense in *their* language rather than being translated so that the full cultural difference in the concepts in question is retained. They are very often powerful enough, at least for a while, to require that that be done.

This problem of translation between culturally differing groups is what Kuhn called attention to in noting that when there is a substantial paradigm difference, as in the case of a paradigm shift, the languages in which scientific work is conducted cannot be translated into one another. If the groups are in fact independent, then there is a translation problem and the same dynamic—the question, you might say, of whose categories will be respected—comes into play.

So what seem like quite reasonable requests for a little clarification are the playing out of a familiar ritual, which occurs whenever quantitative workers in education, psychology, and sociology decide that they will have to pay attention to work of other kinds and then try to coopt that work by making it answer to their criteria, criteria like reliability and validity, rather than to the criteria I proposed, commonly used by qualitative workers. I would say that I wasn't *not dealing* with validity, but *was*, rather, *dealing* with something else that seems as fundamental to me as validity does to others.

This will all sound at odds with my fundamental belief, expressed in the paper, that the two styles of work actually share the same, or a very similar, epistemology. I do believe that's true. But I also think that some workers get fixated on specific procedures (not the same thing as epistemology), act as I have described with respect to those procedures, and have this same feeling that other styles of work must be justified by reference to how well they accomplish what those procedures are supposed to accomplish.

Finally, some people asked how one could tell good from bad or better from worse in qualitative work. I've suggested one answer in the criteria already discussed. Work that is based on careful, close-up observation of a wide variety of matters that bear on the question under investigation is better than work which relies on inference and more remote kinds of observations. That's a criterion. One reason *Street Corner Society* (Whyte 1981) is widely recognized as a masterwork of social science research is that it satisfies this criterion; William Foote Whyte knew what he was talking about, he had observed the social organization he analyzed in minute detail over a long time, and had looked not only at the interactions of a few "corner boys" but also at the operation of much larger organizations in politics and crime, which impinged on the corner boys' lives.

But something else needs to be said. Many people who are quick to recognize the quality of Whyte's work or of Erving Goffman's studies of social organization are just as quick to say that this kind of thing can only be done by specially gifted people, that only *they* can get these remarkable results and, thus, that the methods they have used are not suitable for the development of a science. This recognizes what must be recognized—quality that everyone knows is there—while marginalizing the enterprise that made that quality possible. Goffman was indeed a gifted social scientist, but his gifts expressed themselves within a tradition of thinking and fieldwork that extended from Durkheim through Radcliffe-Brown to Lloyd Warner, as well as from Simmel to Park to Hughes and Blumer. The tradition made his work possible.

That is, however, true of good work in every branch of social science, qualitative or quantitative. Stanley Lieberson, for instance, is a gifted quantitative researcher, but what makes his work outstanding is not that he uses some particular method or that he follows approved procedures correctly, but that he has imagination and can smell a good problem and find a good way to study it. Which is to say that telling good from bad is not as simple as it appears. It's easy enough to tell work that's done badly, and to tell how it was done badly, and where it went off the track. But that in no way means that it is possible, in any version of social science, to write down the recipe for doing work of the highest quality, work that goes beyond mere craft. That's another story. Physicists, who so many social scientists think to imitate, know that. How come we don't?

So these are matters that are deeper than they seem to be, in a variety of ways, and mostly, I think, in organizational ways. I haven't, for reasons I hope to have made clear, answered these questions as the people who asked them hoped. I've explained things in my terms, and I guess they will have to do the translating.

14

Analytic Induction Revisited

Jack Katz

The fundamentals of analytic induction can be stated simply. The researcher is committed to form a perfect relation between data and explanation. When encountering a "negative case"—evidence contradicting the current explanation—the researcher must transform it into a confirming case by revising the definition of either the explaining or the explained phenomenon. The researcher is enjoined to seek negative cases and the resulting opportunity to modify the explanation. There is no methodological value in piling up data of a sort already determined to be consistent with the theory. Quantification therefore plays no logical role.

I used analytic induction throughout my research on the careers of legal assistance lawyers. Legal assistance leaders had often complained about "high turnover" and staff lawyers had often remarked that "two years" represented a benchmark for assessing their careers. Was there, I wondered, a common process of leaving the institution, or "burning out," as the lawyers put it? Was there a concise explanation of when and why staff lawyers would burn out?

My first step was to allocate into groups of short and long tenure all the lawyers who had entered the organization at least two years before the date of my analysis. In effect, the two-year point represented the initial definition of the thing to be explained. Then I looked for background features unique and common to those who remained more than two years, such as education, age, prior experience, political philosophy, work location, ethnicity, and sex. In effect I was looking for factors that would perfectly explain why lawyers were on one list or the other. This did not work, but instead of abandoning the effort I took an obviously artificial tack: I excluded all the confusing cases and drew up two neat lists for comparison, one with lawyers who had stayed more than two years and who had been "activists" before joining legal services, and another with lawyers who had left within two years and who had not been activists. Then I considered "exceptions" one by one, modifying the definition of the explanadum or the explanans in order to fit the "exception." I was manipulating the meaning of the concepts distinguishing the lists in order to restore the perfect correlation which initially characterized them.

It quickly became apparent that I could not hope to explain the difference between those who did and did not stay more than two years. Some lawyers who had stayed more than two years were miserable, as unhappy as some who had left within a few months. Idiosyncratic factors, such as the chance appearance of job offers, might be what really distinguished the two. So I changed the definition of the explanadum to "desiring to stay two years." This definition of the problem provoked new analytic difficulties. Legal Services programs offered staff lawyers a great variety of work settings, from administrative posts, to jobs supervising major litigation, to assignments in neighborhood offices serving walk-in clients. It appeared unlikely that in all of these quite different jobs the same factors would explain the persistence of the desire to remain. So I delimited the explanadum by qualifying it as a "desire to stay in a frustrating place." Through confronting a series of exceptions the explanadum changed again to "involvement in a frustrating place," and then finally to "involvement in an insignificant status." Likewise the definition of the explanans was changed from features of pre-organizational biography to methods of transcending pressures to take on insignificant or routine work, including the use of legal strategies for reform and participation in a collective culture that celebrated the significance of work.

After working this way with sketches of biographies, I developed the concepts further in a two-step process of coding field materials. In this part of the research operation, the codes represented the concept of the explanation, and problems in making coding decisions represented problems in the explanation. First, I altered the codes to fit one-sentence summaries previously made from typed interview and field notes. Then in writing the text, I adjusted the analysis when the quotes extracted directly from the original notes were not what the summaries had led me to expect. When a quotation showed both the presence and absence of involvement in a lawyer's experience at the same time, the concept of involvement had to be further refined; when a section of an interview showed the presence of involvement and the absence of the condition stipulated as explanatory, the explanation had to be revised. Theoretical development continued from early in the research throughout the writing.

Analytic induction used in these ways is a distinctively qualitative methodology, clearly distinguished from methods requiring pre-fixed designs. True, the overriding commitment to seek negative cases is a pre-fixed feature. But the injunction to alter the contents of the theory during data collection gives the research process a distinctive openness. In practice, one does not begin with an hypothesis and then encounter exceptions one by one. Instead, one begins with multiple hypotheses and is confronted with a mass of hostile evidence. Analytic induction permits the researcher to flounder interminably in the choices of: which hypothesis to select out and stick with; then which datum in the dis-confirming mass to select as an "exception" while consciously ignoring tempo-rarily the discouragement of the rest; and then whether to alter the explanans or the explanadum. . . .

Field researchers generally have not embraced analytic induction as a doc-trine. This reluctance appears related to problems historically but not necessarily associated with the method. As originally proposed, analytic induction claimed a superiority over "enumerative induction" by promising perfect correlations and "universal" explanations rather than probabilistic findings. But then very few if any perfect explanations appeared. Yet this embarrassment misconceives the methodology. Analytic induction ought to be evaluated in the same way in which field researchers practically gauge the value of their work. The test is not whether a final state of perfect explanation has been achieved but the *distance* that has been traveled over negative cases and through consequent qualifications from an initial state of knowledge. Analytic induction's quest for perfect explana-tion, or "universals," should be understood as a strategy for research rather than as the ultimate measure of the method. Analytic induction is a method for con-ducting social research, not a perspective from which to evaluate findings. . . .

In addition to their claim of "universal" explanation, early proponents of analytic induction (in particular, Znaniecki 1934) unnecessarily raised hackles by arguing its superiority over "statistical enumeration" for developing "genu-inely causal laws." Against this background, Turner's critique—essentially that the concepts of explaining and explained phenomena in studies using ana-lytic induction shade into each other and suggest tautology—was especially forceful. Analytic induction appeared to produce good definitions at best, not causal explanations.

The case for analytic induction can be made stronger with a number of revi-sions. If we view social life as a continuous symbolic process, we expect our con-cepts to have vague boundaries. If analytic induction follows the contours of experience, it will have ambiguous conceptual fringes. Its independent and dependent variables will inevitably shade into each other, suggesting tautology. But this weakness is only remarkable if exceptional claims are made for the method. Analytic induction and enumerative induction (in other words, survey statistics) differ in the form, not the fact, of uncertain results. For the statistical researcher, practical uncertainty is represented by statements of probabilistic relations; for the analyst of social process, by ambiguities when trying to code borderline cases into one or the other of the "explaining" or "explained" catego-ries. In application to given cases, predictions on the basis of probabilistic expla-nations will sometimes be wrong, and predictions on the basis of explanations of social process sometimes so indeterminate as to be useless. (Turner did not claim that all explanations of analytic induction would be circular, nor that all its predictions would be indeterminate.) . . .

A final difficulty for using the tradition of analytic induction is its apparent emphasis on an epistemology of "induction." What field researchers actually do when they use analytic induction would be described more properly by philosophers of science as "retroduction" than as induction: a "double fitting" or alternating shaping of both observation and explanation, rather than an *ex post facto* discovery of explanatory ideas (Hanson 1958:85ff; Baldamus 1972). To signal both my departure from several aspects of the tradition of analytic induction and my debt to the tradition's essential guide to research practice—the injunction to search exclusively for negative cases—I drop the reference to "induction" in favor of the rubric *analytic research.*

Analytic field studies will not produce "proof," i.e., artifacts of evidence which speak in a standard language or specialized fashion about representativeness, reliability, and so forth. The exclusive commitment to search for negative cases implies that there ought to be a different conceptual point for each reported phenomenon. Each datum reported should make its own substantive and not solely evidentiary contribution to the analysis. But analytic fieldwork does create an elaborate framework which can be used by researchers to assess how well they are doing and by readers to make evaluations. That framework is a social system, which, applied consistently in field research, will: force the researcher to focus on social process as experienced from within; induce research subjects to act toward the researcher as a meaningful member of the native world; enfranchise readers as colleagues competent to make an independent analysis of the relation between data and explanation; and shape a role which subsequent researchers can readily take up for testing substantive findings. This social system can be invoked to spell out answers to a wide variety of methodological questions frequently asked of qualitative field studies. This system of social research relations promotes generalizability, reduces the problem of reactivity, establishes constraints toward reliability, and enhances replicability.

Grounded Theory

Kathy Charmaz

THE LOGIC OF GROUNDED THEORY

What are grounded theory methods? They are a logically consistent set of data collection and analytic procedures aimed to develop theory. Grounded theory methods consist of a set of inductive strategies for analyzing data. That means you start with individual cases, incidents or experiences and develop progressively more abstract conceptual categories to synthesize, to explain and to understand your data and to identify patterned relationships within it. You begin with an area to study. Then, you build your theoretical analysis on what you discover is relevant in the actual worlds that you study within this area.

Grounded theory methods emerged from the fruitful collaboration of sociologists Glaser and Strauss (1965, 1967, 1968; Strauss and Glaser 1970) during the 1960s. In their writing, Glaser and Strauss challenged: (1) the arbitrary division of theory and research; (2) the prevailing view of qualitative research as primarily a precursor to more "rigorous" quantitative methods by claiming the legitimacy of qualitative work in its own right; (3) the belief that qualitative methods were impressionistic and unsystematic; (4) the separation of data collection and analysis phases of research; and (5) the assumption that qualitative research only produced descriptive case-studies rather than theory development. They articulated explicit analytic procedures and research strategies that previously had remained implicit among qualitative researchers. Previously, qualitative researchers had taught generations of students through a combination of mentoring and direct field experience (cf. Rock 1979). Glaser and Strauss changed that oral tradition by offering a clear set of written guidelines for conducting qualitative research. The epistemological assumptions, logic and systematic approach of grounded theory methods reflect Glaser's rigorous quantitative

From Smith, Harré and Van Langenhove (eds.), *Rethinking Methods in Psychology*, 1995, pp. 27–49. Copyright © 1995 Sage Publications Ltd. Reprinted by permission.

training at Columbia University. The intimate link to symbolic interaction (cf. Denzin 1995) stems from Strauss's training at the University of Chicago with Herbert Blumer and Robert Park. Through their influence, Strauss adopted both the pragmatic philosophical tradition with its emphasis on studying process, action and meaning and the Chicago legacy of ethnographic research.

Grounded theory methods provide systematic procedures for shaping and handling rich qualitative materials. The distinguishing characteristics of grounded theory methods (see Charmaz 1983, 1990; Glaser 1978, 1992; Glaser and Strauss 1967; Strauss 1987; Strauss and Corbin 1993) include: (1) simultaneous involvement in data collection and analysis phases of research; (2) creation of analytic codes and categories developed from data, not from preconceived hypotheses; (3) the development of middle-range theories to explain behavior and processes; (4) memo-making, that is, writing analytic notes to explicate and fill out categories, the crucial intermediate step between coding data and writing first drafts of papers; (5) theoretical sampling, that is, sampling for theory construction, not for representativeness of a given population, to check and refine the analyst's emerging conceptual categories; and (6) delay of the literature review. I will address each of these characteristics throughout the chapter.

COLLECTING DATA

Generating Data

Simultaneous involvement in data collection and analysis means that the researcher's emerging analysis shapes his or her data collection procedures. Such simultaneous involvement focuses grounded theory studies and thus not only directs the researcher's efforts, but also fosters his or her taking control of the data. The early analytic work leads the researcher subsequently to collect more data around emerging themes and questions. By simultaneously becoming involved in data collection and analysis, you will avoid the pitfall of amassing volumes of general, unfocused data that both overwhelm you and do not lead to anything new. If you already have collected a substantial amount of data, of course begin with it, but expect to collect additional data on your emerging analytic interests and themes. That way, you can follow up on topics that are explicit in one interview or observation and remain implicit or absent in others. For example, when a woman with multiple sclerosis remarked to me about having "bad days," she said, "I deal with time differently [during a bad day when she felt sick] and time has a different meaning to me" (Charmaz 1991a:52). When we discussed meanings of time, I saw how she connected experiencing time with images of self. On a bad day, her day shortened because all her daily routines— for example, bathing, dressing, exercising, resting—lengthened substantially. As her daily routines stretched, her preferred self shrunk. Until I saw how she defined herself in relation to mundane daily routines, I had not asked interview questions that directly addressed this relationship.[1]

The hallmark of grounded theory studies consists of the researcher deriving his or her analytic categories directly from the data, not from preconceived concepts or hypotheses. Thus, grounded theory methods force the researcher to attend closely to what happens in the empirical world he or she studies. From a constructionist, interpretative perspective, the grounded theory researcher must then study the meanings, intentions and actions of the research participants— whether he or she observes them directly, constructs life histories with them, engages them in intensive interviewing or uses other materials such as clinical case histories or autobiographies.

From the beginning, the researcher actively constructs the data in concert with his or her participants (cf. Charmaz 1990). The first question the researcher must ask is "What is happening here?" (cf. Glaser and Strauss 1967; Glaser 1978, 1992). Perhaps in their enthusiasm to develop an inductive methodology that tightly linked emergent theory and data, Glaser and Strauss (1967; Glaser 1978) imply in their early works that the categories inhere in the data and may even leap out at the researcher. I disagree. Rather, the categories reflect the interaction between the observer and observed. Certainly any observer's worldview, disciplinary assumptions, theoretical proclivities and research interests will influence his or her observations and emerging categories. Grounded theorists attempt to use their background assumptions, proclivities and interests to sensitize them to look for certain issues and processes in their data. Consistent with Blumer's (1969) depiction of sensitizing concepts, grounded theorists often begin their studies with certain research interests and a set of general concepts.[2] For example, I began my studies of people with chronic illnesses with an interest in how they experienced time and how their experiences of illness affected them. My guiding interests brought concepts such as self-concept, identity and duration into the study. But that was only the start. I used those concepts as *points of departure* to look at data, to listen to interviewees and to think analytically about the data. Guiding interests and disciplinary perspectives should provide grounded theorists with such points of departure for developing, rather than limiting, their ideas. Then they develop specific concepts through the research process as they study their data.

What happens if the data do not illuminate the researcher's initial interests? Often, our research topics are sufficiently general that finding interesting data is not a problem, although we find ourselves pursuing unanticipated leads. Grounded theorists evaluate the fit between their initial research interests and their emerging data. They do not force preconceived ideas and theories directly upon their data. Rather, they follow the leads that they define in the data, or design another way of collecting data to try to follow their initial interests. Thus, I started with research interests in time and self-concept but also pursued other topics that my respondents defined as crucial. To understand their concerns, I felt compelled to explore the problematics of disclosing illness, something I had not anticipated. As a result, I studied how, when and why ill people talk about their conditions. Still, my interest in time alerted me to see if their modes of informing others about their conditions changed over time.

What kind of data should you gather for grounded theory studies? Rich, detailed data give you explicit materials with which to work. When I ask for rich, detailed data, I ask for full or "thick" (Geertz 1973a) written descriptions of events observed by researchers, extensive accounts of personal experience from respondents and records that provide narratives of experience (such as transcribed tapes of therapy sessions). Participant observers' fieldnotes, interviewers' transcriptions, patient autobiographies, student journals, may all produce rich, detailed data. It helps if you elaborate upon even detailed raw data such as the typed transcription of a patient conference. Hence, provide the context by describing the structure of the conference, the events leading up to it, the players in it and their unstated concerns (if known or implicit). Similarly, it helps to place a personal interview into perspective by adding a description of the situation, the interaction, the person's affect and your perception of how the interview went. In any case, you need thorough textual renderings of your materials so that you have data that you can study. In short, get as much material down on paper as possible.

Rich data afford views of human experience that etiquette, social conventions and inaccessibility hide or minimize in ordinary discourse. Hence, rich data reveal thoughts, feelings and actions as well as context and structure. In my research, I found that respondents' stories about illness often tumbled out nonstop. For example, one woman stated:

> If you have lupus, I mean one day it's my liver; one day it's my joints; one day it's my head, and it's like people really think you're a hypochondriac if you keep complaining about different ailments. . . . It's like you don't want to say anything because people are going to start thinking, you know, "God, don't go near her, all she is . . . is complaining about this." And I think that's why I never say anything because I feel like everything I have is related one way or another to the lupus but most of the people don't know I have lupus, and even those that do are not going to believe that ten different ailments are the same thing. And I don't want anybody saying, you know, [that] they don't want to come around me because I complain. (Charmaz 1991a:114–15)

Rich data afford the researcher a thorough knowledge of the empirical world or problem that he or she studies. By having this kind of data, grounded theorists therefore can more readily discern what participants mean and how they define their experiences. Thus, you begin your interpretations of the data from the respondent's point of view. What you see in the data may not exactly replicate what participants view as going on because you bring different perspectives and concerns to it. (Here I adopt the positivist assumption that it is the researcher's responsibility to find what is "there" and that it is possible to do so because we already share or can learn to share the language and meanings of those we study.) Having rich data means having detailed texts that allow you to trace events, delineate processes and make comparisons.

The data gathered in grounded theory research become increasingly more focused because the researcher engages in data analysis while collecting data. That data analysis drives subsequent data collection. *The grounded theorist's simultaneous involvement in data-gathering and analysis is explicitly aimed towards developing theory.* Thus, an interviewer will adapt his or her initial interview guide to add areas to explore and to delete questions that have not been fruitful. Many qualitative methodologists refine their questions and follow leads (see Atkinson 1990, 1992; Berg 1989; Gubrium 1988; Hammersley and Atkinson 1983; Lofland 1976; Lofland and Lofland 1995; Seidman 1991; Taylor and Bogdan 1984). But grounded theorists do so to develop their emerging theoretical categories (see Abrahamson and Mizrahi 1994; Biernacki 1986; Charmaz 1990; Glaser 1978; Strauss 1987). Others may do so to gain "thick description" (Geertz 1973a) of concrete behavior without necessarily looking for thick description that fills out, extends or refines theoretical concepts or enables the researcher to make theoretical connections. In contrast, grounded theorists ask theoretical questions of their thick description. For example, I first became aware of respondents' difficulties about disclosing illness 15 years ago when I interviewed several young adults who agonized over telling roommates, acquaintances and dates about their conditions. Rather than only obtaining thick description about these difficulties in disclosing, I began to ask myself analytical questions about disclosing as a process and then gathered data that illuminated that process. Among these questions included:

1. What are the properties of disclosing?
2. Which social psychological conditions foster disclosing? Which inhibit it?
3. How does disclosing compare with other forms of telling?
4. How, if at all, does disclosing change after the person becomes accustomed to his or her diagnosis?
5. What strategies, if any, do people use to disclose? When do they use them?

Despite its analytic thrust, grounded theory researchers can both gain thick description and foster theoretical development by listening closely to their respondents, attempting to learn the unstated or assumed meanings of their statements and shaping their emerging research questions to obtain data that illuminate their theoretical categories.

Making Meanings Explicit

Grounded theorists aim to analyze processes in their data and thus aim to move away from static analyses. Our emphasis on what people are doing also leads to understanding multiple layers of meanings of their actions. These layers could include the person's (1) stated explanation of his or her action, (2) unstated assumptions about it, (3) intentions for engaging in it, as well as (4) its effects on others and (5) consequences for further individual action and interpersonal relations. Throughout the research process, looking at action in relation to meaning helps the researcher to obtain thick description and to develop categories. How does the researcher study meaning?

One view held by some grounded theorists is that meanings can readily be discovered in the research setting. Glaser (1992) states that the significant issues in the field setting, and therefore the significant data, will be readily apparent to the researcher. He believes that anything other than that preconceives the ensuing research. Unlike Glaser, I assume that the interaction between the researcher and the researched *produces* the data, and therefore the meanings that the researcher observes and defines. A researcher has topics to pursue and research participants have goals, thoughts, feelings and actions. Your research questions and mode of inquiry will shape your subsequent data and analysis. That is why you must become self-aware about why and how you gather your data. You can learn to sense when you are gathering rich, useful data that do not undermine or demean your respondent(s). Not surprisingly, then, I believe the grounded theory method works best when the grounded theorist engages in the data collection as well as the data analysis phases of research. That way, you can explore nuances of meaning and process that hired hands might easily miss.

Certainly respondents' stories may tumble out or the main process in an observational setting may jump out at you. But sometimes neither are the stories so forthcoming nor is the main process so obvious. Even if they are, the researcher may need to do more work to discover the subtlety and complexity of respondents' intentions and actions. Closer study and often direct questioning is needed. For example, we do not have a highly developed language with which to talk about time. Thus, many of my research participants' attitudes towards and actions concerning time were unspoken and taken for granted. Yet their stories about illness often were clearly located in conceptions of time and implicitly referred to qualities of experienced time. For example, the woman's statement above referred to the quality and unevenness of her days. If the researcher plans to explore such areas, then he or she often needs to devise ways to make relevant observations or to construct questions that will foster pertinent responses. To illustrate, I asked my respondents questions like, "As you look back on your illness, which events stand out in your mind?", "What is a typical weekday like for you"? Glaser (1992) might say I force the data here by asking preconceived questions of it. Instead, I *generate* data by investigating aspects of life that the research participant takes for granted. At whatever level you attend to your participants' meanings, intentions and actions, you can create a coherent analysis by using grounded theory methods. Hence, the method is useful for fact-finding descriptive studies as well as more conceptually developed theoretical statements.

Perhaps the most important basic rule for a grounded theorist is: *study your emerging data* (Charmaz 1983; Glaser 1978). By studying your data you will become much more aware of your respondents' implicit meanings and taken-for-granted concerns. As a novice, you can best study your data from the very start by transcribing your audiotapes yourself or through writing your own fieldnotes, rather than, say, dictating them to someone else. By studying your data, you learn nuances of your research participants' language and meanings. Thus, you learn to define the directions in which your data can take you. Studying interview audiotapes, for example, prompts you to attend closely to your respondents' feelings and views. Charles Horton Cooley (1902) pointed out that we live in the minds of others and they live in ours. Your respondents will live in your mind as you listen carefully over and over to what they say. For example, one student in my class remarked:

> What an impact the words had on me when I sat alone transcribing the tapes. I was more able to hear and feel what these women were saying to me. I realized how, at times, I was preoccupied with thoughts of what my next

question was, how my eye contact was, or hoping we were speaking loud enough for the tape-recorder. (Charmaz 1991b:393)

Paying close attention to respondents' language can help you bridge your research participants' lived experience with your research questions. To do so, you should avoid taking for granted that you share the same meanings as the respondent. For example, my respondents with chronic illnesses often talked about having "good days" and "bad days." Everyone has good days and bad days whether they are talking about work, child care, school or doing research. As a researcher, however, you cannot assume that your views of good days and bad days mean the same thing as your respondents'. So I probed further and asked more questions around my respondents' taken-for-granted meanings of good and bad days, such as: "What does a good day mean to you?"; "Could you describe what a bad day is?"; "What kinds of things do you do on a good day?"; "How do these activities compare with those on a bad day?" I discovered that good days mean "minimal intrusiveness of illness, maximal control over mind, body and actions, and greater choice of activities" (Charmaz 1991a:50). The meaning of good days also extends to increased temporal and spatial horizons, to the quality of the day and to realizing the self one wishes to be. But had I not followed up and asked respondents about the meanings of these terms, their properties would have remained implicit.

Certainly starting the research with strong data-gathering skills helps. The skilled interviewer or observer will know when to ask more questions or make more focused observations. Nevertheless, novice researchers can make remarkable gains in skill during a brief time by attending closely to their methods and by studying their data. By gathering rich data and by making meanings explicit, you will have solid material with which to create your analysis.

CODING THE DATA

The first major analytic phase of the research consists of coding the data. In short, coding is the process of defining what the data are all about. Unlike quantitative coding that means applying preconceived codes (all planned before the researcher even collects data) to the data, qualitative grounded theory coding means *creating* the codes as you study your data. The codes emerge as you study your data. By studying your data, you again interact with them and ask questions of them. (Thus, the interactive nature of grounded theory research is not limited to data collection, but also includes the analytic work.) As a result, the coding process may take you into unforeseen areas and research questions.

Coding is the pivotal link between collecting data and developing an emergent theory to explain these data. The crucial phase of coding leads directly to developing theoretical categories, some of which you may define in your initial codes. To begin your grounded theory analysis, start your initial coding by examining each line of data and defining the actions or events that you see as occurring in it or as represented by it. Nonetheless, line-by-line coding means naming each line of data (see especially Glaser 1978). Hence, line-by-line coding helps you begin to take an analytic stance towards your work. Line-by-line coding keeps you close to your data. You have to study your data to arrive at codes. Through line-by-line coding, you begin to build your analysis, from the ground up without taking off on theoretical flights of fancy (Charmaz 1990). Line-by-line coding also helps you to refrain from imputing your motives, fears or unresolved personal issues to your respondents and to your collected data. Some years ago, a young man in my undergraduate seminar conducted research on adaptation to disability. He had become paraplegic himself when he was hit by a car while bicycling. His ten in-depth interviews were filled with stories of courage, hope and innovation. His analysis of them was a narrative of grief, anger and loss. When I noted that his analysis did not reflect his collected material, he began to realize how his feelings colored his perceptions of other people's disabilities. His was an important realization. However, had he assiduously done line-by-line coding he might have arrived at it before he handed in his paper.

From the standpoint of grounded theory, each idea should earn its way into your analysis (Glaser 1978). If you apply concepts from your discipline, you must be self-critical to ensure that these concepts work. Do these concepts help you to understand and to explicate what is happening in this line of data? If they do not, use other terms that do.

Line-by-line coding forces you to think about the material in new ways that may differ from your research participants' interpretations. Thomas (1993) states that the researcher must take the familiar, routine and mundane and make it unfamiliar and new. Line-by-line coding helps you to see the familiar in new light. It also helps you gain sufficient distance from your and your participants' taken-for-granted assumptions about the material so that you *can* see it in a new light.

If your codes take another view of a process, action or belief than that of your respondent(s), note that. You have to make analytic sense of the material rather than viewing it as, say, only a sequence of events or as description. Your respondent may not. How do you make analytic sense of the rich stories and descriptions you are compiling? First, look for and identify what you see happening in the data. Some basic questions may help:

1. What is going on?
2. What are people doing?
3. What is the person saying?
4. What do these actions and statements take for granted?
5. How do structure and context serve to support, maintain, impede or change these actions and statements?

Try to frame your codes in as specific terms as possible. Make your codes active. By being specific and active you will begin to see processes in the data that otherwise would likely remain implicit. Glaser and Strauss (1967; Glaser 1978, 1992) assume that any observer will find the most significant processes. Perhaps. But what you define in the data also relies in part upon the perspectives that you bring to it. Rather than seeing your perspectives as truth, try to see them as representing one view among many. That way, you will become more aware of the concepts that you employ. For example, try not to assume that respondents repress or deny significant "facts" about their lives. Instead, look for your respondents' understanding of their situations before you judge their attitudes and actions through the assumptions of your perspective. If afterwards you still invoke previously held perspectives as codes, then you will use them more consciously rather than merely automatically. Of course, observers do vary on the codes that they identify, depending on their training and research interests. In the example of line-by-line coding below, my interest in time and self-concept comes through in the first two codes:

Line-by-line coding

shifting symptoms, having inconsistent days	If you have lupus, I mean one day it's my liver; one day it's my joints; one day it's my head, and
interpreting images of self given by others	it's like people really think you're a
avoiding disclosure	hypochondriac if you keep complaining about different ailments. . . . It's like you don't want to say anything because people are going to start
predicting rejection	thinking, you know, "God, don't go near her, all
keeping others unaware	she is—is complaining about this." And I think
seeing symptoms as connected	that's why I never say anything because I feel like everything I have is related one way or
having others unaware	another to the lupus but most of the people don't
anticipating disbelief	know I have lupus, and even those that do are not
controlling others' views	going to believe that ten different ailments are the
avoiding stigma	same thing. And I don't want anybody saying,
assessing potential losses and risks of disclosing	you know, [that] they don't want to come around me because I complain.

Initial codes often range widely across a variety of topics. Because even a short statement or excerpt may address several points, a researcher could use it to illustrate several different categories. I could use the excerpt above to show how avoiding disclosure serves to control identity. I could also use it to show either how a respondent views his or her illness as inexplicable to others or how each day is unpredictable. When seen from the view of multiple interviews, the excerpt reveals the beginnings of becoming progressively more socially and emotionally isolated. Not telling others about illness leads to withdrawing when ill. Most importantly from a grounded theory perspective, initial codes help you to break the data into categories and begin to see processes. Line-by-line coding frees you from "going native," or from becoming so immersed in your respondent's categories or worldview that you fail to look at your data critically and analytically. Being critical about your data does not necessarily mean that you are critical of your research participants. Instead, being critical forces you to ask yourself questions about your data. Such questions include:

1. What process is at issue here?
2. Under which conditions does this process develop?

3. How does the research participant(s) think, feel and act while involved in this process?
4. When, why and how does the process change?
5. What are the consequences of the process?

Line-by-line coding helps you to make decisions about what kinds of data you need to collect next. Thus, you begin to distill the data and frame your inquiry from very early in the data collection. Your line-by-line coding gives you leads to pursue. To illustrate, you may identify an important process in your fifteenth interview. You can go back to your first respondents and see if that process explains events and experiences in their lives or seek new respondents. Hence, your data collection becomes more focused as does your coding.

Focused coding refers to taking earlier codes that continually reappear in your initial coding and using those codes to sift through large amounts of data. Thus, focused coding is less open-ended and more directed than line-by-line coding. It is also considerably more selective and more conceptual (Charmaz 1983; Glaser 1978). Here, you take a limited number of interesting line-by-line codes and you apply them to large amounts of data. By the time you engage in focused coding, you have decided which of your earlier codes make the most analytic sense and categorize your data most accurately and completely. Yet moving to focused coding is not entirely a linear process. As you gather more data, you will find that some respondents or events make explicit what was implicit in earlier respondents' statements or prior events. This kind of "Aha! Now I understand" experience prompts you to return to your earlier data and study them with a fresh eye. It also may prompt you to return to an earlier respondent to explore an event or issue that you may have glossed over before or that may have been too implicit or unstated to see.

In the example below, I select the codes "avoiding disclosure" and "assessing potential losses and risks of disclosing" to capture, synthesize and understand the main themes in the statement. Again, I try to keep the codes active and close to the data:

Focused coding

avoiding disclosure

assessing potential losses and risks of disclosing

If you have lupus, I mean one day it's my liver; one day it's my joints; one day it's my head, and it's like people really think you're a hypochondriac if you keep complaining about different ailments. . . . It's like you don't want to say anything because people are going to start thinking, you know, "God, don't go near her, all she is—is complaining about this." And I think that's why I never say anything because I feel like everything I have is related one way or another to the lupus but most of the people don't know I have lupus, and given those that do are not going to believe that ten different ailments are the same thing. And I don't want anybody saying, you know, [that] they don't want to come around me because I complain.

Focused coding allows you to create and to try out categories for capturing your data. A category is part of your developing analytic framework. By categorizing, you select certain codes as having overriding significance in explicating events or processes in your data. A category may subsume common themes and patterns in several codes. For example, my category of "keeping illness contained" included "packaging illness," that is, treating it "as if it is controlled, delimited, and confined to specific realms, such as private life," and "passing," that is, "concealing illness, maintaining a conventional self-presentation, and performing like unimpaired peers" (Charmaz 1991a:66–68). Again, make your categories as conceptual as possible while simultaneously remaining true to and consistent with your data. I try to make my focused codes active (to reflect what people are doing or what is happening) and brief so that I can view them as potential categories. By keeping codes active, you can see processes more readily. By keeping your focused codes as succinct as possible, you have a head start on creating sharp, clear categories. By raising a code to the level of a category, you treat it more conceptually and analytically. Thus, you go beyond using the code as a descriptive tool to view and synthesize data.

The emphasis on process in grounded theory starts with a substantive process that you develop from your codes. "Keeping illness contained" and "packaging illness" above are two such processes. As they work with their data, grounded theorists try to aim for defining generic processes. The two processes above are embedded in more fundamental, generic processes of personal information control about illness and about choices in disclosing that information. A generic process cuts across different empirical settings and problems; it can be applied to varied substantive areas (Bigus et al. 1994; Prus 1996; Wiseman 1994). Thus, the grounded theorist can elaborate and refine the generic process by gathering more data from the diverse arenas in which the process is evident. For example, personal information control and choices in disclosing are often problematic for homosexuals, sexual abuse survivors, drug users and ex-convicts as well as for people with chronic conditions. By concentrating on developing the generic process, you will more readily discover its properties, specify the conditions under which it develops and look for its consequences.

As you raise the code to a category, you begin (1) to explicate its properties, (2) to specify conditions under which it arises, is maintained and changes, (3) to describe its consequences and (4) to show how this category relates to other categories (cf. Charmaz 1983, 1990; Glaser 1978; Glaser and Strauss 1967). You do all this work in your written memos that I outline below.

Categories may be *in vivo* codes that you take directly from your respondents' discourse or they may represent your theoretical or substantive definition of what is happening in the data. For example, my terms "good days and bad days" and "living one day at a time" came directly from my respondents' voices. In contrast, my categories "recapturing the past" and "time in immersion and immersion in time" reflect my theoretical definitions of actions and events. Further, categories such as "pulling in," "facing dependency" and "making trade-offs" address my respondents' substantive realities of grappling with a serious illness. I created these codes and used them as categories but they reflect my respondents' concerns and actions. Novice researchers may find that they rely most on *in vivo* and substantive codes. Doing so nets a grounded analysis more than a theory. Nonetheless, studying how these codes fit together in categories can help you treat them more theoretically.

As you engage in focused coding, you attempt to build and to clarify your category by examining all the data it covers and by identifying the variations within it and between other categories. You also will become aware of gaps in your analysis. For example, I developed my category of "existing from day to day" when I realized that living one day at a time did not fully cover impoverished people's level of desperation. The finished narrative reads:

> Existing from day to day occurs when a person plummets into continued crises that rip life apart. It reflects a loss of control of health and the wherewithal to keep life together.
>
> Existing from day to day means constant struggle for daily survival. Poverty and lack of support contribute to and complicate that struggle. Hence, poor and isolated people usually plummet further and faster than affluent individuals with concerned families. Loss of control extends to being unable to obtain necessities—food, shelter, heat, medical care.
>
> The struggle to exist keeps people in the present, especially if they have continued problems in getting the basic necessities that middle-class adults take for granted. Yet other problems can assume much greater significance for these people than their illness—a violent husband, a runaway child, an alcoholic spouse, the overdue rent.
>
> Living one day at a time differs from existing from day to day. Living one day at a time provides a strategy for controlling emotions, managing life, dimming the future, and getting through a troublesome period. It involves managing stress, illness, or regimen, and dealing with these things each day to control them as best as one can. It means concentrating on the here and now and relinquishing other goals, pursuits, and obligations. (Charmaz 1991a:185)

Note the comparisons between the two categories above. To generate categories through focused coding, you need to make comparisons between data, incidents, contexts and concepts. It helps to make the following comparisons: (1) comparing different people (such as their beliefs, situations, actions, accounts or experiences); (2) comparing data from the same individuals with themselves at different points in time; and (3) comparing categories in the data with other categories (cf. Charmaz 1983; Glaser 1978). As I compared different people's experiences, I realized that some people's situations forced them into the present. I then started to look at how my rendering of living one day at a time did not apply to them. I reviewed earlier interviews and began to look for published accounts that might clarify the comparison. As is evident in the distinctions between these two categories above, focused coding prompts you to begin to see the relationships and patterns between categories.

MEMO-WRITING

Memo-writing is the intermediate step between coding and the first draft of your completed analysis. Memo-writing helps you to elaborate processes, assumptions and actions that are subsumed under your code. When memo-writing, you begin to look at your coding as processes to explore rather than as solely ways to sort data into topics. Making your codes as active as possible from the start enables you to define how various categories are connected in an overall process. Many qualitative researchers who do not write memos become lost in mountains of data and cannot make sense of them.

Grounded theory methods aim towards discovering and defining processes. In that sense, these researchers look for patterns, even when focusing on a single case or individual (see Strauss and Glaser 1970). Because they stress identifying patterns, grounded theorists typically use their respondents' stories to illustrate points—rather than to provide complete portrayals of their lives.[3] Bring your raw data right into your memo so that you preserve the most telling examples of your ideas from the very start of your analytic work. Provide enough verbatim material to ground the abstract analysis fully. By bringing verbatim material from different sources into your memo-writing, you can more readily make precise comparisons. Thus, memo-writing helps you to go beyond individual cases and to define patterns.

Memo-writing consists of taking your categories apart by breaking them into their components. Define your category as carefully as possible. That means you identify its properties or characteristics, look for its underlying assumptions and show how and when the category develops and changes. To illustrate, I found that people frequently referred to living one day at a time when they suffered a medical crisis or faced continued uncertainty. So I began to ask questions about what living one day at a time was like for them. From their responses as well as from published autobiographical accounts, I began to define the category and its characteristics. The term "living one day at a time" condenses a whole series of implicit meanings and assumptions. It becomes a strategy for handling unruly feelings, for exerting some control over a life now uncontrollable, for facing uncertainty and for handling a conceivably foreshortened future. Memo-writing spurs you to start digging into implicit, unstated and condensed meanings.

You probably wonder when you should start writing memos. Begin as soon as you have some interesting ideas and categories that you wish to pursue. If you are at a loss about what to write about, look for the codes that you have used repeatedly in your earlier data collection. Then start elaborating on these codes. Keep collecting data, keep coding and keep refining your ideas through writing more and further developed memos. Some researchers who use grounded theory methods discover a few interesting findings early in their data collection and then truncate their research. They do not achieve the "intimate familiarity" that Lofland and Lofland (1995) avow meets the standards for good qualitative research. You need to show that you have covered your topic in-depth by having sufficient cases to explore and to elaborate your categories fully.[4]

Memo-writing should free you to explore your ideas about your categories. Treat memos as preliminary, partial and immanently correctable. Just note where you are on firm ground and where you are making conjectures. Then go back to the field to check your conjectures. Memo-writing is much like free-writing or pre-writing (Elbow 1981; see also Becker 1986). You can do it for your eyes only and use it to help you think about your data. Do not worry about verb tense, overuse of prepositional phrases, or lengthy sentences at this point. Just get your ideas down as quickly and clearly as you can. You are writing to render the data, not to communicate them to an audience. Later, after you turn your memo into a section of a paper, you can start revising the material to make it accessible to a reader. Writing memos quickly without editing them gives you the added bonus of developing and preserving your own voice in your writing. Hence, your writing will read as if a living, thinking, feeling human being wrote it rather than a dead social scientist. From the beginning, you can write memos at different levels of abstraction—from the concrete to the highly theoretical. Some of your memos will find their way directly into your first draft of your analysis. Others you can set aside to develop later into a different focus.

Much of your memo-writing should be directed to making comparisons, what Glaser and Strauss (1967) call "constant comparative methods." Hence, you compare one respondent's beliefs, stance and actions with another respondent's, or one experience with another. If you have longitudinal data, compare a respondent's response, experience or situation at one point in time with that at another time. Then, as you become more analytic, start to make detailed comparisons between categories and then between concepts. Through memo-writing, you clarify which categories are major and which are more minor. Thus, memo-writing helps you to direct the shape and form of your emergent analysis from the very early stages of your research.

At each more analytic and abstract level of memo-writing, bring your data along with you right into your analysis. Build your analysis in the memo upon your data. Bringing your data into successive levels of memo-writing ultimately saves time because then you do not have to dig through stacks of material to illustrate your points. The following excerpt serves as an example of memo-writing taken from my own research.

Example of memo-writing

Living one day at a time means dealing with illness on a day-to-day basis, holding future plans and even ordinary activities in abeyance while the person and, often, others deal with illness. When living one day at a time, the person feels that his or her future remains unsettled, that he or she cannot foresee the future or if there will be a future. Living one day at a time allows the person to focus on illness, treatment and regimen without becoming entirely immobilized by fear or future implications. By concentrating on the present, the person can avoid or minimize thinking about death and the possibility of dying.

Relation to Time Perspective

The felt need to live one day at a time often drastically alters a person's time perspective. Living one day at a time pulls the person into the present and pushes back past futures (the futures the person projected before illness or

> before this round of illness) so that they recede without mourning [their loss]. These past futures can slip away, perhaps almost unnoticed. [I then go and compare three respondents' situations, statements and time perspectives.]

Memo-making leads directly to theoretical sampling, that is, collecting more data to clarify your ideas and to plan how to fit them together. Here, you go back and sample for the purpose of *developing* your emerging theory, not for increasing the generalizability of your results. When I was trying to figure out how people with chronic illnesses defined the passage of time, I intentionally went back to several people I had interviewed before and asked them more focused questions about how they perceived times of earlier crisis and when time seemed to slow, quicken, drift or drag. When an experience resonated with an individual, he or she could respond to even esoteric questions. For example, when I studied their stories, I realized that chronically ill adults implicitly located their self-concepts in the past, present or future. These timeframes reflected the form and content of self and mirrored hopes and dreams for self as well as beliefs and understandings about self. Hence, I made "the self in time" a major category. Thereafter, I explicitly asked more people if they saw themselves in the past, present or future. An elderly working-class woman said without hesitation:

> I see myself in the future now. If you'd asked where I saw myself eight months ago, I would have said, "the past." I was so angry then because I had been so active. And to go downhill as fast as I did—I felt life had been awfully cruel to me. Now I see myself in the future because there's something the Lord wants me to do. Here I sit all crumpled in this chair not being able to do anything for myself and still there's a purpose for me to be here. [Laughs.] I wonder what it could be. (Charmaz 1991a:256)

Theoretical sampling helps you to fill out your categories, to discover variation within them and to define gaps between them. Theoretical sampling relies on comparative methods. Through using comparative methods, you can define the properties of your categories and specify the conditions under which they are linked to other categories. In this way, you raise your categories to concepts in your emerging theory. By the time you need to conduct theoretical sampling, you will have developed a set of categories that you have already found to be relevant and useful to explain your data. After you decide that these categories best explain what is happening in your study, treat them as concepts. In this sense, these concepts are useful to understand many incidents or issues in your data (cf. Strauss and Corbin 1990). I recommend conducting theoretical sampling later in the research to ensure that you have already defined relevant issues and allowed significant data to emerge. Otherwise, early theoretical sampling may bring premature closure to your analysis.

Through theoretical sampling, you will likely discover variation within the process you are analyzing. When conducting theoretical sampling, you are much more selective than before about whom you obtain data from and what you seek from these individuals. You may focus on certain experiences, events or issues, not on individuals per se, because you want to develop your theoretical categories and need to define how and when they vary. However, observing or talking with individuals is the likely way in which you gain more knowledge about the experiences, events or issues that you seek to treat theoretically. For example, one of my main categories was "immersion in illness" (Charmaz 1991a). Major properties of immersion include recasting life around illness, slipping into illness routines, pulling into one's inner circle, facing dependency and experiencing an altered (slowed) time perspective. However, not everyone's time perspective changed. How could I account for that?

By going back through my data, I gained some leads. Then I talked with more people about specific experiences and events. Theoretical sampling helped me to refine the analysis and make it more complex. I then added a category "variations in immersion" that begins as follows and then goes on to detail each remaining point:

> A lengthy immersion in illness shapes daily life and affects how one experiences time. Conversely, ways of experiencing time dialectically affect the qualities of immersion in illness. The picture above of immersion and time has sharp outlines. What sources of variation soften or alter the picture of immersion and time? The picture may vary according to the person's (1) type of illness, (2) kind of medication, (3) earlier time perspective, (4) life situation, and (5) goals.

> The type of illness shapes the experience and way of relating to time. Clearly trying to manage diabetes necessitates gaining a heightened awareness of timing the daily routines. But the effects of the illness may remain much more subtle. People with Sjogren's syndrome, for example, may have periods of confusion when they feel wholly out of synchrony with the world around them. For them, things happen too quickly, precisely when their bodies and minds function too slowly. Subsequently, they may retreat into routines to protect themselves. Lupus patients usually must retreat because they cannot tolerate the sun. Sara Shaw covered her windows with black blankets when she was extremely ill. Thus, her sense of chronological time became further distorted as day and night merged together into an endless flow of illness. (Charmaz 1991a:93)

Theoretical sampling prompts you to collect further data that pinpoint key issues in your research by defining them explicitly and by identifying their properties and parameters. Your subsequent memo-writing becomes more precise, analytic and incisive. By moving between data collection and analysis in your memo-writing about your theoretical sampling, you will follow leads, check out hunches and refine your ideas. This way you have solid materials and sound ideas with which to work. Having both will give you a sense of confidence in your perceptions of your data and in your developing ideas about them.

After filling out your theoretical categories, and ordering them through sorting the memos you have written about them, you are ready to start writing the first draft of your paper (see Becker 1986; Richardson 1990; Wolcott 1990). As you write, try to explicate your logic and purpose clearly. That may take a draft or two. Then outline your draft to identify your main points and to organize how they fit together. (But do not write your draft from an outline—use your memos.) Your main argument or thesis may not be clear (to you as well as to others) until you write and rework several drafts. As your argument becomes clearer, keep tightening it by reorganizing the sections of your paper around it.

What place do raw data such as interview excerpts or fieldnotes have in the body of your paper? Grounded theorists generally provide enough verbatim material to demonstrate the connection between the data and the analysis, but give more weight to the concepts derived from the data.[5] Their analytic focus typically leads grounded theorists to concentrate on making their theoretical relationships explicit and on subordinating their verbatim material to it (cf. Glaser 1978; Strauss 1987). Unlike most other grounded theorists, I prefer to present many detailed interview quotes and examples in the body of my work. I do so to keep the human story in the forefront of the reader's mind and to make the conceptual analysis more accessible to a wider audience (see, for example, Charmaz 1991a, 1994a, 1994b).

After you have developed your conceptual analysis of the data, then go to the literature in your field and compare how and where your work fits in with it. At this point, you must cover the literature thoroughly and weave it into your work explicitly. Then revise and rework your draft to make it a solid finished paper. Use the writing process to sharpen, clarify and integrate your developing analysis. Through writing and rewriting, you can simultaneously make your analysis more abstract and your rendering and grounding of it more concrete. In short, you hone your abstract analysis to define essential properties, assumptions, relationships and processes while providing sufficient actual data to demonstrate how your analysis is grounded in lived experience.

CONCLUSION

Grounded theory methods contrast with traditional logico-deductive research design. As Glaser and Strauss (1967) noted long ago, grounded theory starts from a different set of assumptions than traditional quantitative research design. The inductive nature of these methods assumes an openness and flexibility of approach. Thus, you follow the leads gained from your view of the data, not from the careful and exhaustive literature review of the traditional research design. A fundamental premise of grounded theory is to let the key issues emerge rather than to force them into preconceived categories. Traditional research design, in contrast, is theory-driven from extant theories in the field. Hence, traditional research design requires the investigator to prestructure each phase of the research process to verify or to refute these extant theories. In short, each step is necessarily preconceived.

The grounded theorist builds the research as it ensues rather than having it completely planned before beginning the data collection. Similarly, you shape and alter the data collection to pursue the most interesting and relevant material. This approach differs sharply from the traditional research design with its structured instruments that are used in the same way with each research subject.

The purpose of grounded theory is to develop a theoretical analysis of the data that fits the data and has relevance to the area of study. The procedures within the method are then aimed to further theory development. Traditional research design generates data, not theory, to test existing theories by logically deducing hypotheses from them. By offering a set of systematic procedures, grounded theory enables qualitative researchers to generate ideas that may later be verified through traditional logico-deductive methods.

***

A version of this paper was presented at the Qualitative Research Conference, "Studying Lived Experience: Symbolic Interaction and Ethnographic Research '94," University of Waterloo, Waterloo, Ontario, 18–21 May 1994. I am indebted to Jennifer Dunn, Sachiko Kuwaura and Jonathan A. Smith for comments on an earlier draft.

***

NOTES

1   Her comment provided a valuable source of *comparison*, along with being something to corroborate. For example, this piece of data allowed me to frame new questions: To what extent do people view themselves as separated from or embedded in their daily routines? Which daily routines? How does sickness affect their view? When do they claim the self that they experience while ill? When do they reject it? For a contrasting view of another person with multiple sclerosis, see Hirsch (1977.169–70).

2   Grounded theorists assume that professional researchers, unlike student initiates, already have a sound footing in their disciplines. That is why they recommend using disciplinary concepts and perspectives to *sensitize* the researcher to look for certain processes and topics, but not to blind them to other issues. So any well-trained researcher already possesses a set of epistemological assumptions about the world, disciplinary perspectives and often an intimate familiarity with the research topic and the literature about it. The point is for any grounded theory researcher to remain as open as possible in the early stages of the research. The use of sensitizing concepts and perspectives provides a place to *start*, not to *end*. Hence, grounded theorists develop their sensitizing concepts in relation to the processes they define in their data. For example, I took the concept of identity and developed a framework of identity levels in an identity hierarchy (Charmaz 1987). In contrast, the logico-deductive model in a traditional model of research necessitates operationalizing the previously established concept as accurately as possible.

3   Recent critics from narrative analysis and postmodernism argue that the grounded theory emphasis on fracturing the data (that is, breaking them up to define their analytic properties) does not allow sufficient attention to the individual (see, for example, Conrad 1990; Riessman 1990). These critics now argue that the task of the social scientist is to reveal the totality of the individual's story. Most individuals I interview do not want their whole stories revealed, or their identities exposed. Nor would they have agreed to participate in the research if telling their stories in entirety had been my intent. To date, grounded theory studies have not focused on individual narratives per se. However, that certainly does not mean that grounded theory methods inherently preclude such a focus.

4   Of course, the thoroughness of your work also depends on whether you are doing it for an undergraduate exercise, a graduate thesis or a professional publication.

5   To date, there is little agreement how much verbatim material is necessary in qualitative research more generally. Some narrative analysts and postmodernists advocate emphasizing the individual's story (see Conrad 1990; Richardson 1992, Riessman 1990) and developing new ways to present it (see, for example, Ellis and Bochner 1992; Richardson 1992). Grounded theory works, in contrast, usually take a more traditional social scientific approach of making arguments, presenting and explicating concepts, and offering evidence for assertions and ideas. But compared to those qualitative studies that primarily synthesize description, grounded theory studies are substantially more analytic and conceptual.

16

Tricks of the Trade

Howard S. Becker

We typically discuss sociological theory in a rarified way, as a subject coordinate with, but not really related to, the way we do research. To be sure, Merton published two famous papers (Merton 1957:85–117) outlining the close relations that ought to obtain between theory and research, but students studying for prelims used them more than working social scientists ever did. Everett Hughes, who oriented his own work to the practical problems of finding out about the world, always threatened to write "a little theory book," containing the essence of his theoretical position and somehow different from the nuggets of sociological generalization contained in his essays and books.

Hughes' students all hoped he would write that theory book, because we knew, when we listened to him and read his work, that we were learning a theory, although we could not say what it was. But he never wrote it. He did not, I think, because he did not have a systematic theory in the style of Talcott Parsons. He had, rather, a theoretically informed way of working, if that distinction conveys anything. His theory was not designed to provide all the conceptual boxes into which the world had to fit. It consisted of a collection of generalizing tricks he used in thinking about society, tricks that helped you interpret and make general sense of data. (The flavor is best conveyed in his essays, collected in Hughes [1971].)

Because his theory consisted of such analytic tricks rather than a Theory, you learned it by hanging around him and learning to use his tricks, the way apprentices learn craft skills by observing journeymen who already know them. Sociologists of science (e.g., Latour and Woolgar 1979; Lynch 1985) have documented how natural scientists work in ways never mentioned in their formal statements of method, hiding "shop floor practice"—what scientists really do—

by the way they talk about it. Sociologists do that too. So theory can most appropriately be dealt with by cataloguing and analyzing the tricks we actually use, sociology's shop floor practice. I will describe some of my favorites, as well as some I learned from Hughes, noting their theoretical relevance as I proceed. I have given them names to serve as mnemonics.

WHOSE STANDARDS?

Participants in the worlds we study are usually very interested in the topics of our research and already have a lot of ideas about them. Similarly, scholars who have already studied those phenomena sometimes preempt the field, so that *their* way of defining the object of study, *their* words, take on a reality that seems to go beyond social definition. We need to be careful not to accept those ideas as reality, however, which we have only to study, measure, and investigate. Susan Reed, for instance, found that mental health professionals often used what she called "extraneous" criteria to decide whether to commit people to hospitals, such criteria as whether or not the patient has a family that is ready to keep him at home. But what makes that criterion extraneous? She classified criteria as extraneous by comparing them to the criteria professionals are supposed, according to applicable law, to use, criteria such as whether the patients are dangerous to themselves or others. But she accepted that distinction as worth making in the way those professionals usually make it.

Extraneous, like a lot of similar adjectives (e.g., "efficient"), only has meaning in relation to some standard. But the standard is not an objective, timeless reality. Someone created it because it did a job they wanted done. In this case, civil libertarians designed a law to protect patients against the arbitrary exercise of the professional power to hospitalize. We always need to ask what the standard is, whose it is, and what interests it furthers (or is thought to further, because the people involved might well not be right). The extraneous criteria professionals use make perfect sense from other points of view: the "therapeutic" (designed to maximize the patient's progress toward mental health) or the "trouble avoidance" (designed to minimize the chance of the patient coming back and causing more work for the professionals).

The analytic trick here consists of noticing that some concept makes a judgment that could be made in some other way, from some other point of view, and then asking whose point of view it expresses and what interests it furthers.

EVERYTHING HAS TO BE SOMEPLACE!

Sociologists like to make generalizations and so like to minimize the ways their "case" differs from other cases. We like to say that our case is "representative," that it resembles many or most other cases of things like it. This lets us argue that we have discovered important general results about some social phenomenon or process.

But, remember, I said "case." Every research site is a case of some general category, and so knowledge about it gives knowledge about a generalized phenomenon. We can pretend that it is just like all other cases, or at least is like them in all relevant ways, but only if we ignore all its local, peculiar characteristics. If our case is located in California, it will differ in some ways from a case located in Michigan or Florida or Alaska, because anything related to or contained in or dependent on (there are a lot of possibilities to choose from) the geographical location necessarily affects what we are studying.

What sort of things? The weather, for one. The student uprisings that took place in California in the 1960s were less likely to have taken place in Minnesota; it makes a difference in the incidence of outdoor demonstrations if you have year long mild weather or if you only have a few months of school before it really gets cold. (Irving Horowitz reminds me that some of the most important episodes of the Russian Revolution took place in the coldest parts of that country, a useful reminder that "influences" or "affects" is not the same as "determines.") Population characteristics also make a difference: whether the population is educated or not, the percentages of various racial groups, the prevalence of particular work skills. These and similar facts are relevant to any questions about stratification processes and to other things indirectly tied to those processes (e.g., the eating habits of the population which in turn might cause characteristic patterns of disease around which a professional culture of physicians might form).

Which things related to where our case is located should we take into account, because it is clear we cannot include everything? That is a tactical question. The provisional answer is that you include anything that tells you it can't be left out by sticking its nose up so that it cannot be ignored. If psychoanalysts tell you self-help groups and lay therapies such as EST successfully compete with them for patients, and those therapies and groups are very common in California, then you know that geography and local cultures cannot be ignored. We accumulate knowledge by finding more and more things that, in this sense, can't be left out, things tied to the local circumstances of the cases we study.

That means that we should do our research so that we can find these local peculiarities and build them into our results. Another good example is Thomas Hennessey's study (Hennessey 1973) of the development of big bands among black musicians between 1917 (the end of World War I, when many black musicians returned from service, where they had played in segregated bands) and 1935 (when the new form of the traveling big band became a national phenomenon). The bands, and the music they played, developed differently depending on where in the country the development occurred and, specifically, on the nature of the black and white populations in those metropolitan centers and the relations between them. New York had sophisticated black and white populations; black musicians learned to read music of all kinds; white audiences were accustomed to having black musicians perform for them, so black musicians performed in a great variety of circumstances, and tailored their music to the occasion. Atlanta musicians were much less schooled in conventional European music and mainly played for tent shows for the black population.

THINGS ARE JUST PEOPLE DOING STUFF TOGETHER

Physical objects, and more intangible social objects, while real enough physically, do not have "objective" properties. We give them those properties, for social purposes, by recognizing that they have them. Sociologists often assume that the physical properties of an object constrain what the people involved with it can do, but that almost invariably means that those properties are constraining if, and only if, people use the object the way everyone recognizes it is usually used. A drug may have measurable effects on the central nervous system, but it won't get you high if you do not recognize those effects that way. I suppose there are limits to this; no one can breathe underwater forever (although as soon as I say that I can think of five ways that they probably could, or at least convince others that they had).

The point is not philosophical but rather to recognize and look for the way people define physical objects as usable in only one or a few ways. (Creativity training, brainstorming, and similar exercises get people to redefine or undefine common objects so that they recognize this in a practical way.) We see these definitions in operation by looking for those situations (and we can always find them) in which the object appears not to have its normal properties, as when a narcotic drug does not get someone high or cause addiction. Then we can see that the constraints are essentially social.

While true of such physical objects as drugs or chairs, this is especially a property of social objects. Elihu Gerson likes to show that making a certain kind of argument leaves opponents boxed in so that they *have* to respond in a certain way. If you get opponents in an argument to accept your premises they then *must* accept your conclusion. I like to counter that that only works when the people involved have accepted certain ideas about what and who requires answering; anyone who can ignore those ideas need not respond properly. An opponent in an argument who does not mind appearing illogical or arbitrary can ignore your clever attempts to box him in. Hughes used to talk about upper-class people who were completely impervious to all interviewing tactics (like keeping silent until the interviewee felt compelled to speak) that relied on the necessity of being minimally polite to others. Parents whose children catch them in a logical contradiction, of course, often end discussions with "Because I'm the mommy, that's why!"

Because people usually successfully treat objects as though they had stable properties, we need to account for how they do that. Objects continue to have the same properties when people continue to think of them, and define them jointly, in the same way. Doing that makes joint activity much easier and anyone who wants to change the definition may have to pay a substantial price, so we usually accept current definitions of objects.

Objects, then, are congealed social agreements or, rather, congealed moments in the history of people doing things together. The analytic trick consists of finding places where that agreement has produced a different object than the one we are used to, seeing how objects thus get their properties from all the twists and turns of social process, and building that process into our theorizing.

OR ELSE WHAT?

Social scientists often use the imperative—locutions like "must" or "will have to"—in reference to social organizations or social events: "every social organization must take care of limiting its boundaries" or "every social organization must control deviance."

It is useful, when you hear such phrases, to ask "Or else what?" Because the source of the necessity is never as obvious as such statements make it seem. The use of the imperative suggests inevitability. If an organization "must," well, it just "must," that's all. The implication (sometimes stated explicitly in stern functionalist tracts) is that otherwise it will cease to exist. Or that the necessity is a matter of logic, almost a matter of definition.

Asking "Or else what?" smokes out the conditions under which the necessity holds. Nothing is ever *that* necessary. It is just necessary if certain other things are to happen. "An organization must attend to its boundaries or it will get confused with other organizations." All right, organizations sometimes get confused with other organizations. So what? "If it gets confused, it won't be able to do its work efficiently." I see. Who said it had to do that work and who set the criterion of efficiency by which it should be evaluated. "What are you, some kind of nut?"

Such statements of necessity are really ways of focusing on a problem. If I say an organization must punish deviance or its norms will cease to be effective, that is just a way of saying that some organizations will have ineffective norms. That should not be mistaken for a proposition, let alone a proof, that organizations in that condition can't continue to exist. It's a way of making the problem of the development of ineffective norms salient. But only a part of that problem. Treating the punishment of deviance as a necessity makes the only real problem that of avoiding a breakdown of norms. Sociology does not require that we treat that as something to be avoided at all costs. Only our moral and political commitments can do that.

Focusing on one possible outcome makes everything else a residual category. If I say that organizations must punish deviance in order to be effective I treat anything other than being effective as a residual category not worth going into. It divides the possibilities into being effective and—who cares what else, it doesn't make any difference. But the other possibilities are worth analysis because, after all, many interesting states, worthy of our attention, lie between perfect organizational efficiency and limbo. The choice of outcomes to be interested in is political. We need not be interested in bureaucracies that act like feudal baronies, but our lack of interest is not dictated by the requirements of sociology as a science. Relegating social phenomena to residual categories defines them as not worth thinking about, knowing about, or allowing to be.

It is similar with definitional forms of the gambit. Sometimes analysts using the imperative will say, and may mean, that the point is not that you cannot have some other form than perfect efficiency, or survival, but rather that they want to define that as the subject of study and the phenomenon must have that character or else they are not interested in it. That is subject to the same complaint. Why shouldn't we be interested in a full range of possibilities? This is not the same as saying that you have to be interested in everything, which is always dismissed as counseling unreachable perfection. It is just saying that you want to deal with the question already raised in a complete way.

EVERYTHING IS POSSIBLE

This leads to a related trick, one Everett Hughes taught me. He liked to quote the hero of Robert Musil's novel, *The Man Without Qualities*, saying "Well, after all, it could have been otherwise." We should not assume that anything is impossible, simply could not happen. Rather, we ought to imagine the wildest possibilities and then wonder why they do not happen. The conventional view is that "unusual" things do not happen unless there is some special reason for them to happen. "How can we account for the breakdown of social norms?" The trick here is to take the opposite view, assuming that everything is equally likely to happen and asking why it does not. "Of course social norms break down. How can we account for their persistence for more than ten minutes?"

One thing you learn from such an exercise is that, more often than not, the weirdest thing you could imagine actually happens or has happened, so that you need not imagine it. You have real cases to investigate (probably not where you thought they would turn up). But even if you find the cases in fiction or science fiction they can serve the same theoretical purpose, which is to imagine under what circumstances "unusual events" happen, and what obstacles prevent them from happening all the time.

Some other names for this trick might be: "look at the whole table, not just a few of the cells," or "Find the full range of cases, not just the few that are popular at the moment." Each of those names points to a situation in which social scientists fail to use this trick.

CONCEPTS ARE GENERALIZATIONS

Concepts are not just ideas, or speculations, or matters of definition, though they seem to be all of those things. In fact, concepts are empirical generalizations, which need to be tested and refined on the basis of empirical research results. Let me explain it this way.

We commonly have difficulty applying concepts to real cases of social phenomena: they sort of fit, but not exactly. That is because we seldom define phenomena by one unambiguous criterion. We do not say "If it has a trunk, it's an elephant, and that's that," or "If people exchange goods on the basis of price, that's a market." If we talked that way, we would know for sure whether a case was or was not one of the things we were interested in.

Concepts that interest us, however, usually have multiple criteria. Max Weber did not define bureaucracy by one criterion. He gave a long list of characteristic features: the existence of written files, jobs defined as careers, decisions made by rules, and so on. Similarly, social scientists usually define culture with multiple criteria: shared understandings, handed down between generations, coherent, embodying values, and so on.

In the world, however, phenomena seldom have all the attributes they should have to be, unambiguously, members of a class defined by multiple criteria. An organization has written files, and makes decisions by strict rules, but has no career paths for functionaries. Is it a bureaucracy, or not? A group's members share understandings but invent them on the spot instead of handing them down from generation to generation. Is that culture, or not?

The first problem this creates is that these descriptive titles are seldom neutral, but rather are terms of praise or blame. "Culture" is almost always good, "bureaucracy" is almost always bad. So we care, beyond technical theoretical considerations, whether we can say that a group has culture or not. If it's a "bad" group (e.g., a delinquent gang), some social scientists will not want to give it the honor of having real "culture"; they want to save that word for praiseworthy organizations (see the discussion in Kornhauser, 1978).

Another problem is more technical. Suppose you have x criteria for an object, and you call objects that have all x criteria O. What do you call the objects that have x-1 or x-2 or x-n of the criteria? The simple solution is to call them *not-O* and ignore their differences. But that is often unsatisfactory because hardly any of the objects we study have all the criteria; instead they have varying mixtures of them, what Wittgenstein called "family resemblances." They are similar, but not identical as molecules of copper are. We can, of course, give every combination of possibilities a name and let it go at that, or use some sort of Lazarsfeldian "reduction of a property space" technique (Barton 1955; Lazarsfeld 1972). In fact, we seldom do, because these devices quickly generate a very large number of possibilities (which is why Glazer and Strauss [1965] did not generate all the logically possible kinds of awareness contexts, although they talked as though they would).

So concepts like bureaucracy are really, as we use them, generalizations which say: "Look, these x criteria actually go together, more or less, all the time, enough so that we can pretend that they are all there in every Object O even though almost all Os in fact just have most, not all, of them." That makes a problem because you end up with a number of cases that do not fit, do not act as your theory says they will, precisely because they are missing an important attribute that is responsible for that aspect of the behavior of O.

We can usually finesse that, because the number of cases is small or because the objects we collected do not lack attributes that are important for the problem we are pursuing. But when we cannot, we should recognize that our "concept" was not just an idea but an empirical generalization that said that all those criteria always went together.

A good example from the world of practical affairs has to do with the concept of "living" somewhere. When the 1960 Census failed to count a large number of young black males, the political consequences forced statisticians and survey researchers to take the problem seriously. The practical question confronting the research committee considering this problem (Parsons 1972:57–77) was how to conduct the next Census so as to count the people who had been missed the last time. The U.S. Census must count people where they live, for purposes of political representation, so the question became a double one: how can we find them *where they live* so that they will fill out our forms, and what does it mean to live somewhere (because if we understand what it means to live somewhere we will know how to reach them)?

The expert committees' discussions revealed a profound ambiguity in the notion of living somewhere. What does it mean to live somewhere? For every criterion proposed, you could imagine a perfectly reasonable exception. You live where you sleep: if I am on vacation in Mexico do I live in Mexico? It is where you usually sleep: I am a traveling salesman, I do not usually sleep anywhere in particular. It is where you get your mail: many people get the mail at General Delivery or the City Lights Book Store in San Francisco, but they do not live in those places. It is where you can always be reached: for me that is the Sociology Department at Northwestern, but I certainly do not live there. It is where you keep your clothes, it is where . . .

For most people, most of the time, all those places are the same place. But for most people sometimes, and for some people all the time, they are not: they keep their clothes one place and sleep in another. For them the concept is just not adequate and, if we want to take them into account, we have to break the concept down into its component indicators and treat each one separately. We have, in other words, to realize that the empirical generalization embodied in the concept is not true: all those criteria do not go together all the time.

You can treat that as a technical problem if you want, but it is more productive to make it the jumping off point for expanding and complicating your theory of the world. Isn't it interesting to know that "living somewhere" is that complicated? It should be.

Ethnography's Warrants

Jack Katz

Ethnographers must find a raison d'être in response to a powerful paradox. On one hand, the ethnographic method is distinctively committed to displaying social realities as they are lived, experienced, understood, and familiar to the people studied. Statistical social research, by contrast, is particularly successful when it can demonstrate that features in individuals' backgrounds (e.g., birth order, geopolitical region of residence, parents' education, gender, race) pattern their behavior even while they remain unaware of the influence. Statistical analysts have reason to celebrate when their subjects, citing their own experience, display astonishment or vehemently object to research findings, as such reactions only prove that special methods, inaccessible to the layperson, are necessary to uncover fundamental realities. For the researcher working with large quantitative data sets, such "counterintuitive" findings are delightful resources for responding to the common criticism that sociology only documents common sense. Ethnographers faced with similar reactions from their subjects have good reason to be unnerved. If ethnographic descriptions do not fit the texture of experience as lived by research subjects, then they may be useful only as projections of the researcher's imagination. Few ethnographers have created a style of analysis or a cult of personality sufficiently robust to make that an effective warrant.[1]

But if ethnography must describe its findings as matters of everyday experience to its subjects, then the other horn of the dilemma pops up: Why are realities that are obvious to the subjects not also obvious to the ethnographer's audience? All ethnography is haunted by the paradox that its distinctive methodological respect for its subjects' meanings implies that its labors are gratuitous. Put in the form of a question addressed to the ethnographer: If all you have to offer is just a description of commonsense reality, then what is your contribu-

From *Sociological Methods & Research*, Vol. 25, No. 4, pp. 391–423. Copyright © 1997 Sage Publications, Inc. Reprinted by permission.

tion? If you claim to describe what everyone studied already knows, then who needs you?

Such questions are instances of a general challenge that ethnographers face: establishing a warrant for their research. Without a warrant for a study, no matter how beautifully one's empirical claims may be established, one still may be bowled over by the question "So what?" or "Who cares?" What distinguishes ethnography as a research practice is not only that the process of inquiry must execute a warrant well (e.g., by gathering data that are nuanced, densely textured, locally grounded, meaningful to the subjects, etc.) but also that ethnographies risk being considered banal unless they discover, in the data-gathering process itself, grounds to argue that there is a need for the study in the first place.

Within the vast field of ethnographic study, there are many subgenres. These may be differentiated by noting the kind of bridging work by which ethnographers connect their subjects to their audience. The picture that emerges is far more complex than the one drawn by Mills (1963) when he attributed the motivation of many of the early studies of social problems to the social distance between immigrant, poor and working class, urban, often Catholic subjects and the native-born Protestant, middle class, rural or small-town origins of the sociologists, many of whom came from ministers' families. But Mills's underlying theme about the sociology of sociological knowledge remains valid; much of the market for ethnography is built on a sense of radical distance between the "them" about whom the ethnographer writes and the "us" to whom ethnographic texts are directed.

Perhaps the single most common warrant for sociological ethnography is that what is obvious to the subjects has been kept systematically beyond the cognitive reach of the ethnographer's audience because of the moral character of the social life under investigation. The moral reputation of a set of people or a type of activity, as either deviant and disreputable or especially respectable and worthy of deference, can be invoked as a warrant for ethnography because such a moral status, considered as a social fact rather than as a spiritual reality, implies that social forces systematically maintain social distance between the ethnographer's subjects and his or her audience—an audience that can be presumed to be largely middle class, university educated, and, if not wholly conventional in lifestyle, then still of no uniformly extraordinary moral stripe. Thus a close and unprecedented description of any practice or population that is either, on one hand, especially low, despised, or fascinated with troublemaking or, on the other, especially elite, dripping with respectability, or charismatically inspired, should make a fair bid for attention.

In this article I describe the fieldwork challenges that ethnographers systematically confront when they pursue the most common strategies for warranting research on people and practices that are considered socially to be either deviant or worthy of special deference. With respect to subjects reputed to be deviant, I first distinguish *bohemian* and *normalizing* portraits of subjects and argue that ethnographers routinely struggle with specific problems of data analysis when attempting either of these alternative, morally significant depictions. Next

I distinguish between portraying the *social framing* or the *context-specific* behavior of people who are regarded socially as unique in some morally positive respect. I argue that in pursuing either of these alternatives, the ethnographer typically either *deconstructs* the perspectives in which outsiders lend deference or *debunks* the pretensions of his or her subjects. Then I describe a *naturalistic* approach as a third, more comprehensive strategy for ethnographic research.

In addition to clarifying alternative ways in which to warrant the study of morally exceptional subjects, my goal is to introduce the idea of the warrant as a general methodological concern that is relevant for all ethnographies. In the final section, I briefly note several warrants that are applicable to a more general range of ethnographic research subjects. Ethnographic methodology is bedeviled by doubts that are both blunt and frequently unstated. But once made explicit, the challenge of "So what?" calls out numerous, mutually supportive answers.

DANGEROUS SOCIAL AREAS AND MORALLY PERVERSE PEOPLE

A provocative social distance obtains when the people and places studied are thought to pose risks to nonnatives of such a magnitude that they can gaze only from afar and through a veil of mystery that is sustained rather than dispelled by the glimpses provided by journalism, routine police reports, and periodic riots. It is thus not by accident that deviance, social disorganization, and neighborhoods that are regarded as breeding grounds for social pathology consistently have been a focus of ethnographic inquiry in sociology. Not only do funding sources disproportionately support ethnographic research on deviance, but would-be ethnographers searching for topics to study can easily appreciate that, by choosing a terrain with a deviant reputation, they will avoid the wonder, confusion, and indulgent pity that they can anticipate from family, friends, and academic critics if they choose to study something that calls for no special moral notice— topics such as why Jews in American cities have favored Chinese restaurants (Tuchman and Levine 1993), how people play fantasy games (Fine 1983), or what people on rollerskates must do to get around on city streets (Wolfinger 1995).[2]

Normalizing and Bohemian Portraits

The fact that a study may be conducted under the auspices of a conventional belief that the subjects are scary or troublemaking does not necessarily build in a bias to sustain the beliefs that justify the study in the first place. On the contrary, one of the most common ways to warrant ethnographic research is to produce a text that demonstrates that the anxieties behind conventional opinion are unfounded. An area thought to be a slum, in the sense of an area suffering from the effects of social disorganization, is shown to be governed by an elaborate internal order (Gans 1982; Suttles 1968; Whyte 1955). A practice such as heroin use, depicted in popular culture as enslaving, is shown to be governed by cycles of abstinence and relapse (Ray 1964). Seen up close, street-corner men (Anderson 1978) and adolescent gang members (Klein 1971) often seem to live lives that are more banal than frightening. Again and again, ethnographers claim to have made a novel contribution by asserting that groups conventionally thought to be deviant actually are serving conventional motives or at least conducting deviance via familiar social conventions.

It is relatively rare for an ethnography to confirm that an area of social life is indeed as physically unnerving as, or even more morally perverse than, conventional views would have it. But there are some examples. Recent ethnographic accounts of crack houses depict them as cubicles in which humanity is tortured and degraded to such extremes that the everyday realities would blend in as natural only if they were configured as a patch in a painting by Hieronymus Bosch or in a poetic nook of Dante's imagination (Ratner 1993). Polsky (1967) described hustlers in pool halls and beats in coffee houses as morally unconventional and proud of it. Burglars recently have been depicted as desperately poor, but the pressure of their poverty is shown to be the recurrent result of the very illicit "partying" that they are desperate to rejoin (Wright and Decker 1994). Middle class, well-educated women are found to get pregnant and have abortions not, as much conventional opinion would have it, from ignorance, unavailability of contraception, or psychological resistance but rather by making "a de facto choice of abortion as a method of fertility control" (Luker 1975). This choice becomes understandable only when one appreciates that, in the precise social situations and sequential contexts in which the choice is exercised, there is not only a range of costs to contraception but also, and in ways outsiders might judge to be morally perverse, brief but fateful appreciations of the benefits of pregnancy.

Ethnographies that are warranted by the deviant social reputations of their subjects may undermine or promote a sense of social distance. Using an outdated and thus presumably innocuous term, we might dub as *bohemian* those studies that find that the moral fabric of subjects' lives is more deviant than conventional opinion had imagined. The tendency to document "them" as essentially like "us" but living in troubled circumstances with which "we" need not struggle might be referred to as "normalizing."

Whether the bohemian or the normalizing view is more correct for any given area of socially defined deviance is not simply a matter of the author's or the readers' preferences and values. Ethnographic research on deviance owes much of its methodological strength to the powerful ways in which the social realities of subjects' worlds resist the imposition of the researcher's own moral preferences. Bohemian and normalizing portraits face different but equally insistent methodological challenges, and both risk equally systematic, if different, sources of error.

Bohemian studies risk romanticizing (or, borrowing a term from anthropologists' critiques of anthropology, "exoticizing") their subjects. Klein (1995) documented a tendency in popular culture to exaggerate the depth of the social reality of adolescent gang culture. Outsiders commonly read the symbols of gang life (e.g., graffiti, hand gestures, clothing styles, dramatic acts of violence) as indicating that gang members live in vibrantly distinctive ways. But sometimes what initially appears to be the tip of an iceberg is, when carefully investigated, only a cold tip.

For various reasons, in Los Angeles and other gang-plagued cities, the police and often the liberal urban public want to believe that gang culture organizes much of youth violence. But youth violence rates do not vary among cities or over time in relationship to the perception of gang organization. What gangs more obviously organize are two related patterns of urban American life. One is a pattern of large-scale, constitutionally improper police interventions. The other is a public understanding of a disconcertingly high level of youth violence in parts of the city's population that are especially difficult to comprehend, namely the culturally foreign and politically muted neighborhoods. If gangs do not in fact increase the tendency to violence among young minority men in urban poverty areas, still the idea of the gang effectively explains otherwise incomprehensible incidents of peer-directed violence and addresses the public's anxieties over growing sections of the population that maintain a low profile in representative politics.

The point is that ethnographic methods, by looking beyond symbols to everyday realities, will reveal and can correct errors of romanticization. The error of romanticization is that of falsely suggesting that an inspiring culture diffusely and powerfully organizes behavior along deviant lines. Such errors are commonly betrayed in ethnographic texts that fail to describe how the subjects make situated use of deviant themes in their everyday lives.

The errors of the normalizing view are similarly detectable by examining the extent to which the research has met the ethnographic challenge to document local meanings. For historically emergent reasons, this direction of error has come to loom especially large in the current generation of ethnographic work. The avoidance of this error currently is a major pedagogical challenge.

A generation ago, Becker (1967) argued that the researcher of deviance naturally colored his or her research, depending on the "side" he or she took as a practical matter when conducting the research. If one uses officially collected statistics, then one operates from a perspective fashioned by those in power. Ethnography distinctively offers the opportunity to convey local meaning, that is, the meaning of subjects' actions to the subjects. Ethnographies of deviance, to the extent that they describe the perspectives of those "below," should be expected to highlight the distortions of views imposed from "above."

An exception, Becker (1967) pointed out, is when the moral status of the putatively deviant group has become politicized. Then the "deviants," or others acting on their behalf, are likely to have produced and disseminated a portrait of themselves that is far more favorable than what an innocently motivated ethnographer is likely to describe. Becker was writing early in a powerful trend. In 1979, John Kitsuse, in his presidential address to the Society for the Study of Social Problems, offered a commentary whose implications for the ethnographic study of deviance have still to be fully appreciated (Kitsuse 1980). Kitsuse was writing during times when the civil rights movement was proliferating beyond race to offer political power to a seemingly endless series of groups that had long suffered under reputations as deviant. Groups that had hidden "in the closet" were now publicly organizing to demand an end to official sanctions and a destruction of the harmful stereotypes on which they were based.

For the ethnographic research community, the institutional successes of the civil rights movements have fundamentally revised the warrant that, since the Progressive Era, had consistently underwritten the study of deviant populations. In the period between the papers delivered by Becker (1967) and Kitsuse (1980), new social actors were rapidly emerging specifically to filter "our" perceptions of "them." One after the other, stigmatized groups were deputizing specialized agents to provide the preferred political spin on the appearance that is conveyed to the general public. As a result, the political thrust of the ethnographer's work has developed a profound ambivalence. Now any account of the everyday realities in social worlds whose members are battling reputations as deviant is likely to uncover realities that the group's public relations agents will find embarrassing and counterproductive.

There may be no greater challenge to the quality of ethnographic research today than appreciating and thinking through the response to this challenge. A group's social reputation as deviant still serves as a powerful warrant for doing ethnography because life behind a deviant label is likely to be in some respects different, if only because of the distinctive challenges that a reputation for deviance brings along with it. But as a matter of politics, the ethnographic researcher who moves onto "deviant" turf is apt to find that he or she has unwittingly moved into the service of those who will find bohemian portraits useful for repressive purposes. Because sociological ethnographers almost always want to benefit the interests of the people they study, the predictable result is an intense conflict.[3]

Behind the public relations lines, members of "deviant" groups perceive, respond to, and often undermine the images that the researcher may assume best serve the subjects' interests. The participant observer who hangs out on Los Angeles street corners where illegal immigrants seek work may hear them talk about the availability of public benefits in tones that sound joyfully cynical. A researcher who observes from inside gay rights organizations will see interactions in which erotic themes and *femme* stereotypes are engaged playfully in ways that would give comfort to conservative critics. An observer of young women who wear very short skirts as part of the uniforms in which they serve hamburgers on roller skates to restaurant clients may expect to find a management bent on sexual exploitation and an emotionally suffering female staff; but, in Los Angeles at least, what ethnographers are likely to find is that the employees shorten their skirts in defiance of management policy, that their sisters and mothers celebrate their costumes as cute, and that the job is a natural extension of their prior careers as high school cheerleaders.

Confronted with such material, the ethnographer realizes that it will not be easy to present fieldnotes that will warrant the study simply as a demonstration that outsiders have failed to appreciate how much the subjects are abused by inaccurate stereotypes. But to explore fully the subjects' subculture is to risk putting oneself effectively in the employ of repressive outside forces. A common response is to cut the embarrassing material from the presented data and to make up for what has been removed by rhetorical argumentation about repression elsewhere in the social system—repression that understandably encourages undocumented migrant workers to cynicism, that brings a gallows humor to gay rights groups, and that encourages young women to exploit their physical appearance long before capitalism lays its mercenary hands directly on them.

Whatever the empirical basis of such arguments, they point to times and places in the subjects' lives that are beyond the ethnographer's reach. The methodological strength of ethnography is revealed, not necessarily in the avoidance of political or moral bias in the construction of texts but rather in the textually transparent escape from firsthand data to ringing rhetoric when significant steps must be made in the analysis. Like the research design in survey and laboratory experimental work, the ethnographic warrant does not guarantee a loyal execution of the research act, but it does distinguish between matters of relevance and irrelevance, separate documentation from exhortation, and create a frame for investigation that provides readers with a perspective for evaluation that is independent of the researcher's preferences.

To the extent that the warrant for an ethnography is that it describes social areas that are conventionally thought to be deviant, the value of the study will wax and wane depending on the fate of conventional belief. The place of marijuana in contemporary popular culture no longer fits the exotic and bohemian images of the 1950s, and so an essay on the process of learning to smoke marijuana no longer has the same bridging mandate to fulfill that it once had. It is now hard to appreciate the sense of dread that middle class readers apparently had about the Boston street corners described by Whyte (1955). By the 1960s, such Italian city neighborhoods had become favored tourist spots, and it was black and Spanish-speaking neighborhoods that were thought to be dangerous (Vidich 1992). Whyte's study, if conducted today in the North End, might still be warranted, but the nature of the warrant would have to be different.[4] Because the social distance between particular ethnographic subjects and the audience for ethnography may diminish greatly over time, the ethnographer is well advised to become self-conscious about the entire range of warrants that may sustain his or her work.

SOCIAL WORLDS OF THE ELITE AND THE ADMIRED

If the status of a group or practice as deviant provides a firm warrant for ethnographic research, then so too, for related reasons, does the self-proclaimed or imputed status of a group or practice as elite—especially powerful, charismatically inspired, possessing a rare sensibility, or otherwise worthy of great deference. Getting "behind the scenes" is a compelling basis for inquiry whether the challenging distance is created by dread and deviousness or by respectability and a privileged insularity.

The penumbra of charisma that surrounds many high-status positions in society is a reliably provocative dare for ethnographic research. Thus Morrill (1995) effectively addressed the warrant for his book on conflict management among corporate executives by asking "Why study up?" and answering,

> Despite the lack of close-up scholarly studies of executives, their folk hero status in American society has begotten voluminous popular and prescrip-

> tive literatures ... Much of the popular literature fits into what one business scholar calls the "great man school." ... To some degree, all of these sources convey the image of corporate executives as twentieth century Napoleonic men on white horses. ... Executives in their memoirs and autobiographies portray themselves as risk takers, mavericks, and visionaries and as hugely successful in nearly all their endeavors. It is as if executive life were a series of one-man plays (and they are typically about men) brought to life through the sheer force of the protagonist's will. (9–10)

With such powerful myths touted on best-seller lists, Morrill could be confident of success even if he found nothing more than what ethnographers always find: that people act collaboratively and that what outsiders think of as the product of individual personality is in fact the result of social interaction.

But the ethnographer of elites does not always have such a sure bet. Groups that seem elite and privileged in the eyes of people who look on from one position in society may seem unexceptional and may appear to enjoy no special deference in the eyes of people who look on from other standpoints. One of the dangers that an ethnographer faces in studying a group that he or she considers elite is that, to the ethnographer's readers, the group may be familiar and not particularly noteworthy.

It is especially likely that the subjects will see themselves as less privileged than outsiders may imagine because their outlook on stratification is developed from their own position vis-à-vis other groups. An ethnographer who studies a group or social area that has been labeled as deviant by popular culture, by the repeated enforcement actions of the criminal justice system, and by social welfare agencies' activities has something important to say if he or she finds that as a matter of everyday culture and in the patterns of routine social organization, nothing unusual is happening. Less obvious is the contribution made by a description of normality as the tenor of work life among highly paid professionals, university scientists, religious leaders, or powerful politicians.

The problems of warranting studies of elites are not due primarily to the subjectivity of judging who and what is privileged and respectable. The reality of exceptionally high moral status is as objectively grounded as that of deviant status. As with deviance and disrepute, charisma and exceptional respectability exist as sociological facts to the extent that people and practices are treated in ways that sustain those special moral imputations (Katz 1975). For elites, this typically means such matters as the right to exploit a monopolistic license and ready access to exceptional financial investments by a supporting community.

While people in privileged positions enjoy unique abilities to operate outside of otherwise routine forms of oversight, in contemporary society they also are routinely engaged in describing and explaining their everyday practices. Lawyers who have the power to charge clients $500 an hour also have the obligation to describe their work in 10-minute segments and to log each work-related phone call. The problems of establishing an ethnographic warrant for studying elites are rooted in the culture of rationality that underpins such institutionalized accounting practices.

Thus it is a common experience in studying lawyers, for example, that they convey to ethnographers their wonder at what the researcher could possibly discover given that they already specify and record the nature and reasons for their actions in documents produced for clients, courts, and regulatory agencies. Likewise, scientists in laboratories are centrally occupied with formally explaining the results of their professional action before the ethnographer shows up. Their everyday research practices are undertaken with a constant attention to the implications for reports that will be written (Latour and Woolgar 1986). Doctors may be surprisingly unconcerned with what an ethnographic investigation might find because they already are conditioned to be concerned with what outside critics may find, as indicated by the size of the malpractice premiums they must pay. Subjects in elite positions have good reason to be disarmingly indifferent to ethnographic research.

It is common to remark that ethnographers tend to study down and to explain that tendency by referring to the self-protective secrecy of elites. But ethnographers who have studied people in elite positions do not support the view that their subjects are especially inaccessible (Ostrander 1993). Paradoxically, the relative lack of studies of people in elite positions may have less to do with their secrecy than with their institutionalized openness.[5]

The challenge of this openness goes directly to the ethnographic warrant. In effect, the ethnographer is told by the elite subject, "Here is what we do and why we do it," and then the ethnographer is asked, "What is there about us that we are not already the experts in knowing?" The problem is especially severe with elite or charismatic groups because they claim a moral autonomy, a special knowledge (e.g., medical, legal, scientific) or a special sensibility (e.g., religious, artistic) that cannot be reduced to conventional dimensions of social life. Unless the ethnographer can clarify for the subjects how he or she will advance their understanding of their own world, the implication may easily arise that the study is a hunt to uncover material to embarrass the subjects by undermining their public image.

Thus a moral problem arises for the ethnographer of elites that complements the problem faced by the researcher who would study a group that he or she regards as unjustly labeled deviant. If the thrust of the research is to debunk the respectable group, then the researcher will be pressed to dissemble in order to proceed. If the thrust of the research sustains the group's claims of moral autonomy, then it may not be clear why the group itself, rather than an outsider/sociologist, is not the best source for information on its ways and whys. In this latter case, the challenge of the warrant is restated: Why should we think that we, or anyone else, need you to study us? A common practical resolution to this dilemma is for the ethnographer to be massaged by the subjects into the model of a science writer who popularizes knowledge that is too esoteric in its natural form for the lay public to understand. But that will not satisfy the ethnographer's own professional research audience, and so the dilemma of dissembling arises again, albeit in less stark moral forms, because in this case the ethnographer's "cover" has been designed by the subjects.

Even if the moral dilemma is resolved when the researcher is invited to play an emissary role, the ethnographer of elite subjects still faces a severe challenge in establishing a warrant for the research. On one hand, if the ethnographer takes as data the special knowledge that the subject group claims, then on what basis can the ethnographer claim to understand more than experienced practitioners already know? On the other hand, if the ethnographer skirts distinctive features of the subjects' culture and practices and treats social relational phenomena in terms applicable to any social world, then what is the relevance of the subject group's special status for the researcher's sociological analysis?

Social Framing and Context-Specific Accounts

Ethnographies of elite worlds can be sorted out with respect to their response to this dilemma. One approach, which may be characterized as *social framing*, avoids describing culturally distinctive matters in favor of analyzing the social relations that set up and support the subjects' world. Consider the study of musical work and careers. Making music and developing a career as a musician might be considered charismatic or at least as requiring a special competency, but one can study musicians' social worlds sociologically without describing the practice of any of the music itself. Thus one can describe the relations that musicians create with each other and with their audiences to set the stage to play their music (Becker 1963), and one can analyze turning points and contingencies in musicians' careers (Faulkner 1985). Such work neither debunks nor explicates the unique sensibilities that presumably characterize this artistic social world. The authors only implicitly address readers' assumptions about the special sensibilities of musicians. Explicitly, such studies are offered as relevant to sociologies of work and careers.

An alternative approach might be characterized as *context specific*, and this approach in turn has its subtypes. Ethnographies become studies in folklore when they describe local cultures without addressing either social relations within the examined world or the contingencies of the production of its distinctive culture. Ethnographies become *ethnomethodological* when they focus exclusively on the sequential production of what it is that practitioners of esoteric competencies distinctively and in detail do. In contrast to social research that uses standardized and preset definitions of variables, ethnography is uniquely able to enter the culturally specific world of subjects. But once the researcher begins to make descriptive use of the culturally autonomous language of elite or charismatic practices, sociological readers are likely to get glassy-eyed and, for their part, expert practitioners may not grant that they have learned anything new. Thus David Sudnow's monographs on his solo piano playing became, for sociologists who were not themselves musicians, exercises in applied philosophy more than contributions to sociological theory (Sudnow 1978, 1979), and they left music critics unimpressed by Sudnow's admittedly accurate explication of what practitioners tacitly know (Lipman 1979; Rothstein 1979). Ethnomethodological studies in which the sociologist attempts to represent the perspective of a competent practitioner in worlds of science risk a similar fate (Lynch 1985).

In ethnomethodological ethnography, the effort to make substantive statements about the social relations that frame esoteric work is eschewed as reducing or glossing what is distinctive to the social domain at issue. But in making a bow to the need to be "loyal to the phenomenon," the researcher may abandon the sociological audience. Studies of this type risk becoming exercises in applying the ideas of figures such as Maurice Merleau-Ponty, Alfred Schutz, and Ludwig Wittgenstein, philosophers who pointed the way toward new forms of empirical investigation but did not invite sociological research to reform philosophy.

I have argued that, in fashioning a warrant to study subjects conventionally regarded as morally exceptional, ethnographers predictably swing between characteristic forms of error. The ethnographer of people who are thought to deserve some special deference, for example, risks missing what is culturally distinctive about the research target if he or she focuses on matters of social framing. If the focus is on what is culturally distinctive, then the ethnographer risks losing a sociological audience. There are two common ways to maneuver around these risks. Both focus directly on the social distance that creates a special status for their subjects.

Debunking Charisma and Deconstructing Deference

First, the research can reveal behind-the-scenes matters that undermine historic presumptions of honor and special sensibility. Elite lawyers may be shown to aid their clients to destroy evidence sought by criminal investigators (Manin 1985). The households of the socially and financially elite may be found to display images that are substantially similar to those displayed in households of socially lower and presumably less refined tastes (Halle 1993). Surgeons may be described as no more morally sensitive to the objects of their work than were the butchers from which modern surgeons evolved (Millman 1977). Close description of the practices of futures traders may explode the mystique of supposedly great technical complexity and high pressure that is sustained by outsiders who are overly impressed with the size of the financial stakes (Abolafia 1996). Participant observation research on medical students may reveal that their youthful idealism remains sturdy with respect to matters outside of immediate demands but that, in the context of everyday work, a professional cynicism quickly begins to take hold (Becker, Geer, Hughes, and Strauss 1961).

Less frequently, the debunking light of ethnography is thrown in the opposite direction, onto the perspectives that create elite statuses and institutions of charisma. Two important examples are Becker's (1982) work on art and Latour's work in science studies. Becker in effect sides with the artist in a bemused skepticism about the imputations that would set art worlds apart as uniquely refined, inspired, or inherently transcendent. His work gives pause to the adulation of art in several ways. One is by documenting the essential similarity of activities regarded as art and those regarded as craft. As with his work on deviance, Becker indicates that the labeling process, which he demonstrates in several instances to be dependent on historical contingencies, is arbitrarily related to the nature of the activities and products that are labeled arts and crafts. What was a craft at one point in history comes to be regarded as an art at another, and vice versa.

Another thread of the argument is the appreciation of the multitude of actors and activities that must be fit together for an art product to be recognized as such. The taste and practical pressures on gallery owners, the inventiveness of firms that create new paints, and even the physical labor of the carpenters and electricians whose work puts an art object in a place and light to be admired all not only are essential to the emergence of work as publicly recognized art but also may entail acumen, discriminating judgment, and idiosyncratic talents that may exceed the qualities of the person admired as "the artist." A thickly textured ethnographic description of "art as collective action" makes a powerful case that the attribution of artistic status to particular people and objects says something more specifically about the needs and fantasies of the admiring public than about the distinctiveness of the people and things admired. Himself a musician and photographer, Becker cannot fairly be said to be debunking the pretensions of those regarded as artists. His message emanates from a classic ethnographer's stance at the side of the subjects and looking out wondering why it is that outsiders make such emphatically misguided sense of what artists do.

Latour has taken the implications of this ethnographic perspective a step further in his studies of science. Beginning with his ethnography, carried out in collaboration with Woolgar, of the Salk laboratory (Latour and Woolgar 1986), and continuing through his ambitious essay, *We Have Never Been Modern*, Latour (1993) has taken on a series of assumptions about ontological separations between science and the humanities, between reason and passion, and among people, nonhuman animals, and inanimate things.

For our purposes, it is enough to note that Latour's appreciation of the practical workings of scientific activity is not necessarily an attack on the scientists' pretensions. Scientists go beyond and undermine the apparently rigid control of explicit research designs and reports in many senses. Research designs help scientists get funding. They portray a purposiveness and a force of rational control that inspires nonscientists to make similar commitments, a point that Latour (1988) makes in his analysis of Pasteur's importance for the rise of anti-Prussian militarism in France. Research designs also guide the ad hoc and otherwise chaotic problem-solving of everyday scientific practice so that they fit a post hoc framework of rational predesign. But scientists are pragmatists, not charlatans, and they do not worry that research designs may not control research practice empirically. That outsiders may, for their own independent purposes, wish to believe that research designs govern the actual conduct of research practice is a problem in the frame of mind that would distinguish itself as rational and modern as opposed to some imagined irrational and premodern epoch in human history.

Whether Latour is "right" is not the issue here. Our concern is to clarify the warrants that ethnographers may establish when they study social worlds that are deemed to be morally exceptional. One powerful warrant is that of the debunking ethnography, but the debunking need not be of those considered to be elite. With Latour, the debunking blow is executed not to bring scientists down to earth but rather to deconstruct taken-for-granted distinctions among political, empirical, moral, rational, and sensual realms. (Latour's radicalism holds that these distinctions, when imagined to have empirical and existential justifications, can set up terrifying authoritative centers of practically autonomous power.)

NATURALISTIC STUDIES OF THE MORALLY EXCEPTIONAL

I have reviewed two sets of strategies for warranting ethnographic research on prestigious, charismatic, or admired subjects. The first pair of alternatives is to focus on social framing versus local culture. The second pair of alternatives debunks the social distance that sets elites apart. There is a third, rarely attempted way in which to warrant the ethnographic study of elites, and it parallels a way in which to warrant the study of deviants that also is rarely executed. This is a naturalistic approach, sometimes more and sometimes less phenomenological in its execution, that evokes the distinctive social interactions and the unique cultures that create genuinely exceptional sensibilities.

Studies of especially respected groups such as surgeons follow this path when they describe, in a manner that is neither debunking nor adulating, the distinctive moral codes with which the group recognizes, sanctions, and covers up its errors (Bosk 1979). In the study of deviants, naturalism may mean documenting the special understandings, distinctive interactional competencies, and sensual attractions that motivate deviance. With respect to the worlds of street criminals, for example, this could mean all of the following: revealing interactional knowledge that is acquired only through the repeated practice of violently attacking other people (Athens 1980), describing ways of being "bad" that cannot be reduced to familiar rationalities or to conventional goals such as material gain, and conveying the animating spirits that the serious pursuit of evil may conjure up for the subjects (Katz 1988).

A complementary contribution may be achieved in the study of subjects who identify with exceptionally positive moral themes. In his studies of Catholic charismatic healers, Csordas (1994) provided a good example. Csordas does not skirt their claims of distinctive religious sensibility. He takes up the description and analysis of his subjects' distinctive processes of imagination, memory, language, and emotion, emphasizing such matters as posture and movement in ritual practices, through which the forces of charismatic healing are conjured up. Writing neither as a debunker nor as a believer, he reveals how a curative religious spirituality is embodied in particular interactional forms that are special versions of universal processes.

An ethnography that takes this third path and respects the authenticity of morally exceptional phenomena need not convey a tone of ridicule or offer the ethnographer's personal embrace of the subjects' moral perspectives. The ethnographer takes up the construction of compelling forces of deviance or respectability, or how the subjects create for themselves not only the representation of negative and positive spirits but also ways of acting, understanding, and feeling that are otherwise unobtainable.[6] Deviant or elite (or, for charismatics, "elect") status is treated not only as authentic but also as a socially constructed framework with which the subjects must cope. Thus one looks to the deviant to learn about the special strategic interaction that one masters to cope with a stigmatized identity (Goffman 1963a), and one looks to a charismatic group to understand the machinations by which a set of people can sustain commitments to beliefs in their sacred status while living within a mundane world that ridicules the group's religious and curative claims. Indeed, Csordas (1997) made understandable the appeal to middle class Americans of Pentecostal religion as a way in which to add a distinctively resonant dimension to otherwise mundane aspects of everyday life. His analysis has utility for a genuinely nondebunking, nonconfiming, and yet empirically falsifiable explanation of the appeal of New Age culture in general.

THE RANGE OF WARRANTS AND
THE SILENCES THAT HAUNT ETHNOGRAPHY

The warrant is an especially troublesome methodological challenge for sociological ethnographers as compared to anthropologists. Sociological ethnographers have been more vulnerable to the question "Who needs that study?" because they have studied their own societies and, since the beginnings of academic ethnography in the early decades of the twentieth century, sociologists' own societies have maintained various rival, nonethnographic means of describing themselves, namely novels and journalistic exposés, the files of social reform agencies, interest group documentation, and official records made by governmental organizations. As similar homegrown institutions have developed for self-description in the societies studied by anthropologists, the warrants that anthropologists had become accustomed to exercising have come into question in ways that sociological ethnographers have long faced.[7]

But even when local voices rise to contest the monopolistic license that anthropologists have exercised in depicting far-flung landscapes and conveying them to a home market, the reach of local voices is relatively limited. The intended audience for the social or cultural anthropologist's writings still generally does not reside in or comprehend the language of the society being described. The anthropological ethnographer's audience usually lacks access to many of the alternative sources of knowledge with which the sociological ethnographer must compete if he or she is to maintain a license in good standing. In effect, the anthropologist can more readily take for granted the social distance between subjects and audience that the sociological ethnographer often must construct as a substantive feature of his or her text. "Foreignness" is a magic methodological wand that anthropologists are, on the whole, still freer to wave, however ferocious the contests that have developed in recent decades over the rightful ownership of that wand.[8] Sociological ethnography more often must bootstrap its legitimacy by establishing the foreignness of a domestically located social world.

Among sociologists, the warrant is a distinctive methodological challenge for ethnographers. In part because ethnographers usually do not lay out their warrant simply and quickly in an introductory page or chapter, ethnographies often seem somehow less rigorous or scientific than studies that start by setting rival hypotheses against each other and promising a data duel that will produce a clear winner. Ethnographers routinely must finesse their way into the field, gaining support from funding agencies and dissertation committees on the queasy and inarticulate promise of documenting something that only needs documentation because no one has good evidence that it exists. In ethnographic research, the challenge of providing a warrant is largely a matter of anticipatorily responding to a series of potentially killing silences: the silence of readers who never pick up one's text in the first place because it does not address a clear controversy, the silence of readers who abandon reading because they do not find a compelling point, and the silence of readers who grasp a text only to fulfill obligations in hiring or publication review processes and are too polite or too shy of open controversy to make explicit their blunt sense of "So what?"

Another dangerous silence addresses issues of evidence. In search of an accurate account of social life, the ethnographer changes questions, approaches, methods of recording, and so on, constantly adapting research practices to find and fit the substance of inquiry. As such, ethnographic methods do not allow the researcher to answer questions about reliability, representativeness, reactivity, and replicability in the ways that have become standardized in traditions of quantitative research based on fixed research designs.[9] The rhetoric of "proof" is habitually begged off by ethnographers.

Faced with all these forms of systematic silence, what can the ethnographer say to articulate a warrant for his or her research? In addition to exploiting the moral status of their subjects, ethnographers traditionally have turned to five other frequently complementary justifications for the flexibility of their research practices.

Historically Emergent Social Phenomena

In addition to the first general warrant reviewed in this article—a demonstration that the ethnographer has found meanings of people's conduct that have been kept hidden because of moral condemnation or deference—a second type of warrant is invoked when the ethnographer claims to have located historically new phenomena. "High-tech" jobs have been understood to call for ethnographies that could provide indications of the fate of working class identity in occupational contexts far different from the factory settings that social class analysis has long presumed (Halle 1984). When computer technology brought new forms of play into children's lives, ethnographers perceived the need to map out this new area of culture and interaction (Sudnow 1983). When new forms of suburban housing communities arose at mid-century, ethnographers responded to the implicit call for studies of their potentially novel patterns of social life (Gans 1967).

It should be recalled that sociological ethnography emerged in the United States in the context of the then unprecedented growth of urban immigrant Chicago. Researchers introduced study after study by suggesting that new social realities and new forms of social problems were taking shape. The need to map out new urban realities led to a collective justification of individual studies of social areas and social types as contributing to a "mosaic" of the city (Becker 1966).

In recent decades, there has been a continual succession of new social problems that have justified waves of ethnographic research. Prominent examples are AIDS (Weitz 1991), crack cocaine (Williams 1992), and an explosion in homelessness (Snow and Anderson 1993). New forms of charisma also establish strong warrants for ethnography. The wave of Christian Pentecostalism in this country and in the Third World makes a compelling case for ethnographic investigation. An unprecedented increase in the scale of social organization and economic individualism in high-powered law firms may be confidently taken as a warrant for a new ethnography of elite law practices. What happens to the "professionalism" of corporate law firms when the intimate workings of ethics of honor are challenged by the impersonality that may be required to manage staffs that number in the hundreds? (To find out, see Nelson 1988.) Scandals over massive bank failures related to the sale of "junk bonds" and overmanipulation on futures and options markets have been appreciated as warranting the ethnographic study of the normal operations of these relatively new social worlds of financing and investment (see Abolafia 1996).

The A Fortiori Logic of Theoretically Strategic Sites

A third common form of a substantive warrant for sociological ethnography is the ethnographer's documentation of how people in a certain time and place are confronting exceptionally vivid interactional challenges or devising rarely occurring but generally relevant interactional solutions. In the "second Chicago school" of the 1940s and 1950s (Fine 1995), the students of Everett C. Hughes and Herbert Blumer seemed to intuit this warrant as a guide for their occupationally focused ethnographic studies. Often, after entering a field site for any number of extraneous reasons (e.g., family connections, the need to make money) and gathering data without a clear guiding definition of the substantive issues, an ethnographer would identify a social process for which the site just happened to be a brilliantly strategic data source. Research on janitors became appreciated as an especially useful focus for information on "status dilemmas" or how people who are put in positions of practical control manage interaction with others who are their superiors in prestige and respectability (Gold 1952).[10] Observations of doctors became appreciated as a ground on which to test Weberian notions of the exercise of control among status equals in a bureaucracy (Freidson and Rhea 1963). The social world of the taxicab driver, with its constantly recurring, brief, one-shot relations with clients, was characterized as a wonderful place in which to study how moral constraints limit what one might expect to be an utterly crass performance of a mundane role (Davis 1959). All of these studies play to the a fortiori argument that patterns of social life that are systematically present in analytically extreme circumstances also should be present, although in diluted and obscured forms, in more commonly occurring, less theoretically "pure" circumstances.

Appreciating the rich possibilities for strategic analyses, ethnographers often have focused on distinctive features of the work of people who, as a routine part of their occupational responsibilities, interact with people they label as deviant. Studies of such work often turn up practices, feelings, and cultural phenomena that are generally occurring but are especially vivid in the context of work with deviants. Thus those who work with deviants often must do what they regard as "dirty work," a category that has salience wherever work is governed by a moral division of labor (Emerson and Pollner 1976). And what work institution is not? As Hughes (1971) wrote, "It is hard to imagine an occupation in which one does not appear . . . to be practically compelled to play a role of which he thinks he ought to be a little ashamed morally" (343).

Bosk (1979) explicitly considered the strategic value of studying the social management and meanings of mistakes made by surgeons in "an elite, academic environment":

> Increased accountability is generic to surgery . . . Both formal and informal mechanisms for achieving accountability are more available in elite than in nonelite settings. . . . In elite settings the practice of surgery focuses on difficult surgical cases that represent what is presumptively the "cutting edge" of the field. . . . Where preeminence is unquestioned, there may be a greater willingness to explore the reasons for failure. . . . My site selection limits the universe to which I can generalize, but at the same time it provides a setting in which controls are both salient and displayed in their most primitive form. It allows us to see most clearly what surgeons consider an error, why they use this definition, and how they enforce it. (31–32)

One need not be a sociologist to appreciate that an ethnography is warranted when circumstances turn up an especially compelling case. Laboratory psychologists interested in studying *cognitive dissonance*, the psychological processes that emerge when belief and perception conflict, produced a celebrated ethnographic study when they came across a group of believers who were awaiting the end of the world on a specific date. Although *When Prophecy Fails* (Festinger, Rieken, and Schacter 1956) was a study of a group enthralled by charisma, charisma was important to the ethnographic warrant not in its own right, but rather as predictably setting up a strategic test of cognitive dissonance. In a wholly different substantive area, but with an analogous application of the ethnographic warrant, Wacquant (1995) recently showed how, for young boxers and their older trainers as well, the city gym has a fascinating charm that sustains participants' motivations far beyond what any practical calculation of personal material advantage could justify. The institutional charisma of the boxing gym[11] makes it a strategic site for a novel examination of the relationship of violence, poverty, and masculine and black identity in the contemporary inner-city ghetto.

Needs for Narratives

A fourth way to warrant ethnographies is to describe people acting in ways that build previously undetected personal and communal life stories. This is perhaps the single most compelling warrant for ethnography: the telling of the story of how people, through collaborative and indirectly interdependent behavior, create the ongoing character of particular social places and practices. It may be, as some recent commentary on quantitative research suggests, that key issues of causal explanations are being finessed whenever research reports—even those that summarize huge numbers of quantified cases—are not readable as narratives; "'cases' in standard quantitative methods . . . lose their complexity and their narrative order" (Abbott 1992:53). If so, then no social research is complete without an ethnographic treatment of its subject matter.

The narrative warrant for ethnography is deeply, even existentially, underwritten. As individuals, we all may search for the naturally hidden stories of our early associations to comprehend ways of acting and understanding that became matters of habit long before we could focus self-consciously on social interaction (see, e.g., Agamben 1993). In our everyday conduct, we are routinely indifferent to the multifaceted contributions of multiple others to the thoughts, phrases, and life strategies that we refer to as our "own." As some of Garfinkel's (1967) famous "experiments" demonstrated, social life would be impossible without the artifice of such a seemingly natural egocentrism. All organizations develop investments in ways of hiding and denying collective responsibility for the sometimes untoward results of their members' activities (Katz 1977). There are systematic biographical, social interactional, and corporate organizational reasons that stories go untold until ethnographers take on the task.

Ethnographies have a widely recognized ability to depict communal realities that become visible only when one documents the collective acts through which people subtly fit their lives together over time. Erikson's (1976) study of the consequences of a destructive flood in an Appalachian mining community and Harper's (1992) study of Willy, an upstate New York auto mechanic and farm tool repairman, are two complementary examples of exceptional narrative achievements in ethnography.

Erikson (1976) artfully evokes the loss in the flood of something that had always existed in an enigmatically invisible manner: a taciturn community of presumptive mutual understanding and support.

Harper (1992) brings out the interdependencies that are served by the work of Willy, a Saab and tractor repairman who runs a shop next to his home in an area of rural poverty in upstate New York. His clients may visit only occasionally, and then they may hang around his shop silently for hours without providing the ethnographer with much recordable data, but the ingenuity and care that Willy exercises, in a "hands-on" way that Harper conveys in the photographs that accompany his text, enter their lives in profoundly significant ways. It might be months or even years later before a client could appreciate how, in repairing a farm tool, Willy had anticipated the tests that the tool would face when put to work in an unusually demanding terrain. Willy kept his shop going by keeping decades-old tractors going. Harper's close account reveals that Willy obviously was not getting rich but was subtly sustaining a richness of associations without which much of rural social life in upstate New York could not practically survive.

Summary Images and Policy Relevance

A fifth common ethnographic warrant is to transform understandings about a pattern of action, a set of people, or a social institution by describing the object of study more processually and more fully in social context than do the representations produced routinely by the people studied and more, than had been the case in previous research. The result is not simply to dismantle bad stereotypes but rather to construct good stereotypes by producing a more holistic and satisfying summary view of the subject. In revising the prevailing summary images of types of people and types of social places, ethnography at times plays a role of unappreciated significance as a vigorous form of *policy research.*

In policy discussions, quantifiable data (e.g., the percentage of recidivism within a treatment group, the costs of environmental pollution, the amount of taxes paid by illegal aliens, the frequency of illegitimate births among different sectors of the population, the rate of crime before and after penalties are changed) have great rhetorical utility. To make a significant contribution, it is sufficient to show, for example, that a given policy reduces pollution, increases the employment rates of women who have been on welfare, or reduces school dropouts and raises test scores. Who could be in favor of increasing pollution and dropout rates or of reducing test scores and the employment of low-income populations? Policy research, as conventionally defined, is geared to produce the summary indicators on which policy debates thrive.

The relative value of ethnographic research takes on a different light when we ask a question that is not commonly addressed in reports of policy research: How are policy views actually formed? Where is the evidence that policies that depend on public and official support for school financing, gun control, and immigrants' rights are in fact affected by findings on test scores, crime rates, and tax contributions? If directions of policy change routinely run independently of the signals of policy research, then perhaps there are severe restrictions on the social worlds within which policy research is treated seriously. Studies demonstrating the lack of deterrence of given increments in criminal punishment or studies showing high rates of accidental injury from guns that are kept in the home, may define the relevant issues so narrowly as virtually to guarantee the practical irrelevance of their results to those who are not already convinced of the resulting policy recommendations. If what is more fundamentally at stake in these public debates is the meaning of guns and criminal punishment for promoting an enhanced sense of control in the everyday lives of gun owners and capital punishment supporters, then it will require ethnographic research to document these concerns in their local contexts, to discover their situational contingencies, and to suggest how they may be effectively altered by public policies.

If public views about public school education, immigrants' lifestyles, the motivations of criminals and gun owners, and the like all depend profoundly on stereotypes, then research may be most relevant to policy when it works to reshape the prevailing summary image of the type of person involved. The impact on policy of ethnographic research is not easily evaluated and can easily be exaggerated. Intellectual currents in ethnographic research run closely with the general history of social thought inside and outside of academia. Revisions in the images of types of peoples and places often are promoted simultaneously by ethnographic research and by changes in popular culture. But the warrant for ethnographic research as policy relevant is no less proven than is that for research that proceeds directly under that banner, and some overlap with trends in popular culture may be essential if any social research is to have rhetorical efficacy.

The case for the policy relevance of the studies of Suttles (1968) and Gans (1962) in urging a rethinking of urban renewal policies is at least as compelling as that for the generation of research that has futilely promoted gun control and attacked capital punishment. Becker's (1953) ethnographic portrait of marijuana users certainly was not independently effective in reducing confinement penalties for marijuana use; however, because it addressed the essential nature of use and the stereotype of the user in a memorable qualitative portrait, it became one of the most widely used readings in college social science courses, where it helped revise opinion on the dangers of marijuana among the more educated and, later in his mass readers' lives, the more powerful citizenry. One of the most effective policy researchers in the history of sociology was Erving Goffman, whose ethnographic portrait of "total institutions" (Goffman 1961) was a contemporaneous and scholarly complement to popular novels/movies such as Kesey's (1962) *One Flew Over the Cuckoo's Nest*. Such works helped each other's appeal, and jointly they helped reshape a generation's summary understanding of the human quality of life in mental hospitals and prisons. Goffman's writings, which were cited prominently in federal court cases that recognized constitutional objections to aspects of involuntary confinement, gave officials a respectable source of authority for policy changes that were, no doubt, multiply determined.

Methodological Exemplars

Another warrant to which an ethnography may appeal is that of serving as a methodological exemplar that shows how extraordinarily well an ethnography can be executed. The police cannot execute a search warrant with such sensitive civility that professional excellence in the execution justifies an otherwise unwarranted intervention, but sociologists may make enviable and timeless claims to professional attentions if they carry out research with unprecedented imagination. Ethnographic methodology may be exemplary because of the way in which the researcher exploits naturally occurring resources as data, the way in which data are evaluated, or the way in which data are presented. Respective examples would be Thomas's (1923) use of personal documents to study lonely young women in the big city, the weighting of fieldwork evidence by Becker et al. (1961) in their study of medical students, and Harper's (1982) use of photographs to portray the life of a railroad tramp. Studies that are exemplary for their methodology remain invaluable resources for ethnographic research training, independent of the usefulness of their studies' findings.

ETHNOGRAPHY'S WARRANTS

As an initial effort to draw attention to the subject of ethnographic warrants, this article has notable limits. I have explored at length only the warrants for studies of people and practices thought to be deviant or to deserve special deference. I tested my analysis of ethnographic warrants only against the contents of the various incarnations of the journal now known as *Contemporary Ethnography*, against books reviewed in major sociology journals in recent years, and against my bookshelves. As a set, the six warrants I have identified may not be exhaustive.

It also may be seen as a limitation that the various types of warrants specified here obviously are not mutually exclusive. Any given study usually will rest on more than one type of warrant. There is no compelling reason why authors should separate their writings by warrants; it is common for chapters in a given monograph to speak to different warrants with the result that the ethnography as a whole rests solidly on overlapping justifications. But the potential for overlap indicates one of the advantages of being self-conscious about warrants. In selecting research topics and designing a focus in the field, ethnographers might consider that the more warrants a study can satisfy, the more effectively it may make a claim for readers' attention. If ethnographers are unlikely to discipline the design of their research so that they satisfy all possible warrants, then it still should be helpful to appreciate that they have many mutually supportive bases to speak into the silences that challenge the logic of their methods.

***

Author's Note: For very thoughtful and surprisingly patient advice, I thank Malin Åkerström, Howard S. Becker, Thomas Csordas, Robert M. Emerson, Jonathan Friedman, David Heise, Margarethe Kusenbach, David Snow, and anonymous reviewers for this journal.

***

NOTES

[1] The outstanding example of a possibly overly charming style of ethnographic writing is the work of Lévi-Strauss, who usually does not provide evidence that the cognitive systematics of his analyses of cultural texts are systematically grounded in his subjects' actual practices of storytelling, much less in their lived social relations. It is not as obvious that the neatly complementary, dialectical structures of the myths he analyzes are as charming to the peoples he has studied as they are to his readers. There is thus a disturbing character to the photographs that he took of his subjects in the 1930s (Lévi-Strauss 1995), as readers are led to wonder about the relationship between the elegant dialectical precision of the ideational structures of their myths and the flesh-and-blood reality of his subjects' lives.

[2] Each of these studies, I rush to note, speaks robustly to one or more of the morally less vivid, but often intellectually more creative, warrants that are noted in the conclusion of this article.

[3] Struggles with such conflicts abound in the paradoxically titled volume, *Ethnography Unbound* (Burawoy 1991).

[4] One might, for example, find it warranted to document, as historically new phenomena, the social realities of an urban ethnic population that once was dominant but that has become marginalized by the population growth in the neighborhood of other ethnic groups that currently are suspect in the public's regard (Rieder 1985).

[5] It is not clear whether a "vouching" process is any more or less necessary to get access to people reputed to be elite than to study people who carry deviant labels. On questions of access to elites, qualitative sociologists would do well to keep some quantitative factors in mind. The most fundamental reason that elites pose special difficulties for ethnographic study is that by definition there are relatively few of them. If one is rebuffed in the attempt to study social life on an inner-city ghetto street corner, then there are lots of alternatives. But if one wants to study the small group that presumably governs a given city, then a rebuff may be much more disturbing even if it is much less likely to occur because there is nowhere else to go.

[6] The same three choices confront all areas of sociological investigation. Consider the study of sex and race. Most commonly, they are treated as *ascribed* statuses in quantitative studies that take for granted the existence of sex and race as personal attributes and research their relationship to other features of subjects' social lives, whether those other features be how others treat the subjects or how the subjects themselves act. Less often, ethnographers treat sex and race as *achieved* statuses by describing how one learns a particular cultural version of being male or female, black, white, Chicano, and the like, analyzing how power relations press one to act in certain scripted versions of these identities, and identifying the social contingencies of acting in sex- and race-distinctive ways. The third alternative is to appreciate a personal accomplishment that might be called *the achievement of ascription*: how people come to take on not only what cross-cultural research shows to be obviously achieved features of personal identity but also natural or un-self-consciously practiced and distinctive ways in which to be, for example, male or female. This third alternative calls especially for ethnographic research because of the biographical, behind-the-scenes, personally detailed, and nuanced contextual analysis that is required to see how one comes to take for granted distinctive perspectives and sensibilities as part of one's everyday practices.

[7] The genre of sociological ethnography was born only after other forms of social self-description had created an intellectual space for a contrasting form of inquiry. Before the twentieth century, ethnographic work was performed by authors who were known not primarily as ethnographers but rather as writers of biographies, publishers of diaries, far-flung correspondents contributing lengthy essays to newspapers, social reformers, and the like. The early issues of the *American Journal of Sociology*, and the sources used by early American sociologists such as Robert Park and W. I. Thomas, reflected the birth of sociology on this terrain of emerging differentiation among various forms of inquiry, reflection, and commentary. As Jonathan Friedman reminds me, anthropology also was pressed to clarify a warrant for a new form of representing social life by the writings of missionaries and other prior travelers abroad. The difference between the disciplines is a matter of degree. For early ethnography in both sociology and anthropology, the metaphor of "science" was crucial for laying claim to a new intellectual field. For further discussion of differences in the development and contexts of ethnography in anthropology and sociology, see Snow and Morrill (1993).

[8] See, for example, the debate between Sahlins (1995) and Obeyesekere (1992).

[9] But qualitative research has its own, too often neglected answers for these methodological questions. See Katz (1983).

[10] One respondent's memorable representation of the dialectic: "when you show the tenants that you have a clean character and are respectable, you can train them to be good tenants; that's what's really important in being a success" (Gold 1952:488).

[11] Shils (1975) extended the concept of charisma to institutions. Wacquant (1995) showed that the boxing gym is a surprisingly apt example because it is a social place that, for the young boxers and older trainers who make up its life, deserves unique respect and deference.

18

Techniques of Validation in Qualitative Research
A Critical Commentary

Michael Bloor

INTRODUCTION

In 1903 Blondlot, the French physicist and member of the Academy of Sciences, reported the sensational discovery of a phenomenon that he called N-rays, with properties analogous to, but distinct from, X-rays. His report of his experiments led other scientists to seek to also generate the N-rays in their laboratories, but their attempts were wholly unsuccessful. The failure to reproduce Blondlot's findings eventually led one distinguished physicist, R. W. Wood, to visit Blondlot at his laboratory and to observe him at work. Eventually, it was agreed that the N-rays did not exist, they were mere epiphenomena derived from faulty observation, faulty experimental technique, and inadequate laboratory measurement instruments and equipment.

This story (told at greater length in D. Bloor's *Knowledge and Social Imagery* [1976]) is a common one in the history and philosophy of science. Findings in the natural sciences are validated or verified by their *replication* by a second independent investigator: research reports to the scientific community must carry enough information on the successful experiment to allow the identical circumstances of the experiment to be repeated independently by other members of the scientific community, so that the same results can be observed. Unless findings in the natural sciences can be replicated, they have no validity.

In sociology, in contrast, validation cannot occur through subsequent replication, since identical social circumstances cannot be recreated outside the laboratory.

Social life contains elements which are generalizable across settings (thus providing for the possibility of the social sciences) and other elements which are particular to given settings (thus forever limiting the predictive power of the social sciences). To the journalist, for example, there may be arresting parallels between the increase in heroin consumption in some of the ex-coalfield communities of South Wales in the mid-nineties and the earlier explosion in heroin use in some U.K. cities like Glasgow in the early eighties: the disappearance of employment opportunities for young males, the ready availability of cheap heroin, and so on. But careful observation suggests a number of differences as well as parallels between the nineties and eighties epidemics (the use of heroin in the nineties within a poly-drug culture, with opiates available alongside a wide range of other drugs such as ecstasy and amphetamines; the recent growth of drug treatment services; and so on), all of which makes the nineties epidemic an inadequate testing ground for analyses of the eighties epidemic. History, contrary to popular opinion, never repeats itself.

Instead of the replication of findings across settings, sociologists (and anthropologists) have developed two main techniques which may be considered as alternative methods of validation. The first of these is "triangulation" (Denzin 1978), whereby findings may be judged valid when different and contrasting methods of data collection yield identical findings on the same research subjects: a case of replication within the same setting, rather than replication across settings. The second technique, or rather array of related techniques, judges findings to be valid by demonstrating a correspondence between the analyst's findings and the understandings of members of the collectivity being analyzed. The objective of this chapter will be to comment critically on these sociological validation techniques. Referring to three different empirical studies conducted by the author, it will be argued that all these techniques yield data that are *relevant* to issues of validity in that they provide an occasion and a spur for the re-examination of findings. Nevertheless, it will be seen that they are merely relevant to, rather than constitutive of, validation: all data are shaped by the circumstances of their production and different data produced by different research procedures cannot be treated as equivalent for the purpose of corroboration.

TRIANGULATION: REPLICATING CHALK WITH CHEESE?

The term "triangulation," like Glaser and Strauss's (1967) term "grounded theory," has become somewhat overloaded with meanings and abused by uncritical usage. Denzin, who took the term from Webb (1966), referred to four basic types of triangulation with a range of sub-types, but most commentators have concentrated their attention on the sub-type Denzin calls "between-method triangulation . . . the combination of two or more different research strategies in the study of the same empirical units" (Denzin 1978:302). Validity is claimed because replication of the findings by different methods minimizes the possibility that the findings may be the result of particular measurement biases.

There is much to commend in Denzin's approach and a commitment to methodological pluralism is clearly one mark of the careful investigator. Denzin, the symbolic interactionist, although quoting Webb on triangulation as a test of validity, himself usually (but not universally) steers clear of terms like "validation" or "replication." But statements such as "archival analysis ... may additionally be used to validate respondents' reports during the interviewing period" (303) have provided some warrant for subsequent sociologists to interpret triangulation as a test of validity. There is sufficient ambiguity in Denzin's analysis to allow the popular view that has grown up which treats triangulation as a validation exercise.

The difficulties in treating triangulation as a validation exercise are several. One such difficulty is a matter of logic and needs no empirical illustration. If it is accepted that there are horses for courses and that, for any given topic, there will be one best method of investigation, then triangulation may be said to involve juxtaposing findings gathered by the best available method with findings generated by an inferior method. There seems no difficulty in this, at first sight, when both sets of findings agree. But a problem arises when the two sets of findings are at odds: should the findings from the best available method be set aside on the basis of evidence generated by an inferior method? Logically, there seems little justification for this, but the exercise cannot be a test of validity only when the findings are corroborated and not when the findings are confounded.

The above seems a serious objection, but in practice it will rarely be encountered, because findings collected by different methods will rarely be of such a character that they can be readily compared so as to pronounce them to be matched or mismatched.

All research findings are shaped by the circumstances of their production, so findings collected by different methods will differ in their form and specificity to a degree that will make their direct comparison problematic.

An illustration will make the point with more clarity. In the course of an investigation of death certification practices in a Scottish city (M. Bloor 1991, 1995), I conducted in-depth interviews with a sample of local clinicians whose responsibilities embraced frequent certifications of deaths (general practitioners with responsibilities for old people's homes, junior hospital doctors working on geriatric or psychogeriatric wards, forensic pathologists, police surgeons, and the like). At the conclusion of the interviews I asked the respondents if they would, at their leisure, read a series of detailed case summaries that I had prepared and fill out dummy death certificates based on those dummy cases. One of the major objectives of the research was to investigate whether there were systematic differences between individuals in their death certification practices, such that these differences might contribute to local differences in specific-cause mortality rates.

In principle, there was an opportunity here to corroborate respondents' descriptions of their certification practices at interview with their responses to the dummy cases. In practice, there was a strong tendency for the clinicians to describe their certification behavior during the interviews in terms that were much more general than the specific combinations of symptoms and circumstances found in the case summaries. These differences in the specificity of the two sets of data are such that the analyst is seeking to compare chalk with cheese. For example, here is an extract from the transcript of an interview with a general practitioner who was frequently responsible for certifying deaths occurring in his local Old People's Home:

> MB: Uh-huh. Yes. Would some of these cases be dementing patients?
> GP: Some. Oh yes, I mean they weren't all 100 percent alert, rational people [. . .] But it may not necessarily have appeared on the certificate [. . .]
> MB: If it did appear on your certificate, would it be in Section I or Section II?
> GP: I think probably it would've been Section II [. . .]. I think probably it would be a question of keeping the certification as simple as possible and the things which really had little relevance to the terminal condition, let's put it that way, perhaps not mentioned on the certificate.
> MB: Yes. So perhaps you wouldn't use Section II very much?
> GP: Not very often.

Two of the six dummy cases given to the respondent for certification embraced descriptions of symptoms consistent with dementia or Alzheimer's disease. In one case the GP made no mention of the symptoms on the dummy certificate; in the other case, the GP entered "Alzheimer's Syndrome" in Section II of the certificate (Section II is for the recording of "other significant conditions contributing to death but not relating to the disease or condition causing it"). Here is the dummy case and certificate in question:

> Case 5
> An 86-year-old man has required an indwelling Foley catheter for three years because of urinary incontinence. He is frequently confused during the day and has no recollection of recent events. He requires assistance in dressing and feeding. Two days ago he became unresponsive and was admitted to your ward. He appeared to be hyper-ventilating, although his urine was cloudy, he had no fever and examination of the chest and heart were normal. You prescribed amoxicillin for a presumed urinary tract infection, but despite this the patient became hypotensive and died early this morning.
>
> Cause of Death
> Section I: renal failure due to urinary tract infection
> Section II: Alzheimer Syndrome

It can be seen that the information gleaned in the interview and the results of the dummy certification exercise are superficially consistent. But this consistency may well be an artifact of, on the one hand, the general terminology ("probably," "not very often") used by the respondent in the interview, and on the other hand, the very limited representation of the possible range of dementing symptoms and the possible combinations with other symptoms found in the much more specific dummy cases. Relatedly, any apparent discrepancy between practice reported at interview and practice found on the dummy certificates could be explained by these differences of specificity: a dummy certificate that seemed to conflict with a reported general rule could be explained by the fact that general rules are always defeasible, always subject to qualification in the light of specific circumstances.

Of course, the interviewer may be aware of this tendency of interviewees to over-generalize and the interviewer may seek consciously to compensate by exploring the contingent and qualified applications of general rules of conduct. But such explorations can only be partial, because no interviewee would tolerate interviews long enough to explore all relevant and specific facets of his or her routine practices. In the interview reported above, it will be readily appreciated that the discussion of certification practice with respect to symptoms of dementia was already quite extensive in an interview that was meant to range over the whole of the respondent's certification practice. By the same token, the study of detailed dummy case summaries and the completion of dummy certificates is a time-consuming activity and few interviewees will tolerate the completion of more than a dozen or so. In fact, respondents were only asked to complete six in this study. Since it would take possibly a dozen different case summaries to explore adequately a clinician's certification practice in relation to even a single constellation of symptoms (be it dementia or cancer), it can be seen that systematic corroboration of findings by these two different methods is not possible, due to sheer exigencies of time. As Denzin and others have stated, methodological pluralism allows new light to be shed on topics and allows different facets of problems to be explored, so the mix of different methods has an interactive impact. However, this mix of methods does not allow validity tests on findings.

MEMBER VALIDATION: C'EST MAGNIFIQUE, MAIS CE N'EST PAS L'ACCORD

Member validation is a term used to denote an array of techniques which purport to validate findings by demonstrating a correspondence between the researcher's analysis and collectivity members' descriptions of their social worlds. Critical discussions of these techniques can be found in Emerson (1981). Without being exhaustive, we can note that such techniques may include the following: firstly, the validation of the researcher's taxonomies by the attempted prediction of members' descriptions in the field (see, for example, Frake 1961); secondly, the validation of the researcher's analysis by the demonstrated ability of the researcher to "pass" as a member (see, for example, Douglas 1976); and thirdly, the validation of the researcher's analysis by asking collectivity members to judge the adequacy of the researcher's analysis, taking results back to the field and asking "if the members recognize, understand and accept one's description" (Douglas 1976:131). It is with exercises of the latter type that I shall be concerned here.

A philosophical justification for member validation exercises can be found in the work of the phenomenologist, Alfred Schutz, who pointed out the several continuities between the "commonsense thinking" of community members and the "scientific thinking" of the social scientist. All scientific thinking has its roots in commonsense thinking (if it did not, then it would be dismissed out of hand as non-sense) and collectivity members may be required periodically to provide accounts of their behavior which may be similar in purpose to scientific accounts. Schutz's "postulate of adequacy" famously required that scientific propositions be understandable to members themselves (Schutz 1962). Giddens (1976) has castigated Schutz's postulate as an unreasonable *requirement* for social scientific thinking, without denying the linkages between such thinking and commonsense. Member validation may be acknowledged to be an unreasonable *requirement* while simultaneously being seen as effective *corroboration* of a scientific proposition.

But corroboration too is problematic. The same considerations which cast doubt on the veracity of initial findings will also apply to an exercise to validate those findings: just as the initial findings are shaped by the circumstances of their production, problematized by the frailties of methodologies, so also the results of the validation exercise will be shaped by the data-gathering process itself, by the methods used to elicit members' reactions to the initial findings. Member validation is not immaculately produced. This point can be empirically demonstrated by reference to two different exercises where I undertook to feed research results back to research subjects and where I monitored their reactions.

One exercise was undertaken in the context of an observational study of variations in medical decision-making, where I attempted to differentiate the decision rules and search procedures used by different ENT (Ear, Nose and Throat) surgeons when assessing children in out-patient clinics for possible adeno-tonsillectomy (see M. Bloor 1976). In this exercise I wrote a detailed report for each surgeon of what I believed their assessment practices to be and then requested the opportunity to go through each surgeon's reactions to the report in a taped interview.

The second exercise was undertaken in the context of a series of linked studies of therapeutic communities (M. Bloor et al. 1988). In the second exercise, although some interviews were conducted, many collectivity members fed back their reactions to my draft research reports in "focus groups" (Morgan 1988), audio-recorded group discussions with the focused task of responding to my pre-circulated report. A focus group format was preferred both on economy grounds and on the grounds of circumventing "interviewer effects," the witting or unwitting shaping of interviewee responses by the interviewer. The topics of the draft reports varied from therapeutic community to therapeutic community. In one community study the report centered on the relationship of the informal patient culture to the formal group treatment program: this topic was explored by two focus groups, one group of patients (all of them ex-patients by the time the analysis was completed and the draft report was written) and one group of staff members; one ex-patient was interviewed separately (see below). In another community study the report centered on contrasts in staff practices between two halfway house communities for disturbed adolescents; this topic was explored by a focus group for the staff members of one house and individual interviews and correspondence with the staff of the second house (who had dispersed soon after the completion of fieldwork). In a fourth community, providing "foster family" care for adolescents who were disturbed and/or had learning difficulties, individual interviews were conducted with both continuing and ex-staff members.

Turning to the results of the member validation exercises, members' responses, on occasion, can be extremely gratifying. Thus, from one of the surgeons:

> Surgeon A: It reads very well. I thought it was fine.
> MB: So you felt it quite accurately reflected your ... ?
> Surgeon A: Oh yes. I thought it reflected very well. I thought it read well and it was as good a summary as I could have given myself. It was perfectly alright.
> MB: What about any omissions? You think there's anything significant omitted from it?
> Surgeon A: I don't think so. It covers it very well. Obviously in such a diffuse subject you can't get every detail in, but I would have thought it was very fair. It read well: I would be perfectly satisfied to initial that as being okay.

And from a participant in the halfway house focus group:

> You were certainly close enough for me to burst out laughing, a lot of the time reading it—incidents that you must have been involved in too. Certainly, you got across the essence of certain things that were happening, things that I remember but never actually put into words before. It was very clearly put down ... I don't think you've got the wrong end of the stick about anything. I don't think there's anything that's been misrepresented.

One member described reading the report as like catching sight of himself in the mirror, while another reported that when he read the report he was sometimes embarrassed by the events it recalled, an effect that he ascribed to the honesty of the research description. Some members said that they used the report to give new and enhanced meaning to previously imperfectly understood events and others found within the report handy terminologies and descriptions that they adopted for their own. As in Giddens' (1976) analysis of the "double hermeneutic," sociological descriptions may come actually to constitute the reality they purport to describe:

> Nigel: This term "reality confrontation"—I think that's the essence [of staff practice], a very central part of it. To have that named, that was the most important thing,
> Una: Yeah, we went round [after we'd read the report] congratulating ourselves for doing "reality confrontation."

Moreover, where member assent was withheld or only conditionally granted, there existed the means to explore the disagreement and modify the analysis. The following very detailed comments from a surgeon led to a re-analysis of his cases and some modifications in the report, when it became evident that the particular limited constellations of symptoms he was describing had not occurred in the out-patient clinic sample of cases that I had observed him to assess:

> Surgeon B: Well, I read it through previously, as you know, and I read it through again before you came this morning. It's very interesting, it's very good, and it's very carefully done. There are one or two points, you know, I'd be a bit doubtful about. It's very good really. I think it's an excellent thing.
> Here we are: paragraph 8, page 5. It says: "It may be that otitis media is cumulatively but not separately important as an indication for tonsillec-

tomy." Yes, I quite agree this is so. I would certainly agree with that. I wouldn't say "may be," I think it is so.

[. . .] Okay, there's one over the page, paragraph 12. You said: "Thus secretory otitis was not, of itself, an indication for adenoidectomy unless there was consequent conductive hearing loss." I wouldn't agree with that. I think it may well be, even if the hearing was normal [. . .]

But these morale-boosting encomiums and careful corrections are only half the picture. By no means all the surgeons had read their reports with the attention and precision of Surgeon B. Members were required to study a document line by line and to deliberate on its relationship to their own beliefs and practices; the requirement is an unusual one outside of academic circles and demands more commitment and effort than some members were prepared for. One staff member in the "foster family" community confessed that he simply skipped through the report to read the fieldnote extracts in which he played a part. In other members, paradoxically, too great a commitment might be encountered, eroding the possibility of judgement. Thus, for two members of one staff focus group, my report was defective because it failed to make any reference to the psycho-dynamic concepts on which they based their daily practice:

. . . it seemed to be naive, that was my feeling [. . .] I felt a lot of the . . . I think, well-understood concepts that I base the way I work on weren't being acknowledged (yes, yes) . . . Can I . . . ? Can I say that my comment on naivety is on the basis of what I conceive of as what I'm doing . . . I'm not saying the paper's naive. The concepts that I hold, it seems, we didn't share.

Emerson and Pollner (1988) recount how their attempts to feedback their findings on the workings of mobile psychiatric emergency teams (PET) were bedevilled by fears of cut-backs being imposed on the service, so committed PET workers were unwilling to countenance any research findings that might be construed as critical of the service and be used as ammunition for service cuts. As Emerson and Pollner point out, a member validation exercise is never context-free: it is situated within the world of collectivity members and is expressive of that world.

Furthermore, the contexts in which members view researchers' findings are subject to constant change. In one therapeutic community some staff members were at pains to stress that practice had changed appreciably since the fieldwork period to which the report related.

Enid: I saw a lot of stuff clearer and I saw a lot of stuff that was out-of-date. It made me happy but it also made me realize we'd moved on.

Nigel: It was nice to read it as a measure of where we are now.

Relatedly, the staff member who had previously described my report as naive happened to be the friend of a friend. Intrigued to see if his views had changed over time, some two years later I arranged to meet over a drink to talk over old times. Indeed, his views had shifted in the intervening two years. He no longer felt that the study was defective in its failure to attend to a psycho-dynamic perspective: there was a distinct psycho-dynamic perspective on the matter, but he now believed that to try and incorporate that perspective would have entailed a different study. He felt that the academic article that I had written (M. Bloor 1981), based on the draft report, should be required reading for new staff entering the community. Members' responses to researchers' accounts are provisional and subject to change. But it is by no means always the case that distance lends enchantment to the member's eye: one surgeon who had pronounced himself well satisfied with my report of his assessment practices was anything but enchanted when he later read my comparative account of different surgeons' practices; he wrote a highly critical letter to my then research director.

Still more confusingly, not only is member endorsement provisional and subject to change, it is also perfectly possible for members to endorse a researcher's account in terms which the researcher would find unacceptable. The member may read into the account meanings of which the researcher is unaware. Or aspects of the research which the researcher feels to be of relatively minor importance may be dragged center-stage by the member while the researcher's supposed central topic is disregarded. For example, one ex-patient paid little attention to my supposed central argument about the latently conflicting nature of prescriptions for patient behavior. Instead, she kept returning to what for me had been a minor issue and what for her was of central importance: namely, the role of the patient culture in rewarding patients for their progress in group therapy. Uncomfortably, I found my analysis being endorsed for the wrong reasons. Clearly, the member's purposes at hand are not the researcher's. Members' accounts of their social worlds will differ from researchers' accounts because those purposes at hand will differ. In the same way, members may read a researcher's account with different purposes from those wished upon them by the researcher. It is therefore unsurprising if members should find within the researcher's account topics and interpretations which the researcher had discounted or was unaware of. In the staff focus groups, the participants' expertise in interpretation naturally led them, on occasion, into using my report as a vehicle for interpreting my feelings about their communities and themselves:

> Oliver: Can I ask you a very awkward question? How did you come out of the day hospital feeling about therapeutic communities and the day hospital staff?
>
> MB: How do I feel about the staff here? I felt, um, you know, that . . .
>
> Oliver: When someone asks you that, you shouldn't answer it (laughter). I'll tell you why I asked you: I felt it was a bit cynical at times. That was all. That was just reading it as an outsider.

And from the other staff focus group:

> Una: When I was reading it I couldn't help thinking that the way you were writing it was in some ways slightly more critical of the "Beeches" [the other halfway house) approach than of "Ashley" [Una's halfway house]. Reading it, I was thinking: "Yes, Mick's thinking the same as I'm thinking here."

Of course, there is an irony here. While the tendency of members to interpret rather than judge sociological accounts seems an unhelpful complication in member validation exercises, the indexical nature of members' responses, as

Emerson and Pollner have shown, requires an interpretative effort on the part of researchers to interpret the sense of those responses. One possible frame of interpretation is the social situation in which the response is produced: all encounters between researchers and researched are species of social relationships governed by conventions of politeness and etiquette; in the case of ethnographic research the relationship in question may well embrace fondness and mutual regard. Fieldwork methods and fieldwork relations will shape the nature and content of members' responses. In the exchange below the surgeon, with exemplary courtesy, struggles to maintain a harmonious exchange despite a seemingly serious dispute about an important aspect of his daily work:

> Surgeon C: . . . But I would be very surprised at this. And very reluctant to talk people into an operation.
> MB: Yes. There were . . . I got the impression that it wasn't so much cases where the patient manifested reluctance, but where they denied a history of sore throats say, but the symptomatology was of what they would call recurrent colds or something of that nature.
> Surgeon C: Um. Fair enough, okay.
> MB: Well, I'm, I'm, er . . .
> Surgeon C: (laughter) Well, I don't know. But seeing it in cold print like that . . . I, I say: "Did I, in the absence of a history of sore throats, say that the tonsils have got to come out?" Must have done, must have done, obviously.
> MB: But that's, that's the sort of . . .
> Surgeon C: . . . That's an interesting point . . .
> MB: But it's your impressions of that report, whether you feel it corresponds to your own impressions of your practice that I'm looking for. So . . .
> Surgeon C: Yeah. I would have thought I would say "Oh well there's nothing really of any trouble—you can run along dear." But if you have observed this, then this is of value I know what you mean: there's often, sometimes . . . they say "Oh he's not had any trouble with his throat." And yet they've arrived on your doorstep. So they must have something wrong (um), their own doctor [general practitioner] must . . . (um). Never mind, okay, leave it.
> MB: Well . . .
> Surgeon C: . . . Does that? . . . No, leave it, this is quite valuable to us, I mean. Because, if you . . . (well) this is your . . . this synthesis . . .

In my report on his assessment practice, I had stated that he was prepared to operate on children whose parents denied any history of sore throats, provided there was examination evidence of tonsillar infection. This clearly failed to correspond to his own experience, but the surgeon courteously struggled to repair any conversational breach or dispute by a variety of means—trying to move us on to fresh topics, generously conceding primacy to my observations over his experience, and offering an interpretation that would reconcile the two viewpoints (that a child's parents might deny an indicative history, but the fact of the child having been referred to his outpatient clinic suggested that the referring GP thought there was an indicative history). A member validation exercise is not a scientific test but a social event, constrained in this case by the social dictates of polite conversation and shaped by the biographies and circumstances of the discussants.

It was an awareness of the impact of the interview format on the validation exercise (and, in particular, an awareness of my own role as interviewer) which led me to adopt a focus group format in the later therapeutic communities study. But focus groups too are social events (even if the researcher is less socially prominent). In the ex-patient focus group the oldest of the ex-patients adopted a chair-like role. In similar fashion, a consultant psychiatrist adopted a chair-like role in one of the staff focus groups. Thus, immediately following his colleagues' remarks on my naivety for neglecting psychodynamic interpretations, the consultant exercised a moderating influence:

> This is a tricky one. I think it deserves some thought because you after all, as you state very clearly in your introduction, came in as a participant observer. And I think that role is a difficult one to hold. Err. And how far do you go one way or the other? I think it's a courageous thing to do really, because, err, it's like being in the middle of the road—you get run down by both sides of the traffic (laughter) . . .

Focus groups are free of interviewer biases but they are more subject than interviews to participation biases. The group of ex-patients were willing to take part in a focus group because they and I had become close to each other in the course of my fieldwork and their treatment: they were committed to me on a personal basis and committed to making retrospective sense of their treatment experience. But I was aware that not all ex-patients would view the therapeutic community from the same standpoint and so I made an effort to find and speak to some ex-patients whose treatment experience had been less positive and (unlike my focus group participants) had left the therapeutic community abruptly and prematurely. One such ex-patient (whom I interviewed) made a most valuable remark. The group therapy program operated on a five-day-week basis, but I only attended for three days per week (varying the actual days of my attendance). The interviewee reminisced, to my surprise, that on the days that I attended the patients had seemed a much more cohesive group; when I was absent the patients had seemed more cliquish and divided. He was inclined to attribute this to my alleged sunny manner, but I immediately divined a more painful explanation: it seemed to me that as an assiduous student of the patient culture I had always sought to talk to the whole cross-spectrum of patients in the community, regardless of cliques or favor; in so doing, it seemed that I taken an important bridging role in shaping the very patient culture that I had sought to study.

Of course, this important (if mortifying) information was not part of the member validation exercise: it simply arose in the course of the exercise. It was by no means the only important information gleaned as an incidental aspect of the member validation exercises. Indeed, much of the material on members' responses which seems problematic if viewed from the standpoint of a verification exercise, can be viewed instead as further important data, an occasion for extending and elaborating the researcher's analysis. Members' responses to researchers' accounts are not a test of those accounts, but rather they are additional material for analysis all the more valuable for being topically related to earlier data but produced by different methods and under different auspices.

And finally, feeding back findings to one's research subjects can have other incidental advantages beside the generation of additional research data. It can be an opportunity for researchers to offer thanks and recompense to research subjects (some may feel that etiquette demands this kind of personal feedback wherever such feedback is practical). It can be an opportunity for researcher and researched to deliberate on the policy and service implications of the research. And it can also ease access negotiations where research subjects know that they will have prior sight of the researcher's findings. Member validation is a many splendored thing, but it is not validation.

CONCLUSION

As Emerson and Pollner (1988) have suggested with respect to member validation, there are pendular swings of fashion in qualitative research methods. Classical sociology took it as axiomatic that collectivity members could not know their social worlds as well as researchers. Subsequently, it was argued that the voice of the member could be the absolute and final arbiter of the researcher's account. More recently, the pendulum has swung back with the analysis of the numerous difficulties in member validation exercises. Triangulation is another technique subject to the vagaries of fashion. Currently, it has become almost routine practice for sociological research grant applicants in the U.K. to bolster their claims to methodological rigor by referring to their planned triangulation of methods. These claims may be overblown where they imply that findings may be validated through triangulation.

It has been my argument that neither triangulation nor member validation can be regarded as tests of research findings. A series of particular difficulties with each technique have been outlined and exampled (difficulties in response to noncorroboration, problems of test adequacy in cases of corroboration, problems of comparability, and so forth). All these particular difficulties have their roots in one general unwarranted assumption, namely that techniques of validation can be treated as unproblematically generated, whereas in practice (and as illustrated) all validating techniques are social products, constituted through particular and variable methodological processes. The very methodological frailties which lead sociologists to search for validating evidence are also present in the generation of that validating evidence. This has two consequences: firstly, it means that findings and validating evidence (be it triangulation or members' responses) may not be directly comparable since the different circumstances of their production have generated differences between them of specificity and of topical focus; and secondly, it means that the truth value will be unclear of any corroboration or non-corroboration that is found, because this may be a mere artifact of methodological inadequacies.

However, the conclusion that there can be no tests of validity should in no way weaken the case for practicing either triangulation or gathering members' responses to findings. Neither technique can validate findings, but both techniques can be said to be *relevant* to the issue of validity, insofar as both techniques may yield new data which throw fresh light on the investigation and which provide a spur for deeper and richer analyses. Triangulation and member validation both allow the researcher to reconsider his or her initial analyses from a novel standpoint: it is not just that additional data are available for study, but also that these additional data may alter the researcher's perception of the initial data. Since one important aspect of this reconsideration is an enhanced awareness of possible methodological biases, it can be seen that these so-called validation techniques may be potent agents for reflexive awareness, for an enhanced understanding of how research findings are constituted in the creative process of the research, rather than being pre-existent and simply awaiting discovery. Validation techniques are not tests, but opportunities for reflexive elaboration (Emerson 1981).

Of course, this reading of the analytic process might be thought unsatisfactory in that it is both progressive and indeterminate, in that elaboration may proceed indefinitely with no final authoritative analysis being achievable. In effect, the analytic process becomes that termed by Cicourel "indefinite triangulation":

> I use the expression "indefinite triangulation" to suggest that every procedure that seems to "lock in" evidence, thus to claim a level of adequacy, can itself be subjected to the same sort of analysis that will in turn produce yet another indefinite arrangement of new particulars, or a rearrangement of previously established particulars in "authoritative," "final," "formal" accounts. The indefinite triangulation notion attempts to make visible the practicality and inherent reflexivity of everyday accounts. The elaboration of circumstances and particulars of an occasion can be subjected to an indefinite re-elaboration of the "same" or "new" circumstances and particulars (Cicourel 1974a:124).

However, the necessary residual indeterminacy of sociological analyses poses no problems for the phenomenologist, since it merely mirrors the necessary residual indeterminacy of all commonsense thinking, to which the constructs of social science are indissolubly linked. Just as a member's commonsense thinking about the social world has only that degree of clarity and specificity required for the member's current purpose at hand, so the degree of elaborateness of the researcher's analysis will depend on the researcher's current purpose at hand. It is the researcher's interests and systems of relevance that will determine the practical limits of his or her analysis (Schutz 1970). Techniques of validation provide valuable additional material for analysis and perform further useful functions (such as easing research access), but they do not set the bounds of the analytic task; those bounds are set not by any technical test or procedure, but by a mix of relevances stretching from the researcher's own intellectual curiosity and scrupulousness to external constraints such as funding limits, supervisory stipulations and (not least!) publishing deadlines.

***

All the studies reported on here were conducted with the support of the Medical Research Council. The work on member validation has been much influenced by my correspondence with Bob Emerson, who provided thoughtful editorial comments on an earlier contribution to this topic (Bloor 1983).

References

Abbott, Andrew. 1992. "What Do Cases Do? Some Notes on Activity in Sociological Analysis." In *What Is a Case? Exploring the Foundations of Social Inquiry*, ed. C. C. Ragin and H. S. Becker. Cambridge, UK: Cambridge University Press, pp. 53–82.

Abolafia, Mitchel Y. 1996. *Making Markets: Opportunism and Restraint on Wall Street.* Cambridge, MA: Harvard University Press.

Abrahamson, J. S., and T. Mizrahi. 1994. "Examining Social Work/Physician Collaboration: An Application of Grounded Theory Methods." In *Qualitative Studies in Social Work*, ed. C. K. Riessman. Newbury Park, CA: Sage.

Abramson, A. 1993. "Between Autobiography and Method: Being Male, Seeing Myth and the Analysis of Structures of Gender and Sexuality in the Eastern Interior of Fiji." In *Gendered Fields: Women, Men and Ethnography*, ed. D. Bell, P. Caplan and W. J. Karim. London: Routledge & Kegan Paul, pp. 63–77.

Adams, Laura L. 1999. "The Mascot Researcher: Identity, Power and Knowledge in Fieldwork." *Journal of Contemporary Ethnography* 28:331–63.

Adler, Patricia A. 1985. *Wheeling and Dealing.* New York: Columbia University Press.

Adler, Patricia A., and Peter Adler, 1987. *Membership Roles in Field Research.* Newbury Park, CA: Sage.

Agamben, Giorgio. 1993. *Infancy and History.* Translated by Liz Heron. London: Verso.

Agar, Michael H. 1973. *Ripping and Running: A Formal Ethnography of Urban Heroin Addicts.* New York: Seminar Press.

Agar, Michael H. 1980. *The Professional Stranger: An Informal Introduction to Ethnography.* New York: Academic Press.

Ainsworth, Janet. 1993. "In a Different Register: The Pragmatics of Powerlessness in Police Interrogation." *Yale Law Journal* 103:259–322.

Aldridge, Alan. 1993. "Negotiating Status: Social Scientists and Anglican Clergy." *Journal of Contemporary Ethnography* 22:97–112.

Altheide, David L., and John M. Johnson. 1994. "Criteria for Assessing Interpretive Validity in Qualitative Research." In *Handbook of Qualitative Sociology*, ed. N. K. Denzin and Y. Lincoln. Thousand Oaks, CA: Sage, pp. 485–99.

Amadiume, Ifi. 1993. "The Mouth That Spoke a Falsehood Will Later speak the Truth: Going Home to the Field in Eastern Nigeria." In *Gendered Fields: Women, Men and Ethnography*, ed. D. Bell, P. Caplan and W. J. Karim. London: Routledge & Kegan Paul, pp. 182–98.

Amnesty International. 1990. "Allegations of Police Torture in Chicago, Illinois." December 1990.

Anderson, Elijah. 1978. *A Place on the Corner*. Chicago: University of Chicago Press.

Anderson, Elijah. 1990. *Streetwise: Race, Class and Change in an Urban Community*. Chicago: University of Chicago Press.

Anderson, Nels. 1923/1961. *The Hobo: The Sociology of the Homeless Man*. Chicago: University of Chicago Press.

Angrosino, Michael V. 1986. "Son and Lover: The Anthropologist as Non-Threatening Male." In *Self, Sex and Gender in Cross-Cultural Fieldwork*, ed. T. L. Whitehead and M. E. Conaway. Urbana: University of Illinois Press, pp. 64–83.

Anspach, Renee R. 1993. *Deciding Who Lives: Fateful Choices in the Intensive-Care Nursery*. Berkeley and Los Angeles: University of California Press.

Appell, George. 1978. *Ethical Dilemmas in Anthropological Inquiry: A Case Book*. Waltham, MA: Crossroads.

Arendell, Terry. 1997. "Reflections on the Researcher-Researched Relationship: A Woman Interviewing Men." *Qualitative Sociology* 20:341–68.

Asad, Talal, ed. 1973. *Anthropology and the Colonial Encounter*. London: Ithaca Press.

Asad, Talal. 1986. "The Concept of Cultural Translation in British Social Anthropology." In *Writing Culture: The Poetics and Politics of Ethnography*, ed. J. Clifford and G. E. Marcus. Berkeley: University of California Press, pp. 141–64.

Athens, Lonnie H. 1980. *Violent Criminal Acts and Actors*. London: Routledge & Kegan Paul.

Athens, Lonnie H. 1984. "Scientific Criteria for Evaluating Qualitative Studies." In *Studies in Symbolic Interaction*, v. 5, ed. N. K. Denzin. Greenwich, CT: JAI Press.

Atkinson, J. M. 1978. *Discovering Suicide: Studies in the Social Organization of Sudden Death*. London: Macmillan.

Atkinson, Paul. 1983. "Writing Ethnography." In *Kultur und Institution*, ed. H. J. Helle. Berlin: Duncker und Humblot.

Atkinson, Paul. 1988. "Ethnomethodology: A Critical Review." *Annual Review of Sociology* 14:441–65.

Atkinson, Paul. 1990. *The Ethnographic Imagination: Textual Constructions of Reality*. New York: Routledge.

Atkinson, Paul. 1992. *Understanding Ethnographic Texts*. Newbury Park, CA: Sage.

Auerbach, Erich. 1953. *Mimesis: The Representation of Reality in Western Literature*. Princeton, NJ: Princeton University Press.

Austin, Regina. 1994. "'An Honest Living': Street Vendors, Municipal Regulation, and the Black Public Sphere." *Yale Law Journal* 103:2119–31.

Austin, Regina. 1995. "Social Inequality, Physical Restraints on Mobility, and the Black Public Sphere." Paper presented at *An American Dilemma* Revisited: Fiftieth Anniversary Conference, Harvard University.

Baca Zinn, Maxine. 1979a. "Field Research in Minority Communities: Ethical, Methodological and Political Observations by an Insider." *Social Problems* 27:209–19.

Baca Zinn, Maxine. 1979b. "Qualitative Methods in Family Research: A Look Inside Chicano Families." Annual Meetings of the Western Social Science Association, Lake Tahoe, NV.

Bachnik, Jane M. 1978. "Inside and Outside the Japanese Household (*Ie*): A Contextual Approach to Japanese Social Organization." Ph.D. dissertation, Department of Anthropology, Harvard University.

Bachnik, Jane M. 1982. *Deixis and Self/Other Reference in Japanese Discourse.* Working Papers in Sociolinguistics 99. Austin, TX: Southwest Educational Development Laboratory.

Back, Les. 1993. "Gendered Participation: Masculinity and Fieldwork in a South London Adolescent Community." In *Gendered Fields: Women, Men and Ethnography*, ed. D. Bell, P. Caplan and W. J. Karim. London: Routledge & Kegan Paul, pp. 215–33.

Baldamus, W. 1972. "The Role of Discoveries in Social Science." In *The Rules of the Game: Cross-Disciplinary Essays on Models in Scholarly Thought*, ed. T. Shanin. London: Tavistock, pp. 276–302.

Barnes, J. A. 1967. "Some Ethical Problems in Modern Field Work." In *Anthropologists in the Field*, ed. D. C. Jongmans and P. Gutkind. Assen, The Netherlands: Van Gorcum, pp. 193–213.

Barthes, Roland. 1968. "L'Effect de Réel." *Communications* 11:84–89.

Barton, Allen H. 1955. "The Concept of Property—Space in Social Research." In *The Language of Social Research*, ed. P. F. Lazarsfeld and M. Rosenberg. Glencoe, IL: Free Press, pp. 40–53.

Becker, Howard S. 1953. "Becoming a Marihuana User." *American Journal of Sociology* 59:235–42.

Becker, Howard S. 1958. "Problems of Inference and Proof in Participant-Observation." *American Sociological Review* 23:652–60.

Becker, Howard S. 1963. "The Culture of a Deviant Group: The Dance Musician." Pp. 79–100 in *Outsiders: Studies in the Sociology of Deviance*. New York: Free Press.

Becker, Howard S. 1964. "Problems in the Publication of Field Studies." In *Reflections on Community Studies*, eds. A. J. Vidich, J. Bensman, and M. R. Stein. New York: Wiley, pp. 267–84.

Becker, Howard S. 1966. "Introduction to the Jack-Roller." In *The Jack-Roller: A Delinquent Boy's Own Story*, Clifford R. Shaw. Chicago: University of Chicago Press, pp. v–xviii.

Becker, Howard S. 1967. "Whose Side Are We On?" *Social Problems* 14:239–48.

Becker, Howard S. 1970a. *Sociological Work: Method and Substance*. Chicago: Aldine.

Becker, Howard S. 1970b. "Practitioners of Vice and Crime." In *Pathways to Data*, ed. R. W. Habenstein. Chicago: Aldine, pp. 30–49.

Becker, Howard S. 1982. *Art Worlds*. Berkeley and Los Angeles: University of California Press.

Becker, Howard S. 1986a. *Doing Things Together*. Evanston, IL: Northwestern University Press.

Becker, Howard S. 1986b. *Writing for Social Scientists*. Chicago: University of Chicago Press.

Becker, Howard S. 1996. "The Epistemology of Qualitative Research." In *Ethnography and Human Development*, ed. R. Jessor, A. Colby, and R. Schweder. Chicago: University of Chicago Press, pp. 53–71.

Becker, Howard S. 1998. *Tricks of the Trade: How to Think about Your Research While You're Doing It*. Chicago: University of Chicago Press.

Becker, Howard S., Blanche Geer, Everett C. Hughes, and Anselm L. Strauss. 1961. *Boys in White: Student Culture in Medical School*. Chicago: University of Chicago Press.

Behar, Ruth, and Deborah A. Gordon. 1995. *Women Writing Culture*. Berkeley: University of California Press.

Bell, David. 1990. *Husserl*. London: Routledge.

Bell, Diane. 1993a. "Introduction 1: The Context." In *Gendered Fields: Women, Men and Ethnography*, ed. D. Bell, P. Caplan and W. J. Karim. London: Routledge & Kegan Paul, pp. 1–18.

Bell, Diane. 1993b. "Yes, Virginia, There is a Feminist Ethnography: Reflections from Three Australian Fields." In *Gendered Fields: Women, Men and Ethnography*, ed. D. Bell, P. Caplan and W. J. Karim. London: Routledge & Kegan Paul, pp. 28–43.

Bennett, James. 1981. *Oral History and Delinquency: The Rhetoric of Criminology*. Chicago: University of Chicago Press.

Bennett, John W. 1946. "The Interpretation of Pueblo Culture: A Question of Values." *Southwestern Journal of Anthropology* 2:361–74.

Berg, Bruce L. 1989. *Qualitative Research Methods for the Social Sciences*. Boston: Allyn and Bacon.

Berger, Bennett 1981. *The Survival of a Counterculture: Ideological Work and Everyday Life Among Rural Communards*. Berkeley: University of California Press.

Berger, Peter, and Thomas Luckmann. 1966. *The Social Construction of Reality*. Harmondsworth: Penguin.

Bernstein, Gail L. 1983. *Haruko's World: A Japanese Farm Woman and Her Community*. Stanford: Stanford University Press.

Bernstein, Richard J. 1983. *Beyond Objectivism and Relativism*. Philadelphia: University of Pennsylvania Press.

Berreman, Gerald D. 1962. *Behind Many Masks*. Monograph No. 4, Chicago: Society for Applied Anthropology.

Berreman, Gerald D. 1968. "Ethnography: Method and Product." In *Introduction to Cultural Anthropology: Essays in the Scope and Methods of the Science of Man*, ed. J. A. Clifton. Boston: Houghton Mifflin, pp. 337–73.

Best, Joel. 1995. "Lost in the Ozone Again: The Postmodernist Fad and Interactionist Foibles." *Studies in Symbolic Interaction* 17:125–30.

Bhavnani, Kum Kum. 1993. "Tracing the Contours: Feminist Research and Feminist Objectivity." *Woman's Studies International Forum* 16:95–104.

Biernacki, Patrick L. 1986. *Pathways from Heroin Addiction: Recovery without Treatment*. Philadelphia: Temple University Press.

Bigus, O. E., S. C. Hadden and Barney G. Glaser. 1994. "The Study of Basic Social Processses." In *More Grounded Theory Methodology: A Reader*, ed. B. G. Glaser. Mill Valley, CA: Sociology Press.

Bittner, Egon. 1973. "Objectivity and Realism in Sociology." In *Phenomenological Sociology: Issues and Applications*, ed. G. Psathas. New York: Wiley, pp. 109–25.

Bittner, Egon, and Harold Garfinkel. 1967. "'Good' Organizational Reasons for 'Bad' Organizational Records." In *Studies in Ethnomethodology*, H. Garfinkel. Englewood Cliffs, NJ: Prentice-Hall, pp. 186–207.

Black, Donald. 1980. *The Manners and Customs of the Police*. New York: Academic Press.

Blanchard, D. 1979. "Beyond Empathy: The Emergence of Action Anthropology in the Life and Career of Sol Tax." In *Currents in Anthropology: Essays in Honor of Sol Tax*, ed. R. Hinshaw. The Hague: Mouton, pp. 419–34.

Blauner, Robert. 1977. "Forward." David Wellman, *Portraits of White Racism*. Cambridge, UK: Cambridge University Press.

Blauner, Robert, and David Wellman. 1973. "Toward the Decolonization of Social Research." In *The Death of White Sociology*, ed. J. A. Ladner. New York: Vintage Books.

Bloor, David. 1976. *Knowledge and Social Imagery*. London: Routledge & Kegan Paul.

Bloor, Michael. 1976. "Bishop Berkeley and the Adeno-Tonsillectomy Enigma: An Exploration of Variation in the Social Construction of Medical Disposals." *Sociology* 10:43–61.

Bloor, Michael. 1981. "Therapeutic Paradox—the Patient Culture and Formal Treatment Programme in a Therapeutic Community." *British Journal of Medical Psychology* 54:359–69.

Bloor, Michael. 1983. "Notes on Member Validation." In *Contemporary Field Research: A Collection of Readings*, ed. R. M. Emerson. Boston: Little, Brown, pp. 156–72.

Bloor, Michael. 1991. "A Minor Office: The Variable and Socially Constructed Character of Death Certification in a Scottish City." *Journal of Health and Social Behavior* 32:273–87.

Bloor, Michael. 1995. "Scrutiny and Routine: Medical Decision-Making and Death Certification Practice." In *Qualitative Studies in Medical Care*, ed. M. Bloor and P. Taraborrelli. Aldershot: Avebury.

Bloor, Michael, N. McKeganey, and D. Fonkert. 1988. *One Foot in Eden: A Sociology Study of the Range of Therapeutic Community Practice*. London: Routledge & Kegan Paul.

Blum, Richard. 1972. *Deceivers and Deceived: Observations on Confidence Men and Their Victims, Informants and Their Quarry, Political and Industrial Spies and Ordinary Citizens*. Springfield IL: Charles C. Thomas.

Blumer, Herbert. 1939. *An Appraisal of Thomas and Znaniecki's The Polish Peasant in Europe and America*. New York: Social Science Research Council.

Blumer, Herbert. 1969. *Symbolic Interactionism: Perspective and Method*. Englewood Cliffs, NJ: Prentice-Hall.

Boas, Franz. 1911. *Handbook of American Indian Languages*. Washington, DC: Bureau of American Ethnology, Bulletin 40.

Boelen, W. A. Marianne. 1992. "Street Corner Society: Cornerville Revisited." *Journal of Contemporary Ethnography* 21:11–51.

Bogdan, Robert, and Steven J. Taylor. 1975. *Introduction to Qualitative Research Methods: A Phenomenological Approach to the Social Sciences*. New York: Wiley.

Booth, Charles. 1902. *Life and Labour of the People of London*. London: Macmillan.

Booth, Wayne. 1961. *The Rhetoric of Fiction*. Chicago: University of Chicago Press.

Bosk, Charles L. 1979. *Forgive and Remember: Managing Medical Failure*. Chicago: University of Chicago Press.

Bosk, Charles L. 1992. *All God's Mistakes: Genetic Counseling in a Pediatric Hospital*. Chicago: University of Chicago Press.

Bott, Elizabeth. 1957. *Family and Social Network*. New York: Free Press.

Bourdieu, Pierre, and Jean-Claude Passeron. 1977/1980. *Reproduction in Education, Culture, and Society*. London: Sage.

Brajuha, Mario, and Lyle Hallowell. 1986. "Legal Intrusion and the Politics of Fieldwork." *Urban Life* 14:454–78.

Briggs, Jean L. 1970. *Never in Anger: Portrait of an Eskimo Family*. Cambridge, MA: Harvard University Press.

Briggs, Jean L. 1986. "Kapluna Daughter." In *Women in the Field: Anthropological Experiences*, ed. P. Golde. Berkeley: University of California Press, pp. 19–44.

British Association for the Advancement of Sciences. 1874. *Notes and Queries in Anthropology, for the Use of Travellers and Residents in Uncivilized Lands*. London.

British Association for the Advancement of Sciences. 1912. *Notes and Queries in Anthropology*. 4th edition.

Broadhead, Robert S., and Kathryn J. Fox. 1990. "Takin' It to the Streets: AIDS Outreach as Ethnography." *Journal of Contemporary Ethnography* 19:322–48.

Brown, Karen McCarthy. 1985. "On Feminist Methodology." *Journal of Feminist Studies in Religion* 1:76–79.

Browne, Joy. 1976. "Fieldwork for Fun and Profit." In *The Research Experience*, ed. M. P. Gordon. Itasca, IL: F. E. Peacock, pp. 77–84.

Bruner, Edward M. 1986. "Ethnography as Narrative." In *The Anthropology of Experience*, ed. V. Turner and E. M. Bruner. Urbana: University of Illinois Press, pp. 137–55.

Bruner, Edward M. 1993. "Introduction: The Ethnographic Self and the Personal Self." In *Anthropology and Literature*, ed. P. Benson. Urbana: University of Illinois Press, pp. 1–26.

Bucher, Rue, and Leonard Schatzman. 1962. "The Logic of the State Hospital." *Social Problems* 9:337–49.

Bulmer, Martin. 1979. "Concepts in the Analysis of Qualitative Data: A Symposium." *Sociological Review* 27:651–77.

Bulmer, Martin. 1984. *The Chicago School of Sociology: Institutionalization, Diversity, and the Rise of Sociological Research*. Chicago: University of Chicago Press.

Burawoy, Michael. 1991. *Ethnography Unbound: Power and Resistance in the Modern Metropolis*. Berkeley and Los Angeles: University of California Press.

Burgess, Ernest W. 1961. "Social Planning and Race Relations." In *Race Relations: Problems and Theory—Essays in Honor of Robert E. Park*, ed. J. Masuoka and P. Valien. Chapel Hill: University of North Carolina Press.

Burke, Kenneth. 1945. *A Grammar of Motives*. New York: Prentice-Hall.

Burroughs, William. 1966. *Naked Lunch*. New York: Grove Press.

Caplan, Pat. 1993a. "Introduction 2: The Volume." In *Gendered Fields: Women, Men and Ethnography*, ed. D. Bell, P. Caplan and W. J. Karim. London: Routledge 3& Kegan Paul, pp. 168–181.

Caplan, Pat. 1993b. "Learning Gender: Fieldwork in a Tanzanian Coastal Village, 1965–85." In *Gendered Fields: Women, Men and Ethnography*, ed. D. Bell, P. Caplan and W. J. Karim. London: Routledge & Kegan Paul, 19–27.

Cassell, Joan. 1980. "Ethical Principles for Conducting Fieldwork." *American Anthropologist* 82:28–41.

Cassell, Joan. 1988. "The Relationship of Observer to Observed When Studying Up." *Studies in Qualitative Methodology* 1:89–108.

Castaneda, Carlos. 1968. *The Teachings of Don Juan: A Yaqui Way of Knowledge*. Berkeley: University of California Press.

Caudill, William, Frederick C. Redlich, Helen Gilmore, and Eugene Brody. 1952. "Social Structure and Interaction Process on a Psychiatric Ward." *American Journal of Orthopsychiatry* 22:314–34.

Cavan, Sherri. 1966. *Liquor License: An Ethnography of Bar Behavior*. Chicago: Aldine.

Charmaz, Kathy. 1983. "The Grounded Theory Method: An Explication and Interpretation." In *Contemporary Field Research: A Collection of Readings*, ed. R. M. Emerson. Boston: Little, Brown, pp. 109–26.

Charmaz, Kathy. 1987. "Struggling for a Self: Identity Levels of the Chronically Ill." In *Research in the Sociology of Health Care: The Experience and Management of Chronic Illness*, Vol. 6, ed. J. A. Roth and P. Conrad. Greenwich, CT: JAI Press, pp. 283–321.

Charmaz, Kathy. 1990. "'Discovering' Chronic Illness: Using Grounded Theory." *Social Science & Medicine* 30:1161–72.

Charmaz, Kathy. 1991a. *Good Days, Bad Days: The Self in Chronic Illness and Time*. New Brunswick, NJ: Rutgers University Press.

Charmaz, Kathy. 1991b. "Translating Graduate Qualitative Methods into Undergraduate Teaching: Intensive Interviewing as a Case Example." *Teaching Sociology* 19:384–95.

Charmaz, Kathy. 1994a. "Identity Dilemmas of Chronically Ill Men." *The Sociological Quarterly* 35:269–88.

Charmaz, Kathy. 1994b. "Discoveries of Self in Illness." In *Doing Everyday Life: Ethnography as Human Lived Experience*, ed. M. L. Dietz, R. Prus and W. Shaffir. Mississauga, Ontario: Copp Clark Longman, pp. 226–42.

Cicourel, Aaron V. 1964. *Method and Measurement in Sociology*. New York: Free Press.

Cicourel, Aaron V. 1968. *The Social Organization of Juvenile Justice*. New York: Wiley.

Cicourel, Aaron V. 1974a. *Cognitive Sociology: Language and Meaning in Social Interaction*. New York: Free Press.

Cicourel, Aaron V. 1974b. "Interviewing and Memory." In *Pragmatic Aspects of Human Communications*, ed. C. Cherry. Dordrecht, The Netherlands: D. Reidel.

Cicourel, Aaron V. 1978. "Field Research: The Need for Stronger Theory and More Control Over the Data Base." Unpublished paper, University of California, San Diego.

Cicourel, Aaron V., and John I. Kitsuse. 1963. *The Educational Decision-Makers*. Indianapolis: Bobbs Merrill.

Clarke, Lee. 1989. *Acceptable Risk? Making Decisions in a Toxic Environment*. Berkeley: University of California Press.

Clarke, Lee. 1995. "An Unethical Ethics Code?" *The American Sociologist* 26:12–21.

Clarke, Michael. 1975. "Survival in the Field: Implications of Personal Experience in Field Work." *Theory and Society* 2:95–123.

Clifford, James. 1983. "On Ethnographic Authority." *Representations* 1:118–46.

Clifford, James. 1986a. "Introduction: Partial Truths." In *Writing Culture: The Poetics and Politics of Ethnography*, ed. J. Clifford and G. E. Marcus. Berkeley: University of California Press, pp. 1–26.

Clifford, James. 1986b. "On Ethnographic Allegory." In *Writing Culture: The Poetics and Politics of Ethnography*, ed. J. Clifford and G. E. Marcus. Berkeley: University of California Press, pp. 98–121.

Clifford, James. 1990. "Notes on (Field)notes." In *Fieldnotes: The Making of Anthropology*, ed. R. Sanjek. Ithaca, NY: Cornell University Press, pp. 47–70.

Clifford, James. 1997. "Spatial Practices: Fieldwork, Travel, and the Disciplining of Anthropology." In *Anthropological Locations: Boundaries and Grounds for a Field Science*, ed. A. Gupta and J. Ferguson. Berkeley: University of California Press, pp. 185–222.

Clifford, James, and George E. Marcus, eds. 1986. *Writing Culture: The Poetics and Politics of Ethnography*. Berkeley: University of California Press.

Cobb, Edith. 1977. *The Ecology of Imagination in Childhood*. New York: Columbia University Press.

Collins, Patricia H. 1990. *Black Feminist Thought: Knowledge, Consciousness, and the Politics of Empowerment*. Boston: Unwin Hyman.

Colomy, Paul, and J. David Brown. 1995. "Elaboration, Revision, Polemic, and Progress in the Second Chicago School." In *A Second Chicago School? The Development of a Postwar American Sociology*, ed. G. A. Fine. Chicago: University of Chicago Press, pp. 17–81.

Conrad, Peter. 1990. "Qualitative Research on Chronic Illness: A Commentary on Method and Conceptual Development." *Social Science & Medicine* 30:1257–63.

Cooper, Candace. 1990. "A Question of Rape." *San Francisco Examiner*, September 16–17, 1990.

Corsaro, William A. 1985. *Friendship and Peer Culture in the Early Years*. Norwood, NJ: Ablex Publishing.

Crapanzano, Vincent. 1985. *Waiting: The Whites of South Africa*. New York: Random House.

Crapanzano, Vincent. 1986. "Hermes' Dilemma: The Masking of Subversion in Ethnographic Description." In *Writing Culture: The Poetics and Politics of Ethnography*, ed. J. Clifford and G. E. Marcus. Berkeley: University of California Press, pp. 51–76.

Cressey, Donald R. 1953. *Other People's Money: A Study in the Social Psychology of Embezzlement*. Glencoe, IL: Free Press.

Cressey, Paul G. 1932. *The Taxi Dance Hall: A Sociological Study in Commercialized Recreation and City Life*. Chicago: University of Chicago Press.

Csordas, Thomas J. 1994. *The Sacred Self: A Cultural Phenomenology of Charismatic Healing*. Berkeley: University of California Press.

Csordas, Thomas J. 1997. *Language, Charisma, and Creativity: The Ritual Life of a Religious Movement*. Berkeley: University of California Press.

Culler, Jonathan. 1975. *Structuralist Poetics: Structuralism, Linguistics and the Study of Literature*. London: Routledge & Kegan Paul.

Cusick, Philip A. 1973. *Inside High School*. New York: Holt, Rinehart and Winston.

Daniels, Arlene K. 1967. "The Low-Caste Stranger in Social Research." In *Ethics, Politics, and Social Research*, ed. G. Sjoberg. Cambridge, MA: Schenkman, pp. 267–96.

Daniels, Arlene K. 1988. *Invisible Careers: Women Civic Leaders from the Volunteer World*. Chicago: University of Chicago Press.

Davies, Bronwyn. 1982. *Life in the Classroom and Playground: The Accounts of Primary School Children*. Boston: Routledge & Kegan Paul.

Davis, Dona. 1986. "Changing Self-Image: Studying Menopausal Women in a Newfoundland Fishing Village." In *Self, Sex and Gender in Cross-Cultural Fieldwork*, ed. T. L. Whitehead and M. E. Conaway. Urbana: University of Illinois Press, pp. 240–62.

Davis, Fred. 1959. "The Cabdriver and His Fare: Facets of a Fleeting Relationship." *American Journal of Sociology* 65:158–65.

Davis, Murray S. 1971. "'That's Interesting!' Towards a Phenomenology of Sociology and a Sociology of Phenomenology." *Philosophy of the Social Sciences* 1:309–44.

Dean, Lois R. 1954. "Interaction, Reported and Observed: The Case of One Local Union." *Human Organization* 17:36–44.

Deegan, Mary Jo, and John S. Burger. 1978. "George Herbert Mead and Social Reform." *Journal of the History of the Behavioral Sciences* 14:362–72.

Deegan, Mary Jo, and John S. Burger. 1981. "W. I. Thomas and Social Reform: His Work and Writings." *Journal of the History of the Behavioral Sciences* 17:114–25.

den Hollander, A. N. J. 1967. "Social Description: The Problem of Reliability and Validity." In *Anthropologists in the Field*, ed. D. G. Jongmans and P. C. W. Gutkind. Assen: Van Gorcum, pp. 1–34.

Denzin, Norman K. 1970/1978. *The Research Act: A Theoretical Introduction to Sociological Methods*. New York: McGraw-Hill.

Denzin, Norman K. 1989. *Interpretive Interactionism*. Newbury Park, CA: Sage.

Denzin, Norman K. 1990. "The Spaces of Postmodernism: Reading Plummer on Blumer." *Symbolic Interaction* 13:145–54.

Denzin, Norman K. 1995. "Symbolic Interactionism." In *Rethinking Psychology*: Vol. 1—*Conceptual Foundations*, ed. J. Smith, R. Hare and L. Van Langenhove. London: Sage.

Denzin, Norman K. 1997. *Interpretive Ethnography: Ethnographic Practices for the 21st Century*. Thousand Oaks, CA: Sage.

Denzin, Norman K., and Yvonna S. Lincoln, eds. 1994. *Handbook of Qualitative Research*. Thousand Oaks, CA: Sage.

De Quincey, Thomas. 1956 [1971]. *Confessions of an English Opium Eater*. ed. Aletha Hayter. Harmondsworth: Penguin.

Devault, Marjorie L. 1990. "Talking and Listening from Women's Standpoint: Feminist Strategies for Interviewing and Analysis." *Social Problems* 37:96–116.

Devault, Marjorie L. 1999. *Liberating Method: Feminism and Social Research*. Philadelphia: Temple University Press.

Diamond, Timothy. 1992. *Making Gray Gold: Narratives of Nursing Home Care*. Chicago: University of Chicago Press.

Diesing, Paul. 1971. *Patterns of Discovery in the Social Sciences*. Chicago: Aldine-Atherton.

Dingwall, Robert. 1980. "Ethics and Ethnography." *Sociological Review* 28:871–91.

Doi, Takeo. 1986. *The Anatomy of Self*. Tokyo: Kodansha.

Dollard, John. 1937/1949. *Caste and Class in a Southern Town*. Garden City, NY: Doubleday.

Dorst, John D. 1989. *The Written Suburb: An American Site, An Ethnographic Dilemma*. Philadelphia: University of Pennsylvania Press.

Douglas, Jack D. 1972. "Observing Deviance." In *Research on Deviance*, ed. J. D. Douglass. New York: Random House, pp. 3-34.

Douglas, Jack D. 1976. *Investigative Social Research: Individual and Team Field Research.* Beverly Hills, CA: Sage.

Douglas, Jack D., Paul K. Rasmussen, and Carol Ann Flanagan. 1977. *The Nude Beach.* Beverly Hills, CA: Sage.

Du Bois, W. E. B. 1899/1967. *The Philadelphia Negro: A Social Study.* New York: Schocken.

Dumont, Jean-Paul. 1982/1992. *The Headman and I.* Prospect Heights, IL: Waveland Press.

Dunbar, Paul L. 1997. "We Wear the Mask." In *Lyrics of Lowly Life.* Seacaucus, NJ: Citadel Press.

Duneier, Mitchell. 1999. *Sidewalk.* New York: Farrar, Straus and Giroux.

Dwyer, Kevin. 1982. *Moroccan Dialogues: Anthropology in Question.* Baltimore: John Hopkins University Press.

Easterday, Lois, Diana Papademas, Laura Schorr, and Catherine Valentine. 1977. "The Making of a Female Researcher: Role Problems in Field Work." *Urban Life* 6:333–48.

Edmondson, Ricca. 1984. *Rhetoric in Sociology.* London: Macmillan.

Ellis, Carolyn. 1986. *Fisher Folk: Two Communities on Chesapeake Bay.* Lexington: University of Kentucky Press.

Ellis, Carolyn 1991. "Sociological Introspection and Emotional Experience." *Symbolic Interaction* 14:23–50.

Ellis, Carolyn. 1995a. *Final Negotiations: A Story of Love, Loss, and Chronic Illness.* Philadelphia: Temple University Press.

Ellis, Carolyn. 1995b. "Emotional and Ethical Quagmires in Returning to the Field." *Journal of Contemporary Ethnography* 24:68–98.

Ellis, Carolyn, and A. P. Bochner. 1992. "Telling and Performing Personal Stories: The Constraints of Choice in Abortion." In *Investigating Subjectivity: Research on Lived Experience*, ed. C. Ellis and M. G. Flaherty. Newbury Park, CA: Sage, pp. 79–101.

Ellis, Carolyn, and Michael G. Flaherty, eds. 1992. *Investigating Subjectivity: Research on Lived Experience.* Newbury Park, CA: Sage.

Ellis, William R., Jr., and Peter Orleans. 1971. "Race Research: 'Up Against the Wall' in More Ways than One." In *Race, Change and Urban Society*, ed. P. Orleans and W. R. Ellis, Jr. Beverly Hills, CA: Sage.

Emerson, Robert M. 1981. "Observational Field Work." *Annual Review of Sociology* 7:351–78.

Emerson, Robert M., Rachel I. Fretz, and Linda L. Shaw. 1995. *Writing Ethnographic Fieldnotes.* Chicago: University of Chicago Press.

Emerson, Robert M., Rachel I. Fretz, and Linda L. Shaw. 2001. "Participant Observation and Fieldnotes." In *Handbook of Ethnography*, ed. P. Atkinson, A. Coffey, S. Delamont, L. H. Lofland and J. Lofland. London: Sage, pp. 352–68.

Emerson, Robert M., and Melvin Pollner. 1976. "Dirty Work Designations: Their Features and Consequences in a Psychiatric Setting." *Social Problems* 23:243–55.

Emerson, Robert M., and Melvin Pollner. 1988. "On the Uses of Members' Responses to Researchers' Accounts." *Human Organization* 47:189–98.

Emerson, Robert M., and Melvin Pollner. 1992. "Difference and Dialogue: Members' Readings of Ethnographic Texts." In *Perspectives on Social Problems, Vol. 3*, ed. G. Miller and J. A. Holstein. Greenwich, CT: JAI Press, pp. 79–98.

Ericson, Richard V. 1981. *Making Crime: A Study of Detective Work.* Toronto: Butterworth.

Erikson, Kai T. 1967. "A Comment on Disguised Observation in Sociology." *Social Problems* 12:366–73.

Erikson, Kai T. 1976. *Everything in its Path: Destruction of Community in the Buffalo Creek Flood.* New York: Simon and Schuster.

Erikson, Kai T. 1995. "Commentary." *The American Sociologist* 26:4–11.

Erikson, Kai T. 1996. "A Response to Richard Leo." *The American Sociologist* 27:129–30.

Esterberg, Kritsin G. 1997. *Lesbian and Bisexual Identities: Constructing Communities, Constructing Selves.* Philadelphia: Temple University Press.

Estroff, Sue E. 1981. *Making It Crazy: An Ethnography of Psychiatric Clients in an American Community.* Berkeley: University of California Press.

Evans-Pritchard, E. E. 1976. "Some Reminiscences and Reflections on Fieldwork." Appendix IV in *Witchcraft, Oracles and Magic among the Azande* (Abridged). Oxford: Clarendon Press.

Fahim, Hussein, and Katherine Helmer. 1980. "Indigenous Anthropology in Non-Western Countries: A Further Elaboration." *Current Anthropology* 21:644–63.

Fantasia, Rick. 1988. *Cultures of Solidarity: Consciousness, Action and Contemporary American Workers.* Berkeley: University of California Press.

Faulkner, Robert R. 1985. *Hollywood Studio Musicians: Their Work and Careers in the Recording Industry.* Lanham, MD: University Press of America.

Festinger, Leon, Henry W. Riecken, and Stanley Schachter. 1956. *When Prophecy Fails.* New York: Harper & Row.

Feyerabend, Paul K. 1975. *Against Method: Outline of an Anarchistic Theory of Knowledge.* Atlantic Highlands, NJ: Humanities Press.

Fielding, Nigel. 1982. "Observational Research on the National Front." In *Social Research Ethics,* ed. M. Bulmer. London: Macmillan.

Fimrite, Peter. 1994. "Cop to Stand Trial in Assault Charge: Brutality Charged in Laconia." *San Francisco Chronicle,* January 7, 1994.

Fine, Gary A. 1983. *Shared Fantasy: Role-Playing Games as Social Worlds.* Chicago: University of Chicago Press.

Fine, Gary A. 1993. "Ten Lies of Ethnography: Moral Dilemmas in Field Research." *Journal of Contemporary Ethnography* 22:267–94.

Fine, Gary A., ed. 1995. *A Second Chicago School? The Development of a Postwar American Sociology.* Chicago: University of Chicago Press.

Fine, Gary A. 1996. *Kitchens: The Culture of Restaurant Work.* Berkeley and Los Angeles: University of California Press.

Fine, Gary A, and Barry Glassner. 1979. "Participant Observation with Children: Promise and Problems." *Urban Life* 8:153–74.

Fine, Gary A., and Kent L. Sandstrom. 1988. *Knowing Children: Participant Observation with Minors.* Newbury Park, CA: Sage.

Fine, Michelle. 1992. *Disruptive Voices: The Possibilities of Feminist Research.* Ann Arbor: University of Michigan Press.

Finnegan, William. 1998. *Cold New World.* New York: Random House.

Firth, Rosemary. 1972. "From Wife to Anthropologist." In *Crossing Cultural Boundaries,* ed. S. Kimball and J. Watson. San Francisco: Chandler.

Fischer, Ann. 1986. "Field Work in Five Cultures." In *Women in the Field: Anthropological Experiences,* ed. P. Golde. Berkeley: University of California Press, pp. 267–89.

Fleuhr-Lobban, Carolyn, and R. C. Lobban. 1986. "Families, Gender and Methodology in the Sudan." In *Self, Sex and Gender in Cross-Cultural Fieldwork,* ed. T. L. Whitehead and M. E. Conaway. Urbana: University of Illinois Press.

Forrest, Burke. 1986. "Apprentice-Participation: Methodology and the Study of Subjective Reality." *Urban Life* 14:431–53.

Foucault, Michel. 1978. *The History of Sexuality.* New York: Pantheon.

Fowler, Roger. 1977. *Linguistics and the Novel.* London: Methuen.

Frake, Charles O. 1961. "The Diagnosis of Disease among the Subanun of Mindanao." *American Anthropologist* 63:113–32.

Frake, Charles O. 1962a. "The Ethnographic Study of Cognitive Systems." In *Anthropology and Human Behavior*, ed. T. Gladwin and W. C. Sturtevant. Washington: Anthropological Society of Washington, pp. 72–85.

Frake, Charles O. 1962b. "Cultural Ecology and Ethnography." *American Anthropologist* 64:53–59.

Frake, Charles O. 1964a. "Notes on Queries in Ethnography." *American Anthropologist* 66:132–45.

Frake, Charles O. 1964b. "How to Ask for a Drink in Subanun." *American Anthropologist* 66:127–32.

Frake, Charles O. 1975. "How to Enter a Yakan House." In *Sociocultural Dimensions of Language Use*, ed. M. Sanches and B. G. Blount. New York: Academic Press, pp. 25–40.

Freedman, Diane. 1986. "Wife, Widow, Woman: Roles of an Anthropologist in a Transylvanian Village." In *Women in the Field: Anthropological Experiences*, ed. P. Golde. Berkeley: University of California Press, pp. 335–58.

Freeman, Derek. 1983. *Margaret Mead and Samoa: The Making and Unmaking of an Anthropologist.* Cambridge, MA: Harvard University Press.

Freidson, Eliot, and Buford Rhea. 1963. "Processes of Control in a Company of Equals." *Social Problems* 11:119–31.

Friedl, Ernestine. 1986. "Field Work in a Greek Village." In *Women in the Field: Anthropological Experiences*, ed. P. Golde. Berkeley: University of California Press, pp. 195–236.

Frye, Northrop. 1957. *Anatomy of Criticism.* Princeton, NJ: Princeton University Press.

Galliher, John F. 1982. "The Protection of Human Subjects: A Re-examination of the Professional Code of Ethics." In *Social Research Ethics*, ed. M. Bulmer. London: Macmillan, pp. 152–65.

Galliher, John F. 1983. "Social Scientists' Ethical Responsibilities to Superordinates: Looking Upward Meekly." In *Contemporary Field Research: A Collection of Readings*, ed. R. M. Emerson. Boston: Little, Brown, pp. 300–11.

Gamson, Josh. 1989. "Silence, Death, and the Invisible Enemy: AIDS Activism and Social Movement 'Newness'." *Social Problems* 36:351–67.

Gans, Herbert J. 1962. *The Urban Villagers: Group and Class in the Life of Italian-Americans.* New York: Free Press.

Gans, Herbert J. 1967. *The Levittowners: Ways of Life and Politics in a New Suburban Community.* New York: Pantheon.

Gans, Herbert J. 1968. "The Participant-Observer as a Human Being: Observations on the Personal Aspects of Field Work." In *Institutions and the Person*, ed. H. S. Becker, B. Greer, D. Riesman, and R. S. Weiss. Chicago: Aldine, pp. 300–17.

Garfinkel, Harold. 1967. *Studies in Ethnomethodology.* Englewood Cliffs, NJ: Prentice-Hall.

Garfinkel, Harold, Michael Lynch, and Eric Livingston. 1981. "The Work of a Discovering Science Construed with Materials from the Optically Discovered Pulsar." *Philosophy of the Social Sciences* 11:131–58.

Garfinkel, Harold, Eric Livingston, Michael Lynch, Douglas MacBeth, and Albert B. Robillard. 1988. *Respecifying the Natural Sciences as Discovering Sciences of Practical Action, I & II: Doing so Ethnographically by Administering a Schedule of Contingencies in Discussions with Laboratory Scientists and by Hanging around Their Laboratories.* Unpublished manuscript.

Garfinkel, Harold, and Harvey Sacks. 1970. "The Formal Structure of Practical Actions." In *Theoretical Sociology: Perspectives and Developments*, ed. J. C. McKinney and E. A. Tiryakian. New York: Appleton-Century-Crofts, pp. 337–66.

Garfinkel, Harold, and D. Lawrence Wieder. 1992. "Two Incommensurable, Asymmetrically Alternate Technologies of Social Analysis." In *Text in Context: Studies in Ethnomethodology*, ed. G. Watson and R. M. Seiler. Newbury Park, CA: Sage, pp. 175–206.

Geertz, Clifford. 1973a. *The Interpretation of Cultures*. New York: Basic Books.

Geertz, Clifford. 1973b. "Deep Play: Notes on the Balinese Cockfight." In *The Interpretation of Cultures*. New York: Basic Books, pp. 412–53.

Geertz, Clifford. 1976. "From the Native's Point of View: On the Nature of Anthropological Understanding." In *Meaning in Anthropology*, ed. K. H. Basso and H. A. Selby. Albuquerque: University of New Mexico Press, pp. 221–37.

Geertz, Clifford. 1984. "Anti-anti Relativism." *American Anthropologist* 86:263–78.

Geertz, Clifford. 1988. *Works and Lives: The Anthropologist as Author*. Stanford: Stanford University Press.

Geertz, Clifford. 1995. *After the Fact: Two Countries, Four Decades, One Anthropologist*. Cambridge, MA: Harvard University Press.

Gibbons, Don C. 1975. "Unidentified Research Sites and Fictitious Names." *American Sociologist* 10:32–36.

Giddens, Anthony. 1976. *New Rules of Sociological Method*. London: Hutchinson.

Gilbert, G. Nigel, and Michael Mulkay. 1984. *Opening Pandora's Box: A Sociological Analysis of Scientists' Discoveries*. Cambridge, UK: Cambridge University Press.

Glaser, Barney G. 1978. *Theoretical Sensitivity*. Mill Valley, CA: Sociology Press.

Glaser, Barney G. 1992. *Emergence vs. Forcing: Basics of Grounded Theory Analysis*. Mill Valley, CA: Sociology Press.

Glaser, Barney G., and Anselm L. Strauss. 1965. *Awareness of Dying*. Chicago: Aldine.

Glaser, Barney G., and Anselm L. Strauss. 1967. *The Discovery of Grounded Theory: Strategies for Qualitative Research*. Chicago: Aldine.

Glaser, Barney G., and Anselm L. Strauss. 1968. *Time for Dying*. Chicago: Aldine.

Glaser, Barney G., and Anselm L. Strauss. 1971. *Status Passage*. Chicago: Aldine.

Glassner, Barry, and Julia Loughlin. 1987. *Drugs in Adolescent Worlds: Burnouts to Straights*. New York: St. Martin's Press.

Goffman, Erving. 1959. *The Presentation of Self in Everyday Life*. Garden City, NY: Doubleday.

Goffman, Erving. 1961. *Asylums: Essays on the Social Situation of Mental Patients and Other Inmates*. Garden City, NY: Doubleday.

Goffman, Erving. 1963a. *Stigma: Notes on the Management of Spoiled Identity*. Englewood Cliffs, NJ: Prentice-Hall.

Goffman, Erving. 1963b. *Behavior in Public Places: Notes on the Social Organization of Gatherings*. New York: Free Press.

Goffman, Erving. 1967. *Interaction Ritual: Essays on Face-to-Face Behavior*. Chicago: Aldine.

Goffman, Erving. 1989. "On Fieldwork." *Journal of Contemporary Ethnography* 18:123–32.

Gold, Raymond L. 1952. "Janitors versus Tenants: A Status-Income Dilemma." *American Journal of Sociology* 57:486–93.

Gold, Raymond L. 1958. "Roles in Sociological Field Observations." *Social Forces* 36:217–23.

Golde, Peggy, ed. 1986/1970. *Women in the Field: Anthropological Experiences*. Berkeley: University of California Press.

Goldkind, Victor. 1966. "Class Conflict and Cacique in Chan Kom." *Southwestern Journal of Anthropology* 22:325–45.

Goldkind, Victor. 1970. "Anthropologists, Informants and the Achievement of Power in Chan Kom." *Sociologus* 20:17–41.

Gonzalez, Nancie. 1986. "The Anthropologist as Female Head of Household." In *Self, Sex and Gender in Cross-Cultural Fieldwork*, ed. T. L. Whitehead and M. E. Conaway. Urbana: University of Illinois Press, pp. 84–100.

Goode, David. 1986. "Kids, Culture, and Innocents." *Human Studies* 9:83–106.

Goode, David. 1994. *A World without Words: The Social Construction of Children Born Deaf and Blind*. Philadelphia: Temple University Press.

Goode, Eric. 1996. "The Ethics of Deception in Social Research: A Case Study." *Qualitative Sociology* 19:11–33.

Goodenough, Ward H. 1967. "Componential Analysis." *Science* 156:1203–09.

Gould, Leroy, Andrew L. Walker, Lansing E. Crane, and Charles W. Lidz. 1974. *Connections: Notes from the Heroin World*. New Haven, CT: Yale University Press.

Gouldner, Alvin. 1954. *Patterns of Industrial Bureaucracy*. New York: Free Press.

Gruber, J. W. 1970. "Ethnographic Salvage and the Shaping of Anthropology." *American Anthropologist* 72:1289–99.

Guba, E. G., and Y. S. Lincoln. 1982. "Epistemological and Methodological Bases of Naturalistic Inquiry." *Educational Communication and Technology Journal* 30:233–52.

Gubrium, Jaber F. 1986. *Oldtimers and Alzheimer's: The Descriptive Organization of Senility*. Greenwich, CT: JAI Press.

Gubrium, Jaber F. 1988. *Analyzing Field Reality*. Newbury Park, CA: Sage.

Gubrium, Jaber F., and James A. Holstein. 1997. *The New Language of Qualitative Method*. New York: Oxford University Press.

Gubrium, Jaber F., and James A. Holstein. 1998. "Standing Our Middle Ground." *Journal of Contemporary Ethnography* 27:416–21.

Gupta, Akhil, and James Ferguson, eds. 1997a. *Anthropological Locations: Boundaries and Grounds for a Field Science*. Berkeley and Los Angeles: University of California Press.

Gupta, Akhil, and James Ferguson. 1997b. "Discipline and Practice: 'The Field' as Site, Method, and Location in Anthropology." In *Anthropological Locations: Boundaries and Grounds for a Field Science*. Berkeley and Los Angeles: University of California Press, pp. 1–46.

Gusfield, Joseph R. 1976. "The Literary Rhetoric of Science: Comedy and Pathos in Drinking Driver Research." *American Sociological Review* 41:16–34.

Gusfield, Joseph. 1990. "My Life and Soft Times." In *Authors of Their Own Lives: Intellectual Autobiographies of Twenty American Sociologists*, ed. B. M. Berger. Berkeley and Los Angeles: University of California Press, pp. 104–29.

Gussow, Zachary. 1964. "The Observer-Observed Relationship as Information about Structure in Small-Group Research: A Comparative Study of Urban Elementary School Classrooms." *Psychiatry* 27:230–47.

Haddon, Alfred C. 1903. "Anthropology: Its Position and Needs. Presidential Address." *Journal of the Anthropological Institute* 33:11–23.

Hagaman, Dianne. 1996. *How I Learned Not to Be a Photojournalist*. Lexington: University of Kentucky Press.

Hall, Stuart. 1986. "On Postmodernism and Articulation: An Interview with Stuart Hall." In *Cultural Studies*, ed. L. Grossberg, C. Nelson, and P. Treichlelr. New York: Routledge, pp. 277–94.

Halle, David. 1984. *America's Working Man: Work, Home and Politics among Blue-Collar Property Owners*. Chicago: University of Chicago Press.

Halle, David. 1993. *Inside Culture: Art and Class in the American Home*. Chicago: University of Chicago.

Hamabata, Matthews. 1983. "From Household to Economy: The Japanese Family Enterprise." Ph.D. Dissertation, Department of Sociology, Harvard University.

Hamabata, Matthews. 1990. *Crested Kimono: Power and Love in the Japanese Business Family*. Ithaca: Cornell University Press.

Hammersley, Martyn. 1981. "Ideology in the Staffroom? A Critique of False Consciousness." In *Schools, Teachers and Teaching*, ed. L. Barton and S. Walker. Lewes: Falmer.

Hammersley, Martyn. 1989. *The Dilemma of Qualitative Method: Herbert Blumer and the Chicago Tradition*. London: Routledge.

Hammersley, Martyn. 1991. "Some Reflections on Ethnography and Validity." *International Journal of Qualitative Studies in Education*.

Hammersley, Martyn. 1992. *What's Wrong with Ethnography? Methodological Explorations*. London: Routledge.

Hammersley, Martyn. 1998. *Reading Ethnographic Research: A Critical Guide*. Second Edition. London: Longman.

Hammersley, Martyn, and Paul Atkinson. 1995. *Ethnography: Principles in Practice*. Second Edition. London: Routledge.

Hannerz, Ulf. 1969. *Soulside: Inquiries into Ghetto Culture and Community*. New York: Columbia University Press.

Hannerz, Ulf. 1980. *Exploring the City: Inquiries Toward an Urban Anthropology*. New York: Columbia University Press.

Hanson, Norwood R. 1958. *Patterns of Discovery: An Inquiry into the Conceptual Foundations of Science*. Cambridge, UK: Cambridge University Press.

Harper, Douglas. 1982. *Good Company*. Chicago: University of Chicago Press.

Harper, Douglas. 1992. *Working Knowledge: Skill and Community in a Small Shop*. Berkeley: University of California Press.

Harper, Richard H. R. 1998. *Inside the IMF: An Ethnography of Documents, Technology and Organizational Action*. London: Academic Press.

Haug, Frigga, ed. 1987. *Female Sexualization: A Collective Work of Memory*. London: Verso.

Hayano, David M. 1979. "Auto-Ethnography: Paradigms, Problems, and Prospects." *Human Organization* 38:99–104.

Hayano, David M. 1982. *Poker Faces: The Life and Work of Professional Card Players*. Berkeley: University of California Press.

Hearnshaw, Leslie S. 1979. *Cyril Burt, Psychologist*. Ithaca: Cornell University Press.

Heath, Dwight. 1972. "Comment." *Current Anthropology* 13:536.

Heath, S. 1972. *The Nouveau Roman: A Study in the Practice of Writing*. London: Elek.

Hennessey, Thomas. 1973. "From Jazz to Swing: Black Jazz Musicians and Their Music, 1917–1935." Ph.D. Dissertation, Department of History, Northwestern University.

Herskovits, Melville J. 1972. *Cultural Relativism*. New York: Random House.

Hinsley, Curtis M. 1981. *Savages and Scientists: The Smithsonian Institution and the Development of American Anthropology, 1846–1910*. Washington, DC: Smithsonian Institution Press.

Hinsley, Curtis M. 1983. "Ethnographic Charisma and Scientific Routine: Cushing and Fewkes in the American Southwest, 1879–1893." In *Observers Observed: Essays on Ethnographic Fieldwork*, ed. G. W. Stocking, Jr. Madison: University of Wisconsin Press, pp. 53–69.

Hirsch. E. 1977. *Starting Over*. Hanover, MA: Christopher.

Holstein, James A., and Jaber F. Gubrium. 2000. *Constructing the Life Course*. Second Edition. Dix Hills, NY: General Hall.

Holt, A. E. 1926. "Case Records as Data for Studying the Conditioning of Religious Experience by Social Factors." *American Journal of Sociology* 32:227–36.

Honigmann, John J. 1976. "The Personal Approach in Cultural Anthropological Research." *Current Anthropology* 17:243–51.

Horowitz, Irving L. 1967. *The Rise and Fall of Project Camelot*. Cambridge, MA: M.I.T. Press.

Horowitz, Ruth. 1985. *Honor and the American Dream: Culture and Identity in a Chicano Community*. New Brunswick, NJ: Rutgers University Press.

Horowitz, Ruth. 1986. "Remaining an Outsider: Membership as a Threat to Research Rapport." *Urban Life* 14:409–30.

Hughes, Everett C. 1971. *The Sociological Eye: Selected Papers*. Chicago: Aldine.

Humphreys, Laud. 1970/1975. *Tearoom Trade: Impersonal Sex in Public Places*. Chicago: Aldine.

Hunt, Jennifer. 1984. "The Development of Rapport through the Negotiation of Gender in Field Work among Police." *Human Organization* 45:283–96.

Hunt, Jennifer. 1985. "Police Accounts of Normal Force." *Urban Life* 13:315–41.

Hunt, Jennifer C. 1989. *Psychoanalytic Aspects of Fieldwork*. Newbury Park, CA: Sage.

Hutheesing, Otome K. 1993. "Facework of a Female Elder in a Lisu Field, Thailand." In *Gendered Fields: Women, Men and Ethnography*, ed. D. Bell, P. Caplan and W. J. Karim. London: Routledge & Kegan Paul, pp. 93–102.

Jackson, Jean. 1986. "On Trying to be an Amazon." In *Self, Sex and Gender in Cross-Cultural Fieldwork*, ed. T. L. Whitehead and M. E. Conaway. Urbana: University of Illinois Press.

Jackson, Jean. E. 1990a. "'Deja Entendu': The Liminal Qualities of Anthropological Fieldnotes." *Journal of Contemporary Ethnography* 19:8–43.

Jackson, Jean. E. 1990b. "'I Am a Fieldnote': Fieldnotes as a Symbol of Professional Identity." In *Fieldnotes: The Making of Anthropology*, ed. R. Sanjek. Ithaca, NY: Cornell University Press, pp. 3–33.

James, William. 1899. "On a Certain Blindness in Human Beings." In *Talks to Teachers of Psychology: And to Students of Some of Life's Ideals*. New York: Henry Holt, pp. 229–64.

James, William. 1970. *The Meaning of Truth: A Sequel to Pragmatism*. Ann Arbor: University of Michigan Press.

Janowitz, Morris. 1966. "Introduction." In W. I. Thomas, *On Social Organization and Social Personality*. Chicago: University of Chicago Press.

Jarvie, I. C. 1964. *The Revolution in Anthropology*. London: Routledge & Kegan Paul.

Jarvie, I. C. 1983. *Rationality and Relativism*. London: Routledge & Kegan Paul.

Johnson, John M. 1975. *Doing Field Research*. New York: Free Press.

Johnson, Norris Brock. 1986. "Ethnographic Research and Rites of Incorporation: A Sex and Gender-Based Comparison." In *Self, Sex and Gender in Cross-Cultural Fieldwork*, ed. T. L. Whitehead and M. E. Conaway. Urbana: University of Illinois Press, pp. 164–81.

John-Steiner, Vera. 1985. *Notebooks of the Mind: Explorations of Thinking*. New York: Harper and Row.

Johnstone, Barbara. 1990. *Stories, Community, and Place: Narratives from Middle America*. Bloomington: Indiana University Press.

Jules-Rosette, Bennetta. 1975. *Vision and Realities: Aspects of Ritual and Conversion in an African Church*. Ithaca: Cornell University Press.

Junker, Buford H. 1960. *Field Work: An Introduction to the Social Sciences*. Chicago: University of Chicago Press.

Kaplan, John, Jon. R. Waltz, and Roger Park. 1992. *Evidence: Cases and Materials*. Seventh Edition. Westbury, NY: The Foundation Press.

Karim, Wazir J. 1993. "With *Moyand Melur* in Carey Island: More Endangered, More Engendered." In *Gendered Fields: Women, Men and Ethnography*, ed. D. Bell, P. Caplan and W. J. Karim. London: Routledge & Kegan Paul, pp. 78–92.

Karp, Ivan, and Martha B. Kendall. 1982. "Reflexivity in Field Work." In *Explaining Human Behavior: Consciousness, Human Action and Social Structure*, ed. P. F. Secord. Beverly Hills, CA: Sage, pp. 249–73.

Katriel, Tamar. 1987. *"Bexibudim!"*: Ritualized Charing among Israeli Children." *Language and Society* 16:305–20.

Katz, Jack. 1975. "Essences as Moral Identities: On Verifiability and Responsibility in Imputations of Deviance and Charisma." *American Journal of Sociology* 80:1369–90.

Katz, Jack. 1977. "Cover-up and Collective Integrity." *Social Problems* 25:3–17.

Katz, Jack. 1982. *Poor People's Lawyers in Transition*. New Brunswick, NJ: Rutgers University Press.

Katz, Jack. 1983 . "A Theory of Qualitative Methodology." In *Contemporary Field Research*, ed. R. M. Emerson. Boston: Little, Brown, pp. 127–48.

Katz, Jack. 1988. *Seductions of Crime: Moral and Sensual Attractions in Doing Evil*. New York. Basic Books.

Katz, Jack. 1997. "Ethnography's Warrants." *Sociological Methods & Research* 25:391–423.

Katz, Jack. Forthcoming. "Analytic Induction." In *International Encyclopedia of the Social and Behavioral Sciences*, eds. N. J. Smelser and P. B. Baltes. New York: Elsevier Science.

Keating, Peter, ed. 1976. *Into Unknown England, 1866–1913: Selections from the Social Explorers*. Manchester, UK: Manchester University Press.

Kesey, Ken. 1962. *One Flew Over the Cuckoo's Nest*. New York: Viking Press.

Killian, Lewis M., and Sanford Bloomberg. 1975. "Rebirth in a Therapeutic Community: A Case Study." *Psychiatry* 38:39–54.

Kimball, Solon T., and William L. Partridge. 1979. *The Craft of Community Study: Fieldwork Dialogues*. Gainesville: University Presses of Florida.

King, Gary, Robert O. Keohane, and Sidney Verba. 1994. *Designing Social Inquiry*. Princeton, NJ: Princeton University Press.

Kitsuse, John I. 1980. "Coming Out All Over: Deviants and the Politics of Social Problems." *Social Problems* 28:1–13.

Klatch, Rebecca E. 1988. "The Methodological Problems of Studying a Politically Resistant Community." *Studies in Qualitative Methodology* 1:73–88.

Klein, Malcolm W. 1971. *Street Gangs and Street Workers*. Englewood Cliffs, NJ: Prentice-Hall.

Klein, Malcolm W. 1995. *The American Street Gang: Its Nature, Prevalence, and Control*. New York: Oxford University Press.

Kleinman, Sherryl. 1991. "Fieldworker's Feelings: What We Feel, Who We Are, How We Analyze." In *Experiencing Fieldwork*, ed. W. B. Shaffir and R. A. Stebbins. Newbury Park, CA: Sage, pp. 184–95.

Klockars, Carl B. 1977. "Field Ethics for the Life History." In *Street Ethnography*, ed. R. S. Weppner. Beverly Hills, CA: Sage, pp. 201–26.

Klockars, Carl B. 1979. "Dirty Hands and Deviant Subjects." In *Deviance and Decency: The Ethics of Research with Human Subjects*, ed. C. B. Klockars and F. W. O'Connor. Beverly Hills: Sage, pp. 261–82.

Kluckhohn, Florence. 1940. "The Participant Observer Technique in Small Communities." *American Journal of Sociology* 46:331–43.

Kneeland, Timothy, and Carol A. B. Warren. Forthcoming. *Pushbutton Psychiatry: A History of Electroshock in America*. Westport, CT: Greenwood Press.

Kolakowski, L. 1975. *Husserl and the Search for Certitude*. New Haven, CT: Yale University Press.

Kotlowitz, Alex. 1991. *There Are No Children Here*. New York: Doubleday.

Kondo, Dorinne K. 1982. "Work, Family and the Self: A Cultural Analysis of Japanese Family Enterprise." Ph.D. Dissertation, Department of Anthropology, Harvard University.

Kondo, Dorinne K. 1990. *Crafting Selves: Power, Gender, and Discourses of Identity in a Japanese Workplace*. Chicago: University of Chicago Press.

Kornhauser, Ruth R. 1978. *Social Sources of Delinquency: An Appraisal of Analytic Models.* Chicago: University of Chicago Press.

Krieger, Susan. 1979. *Hip Capitalism.* Beverly Hills, CA: Sage.

Krieger, Susan. 1983. *The Mirror Dance: Identity in a Women's Community.* Philadelphia: Temple University Press.

Krieger, Susan. 1991. *Social Science and the Self: Personal Essays on an Art Form.* New Brunswick, NJ: Rutgers University Press.

Kuhn, Thomas S. 1962/1970. *The Structure of Scientific Revolutions.* Chicago: University of Chicago Press.

Lamphere, Louise, Helena Ragone, and Patricia Zavella. 1997. *Situated Lives: Gender and Culture in Everyday Life.* New York: Routledge & Kegan Paul.

Landes, Ruth. 1986. "A Woman Anthropologist in Brazil." In *Women in the Field: Anthropological Experiences,* ed. P. Golde. Berkeley: University of California Press.

Latour, Bruno. 1987. *Science in Action.* Cambridge, MA: Harvard University Press.

Latour, Bruno. 1988. *The Pasteurization of France.* Translated by Alan Sheridan and John Law. Cambridge, MA: Harvard University Press.

Latour, Bruno. 1993. *We Have Never Been Modern.* Translated by Catherine Porter. Cambridge, MA: Harvard University Press.

Latour, Bruno, and Steve Woolgar. 1979. *Laboratory Life: The Construction of Scientific Facts.* Princeton, NJ: Princeton University Press.

Layder, Derek. 1982. "Grounded Theory: A Constructive Critique." *Journal for the Theory of Social Behaviour* 12:103–23.

Lazarsfeld, Paul F. 1972. "Some Remarks on Typological Procedures in Social Research." In *Continuities in the Language of Social Research,* ed. P. F. Lazarsfeld, A. K. Pasanella and M. Rosenberg. Glencoe, IL: Free Press.

Lazarsfeld, Paul F., and M. Rosenberg, eds. 1955. *The Language of Social Research.* Glencoe, IL: Free Press.

Leach, Edmund R. 1976. *Culture and Communication.* Cambridge, UK: Cambridge University Press.

Lebra, Takie. 1976. *Japanese Patterns of Behavior.* Honolulu: University of Hawaii Press.

Lederman, Rena. 1990. "Pretexts for Ethnography: On Reading Fieldnotes." In *Fieldnotes: The Making of Anthropology,* ed. R. E. Sanjek. Ithaca, NY: Cornell University Press, pp. 71–91.

Leiris, Michel. 1950. "L'Ethnographie devant le Colonialisme." *Les Temps Modernes* 58. Reprinted in Brisees, 125–45. Paris: Mercure de France, 1966.

Lemert, Edwin M. 1962. "Paranoia and the Dynamics of Exclusion." *Sociometry* 25:2–25.

Leo, Richard A. 1994a. "Police Interrogations in America: A Study of Violence, Civility, and Social Change. Ph.D. Dissertation, Program in Jurisprudence and Social Policy, University of California, Berkeley.

Leo, Richard A. 1994b. "The Sociologist as Detective: Reflections on the Methodology and Ethics of Fieldwork Inside the Police Interrogation Room." Paper presented to the Department of Sociology, University of California, Los Angeles, October 1994.

Leo, Richard A. 1995. "Trial and Tribulations: Courts, Ethnography and the Need for an Evidentiary Privilege for Academic Researchers." *The American Sociologist* 26:113–34.

Leo, Richard A. 1996. "The Ethics of Deceptive Research Roles Reconsidered: A Response to Kai Erikson." *The American Sociologist* 27:122–28.

Lévi-Strauss, Claude. 1995. *Saudades do Brasil.* Translated by Sylvia Modelski. Seattle, WA: University of Washington Press.

Levy, Charles J. 1968. *Voluntary Servitude: Whites in the Negro Movement.* New York: Appleton-Century-Crofts.

Lewis, Oscar. 1953. "Controls and Experiments in Field Work." In *Anthropology Today*, ed. A. L. Kroeber. Chicago: University of Chicago Press, pp. 452–75.

Liazos, Alexander. 1972. "The Poverty of the Sociology of Deviance: Nuts, Sluts, and Perverts." *Social Problems* 20:103–20.

Lieberson, Stanley. 1992. "Einstein, Renoir, and Greeley: Some Thoughts about Evidence in Sociology." *American Sociological Review* 57:1–15.

Liebow, Elliot. 1967. *Tally's Corner: A Study of Negro Streetcorner Men.* Boston: Little, Brown.

Liebow, Elliot. 1993. *Tell Them Who I Am: The Lives of Homeless Women.* New York: Penguin.

Lincoln, Yvonne S., and Egon G. Guba. 1985. *Naturalistic Inquiry.* Beverly Hills, CA: Sage.

Lindesmith, Alfred R. 1947. *Opiate Addiction.* Bloomington, IN: Principia Press.

Lindesmith, Alfred R. 1968. *Addiction and Opiates.* Chicago: Aldine.

Lipman, Samuel. 1979. "Theory for Two Hands." *New York Times* (December 2):26.

Livingston, Eric. 1986. *Ethnomethodological Foundations of Mathematics.* London, UK: Routledge & Kegan Paul.

Lofland, John. 1966. *Doomsday Cult: A Study of Conversion, Proselytization, and Maintenance of Faith.* Englewood Cliffs, NJ: Prentice-Hall.

Lofland, John. 1971. *Analyzing Social Settings: A Guide to Qualitative Observation and Analysis.* Belmont, CA: Wadsworth.

Lofland, John. 1972. "Editorial Introduction." *Urban Life and Culture* 1:3–5.

Lofland, John. 1974. "Styles of Reporting Qualitative Field Research." *American Sociologist* 9:101–11.

Lofland, John. 1976. *Doing Social Life: The Qualitative Study of Human Interaction in Natural Settings.* New York: Wiley.

Lofland, John. 1987. "Reflections on a Thrice-Named Journal." *Journal of Contemporary Ethnography* 16:25–40.

Lofland, John F., and Robert A. Lejeune. 1960. "Initial Interaction of Newcomers in Alcoholics Anonymous: A Field Experiment in Class Symbols and Socialization." *Social Problems* 8: 102–11.

Lofland, John, and Lyn H. Lofland. 1995. *Analyzing Social Settings: A Guide to Qualitative Observation and Analysis.* Third Edition. Belmont, CA: Wadsworth.

Lohman, Joseph D. 1937. "Participant-Observation in Community Studies." *American Sociological Review* 6:890–98.

Lomax, H., and N. Casey. 1998. "Recording Social Life: Reflexivity and Video Methodology." *Sociological Research Online*, v. 3, n. 2.

Loseke, Donileen R. 1992. *The Battered Woman and Shelters: The Social Construction of Wife Abuse.* Albany, NY: SUNY Press.

Ludlow, Fitz Hugh. 1857 [1975]. *The Hashish Eater*, ed. M. Horowitz. San Francisco: Level Press.

Luff, Donna. 1999. "Doing Social Research—Issues and Dilemmas." *Sociology* 33:678–703.

Luker, Kristin. 1975. *Taking Chances: Abortion and the Decision Not to Contracept.* Berkeley and Los Angeles: University of California Press.

Lundman, Richard J. 1974. "Routine Police Arrest Practices: A Commonweal Perspective." *Social Problems* 22: 127–41.

Lyman, Karen A. 1993. *Day In, Day Out with Alzheimer's: Stress in Caregiving Relationships.* Philadelphia: Temple University Press.

Lynch, Michael. 1985. *Art and Artifact in Laboratory Science: A Study of Shop Work and Shop Talk in a Research Laboratory.* London, UK: Routledge & Kegan Paul.

Lynch, Michael. 1993. *Scientific Practice and Ordinary Action: Ethnomethodology and the Social Studies of Science.* New York: Cambridge University Press.

Lynch, Michael, Eric Livingston, and Harold Garfinkel. 1983. "Temporal Order in Labora-
    tory Work." In *Science Observed: Perspectives on the Social Study of Science*, ed. K. Knorr-
    Cetina and M. Mulkay. London: Sage, pp. 205–38.
Macintyre, Martha. 1993. "Fictive Kinship or Mistaken Identity? Fieldwork on Tubetube
    Island, Papua New Guinea." In *Gendered Fields: Women, Men and Ethnography*, ed. D. Bell,
    P. Caplan and W. J. Karim. London: Routledge and Kegan Paul, pp. 44–62.
Malcolm, Janet. 1990. *The Journalist and the Murderer*. New York: Alfred A. Knopf.
Malinowski, Bronislaw. 1915/1988. "The Natives of Mailu." In *Malinowski among the Magi*, ed.
    M. W. Young. London: Routledge.
Malinowski, Bronislaw. 1922/1984. *Argonauts of the Western Pacific*. Prospect Heights, IL:
    Waveland Press.
Malinowski, Bronislaw. 1929/1987. *The Sexual Life of Savages in Northwestern Melanesia.* Lon-
    don: Harelock Ellis.
Malinowski, Bronislaw. 1935/1965. *Coral Gardens and Their Magic*. Bloomington: Indiana
    University Press.
Malinowski, Bronislaw. 1967. *A Diary in the Strict Sense of the Term*. New York: Harcourt,
    Brace and World.
Mandell, Nancy. 1988. "The Least-Adult Role in Studying Children." *Journal of Contempo-
    rary Ethnography* 16:433–67.
Mann, Kenneth. 1985. *Defending White-Collar Crime*. New Haven, CT: Yale University Press.
Manning, Peter K. 1972. "Observing the Police: Deviants, Respectables and the Law." In
    Research on Deviance, ed. J. Douglas. New York: Random House, pp. 213–68.
Manning, Peter K. 1982. "Analytic Induction." In *Handbook of Social Science Methods: Qualita-
    tive Methods*, ed. R. B. Smith and P. K. Manning. Cambridge, MA: Ballinger.
Maquet, Jacques. 1964. "Objectivity in Anthropology." *Current Anthropology* 5:47–55.
Marcus, George E. 1980. "Rhetoric and the Ethnographic Genre in Anthropological
    Research." *Current Anthropology* 21:507–10.
Marcus, George E. 1994. "What Comes (Just) After 'Post'? The Case of Ethnography." In
    Handbook of Qualitative Research, ed. N. K. Denzin and Y. S. Lincoln. Thousand Oaks,
    CA: Sage, pp. 563–74.
Marcus, George E. 1998. *Ethnography Through Thick and Thin*. Princeton, NJ: Princeton Uni-
    versity Press.
Marcus, George E., and Dick Cushman. 1982. "Ethnographies as Texts." *Annual Review of
    Anthropology* 11:25–69.
Marcus, George, and Michael Fisher. 1986. *Anthropology as Cultural Critique*. Chicago: Uni-
    versity of Chicago Press
Mark, Joan. 1988. *A Stranger in her Native Land: Alice Fletcher and the American Indians*. Lincoln,
    NE: University of Nebraska Press.
Marquart, James W. 1986. "Doing Research in Prison: The Strengths and Weaknesses of
    Participation as a Guard." *Justice Quarterly* 3:15–32.
Marx, Gary T. 1984. "Notes on the Discovery, Collection and Assessment of Hidden and
    Dirty Data." In *Studies in the Sociology of Social Problems*, ed. J. W. Schneider and J. I. Kit-
    suse. Norwood: Ablex Publishing.
Mascia-Lees, Frances E., Patricia Sharpe, and Collen Ballerino Cohen. 1989. "The Postmod-
    ernist Turn in Anthropology: Cautions from a Femininst Perspective." *Signs* 15:7–33.
Matza, David. 1969. *Becoming Deviant*. Englewood Cliffs, NJ: Prentice-Hall.
Maybury-Lewis, David. 1965. *The Savage and the Innocent*. London: Evans.
Maykovich, Minado Murokawa. 1977. "The Difficulties of a Minority Researcher in
    Minority Communities." *Journal of Social Issues* 33:108–19.

McCall, George J., and J. L. Simmons, eds. 1969. *Issues in Participant Observation: A Text and Reader*. Reading, MA: Addison-Wesley.

McCall, Michal, and Howard S. Becker. 1990. "Performance Science." *Social Problems* 37:117–32.

McCurdy, David W. 1976. "The Medicine Man." In *Ethics and Anthropology Dilemmas in Fieldwork*, ed. M. A. Rynkiewich and J. P. Spradley. New York: Wiley.

McKeganey, Neil, and Michael Bloor. 1991. "Spotting the Invisible Man: The Influence of Male Gender on Fieldwork Relations." *British Journal of Sociology* 42:195–210.

McKinney, John C. 1966. *Constructive Typology and Social Theory*. New York: Appleton-Century-Crofts.

Mead, Margaret. 1928. *Coming of Age in Samoa: A Psychological Study of Primitive Youth for Western Civilization*. New York: Mentor.

Mead, Margaret. 1949. *The Mountain Arapesh V. The Record of Unabelin with Rorschach Analysis*. New York: Anthropological Papers of the American Museum of Natural History 41 (Part 3).

Mead, Margaret. 1986. "Field Work in Pacific Islands." In *Women in the Field: Anthropological Experiences*, ed. P. Golde. Berkeley: University of California Press, pp. 293–331.

Mehan, Hugh. 1979. *Learning Lessons: Social Organization in the Classroom*. Cambridge, MA: Harvard University Press.

Mehan, Hugh, and Houston Wood. 1975. *The Reality of Ethnomethodology*. New York: Wiley.

Merton, Robert K. 1957. *Social Theory and Social Structure*. Glencoe, IL: Free Press.

Milgram, Stanley. 1965. "Some Conditions of Obedience and Disobedience to Authority." *Human Relations* 18:57–76.

Miller, Alice. 1983. *The Drama of the Gifted Child*. New York: Basic Books.

Miller, S. M. 1952. "The Participant Observer and 'Over-Rapport'." *American Sociological Review* 17:97–99.

Millman, Marcia. 1977. *The Unkindest Cut: Life in the Backrooms of Medicine*. New York: Morrow.

Mills, C. Wright. 1963. "The Professional Ideology of Social Pathologists." In *Power, Politics and People*, ed. I. L. Horowitz. New York: Ballantine, pp. 523–52.

Mishler, Elliot G. 1979a. "Meaning in Context: Is There Any Other Kind?" *Harvard Educational Review* 49:1–19.

Mishler, Elliot G. 1979b. "'Wou' You Trade Cookies with the Popcorn?' Talk of Trades among Six Year Olds." In *Language, Culture and Society*, ed. O. Garnica and M. King. Oxford: Pergamon, pp. 221–36.

Miyoshi, Masao. 1988. "Against the Native Grain: The Japanese Novel and the 'Postmodern' West." *South Atlantic Quarterly* 87:525–50.

Moeran, Brian. 1985. *Okubu Diary: Portrait of a Japanese Valley*. Stanford: Stanford University Press.

Moeran, Brian. 1990. "Beating about the Brush: An Example of Ethnographic Writing from Japan." In *Localizing Strategies: Regional Traditions of Ethnographic Writing*, ed. R. Fardon. Edinburgh: Scottish Academic Press, pp. 339–57.

Moerman, Michael. 1969. "A Little Knowledge." In *Cognitive Anthropology*, ed. S. A. Tyler. New York: Holt, Rinehart and Winston, pp. 449–69.

Morgan, David. 1988. *Focus Groups*. Beverly Hills, CA: Sage.

Moore, Joan. 1977. "A Case Study of Collaboration: The Chicano Pinto Research Project." *Journal of Social Issues* 33:144–58.

Morrill, Calvin. 1995. *The Executive Way: Conflict Management in Corporations*. Chicago: University of Chicago Press.

Moston, Stephen, Geoffrey M. Stephenson, and Thomas M. Williamson. 1992. "The Effects of Case Characteristics on Suspect Behavior During Police Questioning." *British Journal of Criminology* 32:23–40.

Muir, William. 1977. *Police: Streetcorner Politicians.* Chicago: University of Chicago Press.

Mulkay, Michael. 1985. *The Word and the World: Explorations in the Form of Sociological Analysis.* London: George Allen & Unwin.

Myerhoff, Barbara. 1989. "'So What Do You Want from Us Here?'" In *In the Field: Readings on the Field Research Experience,* ed. C. D. Smith and W. Kornblum. New York: Praeger, pp. 83–90.

Myers, James. 1992. "Nonmainstream Body Modification: Genital Piercing, Branding, Burning, and Cutting." *Journal of Contemporary Ethnography* 21:267–306.

Nader, Laura. 1969. "Up the Anthropologist—Perspectives Gained from Studying Up." In *Reinventing Anthropology,* ed. D. Hymes. New York: Vintage, pp. 284–311.

Nader, Laura. 1986. "From Anguish to Exultation." In *Women in the Field: Anthropological Experiences,* ed. P. Golde. Berkeley: University of California Press, pp. 97–116.

Naroll, Raoul. 1967. "Native Concepts and Cross-Cultural Surveys." *American Anthropologist* 69: 511–12.

Nash, Dennison, and R. Wintrob. 1972. "The Emergence of Self-Consciousness in Ethnography." *Current Anthropology* 13:527–42.

Nelson, Robert L. 1988. *Partners with Power: The Social Transformation of the Large Law Firm.* Berkeley: University of California Press.

Obeyesekere, Gananath. 1992. *The Apotheosis of James Cook: European Mythmaking in the Pacific.* Princeton, NJ: Princeton University Press.

Oboler, Regina. S. 1986. "For Better or Worse: Anthropologists and Husbands in the Field." In *Self, Sex and Gender in Cross-Cultural Fieldwork,* ed. T. L. Whitehead and M. E. Conaway. Urbana: University of Illinois Press, pp. 28–51.

Ohnuki-Tierney, Emiko. 1984. "'Native' Anthropologists." *American Ethnologist* 11:584–86.

Okimoto, Daniel. 1971. *An American in Disguise.* New York: Weatherhill.

Ostrander, Susan A. 1984. *Women of the Upper Class.* Philadelphia: Temple University Press.

Ostrander, Susan A. 1993. "'Surely You're Not in This Just to Be Helpful': Access, Rapport, and Interviews in Three Studies of Elites." *Journal of Contemporary Ethnography* 22:7–27.

Paget, Marianne A. 1990. "Performing the Text." *Journal of Contemporary Ethnography* 19:136–55.

Paley, Vivian G. 1986. "On Listening to What the Children Say." *Harvard Education Review* 56:122–31.

Palmer, Richard E. 1969. *Hermeneutics: Interpretation Theory in Schleiermacher, Dilthey, Heidigger, and Gadamer.* Evanston, IL: Northwestern University Press.

Paredes, Americo. 1977. "On Ethnographic Work among Minority Groups: A Folklorist's Perspective." *New Scholar* 6:1–53.

Park, Robert E. 1915/1952. "The City: Suggestions for the Investigation of Human Behavior in the Urban Environment." In *Human Communities: The City and Human Ecology.* Glencoe, IL: Free Press.

Park, Robert E. 1950. *Race and Culture.* Glencoe, IL: Free Press.

Parsons, Carole W. 1972. *America's Uncounted People: A Report of the National Research Council Advisory Committee on Problems of Census Enumeration.* Washington, DC: National Academy of Sciences.

Paul, Benjamin D. 1953. "Interview Techniques and Field Relationships." In *Anthropology Today,* ed. A. L. Kroeber. Chicago: University of Chicago Press, pp. 430–51.

Peneff, Jean. 1988. "The Observers Observed: French Survey Researchers at Work." *Social Problems* 35:520–35.

Peshkin, Alan. 1986. *God's Choice: The Total World of a Fundamentalist Christian School*. Chicago: University of Chicago Press.

Pike, Kenneth L. 1954/1967. *Language in Relation to a Unified Theory of the Structure of Human Behavior*, Part I. Second Edition. The Hague: Mouton.

Plath, David W. 1980. *Long Engagements*. Stanford: Stanford University Press.

Platt, Jennifer. 1981. "On Interviewing One's Peers." *British Journal of Sociology* 32:75–91.

Platt, Jennifer. 1983. "The Development of the 'Participant Observation' Method in Sociology: Origin Myth and History." *Journal of the History of the Behavioral Sciences* 19:379–93.

Platt, Jennifer. "Theory and Practice in the Development of Sociological Methodology." Unpublished ms.

Polkinghorne, Donald E. 1988. *Narrative Knowing and the Human Sciences*. Albany, NY: SUNY Press.

Pollner, Melvin, and Robert M. Emerson. 1983. "The Dynamics of Inclusion and Distance in Fieldwork Relations." In *Contemporary Field Research: A Collection of Readings*, ed. R. M. Emerson. Boston: Little, Brown, pp. 235–52.

Pollner, Melvin, and Robert M. Emerson. 2001. "Ethnomethodology and Ethnography." In *Handbook of Ethnography*, ed. P. Atkinson, A. Coffey, S. Delamont, L. H. Lofland and J. Lofland. London: Sage, pp. 118–35.

Polsky, Ned. 1967. *Hustlers, Beats, and Others*. Chicago: Aldine.

Polya, George. 1954. *Mathematics and Plausible Reasoning*. Princeton, NJ: Princeton University Press.

Popper, Karl R. 1968. *The Logic of Scientific Discovery*. New York: Harper and Row.

Powdermaker, Hortense. 1939. *After Freedom: A Cultural Study in the Deep South*. New York: Viking Press.

Powdermaker, Hortense. 1966. *Stranger and Friend: The Way of an Anthropologist*. New York: Norton.

Prus, Robert A. 1987. "Generic Social Processes: Maximizing Conceptual Development in Ethnographic Research." *Journal of Contemporary Ethnography* 16:250–93.

Prus, Robert. 1996. *Symbolic Interaction and Ethnographic Research: Intersubjectivity and the Study of Human Lived Experience*. Albany, NY: SUNY Press.

Punch, Maurice. 1986. *The Politics and Ethics of Fieldwork*. Beverly Hills, CA: Sage.

Rabinow, Paul. 1977. *Reflections on Fieldwork in Morocco*. Berkeley: University of California Press.

Ragin, Charles C. 1994. *Constructing Social Research: The Unity and Diversity of Method*. Thousand Oaks, CA: Pine Forge Press.

Ratner, Mitchell S. 1993. *Crack Pipe as Pimp: An Ethnographic Investigation of Sex-for-Crack Exchanges*. New York: Lexington Books.

Ray, Marsh B. 1964. "The Cycle of Abstinence and Relapse among Heroin Addicts." In *The Other Side: Perspectives on Deviance*, ed. H. S. Becker. New York: Free Press, pp. 163–77.

Read, Kenneth E. 1965. *The High Valley*. New York: Scribner.

Redfield, Robert. 1930. *Tepoztlan—A Mexican Village*. Chicago: University of Chicago Press.

Redfield, Robert. 1941. *The Folk Culture of Yucatan*. Chicago: University of Chicago Press.

Redfield, Robert. 1953. *The Primitive World and Its Transformations*. Chicago: University of Chicago Press.

Reiner, Robert. 1985. *The Politics of the Police*. New York: St. Martin's Press.

Reinharz, Shulamit. 1979. *On Becoming a Social Scientist: From Survey Research and Participant Observation to Experiential Analysis*. San Francisco: Jossey-Bass.

Reinharz, Shulamit. 1992. *Feminist Methods in Social Research*. New York: Oxford University Press.

Reiss, Albert J., Jr. 1968. "Police Brutality—Answers to Key Questions." *Transaction* 5:10–19.

Reiss, Albert J., Jr. 1971. *The Police and the Public*. New Haven, CT: Yale University Press.

Reiss, Albert J., Jr. 1985. *Policing a City's Central District: The Laconia Story*. Washington, DC: U.S. Department of Justice, National Institute of Justice.

Rex, J., and R. Moore. 1967. *Race, Community and Conflict*. London: Oxford University Press.

Rich, Adrienne. 1995. *Of Woman Born: Motherhood as Experience and Institution*. New York: W. W. Norton.

Richardson, James T., Mary W. Stewart, and Robert B. Simmonds. 1978. "Researching a Fundamentalist Commune." In *Understanding the New Religions*, ed. J. Needleman and G. Baker. New York: Seabury Press.

Richardson, Laura. 1990a. "Narrative and Sociology." *Journal of Contemporary Ethnography* 19:116–35.

Richardson, Laura. 1990b. *Writing Strategies: Reaching Diverse Audiences*. Newbury Park, CA: Sage.

Richardson, Laura. 1991. "Postmodern Social Theory." *Sociological Theory* 9:173–79.

Richardson, Laura. 1992a. "The Consequences of Poetic Representation: Writing the Other, Writing the Self." In *Investigating Subjectivity: Research on Lived Experience*, ed. C. Ellis and M. G. Flaherty. Newbury Park, CA: Sage, pp. 125–37.

Richardson, Laura. 1992b. "Trash on the Corner: Ethics and Technology." *Journal of Contemporary Ethnography* 21:103–19.

Richardson, Laura. 1994. "Writing: A Method of Inquiry." In *Handbook of Qualitative Research*, ed. N. K. Denzin and Y. S. Lincoln. Thousand Oaks, CA: Sage, pp. 516–29.

Rickert, H. 1986/1902. *The Limits of Concept Formation in Natural Science*. Cambridge, UK: Cambridge University Press.

Ricouer, Paul. 1971. "The Model of the Text: Meaningful Action Considered as a Text." *Social Research* 38:529–62.

Rieder, Jonathan. 1985. *Canarsie: the Jews and Italians of Brooklyn against Liberalism*. Cambridge, MA: Harvard University Press.

Riemer, Jeffrey W. 1977. "Varieties of Opportunistic Research." *Urban Life* 5:467–77.

Riessman, Catherine K. 1987. "When Gender is not Enough: Women Interviewing Women." *Gender and Society* 1:172–207.

Riessman, Catherine. 1990. *Divorce Talk*. New Brunswick, NJ: Rutgers University Press.

Riessman, Catherine. 1993. *Narrative Analysis*. Thousand Oaks, CA: Sage.

Rivers, W. H. R. 1913. "Report on Anthropological Research outside America." In Rivers et al., *Reports upon the Present Condition and Future Needs of the Science of Anthropology*. Washington, DC, pp. 5–28.

Robbins, Thomas, Dick Anthony, and Thomas E. Curtis. 1973. "The Limits of Symbolic Realism: Problems of Empathetic Field Observation in a Sectarian Context." *Journal for the Scientific Study of Religion* 12:259–71.

Robillard, Albert B. 1999. *Meaning of a Disability: The Lived Experience of Paralysis*. Philadelphia: Temple University Press.

Rochford, E. Burke. 1985. *Hare Krishna in America*. New Brunswick, NJ: Rutgers University Press.

Rochford, E. Burke. 1989. "Factionalism, Group Defection, and Schism in the Hare Krishna Movement." *Journal for the Scientific Study of Religion* 28:162–79.

Rochford, E. Burke. 1992. "The Politics of Member Validation: Taking Findings Back to Hare Krishna." In *Perspectives on Social Problems, Volume 3*, ed. G. Miller and J. A. Holstein. Greenwich, CT: JAI Press, pp. 99–116.

Rochford, E. Burke. 1994. "Field Work and Membership in the Hare Krishna." In *Constructions of Deviance: Social Power, Context and Interaction*, ed. P. A. Adler and P. Adler. Belmont, CA: Wadsworth, pp. 56–67.

Rock, Paul. 1979. *The Making of Symbolic Interactionism.* Totowa, NJ: Roman and Littlefield.

Rohner, Ronald P. 1966. "Franz Boas: Ethnographer on the Northwest Coast." In *Pioneers of American Anthropology*, ed. J. Helm. Seattle: University of Washington Press.

Ronai, Carol R. 1992. "The Reflexive Self Through Narrative: A Night in the Life of an Erotic Dancer/Researcher." In *Investigating Subjectivity: Research on Lived Experience*, ed. C. Ellis and M. G. Flaherty. Newbury Park, CA: Sage, pp. 102–24.

Rosenau, Pauline M. 1992. *Post-Modernism and the Social Sciences: Insights, Inroads, and Intrusions.* Princeton, NJ: Princeton University Press.

Rosenhan, David L. 1973. "On Being Sane in Insane Places." *Science* 179:250–58.

Roth, Julius A. 1962. "Comments on 'Secret Observation'" *Social Problems* 9: 282–84.

Rothstein, Edward. 1979. "Winging it on the Keys." *New York Times* (April 19):12, 51.

Sahlins, Marshall. 1995. *How "Natives" Think: About Captain Cook, for Example.* Chicago: University of Chicago Press.

Said, Edward W. 1979. *Orientalism.* New York: Vintage.

Sanchez Jankowski, Martin. 1991. *Islands in the Street: Gangs and American Urban Society.* Berkeley and Los Angeles: University of California Press.

Sandstrom, Kent L. 1990. "Confronting Deadly Disease: The Drama of Identity Construction among Gay Men with AIDS." *Journal of Contemporary Ethnography* 19:271–94.

Sanjek, Roger, ed. 1990a. *Fieldnotes: The Making of Anthropology.* Ithaca, NY: Cornell University Press.

Sanjek, Roger. 1990b. "A Vocabulary for Fieldnotes." In *Fieldnotes: The Making of Anthropology*, ed. R. Sanjek. Ithaca, NY: Cornell University Press, pp. 92–121.

Sanjek, Roger. 1990c. "On Ethnographic Validity." In *Fieldnotes: The Making of Anthropology*, ed. R. Sanjek. Ithaca, NY: Cornell University Press, pp. 385–418.

Saunders, Frances S. 1999. *The Cultural Cold War: The CIA and the World of Arts and Letters.* New York: New Press.

Scarce, Rik. 1994. "(No) Trial (But) Tribulation: When Courts and Ethnography Conflict." *Journal of Contemporary Ethnography* 23:123–49.

Schachtel, Ernest G. 1959. *Metamorphosis.* New York: Basic Books.

Schatzman, Leonard, and Anselm L. Strauss. 1973. *Field Research: Strategies for a Natural Sociology.* Englewood Cliffs, NJ: Prentice-Hall.

Schegloff, Emanuel A. 1987. "Between Micro and Macro: Contexts and Other Connections." In *The Micro-Macro Link*, ed. J. C. Alexander, B. Biesen, R. Munch, and N. J. Smelser. Berkeley and Los Angeles: University of California Press, pp. 207–34.

Schutz, Alfred. 1962. *Collected Papers, Vol. 1: The Problem of Social Reality*, ed. M. Natanson. The Hague: Martinus Nijhoff.

Schutz, Alfred. 1964. *Collected Papers, Vol. 11: Studies in Social Theory*, ed. M. Natanson. The Hague: Martinus Nijhoff.

Schutz, Alfred. 1970. *Reflections on the Problem of Relevance*, ed. R. Zaner. New Haven, CT: Yale University Press.

Schutz, Alfred, and Thomas Luckmann. 1974. *The Structures of the Life-World.* London: Heineman.

Schwartz, Gary, and Don Merten. 1971. "Participant Observation and the Discovery of Meaning." *Philosophy of the Social Sciences* 1:279–98.

Schwartz, Howard, and Jerry Jacobs. 1979. *Qualitative Sociology: A Method to the Madness.* New York: Free Press.

Schwartz, Morris S., and Charlotte G. Schwartz. 1955. "Problems in Participant Observation." *American Journal of Sociology* 60:343–54.

Seidman, Irving. 1991. *Interviewing as Qualitative Research: A Guide for Researchers in Education and the Social Sciences.* New York: Teachers College Press.

Shaffir, William B., and Robert A. Stebbins, eds. 1991. *Experiencing Fieldwork: An Inside View of Qualitative Research.* Newbury Park, CA: Sage.

Shaw, Clifford R. 1931. *The Natural History of a Delinquent Career.* Chicago: University of Chicago Press.

Shils, Edward A. 1975. *Center and Periphery: Essays in Macrosociology.* Chicago: University of Chicago Press.

Silverman, David. 2000. *Doing Qualitative Research: A Practical Handbook.* Thousand Oaks, CA: Sage.

Silverman, David, and Jaber F. Gubrium. 1989. "Introduction." In *The Politics of Field Research: Sociology Beyond Enlightenment,* ed. J. F. Gubrium and D. Silverman. London: Sage, pp. 1–12.

Simon, David. 1991. *Homicide: A Year on the Killing Streets.* Boston: Houghton Mifflin.

Skolnick, Jerome H. 1966. *Justice without Trial: Law Enforcement in Democratic Society.* New York: Wiley.

Skolnick, Jerome H., and Richard A. Leo. 1992. "The Ethics of Deceptive Investigation." *Criminal Justice Ethics* 11:3–12.

Sluckin, Andy. 1981. *Growing Up in the Playground: The Social Development of Children.* London: Routledge & Kegan Paul.

Smith, Charles W. 1981. *The Mind of the Market: A Study of Stock Market Philosophies, Their Uses and Implications.* Totowa, NJ: Rowman and Littlefield.

Smith, Dorothy E. 1988. *The Everyday World as Problematic.* Toronto: University of Toronto Press.

Smith, J. K. 1984. "The Problem of Criteria for Judging Interpretive Inquiry." *Educational Evaluation and Policy Analysis* 6:379–91.

Smith, J. K. 1989. *The Nature of Social and Educational Inquiry: Empiricism versus Interpretation.* Norwood, NJ: Ablex.

Smith, J. K., and L. Heshusius. 1986. "Closing Down the Conversation: The End of the Quantitative-Qualitative Debate among Educational Inquirers." *Educational Researcher* 15:4–12.

Smith, Robert J. 1983. *Japanese Society: Tradition, Self, and the Social Order.* Cambridge, UK: Cambridge University Press.

Snow, David A., 1980. "The Disengagement Process: A Neglected Problem in Participant Observation Research." *Qualitative Sociology* 3:100–22.

Snow, David A., and Leon Anderson. 1993. *Down on Their Luck: A Study of Homeless Street People.* Berkeley and Los Angeles: University of California Press.

Snow, David A. and Calvin Morrill. 1993. "Reflections on Anthropology's Ethnographic Crisis of Faith." *Contemporary Sociology* 22:8–11.

Snow, David A., Robert D. Benford, and Leon Anderson. 1986. "Fieldwork Roles and Information Yield: A Comparison of Alternative Settings and Roles." *Urban Life* 14:377–408.

Sontag, Susan. 1966. "The Anthropologist as Hero." In *Against Interpretation: Other Essays.* New York: Dell, pp. 69–81.

Speier, Matthew. 1976. "The Adult Ideological Viewpoint in Studies of Childhood." In *Rethinking Childhood,* ed. A. Skolnick. Boston: Little, Brown, pp. 168–86.

Spencer, Walter B., and Frank Gillen. 1899/1968. *The Native Tribes of Central Australia.* New York: Dover.

Spradley, James P., and Brenda J. Mann. 1975. *The Cocktail Waitress: Woman's Work in a Man's World.* New York: Alfred A. Knopf.

Stacey, Judith. 1990. *Brave New Families: Stories of Domestic Upheaval in Late Twentieth Century America.* New York: Basic Books.

Stacey, Judith. 1991. "Can There Be a Feminist Ethnography?" In *Women's Words*, ed. S. B. Gluck and D. Patai. New York: Routledge, pp. 111–19.

Stack, Carol. 1974. *All Our Kin: Strategies for Survival in a Black Community*. New York: Harper and Row.

Stern, J. P. 1973. *On Realism*. London: Routledge & Kegan Paul.

Stocking, George W., Jr. 1988. "Before the Falling Out: W.H.R. Rivers on the Relation between Anthropology and Mission Work." *History of Anthropology Newsletter* 15:3–8.

Stocking, George W., Jr. 1992. *The Ethnographer's Magic and Other Essays in the History of Anthropology*. Madison: University of Wisconsin Press.

Stoddard, Kenneth. 1986. "The Presentation of Everyday Life: Some Textual Strategies for 'Adequate Ethnography'." *Urban Life* 15:103–21.

Stone, Gregory P. 1962. "Appearance and the Self." In *Human Behavior and Social Processes: An Interactionist Approach*, ed. A. M. Rose. Boston: Houghton Mifflin, pp. 86–118.

Strauss, Anselm. 1987. *Qualitative Analysis for Social Scientists*. New York: Cambridge University Press.

Strauss, Anselm, and Juliet Corbin. 1990. *Basics of Qualitative Research: Grounded Theory Procedures and Techniques*. Newbury Park, CA: Sage.

Strauss, Anselm, and Juliet Corbin. 1994. "Grounded Theory Methodology: An Overview." In *Handbook of Qualitative Research*, ed. N. K. Denzin and Y. S. Lincoln. Newbury Park, CA: Sage, pp. 273–85.

Strauss, Anselm, and Juliet Corbin, eds. 1997. *Grounded Theory in Practice*. Thousand Oaks, CA: Sage.

Strauss, Anselm, S. Fagerhaugh, B. Suczek, and C. Wiener. 1985. *The Social Organization of Medical Work*. Chicago: University of Chicago Press.

Strauss, Anselm, and Barney G. Glaser. 1970. *Anguish*. Mill Valley, CA: Sociology Press.

Styles, Joseph. 1979. "Insider/Outsider: Researching Gay Baths." *Urban Life* 8:135–52.

Sudarkasa, Niara. 1986. "In a World of Women: Field Work in a Yoruba Community." In *Women in the Field: Anthropological Experiences*, ed. P. Golde. Berkeley: University of California Press, pp. 167–91.

Sudnow, David N. 1967. *Passing On: The Social Organization of Dying*. Englewood Cliffs, NJ: Prentice Hall.

Sudnow, David N. 1978. *Ways of the Hand: the Organization of Improvised Conduct*. Cambridge, MA: Harvard University Press.

Sudnow, David N. 1979. *Talk's Body: A Meditation Between Two Keyboards*. New York: Alfred A. Knopf.

Sudnow, David N. 1983. *Pilgrim in the Microworld*. New York: Warner Books.

Sullivan, Mortimer, Stuart Queen, and Ralph Patrick, Jr. 1958. "Participant Observation as Employed in the Study of a Military Training Program." *American Sociological Review* 23:660–67.

Suppe, Frederick, ed. 1974. *The Structure of Scientific Theories*. Urbana: University of Illinois Press.

Suttles, Gerald D. 1968. *The Social Order of the Slum*. Chicago: University of Chicago Press.

Sykes, Gresham. 1958. *The Society of Captives*. Princeton, NJ: Princeton University Press.

Taylor, Steven J. 1991. "Leaving the Field: Research, Relationships, and Responsibilities." In *Experiencing Fieldwork: An Inside View of Qualitative Research*, ed. W. B. Shaffir and R. A. Stebbins. Newbury Park, CA: Sage, pp. 238–47.

Tennekes, J. 1971. *Anthropology, Relativism and Method*. Assen, The Netherlands: Van Gorcum.

Thomas, Robert J. 1993. "Interviewing Important People in Big Companies." *Journal of Contemporary Ethnography* 22:80–96.

Thomas, William I. 1923/1967. *The Unadjusted Girl*. New York: Harper and Row.

Thomas, William I., and Florian Znaniecki. 1917. *The Polish Peasant in Europe and America*. Chicago: University of Chicago Press.

Thorne, Barrie. 1975a. "Women in the Draft Resistance Movement: A Case Study of Sex Roles and Social Movements." *Sex Roles* 1:179–95.

Thorne, Barrie. 1975b. "Protest and the Problem of Credibility: Uses of Knowledge and Risk-taking in the Draft Resistance Movement of the 1960s." *Social Problems* 23:111–23.

Thorne, Barrie. 1980. "'You Still Takin' Notes?' Fieldwork and Problems of Informed Consent." *Social Problems* 27:284–97.

Thorne, Barrie. 1983. "Political Activist as Participant Observer: Conflicts of Commitment in a Study of the Draft Resistance Movement of the 1960s." In *Contemporary Field Research: A Collection of Readings*, ed. R. M. Emerson. Boston: Little, Brown, pp. 216–34.

Thorne, Barrie. 1993. *Gender Play: Girls and Boys in School*. New Brunswick, NJ: Rutgers University Press.

Thornton, Kelly. 1993. "Police Review Ways They Interrogate in Wake of Court's Slap." *San Diego Union Tribune*, July 28.

Thrasher, Frederic M. 1927/1963. *The Gang: A Study of 1,313 Gangs in Chicago*. Chicago: University of Chicago Press.

Timmermans, Stefan. 1995. "Cui Bono? Institutional Review Board Ethics and Ethnographic Research." *Studies in Symbolic Interaction* 19:153–73.

Todorov, Tzvetan. 1968. "Introduction, Le Vraisemblable." *Communications* 11:1–4.

Tuchman, Gaye, and Harry Gene Levine. 1993. "New York Jews and Chinese Food: The Social Construction of an Ethnic Pattern." *Journal of Contemporary Ethnography* 22:382–407.

Turnbull, Colin M. 1986. "Sex and Gender: The Role of Subjectivity in Field Research." In *Self, Sex and Gender in Cross-Cultural Fieldwork*, ed. T. L. Whitehead and M. E. Conaway. Urbana: University of Illinois Press, pp. 17–27.

Turner, Ralph H. 1947. "The Navy Disbursing Officer as a Bureaucrat." *American Sociological Review* 12:342-48.

Turner, Ralph H. 1953. "The Quest for Universals in Sociological Research." *American Sociological Review* 18 :604–11.

Tyler, Stephen A. 1985. "Ethnography, Intertextuality, and the End of Description." *American Journal of Semiotics* 3:83–98.

Tyler, Stephen A. 1986. "Post-Modern Ethnography: From Document of the Occult to Occult Document." In *Writing Culture: The Poetics and Politics of Ethnography*, ed. J. Clifford and G. Marcus. Berkeley: University of California Press, pp. 122–40.

Valentine, Charles A., and Betty Lou Valentine. 1970. "Making the Scene, Digging the Action, and Telling It Like It Is: Anthropologists at Work in a Dark Ghetto." In *Afro-American Anthropology: Contemporary Perspectives*, ed. N. E. Whitten, Jr., and J. F. Szwed. New York: Free Press.

Van Maanen, John. 1978. "On Watching the Watchers." In *Policing: A View From the Streets*, ed. P. K. Manning and J. Van Maanen. Pacific Palisades, CA: Goodyear, pp. 309–49.

Van Maanen, John. 1983. "The Moral Fix: On the Ethics of Fieldwork." In *Contemporary Field Research*, ed. R. M. Emerson. Boston: Little, Brown, pp. 269–87.

Van Maanen, John. 1988. *Tales of the Field: On Writing Ethnography*. Chicago: University of Chicago Press.

Van Zandt, David E. 1991. *Living in the Children of God*. Princeton, NJ: Princeton University Press.

Vaughan, Diane. 1992. "Theory Elaboration: The Heuristics of Case Analysis." In *What Is a Case? Exploring the Foundations of Social Inquiry*, ed. C. C. Ragin and H. S. Becker. Cambridge: Cambridge University Press, pp. 173–202.

Vera-Sanso, Penny. 1993. "Perception, East and West: A Madras Encounter." In *Gendered Fields: Women, Men and Ethnography*, ed. D. Bell, P. Caplan and W. J. Karim. London: Routledge & Kegan Paul, pp. 159–67.

Vidich, Arthur J. 1955. "Participant Observation and the Collection and Interpretation of Data." *American Sociological Review* 60:354–60.

Vidich, Arthur J. 1992. "Boston's North End: An American Epic." *Journal of Contemporary Ethnography* 21:80–102.

Vidich, Arthur J., and Joseph Bensman. 1954. "The Validity of Field Data." *Human Organization* 13:20–27.

Vidich, Arthur J., and Joseph Bensman. 1958. *Small Town in Mass Society: Class, Power and Religion in a Rural Community*. Revised Edition (1968). Princeton, NJ: Princeton University Press.

Vidich, Arthur J., and Joseph Bensman. 1964. "The Springdale Case: Academic Bureaucrats and Sensitive Townspeople." In *Reflections on Community Studies*, ed. A. J. Vidich, J. Bensman, and M. R. Stein. New York: Wiley, pp. 313–49.

Vidich, Arthur J., Joseph Bensman, and Maurice R. Stein, eds. 1964. *Reflections on Community Studies*. New York: Wiley.

Voget, Fred W. 1975. *A History of Ethnology*. New York: Holt, Rinehart and Winston.

Vogler, Robin J. M. 1993. *The Medicalization of Eating: Social Control in an Eating Disorders Clinic*. Greenwich, CT: JAI Press.

Wacquant, Loic J. D. 1995. "The Pugilistic Point of View: How Boxers Think and Feel about Their Trade." *Theory and Society* 24: 489–535.

Wacquant, Loic J. D. 1998a. "The Prizefighter's Three Bodies." *Ethnos* 63:325–52.

Wacquant, Loic J. D. 1998b. "A Fleshpeddler at Work: Power, Pain and Profit in the Prizefighting Economy." *Theory and Society* 27:1–42.

Wade, Peter. 1993. "Sexuality and Masculinity in Fieldwork among Colombian Blacks." In *Gendered Fields: Women, Men and Ethnography*, ed. D. Bell, P. Caplan and W. J. Karim. London: Routledge & Kegan Paul, pp. 199–214.

Walkerdine, Valerie. 1990. *Schoolgirl Fictions*. New York: Verso.

Warren, Carol A. B. 1972. *Identity and Community in the Gay World*. New York: Wiley.

Warren, Carol A. B. 1977. "Field Work in the Gay World: Issues in Phenomenological Research." *Journal of Social Issues* 33:93–107.

Warren, Carol A. B. 1980. "Data Presentation and the Audience: Responses, Ethics, and Effects." *Urban Life* 9:282–308.

Warren, Carol A. B. 1982. *The Court of Last Resort: Mental Illness and the Law*. Chicago: University of Chicago Press.

Warren, Carol A. B. 1988. *Gender Issues in Field Research*. Newbury Park, CA: Sage.

Warren, Carol A. B. 2000. "Writing the Other, Inscribing the Self." *Qualitative Sociology* 23:183–99.

Warren, Carol A. B., and Jennifer K. Hackney. 2000. *Gender Issues in Ethnography*. Second Edition. Thousand Oaks, CA: Sage.

Warren, Carol A. B., and Paul K. Rasmussen. 1977. "Sex and Gender in Field Research." *Urban Life* 6:349–70.

Wax, Murray L. 1967. "On Misunderstanding Verstehen: A Reply to Abel." *Sociology and Social Research* 51:323–33.

Wax, Murray L. 1972. "Tenting with Malinowski." *American Sociological Review* 37:1–13.

Wax, Murray L. 1980. "Paradoxes of 'Consent' to the Practice of Fieldwork." *Social Problems* 27:272–83.

Wax, Murray L. 1983. "On Fieldworkers and Those Exposed to Fieldwork: Federal Regulations and Moral Issues." In *Contemporary Field Research*, ed. R. M. Emerson. Boston: Little, Brown, pp. 288–99.

Wax, Rosalie H. 1952. "Field Methods and Techniques: Reciprocity as a Field Technique." *Human Organization* 11:34–37.

Wax, Rosalie H. 1960. "Twelve Years Later: An Analysis of Field Experience." In *Human Organization Research*, ed. R. N. Adams and J. J. Preiss. Homewood, IL: Dorsey.

Wax, Rosalie H. 1971. *Doing Fieldwork: Warnings and Advice*. Chicago: University of Chicago Press.

Wax, Rosalie H. 1979. "Gender and Age in Fieldwork and Fieldwork Education: No Good Thing is Done by Any Man Alone." *Social Problems* 26:509–22.

Webb, Beatrice P. 1926. *My Apprenticeship*. New York: Longman, Green.

Webb, Eugene J. 1966. "Unconventionality, Triangulation and Inference." In *Proceedings of the 1966 Invitational Conference on Testing Problems*. Princeton, NJ: Educational Testing Service, pp. 34–43.

Weidman, Hazel H. 1986. "On Ambivalence in the Field." In *Women in the Field: Anthropological Experiences*, ed. P. Golde. Berkeley: University of California Press, pp. 239–63.

Weinberg, Darin. 1997. "The Social Construction of Non-Human Agency: The Case of Mental Disorder." *Social Problems* 44:217–34.

Weitz, Rose. 1991. *Life with AIDS*. New Brunswick, NJ: Rutgers University Press.

Wetzel, Patricia. 1984. "'Uti' and 'Soto' (In-Group and Out-Group): Social Deixis in Japanese." Ph.D. Dissertation, Department of Linguistics, Cornell University.

White, Hayden. 1973. *Metahistory: The Historical Imagination in Nineteenth-Century Europe*. Baltimore: Johns Hopkins University Press.

White, Merry. 1988. *The Japanese Overseas: Can They Go Home Again?* New York: Free Press.

Whitehead, Tony L., and Mary Ellen Conaway. 1986. *Self, Sex and Gender in Cross-Cultural Fieldwork*. Urbana: University of Illinois Press.

Whyte, William F. 1943/1955/1981/1993. *Street Corner Society: The Social Structure of an Italian Slum*. Chicago: University of Chicago Press.

Whyte, William F. 1992. "In Defense of Street Corner Society." *Journal of Contemporary Ethnography* 21:52–68.

Wieder, D. Lawrence. 1969. "The Convict Code: A Study of a Moral Order as a Persuasive Activity." Ph.D. Dissertation, Department of Sociology, University of California, Los Angeles.

Wieder, D. Lawrence. 1974. *Language and Social Reality: The Case of Telling the Convict Code*. The Hague: Mouton.

Williams, Patricia. 1991. *The Alchemy of Race and Rights*. Cambridge, MA: Harvard University Press.

Williams, Terry. 1989. "Exploring the Cocaine Culture." In *In the Field: Readings on the Field Research Experience*, ed. C. D. Smith and W. Kornblum. New York: Praeger, pp. 27–32.

Williams, Terry. 1992. *Crackhouse: Notes from the End of the Line*. Reading, MA: Addison-Wesley.

Williams, Terry, Eloise Dunlap, Bruce D. Johnson and Ansley Hamid. 1992. "Personal Safety in Dangerous Places." *Journal of Contemporary Ethnography* 21:343–74.

Winch, Peter. 1958. *The Idea of a Social Science and its Relation to Philosophy*. London: Routledge & Kegan Paul.

Winch, P. 1964. "Understanding Primitive Society." *American Philosophical Quarterly* 1:307–24.

Wiseman, Jacqueline P. 1970. *Stations of the Lost: The Treatment of Skid Row Alcoholics.* Englewood Cliffs, NJ: Prentice-Hall.

Wiseman, Jacqueline P. 1994. "The Development of Generic Concepts in Qualitative Research Through Cumulative Application." In *More Grounded Theory: A Reader*, ed. B. G. Glaser. Mill Valley, CA: Sociology Press.

Wolcott, Harry F. 1990. *Writing Up Qualitative Research.* Newbury Park, CA: Sage.

Wolf, Margarey. 1992. *A Thrice-Told Tale: Feminism, Postmodernism, and Ethnographic Responsibility.* Stanford: Stanford University Press.

Wolff, Kurt H. 1964. "Surrender and Community Study: The Study of Loma." In *Reflections on Community Studies*, ed. A. J. Vidich, J. Bensman, and M. R. Stein. New York: Wiley, pp. 233–63.

Wolfinger, Nicholas. 1995. "Passing Moments: Some Social Dynamics of Pedestrian Interaction." *Journal of Contemporary Ethnography* 24:323–40.

Woods, Peter. 1979. *The Divided School.* London: Routledge & Kegan Paul.

Wordsworth, William. 1850/1926. *The Prelude: Or Growth of a Poet's Mind.* Oxford: Clarendon.

Wright, Richard, and Scott Decker. 1994. *Burglars on the Job: Streetlife and Residential Break-Ins.* Boston: Northeastern University Press.

Zavella, Patricia. 1996. "Feminist Insider Dilemmas: Constructing Ethnic Identity with 'Chicana' Informants." In *Feminist Dilemmas in Fieldwork*, ed. D. L. Wolfe. Boulder, CO: Westview, pp. 138–69.

Zelditch, Morris, Jr. 1962. "Some Methodological Problems of Field Studies." *American Journal of Sociology* 67:566–76.

Znaniecki, Florian. 1934. *The Method of Sociology.* New York: Farrar and Rinehart.

Zola, Irving K. 1982. *Missing Pieces: A Chronicle of Living with a Disability.* Philadelphia: Temple University Press.

Index

427